PEARSON CUSTOM LIBRARY

ECON 200
James Madison University
Philip Heap

PEARSON

ISBN 10: 1-323-34279-6
ISBN 13: 978-1-323-34279-4

PEARSON

Table of Contents

Economics:
Foundations and Models

From Chapter 1 of *Macroeconomics*, Fifth Edition. R. Glenn Hubbard and Anthony Patrick O'Brien. Copyright © 2015 by Pearson Education, Inc.

Economics:
Foundations and Models

Chapter Outline and Learning Objectives

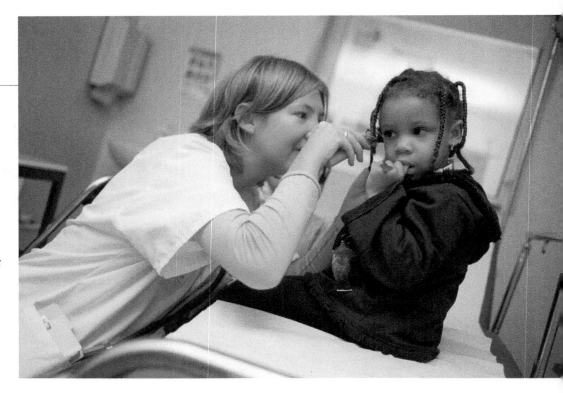

2

Is the Private Doctor's Office Going to Disappear?

Traditionally, most doctors in the United States have worked in private practices that they owned themselves or in partnership with other doctors. Like other businesspeople, a doctor hires workers—nurses, physician's assistants, and receptionists—and buys or rents machinery and equipment. A doctor's income represents the profits from his or her practice, or the difference between the revenue received from patients and their health insurance plans and the costs to the doctor of wages, rent, loans, and insurance.

Increasingly, rather than owning a private practice, many doctors have chosen to work as salaried employees of hospitals. Although in 2000 nearly 60 percent of doctors were in private practice, by 2013 fewer than 40 percent were. What explains the increasing number of doctors who are giving up their private practices to become salaried employees of hospitals? Some doctors choose private practice because they like being their own boss. Other doctors prefer the more regular hours of working for a hospital, where they are less likely to be woken up at 2 A.M. to treat a patient with a medical emergency. Economists believe, though, that the best explanation for doctors abandoning private practice is that the doctors are acting in response to changing *economic incentives*. In fact, one of the key ideas that we will explore in this text is that we can often predict behavior by assuming that people respond to economic incentives.

The economic incentives doctors face have changed in a number of ways. For example, soaring health care costs have led many private insurance companies, as well as the federal and state governments, to reduce the payments they make to doctors in return for treating patients. As a result, doctors in private practice have found their incomes fluctuating, which makes the steady income from a hospital salary more attractive. Congress passed President Barack Obama's package of health care changes in 2010. One rule requires most doctors and hospitals to convert to electronic medical record keeping. Although this change may improve the quality of health care, the computer systems required are expensive. Doctors can avoid this cost by leaving private practice for hospital employment. Other new rules have increased the amount of paperwork doctors must complete to be paid for treating patients.

AN INSIDE LOOK discusses how technological change is affecting medical care.

Sources: Robert Kocher and Nikhil R. Sahni, "Hospitals' Race to Employ Physicians," *New England Journal of Medicine*, Vol. 364, No. 19, May 12, 2011, pp. 1790–1793; Julie Creswell and Reed Abelson, "A Hospital War Reflects a Bind for Doctors in the U.S.," *New York Times*, November 30, 2012; and Scott Gottlieb, "The Doctor Won't See You Now: He's Clocked Out," *Wall Street Journal*, March 14, 2013.

Economics in Your Life

Will There Be Plenty of Jobs Available in the Health Care Industry?

The U.S. Health Resources and Services Administration (HRSA) forecasts that there will be 866,400 doctors in the United States in 2020. The HRSA also forecasts that 922,000 doctors will be needed in 2020. In other words, this federal government agency forecasts that there will be a shortage of about 56,000 doctors in 2020. The U.S. Bureau of Labor Statistics forecasts that 9 of the 20 fastest growing occupations over the next 10 years will be in the medical field. But the availability of these jobs depends on the reliability of the forecasts. What is the basis for the forecasts on the availability of jobs in health care, and how reliable are the forecasts? As you read this chapter, try to answer this question. You can check your answer against the one we provide at the end of this chapter.

I n this text, we use economics to answer questions such as the following:

- How are the prices of goods and services determined?
- Why have health care costs risen so rapidly?
- Why do firms engage in international trade, and how do government policies affect international trade?
- Why does the government control the prices of some goods and services, and what are the effects of those controls?

Economists do not always agree on the answers to every question. In fact, as we will see, economists engage in lively debate on some issues. In addition, new problems and issues are constantly arising. So, economists are always at work developing new methods to analyze economic questions.

All the topics we discuss in this text illustrate a basic fact of life: To attain our goals, we must make choices. We must make choices because we live in a world of **scarcity**, which means that although our wants are *unlimited*, the resources available to fulfill those wants are *limited*. You might like to own a BMW and spend each summer vacationing at five-star European hotels, but unless Bill Gates is a close and generous relative, you probably lack the funds to fulfill these dreams. Every day, you make choices as you spend your limited income on the many goods and services available. The finite amount of time you have also limits your ability to attain your goals. If you spend an hour studying for your economics midterm, you have one hour less to study for your history midterm. Firms and the government are in the same situation as you: They must also attain their goals with limited resources. **Economics** is the study of the choices consumers, business managers, and government officials make to attain their goals, given their scarce resources.

We begin this chapter by discussing three important economic ideas: *People are rational*, *people respond to economic incentives*, and *optimal decisions are made at the margin*. Then, we consider the three fundamental questions that any economy must answer: *What* goods and services will be produced? *How* will the goods and services be produced? and *Who* will receive the goods and services produced? Next, we consider the role of *economic models* in analyzing economic issues. **Economic models** are simplified versions of reality used to analyze real-world economic situations. We will explore why economists use models and how they construct them. Finally, we will discuss the difference between microeconomics and macroeconomics, and we will preview some important economic terms.

Three Key Economic Ideas

As you try to achieve your goals, whether they involve buying a new computer or finding a part-time job, you will interact with other people in *markets*. A **market** is a group of buyers and sellers of a good or service and the institution or arrangement by which they come together to trade. Examples of markets are the markets for smartphones, houses, haircuts, stocks and bonds, and labor. Most of economics involves analyzing what happens in markets.

Scarcity A situation in which unlimited wants exceed the limited resources available to fulfill those wants.

Economics The study of the choices people make to attain their goals, given their scarce resources.

Economic model A simplified version of reality used to analyze real-world economic situations.

1 LEARNING OBJECTIVE

Explain these three key economic ideas: People are rational; people respond to economic incentives; and optimal decisions are made at the margin.

Market A group of buyers and sellers of a good or service and the institution or arrangement by which they come together to trade.

People Are Rational

Economists generally assume that people are rational. This assumption does *not* mean that economists believe everyone knows everything or always makes the "best" decision. It means that economists assume that consumers and firms use all available information as they act to achieve their goals. Rational individuals weigh the benefits and costs of each action, and they choose an action only if the benefits outweigh the costs. For example, if Apple charges a price of $299 for its latest iPhone, economists assume that the managers at Apple have estimated that this price will earn Apple the most profit. The managers may be wrong; perhaps a price of $325 would be more profitable, but economists assume that the managers at Apple have acted rationally, on the basis of the information available to them, in choosing the price. Of course, not everyone behaves rationally all the time. Still, the assumption of rational behavior is very useful in explaining most of the choices that people make.

People Respond to Economic Incentives

Human beings act from a variety of motives, including envy, compassion, and religious belief. While not ignoring other motives, economists emphasize that consumers and firms consistently respond to *economic incentives*. This point may seem obvious, but it is often overlooked. For example, according to an article in the *Wall Street Journal*, the FBI couldn't understand why banks were not taking steps to improve security in the face of an increase in robberies: "FBI officials suggest that banks place uniformed, armed guards outside their doors and install bullet-resistant plastic, known as a 'bandit barrier,' in front of teller windows." FBI officials were surprised that few banks took their advice. But the article also reported that installing bullet-resistant plastic costs $10,000 to $20,000, and a well-trained security guard receives $50,000 per year in salary and benefits. The average loss in a bank robbery is only about $1,200. The economic incentive to banks is clear: It is less costly to put up with bank robberies than to take additional security measures. FBI agents may be surprised by how banks respond to the threat of robberies—but economists are not.

The *Making the Connection* feature discusses a news story or another application related to the chapter material. Read this *Making the Connection* for a discussion of whether people respond to economic incentives even when deciding how much to eat and how much to exercise.

Making the Connection	### Does Health Insurance Give People an Incentive to Become Obese?

Obesity is an increasing problem in the United States. The U.S. Centers for Disease Control and Prevention (CDC) defines obesity for an adult as having a body mass index (BMI) of 30 or greater. The BMI measures a person's weight relative to the person's height. (The exact formula is: $\text{BMI} = (\text{Weight in pounds}/\text{Height in inches}^2 \times 703$.) A BMI of 30 is equivalent to a person 5'4" being 30 pounds overweight. Obesity is related to a variety of diseases, including heart disease, stroke, diabetes, and hypertension.

These two maps show the dramatic increase in obesity between 1994 and 2011. In 1994, in a majority of states between 10 percent and 14 percent of the adult population was obese, and in no state was more than 20 percent of the adult population obese. By 2011, in every state at least 20 percent of the adult population was obese, and in about three-quarters of the states, at least 25 percent of the adult population was obese.

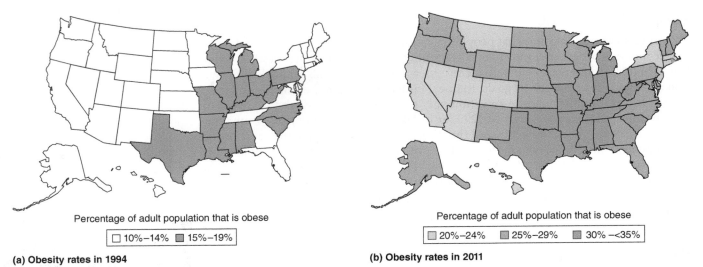

Percentage of adult population that is obese

☐ 10%–14% ■ 15%–19%

(a) Obesity rates in 1994

Percentage of adult population that is obese

☐ 20%–24% ■ 25%–29% ■ 30% –<35%

(b) Obesity rates in 2011

Source: Centers for Disease Control and Prevention, "Prevalence of Self-Reported Obesity among U.S. Adults."

Many people who suffer from obesity have underlying medical conditions. For these people, obesity is an unfortunate medical problem that they cannot control. The fact that obesity is increasing, though, indicates that for some people obesity is the result of diet and lifestyle choices. Potential explanations for the increase in obesity include greater intake of high-calorie fast foods, insufficient exercise, and a decline in the physical activity associated with many jobs. The CDC recommends that teenagers get a minimum of 60 minutes of aerobic exercise per day, a standard that only 15 percent of high school students were meeting in 2013. In 1960, 50 percent of jobs in the United States required at least moderate physical activity. By 2013, only 20 percent of jobs did. As a result, a typical worker was burning off about 130 fewer calories per workday.

In addition to eating too much and not exercising enough, could health insurance be a cause of obesity? Obese people tend to suffer more medical problems and so incur higher medical costs. Obese people with health insurance that will reimburse them for only part of their medical bills or who have no health insurance must pay some or all of these higher medical bills themselves. People with health insurance that covers most of their medical bills will not suffer as large a monetary cost from being obese. In other words, by reducing some of the costs of obesity, health insurance may give people an economic incentive to gain weight.

At first glance, this argument may seem implausible. Some people suffer from medical conditions that can make physical activity difficult or that can cause weight gain even with moderate eating, so they may become obese whether they have health insurance or not. Some people are obese because of poor eating habits or lack of exercise, and they probably don't consider health insurance when deciding whether to have another slice of chocolate cake or to watch television instead of going to the gym. But if economists are correct about the importance of economic incentives, then we would expect that if we hold all other personal characteristics—such as age, gender, and income—constant, people with health insurance will be more likely to be overweight than people without health insurance.

Jay Bhattacharya and Kate Bundorf of Stanford University, Noemi Pace of the University of Venice, and Neeraj Sood of the University of Southern California, have analyzed the effects of health insurance on weight. Using a sample that followed nearly 80,000 people from 1989 to 2004, they found that after controlling for income, education, race, gender, age, and other factors, people with health insurance were significantly more likely to be overweight than people without health insurance. Having private health insurance increased BMI by 1.3 points, and having public health insurance, such as Medicaid, which is a program under which the government provides health care to low-income people, increased BMI by 2.3 points. These findings suggest that people

Response to economic incentive example

respond to economic incentives even when making decisions about what they eat and how much they exercise.

Sources: Centers for Disease Control and Prevention, "Prevalence of Self-Reported Obesity among U.S. Adults," www.cdc .gov; Katherine M. Flegal, Margaret D. Caroll, Cynthia L. Ogden, and Lester R. Curtin, "Prevalence and Trends in Obesity among U.S. Adults, 1999–2008," *Journal of the American Medical Association*, Vol. 303, No. 3, January 20, 2010, pp. 235–241; Jay Bhattacharya, Kate Bundorf, Noemi Pace, and Neeraj Sood, "Does Health Insurance Make You Fat?" in Michael Grossman and Naci H. Mocan, eds., *Economic Aspects of Obesity*, Chicago: University of Chicago Press, 2011; and Tara Parker-Pope, "Less Active at Work, Americans Have Packed on Pounds," *New York Times*, May 25, 2011.

Your Turn: Test your understanding by doing related problems 1.6 and 1.7 at the end of this chapter.

Optimal Decisions Are Made at the Margin

Some decisions are "all or nothing." For instance, when an entrepreneur decides whether to open a new restaurant, she starts the new restaurant or she doesn't. When you decide whether to enter graduate school or to take a job, you enter graduate school or you don't. But rather than being all or nothing, most decisions in life involve doing a little more or a little less. If you are trying to decrease your spending and increase your saving, the decision is not really between saving all the money you earn or spending it all. Rather, many small choices are involved, such as whether to buy a caffè mocha at Starbucks every day or just three times per week.

Economists use the word *marginal* to mean "extra" or "additional." Should you watch another hour of television or spend that hour studying? The *marginal benefit* (*MB*) of watching more television is the additional enjoyment you receive. The *marginal cost* (*MC*) is the lower grade you receive from having studied a little less. Should Apple produce an additional 300,000 iPhones? Firms receive *revenue* from selling goods. Apple's marginal benefit is the additional revenue it receives from selling 300,000 more iPhones. Apple's marginal cost is the additional cost—for wages, parts, and so forth—of producing 300,000 more iPhones. *Economists reason that the optimal decision is to continue any activity up to the point where the marginal benefit equals the marginal cost—* $MB = MC$. Often we apply this rule without consciously thinking about it. Usually you will know whether the additional enjoyment from watching a television program is worth the additional cost involved in not spending that hour studying, without giving the decision a lot of thought. In business situations, however, firms often have to make careful calculations to determine, for example, whether the additional revenue received from increasing production is greater or less than the additional cost of the production. Economists refer to analysis that involves comparing marginal benefits and marginal costs as **marginal analysis**.

Marginal analysis Analysis that involves comparing marginal benefits and marginal costs.

The special feature *Solved Problem* will increase your understanding of the material by leading you through the steps of solving an applied economic problem. After reading the problem, test your understanding by doing the related problems that appear at the end of the chapter. You can also complete Solved Problems on **www.myeconlab.com** and receive tutorial help.

Solved Problem 1

A Doctor Makes a Decision at the Margin

A doctor receives complaints from patients that her office isn't open enough hours. So the doctor asks her office manager to analyze the effect of keeping her office open 9 hours per day rather than 8 hours. The doctor's office manager tells her: "Keeping the office open an extra hour is a good idea because the revenue from your practice will increase by $300,000 per year when the office is open 9 hours per day." Do you agree with the office manager's reasoning? What, if any, additional information do you need to decide whether the doctor should keep her office open an additional hour per day?

Solving the Problem

Step 1: **Review the chapter material.** This problem is about making decisions, so you may want to review the section "Optimal Decisions Are Made at the Margin."

Step 2: **Explain whether you agree with the office manager's reasoning.** We have seen that any activity should be continued to the point where the marginal benefit is equal to the marginal cost. In this case, the doctor should keep her office open up to the point where the additional revenue she receives from seeing more patients is equal to the marginal cost of keeping her office open an additional hour. The office manager has provided information on marginal revenue but not on marginal cost. So the office manager has not provided enough information to make a decision, and you should not agree with the office manager's reasoning.

Step 3: **Explain what additional information you need.** To make a correct decision, you would need information on the marginal cost of remaining open an extra hour per day. The marginal cost would include the additional salary to be paid to the office staff, any additional medical supplies that would be used, as well as any additional electricity or other utilities. The doctor would also need to take into account the nonmonetary cost of spending another hour working rather than spending time with her family and friends or in other leisure activities. The marginal revenue would depend on how many more patients the doctor can see in the extra hour. The doctor should keep her office open an additional hour if the marginal revenue of doing so is greater than the marginal cost. If the marginal cost is greater than the marginal revenue, then the doctor should continue to keep her office open for 8 hours.

Your Turn: For more practice, do related problems 1.8, 1.9, and 1.10 at the end of this chapter.

Discuss how an economy answers these questions: What goods and services will be produced? How will the goods and services be produced? Who will receive the goods and services produced?

Trade-off The idea that, because of scarcity, producing more of one good or service means producing less of another good or service.

Opportunity cost The highest-valued alternative that must be given up to engage in an activity.

The Economic Problem That Every Society Must Solve

Because we live in a world of scarcity, any society faces the *economic problem* that it has only a limited amount of economic resources—such as workers, machines, and raw materials—and so can produce only a limited amount of goods and services. Therefore, every society faces **trade-offs**: Producing more of one good or service means producing less of another good or service. In fact, the best measure of the cost of producing a good or service is the value of what has to be given up to produce it. The **opportunity cost** of any activity—such as producing a good or service—is the highest-valued alternative that must be given up to engage in that activity. The concept of opportunity cost is very important in economics and applies to individuals as much as it does to firms or society as a whole. Consider the example of a doctor who could receive a salary of $100,000 per year working as an employee of a hospital but decides to open his own private practice instead. In that case, the opportunity cost of the physician services he supplies to his own firm is the $100,000 he gives up by not working for the hospital, *even if he does not explicitly pay himself a salary*. As in this example, opportunity costs often do not involve actual payments of money.

Trade-offs force society to make choices when answering the following three fundamental questions:

1. *What* goods and services will be produced?
2. *How* will the goods and services be produced?
3. *Who* will receive the goods and services produced?

We will now briefly introduce each question.

What Goods and Services Will Be Produced?

How will society decide whether to produce more economics textbooks or more Blu-ray players? More daycare facilities or more football stadiums? Of course, "society" does not make decisions; only individuals make decisions. The answer to the question of what will be produced is determined by the choices that consumers, firms, and the government make. Every day, you help decide which goods and services firms will produce when you choose to buy an iPhone instead of a Samsung Galaxy or a caffè mocha rather than a chai tea. Similarly, Apple must choose whether to devote its scarce resources to making more iPhones or more iPads. The federal government must choose whether to spend more of its limited budget on breast cancer research or on repairing highways. In each case, consumers, firms, and the government face the problem of scarcity by trading off one good or service for another. And each choice made comes with an opportunity cost, measured by the value of the best alternative given up.

How Will the Goods and Services Be Produced?

Firms choose how to produce the goods and services they sell. In many cases, firms face a trade-off between using more workers or using more machines. For example, a local service station has to choose whether to provide car repair services using more diagnostic computers and fewer auto mechanics or fewer diagnostic computers and more auto mechanics. Similarly, movie studios have to choose whether to produce animated films using highly skilled animators to draw them by hand or fewer animators and more computers. In deciding whether to move production offshore to China, firms may need to choose between a production method in the United States that uses fewer workers and more machines and a production method in China that uses more workers and fewer machines.

Who Will Receive the Goods and Services Produced?

In the United States, who receives the goods and services produced depends largely on how income is distributed. The higher a person's income, the more goods and services he or she can buy. Often, people are willing to give up some of their income—and, therefore, some of their ability to purchase goods and services—by donating to charities to increase the incomes of poorer people. Each year, Americans donate about $300 billion to charity, or an average donation of $2,650 for each household in the country. An important policy question, however, is whether the government should intervene to make the distribution of income more equal. Such intervention already occurs in the United States, because people with higher incomes pay a larger fraction of their incomes in taxes and because the government makes payments to people with low incomes. There is disagreement over whether the current attempts to redistribute income are sufficient or whether there should be more or less redistribution.

Centrally Planned Economies versus Market Economies

To answer the three questions—what, how, and who—societies organize their economies in two main ways. A society can have a **centrally planned economy** in which the government decides how economic resources will be allocated. Or a society can have a **market economy** in which the decisions of households and firms interacting in markets allocate economic resources.

From 1917 to 1991, the most important centrally planned economy in the world was that of the Soviet Union, which was established when Vladimir Lenin and the Communist Party staged a revolution and took control of the Russian Empire. In the Soviet Union, the government decided what goods to produce, how the goods would be produced, and who would receive the goods. Government employees managed factories and stores. The objective of these managers was to follow the government's orders rather than to satisfy the wants of consumers. Centrally planned economies like that of the Soviet Union have not been successful in producing low-cost, high-quality goods and services. As a result, the standard of living of the average person in a centrally planned economy tends to be low. All centrally planned economies have also been political

Centrally planned economy An economy in which the government decides how economic resources will be allocated.

Market economy An economy in which the decisions of households and firms interacting in markets allocate economic resources.

allocated · distributed

9

dictatorships. Dissatisfaction with low living standards and political repression finally led to the collapse of the Soviet Union in 1991. Today, only North Korea still has a completely centrally planned economy.

All high-income democracies, including the United States, Canada, Japan, and the countries of Western Europe, have market economies. Market economies rely primarily on privately owned firms to produce goods and services and to decide how to produce them. Markets, rather than the government, determine who receives the goods and services produced. In a market economy, firms must produce goods and services that meet the wants of consumers, or the firms will go out of business. In that sense, it is ultimately consumers who decide what goods and services will be produced. Because firms in a market economy compete to offer the highest-quality products at the lowest price, they are under pressure to use the lowest-cost methods of production. For example, in the past 10 years, some U.S. firms have been under pressure to reduce their costs to meet competition from Chinese firms.

In a market economy, the income of an individual is determined by the payments he receives for what he has to sell. If he is a civil engineer, and firms are willing to pay a salary of $85,000 per year for engineers with his training and skills, he will have this amount of income to purchase goods and services. If the engineer also owns a house that he rents out, his income will be even higher. One of the attractive features of markets is that they reward hard work. Generally, the more extensive the training a person has received and the longer the hours the person works, the higher the person's income will be. Of course, luck—both good and bad—also plays a role here, as elsewhere in life. Someone might have a high income because she won the state lottery, while someone else might have a low income because he has severe medical problems. We can conclude that market economies respond to the question: "Who receives the goods and services produced?" with the answer: "Those who are most willing and able to buy them."

The Modern "Mixed" Economy

In the nineteenth and early twentieth centuries, the U.S. government engaged in relatively little regulation of markets for goods and services. Beginning in the middle of the twentieth century, government intervention in the economy dramatically increased in the United States and other market economies. This increase was primarily caused by the high rates of unemployment and business bankruptcies during the Great Depression of the 1930s. Some government intervention was also intended to raise the incomes of the elderly, the sick, and people with limited skills. For example, in the 1930s, the United States established the Social Security system, which provides government payments to retired and disabled workers, and minimum wage legislation, which sets a floor on the wages employers can pay workers in many occupations. In more recent years, government intervention in the economy has also expanded to meet goals such as the protection of the environment, the promotion of civil rights, and the provision of medical care to low-income people and the elderly.

Mixed economy An economy in which most economic decisions result from the interaction of buyers and sellers in markets but in which the government plays a significant role in the allocation of resources.

Some economists argue that the extent of government intervention makes it no longer accurate to refer to the U.S., Canadian, Japanese, and Western European economies as pure market economies. Instead, they should be referred to as *mixed economies*. A **mixed economy** is still primarily a market economy because most economic decisions result from the interaction of buyers and sellers in markets. However, the government plays a significant role in the allocation of resources.

One of the most important developments in the international economy in recent years has been the movement of China from being a centrally planned economy to being a more mixed economy. The Chinese economy suffered decades of economic stagnation following the takeover of the government in 1949 by Mao Zedong and the Communist Party. Although China remains a political dictatorship, the production of most goods and services is now determined in the market rather than by the government. The result has been rapid economic growth that in the future may lead to total production of goods and services in China surpassing total production in the United States.

Efficiency and Equity

Market economies tend to be more efficient than centrally planned economies. There are two types of efficiency. **Productive efficiency** occurs when a good or service is produced at the lowest possible cost. **Allocative efficiency** occurs when production is in accordance with consumer preferences. Markets tend to be efficient because they promote competition and facilitate voluntary exchange. With **voluntary exchange**, both the buyer and the seller of a product are made better off by the transaction. We know that they are both made better off because, otherwise, the buyer would not have agreed to buy the product or the seller would not have agreed to sell it. Productive efficiency is achieved when competition among firms forces them to produce goods and services at the lowest cost. Allocative efficiency is achieved when the combination of competition among firms and voluntary exchange between firms and consumers results in firms producing the mix of goods and services that consumers prefer the most. Competition will force firms to continue producing and selling goods and services as long as the additional benefit to consumers is greater than the additional cost of production. In this way, the mix of goods and services produced will match consumer preferences.

Productive efficiency A situation in which a good or service is produced at the lowest possible cost.

Allocative efficiency A state of the economy in which production is in accordance with consumer preferences; in particular, every good or service is produced up to the point where the last unit provides a marginal benefit to society equal to the marginal cost of producing it.

Voluntary exchange A situation that occurs in markets when both the buyer and the seller of a product are made better off by the transaction.

Although markets promote efficiency, they don't guarantee it. Inefficiency can arise from various sources. To begin with, it may take some time to achieve an efficient outcome. When Blu-ray players were introduced, for example, firms did not instantly achieve productive efficiency. It took several years for firms to discover the lowest-cost method of producing this good. Governments sometimes reduce efficiency by interfering with voluntary exchange in markets. For example, many governments limit the imports of some goods from foreign countries. This limitation reduces efficiency by keeping goods from being produced at the lowest cost. The production of some goods damages the environment. In this case, government intervention can increase efficiency because without such intervention, firms may ignore the costs of environmental damage and thereby fail to produce the goods at the lowest possible cost.

An economically efficient outcome is not necessarily desirable. Many people prefer economic outcomes that they consider fair or equitable, even if those outcomes are less efficient. **Equity** is harder to define than efficiency because there isn't an agreed upon definition of fairness. For some people, equity involves a more equal distribution of economic benefits than would result from an emphasis on efficiency alone. For example, some people support raising taxes on people with higher incomes to provide the funds for programs that aid the poor. Although governments may increase equity by reducing the incomes of high-income people and increasing the incomes of the poor, efficiency may be reduced. People have less incentive to open new businesses, supply labor, and save if the government takes a significant amount of the income they earn from working or saving. The result is that fewer goods and services are produced, and less saving takes place. As this example illustrates, *there is often a trade-off between efficiency and equity*. Government policymakers often confront this trade-off.

Equity The fair distribution of economic benefits.

Economic Models

3 LEARNING OBJECTIVE

Understand the role of models in economic analysis.

Economists rely on economic theories, or models (the words *theory* and *model* are used interchangeably), to analyze real-world issues, such as those involved with health care. As mentioned earlier, economic models are simplified versions of reality. Economists are certainly not alone in relying on models: An engineer may use a computer model of a bridge to help test whether it will withstand high winds, or a biologist may make a physical model of a nucleic acid to better understand its properties. One purpose of economic models is to make economic ideas sufficiently explicit and concrete so that individuals, firms, or the government can use them to make decisions. For example, the model of demand and supply is a simplified version of how the prices of products are determined by the interactions among buyers and sellers in markets.

sufficiently - enough

explicit - stated clearly

Economists use economic models to answer questions. For example, will the United States have a sufficient number of doctors in 2020? For such a complicated question, economists often use several models to examine different aspects of the issue. For example, economists at the U.S. Bureau of Labor Statistics (BLS) build models that allow them to forecast future employment in different occupations. These models allow the BLS to forecast how many doctors there are likely to be at a future date. Economists also use models to forecast the demand for medical services. By separately forecasting the number of doctors and the demand for medical services, these models provide a forecast of whether there will be a sufficient number of doctors in 2020. As mentioned earlier, economists at the U.S. Health Resources and Services Administration (HRSA) have used models to forecast that there will be a shortage of about 56,000 doctors in 2020.

Sometimes economists use an existing model to analyze an issue, but in other cases, they have to develop a new model. To develop a model, economists generally follow these steps:

1. Decide on the assumptions to use in developing the model.
2. Formulate a testable hypothesis.
3. Use economic data to test the hypothesis.
4. Revise the model if it fails to explain the economic data well.
5. Retain the revised model to help answer similar economic questions in the future.

The Role of Assumptions in Economic Models

Any model is based on making assumptions because models have to be simplified to be useful. We cannot analyze an economic issue unless we reduce its complexity. For example, economic models make *behavioral assumptions* about the motives of consumers and firms. Economists assume that consumers will buy the goods and services that will maximize their well-being or their satisfaction. Similarly, economists assume that firms act to maximize their profits. These assumptions are simplifications because they do not describe the motives of every consumer and every firm. How can we know if the assumptions in a model are too simplified or too limiting? We can determine the usefulness of assumptions by forming hypotheses based on the assumptions and then testing the hypotheses using real-world information.

Forming and Testing Hypotheses in Economic Models

Economic variable Something measurable that can have different values, such as the incomes of doctors.

An **economic variable** is something measurable that can have different values, such as the incomes of doctors. In an economic model, a hypothesis is a statement that may be either correct or incorrect about an economic variable. An example of a hypothesis in an economic model is the statement that the falling incomes earned by primary care physicians—often referred to as *family doctors*—will result in a decline in the number of physicians choosing to enter primary care in the United States in 2020. An economic hypothesis is usually about a causal relationship; in this case, the hypothesis states that lower incomes cause, or lead to, fewer doctors entering primary care.

Before we can accept a hypothesis, we have to test it. To test a hypothesis, we analyze statistics on the relevant economic variables. In our example, we would gather statistics on the incomes of family doctors, the number of family doctors, and perhaps other variables as well. Testing a hypothesis can be tricky. For example, showing that the number of family doctors declined at a time when the average income of these doctors declined would not be enough to demonstrate that the decline in income *caused* the decline in the number of family doctors. Just because two things are correlated—that is, they happen at the same time—does not mean that one caused the other. For example, before entering practice, a doctor spends time in a teaching hospital as a resident in his or her field. Teaching hospitals determine how many residencies they will offer in a particular field. Suppose that teaching hospitals decreased the number of residencies in primary care at the same time that the incomes of family doctors were declining. In that case, the declining number of residencies, rather than the declining incomes, might have caused the decline in the number of family doctors. Over a period of time, many economic variables change, which complicates the testing of hypotheses. In fact, when economists disagree about a hypothesis, such as the effect of falling incomes on the number of family doctors, it is often because of disagreements over interpreting the statistical analysis used to test the hypothesis.

Note that hypotheses must be statements that could, in principle, turn out to be incorrect. Statements such as "Increasing the number of family doctors is good" or "Increasing the number of family doctors is bad" are value judgments rather than hypotheses because it is not possible to disprove them.

Economists accept and use an economic model if it leads to hypotheses that are confirmed by statistical analysis. In many cases, the acceptance is tentative, however, pending the gathering of new data or further statistical analysis. In fact, economists often refer to a hypothesis having been "not rejected," rather than having been "accepted," by statistical analysis. But what if statistical analysis clearly rejects a hypothesis? For example, what if a model leads to a hypothesis that declining incomes of family doctors will cause a decline in the number of these doctors, but the data reject this hypothesis? In this case, the model must be reconsidered. It may be that an assumption used in the model was too simplified or too limiting. For example, perhaps the model ignored the fact that family doctors were moving from owning their own practices to becoming salaried employees of hospitals, where they would be freed from the responsibilities involved in running their own businesses. This change in how primary care physicians are employed might explain why the data rejected the hypothesis.

The BLS has analyzed the accuracy of the projections it had made in 1996 of employment levels in 2006. Some projections were quite accurate, while others were less so. For instance, the BLS had projected that 677,917 physicians and surgeons would be employed in 2006, but actual employment was only 633,292, or about 7 percent less than projected. The error with respect to physician's assistants was much larger, with the projection being that 93,485 physician's assistants would be employed in 2006, but actual employment was only 65,628, or about 30 percent less than expected. Analyzing the errors in these projections helps the BLS to improve the models it uses to make projections of occupational employment.

The process of developing models, testing hypotheses, and revising models occurs not just in economics but also in disciplines such as physics, chemistry, and biology. This process is often referred to as the *scientific method*. Economics is a *social science* because it applies the scientific method to the study of the interactions among individuals.

Positive and Normative Analysis

As we build economic models and use them to answer questions, bear in mind the following important distinction: **Positive analysis** is concerned with *what is*, and **normative analysis** is concerned with *what ought to be*. Economics is about positive analysis, which measures the costs and benefits of different courses of action.

Positive analysis Analysis concerned with what is.

Normative analysis Analysis concerned with what ought to be.

We can use the federal government's minimum wage law to compare positive and normative analysis. In 2013, under this law, it was illegal for an employer to hire a worker at a wage less than $7.25 per hour. Without the minimum wage law, some firms and workers would voluntarily agree to a lower wage. Because of the minimum wage law, some workers have difficulty finding jobs, and some firms end up paying more for labor than they otherwise would have. A positive analysis of the federal minimum wage law uses an economic model to estimate how many workers have lost their jobs because of the law, its effect on the costs and profits of businesses, and the gains to workers receiving the minimum wage. After economists complete this positive analysis, the decision as to whether the minimum wage law is a good or a bad idea is a normative one and depends on how people evaluate the trade-off involved. Supporters of the law believe that the losses to employers and workers who are unemployed as a result of the law are more than offset by the gains to workers who receive higher wages than they would without the law. Opponents of the law believe the losses are greater than the gains. The assessment by any individual depends, in part, on that person's values and political views. The positive analysis an economist provides would play a role in the decision but can't by itself decide the issue one way or the other.

The *Don't Let This Happen to You* box alerts you to common pitfalls in thinking about economic ideas. After reading this box, test your understanding by working the related problem that appears at the end of the chapter.

Don't Let This Happen to You

Don't Confuse Positive Analysis with Normative Analysis

"Economic analysis has shown that the minimum wage law is a bad idea because it causes unemployment." Is this statement accurate? As of 2013, the federal minimum wage law prevents employers from hiring workers at a wage of less than $7.25 per hour. This wage is higher than some employers are willing to pay some workers. If there were no minimum wage law, some workers who currently cannot find any firm willing to hire them at $7.25 per hour would be able to find employment at a lower wage. Therefore, positive economic analysis indicates that the minimum wage law causes unemployment (although economists disagree about how much unemployment the minimum wage law causes). But, some workers who have jobs benefit from the minimum wage law because they are paid a higher wage than they otherwise would be. In other words, the minimum wage law creates both losers (the workers who become unemployed and the firms that have to pay higher wages) and winners (the workers who receive higher wages).

Should we value the gains to the winners more than we value the losses to the losers? The answer involves normative analysis. Positive economic analysis can show the consequences of a particular policy, but it cannot tell us whether the policy is "good" or "bad." So, the statement at the beginning of this box is inaccurate.

Your Turn: Test your understanding by doing related problem 3.9 at the end of this chapter.

Economics as a Social Science

Because economics studies the actions of individuals, it is a social science. Economics is therefore similar to other social science disciplines, such as psychology, political science, and sociology. As a social science, economics considers human behavior—particularly decision-making behavior—in every context, not just in the context of business. Economists have studied issues such as how families decide on the number of children to have, why people have difficulty losing weight or attaining other desirable goals, and why people often ignore relevant information when making decisions. Economics also has much to contribute to questions of government policy. Economists have played an important role in formulating government policies in areas such as the environment, health care, and poverty.

Making the Connection

Should Medical School Be Free?

The U.S. population continues to increase, which by itself would increase the demand for medical services. In addition, the average age of the population is rising, and older people need more medical care than do younger people. So, over time, the number of doctors needs to increase. As mentioned at the beginning of this chapter, the U.S. Health Resources and Services Administration (HRSA) estimates that the number of doctors needed to provide patient care will rise from about 805,000 in 2010 to 922,000 in 2020.

Can we be sure that these additional doctors will be available in 2020? The HRSA forecasts that, in fact, there will be a shortage of 56,000 doctors in 2020. The bulk of that shortage is likely to be in primary care physicians, or family doctors. Ordinarily, we expect that when consumers want more of a product, higher wages and salaries and more job openings will attract workers to that industry. For example, during the U.S. housing boom of the mid-2000s, the number of workers in the building trades—carpenters, plumbers, roofers, and others—increased rapidly. But producing more doctors is a long process. After completing his or her undergraduate education, a doctor spends four years in medical school and then three to five years at

Should these medical students have to pay tuition?

a teaching hospital, pursuing a residency in a particular field of medicine. Apparently convinced that hospitals will not train enough doctors unless they get help, Congress contributes $10 billion per year to teaching hospitals, based on the number of residents they train.

Peter Bach of the Sloan-Kettering Cancer Center and Robert Kocher of the Brookings Institution have proposed that medical schools should charge no tuition. They argue that nearly all students graduate from medical school owing money on student loans, with the average student owing more than $160,000. We might expect that these debts, although large, would not deter students from applying to medical school, because in 2013, the average income of physicians was more than $250,000 per year. Bach and Kocher argue, though, that the high cost of medical school has two bad outcomes: Some good students do not apply because they either do not want to be saddled with such large debts or are unable to borrow sufficient money, and many students avoid going into primary care—where average incomes are $190,000—in favor of specialties such as plastic surgery or anesthesiology—where average incomes are $325,000. Teaching hospitals pay doctors a salary of about $50,000 per year during their residencies. Bach and Kocher propose that hospitals continue to pay residents who pursue primary care but not pay residents who specialize. The money that hospitals would otherwise pay to these residents would be paid to medical schools instead to finance the free tuition. The plan would give residents an incentive to pursue primary care rather than to specialize. Critics of the Bach and Kocher proposal have questioned whether many students capable of being admitted to medical school actually are deterred by medical school tuition. They also question whether many residents who intend to specialize would choose primary care instead, even if specializing means they have to borrow to meet living expenses rather than paying for them with a hospital salary.

Like many other policy debates, the debate over whether changes should be made in how medical school is paid for has positive and normative elements. By gathering data and using economic models, we can assess some of the quantitative claims made by each side in the debate: What role does tuition play in a student's decision about whether to attend medical school? Have tuition increases had a large or a small effect on the number of applications to medical school? How do changes in expected future incomes affect the decisions of medical students about which specialty to choose? These are all positive questions, so it is possible to formulate quantitative answers. Ultimately, though, this debate also has a normative element. For instance, some doctors, economists, and policymakers argue that it is important that people living in low-income or rural areas have improved access to health care, so they are willing to support policies that would redirect medical students away from specialized fields and toward primary care. Other doctors, economists, and policymakers believe that medical students who enter specialized fields make a larger contribution to society than do students who enter primary care. A disagreement of this type is unlikely to be resolved by building models and analyzing data because the issue involved is essentially normative.

In 2010, President Obama and Congress enacted the Patient Protection and Affordable Care Act, which made major changes to the U.S. health care system. Most of the changes were in effect by 2014. Additional changes are likely as policymakers grapple with the rapidly escalating costs of health care. Whether Congress and the president will enact policies intended to increase the number of family doctors remains to be seen.

Sources: Uwe E. Reinhardt, "Producing More Primary-Care Doctors," *New York Times*, June 10, 2011; Uwe E. Reinhardt, "The Debt of Medical Students," *New York Times*, September 14, 2012; and Peter B. Bach and Robert Kocher, "Why Medical School Should Be Free," *New York Times*, May 28, 2011.

Your Turn: Test your understanding by doing related problem 3.6 at the end of this chapter.

Microeconomics and Macroeconomics

4 LEARNING OBJECTIVE

Distinguish between microeconomics and macroeconomics.

Economic models can be used to analyze decision making in many areas. We group some of these areas together as *microeconomics* and others as *macroeconomics*. **Microeconomics** is the study of how households and firms make choices, how they interact in markets, and how the government attempts to influence their choices. Microeconomic issues include explaining how consumers react to changes in product prices and how firms decide what prices to charge for the products they sell. Microeconomics

Microeconomics The study of how households and firms make choices, how they interact in markets, and how the government attempts to influence their choices.

Macroeconomics The study of the economy as a whole, including topics such as inflation, unemployment, and economic growth.

also involves policy issues, such as analyzing the most efficient way to reduce teenage smoking, analyzing the costs and benefits of approving the sale of a new prescription drug, and analyzing the most efficient way to reduce air pollution.

Macroeconomics is the study of the economy as a whole, including topics such as inflation, unemployment, and economic growth. Macroeconomic issues include explaining why economies experience periods of recession and increasing unemployment and why, over the long run, some economies have grown much faster than others. Macroeconomics also involves policy issues, such as whether government intervention can reduce the severity of recessions.

The division between microeconomics and macroeconomics is not hard and fast. Many economic situations have *both* a microeconomic and a macroeconomic aspect. For example, the level of total investment by firms in new machinery and equipment helps to determine how rapidly the economy grows—which is a macroeconomic issue. But to understand how much new machinery and equipment firms decide to purchase, we have to analyze the incentives individual firms face—which is a microeconomic issue.

5 LEARNING OBJECTIVE

Define important economic terms.

A Preview of Important Economic Terms

Becoming familiar with certain important terms is a necessary step in learning economics. Here we provide a brief introduction to some of these terms.

- *Firm, company, or business.* A *firm* is an organization that produces a good or service. Most firms produce goods or services to earn profits, but there are also nonprofit firms, such as universities and some hospitals. Economists use the terms *firm, company,* and *business* interchangeably.

- *Entrepreneur.* An *entrepreneur* is someone who operates a business. In a market system, entrepreneurs decide what goods and services to produce and how to produce them. An entrepreneur starting a new business puts his or her own funds at risk. If an entrepreneur is wrong about what consumers want or about the best way to produce goods and services, his or her funds can be lost. Losing money in a failed business is not unusual: In the United States, about half of new businesses close within four years. Without entrepreneurs willing to assume the risk of starting and operating businesses, economic progress would be impossible in a market system.

- *Innovation.* There is a distinction between an *invention* and an *innovation.* An *invention* is a new good or a new process for making a good. An *innovation* is the practical application of an invention. (*Innovation* may also be used more broadly to refer to any significant improvement in a good or in the means of producing a good.) Much time often passes between the appearance of a new idea and its development for widespread use. For example, the Wright brothers first achieved self-propelled flight at Kitty Hawk, North Carolina, in 1903, but the Wright brothers' plane was very crude, and it wasn't until the introduction of the DC-3 by Douglas Aircraft in 1936 that regularly scheduled intercity airline flights became common in the United States. Similarly, the first digital electronic computer—the ENIAC—was developed in 1945, but the first IBM personal computer was not introduced until 1981, and widespread use of computers did not have a significant effect on the productivity of U.S. business until the 1990s.

- *Technology.* A firm's *technology* is the processes it uses to produce goods and services. In the economic sense, a firm's technology depends on many factors, such as the skill of its managers, the training of its workers, and the speed and efficiency of its machinery and equipment.

- *Goods. Goods* are tangible merchandise, such as books, computers, or Blu-ray players.

- *Services. Services* are activities done for others, such as providing haircuts or investment advice.

- *Revenue.* A firm's *revenue* is the total amount received for selling a good or service. We calculate it by multiplying the price per unit by the number of units sold.

- *Profit.* A firm's *profit* is the difference between its revenue and its costs. Economists distinguish between *accounting profit* and *economic profit*. In calculating accounting profit, we exclude the cost of some economic resources that the firm does not pay for explicitly. In calculating economic profit, we include the opportunity cost of all resources used by the firm. When we refer to *profit* in this text, we mean economic profit. It is important not to confuse *profit* with *revenue*.

- *Household.* A *household* consists of all persons occupying a home. Households are suppliers of factors of production—particularly labor—used by firms to make goods and services. Households also demand goods and services produced by firms and governments.

- *Factors of production, economic resources, or inputs.* Firms use *factors of production* to produce goods and services. The main factors of production are labor, capital, natural resources—including land—and entrepreneurial ability. Households earn income by supplying the factors of production to firms. Economists use the terms *factors of production, economic resources,* and *inputs* interchageably.

- *Capital.* In everyday speech, the word *capital* can refer to *financial capital* or to *physical capital*. Financial capital includes stocks and bonds issued by firms, bank accounts, and holdings of money. In economics, though, *capital* refers to physical capital, which includes manufactured goods that are used to produce other goods and services. Examples of physical capital are computers, factory buildings, machine tools, warehouses, and trucks. The total amount of physical capital available in a country is referred to as the country's *capital stock*.

- *Human capital.* *Human capital* refers to the accumulated training and skills that workers possess. For example, college-educated workers generally have more skills and are more productive than workers who have only high school degrees; therefore, college-educated workers have more human capital.

Continued

Economics in Your Life

Will There Be Plenty of Jobs Available in the Health Care Industry?

At the beginning of this chapter, we posed the question: "What is the basis for the forecasts on the availability of jobs in health care, and how reliable are the forecasts?" As the U.S. population increases and as the average age of the population rises, it seems likely that there will be an increase in the number of doctors, nurses, physician's assistants, and other health care workers. The U.S. Bureau of Labor Statistics (BLS) publishes the most widely used occupational forecasts. Economists at the BLS base these forecasts on economic models. The forecasts can be inaccurate, however. For example, in 1996, the BLS forecast that 93,485 physician's assistants would be employed in 2006, when in fact only 65,628 were. The BLS analyzes errors like these in attempting to improve its forecasts. So, it is likely that the BLS's forecasts will become more accurate over time, but it would be a mistake to expect the forecasts to be exact.

Conclusion

Economics is a group of useful ideas about how individuals make choices. Economists have put these ideas into practice by developing economic models. Consumers, business managers, and government policymakers use these models every day to help make choices. In this text, we explore many key economic models and give examples of how to apply them in the real world.

Reading newspapers and other periodicals is an important part of understanding the current business climate and learning how to apply economic concepts to a variety of real-world events. At the end of this chapter, you will see a two-page feature titled *An Inside Look*. This feature consists of an excerpt from an article that relates to the company or economic issue introduced at the start of the chapter and also to the concepts discussed in the chapter. A summary and an analysis with supporting graphs highlight the key economic points of the article. Read *An Inside Look* for a discussion of how technological changes, such as smartphones, affect how doctors provide health care. Test your understanding by answering the *Thinking Critically* questions.

FORBES

The Year 2020: The Doctor Will (NOT) See You Now!

It's the year 2020. 20/20, just like perfect vision.

And interestingly, it's also *your* vision. In today's world of health and wellness, computer-guided laser vision correction is so commonplace that eye glasses are hardly necessary and almost pure fashion. Except for the occasional "Google Glasses" that early innovators still wear as a badge of adoption.

The Exam Room of the Future

Today is the first time you've been to a doctor's office in two years. Yet, surprisingly, you're as compliant and up to date as can be. Over the past two years, you've had several interactions with your doctor including an ECG, simplified physical exam and evaluation of a sore throat. However, these evaluations were done from your home with one of the most essential components of care for both you and your physician—the smartphone. As you arrive, one of the first things you notice is that the waiting room is almost empty. Advances in digital appointments and off site care have changed the practice dynamics significantly. In fact, your family physician sees more patients virtually than in the real world. The digital receptionist acknowledges you by first name as you approach this holographic image. Face recognition has instantly identified you and a thermal scan has checked your body temperature to screen for the potential of any infectious conditions that would immediately shuttle you off to an isolation area.

You pick up an electronic tablet and have a seat in the specific color-coded, pod-like chair that the receptionist has indicated. There are some quick questions to answer on the tablet as electronic sensors built into the chair begin to analyze your weight, blood oxygen, and other key elements of your physiology. You're asked to do some basic tasks including standing, looking into a small scanner and to grasp two sensor handles. The analysis is compared directly with your electronic medical records and prompt questions about unusual changes or variations. Once the basic analysis has been completed, supplemental questions—culled from an extensive clinical database—are asked to preemptively identify health issues and problems that can be addressed much earlier.

You might be surprised to know that most of your "history and-physical" is now complete. An entire "healthprint" is on your physician's desktop. It contains a comprehensive physical exam that has been cross indexed against your past history and a large database of patients. Any outlying concerns can be addressed the good old-fashioned way. But leaving that up to the unpredictable and error-prone abilities of a nurse or doctor can be problematic!

"Looks like you're doing great!" Those are the first words you hear from an actual human—your doctor. And you're done.... But as you leave you can't stop and wonder if this "carwash" type doctor visit is sub-optimal. What happened to the face time and human component of good old-fashioned medicine?

Examining the Exam

Let's take a closer look at what just happened in the future:

- It took 17 minutes—from start to finish. It's effective *and* efficient.
- The analytical and diagnostic acumen of the technology is, in many respects, superior to the physical skill set of your doctor.
- The data used for diagnosis and therapeutic recommendations are always current and reflect the best and brightest thinking in medicine.
- The depth and breadth of the database used for predictive information is massive. No individual physician can ever have the experience, intuition or processing power to come close.
- The human touch is still there—it's just reserved for more specific and valuable use.

Healthcare is in a great state of transition now. Financial concerns, reimbursement and coverage, and an aging population will be powerful drivers of change. Technology will be a beacon of innovation that will help address many of these concerns without the compromise of care. The innovation, and the rate of change, is simply amazing and the future is looking very healthy indeed.

Source: John Nosta, "The Year 2020: The Doctor Will (NOT) See You Now!" *Forbes*, August 15, 2012.

Key Points in the Article

Advances in technology may change the way patients interact with their doctors in 2020. Today, many people visit a doctor's office for routine physical exams or treatment of conditions such as the flu. This article predicts that by the end of this decade, many medical evaluations will be performed via smartphone from the convenience of the patient's home. There will still be occasions when an actual visit to the doctor's office is necessary, so the doctor's office will not disappear, but it will be drastically transformed as a result of technology. These changes, including electronic evaluations and diagnoses based on extensive, current databases, not only will reduce the amount of time required for a typical doctor's appointment but may also dramatically improve the quality of analysis and level of care that patients receive.

Analyzing the News

a Advances in technology continue to change many facets of the economy, and the doctor's office is no exception. Economic incentives are changing for both doctors and patients. Granted, the author of the article is speculating as to how basic medical care will be handled by the end of this decade, but based on ongoing improvements in technology, his ideas read more like fact than fiction. Smartphone technology has improved greatly over the past few years, so it is not hard to imagine these devices playing an ever-increasing role in our everyday lives. Being able to have routine medical tests and diagnoses performed electronically via smartphone will save time and money for doctors, laboratories, and patients, thereby increasing efficiency and potentially reducing costs.

b Imagine a routine trip to the doctor's office taking 17 minutes—from start to finish—and happening only once every two years. No more taking off an entire day from work or school every time a minor ailment arises. (You may not be interested in this improvement now, but your professors and your future employer will appreciate it.) Lost time from work or school can have a negative effect on productivity, decreasing economic efficiency. One key to the scenario presented in the article is that efficiency will be improved without sacrificing quality. The author also argues that the quality of medical care will be enhanced as well. Should this outcome occur, the additional benefits received from this way of delivering medical care would seem to outweigh the additional costs, including having less personal interaction with the doctor.

c The health care industry is changing and, with the passage of the Affordable Care Act in 2010, will continue to change. The chapter opener discusses the increasing number of doctors leaving private practice to become salaried employees of hospitals because of changes in health care laws and financial concerns. Other factors that will significantly affect health care in the coming years and that may also be a reason for doctors choosing hospital employment are the aging population and the increasing number of people covered by health insurance. The figure below shows recent data on the number of people aged 65 and older, the number of uninsured people, and projections for 2020. These numbers indicate a significant increase in demand for health care services in the coming years. Technological innovations such as those discussed in the article could prove invaluable in efficiently providing quality medical care to this growing number of patients.

Thinking Critically

1. One key economic idea is that people respond to economic incentives. Explain how the improvements in technology discussed in the article, along with the expected increase in the demand for health care, may affect the incentives for doctors leaving private practice for employment in hospitals.

2. The article speculates that improvements in technology will increase efficiency in the health care industry without compromising the quality of customer care. Suppose you want to develop an economic model to analyze the relationship between the increased efficiency resulting from the changes in technology used in a doctor's office and the corresponding level of care patients receive. Use information from the article to explain the steps you would take to develop this model.

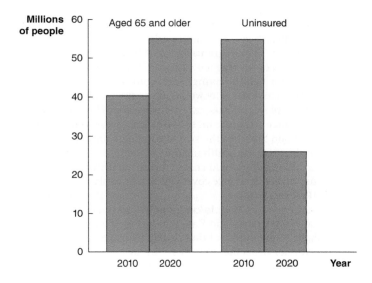

Technological innovations could help increase availability of health care to an aging population and the uninsured.

Data for people aged 65 and older and the uninsured are for 2010 and projected for 2020.

Source: U.S. Census Bureau and Congressional Budget Office.

Chapter Summary and Problems

Key Terms

Allocative efficiency	Economics	Market economy	Positive analysis
Centrally planned economy	Equity	Microeconomics	Productive efficiency
Economic model	Macroeconomics	Mixed economy	Scarcity
Economic variable	Marginal analysis	Normative analysis	Trade-off
	Market	Opportunity cost	Voluntary exchange

Three Key Economic Ideas

LEARNING OBJECTIVE: Explain these three key economic ideas: People are rational; people respond to economic incentives; and optimal decisions are made at the margin.

Summary

Economics is the study of the choices consumers, business managers, and government officials make to attain their goals, given their scarce resources. We must make choices because of **scarcity**, which means that although our wants are unlimited, the resources available to fulfill those wants are limited. Economists assume that people are rational in the sense that consumers and firms use all available information as they take actions intended to achieve their goals. Rational individuals weigh the benefits and costs of each action and choose an action only if the benefits outweigh the costs. Although people act from a variety of motives, ample evidence indicates that they respond to economic incentives. Economists use the word **marginal** to mean extra or additional. The optimal decision is to continue any activity up to the point where the marginal benefit equals the marginal cost.

Visit **www.myeconlab.com** to complete these exercises online and get instant feedback.

Review Questions

1.1 Briefly discuss each of the following economic ideas: People are rational, people respond to economic incentives, and optimal decisions are made at the margin.

1.2 What is scarcity? Why is scarcity central to the study of economics?

Problems and Applications

1.3 Do you agree with the following statement: "The problem with economics is that it assumes that consumers and firms always make the correct decisions. But we know that everyone makes mistakes."

1.4 According to the FBI Bank Crime Statistics, there were more than 5,000 bank robberies in the United States in 2012. The FBI claims that banks have allowed themselves to become easy targets by refusing to install clear acrylic partitions, called *bandit barriers*, that separate bank tellers from the public. According to a special agent with the FBI, "Bandit barriers are a great deterrent. We've talked to guys who rob banks, and as soon as they see a bandit barrier, they go find another bank." Despite this finding, many banks have been reluctant to install these barriers. Wouldn't banks have a strong incentive to install bandit barriers to deter robberies? Why, then, do so many banks not do so?

Sources: "FBI Bank Crime Statistics 2012," www.fbi.gov; and Richard Cowen, "FBI: Banks Are to Blame for Rise in Robberies," NorthJersey .com, March 10, 2009.

1.5 The grading system plays an important role in student learning. In their book *Effective Grading: A Tool for Learning and Assessment in College*, Barbara Walvoord and Virginia Anderson state that "grading infuses everything that happens in the classroom." They also argue that grading "needs to be acknowledged and managed from the first moment that an instructor begins planning a class."

a. How could the grading system a teacher uses affect the incentives of students to learn the course material?

b. If teachers put too little weight in the grading scale on a certain part of the course, such as readings outside the textbook, how might students respond?

c. Teachers often wish that students came to class prepared, having read the upcoming material. How could a teacher design the grading system to motivate students to come to class prepared?

Source: Barbara E. Walvoord and Virginia Johnson Anderson, *Effective Grading: A Tool for Learning and Assessment in College*, 2nd edition, San Francisco: Jossey-Bass, 2010, p. 1.

1.6 **[Related to the** Making the Connection: **Does Health Insurance Give People an Incentive to Become Obese?]** Many universities and corporations offer a health wellness program that helps their employees improve or maintain their health and get paid (a relatively small amount) for doing so. The programs vary but typically consist of employees completing a health assessment, receiving a program for healthy living, and monitoring their monthly health activities. Why would universities and corporations pay employees to take care of themselves? How does health insurance affect the incentive of employees to improve or maintain their health? Would a wellness program increase or decrease the health insurance premiums that an insurance company would charge the university or corporation to provide insurance coverage? Briefly explain.

1.7 **[Related to the** Making the Connection: **Does Health Insurance Give People an Incentive to Become Obese?]** Jay Bhattacharya and Kate Bundorf of Stanford University have found evidence that people who are obese and who work for firms that provide health insurance receive lower wages than workers at those firms who are not obese. At firms that do not provide health insurance, obese workers do not receive lower wages than workers who are not obese.

a. Why might firms that provide workers with health insurance pay a lower wage to obese workers than to workers who are not obese?

b. Is Bhattacharya and Bundorf's finding relevant to the question of whether health insurance provides people with an incentive to become obese? Briefly explain.

Source: Jay Bhattacharya and M. Kate Bundorf, "The Incidence of the Health Care Costs of Obesity," *Journal of Health Economics*, Vol. 28, No. 3, May 2009, pp. 649–658.

1.8 **[Related to** Solved Problem 1**]** In 2013, the president and chief executive officer of McDonald's, Don Thompson, said that McDonald's was considering serving breakfast all day, instead of stopping at 10:30 A.M. on weekdays and 11:00 A.M. on weekends. Several owners of McDonald's restaurants, however, point out that offering breakfast 24 hours a day presents two logistical problems: (1) Burgers and other meats need to be cooked at a higher temperature than eggs, so it would be difficult for employees to set the grill at the right temperature for both foods, and (2) scrambled eggs require employees to continually stir, while hamburgers don't require this attention. In addition, some customers might buy the cheaper breakfast rather than the more expensive lunch or dinner meals. If you were the president and chief executive officer of McDonald's, discuss how you would go about deciding whether to serve breakfast all day. Would your decision have to be all or nothing—either serve breakfast up to 10:30 A.M. or serve breakfast all day? Would you have to serve the entire breakfast menu all day?

Source: Susan Berfield and Leslie Patton, "What's So Hard About a 24/7 McMuffin?" *Bloomberg BusinessWeek*, May 6–12, 2013.

1.9 **[Related to** Solved Problem 1**]** Two students are discussing Solved Problem 1:

> **Joe:** I think the key additional information you need to know in deciding whether the doctor should keep the medical practice open 9 hours per day rather than 8 hours is the amount of profit she is currently making while being open

8 hours. Then, she can compare the profit earned from being open 9 hours with the profit earned from being open 8 hours. This information is more important than the additional revenue and additional cost of being open 1 more hour.

> **Jill:** Actually, Joe, knowing how much profits change when the medical practice stays open 1 more hour is exactly the same as knowing the additional revenue and the additional cost.

Briefly evaluate their discussion.

1.10 **[Related to** Solved Problem 1**]** Late in the semester, a friend tells you, "I was going to drop my psychology course so I could concentrate on my other courses, but I had already put so much time into the course that I decided not to drop it." What do you think of your friend's reasoning? Would it make a difference to your answer if your friend has to pass the psychology course at some point to graduate? Briefly explain.

1.11 In a paper written by Bentley College economists Patricia M. Flynn and Michael A. Quinn, the authors state:

> We find evidence that Economics is a good choice of major for those aspiring to become a CEO [chief executive officer]. When adjusting for size of the pool of graduates, those with undergraduate degrees in Economics are shown to have had a greater likelihood of becoming an S&P 500 CEO than any other major.

A list of famous economics majors published by Marietta College includes business leaders Warren Buffett, Donald Trump, Ted Turner, Diane von Furstenberg, Steve Ballmer, and Sam Walton, as well as former presidents George H.W. Bush, Gerald Ford, and Ronald Reagan. Why might studying economics be particularly good preparation for being the top manager of a corporation or a leader in government?

Sources: Patricia M. Flynn and Michael A. Quinn, "Economics: A Good Choice of Major for Future CEOs," *Social Science Research Network*, November 28, 2006; and *Famous Economics Majors*, Marietta College, Marietta, Ohio, May 15, 2012.

---

2   The Economic Problem That Every Society Must Solve

LEARNING OBJECTIVE: Discuss how an economy answers these questions: What goods and services will be produced? How will the goods and services be produced? Who will receive the goods and services produced?

Summary

Society faces **trade-offs**: Producing more of one good or service means producing less of another good or service. The **opportunity cost** of any activity—such as producing a good or service—is the highest-valued alternative that must be given up to engage in that activity. The choices of consumers, firms, and governments determine what goods and services will be produced. Firms choose how to produce the goods and services they sell. In the United States, who receives the goods and services produced depends largely on how income is distributed in the marketplace. In a **centrally planned economy**, most economic decisions are made by the government. In a **market economy**, most economic decisions are made by consumers and firms. Most economies, including that of the United States, are **mixed economies** in which most economic decisions are made by consumers and firms but in which the government also plays a significant role. There are two types of efficiency: productive efficiency and allocative efficiency. **Productive efficiency** occurs when a good or service is produced at the lowest possible cost. **Allocative efficiency** occurs when production

corresponds with consumer preferences. **Voluntary exchange** is a situation that occurs in markets when both the buyer and the seller of a product are made better off by the transaction. **Equity** is more difficult to define than efficiency, but it usually involves a fair distribution of economic benefits. Government policymakers often face a trade-off between equity and efficiency.

 Visit **www.myeconlab.com** to complete these exercises online and get instant feedback.

Review Questions

2.1 Why does scarcity imply that every society and every individual face trade-offs?

2.2 What are the three economic questions that every society must answer? Briefly discuss the differences in how centrally planned, market, and mixed economies answer these questions?

2.3 What is the difference between productive efficiency and allocative efficiency?

2.4 What is the difference between efficiency and equity? Why do government policymakers often face a trade-off between efficiency and equity?

Problems and Applications

2.5 When the price of Microsoft stock increased more than 27 percent in the first part of 2013, Bill Gates, who owns 436 million shares of Microsoft stock, once again became the world's richest person. Does Bill Gates face scarcity? Does everyone? Are there any exceptions?

Source: "Bill Gates Surpasses Carlos Slim to Become Richest Man in the World," Huffingtonpost.com, May 16, 2013.

2.6 Consider an organization that exists to help the poor. The members of the organization are discussing alternative methods of aiding the poor, when a proponent of one particular method asserts that: "If even one poor person is helped with this method, then all our time and money would have been worth it." If you were a member of the organization, how would you reply to this assertion?

2.7 In a market economy, why does a firm have a strong incentive to be productively efficient and allocatively efficient? What does the firm earn if it is productively and allocatively efficient, and what happens if it is not?

2.8 Would you expect new and better machinery and equipment to be adopted more rapidly in a market economy or in a centrally planned economy? Briefly explain.

2.9 Centrally planned economies have been less efficient than market economies.
  a. Has this difference in efficiency happened by chance, or is there some underlying reason?
  b. If market economies are more economically efficient than centrally planned economies, would there ever be a reason to prefer having a centrally planned economy rather than a market economy?

2.10 Would you expect a centrally planned economy to be better at productive efficiency or allocative efficiency? Briefly explain.

2.11 Leonard Fleck, a philosophy professor at Michigan State University, has written:

> When it comes to health care in America, we have limited resources for unlimited health care needs. We want everything contemporary medical technology can offer that will improve the length or quality of our lives as we age. But as presently healthy taxpayers, we want costs controlled.

Why is it necessary for all economic systems to limit services such as health care? How does a market system prevent people from getting as many goods and services as they want?

Source: Leonard Fleck, *Just Caring: Health Care Rationing and Democratic Deliberation*, New York: Oxford University Press, 2009.

2.12 Suppose that your local police department recovers 100 tickets to a big NASCAR race in a drug raid. Police decide to distribute the tickets to residents and announce that tickets will be given away at 10 A.M. Monday at City Hall.
  a. What groups of people will be most likely to try to get the tickets? Think of specific examples and then generalize.
  b. What is the opportunity cost of distributing the tickets this way?
  c. Productive efficiency occurs when a good or service (such as the distribution of tickets) is produced at the lowest possible cost. Is this an efficient way to distribute the tickets? If possible, think of a more efficient method of distributing the tickets.
  d. Is this an equitable way to distribute the tickets? Explain.

 Economic Models

LEARNING OBJECTIVE: Understand the role of models in economic analysis.

Summary

An **economic variable** is something measurable that can have different values, such as the wages of software programmers. Economists rely on economic models when they apply economic ideas to real-world problems. **Economic models** are simplified versions of reality used to analyze real-world economic situations. Economists accept and use an economic model if it leads to hypotheses that are confirmed by statistical analysis. In many cases, the acceptance is tentative, however, pending the gathering of new data or further statistical analysis. Economics is a *social science* because it applies the scientific method to the study of the interactions among individuals. Economics is concerned with positive analysis rather than normative analysis. **Positive analysis** is concerned with what is. **Normative analysis** is concerned with what ought to be. As a social science, economics considers human behavior in every context of decision making, not just in business.

Visit **www.myeconlab.com** to complete these exercises online and get instant feedback.

Review Questions

3.1 Why do economists use models? How are economic data used to test models?

3.2 Describe the five steps by which economists arrive at a useful economic model.

3.3 What is the difference between normative analysis and positive analysis? Is economics concerned mainly with normative analysis or positive analysis? Briefly explain.

Problems and Applications

3.4 Suppose an economist develops an economic model and finds that "it works great in theory, but it fails in practice." What should the economist do next?

3.5 Dr. Strangelove's theory is that the price of mushrooms is determined by the activity of subatomic particles that exist in another universe parallel to ours. When the subatomic particles are emitted in profusion, the price of mushrooms is high. When subatomic particle emissions are low, the price of mushrooms is also low. How would you go about testing Dr. Strangelove's theory? Discuss whether this theory is useful.

3.6 [Related to the Making the Connection: **Should Medical School Be Free?]** This feature explains that there are both positive and normative elements to the debate over whether medical schools should charge tuition and whether hospitals should continue to pay residents who pursue primary care but not residents who specialize. What economic statistics would be most useful in evaluating the positive elements in this debate? Assuming that these statistics are available or could be gathered, are they likely to resolve the normative issues in this debate?

3.7 [Related to the Chapter Opener**]** In recent years, many doctors have decided to give up running their private practices as small businesses and have become salaried employees of hospitals.
  a. What important differences exist between doctors' private practices and other small businesses, such as restaurants and hardware stores?
  b. How have the economic incentives a doctor faces when considering whether to operate a private practice or become a salaried employee of a hospital changed over the years?

3.8 [Related to the Chapter Opener**]** According to an article in the *New York Times*, hospitals sometimes complain that doctors do not work as hard when they become hospital employees as they do when they operate a private practice. How do the economic incentives a doctor faces to work hard change when the doctor closes a private practice and becomes a salaried employee of a hospital?

Source: Julie Crewell and Reed Abelson, "A Hospital War Reflects a Bind for Doctors in the U.S.," *New York Times*, November 30, 2012.

3.9 [Related to the Don't Let This Happen to You**]** Explain which of the following statements represent positive analysis and which represent normative analysis.
  a. A 50-cent-per-pack tax on cigarettes will lead to a 12 percent reduction in smoking by teenagers.
  b. The federal government should spend more on AIDS research.
  c. Rising wheat prices will increase bread prices.
  d. The price of coffee at Starbucks is too high.

3.10 In the United States, to receive a medical license, a doctor must complete a residency program at a hospital. Hospitals are not free to expand their residency programs in a particular medical specialty without approval from a Residency Review Committee (RRC), which is made up of physicians in that specialty. A hospital that does not abide by the rulings of the RRC runs the risk of losing its accreditation from the Accreditation Council for Graduate Medical Education (ACGME). The ACGME and the RRCs argue that this system makes it possible to ensure that residency programs do not expand to the point where they are not providing residents with high-quality training.
  a. How does this system help protect consumers?
  b. How might this system protect the financial interests of doctors more than the well-being of consumers?
  c. Briefly discuss whether you consider this system to be a good one. Is your conclusion an example of normative economics or of positive economics? Briefly explain.

Sources: Brian Palmer, "We Need More Doctors, Stat!" *Slate*, June 27, 2011; and Sean Nicholson, "Barriers to Entering Medical Specialties," Wharton School, September 2003.

Microeconomics and Macroeconomics
LEARNING OBJECTIVE: Distinguish between microeconomics and macroeconomics.

Summary

Microeconomics is the study of how households and firms make choices, how they interact in markets, and how the government attempts to influence their choices. **Macroeconomics** is the study of the economy as a whole, including topics such as inflation, unemployment, and economic growth.

Visit **www.myeconlab.com** to complete these exercises online and get instant feedback.

Review Question

4.1 Briefly discuss the difference between microeconomics and macroeconomics.

4.2 Is every economic issue either strictly microeconomic or strictly macroeconomic? Briefly explain.

Problems and Applications

4.3 Briefly explain whether each of the following is primarily a microeconomic issue or a macroeconomic issue.
  a. The effect of higher cigarette taxes on the quantity of cigarettes sold.
  b. The effect of higher income taxes on the total amount of consumer spending.
  c. The reasons the economies of East Asian countries grow faster than the economies of sub-Saharan African countries.
  d. The reasons for low rates of profit in the airline industry.

4.4 Briefly explain whether you agree with the following assertion: "Microeconomics is concerned with things that happen in one particular place, such as the unemployment rate in one city. In contrast, macroeconomics is concerned with things that affect the country as a whole, such as how the rate of teenage smoking in the United States would be affected by an increase in the tax on cigarettes."

A Preview of Important Economic Terms
LEARNING OBJECTIVE: Define important economic terms.

Summary

Becoming familiar with important terms is a necessary step in learning economics. These important economic terms include

capital, entrepreneur, factors of production, firm, goods, household, human capital, innovation, profit, revenue, services, and *technology.*

Appendix

Using Graphs and Formulas

Graphs are used to illustrate key economic ideas. Graphs appear not just in economics textbooks but also on Web sites and in newspaper and magazine articles that discuss events in business and economics. Why the heavy use of graphs? Because they serve two useful purposes: (1) They simplify economic ideas, and (2) they make the ideas more concrete so they can be applied to real-world problems. Economic and business issues can be complicated, but a graph can help cut through complications and highlight the key relationships needed to understand the issue. In that sense, a graph can be like a street map.

Suppose you take a bus to New York City to see the Empire State Building. After arriving at the Port Authority Bus Terminal, you will probably use a map similar to the one shown here to find your way to the Empire State Building.

Maps are very familiar to just about everyone, so we don't usually think of them as being simplified versions of reality, but they are. This map does not show much more than the streets in this part of New York City and some of the most important buildings. The names, addresses, and telephone numbers of the people who live and work in the area aren't given. Almost none of the stores and buildings those people work and live in are shown either. The map doesn't indicate which streets allow curbside parking and which don't. In fact, the map shows almost nothing about the messy reality of life in this section of New York City, except how the streets are laid out, which is the essential information you need to get from the Port Authority Bus Terminal to the Empire State Building.

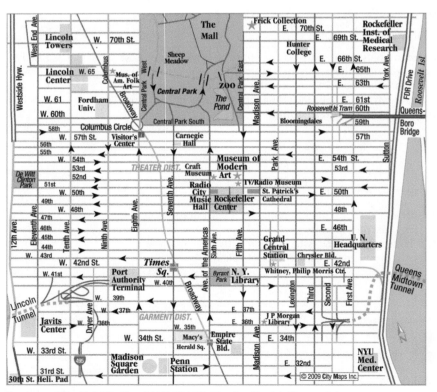

Street map of New York City. Copyright © 2011 City Maps Inc. Reprinted by permission.

Think about someone who says, "I know how to get around in the city, but I just can't figure out how to read a map." It certainly is possible to find your destination in a city without a map, but it's a lot easier with one. The same is true of using graphs in economics. It is possible to arrive at a solution to a real-world problem in economics and business without using graphs, but it is usually a lot easier if you use them.

Often, the difficulty students have with graphs and formulas is a lack of familiarity. With practice, all the graphs and formulas in this text will become familiar to you. Once you are familiar with them, you will be able to use them to analyze problems that would otherwise seem very difficult. What follows is a brief review of how graphs and formulas are used.

Graphs of One Variable

Figure A.1 displays values for *market shares* in the U.S. automobile market, using two common types of graphs. Market shares show the percentage of industry sales accounted for by different firms. In this case, the information is for groups of firms: the "Big Three"—Ford, General Motors, and Chrysler—as well as Japanese, European, and Korean firms. Panel (a) displays the information on market shares as a *bar graph*, where the market share of each group of firms is represented by the height of its bar. Panel (b) displays the same information as a *pie chart*, where the market share of each group of firms is represented by the size of its slice of the pie.

Information on economic variables is also often displayed in *time-series graphs*. Time-series graphs are displayed on a coordinate grid. In a coordinate grid, we can measure the value of one variable along the vertical axis (or *y*-axis) and the value of another variable along the horizontal axis (or *x*-axis). The point where the vertical axis intersects the horizontal axis is called the *origin*. At the origin, the value of both variables is zero. The points on a coordinate grid represent values of the two variables. In Figure A.2, we measure the number of automobiles and trucks sold worldwide by Ford Motor Company on the vertical axis, and we measure time on the horizontal axis. In time-series graphs, the height of the line at each date shows the value of the variable measured on the vertical axis. Both panels of Figure 2 show Ford's worldwide sales during each year from 2001 to 2012. The difference between panel (a) and panel (b) illustrates the importance of the scale used in a time-series graph. In panel (a), the vertical axis starts at 0 and the distance between each value shown is the same. In this panel, the decline in

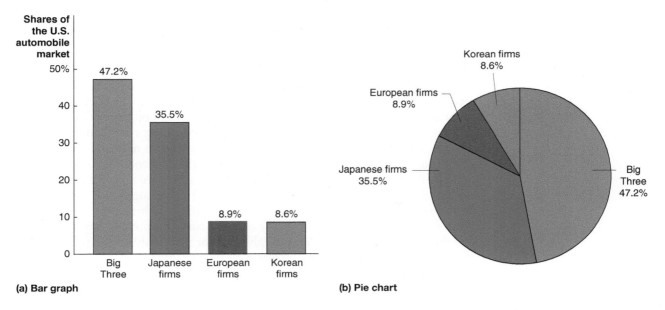

(a) Bar graph

(b) Pie chart

Figure A.1   **Bar Graphs and Pie Charts**

Values for an economic variable are often displayed as a bar graph or a pie chart. In this case, panel (a) shows market share data for the U.S. automobile industry as a bar graph, where the market share of each group of firms is represented by the height of its bar. Panel (b) displays the same information as a pie chart, where the market share of each group of firms is represented by the size of its slice of the pie. **Source:** "Auto Sales," *Wall Street Journal*, May 1, 2013.

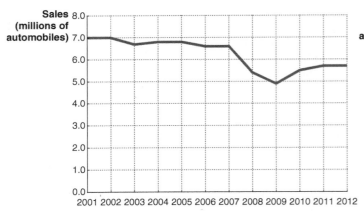

(a) Time-series graph where the scale is not truncated

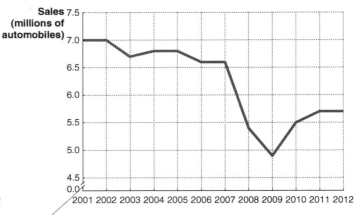

The slashes (//) indicate that the scale on the vertical axis is truncated, which means that some numbers are omitted. The numbers on the vertical axis jump from 0 to 4.5.

(b) Time-series graph with truncated scale

Figure A.2   Time-Series Graphs

Both panels present time-series graphs of Ford Motor Company's worldwide sales during each year from 2001 to 2012. In panel (a), the vertical axis starts at 0 and the distance between each pair of values shown is the same. In panel (b), the scale on the vertical axis is truncated, which means that although it starts at zero, it then jumps to 4.5 million. As a result, the fluctuations in Ford's sales appear smaller in panel (a) than in panel (b).

Source: Ford Motor Company, *Annual Report*, various years.

Ford's sales during 2008 and 2009 appears relatively small. In panel (b), the scale on the vertical axis is truncated, which means that although it starts at zero, it jumps to 4.5 million. As a result, the distance on the vertical axis from 0 to 4.5 million is much smaller than the distance from 4.5 million to 5.0 million. The slashes (//) near the bottom of the axis indicate that the scale is truncated. In panel (b), the decline in Ford's sales during 2008 and 2009 appears much larger than in panel (a). (Technically, the horizontal axis in both panels is also truncated because we start with 2001, not 0.)

Graphs of Two Variables

We often use graphs to show the relationship between two variables. Suppose you are interested in the relationship between the price of a pepperoni pizza and the quantity of pizzas sold per week in the small town of Bryan, Texas. A graph showing the relationship between the price of a good and the quantity of the good demanded at each price is called a *demand curve*. (As we will discuss later, in drawing a demand curve for a good, we have to hold constant any variables other than price that might affect the willingness of consumers to buy the good.) Figure A.3 shows the data collected on price and quantity. The figure shows a two-dimensional grid on which we measure the price of pizza along the *y*-axis and the quantity of pizza sold per week along the *x*-axis. Each point on the grid represents one of the price and quantity combinations listed in the table. We can connect the points to form the demand curve for pizza in Bryan, Texas. Notice that the scales on both axes in the graph are truncated. In this case, truncating the axes allows the graph to illustrate more clearly the relationship between price and quantity by excluding low prices and quantities.

Slopes of Lines

Once you have plotted the data in Figure A.3, you may be interested in how much the quantity of pizza sold increases as the price decreases. The *slope* of a line tells us how much the variable we are measuring on the *y*-axis changes as the variable we are measuring on the *x*-axis changes. We can use the Greek letter delta (Δ) to stand for the

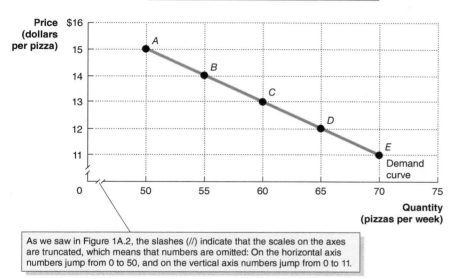

Price (dollars per pizza)	Quantity (pizzas per week)	Points
$15	50	A
14	55	B
13	60	C
12	65	D
11	70	E

As we saw in Figure 1A.2, the slashes (//) indicate that the scales on the axes are truncated, which means that numbers are omitted: On the horizontal axis numbers jump from 0 to 50, and on the vertical axis numbers jump from 0 to 11.

Figure A.3

Plotting Price and Quantity Points in a Graph

The figure shows a two-dimensional grid on which we measure the price of pizza along the vertical axis (or *y*-axis) and the quantity of pizza sold per week along the horizontal axis (or *x*-axis). Each point on the grid represents one of the price and quantity combinations listed in the table. By connecting the points with a line, we can better illustrate the relationship between the two variables.

change in a variable. The slope is sometimes referred to as the rise over the run. So, we have several ways of expressing slope:

$$\text{Slope} = \frac{\text{Change in value on the vertical axis}}{\text{Change in value on the horizontal axis}} = \frac{\Delta y}{\Delta x} = \frac{\text{Rise}}{\text{Run}}.$$

Figure A.4 reproduces the graph from Figure A.3. Because the slope of a straight line is the same at any point, we can use any two points in the figure to calculate the slope of the line. For example, when the price of pizza decreases from $14 to $12, the quantity of pizza sold increases from 55 per week to 65 per week. Therefore, the slope is:

$$\text{Slope} = \frac{\Delta \text{Price of pizza}}{\Delta \text{Quantity of pizza}} = \frac{(\$12 - \$14)}{(65 - 55)} = \frac{-2}{10} = -0.2.$$

The slope of this line shows us how responsive consumers in Bryan, Texas, are to changes in the price of pizza. The larger the value of the slope (ignoring the negative sign), the steeper the line will be, which indicates that not many additional pizzas are sold when the price falls. The smaller the value of the slope, the flatter the line will be, which indicates a greater increase in pizzas sold when the price falls.

Taking into Account More Than Two Variables on a Graph

The demand curve graph in Figure A.4 shows the relationship between the price of pizza and the quantity of pizza demanded, but we know that the quantity of any good demanded depends on more than just the price of the good. For example, the quantity of pizza demanded in a given week in Bryan, Texas, can be affected by other variables—the price of hamburgers, whether an advertising campaign by local pizza parlors has begun that week, and so on. Allowing the values of any other variables to change will cause the position of the demand curve in the graph to change.

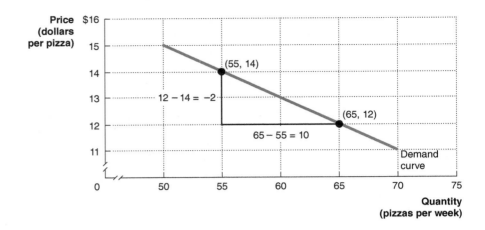

Figure A.4

Calculating the Slope of a Line

We can calculate the slope of a line as the change in the value of the variable on the y-axis divided by the change in the value of the variable on the x-axis. Because the slope of a straight line is constant, we can use any two points in the figure to calculate the slope of the line. For example, when the price of pizza decreases from $14 to $12, the quantity of pizza demanded increases from 55 per week to 65 per week. So, the slope of this line equals −2 divided by 10, or −0.2.

Suppose that the demand curve in Figure A.4 were drawn holding the price of hamburgers constant, at $1.50. If the price of hamburgers rises to $2.00, some consumers will switch from buying hamburgers to buying pizza, and more pizzas will be demanded at every price. The result on the graph will be to shift the line representing the demand curve to the right. Similarly, if the price of hamburgers falls from $1.50 to $1.00, some consumers will switch from buying pizza to buying hamburgers, and fewer pizzas will be demanded at every price. The result on the graph will be to shift the line representing the demand curve to the left.

The table in Figure A.5 shows the effect of a change in the price of hamburgers on the quantity of pizza demanded. On the graph, suppose that at first we are on the line labeled Demand curve₁. If the price of pizza is $14 (point A), an increase in the price of

Figure A.5

Showing Three Variables on a Graph

The demand curve for pizza shows the relationship between the price of pizzas and the quantity of pizzas demanded, *holding constant other factors that might affect the willingness of consumers to buy pizza.* If the price of pizza is $14 (point A), an increase in the price of hamburgers from $1.50 to $2.00 increases the quantity of pizzas demanded from 55 to 60 per week (point B) and shifts us to Demand curve₂. Or, if we start on Demand curve₁ and the price of pizza is $12 (point C), a decrease in the price of hamburgers from $1.50 to $1.00 decreases the quantity of pizza demanded from 65 to 60 per week (point D) and shifts us to Demand curve₃.

	Quantity (pizzas per week)		
Price (dollars per pizza)	When the Price of Hamburgers = $1.00	When the Price of Hamburgers = $1.50	When the Price of Hamburgers = $2.00
$15	45	50	55
14	50	55	60
13	55	60	65
12	60	65	70
11	65	70	75

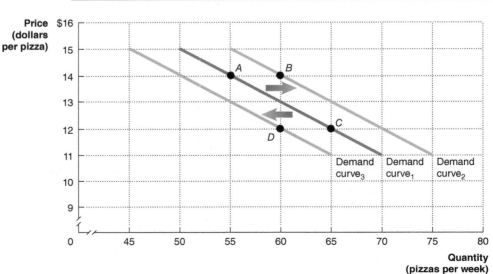

hamburgers from $1.50 to $2.00 increases the quantity of pizzas demanded from 55 to 60 per week (point *B*) and shifts us to Demand curve₂. Or, if we start on Demand curve₁ and the price of pizza is $12 (point *C*), a decrease in the price of hamburgers from $1.50 to $1.00 decreases the quantity of pizzas demanded from 65 to 60 per week (point *D*) and shifts us to Demand curve₃. By shifting the demand curve, we have taken into account the effect of changes in the value of a third variable—the price of hamburgers. We will use this technique of shifting curves to allow for the effects of additional variables many times in this text.

Positive and Negative Relationships

We can use graphs to show the relationships between any two variables. Sometimes the relationship between the variables is *negative*, meaning that as one variable increases in value, the other variable decreases in value. This was the case with the price of pizza and the quantity of pizzas demanded. The relationship between two variables can also be *positive*, meaning that the values of both variables increase or decrease together. For example, when the level of total income—or *disposable personal income*—received by households in the United States increases, the level of total *consumption spending*, which is spending by households on goods and services, also increases. The table in Figure A.6 shows the values (in billions of dollars) for income and consumption spending for 2009–2012. The graph plots the data from the table, with disposable personal income measured along the horizontal axis and consumption spending measured along the vertical axis. Notice that the points for 2010 and 2011 do not all fall exactly on the line. To examine the relationship between two variables, economists often use the straight line that best fits the data.

Determining Cause and Effect

When we graph the relationship between two variables, we usually want to draw conclusions about whether changes in one variable are causing changes in the other variable. Doing so can, however, lead to mistakes. Suppose you graph over the course of a year the number of homes in a neighborhood that have a fire burning in the fireplace and the number of leaves on trees in the neighborhood. You would get a relationship like

Year	Disposable Personal Income (billions of dollars)	Consumption Spending (billions of dollars)
2009	$10,722	$9,846
2010	11,127	10,216
2011	11,549	10,729
2012	11,931	11,120

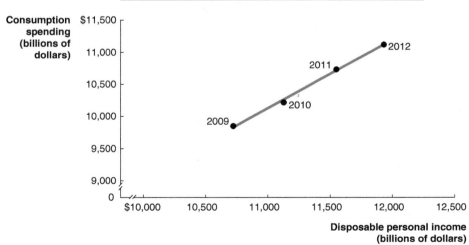

Figure A.6

Graphing the Positive Relationship between Income and Consumption

In a positive relationship between two economic variables, as one variable increases, the other variable also increases. This figure shows the positive relationship between disposable personal income and consumption spending. As disposable personal income in the United States has increased, so has consumption spending.
Source: U.S. Department of Commerce, Bureau of Economic Analysis.

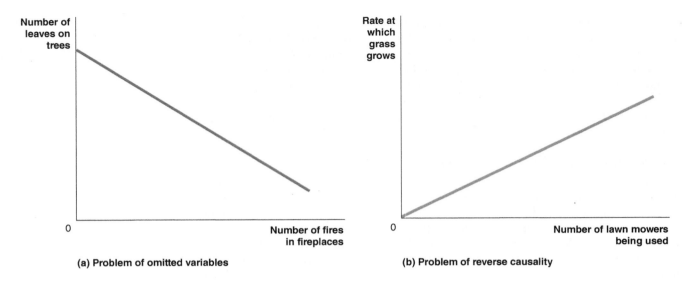

(a) Problem of omitted variables

(b) Problem of reverse causality

Figure A.7   Determining Cause and Effect

Using graphs to draw conclusions about cause and effect can be hazardous. In panel (a), we see that there are fewer leaves on the trees in a neighborhood when many homes have fires burning in their fireplaces. We cannot draw the conclusion that using fireplaces causes the leaves to fall because we have an *omitted* *variable*—the season of the year. In panel (b), we see that more lawn mowers are used in a neighborhood during times when the grass grows rapidly and fewer lawn mowers are used when the grass grows slowly. Concluding that using lawn mowers *causes* the grass to grow faster would be making the error of *reverse causality*.

that shown in panel (a) of Figure A.7: The more fireplaces in use in the neighborhood, the fewer leaves the trees have. Can we draw the conclusion from this graph that using a fireplace causes trees to lose their leaves? We know, of course, that such a conclusion would be incorrect. In spring and summer, there are relatively few fireplaces being used, and the trees are full of leaves. In the fall, as trees begin to lose their leaves, fireplaces are used more frequently. And in winter, many fireplaces are being used and many trees have lost all their leaves. The reason that the graph in Figure A.7 is misleading about cause and effect is that there is obviously an *omitted variable* in the analysis—the season of the year. An omitted variable is one that affects other variables, and its omission can lead to false conclusions about cause and effect.

Although in our example the omitted variable is obvious, there are many debates about cause and effect where the existence of an omitted variable has not been clear. For instance, it has been known for many years that people who smoke cigarettes suffer from higher rates of lung cancer than do nonsmokers. For some time, tobacco companies and some scientists argued that there was an omitted variable—perhaps a failure to exercise or a poor diet—that made some people more likely to smoke and more likely to develop lung cancer. If this omitted variable existed, then the finding that smokers were more likely to develop lung cancer would not have been evidence that smoking *caused* lung cancer. In this case, however, nearly all scientists eventually concluded that the omitted variable did not exist and that, in fact, smoking does cause lung cancer.

A related problem in determining cause and effect is known as *reverse causality*. The error of reverse causality occurs when we conclude that changes in variable X cause changes in variable Y when, in fact, it is actually changes in variable Y that cause changes in variable X. For example, panel (b) of Figure A.7 plots the number of lawn mowers being used in a neighborhood against the rate at which grass on lawns in the neighborhood is growing. We could conclude from this graph that using lawn mowers *causes* the grass to grow faster. We know, however, that in reality, the causality is in the other direction. Rapidly growing grass during the spring and summer causes the increased use of lawn mowers. Slowly growing grass in the fall or winter or during periods of low rainfall causes the decreased use of lawn mowers.

Once again, in our example, the potential error of reverse causality is obvious. In many economic debates, however, cause and effect can be more difficult to determine.

For example, changes in the money supply, or the total amount of money in the economy, tend to occur at the same time as changes in the total amount of income people in the economy earn. A famous debate in economics was about whether the changes in the money supply caused the changes in total income or whether the changes in total income caused the changes in the money supply. Each side in the debate accused the other side of committing the error of reverse causality.

Are Graphs of Economic Relationships Always Straight Lines?

The graphs of relationships between two economic variables that we have drawn so far have been straight lines. The relationship between two variables is *linear* when it can be represented by a straight line. Few economic relationships are actually linear. For example, if we carefully plot data on the price of a product and the quantity demanded at each price, holding constant other variables that affect the quantity demanded, we will usually find a curved—or *nonlinear*—relationship rather than a linear relationship. In practice, however, it is often useful to approximate a nonlinear relationship with a linear relationship. If the relationship is reasonably close to being linear, the analysis is not significantly affected. In addition, it is easier to calculate the slope of a straight line, and it is also easier to calculate the area under a straight line. So, in this text, we often assume that the relationship between two economic variables is linear, even when we know that this assumption is not precisely correct.

Slopes of Nonlinear Curves

In some situations, we need to take into account the nonlinear nature of an economic relationship. For example, panel (a) of Figure A.8 shows the hypothetical relationship between Apple's total cost of producing iPhones and the quantity of iPhones produced. The relationship is curved rather than linear. In this case, the cost of production is increasing at an increasing rate, which often happens in manufacturing. In other words, as we move up the curve, its slope becomes larger. (Remember that with a straight line, the slope is always constant.) To see why, first remember that we calculate the slope of a curve by dividing the change in the variable on the y-axis by the change in the variable on the x-axis. As we move from point A to point B, the quantity produced increases by 1 million iPhones, while the total cost of production increases by $50 million. Farther up the curve, as we move from point C to point D, the change in quantity is the same—1 million iPhones—but the change in the total cost of production is now much larger—$250 million. Because the change in the y variable has increased, while the change in the x variable has remained the same, we know that the slope has increased.

To measure the slope of a nonlinear curve at a particular point, we measure the slope of the line that is tangent to that curve at that point. This tangent line will touch the curve only at that point. We can measure the slope of the tangent line just as we would measure the slope of any other straight line. In panel (b), the tangent line at point B has a slope equal to:

$$\frac{\Delta \text{Cost}}{\Delta \text{Quantity}} = \frac{75}{1} = 75.$$

The tangent line at point C has a slope equal to:

$$\frac{\Delta \text{Cost}}{\Delta \text{Quantity}} = \frac{150}{1} = 150.$$

Once again, we see that the slope of the curve is larger at point C than at point B.

Formulas

We have just seen that graphs are an important economic tool. In this section, we will review several useful formulas and show how to use them to summarize data and to calculate important relationships.

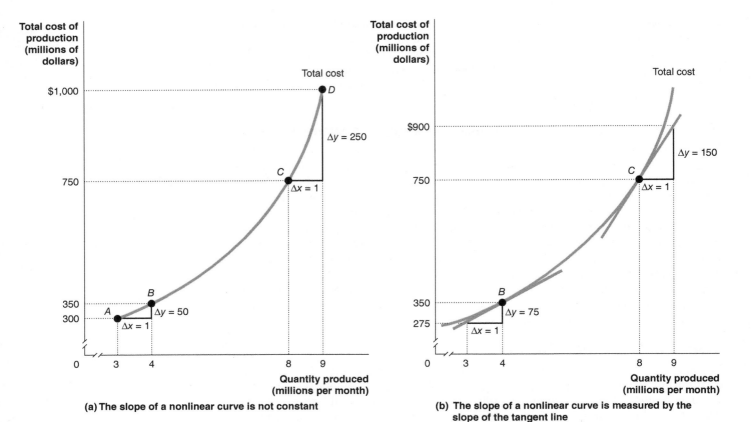

Figure A.8   The Slope of a Nonlinear Curve

The relationship between the quantity of iPhones produced and the total cost of production is curved rather than linear. In panel (a), when we move from point *A* to point *B*, the quantity produced increases by 1 million iPhones, while the total cost of production increases by $50 million. Farther up the curve, as we move from point *C* to point *D*, the change in quantity is the same—1 million iPhones— but the change in the total cost of production is now much larger—$250 million.

Because the change in the *y* variable has increased, while the change in the *x* variable has remained the same, we know that the slope has increased. In panel (b), we measure the slope of the curve at a particular point by calculating the slope of the tangent line at that point. The slope of the tangent line at point *B* is 75, and the slope of the tangent line at point *C* is 150.

Formula for a Percentage Change

One important formula is the percentage change. The *percentage change* is the change in some economic variable, usually from one period to the next, expressed as a percentage. A key macroeconomic measure is the real gross domestic product (GDP). GDP is the value of all the final goods and services produced in a country during a year. "Real" GDP is corrected for the effects of inflation. When economists say that the U.S. economy grew 2.8 percent during 2012, they mean that real GDP was 2.8 percent higher in 2012 than it was in 2011. The formula for making this calculation is:

$$\left(\frac{GDP_{2012} - GDP_{2011}}{GDP_{2011}} \right) \times 100,$$

or, more generally, for any two periods:

$$\text{Percentage change} = \left(\frac{\text{Value in the second period} - \text{Value in the first period}}{\text{Value in the first period}} \right) \times 100.$$

In this case, real GDP was $15,052 billion in 2011 and $15,471 billion in 2012. So, the growth rate of the U.S. economy during 2012 was:

$$\left(\frac{\$15,471 - \$15,052}{\$15,052} \right) \times 100 = 2.8\%.$$

Notice that it doesn't matter that in using the formula, we ignored the fact that GDP is measured in billions of dollars. In fact, when calculating percentage changes, *the units don't matter*. The percentage increase from $15,052 billion to $15,471 billion is exactly the same as the percentage increase from $15,052 to $15,471.

Formulas for the Areas of a Rectangle and a Triangle

Areas that form rectangles and triangles on graphs can have important economic meaning. For example, Figure A.9 shows the demand curve for Pepsi. Suppose that the price is currently $2.00 and that 125,000 bottles of Pepsi are sold at that price. A firm's *total revenue* is equal to the amount it receives from selling its product, or the quantity sold multiplied by the price. In this case, total revenue will equal 125,000 bottles times $2.00 per bottle, or $250,000.

The formula for the area of a rectangle is:

$$\text{Area of a rectangle} = \text{Base} \times \text{Height}.$$

In Figure A.9, the shaded rectangle also represents the firm's total revenue because its area is given by the base of 125,000 bottles multiplied by the price of $2.00 per bottle.

Areas that are triangles can also have economic significance. The formula for the area of a triangle is:

$$\text{Area of a triangle} = \frac{1}{2} \times \text{Base} \times \text{Height}.$$

The shaded area in Figure A.10 is a triangle. The base equals 150,000 − 125,000, or 25,000. Its height equals $2.00 − $1.50, or $0.50. Therefore, its area equals 1/2 × 25,000 × $0.50, or $6,250. Notice that the shaded area is a triangle only if the demand curve is a straight line, or linear. Not all demand curves are linear. However, the formula for the area of a triangle will usually still give a good approximation, even if the demand curve is not linear.

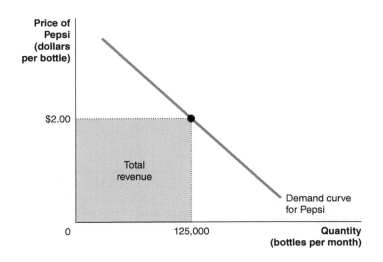

Figure A.9

Showing a Firm's Total Revenue on a Graph

The area of a rectangle is equal to its base multiplied by its height. Total revenue is equal to quantity multiplied by price. Here, total revenue is equal to the quantity of 125,000 bottles times the price of $2.00 per bottle, or $250,000. The area of the shaded rectangle shows the firm's total revenue.

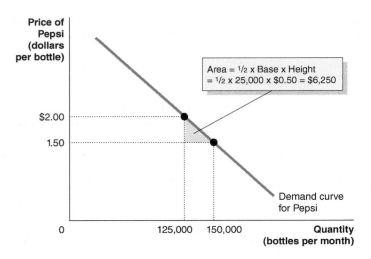

Figure A.10

The Area of a Triangle

The area of a triangle is equal to 1/2 multiplied by its base multiplied by its height. The area of the shaded triangle has a base equal to 150,000 − 125,000, or 25,000, and a height equal to $2.00 − $1.50, or $0.50. Therefore, its area is equal to 1/2 × 25,000 × $0.50, or $6,250.

Summary of Using Formulas

Whenever you use a formula, you should follow these steps:

1. Make sure you understand the economic concept the formula represents.
2. Make sure you are using the correct formula for the problem you are solving.
3. Make sure the number you calculate using the formula is economically reasonable. For example, if you are using a formula to calculate a firm's revenue and your answer is a negative number, you know you made a mistake somewhere.

Using Graphs and Formulas

LEARNING OBJECTIVE: Review the use of graphs and formulas.

Visit www.myeconlab.com to complete these exercises online and get instant feedback.

Problems and Applications

A.1 The following table shows the relationship between the price of custard pies and the number of pies Jacob buys per week:

Price (dollars per pie)	Quantity of pies	Week
$3.00	6	July 2
2.00	7	July 9
5.00	4	July 16
6.00	3	July 23
1.00	8	July 30
4.00	5	August 6

a. Is the relationship between the price of pies and the number of pies Jacob buys a positive relationship or a negative relationship?

b. Plot the data from the table on a graph similar to Figure A.3. Draw a straight line that best fits the points.

c. Calculate the slope of the line.

A.2 The following table gives information on the quantity of glasses of lemonade demanded on sunny and overcast days:

Price (dollars per glass)	Quantity (glasses of lemonade per day)	Weather
$0.80	30	Sunny
0.80	10	Overcast
0.70	40	Sunny
0.70	20	Overcast
0.60	50	Sunny
0.60	30	Overcast
0.50	60	Sunny
0.50	40	Overcast

Plot the data from the table on a graph similar to Figure A.5. Draw two straight lines representing the two demand curves—one for sunny days and one for overcast days.

A.3 Using the information in Figure A.2, calculate the percentage change in Ford's auto sales from one year to the next. During which year did sales fall at the highest rate?

A.4 Real GDP in 2008 was $14,834 billion. Real GDP in 2009 was $14,418 billion. What was the percentage change in real GDP from 2008 to 2009. What do economists call the percentage change in real GDP from one year to the next?

A.5 Assume that the demand curve for Pepsi passes through the following two points:

Price per bottle of Pepsi (in dollars)	Number of bottles demanded
$2.50	100,000
1.25	200,000

a. Draw a graph with a linear demand curve that passes through these two points.

b. Show on the graph the areas representing total revenue at each price. Give the value for total revenue at each price.

A.6 What is the area of the triangle shown in the following figure?

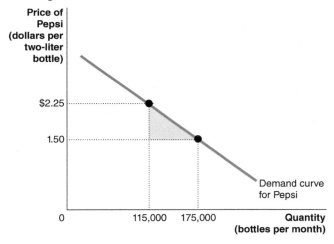

A.7 Calculate the slope of the total cost curve at point A and at point B in the following figure.

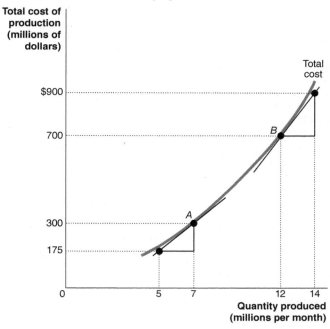

Glossary

Allocative efficiency A state of the economy in which production is in accordance with consumer preferences; in particular, every good or service is produced up to the point where the last unit provides a marginal benefit to society equal to the marginal cost of producing it.

Centrally planned economy An economy in which the government decides how economic resources will be allocated.

Economic model A simplified version of reality used to analyze real-world economic situations.

Economic variable Something measurable that can have different values, such as the incomes of doctors.

Economics The study of the choices people make to attain their goals, given their scarce resources.

Equity The fair distribution of economic benefits.

Macroeconomics The study of the economy as a whole, including topics such as inflation, unemployment, and economic growth.

Marginal analysis Analysis that involves comparing marginal benefits and marginal costs.

Market A group of buyers and sellers of a good or service and the institution or arrangement by which they come together to trade.

Market economy An economy in which the decisions of households and firms interacting in markets allocate economic resources.

Microeconomics The study of how households and firms make choices, how they interact in markets, and how the government attempts to influence their choices.

Mixed economy An economy in which most economic decisions result from the interaction of buyers and sellers in markets but in which the government plays a significant role in the allocation of resources.

Normative analysis Analysis concerned with what ought to be.

Opportunity cost The highest-valued alternative that must be given up to engage in an activity.

Positive analysis Analysis concerned with what is.

Productive efficiency A situation in which a good or service is produced at the lowest possible cost.

Scarcity A situation in which unlimited wants exceed the limited resources available to fulfill those wants.

Trade-off The idea that, because of scarcity, producing more of one good or service means producing less of another good or service.

Voluntary exchange A situation that occurs in markets when both the buyer and the seller of a product are made better off by the transaction.

Credits

Credits are listed in the order of appearance.

Photo

Véronique Burger/Science Source/Photo Researchers, Inc.; Burger/Phanie/SuperStock

Text

John Hechinger, "FBI Presses Banks to Boost Security as Robberies Rise," *Wall Street Journal*, October 8, 2002.

Trade-offs, Comparative Advantage, and the Market System

From Chapter 2 of *Macroeconomics*, Fifth Edition. R. Glenn Hubbard and Anthony Patrick O'Brien. Copyright © 2015 by Pearson Education, Inc.
All rights reserved.

Trade-offs, Comparative Advantage, and the Market System

Chapter Outline and Learning Objectives

1 **Production Possibilities Frontiers and Opportunity Costs**
   Use a production possibilities frontier to analyze opportunity costs and trade-offs.

2 **Comparative Advantage and Trade**
   Describe comparative advantage and explain how it serves as the basis for trade.

3 **The Market System**
   Explain the basic idea of how a market system works.

Managers at Tesla Motors Face Trade-Offs

Are all-electric cars the wave of the future? If you're like most drivers, you probably like the idea of skipping the gas station in favor of powering up your car by plugging it into an electric outlet. Yet, all-electric cars, such as the Chevrolet Volt and Nissan Leaf, have struggled to succeed in the marketplace for two key reasons: (1) The lithium batteries that power electric cars are costly, forcing up the prices of the cars, and (2) available batteries need to be recharged every 300 miles or so, making all-electric cars difficult to use on long trips.

Many people were therefore surprised when Tesla Motors announced in early 2013 that sales of its all-electric cars had been higher than expected and that it had made a profit for the first time. Tesla was founded in 2003 by billionaire Elon Musk, who also started the online payment system PayPal and the private space firm SpaceX. As many investors began to believe that Tesla was likely to become the first successful electric car company, the value of the firm soared to more than $200 billion.

Tesla manufactures its cars in Fremont, California. To compete in the automobile market, Tesla's managers must make many strategic decisions, such as whether to introduce new car models. In 2013, Tesla's only model, the Model S sedan, received the highest car rating ever from *Consumer Reports* and won the 2013 award for World Green Car of the Year. In 2014, Tesla introduced a second model, the Model X, a cross between a sport utility vehicle (SUV) and a minivan. The Model X was designed for families who would otherwise buy traditional gasoline-powered SUVs or minivans.

Tesla's managers must also decide how to sell and service its cars. Most cars are sold through dealerships, which also provide service for those cars. In 2013, however, Tesla had no dealerships. Instead, the company sold all of its cars online and relied on company-owned service centers to provide maintenance and repair services. Some economists have questioned whether Tesla will be able to meet its future sales goals without selling cars through dealerships.

Managers also make smaller-scale decisions. For instance, in scheduling production at its Fremont plant, Tesla's managers must decide each month the quantity of Model S sedans and Model X SUVs to manufacture. Like other decisions managers make, this one involves a trade-off: Producing more of one of these two models means producing fewer of the other.

AN INSIDE LOOK discusses how managers at Mercedes-Benz decide which models to manufacture and why the company chose to partner with Tesla Motors to develop electric-vehicle components.

Sources: Steven Russolillo, "Four Reasons Morgan Stanley Loves Tesla," *Wall Street Journal*, May 14, 2013; and Christopher F. Schuetze, "Will 2013 Be the Year of the Electric Car?" *New York Times*, January 7, 2013.

Economics in Your Life

The Trade-offs When You Buy a Car

When you buy a traditional gasoline-powered car, you probably consider factors such as safety and fuel efficiency. To increase fuel efficiency, automobile manufacturers make cars that are small and light. Large cars absorb more of the impact of an accident than do small cars. As a result, people are usually safer driving large cars than small cars. What can we conclude from these facts about the relationship between safety and fuel efficiency? Under what circumstances would it be possible for automobile manufacturers to make cars that are both safer and more fuel efficient? As you read the chapter, try to answer these questions. You can check your answers against those provided at the end of this chapter.

Scarcity A situation in which unlimited wants exceed the limited resources available to fulfill those wants.

I n a market system, managers at most firms must make decisions like those made by Tesla's managers. These decisions reflect a key fact of economic life: *Scarcity requires trade-offs.* **Scarcity** exists because we have unlimited wants but only limited resources available to fulfill those wants. Goods and services are scarce. So, too, are the economic resources, or *factors of production*—workers, capital, natural resources, and entrepreneurial ability—used to make goods and services. Your time is scarce, which means you face trade-offs: If you spend an hour studying for an economics exam, you have one less hour to spend studying for a psychology exam or going to the movies. If your university decides to use some of its scarce budget to buy new computers for the computer labs, those funds will not be available to buy new books for the library or to resurface the student parking lot. If Tesla decides to devote some of the scarce workers and machinery in its Fremont assembly plant to producing more Model X SUVs, those resources will not be available to produce more Model S sedans.

Households and firms make many of their decisions in markets. Trade is a key activity that takes place in markets. Trade results from the decisions of millions of households and firms spread around the world. By engaging in trade, people can raise their incomes. In this chapter, we provide an overview of how the market system coordinates the independent decisions of these millions of households and firms. We begin our analysis of the economic consequences of scarcity and the working of the market system by introducing an important economic model: the *production possibilities frontier*.

1 LEARNING OBJECTIVE

Use a production possibilities frontier to analyze opportunity costs and trade-offs.

Production possibilities frontier (PPF) A curve showing the maximum attainable combinations of two products that may be produced with available resources and current technology.

Production Possibilities Frontiers and Opportunity Costs

As we saw in the chapter opener, Tesla operates an automobile factory in Fremont, California, where it assembles two car models. Because the firm's resources—workers, machinery, materials, and entrepreneurial skills—are limited, Tesla faces a trade-off: Resources devoted to producing one model are not available for producing the other model. Economic models can be useful in analyzing many questions. We can use a simple model called the *production possibilities frontier* to analyze the trade-offs Tesla faces in its Fremont plant. A **production possibilities frontier (PPF)** is a curve showing the maximum attainable combinations of two products that may be produced with available resources and current technology. In Tesla's case, the company produces only Model S sedans and Model X SUVs at the Fremont plant, using workers, materials, robots, and other machinery.

Graphing the Production Possibilities Frontier

Figure 1 uses a production possibilities frontier to illustrate the trade-offs that Tesla faces. The numbers from the table are plotted in the graph. The line in the graph represents Tesla's production possibilities frontier. If Tesla uses all its resources to produce Model S sedans, it can produce 80 per day—point *A* at one end of the production possibilities frontier. If Tesla uses all its resources to produce Model X SUVs, it can produce 80 per day—point *E* at the other end of the production possibilities frontier. If Tesla devotes resources to producing both vehicles, it could be at a point like *B*, where it produces 60 sedans and 20 SUVs.

All the combinations either on the frontier—like points *A*, *B*, *C*, *D*, and *E*—or inside the frontier—like point *F*—are *attainable* with the resources available. Combinations on the frontier are *efficient* because all available resources are being fully utilized,

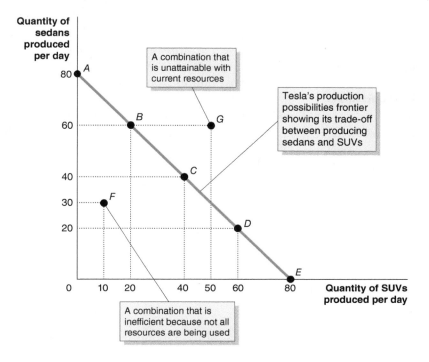

Tesla's Production Choices at Its Fremont Plant

Choice	Quantity of Sedans Produced	Quantity of SUVs Produced
A	80	0
B	60	20
C	40	40
D	20	60
E	0	80

A combination that is unattainable with current resources

Tesla's production possibilities frontier showing its trade-off between producing sedans and SUVs

A combination that is inefficient because not all resources are being used

Figure 1

Tesla's Production Possibilities Frontier

Tesla faces a trade-off: To build one more sedan, it must build one fewer SUV. The production possibilities frontier illustrates the trade-off Tesla faces. Combinations on the production possibilities frontier—like points *A*, *B*, *C*, *D*, and *E*—are *technically efficient* because the maximum output is being obtained from the available resources. Combinations inside the frontier—like point *F*—are *inefficient* because some resources are not being used. Combinations outside the frontier—like point *G*—are *unattainable* with current resources.

and the fewest possible resources are being used to produce a given amount of output. Combinations inside the frontier—like point *F*—are *inefficient* because maximum output is not being obtained from the available resources—perhaps because the assembly line is not operating at its capacity. Tesla might like to be beyond the frontier—at a point like *G*, where it would be producing 60 sedans and 50 SUVs per day—but points beyond the production possibilities frontier are *unattainable*, given the firm's current resources. To produce the combination at *G*, Tesla would need more machines and more workers.

Notice that if Tesla is producing efficiently and is on the production possibilities frontier, the only way to produce more of one vehicle is to produce fewer of the other vehicle. The **opportunity cost** of any activity is the highest-valued alternative that must be given up to engage in that activity. For Tesla, the opportunity cost of producing one more SUV is the number of sedans the company will not be able to produce because it has shifted those resources to producing the SUV. For example, in moving from point *B* to point *C*, the opportunity cost of producing 20 more SUVs per day is the 20 fewer sedans that Tesla can produce.

What point on the production possibilities frontier is best? We can't tell without further information. If consumer demand for SUVs is greater than the demand for sedans, the company is likely to choose a point closer to *E*. If demand for sedans is greater than the demand for SUVs, the company is likely to choose a point closer to *A*.

Opportunity cost The highest-valued alternative that must be given up to engage in an activity.

Solved Problem 1

Drawing a Production Possibilities Frontier for Tesla Motors

Suppose, for simplicity, that during any given week, the machinery and number of workers at Tesla Motors' Fremont plant cannot be increased. So the number of sedans or SUVs the company can produce during the week depends on how many hours are devoted to assembling each of the different models. Assume that SUVs are more difficult to assemble, so if Tesla devotes an hour to assembling sedans, it will produce 15 vehicles, but if Tesla devotes an hour to producing SUVs, it will produce only 10 vehicles. Assume that the plant can run for 8 hours per day.

a. Use the information given to complete the following table:

b. Use the data in the table to draw a production possibilities frontier graph illustrating Tesla's trade-off between assembling sedans and assembling SUVs. Label the vertical axis "Quantity of sedans produced per day." Label the horizontal axis "Quantity of SUVs produced per day." Make sure to label the values where Tesla's production possibilities frontier intersects the vertical and horizontal axes.

c. Label the points representing choice D and choice E. If Tesla is at choice D, what is its opportunity cost of making 10 more SUVs?

| | Hours Spent Making | | Quantity Produced per Day | |
Choice	Sedans	SUVs	Sedans	SUVs
A	8	0	———	———
B	7	1	———	———
C	6	2	———	———
D	5	3	———	———
E	4	4	———	———
F	3	5	———	———
G	2	6	———	———
H	1	7	———	———
I	0	8	———	———

Solving the Problem

Step 1: **Review the chapter material.** This problem is about using production possibilities frontiers to analyze trade-offs, so you may want to review the section "Graphing the Production Possibilities Frontier."

Step 2: **Answer part (a) by filling in the table.** If Tesla can assemble 15 sedans in 1 hour, then with choice A, it can assemble 120 sedans and 0 SUVs. Because Tesla can assemble 10 SUVs in 1 hour, with choice B, it will produce 105 sedans and 10 SUVs. Using similar reasoning, you can fill in the remaining cells in the table as follows:

| | Hours Spent Making | | Quantity Produced per Day | |
Choice	Sedans	SUVs	Sedans	SUVs
A	8	0	120	0
B	7	1	105	10
C	6	2	90	20
D	5	3	75	30
E	4	4	60	40
F	3	5	45	50
G	2	6	30	60
H	1	7	15	70
I	0	8	0	80

Step 3: **Answer part (b) by drawing the production possibilities frontier graph.**
Using the data in the table in Step 2, you should draw a graph that looks like this:

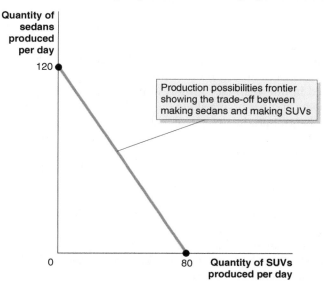

If Tesla devotes all 8 hours to assembling sedans, it will produce 120 sedans.
Therefore, Tesla's production possibilities frontier will intersect the vertical
axis at 120 sedans produced. If Tesla devotes all 8 hours to assembling SUVs,
it will produce 80 SUVs. Therefore, Tesla's production possibilities frontier
will intersect the horizontal axis at 80 SUVs produced.

Step 4: **Answer part (c) by labeling choices _D_ and _E_ on your graph.** The points for
choices _D_ and _E_ can be plotted using the information from the table:

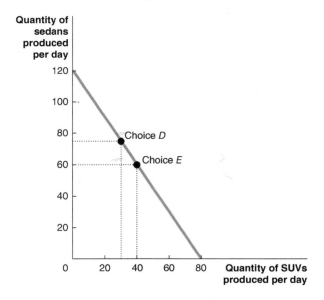

Moving from choice _D_ to choice _E_ increases Tesla's production of SUVs by 10
but lowers its production of sedans by 15. Therefore, Tesla's opportunity cost
of producing 10 more SUVs is making 15 fewer sedans.

Your Turn: For more practice, do related problem 1.10 at the end of this chapter.

Increasing Marginal Opportunity Costs

We can use the production possibilities frontier to explore issues concerning the economy as a whole. Suppose we divide all the goods and services produced in the economy into just two types: military goods and civilian goods. In Figure 2, we let tanks represent military goods and automobiles represent civilian goods. If all the country's resources are devoted to producing military goods, 400 tanks can be produced in one year. If all resources are devoted to producing civilian goods, 500 automobiles can be produced in one year. Devoting resources to producing both goods results in the economy being at other points along the production possibilities frontier.

Notice that this production possibilities frontier is bowed outward rather than being a straight line. Because the curve is bowed out, the opportunity cost of automobiles in terms of tanks depends on where the economy currently is on the production possibilities frontier. For example, to increase automobile production from 0 to 200—moving from point *A* to point *B*— the economy has to give up only 50 tanks. But to increase automobile production by another 200 vehicles—moving from point *B* to point *C*—the economy has to give up 150 tanks.

As the economy moves down the production possibilities frontier, it experiences *increasing marginal opportunity costs* because increasing automobile production by a given quantity requires larger and larger decreases in tank production. Increasing marginal opportunity costs occur because some workers, machines, and other resources are better suited to one use than to another. At point *A*, some resources that are well suited to producing automobiles are forced to produce tanks. Shifting these resources into producing automobiles by moving from point *A* to point *B* allows a substantial increase in automobile production, without much loss of tank production. But as the economy moves down the production possibilities frontier, more and more resources that are better suited to tank production are switched to automobile production. As a result, the increases in automobile production become increasingly smaller, while the decreases in tank production become increasingly larger. We would expect in most situations that production possibilities frontiers will be bowed outward rather than linear as in the Tesla example discussed earlier.

The idea of increasing marginal opportunity costs illustrates an important economic concept: *The more resources already devoted to an activity, the smaller the payoff to devoting additional resources to that activity.* For example, the more hours you have already spent studying economics, the smaller the increase in your test grade from each additional hour you spend—and the greater the opportunity cost of using the hour in that way. The more funds a firm has devoted to research and development during a given year, the smaller the amount of useful knowledge it receives from each additional dollar—and the greater the opportunity cost of using the funds in that way. The more funds the federal government spends cleaning up the environment during a given year, the smaller the reduction in pollution from each additional dollar—and, once again, the greater the opportunity cost of using the funds in that way.

Figure 2

Increasing Marginal Opportunity Costs

As the economy moves down the production possibilities frontier, it experiences *increasing marginal opportunity costs* because increasing automobile production by a given quantity requires larger and larger decreases in tank production. For example, to increase automobile production from 0 to 200—moving from point *A* to point *B*—the economy has to give up only 50 tanks. But to increase automobile production by another 200 vehicles—moving from point *B* to point *C*—the economy has to give up 150 tanks.

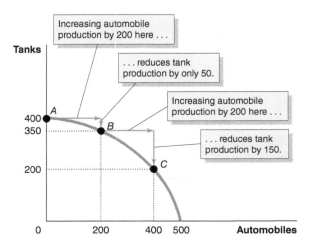

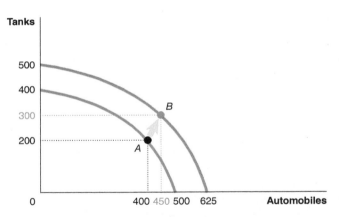

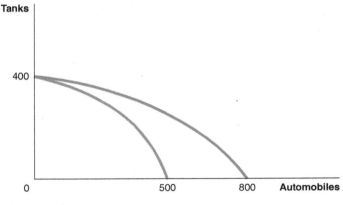

(a) Shifting out the production possibilities frontier

(b) Technological change in the automobile industry

Figure 3 Economic Growth

Panel (a) shows that as more economic resources become available and technological change occurs, the economy can move from point *A* to point *B*, producing more tanks and more automobiles. Panel (b) shows the results of technological change in the automobile industry that increases the quantity of vehicles workers can produce per year while leaving unchanged the maximum quantity of tanks they can produce. Outward shifts in the production possibilities frontier represent *economic growth*.

Economic Growth

At any given time, the total resources available to any economy are fixed. Therefore, if, for example, the United States produces more automobiles, it must produce less of something else—tanks in our example. Over time, though, the resources available to an economy may increase. For example, both the labor force and the capital stock—the amount of machinery and other physical capital available in the country—may increase. The increase in the available labor force and the capital stock shifts the production possibilities frontier outward for the U.S. economy and makes it possible to produce both more automobiles and more tanks. Panel (a) of Figure 3 shows that the economy can move from point *A* to point *B*, producing more tanks and more automobiles.

Similarly, technological change makes it possible to produce more goods with the same number of workers and the same amount of machinery, which also shifts the production possibilities frontier outward. Technological change need not affect all sectors equally. Panel (b) of Figure 3 shows the results of technological change in the automobile industry that increases the quantity of automobiles workers can produce per year while leaving unchanged the quantity of tanks they can produce.

Outward shifts in the production possibilities frontier represent **economic growth** because they allow the economy to increase the production of goods and services, which ultimately raises the standard of living. In the United States and other high-income countries, the market system has aided the process of economic growth, which over the past 200 years has greatly increased the well-being of the average person.

Economic growth The ability of the economy to increase the production of goods and services.

Comparative Advantage and Trade

We can use the concepts of the production possibilities frontier and opportunity costs to understand the basic economic activity of *trade*. Markets are fundamentally about **trade**, which is the act of buying and selling. Sometimes we trade directly, as when children trade one baseball card for another baseball card. But often we trade indirectly: We sell our labor services as, say, an accountant, a salesperson, or a nurse for money, and then we use the money to buy goods and services. Although in these cases trade takes place indirectly, ultimately the accountant, salesperson, or nurse is trading his or her services for food, clothing, and other goods and services. One of the great benefits of trade is that it makes it possible for people to become better off by increasing both their production and their consumption.

Describe comparative advantage and explain how it serves as the basis for trade.

Trade The act of buying and selling.

45

Specialization and Gains from Trade

Consider the following situation: You and your neighbor both have fruit trees on your properties. Initially, suppose you have only apple trees and your neighbor has only cherry trees. In this situation, if you both like apples and cherries, there is an obvious opportunity for both of you to gain from trade: You trade some of your apples for some of your neighbor's cherries, making you both better off. But what if there are apple and cherry trees growing on both of your properties? In that case, there can still be gains from trade. For example, your neighbor might be very good at picking apples, and you might be very good at picking cherries. It would make sense for your neighbor to concentrate on picking apples and for you to concentrate on picking cherries. You can then trade some of the cherries you pick for some of the apples your neighbor picks. But what if your neighbor is actually better at picking both apples and cherries than you are?

We can use production possibilities frontiers (*PPFs*) to show how your neighbor can benefit from trading with you *even though she is better than you are at picking both apples and cherries*. (For simplicity, and because it will not have any effect on the conclusions we draw, we will assume that the *PPFs* in this example are straight lines.) The table in Figure 4 shows how many apples and how many cherries you and your neighbor can pick in one week. The graph in the figure uses the data from the table to construct *PPFs*. Panel (a) shows your *PPF*. If you devote all your time to picking apples, you can pick 20 pounds of apples per week. If you devote all your time to picking cherries, you can pick 20 pounds per week. Panel (b) shows that if your neighbor devotes all her time to picking apples, she can pick 30 pounds. If she devotes all her time to picking cherries, she can pick 60 pounds.

The *PPFs* in Figure 4 show how many apples and cherries you and your neighbor can consume, *without trade*. Suppose that when you don't trade with your neighbor, you pick and consume 8 pounds of apples and 12 pounds of cherries per week. This

	You		Your Neighbor	
	Apples	Cherries	Apples	Cherries
Devote all time to picking apples	20 pounds	0 pounds	30 pounds	0 pounds
Devote all time to picking cherries	0 pounds	20 pounds	0 pounds	60 pounds

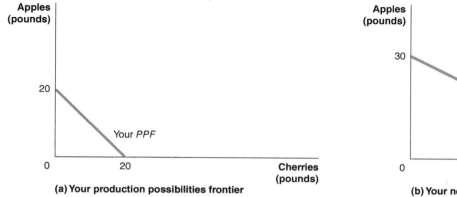

(a) Your production possibilities frontier

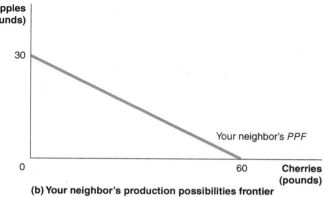

(b) Your neighbor's production possibilities frontier

Figure 4   Production Possibilities for You and Your Neighbor, without Trade

The table shows how many pounds of apples and how many pounds of cherries you and your neighbor can each pick in one week. The graphs use the data from the table to construct *PPFs* for you and your neighbor. Panel (a) shows your *PPF*. If you devote all your time to picking apples and none to picking cherries, you can pick 20 pounds. If you devote all your time to picking cherries, you can pick 20 pounds. Panel (b) shows that if your neighbor devotes all her time to picking apples, she can pick 30 pounds. If she devotes all her time to picking cherries, she can pick 60 pounds.

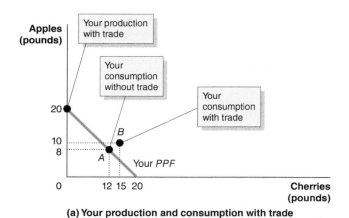
(a) Your production and consumption with trade

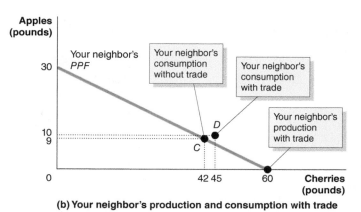
(b) Your neighbor's production and consumption with trade

Figure 5   Gains from Trade

When you don't trade with your neighbor, you pick and consume 8 pounds of apples and 12 pounds of cherries per week—point A in panel (a). When your neighbor doesn't trade with you, she picks and consumes 9 pounds of apples and 42 pounds of cherries per week—point C in panel (b). If you specialize in picking apples, you can pick 20 pounds. If your neighbor specializes in picking cherries, she can pick 60 pounds. If you trade 10 pounds of your apples for 15 pounds of your neighbor's cherries, you will be able to consume 10 pounds of apples and 15 pounds of cherries—point B in panel (a). Your neighbor can now consume 10 pounds of apples and 45 pounds of cherries—point D in panel (b). You and your neighbor are both better off as a result of the trade.

combination of apples and cherries is represented by point A in panel (a) of Figure 5. When your neighbor doesn't trade with you, she picks and consumes 9 pounds of apples and 42 pounds of cherries per week. This combination of apples and cherries is represented by point C in panel (b).

After years of picking and consuming your own apples and cherries, suppose your neighbor comes to you one day with the following proposal: She offers to trade you 15 pounds of her cherries for 10 pounds of your apples the next week. Should you accept this offer? As we can show, you should accept because you will end up with more apples and more cherries to consume. To take advantage of her proposal, you should specialize in picking only apples rather than splitting your time between picking apples and picking cherries. We know specializing will allow you to pick 20 pounds of apples. You can trade 10 pounds of apples to your neighbor for 15 pounds of her cherries. The result is that you will be able to consume 10 pounds of apples and 15 pounds of cherries (point B in panel (a) of Figure 5). You are clearly better off as a result of trading with your neighbor: You can now consume 2 more pounds of apples and 3 more pounds of cherries than you were consuming without trading. You have moved beyond your PPF!

Your neighbor has also benefited from the trade. By specializing in picking only cherries, she can pick 60 pounds. She trades 15 pounds of cherries to you for 10 pounds of apples. She can then consume 10 pounds of apples and 45 pounds of cherries (point D in panel (b) of Figure 5). This combination is 1 more pound of apples and 3 more pounds of cherries than she was consuming before trading with you. She also has moved beyond her PPF. Table 1 summarizes the changes in production and consumption that result from your trade with your neighbor. (In this example, we chose one specific rate of trading cherries for apples—15 pounds of cherries for 10 pounds of apples. There are, however, many other rates of trading cherries for apples that would also make you and your neighbor better off.)

Absolute Advantage versus Comparative Advantage

Perhaps the most remarkable aspect of the preceding example is that your neighbor benefits from trading with you even though she is better than you at picking both apples and cherries. **Absolute advantage** is the ability of an individual, a firm, or a country to produce more of a good or service than competitors, using the same amount of resources. Your neighbor has an absolute advantage over you in picking both apples and

Absolute advantage The ability of an individual, a firm, or a country to produce more of a good or service than competitors, using the same amount of resources.

Table 1

A Summary of the Gains from Trade

	You		Your Neighbor	
	Apples (in pounds)	**Cherries (in pounds)**	**Apples (in pounds)**	**Cherries (in pounds)**
Production *and* consumption *without* trade	8	12	9	42
Production *with* trade	20	0	0	60
Consumption *with* trade	10	15	10	45
Gains from trade (increased consumption)	2	3	1	3

cherries because she can pick more of each fruit than you can in the same amount of time. Although it seems that your neighbor should pick her own apples *and* her own cherries, we have just seen that she is better off specializing in picking cherries and leaving picking apples to you.

We can consider further why both you and your neighbor benefit from specializing in picking only one fruit. First, think about the opportunity cost to each of you of picking the two fruits. We saw from the *PPF* in Figure 4 that if you devoted all your time to picking apples, you would be able to pick 20 pounds of apples per week. As you move down your *PPF* and shift time away from picking apples to picking cherries, you have to give up 1 pound of apples for each pound of cherries you pick (the slope of your *PPF* is −1.) Therefore, your opportunity cost of picking 1 pound of cherries is 1 pound of apples. By the same reasoning, your opportunity cost of picking 1 pound of apples is 1 pound of cherries. Your neighbor's *PPF* has a different slope, so she faces a different trade-off: As she shifts time from picking apples to picking cherries, she has to give up 0.5 pound of apples for every 1 pound of cherries she picks (the slope of your neighbor's *PPF* is −0.5). As she shifts time from picking cherries to picking apples, she gives up 2 pounds of cherries for every 1 pound of apples she picks. Therefore, her opportunity cost of picking 1 pound of apples is 2 pounds of cherries, and her opportunity cost of picking 1 pound of cherries is 0.5 pound of apples.

Table 2 summarizes the opportunity costs for you and your neighbor of picking apples and cherries. Note that even though your neighbor can pick more apples in a week than you can, the *opportunity cost* of picking apples is higher for her than for you because when she picks apples, she gives up more cherries than you do. So, even though she has an absolute advantage over you in picking apples, it is more costly for her to pick apples than it is for you. The table also shows that her opportunity cost of picking cherries is lower than yours. **Comparative advantage** is the ability of an individual, a firm, or a country to produce a good or service at a lower opportunity cost than competitors. In picking apples, your neighbor has an *absolute advantage* over you, while you have a *comparative advantage* over her. Your neighbor has both an absolute advantage and a comparative advantage over you in picking cherries. As we have seen, you are better off specializing in picking apples, and your neighbor is better off specializing in picking cherries.

Comparative advantage The ability of an individual, a firm, or a country to produce a good or service at a lower opportunity cost than competitors.

Comparative Advantage and the Gains from Trade

We have just arrived at an important economic principle: *The basis for trade is comparative advantage, not absolute advantage.* The fastest apple pickers do not necessarily do

Table 2

Opportunity Costs of Picking Apples and Cherries

	Opportunity Cost of Picking 1 Pound of Apples	**Opportunity Cost of Picking 1 Pound of Cherries**
You	1 pound of cherries	1 pound of apples
Your Neighbor	2 pounds of cherries	0.5 pound of apples

Don't Let This Happen to You

Don't Confuse Absolute Advantage and Comparative Advantage

First, make sure you know the definitions:

- **Absolute advantage.** The ability of an individual, a firm, or a country to produce more of a good or service than competitors, using the same amount of resources. In our example, your neighbor has an absolute advantage over you in both picking apples and picking cherries.
- **Comparative advantage.** The ability of an individual, a firm, or a country to produce a good or service at a lower opportunity cost than competitors. In our example, your neighbor has a comparative advantage in picking cherries, but you have a comparative advantage in picking apples.

Keep these two key points in mind:

1. It is possible to have an absolute advantage in producing a good or service without having a comparative advantage. This is the case with your neighbor picking apples.
2. It is possible to have a comparative advantage in producing a good or service without having an absolute advantage. This is the case with your picking apples.

Your Turn: Test your understanding by doing related problem 2.5 at the end of this chapter.

much apple picking. If the fastest apple pickers have a comparative advantage in some other activity—picking cherries, playing Major League Baseball, or being industrial engineers—they are better off specializing in that activity. Individuals, firms, and countries are better off if they specialize in producing goods and services for which they have a comparative advantage and obtain the other goods and services they need by trading.

Solved Problem 2

Comparative Advantage and the Gains from Trade

Suppose that Canada and the United States both produce maple syrup and honey, which are sold for the same price in both countries. These are the combinations of the two goods that each country can produce in one day using the same amounts of capital and labor:

Canada		United States	
Honey (in tons)	Maple Syrup (in tons)	Honey (in tons)	Maple Syrup (in tons)
0	60	0	50
10	45	10	40
20	30	20	30
30	15	30	20
40	0	40	10
		50	0

a. Which country has a comparative advantage in producing maple syrup? Which country has a comparative advantage in producing honey?

b. Suppose that Canada is currently producing 30 tons of honey and 15 tons of maple syrup, and the United States is currently producing 10 tons of honey and 40 tons of maple syrup. Demonstrate that Canada and the United States can both be better off if they specialize in producing only one good and trade for the other.

c. Illustrate your answer to question (b) by drawing a *PPF* for the United States and a *PPF* for Canada. Show on your *PPFs* the combinations of honey and maple syrup produced and consumed in each country before and after trade.

Solving the Problem

Step 1: **Review the chapter material.** This problem is about comparative advantage, so you may want to review the section "Absolute Advantage versus Comparative Advantage."

49

Step 2: **Answer part (a) by calculating which country has a comparative advantage in each activity.** Remember that a country has a comparative advantage in producing a good if it can produce the good at the lowest opportunity cost. When Canada produces 1 more ton of honey, it produces 1.5 tons less of maple syrup. When the United States produces 1 more ton of honey, it produces 1 ton less of maple syrup. Therefore, the United States' opportunity cost of producing honey—1 ton of maple syrup—is lower than Canada's—1.5 tons of maple syrup. When Canada produces 1 more ton of maple syrup, it produces 0.67 ton less of honey. When the United States produces 1 more ton of maple syrup, it produces 1 ton less of honey. Therefore, Canada's opportunity cost of producing maple syrup—0.67 ton of honey—is lower than that of the United States—1 ton of honey. We can conclude that the United States has a comparative advantage in the production of honey and Canada has a comparative advantage in the production of maple syrup.

Step 3: **Answer part (b) by showing that specialization makes Canada and the United States better off.** We know that Canada and the United States should each specialize where it has a comparative advantage. If both countries specialize, Canada will produce 60 tons of maple syrup and 0 tons of honey, and the United States will produce 0 tons of maple syrup and 50 tons of honey. After both countries specialize, the United States could then trade 30 tons of honey to Canada for 40 tons of maple syrup. (Other mutually beneficial trades are possible as well.) We can summarize the results in a table:

	Before Trade		After Trade	
	Honey (in tons)	Maple Syrup (in tons)	Honey (in tons)	Maple Syrup (in tons)
Canada	30	15	30	20
United States	10	40	20	40

The United States is better off after trade because it can consume the same amount of maple syrup and 10 more tons of honey. Canada is better off after trade because it can consume the same amount of honey and 5 more tons of maple syrup.

Step 4: **Answer part (c) by drawing the *PPFs*.**

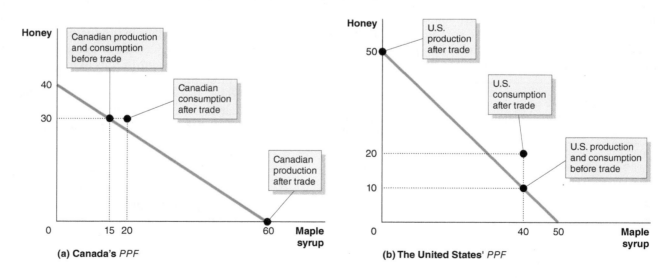

(a) Canada's *PPF*

(b) The United States' *PPF*

Your Turn: For more practice, do related problems 2.6 and 2.7 at the end of this chapter.

Making the Connection

Comparative Advantage, Opportunity Cost, and Housework

Among roommates, married couples, and other people living together, dividing up the household chores can be a source of stress. Traditionally among married couples, women did most of the housework, such as preparing meals, cleaning, and doing the laundry. In 1965, married women with children averaged about 32 hours of housework per week, while married men averaged only 4 hours. Today, women average about 18 hours of housework, while men average about 10 hours.

Housework doesn't seem to be part of buying, selling, and the usual topics of business and economics. In fact, we can use basic economic concepts to analyze housework. Consider first the most efficient way to divide up household chores. Suppose Jack and Jill need to decide how they will get the cooking and laundry done. Assume Jack has an absolute advantage over Jill in both chores, but he has a big advantage over Jill in cooking—he takes much less time to prepare very tasty meals—but is only a little faster than Jill in doing the laundry. In other words, assuming they have the same amount of time available to do housework, Jack has a comparative advantage in cooking, while Jill has a comparative advantage in doing the laundry. So rather than Jack and Jill both doing some of the cooking and some of the laundry, they would be better off if Jack follows his comparative advantage and does all the cooking, while Jill follows her comparative advantage and does all the laundry.

What's the most efficient way to divide up household chores?

Economics can also provide some insight into the decline in the number of hours spent on housework since the 1960s. Combined, men and women now spend more than 20 percent fewer hours on housework. This decline has been partly driven by technology, particularly improvements in household appliances, such as dishwashers and microwave ovens. The decline in the number of hours women devote to housework also reflects the greater job opportunities available to women today compared with the 1960s. The opportunity cost to a woman of spending time on housework and childcare is the wage she gives up by not spending that time in paid work. If a woman could work for an hour at a wage of $20 but spends that hour doing household chores, the opportunity cost of the time spent on chores is $20. As job opportunities for women and the wages those jobs pay have increased, so has the opportunity cost of doing housework. So in addition to taking advantage of improved appliances, many families have found that the cost of hiring specialists in household chores, such as cleaning services and lawn care services, is lower than the cost of the wife (or husband) performing those chores.

As women's wages have risen relative to men's wages, the opportunity cost to women of doing housework has increased more than has the opportunity cost to men. So we would expect that in addition to women devoting fewer hours to housework, the gap between the hours women and men devote would narrow. In fact, between 1965 and 2011, the average number of hours women devote to housework declined from 32 hours per week to 18 hours. The average number of hours women devote to paid work increased from 8 hours per week to 21 hours.

Of course, changes in social attitudes also help explain changes in how men and women allocate their time. But we have seen that the basic economic concepts of comparative advantage and opportunity cost provide important insights into the not-so-wonderful world of household chores.

Sources: Kim Parker and Wendy Wang, "Modern Parenthood: Roles of Moms and Dads Converge as They Balance Work and Family," pewsocialtrends.org, March 13, 2013; Emily Oster, "You're Dividing the Chores Wrong," *Slate*, November 21, 2012; and Ellen Byron, "A Truce in the Chore Wars," *New York Times*, December 4, 2012.

Your Turn: Test your understanding by doing related problems 2.14 and 2.15 at the end of this chapter.

The Market System

We have seen that households, firms, and the government face trade-offs and incur opportunity costs because resources are scarce. We have also seen that trade allows people to specialize according to their comparative advantage. By engaging in trade, people can raise their incomes and their standard of living. Of course, trade in the modern world is much more complex than the examples we have considered so far. Trade today involves the decisions of millions of people around the world. How are the decisions of these millions of people coordinated? In the United States and most other countries, trade is carried out in markets. Markets also determine the answers to the three fundamental questions: What goods and services will be produced? How will the goods and services be produced? and Who will receive the goods and services produced?

Market A group of buyers and sellers of a good or service and the institution or arrangement by which they come together to trade.

Market is a group of buyers and sellers of a good or service and the institution or arrangement by which they come together to trade. Markets take many forms: They can be physical places, such as a local pizza parlor or the New York Stock Exchange, or virtual places, such as eBay or iTunes. In a market, the buyers are demanders of goods or services, and the sellers are suppliers of goods or services. Households and firms interact in two types of markets: *product markets* and *factor markets*. **Product markets** are markets for goods—such as computers—and services—such as medical treatment. In product markets, households are demanders and firms are suppliers. **Factor markets** are markets for the *factors of production*. **Factors of production** are the inputs used to make goods and services. Factors of production are divided into four broad categories:

Product market A market for goods—such as computers—or services—such as medical treatment.

Factor market A market for the factors of production, such as labor, capital, natural resources, and entrepreneurial ability.

Factors of production The inputs used to make goods and services.

- *Labor* includes all types of work, from the part-time labor of teenagers working at McDonald's to the work of senior managers in large corporations.

- *Capital* refers to physical capital, such as computers and machine tools, that is used to produce other goods.

- *Natural resources* include land, water, oil, iron ore, and other raw materials (or "gifts of nature") that are used in producing goods.

- An *entrepreneur* is someone who operates a business. *Entrepreneurial ability* is the ability to bring together the other factors of production to successfully produce and sell goods and services.

The Circular Flow of Income

Two key groups participate in markets:

- A *household* consists of all the individuals in a home. Households are suppliers of factors of production—particularly labor—employed by firms to make goods and services. Households use the income they receive from selling the factors of production to purchase the goods and services supplied by firms. We are familiar with households as suppliers of labor because most people earn most of their income by going to work, meaning they are selling their labor services to firms in the labor market. But households own the other factors of production as well, either directly or indirectly, by owning the firms that own these resources. All firms are owned by households. Small firms, like a neighborhood restaurant, might be owned by one person. Large firms, like Apple, are owned by millions of households that own shares of stock in them. When firms pay profits to the people who own them, the firms are paying for using the capital and natural resources that are supplied to them by those owners. So, we can generalize by saying that in factor markets, households are suppliers and firms are demanders.

- *Firms* are suppliers of goods and services. Firms use the funds they receive from selling goods and services to buy or hire the factors of production needed to make the goods and services.

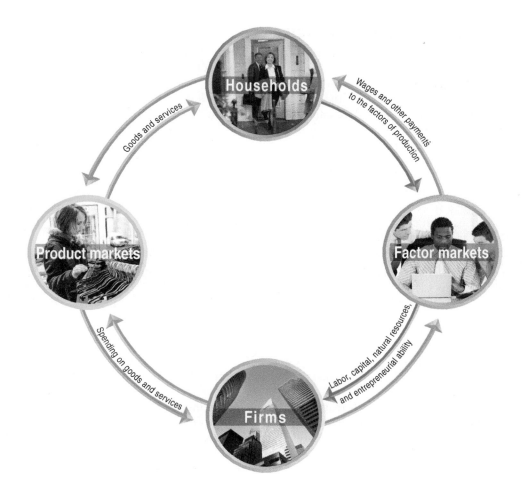

Figure 6

The Circular-Flow Diagram

Households and firms are linked together in a circular flow of production, income, and spending. The blue arrows show the flow of the factors of production. In factor markets, households supply labor, entrepreneurial ability, and other factors of production to firms. Firms use these factors of production to make goods and services that they supply to households in product markets. The red arrows show the flow of goods and services from firms to households. The green arrows show the flow of funds. In factor markets, households receive wages and other payments from firms in exchange for supplying the factors of production. Households use these wages and other payments to purchase goods and services from firms in product markets. Firms sell goods and services to households in product markets, and they use the funds to purchase the factors of production from households in factor markets.

We can use a simple economic model called the **circular-flow diagram** to see how participants in markets are linked. Figure 6 shows that in factor markets, households supply labor and other factors of production in exchange for wages and other payments from firms. In product markets, households use the payments they earn in factor markets to purchase the goods and services supplied by firms. Firms produce these goods and services using the factors of production supplied by households. In the figure, the blue arrows show the flow of factors of production from households through factor markets to firms. The red arrows show the flow of goods and services from firms through product markets to households. The green arrows show the flow of funds from firms through factor markets to households and the flow of spending from households through product markets to firms.

Like all economic models, the circular-flow diagram is a simplified version of reality. For example, Figure 6 leaves out the important role of government in buying goods from firms and in making payments, such as Social Security or unemployment insurance payments, to households. The figure also leaves out the roles played by banks, the stock and bond markets, and other parts of the *financial system* in aiding the flow of funds from lenders to borrowers. Finally, the figure does not show that some goods and services purchased by domestic households are produced in foreign countries and some goods and services produced by domestic firms are sold to foreign households. Despite these simplifications, the circular-flow diagram in Figure 6 is useful for seeing how product markets, factor markets, and their participants are linked together. One of the great wonders of the market system is that it manages to successfully coordinate the independent activities of so many households and firms.

Circular-flow diagram A model that illustrates how participants in markets are linked.

The Gains from Free Markets

Free market A market with few government restrictions on how a good or service can be produced or sold or on how a factor of production can be employed.

A **free market** exists when the government places few restrictions on how goods and services can be produced or sold or on how factors of production can be employed. Governments in all modern economies intervene more than is consistent with a fully free market. In that sense, we can think of the free market as being a benchmark against which we can judge actual economies. There are relatively few government restrictions on economic activities in the United States, Canada, the countries of Western Europe, Hong Kong, Singapore, and Estonia. So these countries come close to the free market benchmark. In countries such as Cuba and North Korea, the free market system has been rejected in favor of centrally planned economies with extensive government control over product and factor markets. Countries that come closest to the free market benchmark have been more successful than countries with centrally planned economies in providing their people with rising living standards.

The Scottish philosopher Adam Smith is considered the father of modern economics because his book *An Inquiry into the Nature and Causes of the Wealth of Nations*, published in 1776, was an early and very influential argument for the free market system. Smith was writing at a time when extensive government restrictions on markets were common. In many parts of Europe, the *guild system* prevailed. Under this system, governments would give guilds, or organizations of producers, the authority to control the production of a good. For example, the shoemakers' guild controlled who was allowed to produce shoes, how many shoes they could produce, and what price they could charge. In France, the cloth makers' guild even dictated the number of threads in the weave of the cloth.

Smith argued that such restrictions reduced the income, or wealth, of a country and its people by restricting the quantity of goods produced. Some people at the time supported the restrictions of the guild system because it was in their financial interest to do so. If you were a member of a guild, the restrictions served to reduce the competition you faced. But other people sincerely believed that the alternative to the guild system was economic chaos. Smith argued that these people were wrong and that a country could enjoy a smoothly functioning economic system if firms were freed from guild restrictions.

The Market Mechanism

In Smith's day, defenders of the guild system worried that if, for instance, the shoemakers' guild did not control shoe production, either too many or too few shoes would be produced. Smith argued that prices would do a better job of coordinating the activities of buyers and sellers than the guilds could. A key to understanding Smith's argument is the assumption that *individuals usually act in a rational, self-interested way*. In particular, individuals take those actions that are most likely to make themselves better off financially. This assumption of rational, self-interested behavior underlies nearly all economic analysis. In fact, economics can be distinguished from other disciplines that study human behavior—such as sociology and psychology—by its emphasis on the assumption of self-interested behavior. Adam Smith understood—as economists today understand—that people's motives can be complex. But when we analyze people in the act of buying and selling, the motivation of financial reward usually provides the best explanation for the actions people take.

For example, suppose that a significant number of consumers switch from buying regular gasoline-powered cars to buying gasoline/electric-powered hybrid cars, such as the Toyota Prius, or all-electric cars, such as the Tesla Model S. Firms will find that they can charge relatively higher prices for hybrid cars and electric cars than they can for regular cars. The self-interest of these firms will lead them to respond to consumers' wishes by producing more hybrid and electric cars and fewer regular cars. Or suppose that consumers decide that they want to eat less bread, pasta, and other foods that are high in carbohydrates. Then the prices firms can charge for bread and pasta will fall.

The self-interest of firms will lead them to produce less bread and pasta, which, in fact, is what has happened over the past 10 years.

Note that for the market mechanism to work in response to changes in consumers' wants, *prices must be flexible*. Changes in *relative prices*—the price of one good or service relative to the prices of other goods or services—provide information, or a signal, to both consumers and firms. For example, during 2010, consumers worldwide increased their demand for cattle and poultry. Because corn is fed to cattle and poultry, prices for corn soared relative to prices for other crops. Many farmers in the United States received this price signal and responded by increasing the amount of corn they planted and decreasing the amount of soybeans and wheat. One Kansas farmer was quoted as saying, "It seemed to me there was $100 to $150 per acre more money in the corn than there was in the beans. That's the kind of math that a lot of guys were using." By 2013, the United States was experiencing record corn crops. Similarly, falling prices for DVDs or music CDs in the 2000s were a signal to movie studios and record companies to devote fewer resources to these products and more resources to making movies and music available online.

In the United States today, governments at the federal, state, and local levels set or regulate the prices of only about 10 to 20 percent of goods and services. The prices of other goods and services are free to change as consumer wants change and as costs of production change.

In the case where consumers want more of a product, and in the case where they want less of a product, the market system responds without a guild or the government giving orders about how much to produce or what price to charge. In a famous phrase, Smith said that firms would be led by the "invisible hand" of the market to provide consumers with what they want. Firms respond *individually* to changes in prices by making decisions that *collectively* end up satisfying the wants of consumers.

<table>
<tr><td>Making
the
Connection</td><td>

A Story of the Market System in Action: How Do You Make an iPad?

Apple produces the iPad. Because Apple's headquarters are in Cupertino, California, it seems reasonable to assume that iPads are also manufactured in that state. A poll by the *New*

</td></tr>
</table>

York Times showed that, in fact, a majority of people interviewed believed that iPads were manufactured in the United States, if not specifically in California. Although engineers at Apple designed the iPad, the company produces none of the components of the iPad, nor does it assemble the components into a finished product. Far from being produced entirely by one company in one country, the iPad requires the coordinated activities of thousands of workers and dozens of firms spread around the world.

Foxconn, which is based in Taiwan, assembles the iPad in factories in Shenzhen and Chengdu, China, and Jundiai, São Paulo, Brazil, and ships them to Apple for sale in the United States. Although Foxconn does final assembly, it doesn't make any of the components and, in fact, charges Apple less than $15 for assembling each iPad.

The following table lists some of the many suppliers of iPad components.

Each of these suppliers in turn relies on its own suppliers. For example, Broadcom designs the touchscreen controller for the iPad and supplies it to Apple, but it does not manufacture the components of the controller or assemble them. To manufacture the components, Broadcom relies on SilTerra, based in Malaysia; SMIC, based in mainland China; and Taiwan Semiconductor Manufacturing Corporation (TSMC) and UMC, based in Taiwan. TSMC's factories are for the most part not in Taiwan but in mainland China and Eastern Europe. To assemble the components, Broadcom uses several companies, including Amkor Technology, based in Chandler, Arizona, and STATS Chip-PAC, based in Singapore.

The market coordinates the activities of the many people spread around the world who contribute to making an iPad.

Firm	Location of the Firm	iPad Component the Firm Supplies
AKM	Japan	Motion sensor
AU Optronics	Taiwan	Display
Broadcom	United States (California)	Touchscreen controller and wireless chip
Cirrus Logic	United States (Texas)	Audio chip
Corning	United States (New York)	Glass screen cover
Elpida	Japan	System memory
SK Hynix	South Korea	Flash memory
Infineon Technologies	Germany	Semiconductors
LG Electronics	South Korea	Display
Quicomm	United Kingdom	Wireless section
Samsung	South Korea	Display, flash memory, and applications processor
Sharp	Japan	Display
STMicroelectronics	France/Italy	Motion sensors
Texas Instruments	United States (Texas)	Touchscreen controller
Toshiba	Japan	Flash memory

All told, an iPad contains hundreds of parts that are designed, manufactured, and assembled by firms around the world. Many of these firms are not even aware of which other firms are also producing components for the iPad. Few of the managers of these firms have met managers of the other firms or shared knowledge of how their particular components are produced. In fact, no one person from Tim Cook, the chief executive officer of Apple, on down possesses the knowledge of how to produce all the components that are assembled into an iPad. Instead, the invisible hand of the market has led these firms to contribute their knowledge and resources to the process that ultimately results in an iPad available for sale in a store in the United States. Apple has so efficiently organized the process of producing the iPad that you can order a custom iPad with a personal engraving and have it delivered from an assembly plant in China or Brazil to your doorstep in the United States in as little as three days.

Sources: Marjorie Connelly, "Poll Finds Consumer Confusion on Where Apple Devices Are Made," *New York Times*, January 25, 2012; Andrew Rassweiler, "New iPad 32GB + 4G Carries $364.35 Bill of Materials," iSuppli.com, March 16, 2012; and Arik Hesseldahl, "Teardown Shows Apple iPad Mini Costs at Least $188 to Build," allthingsd.com, November 3, 2012.

Your Turn: Test your understanding by doing related problems 3.8 and 3.9 at the end of this chapter.

The Role of the Entrepreneur

Entrepreneur Someone who operates a business, bringing together the factors of production—labor, capital, and natural resources—to produce goods and services.

Entrepreneurs are central to the working of the market system. An **entrepreneur** is someone who operates a business. Entrepreneurs first determine what goods and services they believe consumers want and then decide how to produce those goods and services most profitably, using the available factors of production—labor, capital, and natural resources. Successful entrepreneurs are able to search out opportunities to provide new goods and services. Frequently these opportunities are created by new technology. Consumers and existing businesses often do not at first realize that the new technology makes new products feasible. For example, even after the development of the internal combustion engine had made automobiles practicable, Henry Ford remarked, "If I had asked my customers what they wanted, they would have said a faster horse." Because consumers often cannot evaluate a new product before it exists, some of the most successful entrepreneurs, such as the late Steve Jobs of Apple, rarely use *focus groups*, or meetings with consumers in which the consumers are asked what new products they would like to see. Instead, entrepreneurs think of products that consumers may not even realize they need, such as, in Jobs's case, an MP3 player—iPod—or a tablet computer—iPad. Entrepreneurs are important to the economy because they are often responsible for making new products widely available to consumers, as Henry Ford did with the automobile and Steve Jobs did with the iPod.

The firms entrepreneurs found are typically small at first, as Apple and Ford were. Table 3 lists some of the important products entrepreneurs at small firms introduced during the twentieth century.

Entrepreneurs put their own funds at risk when they start businesses. If they are wrong about what consumers want or about the best way to produce goods and services, they can lose those funds. In fact, it is not unusual for entrepreneurs who eventually achieve great success to fail at first. For instance, early in their careers, both Henry Ford and Sakichi Toyoda, who eventually founded the Toyota Motor Corporation, started companies that quickly failed. Research by Richard Freeman of Harvard University has shown that a typical entrepreneur earns less than an employee at a large firm who has the same education and other characteristics. Few entrepreneurs make the fortunes earned by Mark Zuckerberg, Steve Jobs, or Bill Gates.

Product	Inventor
Air conditioning	William Haviland Carrier
Airplane	Orville and Wilbur Wright
Automobile, mass produced	Henry Ford
Biomagnetic imaging	Raymond Damadian
Biosynthetic insulin	Herbert Boyer
DNA fingerprinting	Alec Jeffries
FM radio	Edwin Howard Armstrong
Helicopter	Igor Sikorsky
High-resolution CAT scanner	Robert Ledley
Hydraulic brake	Malcolm Lockheed
Integrated circuit	Jack Kilby
Microprocessor	Ted Hoff
Optical scanner	Everett Franklin Lindquist
Oral contraceptives	Carl Djerassi
Overnight delivery service	Fred Smith
Personal computer	Steve Jobs and Steve Wozniak
Quick-frozen foods	Clarence Birdseye
Safety razor	King Gillette
Soft contact lens	Kevin Tuohy
Solid fuel rocket engine	Robert Goddard
Supercomputer	Seymour Cray
Vacuum tube	Philo Farnsworth
Zipper	Gideon Sundback

Table 3

Important Products Introduced by Entrepreneurs at Small Firms

Source: William J. Baumol, *The Microtheory of Innovative Entrepreneurship*, Princeton, NJ: Princeton University Press, 2010, and various sources. Note that the person who first commercially developed a particular product is sometimes disputed by historians.

Entrepreneurs make a vital contribution to economic growth through their roles in responding to consumer demand and introducing new products. Government policies that encourage entrepreneurship are also likely to increase economic growth and raise the standard of living. In the next section, we consider the legal framework required for a successful market in which entrepreneurs can succeed.

The Legal Basis of a Successful Market System

In a free market, government does not restrict how firms produce and sell goods and services or how they employ factors of production. But the absence of government intervention is not enough for the market system to work well. Government has to take active steps to provide a *legal environment* that will allow markets to operate efficiently.

Protection of Private Property For the market system to work well, individuals must be willing to take risks. Someone with $250,000 can be cautious and keep it safely in a bank—or even in cash, if the person doesn't trust banks. But the market system won't work unless a significant number of people are willing to risk their funds by investing them in businesses. Investing in businesses is risky in any country. Many businesses fail every year in the United States and other high-income countries. But in high-income countries, someone who starts a new business or invests in an existing business doesn't have to worry that the government, the military, or criminal gangs might decide to seize the business or demand payments for not destroying the business. Unfortunately, in many poor countries, owners of businesses are not well protected from having their businesses seized by the government or from having their profits taken by criminals. Where these problems exist, opening a business can be extremely risky. Cash can be concealed easily, but a business is difficult to conceal or move.

(handwritten margin note: market runs by people putting money into the bank but that is risky)

Property rights The rights individuals or firms have to the exclusive use of their property, including the right to buy or sell it.

Property rights are the rights individuals or firms have to the exclusive use of their property, including the right to buy or sell it. Property can be tangible, physical property, such as a store or factory. Property can also be intangible, such as the right to an idea. Two amendments to the U.S. Constitution guarantee property rights: The Fifth Amendment states that the federal government shall not deprive any person "of life, liberty, or property, without due process of law." The Fourteenth Amendment extends this guarantee to the actions of state governments: "No state … shall deprive any person of life, liberty, or property, without due process of law." Similar guarantees exist in every high-income country. Unfortunately, in many developing countries, such guarantees do not exist or are poorly enforced.

In any modern economy, *intellectual property rights* are very important. Intellectual property includes books, films, software, and ideas for new products or new ways of producing products. To protect intellectual property, the federal government grants a *patent* that gives an inventor—often a firm—the exclusive right to produce and sell a new product for a period of 20 years from the date the patent was filed. For instance, because Microsoft has a patent on the Windows operating system, other firms cannot sell their own versions of Windows. The government grants patents to encourage firms to spend money on the research and development necessary to create new products. If other companies could freely copy Windows, Microsoft would not have spent the funds necessary to develop it. Just as a new product or a new method of making a product receives patent protection, new books, films, and software receive *copyright* protection. Under U.S. law, the creator of a book, film, or piece of music has the exclusive right to use the creation during the creator's lifetime. The creator's heirs retain this exclusive right for 50 years after the death of the creator.

In providing copyright protection for only a limited time, Congress provides economic incentives to creators while eventually—after the period of copyright has ended—allowing the creators' works to be freely available. The longer the period of copyright, the more likely it is that some consumers will not gain access to the copyrighted work and the longer the wait before others can use the copyrighted work in their own work, for instance, by writing a sequel to a copyrighted book.

| Making the Connection | ### Who Owns *The Wizard of Oz*? |

The U.S. Congress provides copyright protection to authors to give them an economic incentive to invest the time and effort required to write a book. While a book is under copyright, only the author—or whoever the author sells the copyright to—can legally publish a paper or digital copy of the book. Once the copyright expires, however, the book enters the *public domain* and anyone is free to publish the book. Copies of classic books, such as *Huckleberry Finn* or *Oliver Twist*, are usually available from many publishers.

L. Frank Baum wrote *The Wonderful Wizard of Oz* in 1900. The copyright on the book expired years ago and many publishers now sell their own versions of the book. While these publishers can't claim copyright of Baum's words, because those words are in the public domain, they can claim copyright on a new design of the book or on any new illustrations they create.

A similar situation exists with the famous 1939 MGM film *The Wizard of Oz*. Warner Brothers, which now owns the copyright to the film, does not have a legal right to any of the words or incidents in the film that were taken directly from Baum's book. However, Warner Brothers does have a copyright on any dialogue or incidents that were written specifically for the film as well as the design of the film sets and the actors' costumes. Warner Brothers was aggressive in defending its copyright when Walt Disney announced that it was making a film called *Oz The Great and Powerful*. As a copyright lawyer put it: "The MGM film presented the story in a certain way, and it's those things—the embellishments, the creative decisions—that Disney cannot use."

The Wonderful Wizard of Oz is a classic book from 1900 that became a classic film in 1939. A remake of the film in 2013 raised copyright issues.

Disney had to be careful even in minor details to avoid violating Warner Brothers' copyright. For example, it made the green makeup of the Wicked Witch of the West a different shade from that in the earlier film. Disney also changed the location of the Yellow Brick Road and the name of Munchkin Country to avoid infringing on Warner Brothers' copyright. Shortly before the film was released in early 2013, Disney's lawyers decided that the hairstyles of some of the Munchkins in the completed film had to be digitally altered because they appeared too close to the hairstyles in the earlier film.

Most economists believe that copyrights provide needed protection for authors and creators of movies or other artistic works. However, the roadblocks Warner Brothers placed in the way of Disney making a new *Oz* film show that copyrights may deter others from producing new work that might infringe on a copyrighted work.

Sources: Brooks Barnes, "We Aren't in the Old Kansas, Toto," *New York Times*, February 28, 2013; and Eriq Gardner, "Disney, Warner Bros. Fighting Over 'Wizard of Oz' Trademarks," *Hollywood Reporter*, February 12, 2012.

Your Turn: Test your understanding by doing related problem 3.17 at the end of this chapter.

Enforcement of Contracts and Property Rights Business activity often involves someone agreeing to carry out some action in the future. For example, you may borrow $20,000 to buy a car and promise the bank—by signing a loan contract—that you will pay back the money over the next five years. Or Facebook may sign a licensing agreement with a small technology company, agreeing to use that company's technology for a period of several years in return for a fee. Usually these agreements take the form of legal contracts. For the market system to work, businesses and individuals have to rely on these contracts being carried out. If one party to a legal contract does not fulfill its obligations—perhaps the small company had promised Facebook exclusive use of its technology but then began licensing it to other companies—the other party can go to court to have the agreement enforced. Similarly, if property owners in the United States believe that the federal or state government has violated their rights under the Fifth or Fourteenth Amendments, they can go to court to have their rights enforced.

But going to court to enforce a contract or private property rights will be successful only if the court system is independent and judges are able to make impartial decisions on the basis of the law. In the United States and other high-income countries, the court systems have enough independence from other parts of the government and enough protection from intimidation by outside forces—such as criminal gangs—that they are able to make their decisions based on the law. In many developing countries, the court systems lack this independence and will not provide a remedy if the government violates private property rights or if a person with powerful political connections decides to violate a business contract.

If property rights are not well enforced, fewer goods and services will be produced. This reduces economic efficiency, leaving the economy inside its production possibilities frontier.

Continued

Economics in Your Life

The Trade-offs When You Buy a Car

At the beginning of the chapter, we asked you to think about two questions: With respect to traditional gasoline-powered cars, what is the relationship between safety and fuel efficiency? and Under what circumstances would it be possible for automobile manufacturers to make cars safer and more fuel efficient? To answer the first question, you have to recognize that there is a trade-off between safety and fuel efficiency. With the technology available at any particular time, an automobile manufacturer can increase fuel efficiency by making a car smaller and lighter. But driving a lighter car increases your chances of being injured if you have an accident. The trade-off between safety and fuel efficiency would look much like the relationship in Figure 1. To get more of both safety and gas mileage, automobile makers would have to discover new technologies that allow them to make cars lighter and safer at the same time. Such new technologies would make points like G in Figure 1 attainable.

Conclusion

We have seen that by trading in markets, people are able to specialize and pursue their comparative advantage. Trading on the basis of comparative advantage makes all participants in trade better off. The key role of markets is to facilitate trade. In fact, the market system is a very effective means of coordinating the decisions of millions of consumers, workers, and firms. At the center of the market system is the consumer. To be successful, firms must respond to the desires of consumers. These desires are communicated to firms through prices. To explore how markets work, we must study the behavior of consumers and firms.

Read *An Inside Look* on the next page to explore the trade-offs managers face at luxury carmaker Mercedes-Benz and why the company chose to partner with Tesla Motors to develop electric-vehicle components.

CAR AND DRIVER

Mercedes-Benz Execs Talk 13 New Models, Electric Cars, and Hybrid AMGs

Mercedes-Benz has never had a stronger first quarter in the United States than it has had in 2013, but the German automaker isn't about to slow down. The company is taking strides to secure its position over the long term and to bolster its global sales with 13 all-new new models by 2020. These vehicles aren't just refreshes and redesigns; the Stuttgart-based marque will introduce 13 new nameplates—vehicles without a predecessor. We know there will be the front-drive-based GLA-class crossover and the S-class will add coupe and convertible variants, but the bulk of the plan remains a mystery. Hoping to fill in some of the unknowns, we sat down with four of the most influential executives at Mercedes-Benz: Thomas Weber, head of R&D; Dieter Zetsche, Daimler chairman and head of Mercedes-Benz cars; Jörg Prigl, vice president of small-car development; and Ola Källenius, chairman of Mercedes-Benz AMG. Here's what they had to say about the future of Mercedes:

Car and Driver [C/D]: We're struggling to find 13 obvious holes in the Mercedes-Benz lineup. What kinds of vehicles are coming? Should we expect Mercedes versions of BMW's Gran Turismos?

Thomas Weber: To build such a vehicle is easy. To be successful is the name of the game. You also must be careful not to say a current trend is a trend forever. We will certainly add long-wheelbase models targeting the Asian markets. As we look at these new models, we need to beat our competitors in three areas: design, powertrains, and environmental and safety technologies.

C/D: Is there any concern that the $30,825 CLA250 might dilute the brand image in the U.S. or cannibalize C-class sales?

Dieter Zetsche: Our more-mature, more-affluent customers are very good to us. At the same time, the A-class has an average age drop of 10 years [in Europe]. It's all about striking the right balance. The new S-class will move into Rolls-Royce Ghost territory. Just as we introduce small cars, we keep the light shining on the brand.

Jörg Prigl: If we saw that as a risk, we shouldn't have done the CLA. We are not fighting for the loyal customers we have.

C/D: Electric vehicles have failed to take off in the U.S. Why bring the electric B-class to market?

Prigl: Technology leadership in a potential future drivetrain is a must for us. The partnership with Tesla will help us speed up and beat the competition. If you believe you can do this alone as an automaker, you will fail. The battery cell should not be done by the OEM [Auto Parts]. There should be huge competition among suppliers to get the cell right. The specific know-how for the automaker is in the packaging and the battery management. Tesla provides the complete powertrain for the B-class Electric Drive, but the calibration is split between Tesla and Mercedes-Benz.

C/D: The Geneva auto show was dominated by a pair of hybrid supercars, the McLaren P1 and the Ferrari LaFerrari. At what point will tightening environmental regulations force AMG to adopt hybrid powertrains?

Ola Källenius: The SLS AMG Electric Drive is a glimpse of the future, but we took two steps forward to take one step back. Hybrids are the next logical step, likely in five to seven years. For now, with conventional gas measures we can reduce emissions another 20 percent. The immediate future is relatively clear. Downsize and direct injection is where combustion is headed, but it is inevitable that we will have to electrify these cars.

C/D: Why isn't Mercedes making a big investment in carbon fiber like BMW and the Volkswagen Group have?

Källenius: Carbon fiber is for a hypercar. Taking out weight is a decathlon. You need to work with all the materials. Right now, the industry is at a peak; every new car going forward will shave off weight ….

Source: Eric Tingwall, "Mercedes-Benz Execs Talk 13 New Models, Electric Cars, and Hybrid AMGs," *Car and Driver*, April 10, 2013.

Key Points in the Article

Mercedes is planning 13 new models by 2020, including a new crossover vehicle; new variations of its S-class automobile; redeveloped entry-level vehicles; and the introduction of an electric car. With these new models, the managers at Mercedes are making choices about how to use new designs, upgraded powertrains, and advances in technology to deal with environmental and safety concerns. In addition, these managers have also chosen to partner with Tesla Motors to develop electric-vehicle components. Making the optimal choices will be important for Mercedes to remain one of the most competitive and successful high-end automobile manufacturers in the world.

Analyzing the News

a Automobile manufacturers must decide what type of cars to bring to market. Mercedes has two challenges in introducing a new entry-level car in the United States. First, for a high-end manufacturer like Mercedes, image is very important, and even the perception that the company is catering to a lower-income consumer can be damaging. Second, Mercedes does not want to sacrifice sales of its more profitable C-class models for these new lower-price A-class models. Suppose Mercedes produced only A-class and C-class vehicles and in 2013 had the capability of producing a total of 30,000 vehicles. This capacity is represented by PPF_{2013} in the figure below. This curve shows that Mercedes would have to sacrifice production (and therefore sales) of one type of vehicle to produce more of the other. The executives at Mercedes expect their market to continue to grow, and they do not believe that introducing the new A-class model will take sales away from the C-class. Mercedes will therefore have to produce a larger number of automobiles, which is represented by PPF_{2020} in the figure.

b Despite disappointing sales figures for electric vehicles, Mercedes has decided to introduce its electric B-class model in the U.S. market. Mercedes believes that the market for electric vehicles will grow, and it needs to be at the forefront of development in order to beat the competition. Mercedes faced a trade-off when deciding on the development of its electric vehicle. Rather than build this vehicle completely in-house, Mercedes chose to partner with Tesla, believing that Tesla's experience in producing electric vehicles would be advantageous for both companies and make the B-class a success. In choosing to take advantage of Tesla's expertise and technology, Mercedes gave up some level of control, but it chose this path believing it would increase the potential for building a vehicle that would have strong sales.

c As emissions standards continue to tighten and gas-mileage requirements continue to grow, lighter-weight cars will become a bigger part of our future. One decision Mercedes has made is to *not* invest heavily in lightweight carbon fiber for use in production, but rather to reduce the weight of all materials over the next several years. Here again, Mercedes faced a trade-off between investing in one specific technology and waiting to see what the future holds in terms of other lighter-weight production options that it can use in its manufacturing.

Thinking Critically

1. Suppose that from 2013 to 2020, the resources Mercedes-Benz uses to produce its automobiles remain constant, while improvements in technology in 2020 allow Mercedes to produce the additional quantity of A-class models shown in the figure below, but no additional C-class models. Draw a graph that illustrates this technology change. Be sure to show both the 2013 and new 2020 *PPF*s. What is the opportunity cost to Mercedes-Benz of producing one C-class model in 2013? In 2020?

2. Assume that the figure below accurately represents Mercedes-Benz's *PPF*s for 2013 and 2020, and that in 2020 it has customer orders for 35,000 A-class models and 20,000 C-class models. Explain whether Mercedes can fill all of these orders.

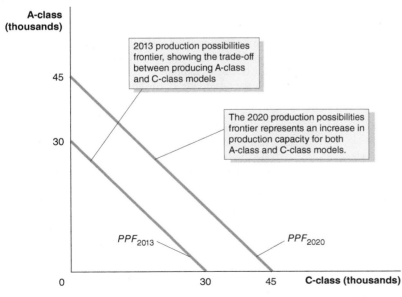

Choosing between producing a Mercedes A-class model and producing a C-class model.

Chapter Summary and Problems

Key Terms

Absolute advantage

Circular-flow diagram

Comparative advantage

Economic growth

Entrepreneur

Factor market

Factors of production

Free market

Market

Opportunity cost

Product market

Production possibilities
frontier (**PPF**)

Property rights

Scarcity

Trade

 Production Possibilities Frontiers and Opportunity Costs
LEARNING OBJECTIVE: Use a production possibilities frontier to analyze opportunity costs and trade-offs.

Summary

The **production possibilities frontier (PPF)** is a curve that shows the maximum attainable combinations of two products that may be produced with available resources. The *PPF* is used to illustrate the trade-offs that arise from **scarcity**. Points on the frontier are technically efficient. Points inside the frontier are inefficient, and points outside the frontier are unattainable. The **opportunity cost** of any activity is the highest-valued alternative that must be given up to engage in that activity. Because of increasing marginal opportunity costs, production possibilities frontiers are usually bowed out rather than straight lines. This illustrates the important economic concept that the more resources that are already devoted to any activity, the smaller the payoff from devoting additional resources to that activity is likely to be. **Economic growth** is illustrated by shifting a production possibilities frontier outward.

Visit **www.myeconlab.com** to complete these exercises online and get instant feedback.

Review Questions

1.1 What do economists mean by *scarcity*? Can you think of anything that is not scarce according to the economic definition?

1.2 What is a production possibilities frontier? How can we show efficiency on a production possibilities frontier? How can we show inefficiency? What causes a production possibilities frontier to shift outward?

1.3 What does increasing marginal opportunity costs mean? What are the implications of this idea for the shape of the production possibilities frontier?

Problems and Applications

1.4 Draw a production possibilities frontier that shows the trade-off between the production of cotton and the production of soybeans.

   a. Show the effect that a prolonged drought would have on the initial production possibilities frontier.

   b. Suppose genetic modification makes soybeans resistant to insects, allowing yields to double. Show the effect of this technological change on the initial production possibilities frontier.

1.5 **[Related to the** Chapter Opener**]** One of the trade-offs Tesla faces is between safety and the maximum range someone can drive an all-electric car before having to recharge it. For example, adding steel to a car makes it safer but also heavier, which results in fewer miles between recharges. Draw a hypothetical production possibilities frontier that Tesla engineers face that shows this trade-off.

1.6 **[Related to** Chapter Opener**]** According to an article on *CNNMoney*, in May 2013 CEO Elon Musk of Tesla Motors announced plans for a large expansion of Tesla's network of supercharger stations by the end of the year. The network of supercharger stations will stretch from Los Angeles to New York and cover most metropolitan areas in the United States and Supercharger stations allow the all-electric cars to be recharged in about an hour. Musk stated that: "It is very important to address this issue of long-distance travel."

   a. Why is it important for Tesla Motors to address the issue of long-distance travel?

   b. Tesla Motors, like other firms, faces many strategic decisions and trade-offs. What would be the opportunity cost to Tesla Motors to expanding the supercharger networks?

Source: Chris Isidore, "Tesla Tripling Supercharger Network for LA to NY Trip," *CNNMoney*, May 31, 2013.

1.7 Suppose you win free tickets to a movie plus all you can eat at the snack bar for free. Would there be a cost to you to attend this movie? Explain.

1.8 Suppose we can divide all the goods produced by an economy into two types: consumption goods and capital goods. Capital goods, such as machinery, equipment, and computers, are goods used to produce other goods.

   a. Use a production possibilities frontier graph to illustrate the trade-off to an economy between producing consumption goods and producing capital goods. Is it likely that the production possibilities frontier in this situation will be a straight line (as in Figure 1) or bowed out (as in Figure 2)? Briefly explain.

   b. Suppose a technological change occurs that has a favorable effect on the production of capital goods but not consumption goods. Show the effect on the production possibilities frontier.

c. Suppose that Lichtenstein and Luxembourg currently have identical production possibilities frontiers but that Lichtenstein devotes only 5 percent of its resources to producing capital goods over each of the next 10 years, while Luxembourg devotes 30 percent. Which country is likely to experience more rapid economic growth in the future? Illustrate using a production possibilities frontier graph. Your graph should include production possibilities frontiers for Lichtenstein and Luxembourg today and in 10 years.

1.9 Use the following production possibilities frontier for a country to answer the questions.

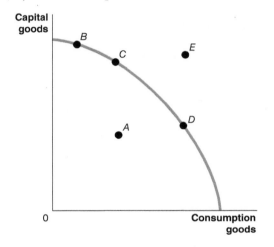

a. Which point or points are unattainable? Briefly explain why.

b. Which point or points are efficient? Briefly explain why.

c. Which point or points are inefficient? Briefly explain why.

d. At which point is the country's future growth rate likely to be the highest? Briefly explain why.

1.10 [**Related to** Solved Problem 1] You have exams in economics and chemistry coming up, and you have 5 hours available for studying. The following table shows the trade-offs you face in allocating the time you will spend in studying each subject:

	Hours Spent Studying		Midterm Score	
Choice	Economics	Chemistry	Economics	Chemistry
A	5	0	95	70
B	4	1	93	78
C	3	2	90	84
D	2	3	86	88
E	1	4	81	90
F	0	5	75	91

a. Use the data in the table to draw a production possibilities frontier graph. Label the vertical axis "Score on economics exam," and label the horizontal axis "Score on chemistry exam." Make sure to label the values where your production possibilities frontier intersects the vertical and horizontal axes.

b. Label the points representing choice C and choice D. If you are at choice C, what is your opportunity cost of increasing your chemistry score by 4 points?

c. Under what circumstances would choice A be a sensible choice?

1.11 Suppose the U.S. president is attempting to decide whether the federal government should spend more on research to find a cure for heart disease. He asks you, one of his economic advisors, to prepare a report discussing the relevant factors he should consider. Use the concepts of opportunity cost and trade-offs to discuss some of the main issues you would deal with in your report.

1.12 Suppose that the federal government is deciding which of two cancer treatment therapies it will allow Medicare to pay for (assuming that only one treatment therapy will be funded): Therapy A, which will prolong the average life span of patients receiving the treatment by 24 months and will cost $750,000 per patient treated, or therapy B, which will prolong the average life span of patients receiving the treatment by 20 months and will cost $25,000 per patient treated. What factors should the federal government take into consideration in making its decision?

1.13 Lawrence Summers served as secretary of the Treasury in the Clinton administration from 1999 to 2001 and as director of the National Economic Council in the Obama administration from 2009 to 2010. He has been quoted as giving the following defense of the economic approach:

> There is nothing morally unattractive about saying: We need to analyze which way of spending money on health care will produce more benefit and which less, and using our money as efficiently as we can. I don't think there is anything immoral about seeking to achieve environmental benefits at the lowest possible costs.

Would it be more ethical to reduce pollution without worrying about the cost, or by taking the cost into account? Briefly explain.

Source: David Wessel, "Precepts from Professor Summers," *Wall Street Journal*, October 17, 2002.

1.14 In *The Wonderful Wizard of Oz* and his other books about the Land of Oz, L. Frank Baum observed that if people's wants were limited enough, most goods would not be scarce. According to Baum, this was the case in Oz:

> There were no poor people in the Land of Oz, because there was no such thing as money.... Each person was given freely by his neighbors whatever he required for his use, which is as much as anyone may reasonably desire. Some tilled the lands and raised great crops of grain, which was divided equally among the whole population, so that all had enough. There were many tailors and dressmakers and shoemakers and the like, who made things that any who desired them might wear. Likewise there were jewelers who made ornaments for the person, which pleased and beautified the people, and these ornaments also were free to those who asked for them. Each man and woman, no

matter what he or she produced for the good of the community, was supplied by the neighbors with food and clothing and a house and furniture and ornaments and games. If by chance the supply ever ran short, more was taken from the great storehouses of the Ruler, which were afterward filled up again when there was more of any article than people needed... .

You will know, by what I have told you here, that the Land of Oz was a remarkable country. I do not suppose such an arrangement would be practical with us.

Do you agree with Baum that the economic system in Oz wouldn't work in the contemporary United States? Briefly explain why or why not.

Source: L. Frank Baum, *The Emerald City of Oz*, 1910, pp. 30–31.

 ## Comparative Advantage and Trade

LEARNING OBJECTIVE: Describe comparative advantage and explain how it serves as the basis for trade.

Summary

Fundamentally, markets are about **trade**, which is the act of buying or selling. People trade on the basis of comparative advantage. An individual, a firm, or a country has a **comparative advantage** in producing a good or service if it can produce the good or service at the lowest opportunity cost. People are usually better off specializing in the activity for which they have a comparative advantage and trading for the other goods and services they need. It is important not to confuse comparative advantage with absolute advantage. An individual, a firm, or a country has an **absolute advantage** in producing a good or service if it can produce more of that good or service using the same amount of resources. It is possible to have an absolute advantage in producing a good or service without having a comparative advantage.

Visit **www.myeconlab.com** to complete these exercises online and get instant feedback.

Review Questions

2.1 What is absolute advantage? What is comparative advantage? Is it possible for a country to have a comparative advantage in producing a good without also having an absolute advantage? Briefly explain.

2.2 What is the basis for trade: absolute advantage or comparative advantage? How can an individual or a country gain from specialization and trade?

Problems and Applications

2.3 Look again at the information in Figure 4. Choose a rate of trading cherries for apples different from the rate used in the text (15 pounds of cherries for 10 pounds of apples) that will allow you and your neighbor to benefit from trading. Prepare a table like Table 1 to illustrate your answer.

2.4 Using the same amount of resources, the United States and Canada can both produce lumberjack shirts and

lumberjack boots, as shown in the following production possibilities frontiers:

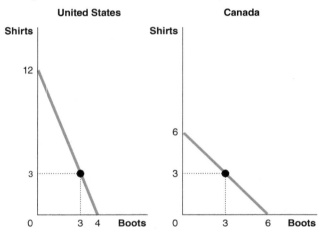

a. Who has a comparative advantage in producing lumberjack boots? Who has a comparative advantage in producing lumberjack shirts? Explain your reasoning.

b. Does either country have an absolute advantage in producing both goods? Explain.

c. Suppose that both countries are currently producing three pairs of boots and three shirts. Show that both can be better off if they each specialize in producing one good and then trade for the other.

2.5 **[Related to** Don't Let This Happen to You**]** In the 1950s, the economist Bela Balassa compared 28 manufacturing industries in the United States and Britain. In every one of the 28 industries, Balassa found that the United States had an absolute advantage. In these circumstances, would there have been any gain to the United States from importing any of these products from Britain? Explain.

2.6 **[Related to** Solved Problem 2**]** Suppose Iran and Iraq both produce oil and olive oil, which are sold for the same prices in both countries. The following table shows the combinations of both goods that each country can produce in a day, measured in thousands of barrels, using the same amounts of capital and labor:

Iraq		Iran	
Oil	Olive Oil	Oil	Olive Oil
0	8	0	4
2	6	1	3
4	4	2	2
6	2	3	1
8	0	4	0

a. Who has the comparative advantage in producing oil? Explain.
b. Can these two countries gain from trading oil and olive oil? Explain.

2.7 **[Related to** Solved Problem 2**]** Suppose that France and Germany both produce schnitzel and wine. The following table shows combinations of the goods that each country can produce in a day:

France		Germany	
Wine (bottles)	Schnitzel (pounds)	Wine (bottles)	Schnitzel (pounds)
0	8	0	15
1	6	1	12
2	4	2	9
3	2	3	6
4	0	4	3
		5	0

a. Who has a comparative advantage in producing wine? Who has a comparative advantage in producing schnitzel?
b. Suppose that France is currently producing 1 bottle of wine and 6 pounds of schnitzel, and Germany is currently producing 3 bottles of wine and 6 pounds of schnitzel. Demonstrate that France and Germany can both be better off if they specialize in producing only one good and then trade for the other.

2.8 Can an individual or a country produce beyond its production possibilities frontier? Can an individual or a country consume beyond its production possibilities frontier? Explain.

2.9 If Nicaragua can produce with the same amount of resources twice as much coffee as Columbia, explain how Columbia could have a comparative advantage in producing coffee.

2.10 Imagine that the next time the Indianapolis Colts play the New England Patriots at Lucas Oil Stadium in Indianapolis, Colts star quarterback Andrew Luck has a temporary lack of judgment and plans to sell Colts memorabilia during the game because he realizes that he can sell five times more Colts products than any other player. Likewise, imagine that you are a creative and effective manager at work and that you tell your employees that during the next six months, you plan to clean the offices because you can clean five times better than the cleaning staff. What error in judgment are both Andrew and you making? Why shouldn't Andrew and you do what you are better than anyone else at doing?

2.11 Is specialization and trade between individuals and countries more about having a job or about obtaining a higher standard of living? Individually, if you go from a situation of not trading with others (you produce everything yourself) to a situation of trading with others, do you still have a job? Does your standard of living increase? Likewise, if a country goes from not trading with other countries to trading with other countries, does it still have jobs? Does its standard of living increase?

2.12 In colonial America, the population was spread thinly over a large area, and transportation costs were very high because it was difficult to ship products by road for more than short distances. As a result, most of the free population lived on small farms, where they not only grew their own food but also usually made their own clothes and very rarely bought or sold anything for money. Explain why the incomes of these farmers were likely to rise as transportation costs fell. Use the concept of comparative advantage in your answer.

2.13 During the 1928 presidential election campaign, Herbert Hoover, the Republican candidate, argued that the United States should import only products that could not be produced here. Do you believe that this would be a good policy? Explain.

2.14 **[Related to the** Making the Connection: **Comparative Advantage, Opportunity Cost, and Housework]** In discussing dividing up household chores, Emily Oster, an economist at the University of Chicago, advises that: "No, you shouldn't always unload the dishwasher because you're better at it." If you are better at unloading the dishwasher, why shouldn't you be the one to unload it?

Source: Emily Oster, "Your're Dividing the Chores Wrong," *Slate*, November 21, 2012.

2.15 **[Related to the** Making the Connection: **Comparative Advantage, Opportunity Cost, and Housework]**According to the U.S. Bureau of Labor Statistics, the amount of time men devote to housework has been increasing, while the amount of time women devote to housework has been decreasing. Briefly explain whether there is an economic explanation for these trends.

Source: U.S. Bureau of Labor Statistics, *American Time Use Survey*.

3 The Market System

LEARNING OBJECTIVE: Explain the basic idea of how a market system works.

Summary

A **market** is a group of buyers and sellers of a good or service and the institution or arrangement by which they come together to trade. **Product markets** are markets for goods and services, such as computers and medical treatment. **Factor markets** are markets for the **factors of production**, such as labor, capital, natural resources, and entrepreneurial ability. A **circular-flow diagram** shows how participants in product markets and factor markets are linked. Adam Smith argued in his 1776 book *The Wealth of Nations* that in a **free market**, where the government does not control the production of goods and services, changes in prices lead firms to produce the goods and services most desired by consumers. If consumers demand more of a good, its price will rise. Firms respond to rising prices by increasing production. If consumers demand less of a good, its price will fall. Firms respond to falling prices by producing less of a good. An **entrepreneur** is someone who operates a business. In the market system, entrepreneurs are responsible for organizing the production of goods and services. The market system will work well only if there is protection for **property rights**, which are the rights of individuals and firms to use their property.

Visit **www.myeconlab.com** to complete these exercises online and get instant feedback.

Review Questions

3.1 What is a circular-flow diagram, and what does it demonstrate?

3.2 What are the two main categories of participants in markets? Which participants are of greatest importance in determining what goods and services are produced?

3.3 What is a free market? In what ways does a free market economy differ from a centrally planned economy?

3.4 What is an entrepreneur? Why do entrepreneurs play a key role in a market system?

3.5 Under what circumstances are firms likely to produce more of a good or service? Under what circumstances are firms likely to produce less of a good or service?

3.6 What are private property rights? What role do they play in the working of a market system? Why are independent courts important for a well-functioning economy?

Problems and Applications

3.7 Identify whether each of the following transactions will take place in the factor market or in the product market and whether households or firms are supplying the good or service or demanding the good or service:

a. George buys a Tesla Model S.

b. Tesla increases employment at its Fremont plant.

c. George works 20 hours per week at McDonald's.

d. George sells the land he owns to McDonald's so that it can build a new restaurant.

3.8 [Related to the Making the Connection: **A Story of the Market System in Action: How Do You Make an iPad?**] In *The Wealth of Nations*, Adam Smith wrote the following (Book I, Chapter II): "It is not from the benevolence

of the butcher, the brewer, or the baker, that we expect our dinner, but from their regard to their own interest." Briefly discuss what he meant by this.

3.9 [Related to the Making the Connection: **A Story of the Market System in Action: How Do You Make an iPad?**] According to an article in the *Wall Street Journal*, the parts contained in the BlackBerry Torch smartphone include a power management chip made by Texas Instruments (United States); a memory chip made by Samsung (South Korea); a GPS receiver made by CSR (United Kingdom); a radio frequency (RF) transceiver made by Dialog Semiconductor (Germany); an RF transceiver made by Renesas (Japan); an application and communications processor made by Marvell (United States); a video image processor made by STMicroelectronics (Switzerland); and plastic and stamped metal parts made by several firms in China. A firm in Mexico carries out final assembly of the Torch before it is shipped to BlackBerry for sale in the United States and other countries. Is it necessary for the managers in all these firms to know how the components of the Torch are manufactured and how the components are assembled into a smartphone? Is it necessary for the chief executive officer (CEO) of BlackBerry to know this information? Briefly explain.

Source: Jennifer Valentino-DeVries and Phred Dvorak, "Piece by Piece: The Suppliers Behind the New BlackBerry Torch Smartphone," *Wall Street Journal*, August 16, 2010.

3.10 In many parts of Europe during the mid-1770s, governments gave guilds, or organizations of producers, the authority to control who was allowed to produce a good, the amount of the good produced, and the price charged for the good. Would you expect more competition among producers in a *guild system* or in a market system? Was the consumer or the producer at the center of the guild system, and which is at the center of the market system? How would the two systems compare over time in terms of innovation of new products and technologies?

3.11 In a speech at the New York University Law School, Federal Reserve Chairman Ben Bernanke stated:

> Writing in the eighteenth century, Adam Smith conceived of the free-market system as an "invisible hand" that harnesses the pursuit of private interest to promote the public good. Smith's conception remains relevant today, notwithstanding the enormous increase in economic complexity since the Industrial Revolution.

Briefly explain the idea of the invisible hand. What is so important about the idea of the invisible hand?

Source: Ben S. Bernanke, "Financial Regulation and the Invisible Hand," speech made at the New York University Law School, New York, New York, April 11, 2007.

3.12 Evaluate the following argument: "Adam Smith's analysis is based on a fundamental flaw: He assumes that people are motivated by self-interest. But this isn't true. I'm not selfish, and most people I know aren't selfish."

3.13 Writing in the *New York Times*, Michael Lewis argued that "a market economy is premised on a system of incentives designed to encourage an ignoble human trait: self-interest." Do you agree that self-interest is an "ignoble human trait"? What incentives does a market system provide to encourage self-interest?

Source: Michael Lewis, "In Defense of the Boom," *New York Times*, October 27, 2002.

3.14 Some economists have been puzzled that although entrepreneurs take on the risk of losing money by starting new businesses, on average their incomes are lower than those of people with similar characteristics who go to work at large firms. Economist William Baumol believes part of the explanation for this puzzle may be that entrepreneurs are like people who buy lottery tickets. On average, people who don't buy lottery tickets are left with more money than people who buy tickets because lotteries take in more money than they give out. Baumol argues that "the masses of purchasers who grab up the [lottery] tickets are not irrational if they receive an adequate payment in another currency: psychic rewards."
   a. What are "psychic rewards"?
   b. What psychic rewards might an entrepreneur receive?
   c. Do you agree with Baumol that an entrepreneur is like someone buying a lottery ticket? Briefly explain.

Source: William J. Baumol, *The Microtheory of Innovative Entrepreneurship*, Princeton, NJ: Princeton University Press, 2010.

3.15 The 2009 International Property Rights Index study states:

> [T]hose developing countries that respect property rights grow on average faster than those that fail to provide sound legal and political environments and protection for physical property rights.

Why would the protection of property rights be likely to increase economic growth in a developing, or low-income, country?

Source: Gaurav Tiwari, "Report: Property Rights Linked to Economic Security," *International Property Rights Index 2012 Report*.

3.16 According to an article on Phillyburbs.com, some farmers in rural Pennsylvania are causing a "stink" by using pig manure for fertilizer. The farmers purchase the pig manure, which is an organic fertilizer, from a nearby pork processing plant and spread it across the fields where they grow corn and soybeans. The article asserts that the farmers switched to pig manure because of the skyrocketing price of chemical fertilizers. Some of the residents of Milford, however, have complained about the smell, but the "farmers are likely protected under Pennsylvania's Right to Farm Act, which allows farmers to engage in practices that are common to agriculture."
   a. What price signal did the farmers respond to in their switch to the organic pig manure fertilizer?
   b. According to the Pennsylvania Right to Farm Act, do the farmers or the townspeople have the property right to the smell of the air around the farms? (Some of the residents did ask the township to urge the farmers to plow under the manure to reduce its stench.)

Source: Amanda Cregan, "Milford Farmers Switch to Pig Manure Causing a Stink for Neighbors," Phillyburbs.com, March 6, 2013.

3.17 **[Related to the** Making the Connection: **Who Owns *The Wizard of Oz*?]** The British historian Thomas Macaulay once remarked that copyrights are "a tax on readers." In what sense are copyrights a tax on readers? If copyrights are a tax on readers, why do governments enact them?

Glossary

Absolute advantage The ability of an individual, a firm, or a country to produce more of a good or service than competitors, using the same amount of resources.

Circular-flow diagram A model that illustrates how participants in markets are linked.

Comparative advantage The ability of an individual, a firm, or a country to produce a good or service at a lower opportunity cost than competitors.

Economic growth The ability of an economy to produce increasing quantities of goods and services.

Entrepreneur Someone who operates a business, bringing together the factors of production—labor, capital, and natural resources—to produce goods and services.

Factor market A market for the factors of production, such as labor, capital, natural resources, and entrepreneurial ability.

Factors of production Labor, capital, natural resources, and other inputs used to produce goods and services.

Free market A market with few government restrictions on how a good or service can be produced or sold or on how a factor of production can be employed.

Market A group of buyers and sellers of a good or service and the institution or arrangement by which they come together to trade.

Opportunity cost The highest-valued alternative that must be given up to engage in an activity.

Product market A market for goods—such as computers—or services—such as medical treatment.

Production possibilities frontier (PPF) A curve showing the maximum attainable combinations of two products that may be produced with available resources and current technology.

Property rights The rights individuals or firms have to the exclusive use of their property, including the right to buy or sell it.

Scarcity A situation in which unlimited wants exceed the limited resources available to fulfill those wants.

Trade The act of buying and selling.

Credits

Credits are listed in the order of appearance.

Photo

Where Prices Come From:
The Interaction of Demand and Supply

From Chapter 3 of *Macroeconomics*, Fifth Edition. R. Glenn Hubbard and Anthony Patrick O'Brien.

Where Prices Come From: The Interaction of Demand and Supply

Chapter Outline and Learning Objectives

1 **The Demand Side of the Market**
Discuss the variables that influence demand.

2 **The Supply Side of the Market**
Discuss the variables that influence supply.

3 **Market Equilibrium: Putting Demand and Supply Together**
Use a graph to illustrate market equilibrium.

4 **The Effect of Demand and Supply Shifts on Equilibrium**
Use demand and supply graphs to predict changes in prices and quantities.

Smartphones: The Indispensible Product?

If you're like most students, professors, and businesspeople, you carry your cellphone or smartphone everywhere you go. With a cellphone, you can make and receive phone calls and text messages. With a smartphone, you can do much more: send and receive e-mails, check Facebook and other social media sites, share photos, and stream videos. By 2013, more than two million smartphones were being sold *per day* worldwide.

Ten years ago, the BlackBerry, sold by the Canadian-based firm Research in Motion, was the only widely used smartphone. The BlackBerry was expensive, though, and most buyers were businesspeople who wanted to send and answer e-mails while away from the office. When Apple introduced the iPhone in 2007, smartphones started to become popular with a wider market of consumers, including students. With the release of the iPhone 3G in 2008, Apple announced that a section of its immensely popular iTunes music and video store would be devoted to applications (or "apps") for the iPhone. Major software companies, as well as individuals writing their first software programs, have posted games, calendars, dictionaries, and many other types of apps to the iTunes store. Apple sold more than 3 million iPhones within a month of launching the iPhone 3G.

Although initially Apple had a commanding share of the smartphone market, competitors soon appeared. Companies such as Samsung, Nokia, HTC, LG, Huawei, Microsoft, Sony, ZTE, and Panasonic introduced smartphones. Most of these manufacturers followed Apple in developing apps or providing users access to online app stores.

The intense competition among firms selling smartphones is a striking example of how the market responds to changes in consumer tastes. As many consumers indicated that they would pay more for a smartphone than a regular cellphone, firms scrambled to meet the demand for smartphones. Although intense competition is not always good news for firms trying to sell products, it is great news for consumers because it increases the available choice of products and lowers the prices consumers pay for those products.

AN INSIDE LOOK discusses how Google faced the problem of not having enough of its Nexus 4 smartphones to meet customer demand, while Apple worried about overproduction of its iPhone 5.

Sources: Brian X. Chen, "Smartphones Finally Surpass the Feature Phone," *New York Times*, April 26, 2013; Eric Pfanner, "Competition Designed to Spread Basic Technologies," *New York Times*, April 18, 2013; and Brad Reed, "A Brief History of Smartphones," pcworld.com, June 18, 2010.

Economics in Your Life

Will You Buy an Apple iPhone or a Samsung Galaxy?

Suppose you want to buy a smartphone and are choosing between an Apple iPhone and a Samsung Galaxy S. If you buy an iPhone, you will have access to more applications—or "apps"—that can increase the enjoyment and performance of your smartphone. In addition, the iPhone is thin, lightweight, and sleek looking. One strategy Samsung can use to overcome these advantages is to compete based on price and value. Would you choose to buy a Galaxy S if it had a lower price than a comparable iPhone? If your income increased, would it affect your decision about which smartphone to buy? As you read this chapter, try to answer these questions. You can check your answers against those we provide at the end of this chapter.

I n this chapter, we explore the model of demand and supply, which is the most powerful tool in economics.

Because economic models rely on assumptions, the models are simplifications of reality. In some cases, the assumptions of a model may not seem to describe exactly the economic situation being analyzed. For example, the model of demand and supply assumes that we are analyzing a **perfectly competitive market**, which is a market where there are many buyers and sellers, all the products sold are identical, and there are no barriers to new firms entering the market. These assumptions are very restrictive and apply exactly to only a few markets, such as the markets for wheat and other agricultural products. Experience has shown, however, that the model of demand and supply can be very useful in analyzing markets where competition among sellers is intense, even if there are relatively few sellers and the products being sold are not identical. In fact, in recent studies, the model of demand and supply has been successful in analyzing markets with as few as four buyers and four sellers. In the end, the usefulness of a model depends on how well it can predict outcomes in a market. As we will see in this chapter, this model is often successful in predicting changes in quantities and prices in many markets.

We begin studying the model of demand and supply by discussing consumers and the demand side of the market, before turning to firms and the supply side. Throughout this text, we will apply this model to understand business, the economy, and economic policy.

Perfectly competitive market A market that meets the conditions of (1) many buyers and sellers, (2) all firms selling identical products, and (3) no barriers to new firms entering the market.

The Demand Side of the Market

1 LEARNING OBJECTIVE

Discuss the variables that influence demand.

In a market system consumers ultimately determine which goods and services will be produced. The most successful businesses are the ones that respond best to consumer demand. But what determines consumer demand for a product? Certainly, many factors influence the willingness of consumers to buy a particular product. For example, consumers who are considering buying a smartphone, such as an Apple iPhone or a Samsung Galaxy S, will make their decisions based on, among other factors, the income they have available to spend and the effectiveness of the advertising campaigns of the companies that sell smartphones. The main factor in most consumer decisions, though, is the price of the product. So, it makes sense to begin with price when analyzing how consumers decide to buy a product. It is important to note that when we discuss demand, we are considering not what a consumer *wants* to buy but what the consumer is both willing and *able* to buy.

Demand Schedules and Demand Curves

Demand schedule A table that shows the relationship between the price of a product and the quantity of the product demanded.

Quantity demanded The amount of a good or service that a consumer is willing and able to purchase at a given price.

Demand curve A curve that shows the relationship between the price of a product and the quantity of the product demanded.

Market demand The demand by all the consumers of a given good or service.

Tables that show the relationship between the price of a product and the quantity of the product demanded are called **demand schedules**. The table in Figure 1 shows the number of smartphones consumers would be willing to buy over the course of a week at five different prices. The amount of a good or service that a consumer is willing and able to purchase at a given price is called the **quantity demanded**. The graph in Figure 1 plots the numbers from the table as a **demand curve**, which shows the relationship between the price of a product and the quantity of the product demanded. (Note that, for convenience, we made the demand curve in Figure 1 a straight line, or linear. There is no reason that all demand curves need to be straight lines.) The demand curve in Figure 1 shows the **market demand**, which is the demand by all the consumers of a given good or service. The market for a product, such as restaurant meals, that is sold locally would include all the consumers in a city or a relatively small area. The market for a product, such as smartphones, that is sold internationally would include all the consumers in the world.

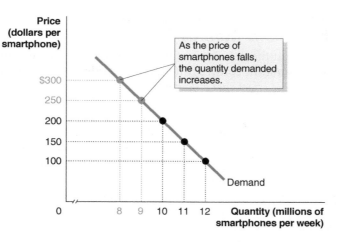

Figure 1

A Demand Schedule and Demand Curve

As the price changes, consumers change the quantity of smartphones they are willing to buy. We can show this as a *demand schedule* in a table or as a *demand curve* on a graph. The table and graph both show that as the price of smartphones falls, the quantity demanded increases. When the price of smartphones is $300, consumers buy 8 million smartphones per week. When the price falls to $250, consumers buy 9 million. Therefore, the demand curve for smartphones is downward sloping.

The demand curve in Figure 1 slopes downward because consumers will buy more smartphones as the price falls. When the price of smartphones is $300, consumers buy 8 million smartphones per week. When the price falls to $250, consumers buy 9 million. Buyers demand a larger quantity of a product as the price falls because the product becomes less expensive relative to other products and because they can afford to buy more at a lower price.

The Law of Demand

The inverse relationship between the price of a product and the quantity of the product demanded is called the **law of demand**: Holding everything else constant, when the price of a product falls, the quantity demanded of the product will increase, and when the price of a product rises, the quantity demanded of the product will decrease. The law of demand holds for any market demand curve. Economists have found only a very few exceptions to this law.

Law of demand The rule that, holding everything else constant, when the price of a product falls, the quantity demanded of the product will increase, and when the price of a product rises, the quantity demanded of the product will decrease.

What Explains the Law of Demand?

It makes sense that consumers will buy more of a good when its price falls and less of a good when its price rises, but let's look more closely at why this result holds. When the price of a product falls, consumers buy a larger quantity because of the *substitution effect* and the *income effect*.

Substitution Effect The **substitution effect** refers to the change in the quantity demanded of a good that results from a change in price making the good more or less expensive *relative* to other goods that are *substitutes*. When the price of smartphones falls, people will substitute buying smartphones for other goods, such as regular cellphones or even tablet computers, such as the iPad.

Substitution effect The change in the quantity demanded of a good that results from a change in price making the good more or less expensive relative to other goods that are substitutes.

Income Effect The **income effect** of a price change refers to the change in the quantity demanded of a good that results from the effect of a change in the good's price on consumers' *purchasing power*. Purchasing power is the quantity of goods a consumer can buy with a fixed amount of income. When the price of a good falls, the increased purchasing power of consumers' incomes will usually lead them to purchase a larger quantity of the good. When the price of a good rises, the decreased purchasing power of consumers' incomes will usually lead them to purchase a smaller quantity of the good.

Income effect The change in the quantity demanded of a good that results from the effect of a change in the good's price on consumers' purchasing power.

Note that although we can analyze them separately, the substitution effect and the income effect occur simultaneously whenever a price changes. So, a fall in the price of smartphones leads consumers to buy more smartphones both because the smartphones are now less expensive relative to substitute products and because the purchasing power of consumers' incomes has increased.

Holding Everything Else Constant: The *Ceteris paribus* Condition

Notice that the definition of the law of demand contains the phrase *holding everything else constant*. In constructing the market demand curve for smartphones, we focused only on the effect that changes in the price of smartphones would have on the quantity consumers would be willing and able to buy. We were holding constant other variables that might affect the willingness of consumers to buy smartphones. Economists refer to the necessity of holding all variables other than price constant in constructing a demand curve as the **ceteris paribus** condition. *Ceteris paribus* means "all else equal" in Latin.

What would happen if we allowed a change in a variable—other than price—that might affect the willingness of consumers to buy smartphones? Consumers would then change the quantity they demanded at each price. We can illustrate this effect by shifting the market demand curve. A shift of a demand curve is *an increase or a decrease in demand*. A movement along a demand curve is *an increase or a decrease in the quantity demanded*. As Figure 2 shows, we shift the demand curve to the right if consumers decide to buy more smartphones at each price, and we shift the demand curve to the left if consumers decide to buy less at each price.

Ceteris paribus ("all else equal") condition The requirement that when analyzing the relationship between two variables—such as price and quantity demanded—other variables must be held constant.

Variables That Shift Market Demand

Many variables other than price can influence market demand. These five are the most important:

- Income
- Prices of related goods
- Tastes
- Population and demographics
- Expected future prices

We next discuss how changes in each of these variables affect the market demand curve.

Income The income that consumers have available to spend affects their willingness and ability to buy a good. Suppose that the market demand curve in Figure 1 represents the willingness of consumers to buy smartphones when average household income is $50,000. If average household income rises to $52,000, the demand for smartphones will increase, which we show by shifting the demand curve to the right. A good is a **normal good** when the demand for the good increases following a rise in

Normal good A good for which the demand increases as income rises and decreases as income falls.

Figure 2

Shifting the Demand Curve

When consumers increase the quantity of a product they want to buy at a given price, the demand curve shifts to the right, from D_1 to D_2. When consumers decrease the quantity of a product they want to buy at a given price, the demand curve shifts to the left, from D_1 to D_3.

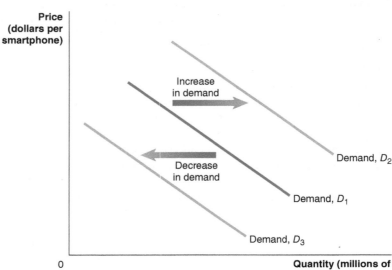

income and decreases following a fall in income. Most goods are normal goods, but the demand for some goods falls when income rises and rises when income falls. For instance, as your income rises, you might buy less canned tuna or fewer instant noodles and buy more shrimp or whole grain pasta. A good is an **inferior good** when the demand for the good decreases following a rise in income and increases following a fall in income. So, for you, canned tuna and instant noodles would be examples of inferior goods—not because they are of low quality but because you buy less of them as your income increases.

Inferior good A good for which the demand increases as income falls and decreases as income rises.

Prices of Related Goods The prices of other goods can also affect consumers' demand for a product. Consumers who would use a smartphone primarily for making phone calls could use a regular cellphone instead. Consumers who would use a smartphone to answer e-mails or surf the Web could use a tablet computer instead. Goods and services that can be used for the same purpose are called **substitutes**. When two goods are substitutes, the more you buy of one, the less you will buy of the other. A decrease in the price of a substitute causes the demand curve for a good to shift to the left. An increase in the price of a substitute causes the demand curve for a good to shift to the right.

Substitutes Goods and services that can be used for the same purpose.

Suppose that the market demand curve in Figure 1 represents the willingness and ability of consumers to buy smartphones during a week when the average price of tablet computers is $700. If the average price of tablets falls to $600, how will the market demand for smartphones change? Consumers will demand fewer smartphones at every price. We show this change by shifting the demand curve for smartphones to the left.

| Making the Connection | Are Tablet Computers Substitutes for E-Readers? |

Two products are rarely perfect substitutes for each other in the sense that consumers use them for exactly the same purpose. For example, if you want to read e-books, you would buy an e-reader, such as Barnes & Noble's Nook, Amazon's Kindle, or Kobo's Aura HD. If you want to send and receive e-mails, check your Facebook page, or watch a video, you would probably buy a tablet computer, such as Apple's iPad or Samsung's Galaxy Tab. Although you could use tablet computers to read e-books, tablets have higher prices and are often heavier than e-readers, which makes them less comfortable to hold for an extended period of reading. In addition, tablets typically don't display text as sharply as e-readers.

So e-readers and tablets are substitutes—but they aren't perfect substitutes. To correctly forecast sales and produce the correct quantity of e-readers, firms that produce them need to evaluate how close a substitute consumers consider e-readers and tablets to be. If people who read a lot of e-books strongly prefer e-readers to tablets, then e-reader sales are likely to be higher than if those people consider e-readers and tablets close substitutes.

By 2013, it had become clear that consumers considered the two products close substitutes. E-reader sales were falling much faster than many industry analysts had been expecting. Although 23 million e-readers were sold worldwide in 2011, only 16 million were sold in 2012, and as few as 5.8 million were expected to be sold in 2013. In July 2013, Barnes & Noble's CEO William Lynch resigned after losses from selling the Nook e-reader more than offset the company's profits from its retail stores. As one analyst explained: "It's looking like e-readers were a device for a particular moment in time that, more rapidly than we or anyone else thought, has been replaced by a new technology." Unfortunately for firms selling e-readers, consumers decided that tablets were a close substitute.

By 2013, many consumers saw the tablet computer as a close substitute for the e-reader.

Sources: Jeffrey A. Trachtenberg, "Barnes & Noble Pulls Back After Losses In Tablet Wars," *Wall Street Journal*, June 25, 2013; Brian X. Chen, "E-Reader Market Shrinks Faster Than Many Predicted," *New York Times*, December 20, 2012; Tom Gara, "The Future of the Nook," *Wall Street Journal*, May 9, 2013; Erik Sofge, "The Best E-Reader: Kobo's Aura HD," *Wall Street Journal*, May 3, 2013; and Tom Gara, "One More Casualty Of Barnes & Noble's Nook Problems: Its CEO," *Wall Street Journal*, July 8, 2013.

Your Turn: Test your understanding by doing related problem 1.12 at the end of this chapter.

Complements Goods and services that are used together.

Goods and services that are used together—such as hot dogs and hot dog buns—are called **complements**. When two goods are complements, the more consumers buy of one, the more they will buy of the other. A decrease in the price of a complement causes the demand curve for a good to shift to the right. An increase in the price of a complement causes the demand curve for a good to shift to the left.

Many people use applications, or "apps," on their smartphones. So, smartphones and apps are complements. Suppose the market demand curve in Figure 1 represents the willingness of consumers to buy smartphones at a time when the average price of an app is $2.99. If the average price of apps falls to $0.99, consumers will buy more apps *and* more smartphones, and the demand curve for smartphones will shift to the right.

Tastes Consumers can be influenced by an advertising campaign for a product. If Apple, Samsung, LG, and other firms making smartphones begin to advertise heavily, consumers are more likely to buy smartphones at every price, and the demand curve will shift to the right. An economist would say that the advertising campaign has affected consumers' *taste* for smartphones. Taste is a catchall category that refers to the many subjective elements that can enter into a consumer's decision to buy a product. A consumer's taste for a product can change for many reasons. Sometimes trends play a substantial role. For example, the popularity of low-carbohydrate diets caused a decline in demand for some goods, such as bread and donuts, and an increase in demand for beef. In general, when consumers' taste for a product increases, the demand curve will shift to the right, and when consumers' taste decreases, the demand curve will shift to the left.

Demographics The characteristics of a population with respect to age, race, and gender.

Population and Demographics As the population of a country increases, the number of consumers and the demand for most products will increase. The **demographics** of a population refers to its characteristics, with respect to age, race, and gender. As the demographics of a country or region change, the demand for particular goods will increase or decrease because different categories of people tend to have different preferences for those goods. For instance, Hispanics are expected to increase from 17 percent of the U.S. population in 2012 to 29 percent in 2050. This increase will expand demand for Spanish-language books and cable television channels, among other goods and services.

| Making the Connection | **Coke and Pepsi Are Hit by U.S. Demographics** |

Traditionally, consumption of soft drinks, such as Coca-Cola and Pepsi-Cola, has been much higher among people aged 30 and below than among older consumers. For many years, the demographics of soft drink consumption did not pose a problem for U.S. soft drink companies. As one generation aged and moved on to drinking coffee, tea, and other beverages, another generation of soft drink buyers took its place. In recent years, though, soft drink companies have begun to experience gradually decreasing sales in the United States.

One reason for declining soft drink sales is that the average age of the U.S. population is increasing. Following the end of World War II in 1945, the United States experienced a "baby boom," as birthrates rose and remained high through the early 1960s. Falling birthrates after 1965 mean that the baby boom generation is larger than the generations before and after it. As the baby boomers have aged and reduced their soft drink consumption, the generations that have followed have been smaller.

Even worse news for the soft drink companies is that younger consumers are not buying as much Coke, Pepsi, and other soft drinks as their parents and grandparents did. Younger consumers are more likely to buy energy drinks, water, juice, coffee, or tea than past generations. Part of the move away from soda is due to increased publicity about the potential health problems resulting from drinking soda. Some public health advocates argue that the amount of added sugars in many soft drinks make them unsafe and have called on the federal government to regulate the ingredients in soft

Younger consumers are buying more water and juice and less Coke and Pepsi than previous generations.

drinks. Many schools have reduced the availability of sodas in cafeterias and vending machines. As a result, consumption per person of carbonated soft drinks declined by more than 15 percent in the United States between 2005 and 2013. In early 2013, Pepsi announced that in just the past year, its soda sales in North America had declined by about 5 percent. The double problem of an aging population and a younger population not as inclined to drink soda led an article in the *Wall Street Journal* to ask: "Is This the End of the Soft-Drink Era?"

There were, however, some rays of sunshine for U.S. soft drink companies. Although demographics were hurting the demand for soft drinks in the United States, a growing population of young people worldwide meant that the global demand for soft drinks, particularly in developing countries, was increasing. U.S. soft drink companies responded to this opportunity. Coca-Cola announced a multiyear plan to increase sales in foreign markets, including investments of $5 billion in new bottling plants in India and $4 billion in China. As Indra K. Nooyi, PepsiCo's chairman and chief executive officer, put it in the company's *Annual Report*: "Looking back to 2006, emerging and developing markets accounted for 24 percent of our net revenue; in 2012, they represented 35 percent of our net revenue. And over the long term, we are looking to grow our business in these markets at high single digits to low double digits."

Clearly, soft drink companies needed to be aware of the effects of changing demographics on the demand for their products.

Sources: Mike Esterl, "Is This the End of the Soft-Drink Era?" *Wall Street Journal*, January 18, 2013; "PepsiCo Beats Expectations Despite Soda Struggles," Associated Press, April 13, 2013; PepsiCo, *2012 Annual Report*, www.pepsico.com /annual12/; and Stephanie Strom, "Health Officials Urge F.D.A. to Limit Sweeteners in Sodas," *New York Times*, February 13, 2013.

Your Turn: Test your understanding by doing related problem 1.13 at the end of this chapter.

Expected Future Prices Consumers choose not only which products to buy but also when to buy them. For instance, if enough consumers become convinced that houses will be selling for lower prices in three months, the demand for houses will decrease now, as some consumers postpone their purchases to wait for the expected price decrease. Alternatively, if enough consumers become convinced that the price of houses will be higher in three months, the demand for houses will increase now, as some consumers try to beat the expected price increase.

Table 1 summarizes the most important variables that cause market demand curves to shift. Note that the table shows the shift in the demand curve that results from an *increase* in each of the variables. A *decrease* in these variables would cause the demand curve to shift in the opposite direction.

A Change in Demand versus a Change in Quantity Demanded

It is important to understand the difference between a *change in demand* and a *change in quantity demanded*. A change in demand refers to a shift of the demand curve. A shift occurs if there is a change in one of the variables—*other than the price of the product*—that affects the willingness of consumers to buy the product. A change in quantity demanded refers to a movement along the demand curve as a result of a change in the product's price. Figure 3 illustrates this important distinction. If the price of smartphones falls from $300 to $250, the result will be a movement along the demand curve from point A to point B—an increase in quantity demanded from 8 million to 9 million. If consumers' incomes increase, or if another factor changes that makes consumers want more of the product at every price, the demand curve will shift to the right—an increase in demand. In this case, the increase in demand from D_1 to D_2 causes the quantity of smartphones demanded at a price of $300 to increase from 8 million at point A to 10 million at point C.

Table 1

Variables That Shift Market Demand Curves

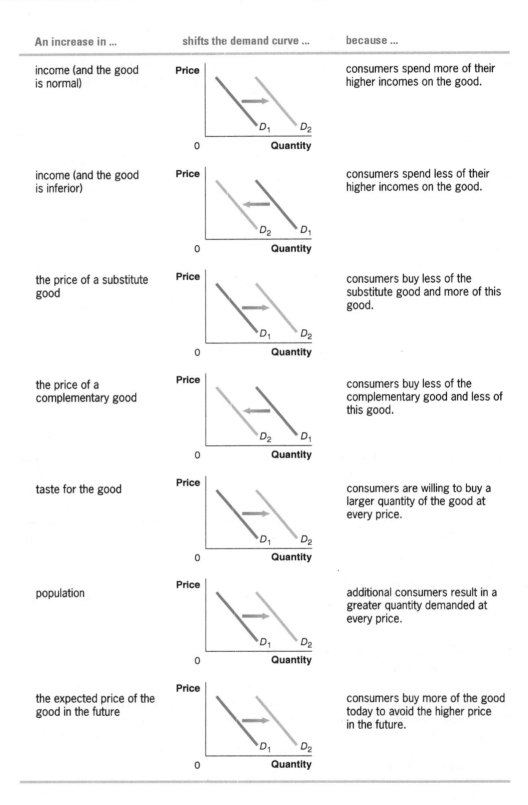

An increase in ...	shifts the demand curve ...	because ...
income (and the good is normal)		consumers spend more of their higher incomes on the good.
income (and the good is inferior)		consumers spend less of their higher incomes on the good.
the price of a substitute good		consumers buy less of the substitute good and more of this good.
the price of a complementary good		consumers buy less of the complementary good and less of this good.
taste for the good		consumers are willing to buy a larger quantity of the good at every price.
population		additional consumers result in a greater quantity demanded at every price.
the expected price of the good in the future		consumers buy more of the good today to avoid the higher price in the future.

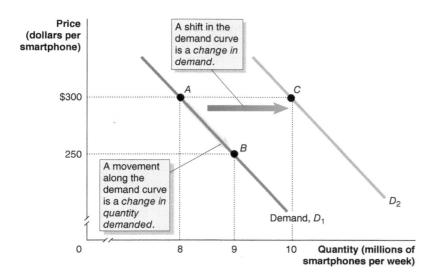

Price (dollars per smartphone)

A shift in the demand curve is a *change in demand*.

$300

A

C

250

B

A movement along the demand curve is a *change in quantity demanded*.

D_2

Demand, D_1

0   8   9   10   **Quantity (millions of smartphones per week)**

Figure 3

A Change in Demand versus a Change in Quantity Demanded

If the price of smartphones falls from \$300 to \$250, the result will be a movement along the demand curve from point A to point B—an increase in quantity demanded from 8 million to 9 million. If consumers' incomes increase, or if another factor changes that makes consumers want more of the product at every price, the demand curve will shift to the right—an increase in demand. In this case, the increase in demand from D_1 to D_2 causes the quantity of smartphones demanded at a price of \$300 to increase from 8 million at point A to 10 million at point C.

Making the Connection

Forecasting the Demand for iPhones

One of the most important decisions that managers of any large firm face is which new products to develop. A firm must devote people, time, and money to design a new product, negotiate with suppliers, formulate a marketing campaign, and perform many other tasks. But any firm has only limited resources and so faces a trade-off: Resources used to develop one product will not be available to develop another product. Ultimately, the products a firm chooses to develop will be those that it believes will be the most profitable. So, to decide which products to develop, firms need to forecast the demand for those products.

David Sobotta, who worked at Apple for 20 years and eventually became its national sales manager, has described discussions at Apple during 2002 about whether to develop a tablet computer. According to Sobotta, representatives of the U.S. National Institutes of

Will demand for iPhones continue to grow despite increasing competition?

Health urged Apple to develop a tablet computer, arguing that it would be particularly useful to doctors, nurses, and hospitals. In 2001, Bill Gates, chairman of Microsoft, had predicted that "within five years … [tablet PCs] will be the most popular form of PC sold in America." Apple's managers decided not to develop a tablet computer, however, because they believed the technology available at that time was too complex for an average computer user, and they also believed that the demand from doctors and nurses would be small. Apple's forecast was correct. Despite Bill Gates's prediction, in 2006 tablet computers made up only 1 percent of the computer market. According to Sobotta, "Apple executives had a theory that the route to success will not be through selling thousands of relatively expensive things, but millions of very inexpensive things like iPods."

Apple continued to work on smartphones, developing the technology to eliminate keyboards in favor of touchscreen displays. Rather than proceeding immediately to build a tablet computer, Steve Jobs, then Apple's CEO, realized he could use this technology in a different way: "I thought 'My God we can build a phone out of this.'" From its introduction in 2007, the iPhone was an immediate success. By mid-2013, Apple had sold more than 350 million iPhones worldwide.

As Apple attempts to forecast demand for its iPhone, it needs to consider two factors: competition from other firms producing smartphones and competition from substitute goods. By 2013, industry analysts were divided as to whether Apple would be able to maintain its share of the smartphone market in the face of increasing competition from other firms. The outlook for substitute goods was also mixed. Smartphones were an increasing share of the overall worldwide cellphone market. Many consumers were shifting from regular cellphones and music players, such as iPods, to smartphones. The increasing availability of apps, including new mobile payment apps that can be used in place of credit cards, was increasing the usefulness of smartphones. Some consumers, though, preferred the use of tablets, such as Apple's iPad or Samsung's Galaxy Tab, with their larger screens, for checking e-mails or surfing the Web. Installing the Skype app even made it possible to use a tablet to make phone calls.

Taking these factors together, Apple was optimistic that its iPhone sales would double by 2016 in comparison with 2012. As any firm does in forecasting demand, Apple faced a trade-off: If it was too cautious in expanding capacity or buying components for smartphones, other firms might seize a large share of the market. But, if Apple was too optimistic, it ran the risk of spending on capacity to produce more units than it could actually sell—an outcome that might turn potential profits into losses. Apple spent several billion dollars to buy large quantities of motion sensors, screens, and other components from suppliers. That will be money well spent … if the forecast of demand turns out to be accurate. Time will tell whether the future demand for smartphones will be as large as Apple and other firms were forecasting.

Source: "Apple Reports Second Quarter Results: 37.4 Million iPhones Sold; 19.5 Million iPads Sold," www.apple.com, April 23, 2013; Jérémie Bouchaud, "Apple and Samsung Are Top Buyers of MEMS Motion Sensors in Handsets and Tablets," www.isuppli.com, April 1, 2013; Jay Yarow, "CITI: Apple Is Pretty Much Doomed," www.businessinsider.com, March 6, 2013; David Sobotta, "What Jobs Told Me on the iPhone," *Guardian* (London), January 3, 2007; "Jobs Says iPad Idea Came Before iPhone," Associated Press, January 2, 2010; and "More Smartphones Were Shipped in Q1 2013 Than Feature Phones, an Industry First According to IDC," www.idc.com, April 25, 2013.

Your Turn: Test your understanding by doing related problem 1.17 at the end of this chapter.

---

2 LEARNING OBJECTIVE

Discuss the variables that influence supply.

Quantity supplied The amount of a good or service that a firm is willing and able to supply at a given price.

Supply schedule A table that shows the relationship between the price of a product and the quantity of the product supplied.

Supply curve A curve that shows the relationship between the price of a product and the quantity of the product supplied.

The Supply Side of the Market

Just as many variables influence the willingness and ability of consumers to buy a particular good or service, many variables influence the willingness and ability of firms to sell a good or service. The most important of these variables is price. The amount of a good or service that a firm is willing and able to supply at a given price is the **quantity supplied**. Holding other variables constant, when the price of a good rises, producing the good is more profitable, and the quantity supplied will increase. When the price of a good falls, selling the good is less profitable, and the quantity supplied will decrease. In addition, devoting more and more resources to the production of a good results in increasing marginal costs. If, for example, Apple, Samsung, LG, and other firms increase production of smartphones during a given time period, they are likely to find that the cost of producing additional smartphones increases as their suppliers run existing factories for longer hours and pay higher prices for components and higher wages for workers. With higher marginal costs, firms will supply a larger quantity only if the price is higher.

Supply Schedules and Supply Curves

A **supply schedule** is a table that shows the relationship between the price of a product and the quantity of the product supplied. The table in Figure 4 is a supply schedule showing the quantity of smartphones that firms would be willing to supply per month at different prices. The graph in Figure 4 plots the numbers from the table as a **supply curve**, which shows the relationship between the price of a product and the quantity of

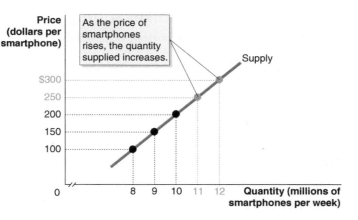

Supply Schedule	
Price (dollars per smartphone)	Quantity (millions of smartphones per week)
$300	12
250	11
200	10
150	9
100	8

Figure 4

A Supply Schedule and Supply Curve

As the price changes, Apple, Samsung, LG, and other firms producing smartphones change the quantity they are willing to supply. We can show this as a *supply schedule* in a table or as a *supply curve* on a graph. The supply schedule and supply curve both show that as the price of smartphones rises, firms will increase the quantity they supply. At a price of $250 per smartphone, firms will supply 11 million smartphones per week. At a price of $300, firms will supply 12 million.

the product supplied. The supply schedule and supply curve both show that as the price of smartphones rises, firms will increase the quantity they supply. At a price of $250 per smartphone, firms will supply 11 million smartphones per week. At a higher price of $300, firms will supply 12 million. (Once again, we are assuming for convenience that the supply curve is a straight line, even though not all supply curves are actually straight lines.)

The Law of Supply

The *market supply curve* in Figure 4 is upward sloping. We expect most supply curves to be upward sloping, according to the **law of supply**, which states that, holding everything else constant, increases in price cause increases in the quantity supplied, and decreases in price cause decreases in the quantity supplied. Notice that the definition of the law of supply—like the definition of the law of demand—contains the phrase *holding everything else constant*. If only the price of the product changes, there is a movement along the supply curve, which is *an increase or a decrease in the quantity supplied*. As Figure 5 shows, if any other variable that affects the willingness of firms to supply a good changes, the supply curve will shift, which is *an increase or a decrease in supply*. When firms increase the quantity of a product they want to sell at a given price, the supply curve shifts to the right. The shift from S_1 to S_3 represents *an increase in supply*. When firms decrease the quantity of a product they want to sell at a given price, the supply curve shifts to the left. The shift from S_1 to S_2 represents *a decrease in supply*.

Law of supply The rule that, holding everything else constant, increases in price cause increases in the quantity supplied, and decreases in price cause decreases in the quantity supplied.

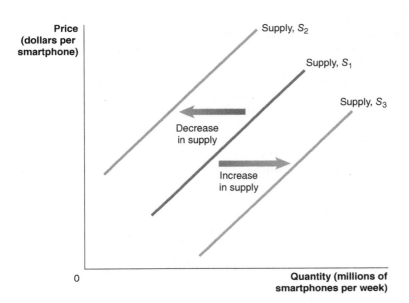

Figure 5

Shifting the Supply Curve

When firms increase the quantity of a product they want to sell at a given price, the supply curve shifts to the right. The shift from S_1 to S_3 represents an *increase in supply*. When firms decrease the quantity of a product they want to sell at a given price, the supply curve shifts to the left. The shift from S_1 to S_2 represents a *decrease in supply*.

Variables That Shift Market Supply

The following are the most important variables that shift market supply:

- Prices of inputs
- Technological change
- Prices of substitutes in production
- Number of firms in the market
- Expected future prices

We next discuss how changes in each of these variables affect the market supply curve.

Prices of Inputs The factor most likely to cause the supply curve for a product to shift is a change in the price of an *input*. An input is anything used in the production of a good or service. For instance, if the price of a component of smartphones, such as memory chips, rises, the cost of producing smartphones will increase, and smartphones will be less profitable at every price. The supply of smartphones will decline, and the market supply curve for smartphones will shift to the left. Similarly, if the price of an input declines, the supply of smartphones will increase, and the market supply curve will shift to the right.

Technological change A positive or negative change in the ability of a firm to produce a given level of output with a given quantity of inputs.

Technological Change A second factor that causes a change in supply is **technological change**, which is a positive or negative change in the ability of a firm to produce a given level of output with a given quantity of inputs. Positive technological change occurs whenever a firm is able to produce more output using the same amount of inputs. In other words, the *productivity* of the firm's workers or machines has increased. If a firm can produce more output with the same amount of inputs, its costs will be lower, and the good will be more profitable to produce at any given price. As a result, when positive technological change occurs, the firm will increase the quantity supplied at every price, and its supply curve will shift to the right.

Negative technological change is relatively rare, although it could result from an earthquake or another natural disaster or from a war that reduces the ability of firms to supply as much output with a given amount of inputs. Negative technological change will raise firms' costs, and firms will earn lower profits from producing the good. Therefore, negative technological change will cause the market supply curve to shift to the left.

Prices of Substitutes in Production Firms often choose which good or service they will produce. Alternative products that a firm could produce are called *substitutes in production*. Many of the firms that produce smartphones also produce other consumer electronics. For example, Apple produces the iPad and Samsung produces the Galaxy Tab. These products typically use similar components and are often assembled in the same factories. If the price of smartphones increases relative to the price of tablet computers, smartphones will become more profitable, and Apple, Samsung, and other firms making smartphones will shift some of their productive capacity from tablets toward smartphones. The firms will offer more smartphones for sale at every price, so the supply curve for smartphones will shift to the right.

Number of Firms in the Market A change in the number of firms in the market will change supply. When new firms *enter* a market, the supply curve shifts to the right, and when existing firms leave, or *exit*, a market, the supply curve shifts to the left. In 2013, for instance, Amazon was widely expected to enter the market for smartphones. Amazon's entry will shift the market supply curve for smartphones to the right.

Expected Future Prices If a firm expects that the price of its product will be higher in the future, it has an incentive to decrease supply now and increase it in the future. For instance, if Apple believes that prices for smartphones are temporarily low—perhaps because of a recession—it may store some of its production today to sell later on, when it expects prices to be higher.

Table 2

Variables That Shift Market Supply Curves

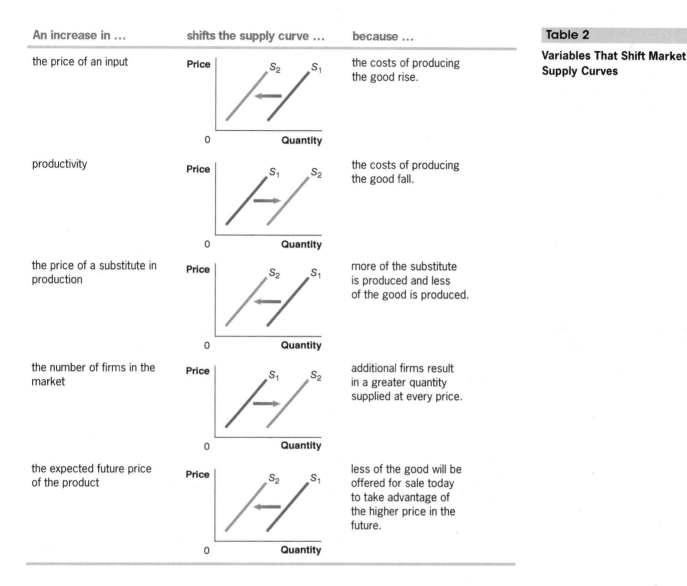

An increase in ...	shifts the supply curve ...	because ...
the price of an input		the costs of producing the good rise.
productivity		the costs of producing the good fall.
the price of a substitute in production		more of the substitute is produced and less of the good is produced.
the number of firms in the market		additional firms result in a greater quantity supplied at every price.
the expected future price of the product		less of the good will be offered for sale today to take advantage of the higher price in the future.

Table 2 summarizes the most important variables that cause market supply curves to shift. Note that the table shows the shift in the supply curve that results from an *increase* in each of the variables. A *decrease* in these variables would cause the supply curve to shift in the opposite direction.

A Change in Supply versus a Change in Quantity Supplied

We noted earlier the important difference between a change in demand and a change in quantity demanded. There is a similar difference between a *change in supply* and a *change in quantity supplied*. A change in supply refers to a shift of the supply curve. The supply curve will shift when there is a change in one of the variables—*other than the price of the product*—that affects the willingness of suppliers to sell the product. A change in quantity supplied refers to a movement along the supply curve as a result of a change in the product's price. Figure 6 illustrates this important distinction. If the price of smartphones rises from $200 to $250, the result will be a movement up the supply curve from point *A* to point *B*—an increase in quantity supplied from 10 million to 11 million. If the price of an input decreases, or if another factor changes that causes sellers to supply more of a product at every price, the supply curve will shift to the right—an increase in supply. In this case, the increase in supply from S_1 to S_2 causes the quantity of smartphones supplied at a price of $250 to increase from 11 million at point *B* to 13 million at point *C*.

Figure 6

A Change in Supply versus a Change in Quantity Supplied

If the price of smartphones rises from $200 to $250, the result will be a movement up the supply curve from point *A* to point *B*—an increase in quantity supplied by Apple, Samsung, Nokia, and other firms from 10 million to 11 million. If the price of an input decreases, or if another factor changes that causes sellers to supply more of the product at every price, the supply curve will shift to the right—an increase in supply. In this case, the increase in supply from S_1 to S_2 causes the quantity of smartphones supplied at a price of $250 to increase from 11 million at point *B* to 13 million at point *C*.

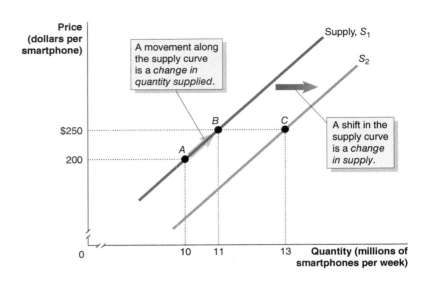

Use a graph to illustrate market equilibrium.

Market equilibrium A situation in which quantity demanded equals quantity supplied.

Competitive market equilibrium A market equilibrium with many buyers and sellers.

Market Equilibrium: Putting Demand and Supply Together

The purpose of markets is to bring buyers and sellers together. Instead of being chaotic and disorderly, the interaction of buyers and sellers in markets ultimately results in firms being led to produce the goods and services that consumers want most. To understand how this process happens, we first need to see how markets work to reconcile the plans of buyers and sellers.

In Figure 7, we bring together the market demand curve and the market supply curve for smartphones. Notice that the demand curve crosses the supply curve at only one point. This point represents a price of $200 and a quantity of 10 million smartphones per week. Only at this point of **market equilibrium** is the quantity of smartphones consumers are willing and able to buy equal to the quantity of smartphones firms are willing and able to sell. In this case, the *equilibrium price* is $200, and the *equilibrium quantity* is 10 million. As we noted at the beginning of the chapter, markets that have many buyers and sellers are competitive markets, and equilibrium in these markets is a **competitive market equilibrium**. In the market for smartphones, there are many buyers but only about 20 firms. Whether 20 firms are enough for our model of demand and supply to apply to this

Figure 7

Market Equilibrium

Where the demand curve crosses the supply curve determines market equilibrium. In this case, the demand curve for smartphones crosses the supply curve at a price of $200 and a quantity of 10 million smartphones. Only at this point is the quantity of smartphones consumers are willing to buy equal to the quantity that Apple, Samsung, LG, and other firms are willing to sell: The quantity demanded is equal to the quantity supplied.

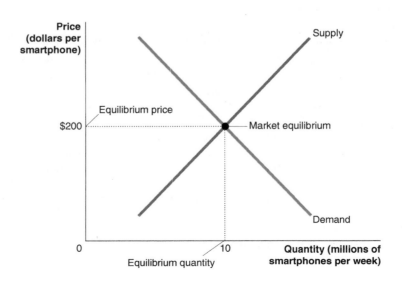

market is a matter of judgment. In this chapter, we are assuming that the market for smartphones has enough sellers to be competitive.

How Markets Eliminate Surpluses and Shortages

A market that is not in equilibrium moves toward equilibrium. Once a market is in equilibrium, it remains in equilibrium. To see why, consider what happens if a market is not in equilibrium. Suppose that the price in the market for smartphones was $250 rather than the equilibrium price of $200. As Figure 8 shows, at a price of $250, the quantity of smartphones supplied would be 11 million, and the quantity of smartphones demanded would be 9 million. When the quantity supplied is greater than the quantity demanded, there is a **surplus** in the market. In this case, the surplus is equal to 2 million smartphones (11 million − 9 million = 2 million). When there is a surplus, firms will have unsold goods piling up, which gives them an incentive to increase their sales by cutting the price. Cutting the price will simultaneously increase the quantity demanded and decrease the quantity supplied. This adjustment will reduce the surplus, but as long as the price is above $200, there will be a surplus, and downward pressure on the price will continue. Only when the price falls to $200 will the market be in equilibrium.

If, however, the price were $100, the quantity demanded would be 12 million, and the quantity supplied would be 8 million, as shown in Figure 8. When the quantity demanded is greater than the quantity supplied, there is a **shortage** in the market. In this case, the shortage is equal to 4 million smartphones (12 million − 8 million = 4 million). When a shortage occurs, some consumers will be unable to buy smartphones at the current price. In this situation, firms will realize that they can raise the price without losing sales. A higher price will simultaneously increase the quantity supplied and decrease the quantity demanded. This adjustment will reduce the shortage, but as long as the price is below $200, there will be a shortage, and upward pressure on the price will continue. Only when the price rises to $200 will the market be in equilibrium.

At a competitive market equilibrium, all consumers willing to pay the market price will be able to buy as much of the product as they want, and all firms willing to accept the market price will be able to sell as much of the product as they want. As a result, there will be no reason for the price to change unless either the demand curve or the supply curve shifts.

Surplus A situation in which the quantity supplied is greater than the quantity demanded.

Shortage A situation in which the quantity demanded is greater than the quantity supplied.

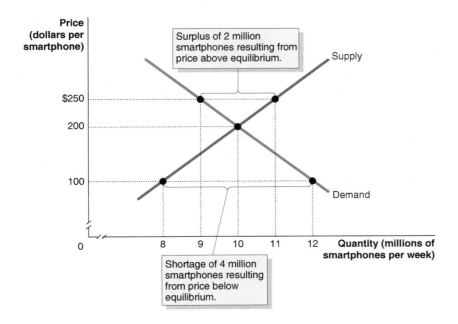

Figure 8

The Effect of Surpluses and Shortages on the Market Price

When the market price is above equilibrium, there will be a *surplus*. A price of $250 for smartphones results in 11 million smartphones being supplied but only 9 million being demanded, or a surplus of 2 million. As Apple, Nokia, LG, and other firms cut the price to dispose of the surplus, the price will fall to the equilibrium of $200. When the market price is below equilibrium, there will be a *shortage*. A price of $100 results in 12 million smartphones being demanded but only 8 million being supplied, or a shortage of 4 million. As firms find that consumers who are unable to find smartphones available for sale are willing to pay higher prices to get them, the price will rise to the equilibrium of $200.

Demand and Supply Both Count

Keep in mind that the interaction of demand and supply determines the equilibrium price. Neither consumers nor firms can dictate what the equilibrium price will be. No firm can sell anything at any price unless it can find a willing buyer, and no consumer can buy anything at any price without finding a willing seller.

Solved Problem 3

Demand and Supply Both Count: A Tale of Two Letters

Which letter is likely to be worth more: one written by Abraham Lincoln or one written by his assassin, John Wilkes Booth? Lincoln is one of the greatest presidents, and many people collect anything he wrote. The demand for letters written by Lincoln surely would seem to be much greater than the demand for letters written by Booth. Yet, when R.M. Smythe and Co. auctioned off on the same day a letter written by Lincoln and a letter written by Booth, the Booth letter sold for $31,050, and the Lincoln letter sold for only $21,850. Use a demand and supply graph to explain how the Booth letter has a higher market price than the Lincoln letter, even though the demand for letters written by Lincoln is greater than the demand for letters written by Booth.

Solving the Problem

Step 1: **Review the chapter material.** This problem is about prices being determined at market equilibrium, so you may want to review the section "Market Equilibrium: Putting Demand and Supply Together."

Step 2: **Draw demand curves that illustrate the greater demand for Lincoln's letters.** Begin by drawing two demand curves. Label one "Demand for Lincoln's letters" and the other "Demand for Booth's letters." Make sure that the Lincoln demand curve is much farther to the right than the Booth demand curve.

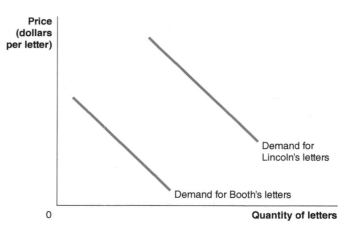

Step 3: **Draw supply curves that illustrate the equilibrium price of Booth's letters being higher than the equilibrium price of Lincoln's letters.** Based on the demand curves you have just drawn, think about how it might be possible for the market price of Lincoln's letters to be lower than the market price of Booth's letters. This outcome can occur only if the supply of Lincoln's letters is much greater than the supply of Booth's letters. Draw on your graph a supply curve for Lincoln's letters and a supply curve for Booth's letters that will result in an equilibrium price of Booth's letters of $31,050 and an equilibrium price of Lincoln's letters of $21,850. You have now solved the problem.

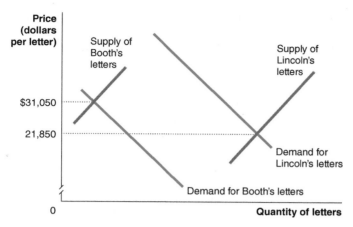

Extra Credit: The explanation for this puzzle is that both demand and supply count when determining market price. The demand for Lincoln's letters is much greater than the demand for Booth's letters, but the supply of Booth's letters is very small. Historians believe that only eight letters written by Booth exist today. (Note that the supply curves for letters written by Booth and by Lincoln are upward sloping, even though only a fixed number of each of these letters is available and, obviously, no more can be produced. The upward slope of the supply curves occurs because the higher the price, the larger the quantity of letters that will be offered for sale by people who currently own them.)

Your Turn: For more practice, do related problems 3.5, 3.6, and 3.7 at the end of this chapter.

The Effect of Demand and Supply Shifts on Equilibrium

4 LEARNING OBJECTIVE

Use demand and supply graphs to predict changes in prices and quantities.

We have seen that the interaction of demand and supply in markets determines the quantity of a good that is produced and the price at which it is sold. We have also seen that several variables cause demand curves to shift and other variables cause supply curves to shift. As a result, demand and supply curves in most markets are constantly shifting, and the prices and quantities that represent equilibrium are constantly changing. In this section, we look at how shifts in demand and supply curves affect equilibrium price and quantity.

The Effect of Shifts in Supply on Equilibrium

If Amazon enters the market for smartphones, the market supply curve for smartphones will shift to the right. Figure 9 shows the supply curve shifting from S_1 to S_2.

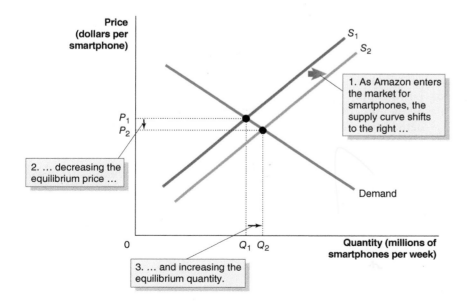

Figure 9

The Effect of an Increase in Supply on Equilibrium

If a firm enters a market, as Amazon is expected to enter the market for smartphones, the equilibrium price will fall, and the equilibrium quantity will rise:

1. As Amazon enters the market for smartphones, a larger quantity of smartphones will be supplied at every price, so the market supply curve shifts to the right, from S_1 to S_2, which causes a surplus of smartphones at the original price, P_1.

2. The equilibrium price falls from P_1 to P_2.

3. The equilibrium quantity rises from Q_1 to Q_2.

When the supply curve shifts to the right, there will be a surplus at the original equilibrium price, P_1. The surplus is eliminated as the equilibrium price falls to P_2, and the equilibrium quantity rises from Q_1 to Q_2. If an existing firm exits the market, the supply curve will shift to the left, causing the equilibrium price to rise and the equilibrium quantity to fall.

Making the Connection	**The Falling Price of Blu-ray Players**

The technology for playing prerecorded movies has progressed rapidly during the past 30 years. Video cassette recorders (VCRs) were introduced in Japan in 1976 and in the United States in 1977. As the first way of recording TV programs or playing prerecorded movies, VHS players were immensely popular. In 1997, though, digital video disc (DVD) players became available in the United States. DVDs could store more information than could the VHS tapes played on VCRs and could produce a crisper picture. Within a few years, sales of DVD players were greater than sales of VCRs, and by 2006 the movie studios had stopped releasing films on VHS tapes. In 2006, Blu-ray players were introduced. Because Blu-ray discs can store up to 50 gigabytes of data, compared with fewer than 5 gigabytes on a typical DVD, Blu-ray players can reproduce high-definition images that DVD players cannot.

When firms began selling VCRs, DVD players, and Blu-ray players, they initially charged high prices that declined rapidly within a few years. As this figure shows, the average price of a Blu-ray player was about $800 in May 2006, but it had declined to about $95 in 2013. Sales of Blu-ray players rose from about 425,000 in 2006 to 13.3 million in 2013. The figure shows that the decline in price and increase in quantity resulted from a large shift to the right of the supply curve. The supply curve in 2013 was much farther to the right than the supply curve in 2006 for two reasons: First, after Samsung introduced the first Blu-ray player—at a price of $999—other firms entered the industry, increasing the quantity supplied at every price. Second, the prices of the parts used in manufacturing Blu-ray players, particularly the laser components, declined sharply. As the cost of manufacturing the players declined, the quantity supplied at every price increased.

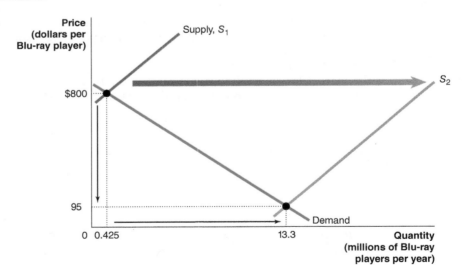

Source: Sarah McBride, "New DVD Players Resolve Battle of Formats," *Wall Street Journal*, January 4, 2007; Yukari Iwatani Kane and Miguel Bustillo, "Dreaming of a Blu Christmas," *Wall Street Journal*, December 23, 2009; and "DEG 2012 Year-End Home Entertainment Report," www.degonline.org.

Your Turn: Test your understanding by doing related problem 4.5 at the end of this chapter.

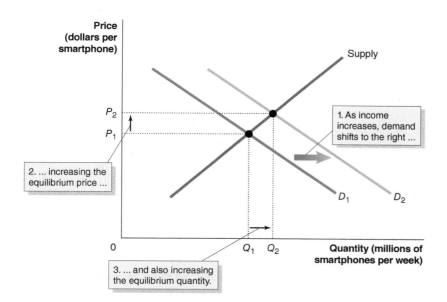

Figure 10

The Effect of an Increase in Demand on Equilibrium

Increases in income will cause the equilibrium price and quantity to rise:
1. Because smartphones are a normal good, as income increases, the quantity demanded increases at every price, and the market demand curve shifts to the right, from D_1 to D_2, which causes a shortage of smartphones at the original price, P_1.
2. The equilibrium price rises from P_1 to P_2.
3. The equilibrium quantity rises from Q_1 to Q_2.

The Effect of Shifts in Demand on Equilibrium

Because smartphones are a normal good, when incomes increase, the market demand curve shifts to the right. Figure 10 shows the effect of a demand curve shifting to the right, from D_1 to D_2. This shift causes a shortage at the original equilibrium price, P_1. To eliminate the shortage, the equilibrium price rises to P_2, and the equilibrium quantity rises from Q_1 to Q_2. In contrast, if the price of a substitute good, such as tablet computers, were to fall, the demand for smartphones would decrease, shifting the demand curve to the left. When the demand curve shifts to the left, both the equilibrium price and quantity will decrease.

The Effect of Shifts in Demand and Supply over Time

Whenever only demand or only supply shifts, we can easily predict the effect on equilibrium price and quantity. But, what happens if *both* curves shift? For instance, in many markets, the demand curve shifts to the right over time as population and income increase. The supply curve also often shifts to the right as new firms enter the market and positive technological change occurs. Whether the equilibrium price in a market rises or falls over time depends on whether demand shifts to the right more than does supply. Panel (a) of Figure 11 shows that when demand shifts to the right more than supply, the equilibrium price rises, while panel (b) shows that when supply shifts to the right more than demand, the equilibrium price falls.

Table 3 summarizes all possible combinations of shifts in demand and supply over time and the effects of the shifts on equilibrium price (*P*) and quantity (*Q*). For example, the entry in red in the table shows that if the demand curve shifts to the right and the supply curve also shifts to the right, the equilibrium quantity will increase, while the equilibrium price may increase, decrease, or remain unchanged. To make sure you understand each entry in the table, draw demand and supply graphs to check whether you can reproduce the predicted changes in equilibrium price and quantity. If the entry in the table says the predicted change in equilibrium price or quantity can be either an increase or a decrease, draw two graphs similar to panels (a) and (b) of Figure 11, one showing the equilibrium price or quantity increasing and the other showing it decreasing. Note also that in the ambiguous cases where either price or quantity might increase or decrease, it is also possible that price or quantity might remain unchanged. Be sure you understand why this is true.

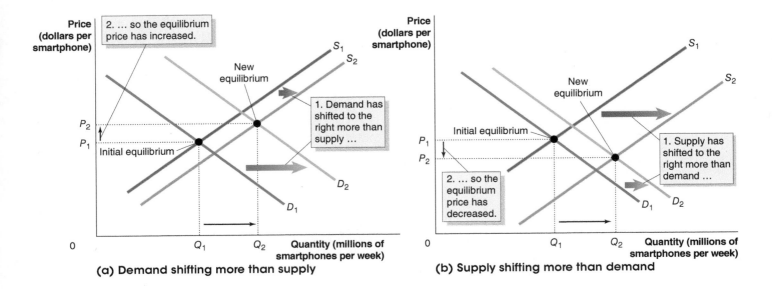

Figure 11 **Shifts in Demand and Supply over Time**

Whether the price of a product rises or falls over time depends on whether demand shifts to the right more than supply.

In panel (a), demand shifts to the right more than supply, and the equilibrium price rises:

1. Demand shifts to the right more than supply.
2. The equilibrium price rises from P_1 to P_2.

In panel (b), supply shifts to the right more than demand, and the equilibrium price falls:

1. Supply shifts to the right more than demand.
2. The equilibrium price falls from P_1 to P_2.

Table 3 **How Shifts in Demand and Supply Affect Equilibrium Price (P) and Quantity (Q)**	**Supply Curve Unchanged**	**Supply Curve Shifts to the Right**	**Supply Curve Shifts to the Left**
Demand Curve Unchanged	Q unchanged P unchanged	Q increases P decreases	Q decreases P increases
Demand Curve Shifts to the Right	Q increases P increases	Q increases P increases or decreases	Q increases or decreases P increases
Demand Curve Shifts to the Left	Q decreases P decreases	Q increases or decreases P decreases	Q decreases P increases or decreases

Solved Problem 4

What Has Caused the Decline in Beef Consumption?

Whether you like to eat hamburger or roast beef, the source of the meat is a farmer who raises cattle. An article in the *New York Times* discussed how the cost to farmers of raising cattle for beef had been increasing. At the same time, consumer tastes had been changing, leading to a decline in the demand for beef. Use demand and supply graphs to illustrate your answers to the following questions:

a. Can we use this information to be certain whether the equilibrium quantity of beef will increase or decrease?

b. Can we use this information to be certain whether the equilibrium price of beef will increase or decrease?

Solving the Problem

Step 1: **Review the chapter material.** This problem is about how shifts in demand and supply curves affect the equilibrium price, so you may want to review the section "The Effect of Shifts in Demand and Supply over Time."

Step 2: **Answer part (a) using demand and supply analysis.** You are given the information that consumer tastes have changed, leading to a decline in demand for beef. So, the demand curve for beef has shifted to the left. You are also given the information that the cost of raising beef has increased. So, the supply curve for beef has also shifted to the left. The following graph shows both these shifts:

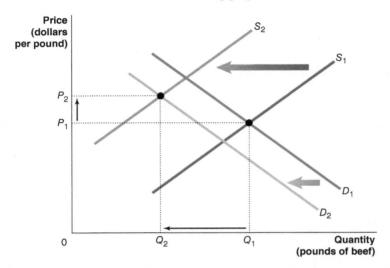

As Table 3 summarizes, if the demand curve and the supply curve both shift to the left, the equilibrium quantity must decrease. Therefore, we can answer part (a) by stating that we are certain that the equilibrium quantity of beef will decrease.

Step 3: **Answer part (b) using demand and supply analysis.** The graph we drew in Step 2 showed the equilibrium price of beef increasing. But given the information provided, the following graph would also be correct:

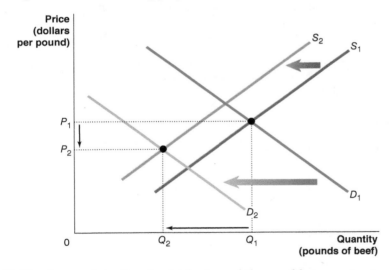

Unlike the graph in Step 2, which showed the equilibrium price increasing, this graph shows the equilibrium price decreasing. The uncertainty about whether the equilibrium price will increase or decrease is consistent with what we saw in Table 3 when the demand curve and the supply curve both shift to the left. Therefore, we can answer part (b) by stating that we cannot be certain whether the equilibrium price of beef will increase or decrease.

Extra Credit: During 2012 and 2013, the equilibrium quantity of beef decreased while the equilibrium price of beef increased. We can conclude that *both* the decrease in demand for beef and the decrease in the supply of beef contributed to the decline in beef consumption. That the price of beef rose indicates that the decrease in supply had a larger effect on equilibrium in the beef market than did the decrease in demand.

Sources: Theopolis Waters, "US Beef Prices Set New High as Spring Barbecue Season Heats Up," www.reuters.com, May 3, 2013; and Mark Bittman, "We're Eating Less Meat. Why?" *New York Times*, January 10, 2012.

Your Turn: For more practice, do related problems 4.6, 4.7, and 4.8 at the end of this chapter.

Shifts in a Curve versus Movements along a Curve

When analyzing markets using demand and supply curves, it is important to remember that *when a shift in a demand or supply curve causes a change in equilibrium price, the change in price does not cause a further shift in demand or supply.* Suppose an increase in

Don't Let This Happen to You

Remember: A Change in a Good's Price Does *Not* Cause the Demand or Supply Curve to Shift

Suppose a student is asked to draw a demand and supply graph to illustrate how an increase in the price of oranges would affect the market for apples, with other variables being constant. He draws the graph on the left and explains it as follows: "Because apples and oranges are substitutes, an increase in the price of oranges will cause an initial shift to the right in the demand curve for apples, from D_1 to D_2. However, because this initial shift in the demand curve for apples results in a higher price for apples, P_2, consumers will find apples less desirable, and the demand curve will shift to the left, from D_2 to D_3, resulting in a final equilibrium price of P_3." Do you agree or disagree with the student's analysis?

You should disagree. The student has correctly understood that an increase in the price of oranges will cause the demand curve for apples to shift to the right. But, the second demand curve shift the student describes, from D_2

to D_3, will not take place. Changes in the price of a product do not result in shifts in the product's demand curve. Changes in the price of a product result only in movements along a demand curve.

The graph on the right shows the correct analysis. The increase in the price of oranges causes the demand curve for apples to increase from D_1 to D_2. At the original price, P_1, the increase in demand initially results in a shortage of apples equal to $Q_3 - Q_1$. But, as we have seen, a shortage causes the price to increase until the shortage is eliminated. In this case, the price will rise to P_2, where both the quantity demanded and the quantity supplied are equal to Q_2. Notice that the increase in price causes a decrease in the *quantity demanded*, from Q_3 to Q_2, but does *not* cause a decrease in demand.

Your Turn: Test your understanding by doing related problems 4.13 and 4.14 at the end of this chapter.

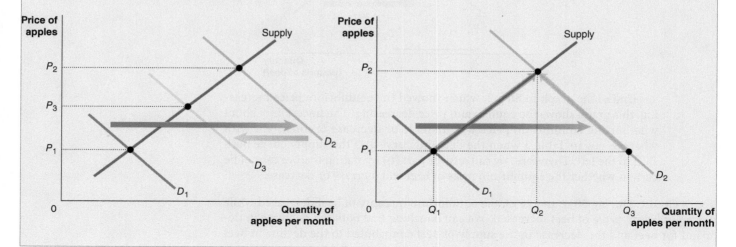

supply causes the price of a good to fall, while everything else that affects the willingness of consumers to buy the good is constant. The result will be an increase in the quantity demanded but not an increase in demand. For demand to increase, the whole curve must shift. The point is the same for supply: If the price of the good falls but everything else that affects the willingness of sellers to supply the good is constant, the quantity supplied decreases, but the supply does not. For supply to decrease, the whole curve must shift.

Continued

Economics in Your Life

Will You Buy an Apple iPhone or a Samsung Galaxy?

At the beginning of this chapter, we asked you to consider two questions: Would you choose to buy a Samsung Galaxy S if it had a lower price than a comparable Apple iPhone? and Would your decision be affected if your income increased? To determine the answer to the first question, you have to recognize that the iPhone and the Galaxy S are substitutes. If you consider the two smartphones to be close substitutes, then you are likely to buy the one with the lower price. In the market, if consumers generally believe that the iPhone and the Galaxy S are close substitutes, a fall in the price of the iPhone will increase the quantity of iPhones demanded and decrease the demand for Galaxy Ss. Suppose that you are currently leaning toward buying the Galaxy S because its price is lower than the price of the iPhone. If an increase in your income would cause you to change your decision and buy the iPhone, then the Galaxy S is an inferior good for you.

Conclusion

The interaction of demand and supply determines market equilibrium. The model of demand and supply is a powerful tool for predicting how changes in the actions of consumers and firms will cause changes in equilibrium prices and quantities. As we have seen in this chapter, we can use the model to analyze markets that do not meet all the requirements for being perfectly competitive. As long as there is intense competition among sellers, the model of demand and supply can often successfully predict changes in prices and quantities.

Read *An Inside Look* on the next page for a discussion of how Google dealt with the problem of not having enough of its Nexus 4 smartphones to meet customer demand, and how Apple dealt with overproduction of its iPhone 5.

MOTLEY FOOL

Google's Smartphone Production Problems

Predicting mobile computing sales is a tough one, especially when rolling out a relatively new product. Unless the production numbers match sales expectations perfectly, investors are going to be disappointed. Just ask **Apple** (NASDAQ: AAPL).

On Monday [January 14, 2013], Apple cut orders from its iPhone 5 manufacturers by as much as half due to lack of demand. Forget that production changes often occur after the busy holiday shopping season, or that Apple could have previously placed massive orders to adjust supply chain problems with its new iPhone, or any other fair reason. Investors weren't interested. Apple stock proceeded to drop over 3%, and remains below $500 a share.

Google (NASDAQ: GOOG) and its Nexus 4 smartphone partner LG have found themselves in a similar situation as Apple, though on the opposite end of the spectrum. The problem for Google is too much demand internationally for its low-cost smartphone. It took all of 20 minutes for Google's Play store to sell out of what was then its new Nexus 4 for the international market, and the backlog of orders isn't improving.

He said, she said

In response to concerns about production keeping up with Nexus 4 demand, a director in Google's U.K. offices said, "Supplies with the manufacturer [LG] are erratic," not exactly a glowing recommendation for LG. One estimate put the number of Google Nexus 4 sales since its release a couple of months ago at 370,000; not bad, but paltry compared to Apple and Samsung numbers. So, when in doubt, apparently you blame the supplier.

However, LG isn't taking Google's insinuations about production problems lying down. In a recent interview, an LG executive pulled no punches when asked what the problems were in keeping Nexus 4 phones in stock. According to the LG exec, Google underestimated demand, particularly in the U.K. and Germany, by as much as 10 times the number of Nexus 4's needed to fill orders.

The price for being wrong

The impact of its Nexus 4 supply issues on Google's bottom line will be negligible when it announces earnings Jan. 22. The Nexus is, after all, relatively new to market and Google certainly has other sources of revenue. But Google's inability to meet demand will hurt its share price in the near term, but will be little more than a hiccup in the overall scheme of things.

The flip side of Google's production issue is Apple. According to estimates, Apple sold around 50 million smartphones in the recently completed Q4 of 2012. But because of declining sales expectations this quarter, Apple cut component deliveries and its share price got beaten down. Can you imagine if Apple planned for 40 million units, and were then forced to announce a ramp-up in production to meet demand for 10 more million iPhones? You can bet share prices would have soared.

Is it any wonder **Microsoft** (NASDAQ: MSFT) hasn't released sales data for its Surface tablet, or why it was initially rolled out on such a minimal basis, with temporary retail outlets? If Microsoft CEO Steve Ballmer had shot for the moon relative to Surface sales, and didn't meet those lofty expectations, he'd feel the wrath of shareholders all the way up in Redmond, Wa. Of course, if Ballmer undershot expectations, and then was having production difficulty filling orders, shareholders would again be on the warpath.

When it's said and done, supply and demand forecasting isn't an exact science. Sure, there's information that can be gleaned from changes in orders and amounts, but let's keep it in perspective. Do Google's issues with LG threaten to derail the online leader? Of course not. Take the 4% drop in Google's share price the past week for what it is: an opportunity.

Source: Tim Brugger, "Google's Smartphone Production Problems," *Motley Fool*, January 18, 2013.

Key Points in the Article

The demand for Google's Nexus 4 smartphone and the production problems prevented the company from supplying enough of the product to fill its orders. Google blamed the shortage on the phone's manufacturer, LG, while LG executives claimed that Google severely underestimated demand for the smartphone, especially in some European markets. Although Google was dealing with the problem of underproduction, Apple was worried about overproduction of its iPhone 5. In January 2013, Apple cut orders from its iPhone 5 manufacturers by as much as half due to falling demand. For both Google and Apple, the production issues resulted in declines in the companies' stock prices.

Analyzing the News

(a) At the beginning of 2013, Apple and Google found themselves dealing with significant, but different, demand and supply issues. Apple reduced its orders of iPhone 5s from its manufacturers by as much as 50 percent due to insufficient demand, while Google sought ways to increase production of its Nexus 4 due to high demand. Both companies misjudged the demand for their smartphones. Figure 1 below shows a decrease in demand as a shift to the left of the

demand curve from D_1 to D_3, which illustrates the situation Apple faced for its iPhone 5. All else equal, a decrease in demand would decrease equilibrium price from P_1 to P_3 and decrease equilibrium quantity from Q_1 to Q_3. Google faced an increase in demand for the Nexus 4, which is represented in Figure 1 by a shift to the right of the demand curve from D_1 to D_2. All else equal, an increase in demand would increase equilibrium price from P_1 to P_2 and increase equilibrium quantity from Q_1 to Q_2.

(b) On the supply side, Google blamed the Nexus 4 manufacturer, LG, for not being able to supply enough product, and LG blamed Google for underestimating Nexus 4 sales. Regardless of which company was ultimately at fault, Google needed to increase the supply of its smartphones to meet the growing demand. By blaming Google for the supply problem, the executives at LG implied that their company had the capability of producing enough smartphones to cover the backlog of orders, so increasing the supply of Nexus 4 phones would apparently not be an issue on the manufacturing end. An increase in supply, which Google needed, is represented in Figure 2 by a shift from S_1 to S_2. All else equal, an increase in supply would decrease the equilibrium price from P_1 to P_3 and increase the equilibrium quantity from Q_1 to Q_2.

(c) Apple expected sales of its iPhone 5 to decline in the first quarter of 2013 and chose to cut production of its smartphone in light of this expectation. A decrease in supply, such as Apple's reduction in production, is represented in Figure 2 by a shift from S_1 to S_3. All else equal, a decrease in supply would increase the equilibrium price from P_1 to P_2 and decrease the equilibrium quantity from Q_1 to Q_3.

Thinking Critically

1. Draw a demand and supply graph for the smartphone market. Show the change in the equilibrium price and quantity after Amazon enters the market by selling a smartphone.

2. Suppose that the federal government starts a new program that offers to reimburse low-income people for half the price of a new smartphone. Use a demand and supply graph of the smartphone market to show the effect on equilibrium price and quantity as a result of Amazon entering the market and the government beginning this program. Can we be sure whether the equilibrium quantity of smartphones will increase? Can we be sure whether the equilibrium price of smartphones will increase? Briefly explain.

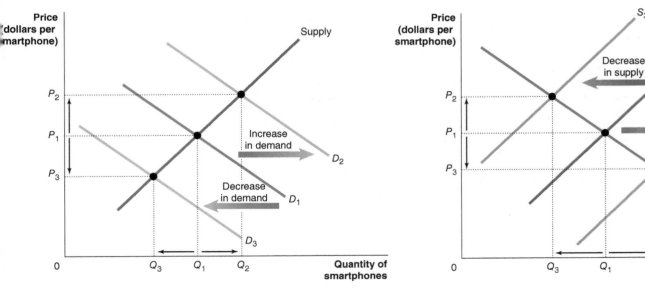

Figure 1

An increase in demand for smartphones shifts the demand curve to the right. All else equal, equilibrium price and equilibrium quantity both increase. A decrease in demand would have the opposite effect.

Figure 2

An increase in supply of smartphones shifts the supply curve to the right. All else equal, equilibrium price decreases and equilibrium quantity increases. A decrease in supply would have the opposite effect.

Chapter Summary and Problems

Key Terms

Ceteris paribus ("all else equal") condition

Competitive market equilibrium

Complements

Demand curve

Demand schedule

Demographics

Income effect

Inferior good

Law of demand

Law of supply

Market demand

Market equilibrium

Normal good

Perfectly competitive market

Quantity demanded

Quantity supplied

Shortage

Substitutes

Substitution effect

Supply curve

Supply schedule

Surplus

Technological change

The Demand Side of the Market

LEARNING OBJECTIVE: Discuss the variables that influence demand.

Summary

The model of demand and supply is the most powerful tool in economics. The model applies exactly only to **perfectly competitive markets**, where there are many buyers and sellers, all the products sold are identical, and there are no barriers to new sellers entering the market. But, the model can also be useful in analyzing markets that don't meet all these requirements. The **quantity demanded** is the amount of a good or service that a consumer is willing and able to purchase at a given price. A **demand schedule** is a table that shows the relationship between the price of a product and the quantity of the product demanded. A **demand curve** is a graph that shows the relationship between the price of a product and the quantity of the product demanded. **Market demand** is the demand by all consumers of a given good or service. The **law of demand** states that *ceteris paribus*—holding everything else constant—the quantity of a product demanded increases when the price falls and decreases when the price rises. Demand curves slope downward because of the **substitution effect**, which is the change in quantity demanded that results from a price change making one good more or less expensive relative to another good, and the income effect, which is the change in quantity demanded of a good that results from the effect of a change in the good's price on consumer purchasing power. Changes in income, the prices of related goods, tastes, population and demographics, and expected future prices all cause the demand curve to shift. **Substitutes** are goods that can be used for the same purpose. **Complements** are goods that are used together. A **normal good** is a good for which demand increases as income increases. An **inferior good** is a good for which demand decreases as income increases. **Demographics** refers to the characteristics of a population with respect to age, race, and gender. A change in demand refers to a shift of the demand curve. A change in quantity demanded refers to a movement along the demand curve as a result of a change in the product's price.

Visit **www.myeconlab.com** to complete these exercises online and get instant feedback.

Review Questions

1.1 What is a demand schedule? What is a demand curve?

1.2 What do economists mean when they use the Latin expression *ceteris paribus*?

1.3 What is the difference between a change in demand and a change in quantity demanded?

1.4 What is the law of demand? Use the substitution effect and the income effect to explain why an increase in the price of a product causes a decrease in the quantity demanded.

1.5 What are the main variables that will cause the demand curve to shift? Give an example of each.

Problems and Applications

1.6 For each of the following pairs of products, state which are complements, which are substitutes, and which are unrelated.
   a. New cars and used cars
   b. Houses and washing machines
   c. UGG boots and Kindle e-readers
   d. iPads and Kindle e-readers

1.7 **[Related to the** Chapter Opener**]** When smartphones based on the Android operating system were first introduced, there were relatively few applications, or "apps," available for them. Now, there are many more apps available for Android-based smartphones. Are these apps substitutes or complements for smartphones? How has the increase in the availability of apps for these smartphones affected the demand for Apple iPhones? Briefly explain.

1.8 **[Related to the** Chapter Opener**]** Smart TVs, unlike traditional TVs, can connect directly to the Internet. Smart TVs made up 27 percent of all televisions sold worldwide in 2012.
   a. Should smart TVs be considered a substitute good for smartphones? Briefly explain.
   b. If smart TVs are a substitute for smartphones, how would a decline in the price of smart TVs affect the demand curve for smartphones? Include a graph in your answer.

   Source: Greg Tarr, "Smart TVs Rise to 27% of TV Shipments," www.twice.com, February 21, 2013.

1.9 State whether each of the following events will result in a movement along the demand curve for McDonald's Big Mac hamburgers or whether it will cause the curve to shift. If the demand curve shifts, indicate whether it will shift to the left or to the right and draw a graph to illustrate the shift.
   a. The price of Burger King's Whopper hamburger declines.
   b. McDonald's distributes coupons for $1.00 off the purchase of a Big Mac.

c. Because of a shortage of potatoes, the price of French fries increases.

d. Fast-food restaurants post nutrition warning labels.

e. The U.S. economy enters a period of rapid growth in incomes.

1.10 Suppose that the following table shows the quantity demanded of UGG boots at five different prices in 2014 and 2015:

| Price | Quantity Demanded (thousands of pairs of boots) | |
	2014	2015
$160	5,000	4,000
170	4,500	3,500
180	4,000	3,000
190	3,500	2,500
200	3,000	2,000

Name two different variables that could cause the quantity demanded of UGG boots to change from 2014 to 2015 as indicated in the table.

1.11 Suppose that the curves in the following graph represent two demand curves for traditional wings (basket of six) at Buffalo Wild Wings. What would cause a movement from point A to point B on D_1? Name two variables that would cause a movement from point A to point C.

1.12 [Related to the Making the Connection: **Are Tablet Computers Substitutes for E-Readers?**] Are smartphones a closer substitute for tablet computers, such as the iPad, or for e-readers, such as the Kindle? Briefly explain.

1.13 [Related to the Making the Connection: **Coke and Pepsi Are Hit by U.S. Demographics**] Since 1979, China has had a policy that allows couples to have only one child. This policy has caused a change in the demographics of China. Between 1980 and 2011, the share of the population under age 14 decreased from 36 percent to 19 percent. And, as parents attempt to ensure that the lone child is a son, the number of newborn

males relative to females has increased. Choose three goods and explain how the demand for them has been affected by China's one-child policy.

Sources: World Bank, *World Development Indicators*, May 2013; and "China's Family Planning: Illegal Children Will Be Confiscated" and "China's Population: Only and Lonely," *Economist*, July 21, 2011.

1.14 Suppose the following table shows the price of a base model Toyota Prius hybrid and the quantity of Priuses sold for three years. Do these data indicate that the demand curve for Priuses is upward sloping? Explain.

Year	Price	Quantity
2012	$31,880	35,265
2013	30,550	33,250
2014	33,250	36,466

1.15 The following statement appeared in an article in the *New York Times* on the effects of changes in college tuition: "Some private colleges said that applications actually increased when they bolstered prices, apparently because families equated higher prices with quality." If applications increased when these colleges raised the tuition price they charged, did these colleges face upward sloping demand curves? Briefly explain.

Source: Andrew Martin, "Colleges Expect Lower Enrollment," *New York Times*, January 10, 2013.

1.16 Richard Posner is a federal court judge who also writes on economic topics. A newspaper reporter summarized Posner's views on the effect of online bookstores and e-books on the demand for books:

> Posner's [argument] is that the disappearance of bookstores is to be celebrated and not mourned, partly because e-books and online stores will reduce the cost of books and thus drive up demand for them.

Do you agree with Posner's statement, as given by the reporter? Briefly explain.

Source: Christopher Shea, "Judge Posner Hails the Demise of Bookstores," *Wall Street Journal*, January 13, 2011.

1.17 [Related to the Making the Connection: **Forecasting the Demand for iPhones**] An article in the *Wall Street Journal* in 2013 was titled "In India, iPhone Lags Far Behind." According to the article, the difficulty Apple was having selling iPhones in India was "no small matter as Apple's growth slows in the U.S. and other mature markets."

a. What does the article mean by "mature markets"?

b. Why would sales of iPhones be likely to be slower in mature markets than in countries such as India?

c. Would forecasting sales in mature markets be easier or harder than forecasting sales in countries such as India? Briefly explain.

Source: Dhanya Ann Thoppil, Amol Sharma, and Jessica E. Lessin, "In India, iPhone Lags Far Behind," *Wall Street Journal*, February 26, 2013.

The Supply Side of the Market

2

LEARNING OBJECTIVE: Discuss the variables that influence supply.

Summary

The **quantity supplied** is the amount of a good that a firm is willing and able to supply at a given price. A **supply schedule** is a table that shows the relationship between the price of a product and

the quantity of the product supplied. A **supply curve** is a curve that shows the relationship between the price of a product and the quantity of the product supplied. When the price of a product rises, producing the product is more profitable, and a greater amount will be supplied. The **law of supply** states that, holding everything else constant, the quantity of a product supplied increases when the price rises and decreases when the price falls. Changes in the prices of inputs, technology, the prices of substitutes in production, expected future prices, and the number of firms in a market all cause the supply curve to shift. **Technological change** is a positive or negative change in the ability of a firm to produce a given level of output with a given quantity of inputs. A change in supply refers to a shift of the supply curve. A change in quantity supplied refers to a movement along the supply curve as a result of a change in the product's price.

Visit **www.myeconlab.com** to complete these exercises online and get instant feedback.

Review Questions

2.1 What is a supply schedule? What is a supply curve?

2.2 What is the difference between a change in supply and a change in the quantity supplied?

2.3 What is the law of supply? What are the main variables that will cause a supply curve to shift? Give an example of each.

Problems and Applications

2.4 Briefly explain whether each of the following statements describes a change in supply or a change in the quantity supplied:

   a. To take advantage of high prices for snow shovels during a snowy winter, Alexander Shovels, Inc., decides to increase output.

   b. The success of the Apple iPhone leads more firms to begin producing smartphones.

   c. In the six months following the Japanese earthquake and tsunami in 2011, production of automobiles in Japan declined by 20 percent.

2.5 Suppose that the curves in the following graph represent two supply curves for traditional wings (basket of six) at Buffalo Wild Wings. What would cause a movement from point A to point B on S_1? Name two variables that would cause a movement from point A to point C.

2.6 Suppose that the following table shows the quantity supplied of UGG boots at five different prices in 2014 and 2015:

	Quantity Supplied (thousands of pairs of boots)	
Price	2014	2015
$160	3,000	2,000
170	3,500	2,500
180	4,000	3,000
190	4,500	3,500
200	5,000	4,000

Name two different variables that would cause the quantity supplied of UGG boots to change from 2014 to 2015 as indicated in the table.

2.7 Will each firm in the smartphone industry always supply the same quantity as every other firm at each price? What factors might cause the quantity of smartphones supplied by different firms to be different at a particular price?

2.8 If the price of a good increases, is the increase in the quantity of the good supplied likely to be smaller or larger, the longer the time period being considered? Briefly explain.

---

3   Market Equilibrium: Putting Demand and Supply Together

LEARNING OBJECTIVE: Use a graph to illustrate market equilibrium.

Summary

Market equilibrium occurs where the demand curve intersects the supply curve. A **competitive market equilibrium** has a market equilibrium with many buyers and sellers. Only at this point is the quantity demanded equal to the quantity supplied. Prices above equilibrium result in **surpluses**, with the quantity supplied being greater than the quantity demanded. Surpluses cause the market price to fall. Prices below equilibrium result in **shortages**, with the quantity demanded being greater than the quantity supplied. Shortages cause the market price to rise.

Visit **www.myeconlab.com** to complete these exercises online and get instant feedback.

Review Questions

3.1 What do economists mean by *market equilibrium*?

3.2 What do economists mean by a *shortage*? By a *surplus*?

3.3 What happens in a market if the current price is above the equilibrium price? What happens if the current price is below the equilibrium price?

Problems and Applications

3.4 Briefly explain whether you agree with the following statement: "When there is a shortage of a good, consumers eventually give up trying to buy it, so the demand for the good declines, and the price falls until the market is finally in equilibrium."

3.5 **[Related to** Solved Problem 3**]** In *The Wealth of Nations*, Adam Smith discussed what has come to be known as the "diamond and water paradox":

Nothing is more useful than water: but it will purchase scarce anything; scarce anything can be had in exchange for it. A diamond, on the contrary, has scarce any value in use; but a very great quantity of other goods may frequently be had in exchange for it.

Graph the market for diamonds and the market for water. Show how it is possible for the price of water to be much lower than the price of diamonds, even though the demand for water is much greater than the demand for diamonds.

Source: Adam Smith, *An Inquiry into the Nature and Causes of the Wealth of Nations*, Vol. I, Oxford, UK: Oxford University Press, 1976; original edition, 1776.

3.6 **[Related to** Solved Problem 3**]** An article discusses the market for autographs by Mickey Mantle, the superstar centerfielder for the New York Yankees during the 1950s and 1960s: "At card shows, golf outings, charity dinners, Mr. Mantle signed his name over and over." One expert on sport autographs is quoted as saying, "He was a real good signer.... He is not rare." Yet the article quotes another expert as saying, "Mr. Mantle's autograph ranks No. 3 of most-popular autographs, behind Babe Ruth and Muhammad Ali." A baseball signed by Mantle is likely to sell for the relatively high price of $250 to $400. By contrast, baseballs signed by Whitey Ford, a teammate of Mantle's on the Yankees, typically sell for less than $150. Use one graph to show both the demand and supply for autographs by Whitey Ford and the demand and supply for autographs by Mickey Mantle. Show how it is possible for the price of Mantle's autographs to be higher than the price of Ford's autographs, even though the supply of Mantle autographs is larger than the supply of Ford autographs.

Source: Beth DeCarbo, "Mantle Autographs Not Rare, but Collectors Don't Care," *Wall Street Journal*, August 4, 2008.

3.7 **[Related to** Solved Problem 3**]** Comic book fans eagerly compete to buy copies of *Amazing Fantasy* No. 15, which contains the first appearance of the superhero Spider-Man. At the same time the publisher printed copies of the comic for the U.S. market, with the price printed on the cover in cents, it printed copies for the U.K. market, with the price printed on the cover in British pence. About 10 times as many U.S. copies of *Amazing Fantasy* No. 15 have survived as U.K. copies. Yet in auctions that occurred at about the same time in 2013, a U.S. copy sold for $29,000, while a U.K. copy in the same condition sold for only $10,755. Use a demand and supply graph to explain how the U.S. version of the comic has a higher price than the U.K. version, even though the supply of the U.S. version is so much greater than the supply of the U.K. version.

Source: Auction price data from: *GPA Analysis for CGC Comics*, www.comics.gpanalysis.com.

3.8 If a market is in equilibrium, is it necessarily true that all buyers and sellers are satisfied with the market price? Briefly explain.

3.9 During 2013, an article in the *Wall Street Journal* stated: "Steel prices have slumped this month, setting off a scramble among steelmakers to maintain prices … despite a nationwide glut."
a. What does the article mean by a "glut"? What does a glut imply about the quantity demanded of steel relative to the quantity supplied?
b. Why would steel prices slump if there is a glut in the steel market?
c. Is it likely that steel companies would succeed in maintaining steel prices in the face of a glut in the market? Briefly explain.

Source: John W. Miller, "Steelmakers Pinched by Price Plunge," *Wall Street Journal*, April 26, 2013.

---

 4 **The Effect of Demand and Supply Shifts on Equilibrium**
LEARNING OBJECTIVE: Use demand and supply graphs to predict changes in prices and quantities.

Summary

In most markets, demand and supply curves shift frequently, causing changes in equilibrium prices and quantities. Over time, if demand increases more than supply, equilibrium price will rise. If supply increases more than demand, equilibrium price will fall.

Visit **www.myeconlab.com** to complete these exercises online and get instant feedback.

Review Questions

4.1 Draw a demand and supply graph to show the effect on the equilibrium price in a market in the following situations:
a. The demand curve shifts to the right.
b. The supply curve shifts to the left.

4.2 If, over time, the demand curve for a product shifts to the right more than the supply curve does, what will happen to the equilibrium price? What will happen to the equilibrium price if the supply curve shifts to the right more than the demand curve? For each case, draw a demand and supply graph to illustrate your answer.

Problems and Applications

4.3 According to an article in the *Wall Street Journal*, one of the effects of an increase in the demand for corn was a decline in the number of U.S. farmers growing rice: "The number of acres dedicated to rice likely will decline 3% this spring compared with last year, to 2.61 million acres." Use a demand and supply graph to analyze the effect on the equilibrium price of rice resulting from the increase in the demand for corn.

Source: Owen Fletcher, "Farmers Lose Their Taste for Rice," *Wall Street Journal*, April 1, 2013.

4.4 According to an article on the wine market in the *Wall Street Journal*, "many farmers in recent years stopped planting new [grape] vines, and some even switched to nuts, vegetables and other fruit." But at the same time, "Americans kept drinking more wine." Use demand and supply graphs to illustrate your answers to the following questions:
a. Can we use this information to be certain whether the equilibrium quantity of wine will increase or decrease?
b. Can we use this information to be certain whether the equilibrium price of wine will increase or decrease?

Source: Mike Esterl, "Fewer Grapes, More Drinkers," *Wall Street Journal*, June 8, 2012.

4.5 **[Related to the** Making the Connection**]** More than half of homes in the United States are heated by burning natural gas. According to an article in the *Wall Street Journal*, demand for natural gas decreased during the winter of 2012 because of unusually warm weather. At the same time, "robust production [of natural gas] from U.S. shale fields has created record supplies." Use demand and supply graphs to illustrate your answers to the following questions:

101

a. Can we use this information to be certain whether the equilibrium quantity of natural gas increased or decreased?

b. Can we use this information to be certain whether the equilibrium price of natural gas increased or decreased?

Source: Christian Berthelsen, "Natural-Gas Futures Slide," *Wall Street Journal*, January 11, 2012.

4.6 **[Related to** Solved Problem 4**]** The demand for watermelons is highest during summer and lowest during winter. Yet, watermelon prices are normally lower in summer than in winter. Use a demand and supply graph to demonstrate how this is possible. Be sure to carefully label the curves in your graph and to clearly indicate the equilibrium summer price and the equilibrium winter price.

4.7 **[Related to** Solved Problem 4**]** According to one observer of the lobster market: "After Labor Day, when the vacationers have gone home, the lobstermen usually have a month or more of good fishing conditions, except for the occasional hurricane." Use a demand and supply graph to explain whether lobster prices are likely to be higher or lower during the fall than during the summer.

Source: Jay Harlow, "Lobster: An Affordable Luxury," www.Sallybernstein.com.

4.8 **[Related to** Solved Problem 4**]** An article in the *Wall Street Journal* discussed the market for gasoline in the United States during the summer of 2013. Compared with the previous summer, the article stated that there will be "lower demand, as cars become more efficient" and "growth in oil production from hydraulic fracturing of shale deposits in the U.S."

a. Draw a demand and supply graph of the market for gasoline to analyze the situation described in this article. Be sure to indicate the equilibrium price and quantity of gasoline in the summer of 2012, the equilibrium price and quantity of gasoline in the summer of 2013, and any shifts in the demand curve and supply curve for gasoline.

b. Can you be certain from your analysis whether the equilibrium price of gasoline would increase or decrease? Can you be certain whether the equilibrium quantity of gasoline would increase or decrease? Briefly explain.

Source: Ángel González, "Drivers Can Expect a Break On Summer Gas Prices," *Wall Street Journal*, April 14, 2013.

4.9 Years ago, an apple producer argued that the United States should enact a tariff, or a tax, on imports of bananas. His reasoning was that "the enormous imports of cheap bananas into the United States tend to curtail the domestic consumption of fresh fruits produced in the United States."

a. Was the apple producer assuming that apples and bananas are substitutes or complements? Briefly explain.

b. If a tariff on bananas acts as an increase in the cost of supplying bananas in the United States, use two demand and supply graphs to show the effects of the apple producer's proposal. One graph should show the effect on the banana market in the United States, and the other graph should show the effect on the apple market in the United States. Be sure to label the change in equilibrium price and quantity in each market and any shifts in the demand and supply curves.

Source: Douglas A. Irwin, *Peddling Protectionism: Smoot-Hawley and the Great Depression*, Princeton, NJ: Princeton University Press, 2011, p. 22.

4.10 An article in the *Wall Street Journal* noted that the demand for video Internet advertising was increasing at the same time that the number of Internet sites accepting advertising was also increasing. After reading the article, a student argues: "From this information, we know that the price of Internet ads should rise, but we don't know whether the total quantity of Internet ads will increase or decrease." Is the student's analysis correct? Illustrate your answer with a demand and supply graph.

Source: Suzanne Vranica, "Web Video: Bigger and Less Profitable," *Wall Street Journal*, March 14, 2013.

4.11 Historically, the production of many perishable foods, such as dairy products, was highly seasonal. As the supply of those products fluctuated, prices tended to fluctuate tremendously—typically by 25 to 50 percent or more—over the course of the year. One effect of mechanical refrigeration, which was commercialized on a large scale in the last decade of the nineteenth century, was that suppliers could store perishables from one season to the next. Economists have estimated that as a result of refrigerated storage, wholesale prices rose by roughly 10 percent during peak supply periods, while they fell by almost the same amount during the off season. Use a demand and supply graph for each season to illustrate how refrigeration affected the market for perishable food.

Source: Lee A. Craig, Barry Goodwin, and Thomas Grennes, "The Effect of Mechanical Refrigeration on Nutrition in the U.S.," *Social Science History*, Vol. 28, No. 2, Summer 2004, pp. 327–328.

4.12 If the equilibrium price and quantity of a product were $100 and 1,000 units per month in 2013 and are $150 and 800 units per month in 2014, did this product experience a larger shift in its demand curve or supply curve from 2013 to 2014? Briefly explain.

4.13 **[Related to the** Don't Let This Happen to You**]** A student writes the following: "Increased production leads to a lower price, which in turn increases demand." Do you agree with his reasoning? Briefly explain.

4.14 **[Related to the** Don't Let This Happen to You**]** A student was asked to draw a demand and supply graph to illustrate the effect on the market for smartphones of a fall in the price of displays used in smartphones, holding everything else constant. She drew the following graph and explained it as follows:

Displays are an input to smartphones, so a fall in the price of displays will cause the supply curve for smartphones to shift to the right (from S_1 to S_2). Because this shift in the supply curve results in a lower price (P_2), consumers will want to buy more smartphones, and the demand curve will shift to the right (from D_1 to D_2). We know that

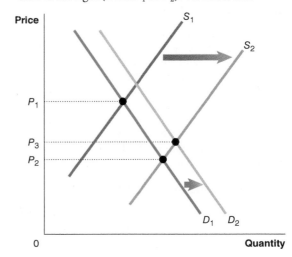

more smartphones will be sold, but we can't be sure whether the price of smartphones will rise or fall. That depends on whether the supply curve or the demand curve has shifted farther to the right. I assume that the effect on supply is greater than the effect on demand, so I show the final equilibrium price (P_3) as being lower than the initial equilibrium price (P_1).

Explain whether you agree or disagree with the student's analysis. Be careful to explain exactly what—if anything—you find wrong with her analysis.

4.15 Following are four graphs and four market scenarios, each of which would cause either a movement along the supply curve for Pepsi or a shift of the supply curve. Match each scenario with the appropriate graph.
   a. A decrease in the supply of Coke
   b. A drop in the average household income in the United States from $52,000 to $50,000
   c. An improvement in soft drink bottling technology
   d. An increase in the prices of sugar and high-fructose corn syrup

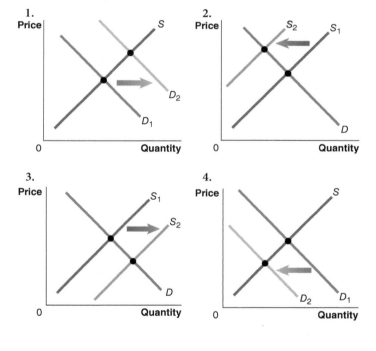

4.16 Proposals have been made to increase government regulation of firms providing childcare services by, for instance, setting education requirements for childcare workers. Suppose that these regulations increase the quality of childcare and cause the demand for childcare services to increase. At the same time, assume that complying with the new government regulations increases the costs of firms providing childcare services. Draw a demand and supply graph to illustrate the effects of these changes in the market for childcare services. Briefly explain whether the total quantity of childcare services purchased will increase or decrease as a result of regulation.

4.17 Which of the following graphs best represents what happens in the market for hotel rooms at a ski resort during the winter? Briefly explain. From the graph that you picked, what would be the result during the winter if hotel rates stayed at their summer level?

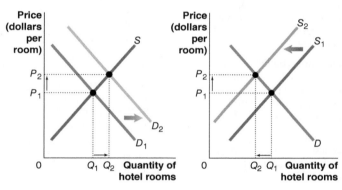

4.18 The following graphs show the supply and demand curves for two markets. One of the markets is for Tesla automobiles, and the other is for a cancer-fighting drug, without which lung cancer patients will die. Briefly explain which graph most likely represents which market.

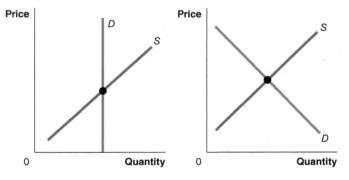

Glossary

Ceteris paribus **("all else equal") condition** The requirement that when analyzing the relationship between two variables—such as price and quantity demanded— other variables must be held constant.

Competitive market equilibrium A market equilibrium with many buyers and sellers.

Complements Goods and services that are used together.

Demand curve A curve that shows the relationship between the price of a product and the quantity of the product demanded.

Demand schedule A table that shows the relationship between the price of a product and the quantity of the product demanded.

Demographics The characteristics of a population with respect to age, race, and gender.

Income effect The change in the quantity demanded of a good that results from the effect of a change in the good's price on consumers' purchasing power, holding all other factors constant.

Inferior good A good for which the demand increases as income falls and decreases as income rises.

Law of demand The rule that, holding everything else constant, when the price of a product falls, the quantity demanded of the product will increase, and when the price of a product rises, the quantity demanded of the product will decrease.

Law of supply The rule that, holding everything else constant, increases in price cause increases in the quantity supplied, and decreases in price cause decreases in the quantity supplied.

Market demand The demand by all the consumers of a given good or service.

Market equilibrium A situation in which quantity demanded equals quantity supplied.

Normal good A good for which the demand increases as income rises and decreases as income falls.

Perfectly competitive market A market that meets the conditions of (1) many buyers and sellers, (2) all firms selling identical products, and (3) no barriers to new firms entering the market.

Quantity demanded The amount of a good or service that a consumer is willing and able to purchase at a given price.

Quantity supplied The amount of a good or service that a firm is willing and able to supply at a given price.

Shortage A situation in which the quantity demanded is greater than the quantity supplied.

Substitutes Goods and services that can be used for the same purpose.

Substitution effect The change in the quantity demanded of a good that results from a change in price making the good more or less expensive relative to other goods that are substitutes.

Supply curve A curve that shows the relationship between the price of a product and the quantity of the product supplied.

Supply schedule A table that shows the relationship between the price of a product and the quantity of the product supplied.

Surplus A situation in which the quantity supplied is greater than the quantity demanded.

Technological change A change in the ability of a firm to produce a given level of output with a given quantity of inputs.

Credits

Credits are listed in the order of appearance.

Photo

Ariel Skelley/Blend Images/Corbis; Wavebreak Media/Thinkstock; Eric Audras/Alamy; Susanna Bates/EPA/Landov

Economic Growth, the Financial System, and Business Cycles

From Chapter 10 of *Macroeconomics*, Fifth Edition. R. Glenn Hubbard and Anthony Patrick O'Brien. Copyright © 2015 by Pearson Education, Inc.
All rights reserved.

Economic Growth, the Financial System, and Business Cycles

Chapter Outline and Learning Objectives

1 **Long-Run Economic Growth**
   Discuss the importance of long-run economic growth.

2 **Saving, Investment, and the Financial System**
   Discuss the role of the financial system in facilitating long-run economic growth.

3 **The Business Cycle**
   Explain what happens during the business cycle.

Economic Growth and the Business Cycle at Whirlpool

In 1911, Louis and Emory Upton and Lowell Bassford formed the Upton Machine Company in Benton Harbor, Michigan, to produce the first electric washing machine. The company later became the Whirlpool Corporation, which today is the world's leading manufacturer of home appliances. In 2012, Whirlpool had more than 68,000 employees and $18 billion in revenue. Whirlpool's experiences have mirrored two key macroeconomic facts: In the long run, the U.S. economy has experienced economic growth, and in the short run, the economy has experienced a series of business cycles. Whirlpool has also experienced growth over the long run, while being affected by the business cycle.

Just as advances in transportation, communication, and computing technology have led to improvements in the standard of living over the past century, so too have improvements in household technology. In 1900, only 3 percent of families lived in homes with electric lights and no families had electric washing machines, dishwashers, or refrigerators. Most families cooked on coal- or wood-burning stoves. Today, nearly all families have electric washing machines and refrigerators, as well as electric or natural gas stoves, and about two-thirds have dishwashers. Valerie Ramey, an economist at the University of California, San Diego, has estimated that today adult women spend an average of 18 fewer hours each week on household chores than they did in 1900. New and improved technology to perform household chores has given women the opportunity to pursue careers outside the home and allowed both women and men time to enjoy more leisure activities.

The housing market collapse that led to the recession of 2007–2009 caused a sharp decline in the demand for durable goods, including household appliances. Although Whirlpool and other appliance makers lowered prices to boost sales during the recession, real consumer expenditures for household appliances fell each year from 2007 to 2009. As the economy recovered from the recession, spending on durable goods rose. By 2013, Jeff Fettig, Whirlpool's chief executive officer (CEO), was able to report: "We expect to see moderately higher revenue growth, due to continued strength in U.S. housing and improving demand trends internationally."

In this chapter, we provide an overview of long-run growth and the business cycle and discuss their importance for firms, consumers, and the economy as a whole.

Sources: Bob Tita, "Whirlpool Stung by U.S. Sales," *Wall Street Journal*, April 24, 2013; Valerie A. Ramey, "Time Spent in Home Production in the 20th Century United States," *Journal of Economic History*, Vol. 69, No. 1, March 2009, pp. 1–47; U.S. Energy Information Administration, *Residential Energy Consumption Survey*, www.eia.gov/consumption/residential/index.cfm; and www.whirlpoolcorp.com.

Economics in Your Life

Do You Help the Economy More if You Spend or if You Save?

Suppose that you have received an income tax refund check from the U.S. government. You are not sure what to do with the money, so you ask your two roommates for advice. One roommate tells you that if you want to help the economy, you should save all the money because a country's economic growth depends on the amount of saving by households. The other roommate disagrees and advises you to spend all the money because consumer spending is a major component of gross domestic product (GDP), and your spending would help increase production and create more jobs. Which of your two roommates is right? As you read this chapter, try to answer this question. You can check your answer against the one we provide at the end of this chapter.

A successful economy is capable of increasing production of goods and services faster than the growth in population. Attaining this level of growth is the only way that the standard of living of the average person in a country can increase. Unfortunately, some economies around the world are not growing at all or are growing very slowly. Most people in those countries live on about the same levels of income as their ancestors did decades, or even centuries, ago. In the United States and other developed countries, however, incomes and living standards are much higher today than they were 50 years ago. An important macroeconomic topic is why some countries grow much faster than others.

As we will see, one determinant of economic growth is the ability of firms to expand their operations, buy additional equipment, train workers, and adopt new technologies. To carry out these activities, firms must acquire funds from households, either directly through financial markets—such as the stock and bond markets—or indirectly through financial intermediaries—such as banks. Financial markets and financial intermediaries together comprise the *financial system*. In this chapter, we present an overview of the financial system and see how funds flow from households to firms through the *market for loanable funds*.

Since at least the early nineteenth century, the U.S. economy has experienced periods of expanding production and employment followed by periods of recession during which production and employment decline. These alternating periods of expansion and recession are called the **business cycle**. The business cycle is not uniform: Each period of expansion is not the same length, nor is each period of recession, but every period of expansion in U.S. history has been followed by a period of recession, and every period of recession has been followed by a period of expansion.

In this chapter, we begin to explore two key aspects of macroeconomics: the long-run growth that has steadily raised living standards in the United States and the short-run fluctuations of the business cycle.

Business cycle Alternating periods of economic expansion and economic recession.

1 LEARNING OBJECTIVE

Discuss the importance of long-run economic growth.

Long-Run Economic Growth

Most people in the United States, Western Europe, Japan, and other high-income countries expect that over time, their standard of living will improve. They expect that year after year, firms will introduce new and improved products, new prescription drugs and better surgical techniques will overcome more diseases, and their ability to afford these goods and services will increase. For most people, these are reasonable expectations.

In 1900, the United States was already enjoying the highest standard of living in the world. Yet in that year, only 3 percent of U.S. homes had electricity, only 15 percent had indoor flush toilets, and only 25 percent had running water. The lack of running water meant that before people could cook or bathe, they had to pump water from wells and haul it to their homes in buckets—on average about 10,000 gallons per year per family. Not surprisingly, water consumption averaged only about 5 gallons per person per day, compared with about 150 gallons today. The result was that people washed themselves and their clothing only infrequently. A majority of families living in cities had to use outdoor toilets, which they shared with other families. Diseases such as smallpox, typhus, dysentery, and cholera were still common. In 1900, 5,000 of the 45,000 children born in Chicago died before their first birthday. Life expectancy at birth was about 47 years, compared with 79 years in 2013. Few families had electric lights, relying instead on burning candles or burning kerosene or coal oil in lamps. Many homes were heated in the winter by burning coal, which contributed to the severe pollution that fouled the air of most

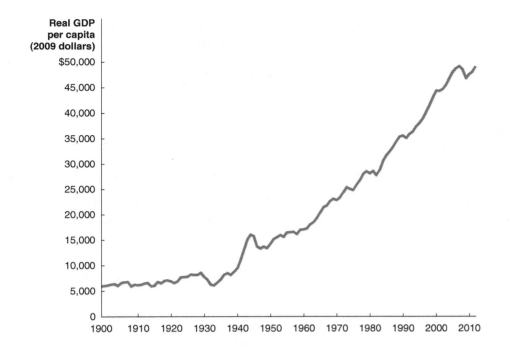

Figure 1

The Growth in Real GDP per Capita, 1900–2012

Measured in 2009 dollars, real GDP per capita in the United States grew from about $6,000 in 1900 to about $49,200 in 2012. An average American in 2012 could buy more than eight times as many goods and services as an average American in 1900.
Sources: Samuel H. Williamson, "What Was the U.S. GDP Then?" MeasuringWorth, August 2013; and U.S. Bureau of Economic Analysis.

large cities. In 1900, there were no modern appliances, so housework was time consuming and physically demanding. The typical American homemaker baked a half-ton of bread per year.

The process of **long-run economic growth** brought the typical American from the standard of living of 1900 to the standard of living of today. The best measure of the standard of living is real GDP per person, which is usually called *real GDP per capita*. So, we measure long-run economic growth by increases in real GDP per capita over long periods of time, generally decades or more. We use real GDP rather than nominal GDP to adjust for changes in the price level over time. Figure 1 shows the growth in real GDP per capita in the United States from 1900 to 2012. The figure shows that the trend in real GDP per capita is strongly upward, although it fluctuates in the short run because of the business cycle. It is the upward trend in real GDP per capita that we focus on when discussing long-run economic growth.

The values in Figure 1 are measured in prices of 2009, so they represent constant amounts of purchasing power. In 1900, real GDP per capita was about $6,000. More than a century later, in 2012, it had risen to about $49,200, which means that an average American in 2012 could purchase more than eight times as many goods and services as an average American in 1900. Large as it is, this increase in real GDP per capita actually understates the true increase in the standard of living of Americans in 2012 compared with 1900. Many of today's goods and services were not available in 1900. For example, if you lived in 1900 and became ill with a serious infection, you could not purchase antibiotics to treat your illness—no matter how high your income. You might have died from an illness for which even a very poor person in today's society could receive effective medical treatment. Of course, the quantity of goods and services that a person can buy is not a perfect measure of how happy or contented that person may be. A person's happiness also depends on education, health, spiritual well-being, and many other factors ignored in calculating GDP. Nevertheless, economists rely heavily on comparisons of real GDP per capita because it is the best means of comparing the performance of one economy over time or the performance of different economies at any particular time.

Long-run economic growth The process by which rising productivity increases the average standard of living.

The Connection between Economic Prosperity and Health

We can see the direct effect of economic growth on living standards by looking at improvements in health in high-income countries over the past 100 years. The research of the late Robert Fogel, winner of the Nobel Prize in Economics, highlights the close connection between economic growth, improvements in technology, and improvements in human physiology. One important measure of health is life expectancy at birth. As the following graph shows, in 1900, life expectancy was less than 50 years in the United States, the United Kingdom, and France. Today, life expectancy is about 80 years. Although life expectancies in the lowest-income countries remain very short, some countries that have begun to experience economic growth have seen dramatic increases in life expectancies. For example, life expectancy in India has more than doubled from 27 years in 1900 to 67 years today.

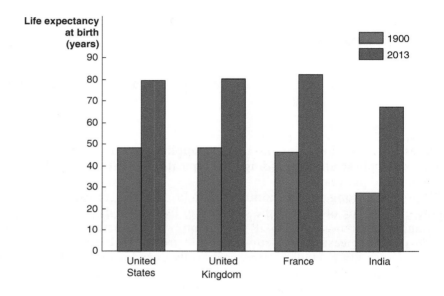

Many economists believe there is a link between health and economic growth. In the United States and Western Europe during the nineteenth century, improvements in agricultural technology and rising incomes led to dramatic improvements in the nutrition of the average person. The development of the germ theory of disease and technological progress in the purification of water in the late nineteenth century led to sharp declines in sickness due to waterborne diseases. As people became taller, stronger, and less susceptible to disease, they also became more productive. Today, economists studying economic development have put increasing emphasis on the need for low-income countries to reduce disease and increase nutrition if they are to experience economic growth.

Many researchers believe that the state of human physiology will continue to improve as technology advances. In high-income countries, life expectancy at birth is expected to rise from about 80 years today to about 90 years by the middle of the twenty-first century. Technological advances will continue to reduce the average number of hours worked per day and the number of years an average person spends in the paid workforce. Individuals spend about 10 hours per day sleeping, eating, and bathing. Their remaining "discretionary hours" are divided between paid work and leisure. The following graph is based on estimates by Robert Fogel that contrast how individuals in the United States will divide their time in 2040 compared with 1880 and 1995. Not only will technology and economic growth allow people in the near future to live longer lives, but a much smaller fraction of those lives will need to be spent at paid work.

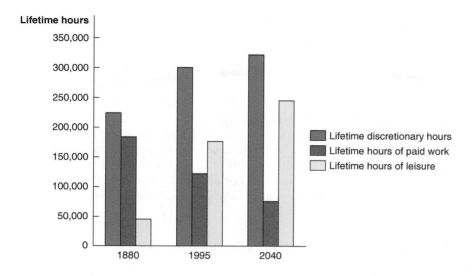

Sources: Robert William Fogel, *The Escape from Hunger and Premature Death, 1700–2100*, New York: Cambridge University Press, 2004; and U.S. Central Intelligence Agency, *The 2013 World Factbook*, online version.

Your Turn: Test your understanding by doing related problem 1.7 at the end of this chapter.

Calculating Growth Rates and the Rule of 70

The growth rate of real GDP or real GDP per capita during a particular year is equal to the percentage change from the previous year. For example, measured in 2009 prices, real GDP equaled $15,052 billion in 2011 and rose to $15,471 billion in 2012. We calculate the growth of real GDP in 2012 as:

$$\left(\frac{\$15{,}471 \text{ billion} - \$15{,}052 \text{ billion}}{\$15{,}052 \text{ billion}} \right) \times 100 = 2.8\%.$$

For longer periods of time, we can use the *average annual growth rate*. For example, real GDP in the United States was $2,182 billion in 1950 and $15,471 billion in 2012. To find the average annual growth rate during this 62-year period, we compute the annual growth rate that would result in $2,182 billion increasing to $15,471 billion over 62 years. In this case, the growth rate is 3.2 percent. That is, if $2,182 billion grows at an average rate of 3.2 percent per year, after 62 years, it will have grown to $15,471 billion.

For shorter periods of time, we get approximately the same answer by averaging the growth rate for each year. For example, real GDP in the United States grew by 2.5 percent in 2010, 1.8 percent in 2011, and 2.8 percent in 2012. So, the average annual growth rate of real GDP for the period 2010–2012 was 2.4 percent, which is the average of the three annual growth rates:

$$\frac{2.5\% + 1.8\% + 2.8\%}{3} = 2.4\%.$$

Finally, when discussing long-run economic growth, we usually shorten "average annual growth rate" to "growth rate."

We can judge how rapidly an economic variable is growing by calculating the number of years it would take to double. For example, if real GDP per capita in a country doubles, say, every 20 years, most people in the country will experience significant increases in their standard of living over the course of their lives. If real GDP per capita doubles only every 100 years, increases in the standard of living will occur too slowly to notice. One easy way to calculate approximately how many years it will take real GDP per capita to double is to use the *rule of 70*. The formula for the rule of 70 is:

$$\text{Number of years to double} = \frac{70}{\text{Growth rate}}.$$

For example, if real GDP per capita is growing at a rate of 5 percent per year, it will double in $70/5 = 14$ years. If real GDP per capita is growing at a rate of 2 percent per year, it will take $70/2 = 35$ years to double. These examples illustrate an important point: Small differences in growth rates can have large effects on how rapidly the standard of living in a country increases. Finally, notice that the rule of 70 applies not just to growth in real GDP per capita but to growth in any variable. For example, if you invest $1,000 in the stock market, and your investment grows at an average annual rate of 7 percent, your investment will double to $2,000 in 10 years.

What Determines the Rate of Long-Run Growth?

Labor productivity The quantity of goods and services that can be produced by one worker or by one hour of work.

A key point in explaining long-run growth is that *increases in real GDP per capita depend on increases in labor productivity*. **Labor productivity** is the quantity of goods and services that can be produced by one worker or by one hour of work. In analyzing long-run growth, economists usually measure labor productivity as output per hour of work to avoid the effects of fluctuations in the length of the workday and in the fraction of the population employed. If the quantity of goods and services consumed by the average person is to increase, the quantity of goods and services produced per hour of work must also increase. Why in 2012 was the average American able to consume more than eight times as many goods and services as the average American in 1900? Because the average American worker in 2012 was eight times as productive as the average American worker in 1900.

If increases in labor productivity are the key to long-run economic growth, what causes labor productivity to increase? Economists believe two key factors determine labor productivity: the quantity of capital per hour worked and the level of technology. Therefore, economic growth occurs if the quantity of capital per hour worked increases and if there is technological change.

Increases in Capital per Hour Worked Workers today in high-income countries such as the United States have more physical capital available than workers in low-income countries or workers in the high-income countries of 100 years ago. **Capital** refers to manufactured goods that are used to produce other goods and services. Examples of capital are computers, factory buildings, machine tools, warehouses, and trucks. The total amount of physical capital available in a country is known as the country's *capital stock*.

Capital Manufactured goods that are used to produce other goods and services.

As the amount of capital per hour worked increases, worker productivity increases. An accountant who records a firm's revenues and costs using Excel is more productive than an accountant who uses only pen and paper. A worker who uses a backhoe can excavate more earth than a worker who uses only a shovel.

Human capital refers to the accumulated knowledge and skills workers acquire from education and training or from their life experiences. For example, workers with a college education generally have more skills and are more productive than workers who have only a high school degree. Increases in human capital are particularly important in stimulating economic growth.

Technological Change Economic growth depends more on *technological change* than on increases in capital per hour worked. *Technology* refers to the processes a firm uses to turn inputs into outputs of goods and services. Technological change is an increase in the quantity of output firms can produce, using a given quantity of inputs. Technological change can come from many sources. For example, a firm's managers may rearrange a factory floor or the layout of a retail store to increase production and sales. Most technological change, however, is embodied in new machinery, equipment, or software.

A very important point is that just accumulating more inputs—such as labor, capital, and natural resources—will not ensure that an economy experiences economic growth unless technological change also occurs. For example, the Soviet Union failed to maintain a high rate of economic growth, even though it continued to increase the quantity of capital available per hour worked, because it experienced relatively little technological change.

Entrepreneurs are critical for implementing technological change. An entrepreneur is someone who operates a business, bringing together the factors of production—labor, capital, and natural resources—to produce goods and services. In a market economy, entrepreneurs make the crucial decisions about whether to introduce new technology to produce better or lower-cost products. Entrepreneurs also decide whether to allocate a firm's resources to research and development that can result in new technologies. One of the difficulties centrally planned economies have in sustaining economic growth is that managers employed by the government are usually much slower to develop and adopt new technologies than are entrepreneurs in a market system.

Solved Problem 1

Explaining Economic Growth in Singapore

Between 1960 and 1995, real GDP per capita in Singapore grew at an average annual rate of 6.2 percent. This very rapid growth rate results in the level of real GDP per capita doubling about every 11.3 years. In 1995, Alwyn Young of the London School of Economics published an article in which he argued that Singapore's growth depended more on increases in capital per hour worked, increases in the labor force participation rate, and the transfer of workers from agricultural to nonagricultural jobs than on technological change. If Young's analysis was correct, predict what was likely to happen to Singapore's growth rate in the years after 1995.

Solving the Problem

Step 1: Review the chapter material. This problem is about what determines the rate of long-run growth, so you may want to review the section "What Determines the Rate of Long-Run Growth?."

Step 2: Predict what happened to the growth rate in Singapore after 1995. As countries begin to develop, they often experience an increase in the labor force participation rate, as workers who are not part of the paid labor force respond to rising wage rates. Many workers also leave the agricultural sector—where output per hour worked is often low—for the nonagricultural sector. These changes increase real GDP per capita, but they are "one-shot" changes that eventually come to an end, as the labor force participation rate and the fraction of the labor force outside agriculture both approach the levels found in high-income countries. Similarly, as we already noted, increases in capital per hour worked cannot sustain high rates of economic growth unless they are accompanied by technological change.

We can conclude that Singapore was unlikely to sustain its high growth rates in the years after 1995. In fact, from 1996 to 2012, the growth of real GDP per capita slowed to an average rate of 3.0 percent per year. Although this growth rate is comparable to rates experienced in high-income countries, such as the United States, it leads to a doubling of real GDP per capita only about every 23 years rather than about every 11 years.

Sources: Alwyn Young, "The Tyranny of Numbers: Confronting the Statistical Realities of the East Asian Growth Experience," *Quarterly Journal of Economics*, Vol. 110, No. 3, August 1995, pp. 641–680; and International Monetary Fund, *World Economic Outlook Database*, April 2013.

Your Turn: For more practice, do related problem 1.11 at the end of this chapter.

Finally, an additional requirement for economic growth is that the government must provide secure rights to private property. A market system cannot function unless rights to private property are secure. In addition, the government can aid economic growth by establishing an independent court system that enforces contracts between private individuals. Many economists would also say that the government has a role in facilitating the development of an efficient financial system, as well as systems of education, transportation, and communication. Economist Richard Sylla of New York University has argued that every country that has experienced economic growth first experienced a "financial revolution." For example, before the United States was able to experience significant economic growth in the early nineteenth century, the country's banking and monetary systems were reformed under the guidance of Alexander Hamilton, who was appointed the country's first secretary of the Treasury in 1789. Without supportive government policies, long-run economic growth is unlikely to occur.

| Making the Connection | Can India Sustain Its Rapid Growth? |

Can India Sustain Its Rapid Growth?

When you have a computer problem and need technical support, the person who takes your call may well be in India. In addition to information technology, in recent years Indian firms have made gains in the global markets for steel, oil, and automobiles, among other goods.

To many people in the United States, the rapid economic rise of India was unexpected. As the following figure shows, Indian real GDP per capita increased very slowly up to the time India became independent from England in 1947. As a result, in 1950 India was desperately poor. India's real GDP per capita in 1950 was less than $1,000 measured in 2013 dollars, or less than 7 percent of 1950 U.S. real GDP per capita. During the first 40 years of independence, India's growth rate increased but was still too slow to significantly reduce the country's poverty. Recent years tell a much different story, however. In 1991, the Indian government decided to scale back central planning, reduce regulations, and introduce market-based reforms. The result was that the growth rate doubled over the following decade. In the most recent 10 years, growth has been even more rapid.

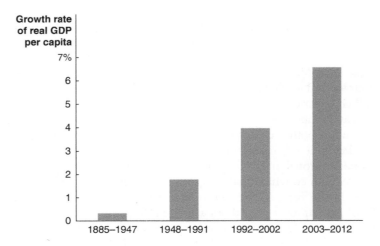

Still, India remains a very poor country. More than half of its population of 1.2 billion are employed in agriculture and many can barely produce enough to feed themselves. Infant mortality remains high, and nearly half of all adult women and one-quarter of adult men are unable to read and write. The rapid economic growth that began in 1991 will have to continue in the coming decades if the average person in India is eventually to enjoy a standard of living equal to that in the United States and other high-income countries. But can India continue its rapid growth?

Some economists and policymakers worry that India's growth rates may begin to decline, leaving hundreds of millions of its people stuck in deep poverty. These economists point to several problems facing the Indian economy. The public education system has struggled to provide basic instruction, particularly in rural and poorer urban areas. India's expenditures on education rank it 131 out of 173 countries, which is far below the level in most successful developing countries. As a result, many adults lack the basic skills needed for a productive workforce. Even many high school and college graduates lack the skills to work in firms that compete in global markets. High rates of infectious disease also reduce the productivity of the workforce. Barely more than half of urban residents have access to modern sewage systems, and fewer than one-quarter of rural residents do. In general, India has struggled to meet its infrastructure needs, as highways, bridges, and its train system—which dates from the British colonial period—have deteriorated.

India also suffers from political problems with ethnic, religious, cultural, and geographic divisions often making it difficult for the government to successfully implement policy reforms. Many observers believe that government corruption has increased, making it more difficult for businesses to obtain the permits necessary to operate. One estimate puts the size of the underground economy at more than 50 percent of GDP. Some economists and policymakers also worry about the slowing pace of market-oriented reforms and urge the government to allow greater foreign investment in the financial and retail sectors. Greater foreign investment would allow these sectors to gain access to new technology and to increase productivity.

The economic progress India has made in the past 20 years has already lifted hundreds of millions of people out of poverty. For that progress to continue, however, many economists believe that the Indian government will need to upgrade infrastructure, improve the provision of educational and health services, and renew its commitment to the rule of law and to market-based reforms.

Sources: Amartya Sen, "Why India Trails China," *New York Times*, June 19, 2013; Neha Thirani, "Where Is the Indian Economy Headed?" *New York Times*, January 10, 2013; Geeta Anand, "India Graduates Millions, but Too Few Are Fit to Hire," *Wall Street Journal*, April 5, 2011; Paul Beckett, "In India, Doubts Gather over Rising Giant's Course," *Wall Street Journal*, March 30 2011; data in graph are authors' calculations from the Maddison Project database www.ggdc.net/maddison/maddison-project/home.htm; and International Monetary Fund, *World Economic Outlook Database*.

Your Turn: Test your understanding by doing related problems 1.13 and 1.14 at the end of this chapter.

Potential GDP

Because economists take a long-run perspective in discussing economic growth, the concept of *potential GDP* is useful. **Potential GDP** is the level of real GDP attained when all firms are producing at capacity. The capacity of a firm is *not* the maximum output the firm is capable of producing. A Whirlpool factory could operate 24 hours per day for 52 weeks per year and would be at its maximum production level. The factory's capacity, however, is measured by its production when operating on normal hours, using a normal workforce. If all firms in the economy were operating at capacity, the level of total production of final goods and services would equal potential GDP. Potential GDP increases over time as the labor force grows, new factories and office buildings are built, new machinery and equipment are installed, and technological change takes place.

From 1949 to 2013, potential GDP in the United States grew at an average annual rate of 3.2 percent. In other words, each year on average the capacity of the economy to produce final goods and services expanded by 3.2 percent. The *actual* level of real GDP increased by more or less than 3.2 percent as the economy moved through the business cycle. Figure 2 shows movements in actual and potential GDP for the years since 1989. The red line represents potential GDP, and the blue line represents actual real GDP. Notice that in each of the three recessions since 1989, actual real GDP has fallen below potential GDP. During the 2007–2009 recession, the gap between actual real GDP and potential GDP was particularly large, which is an indication of the severity of the recession.

Potential GDP The level of real GDP attained when all firms are producing at capacity.

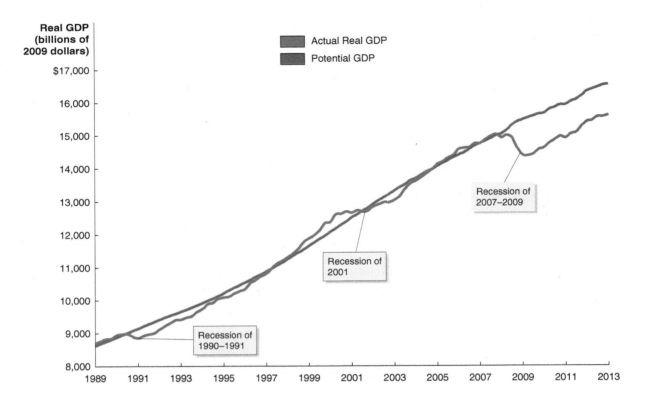

Figure 2   Actual and Potential GDP

Potential GDP increases every year as the labor force and the capital stock grow and technological change occurs. The red line represents potential GDP, and the blue line represents actual real GDP. During the three recessions since 1989, actual real GDP has been less than potential GDP.
Source: Federal Reserve Bank of St. Louis.

2 LEARNING OBJECTIVE

Discuss the role of the financial system in facilitating long-run economic growth.

Saving, Investment, and the Financial System

The process of economic growth depends on the ability of firms to expand their operations, buy additional equipment, train workers, and adopt new technologies. Firms can finance some of these activities from *retained earnings*, which are profits that are reinvested in the firm rather than paid to the firm's owners. For many firms, retained earnings are not sufficient to finance the rapid expansion required in economies experiencing high rates of economic growth. Firms can acquire funds from households, either directly through financial markets—such as the stock and bond markets—or indirectly through financial intermediaries—such as banks. Financial markets and financial intermediaries together comprise the **financial system**. Without a well-functioning financial system, economic growth is impossible because firms will be unable to expand and adopt new technologies. As we noted earlier, no country without a well-developed financial system has been able to sustain high levels of economic growth.

Financial system The system of financial markets and financial intermediaries through which firms acquire funds from households.

An Overview of the Financial System

The financial system channels funds from savers to borrowers and channels returns on the borrowed funds back to savers. In **financial markets,** such as the stock market or the bond market, firms raise funds by selling financial securities directly to savers. A *financial security* is a document—sometimes in electronic form—that states the terms under which funds pass from the buyer of the security—who is providing funds—to the seller. *Stocks* are financial securities that represent partial ownership of a firm. If you buy one share of stock in Whirlpool, you become one of millions of owners of that firm. *Bonds* are financial securities that represent promises to repay a

Financial markets Markets where financial securities, such as stocks and bonds, are bought and sold.

fixed amount of funds. When Whirlpool sells a bond, the firm promises to pay the purchaser of the bond an interest payment each year for the term of the bond, as well as a final payment of the amount of the loan.

Financial intermediaries, such as banks, mutual funds, pension funds, and insurance companies, act as go-betweens for borrowers and lenders. In effect, financial intermediaries borrow funds from savers and lend them to borrowers. When you deposit funds in your checking account, you are lending your funds to the bank. The bank may lend your funds (together with the funds of other savers) to an entrepreneur who wants to start a business. Suppose Lena wants to open a laundry. Rather than you lending money directly to Lena's Laundry, the bank acts as a go-between for you and Lena. Intermediaries pool the funds of many small savers to lend to many individual borrowers. The intermediaries pay interest to savers in exchange for the use of savers' funds and earn a profit by lending money to borrowers and charging borrowers a higher rate of interest on the loans. For example, a bank might pay you as a depositor a 2 percent rate of interest, while it lends the money to Lena's Laundry at a 6 percent rate of interest.

Banks, mutual funds, pension funds, and insurance companies also make investments in stocks and bonds on behalf of savers. For example, *mutual funds* sell shares to savers and then use the funds to buy a portfolio of stocks, bonds, mortgages, and other financial securities. Large mutual fund companies, such as Fidelity, Vanguard, and Dreyfus, offer many stock and bond funds. Some funds hold a wide range of stocks or bonds; others specialize in securities issued by a particular industry or sector, such as health care; and others invest as index funds in fixed market baskets of securities, such as shares of the Standard & Poor's 500 firms. Over the past 30 years, the role of mutual funds in the financial system has increased dramatically. Today, competition among hundreds of mutual fund firms gives investors thousands of funds from which to choose.

In addition to matching households that have excess funds with firms that want to borrow funds, the financial system provides three key services for savers and borrowers: risk sharing, liquidity, and information. *Risk* is the chance that the value of a financial security will change relative to what you expect. For example, you may buy a share of stock in Whirlpool at a price of $125, only to have the price fall to $20. Most individual savers are not gamblers and seek a steady return on their savings rather than erratic swings between high and low earnings. The financial system provides risk sharing by allowing savers to spread their money among many financial investments. For example, you can divide your money among a bank certificate of deposit, individual bonds, and a stock mutual fund.

Liquidity is the ease with which a financial security can be exchanged for money. The financial system provides the service of liquidity by offering savers markets where they can sell their holdings of financial securities. For example, savers can easily sell their holdings of the stocks and bonds issued by large corporations on the major stock and bond markets.

A third service that the financial system provides savers is the collection and communication of *information*, or facts about borrowers and expectations about returns on financial securities. For example, Lena's Laundry may want to borrow $10,000 from you. Finding out what Lena intends to do with the funds and how likely she is to pay you back may be costly and time-consuming. By depositing $10,000 in the bank, you are, in effect, allowing the bank to gather this information for you. Because banks specialize in gathering information on borrowers, they are able to do it faster and at a lower cost than can individual savers. The financial system plays an important role in communicating information. If you read a news story announcing that an automobile firm has invented a car with an engine that runs on water, how would you determine the effect of that discovery on the firm's profits? Financial markets do the job for you by incorporating information into the prices of stocks, bonds, and other financial securities. In this example, the expectation of higher future profits would boost the prices of the automobile firm's stock and bonds.

Financial intermediaries Firms, such as banks, mutual funds, pension funds, and insurance companies, that borrow funds from savers and lend them to borrowers.

The Macroeconomics of Saving and Investment

As we have seen, the funds available to firms through the financial system come from saving. When firms use funds to purchase machinery, factories, and office buildings, they are engaging in investment. In this section, we explore the macroeconomics of saving and investment. A key point we will develop is that *the total value of saving in the economy must equal the total value of investment.* National income accounting refers to the methods the Bureau of Economic Analysis uses to keep track of total production and total income in the economy. We can use some relationships from national income accounting to understand why total saving must equal total investment.

We begin with the relationship between GDP (Y) and its components, consumption (C), investment (I), government purchases (G), and net exports (NX):

$$Y = C + I + G + NX.$$

Remember that GDP is a measure of both total production in the economy and total income.

In an *open economy*, there is interaction with other economies in terms of both trading of goods and services and borrowing and lending. All economies today are open economies, although they vary significantly in the extent of their openness. In a *closed economy*, there is no trading or borrowing and lending with other economies. For simplicity, we will develop the relationship between saving and investment for a closed economy, which allows us to focus on the most important points in a simpler framework.

In a closed economy, net exports are zero, so we can rewrite the relationship between GDP and its components as:

$$Y = C + I + G.$$

If we rearrange this relationship, we have an expression for investment in terms of the other variables:

$$I = Y - C - G.$$

This expression tells us that in a closed economy, investment spending is equal to total income minus consumption spending and minus government purchases.

We can also derive an expression for total saving. *Private saving* is equal to what households retain of their income after purchasing goods and services (C) and paying taxes (T). Households receive income for supplying the factors of production to firms. This portion of household income is equal to Y. Households also receive income from government in the form of *transfer payments* (TR), which include Social Security payments and unemployment insurance payments. We can write an expression for private saving ($S_{Private}$):

$$S_{Private} = Y + TR - C - T.$$

The government also engages in saving. *Public saving* (S_{Public}) equals the amount of tax revenue the government retains after paying for government purchases and making transfer payments to households:

$$S_{Public} = T - G - TR.$$

So, total saving in the economy (S) is equal to the sum of private saving and public saving:

$$S = S_{Private} + S_{Public},$$

or:

$$S = (Y + TR - C - T) + (T - G - TR),$$

or:

$$S = Y - C - G.$$

The right side of this expression is identical to the expression we derived earlier for investment spending. So, we can conclude that total saving must equal total investment:

$$S = I.$$

When the government spends the same amount that it collects in taxes, there is a *balanced budget*. When the government spends more than it collects in taxes, there is a *budget deficit*. In the case of a deficit, T is less than $G + TR$, which means that public saving is negative. Negative saving is also known as *dissaving*. How can public saving be negative? When the federal government runs a budget deficit, the U.S. Department of the Treasury sells Treasury bonds to borrow the money necessary to fund the gap between taxes and spending. In this case, rather than adding to the total amount of saving available to be borrowed for investment spending, the government is subtracting from it. (Notice that if households borrow more than they save, the total amount of saving will also fall.) With less saving, investment must also be lower. We can conclude that, holding constant all other factors, there is a lower level of investment spending in the economy when there is a budget deficit than when there is a balanced budget.

When the government spends less than it collects in taxes, there is a *budget surplus*. A budget surplus increases public saving and the total level of saving in the economy. A higher level of saving results in a higher level of investment spending. Therefore, holding constant all other factors, there is a higher level of investment spending in the economy when there is a budget surplus than when there is a balanced budget.

The U.S. federal government has experienced dramatic swings in the state of its budget over the past 20 years. In 1992, the federal budget deficit was $297.4 billion. The federal budget had a surplus of $189.5 billion in 2000, but a sharp decline in taxes and increase in government spending resulting from the recession of 2007–2009 led to a record budget deficit of $1.4 trillion in 2009. By 2013, the budget deficit had declined to less than $700 billion.

The Market for Loanable Funds

We have seen that the value of total saving must equal the value of total investment, but we have not yet discussed how this equality is actually brought about in the financial system. We can think of the financial system as being composed of many markets through which funds flow from lenders to borrowers: the market for certificates of deposit at banks, the market for stocks, the market for bonds, the market for mutual fund shares, and so on. For simplicity, we can combine these markets into a single market for *loanable funds*. In the model of the **market for loanable funds**, the interaction of borrowers and lenders determines the market interest rate and the quantity of loanable funds exchanged. Firms can also borrow from savers in other countries. For the remainder of this chapter, we will assume that there are no interactions between households and firms in the United States and those in other countries.

Market for loanable funds The interaction of borrowers and lenders that determines the market interest rate and the quantity of loanable funds exchanged.

Demand and Supply in the Loanable Funds Market The demand for loanable funds is determined by the willingness of firms to borrow money to engage in new investment projects, such as building new factories or carrying out research and development of new products. In determining whether to borrow funds, firms compare the return they expect to make on an investment with the interest rate they must pay to borrow the necessary funds. For example, if Home Depot is considering opening several new stores and expects to earn a return of 12 percent on its investment, the investment will be profitable if Home Depot can borrow the funds at an interest rate of 8 percent but will not be profitable if the interest rate is 15 percent. In Figure 3, the demand for loanable funds is downward sloping because the lower the interest rate, the more investment projects firms can profitably undertake, and the greater the quantity of loanable funds they will demand.

The supply of loanable funds is determined by the willingness of households to save and by the extent of government saving or dissaving. When households save, they reduce the amount of goods and services they can consume and enjoy today. The willingness

Figure 3

The Market for Loanable Funds

The demand for loanable funds is determined by the willingness of firms to borrow money to engage in new investment projects. The supply of loanable funds is determined by the willingness of households to save and by the extent of government saving or dissaving. Equilibrium in the market for loanable funds determines the real interest rate and the quantity of loanable funds exchanged.

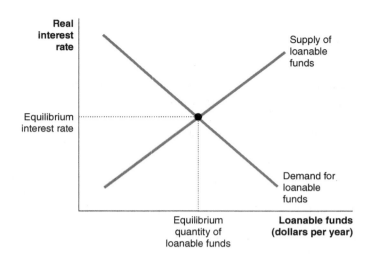

of households to save rather than consume their incomes today will be determined in part by the interest rate they receive when they lend their savings. The higher the interest rate, the greater the reward for saving and the larger the amount of funds households will save. Therefore, the supply curve for loanable funds in Figure 3 is upward sloping because the higher the interest rate, the greater the quantity of saving supplied.

Recall the distinction between the *nominal interest rate* and the *real interest rate*. The nominal interest rate is the stated interest rate on a loan. The real interest rate corrects the nominal interest rate for the effect of inflation and is equal to the nominal interest rate minus the inflation rate. Because both borrowers and lenders are interested in the real interest rate they will receive or pay, equilibrium in the market for loanable funds determines the real interest rate rather than the nominal interest rate.

| Making the Connection | **Ebenezer Scrooge: Accidental Promoter of Economic Growth?** |

Ebenezer Scrooge's name has become synonymous with miserliness. Before his reform at the end of Charles Dickens's *A Christmas Carol*, Scrooge is extraordinarily reluctant to spend money. Although he earns a substantial income, he lives in a cold, dark house that he refuses to heat or light adequately, and he eats a meager diet of gruel because he refuses to buy more expensive food. Throughout most of the book, Dickens portrays Scrooge's behavior in an unfavorable way. Only at the end of the book, when the reformed Scrooge begins to spend lavishly on himself and others, does Dickens praise his behavior.

As economist Steven Landsburg of the University of Rochester points out, however, economically speaking, it may be the pre-reform Scrooge who is more worthy of praise:

> In this whole world, there is nobody more generous than the miser—the man who could deplete the world's resources but chooses not to. The only difference between miserliness and philanthropy is that the philanthropist serves a favored few while the miser spreads his largess far and wide.

We can extend Landsburg's discussion to consider whether the actions of the pre-reform Scrooge or the actions of the post-reform Scrooge are more helpful to economic growth. Pre-reform Scrooge spends very little, investing most of his income in the financial markets. These funds became available for firms to borrow to build new factories and to carry out research and development. Post-reform Scrooge spends much more—and saves much less. Funds that he had previously saved are now spent on food for Bob Cratchit's family and on "making merry" at Christmas. In other words, the

Who was better for economic growth: Scrooge the saver or Scrooge the spender?

actions of post-reform Scrooge contribute to more consumption goods being produced and fewer investment goods. We can conclude that Scrooge's reform caused economic growth to slow down—if only by a little. The larger point is, of course, that savers provide the funds that are indispensable for the investment spending that economic growth requires, and the only way to save is to not consume.

Source: Steven Landsburg, "What I Like About Scrooge," *Slate*, December 9, 2004.

Your Turn: Test your understanding by doing related problem 2.16 at the end of this chapter.

Explaining Movements in Saving, Investment, and Interest Rates

Equilibrium in the market for loanable funds determines the quantity of loanable funds that will flow from lenders to borrowers each period. Equilibrium also determines the real interest rate that lenders will receive and that borrowers must pay. We draw the demand curve for loanable funds by holding constant all factors, other than the interest rate, that affect the willingness of borrowers to demand funds. We draw the supply curve by holding constant all factors, other than the interest rate, that affect the willingness of lenders to supply funds. A shift in either the demand curve or the supply curve will change the equilibrium interest rate and the equilibrium quantity of loanable funds.

If, for example, the profitability of new investment increases due to technological change or because the government reduces corporate taxes, firms will increase their demand for loanable funds. Figure 4 shows the effect of an increase in demand in the market for loanable funds. As in the markets for goods and services, an increase in demand in the market for loanable funds shifts the demand curve to the right. In the new equilibrium, the interest rate increases from i_1 to i_2, and the equilibrium quantity of loanable funds increases from L_1 to L_2. Notice that an increase in the quantity of loanable funds means that both the quantity of saving by households and the quantity of investment by firms have increased. Increasing investment increases the capital stock and the quantity of capital per hour worked, helping to increase economic growth.

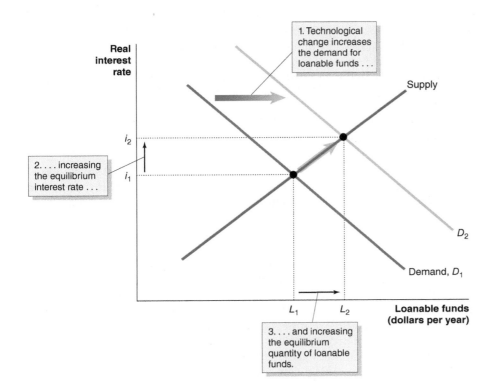

Figure 4

An Increase in the Demand for Loanable Funds

An increase in the demand for loanable funds increases the equilibrium interest rate from i_1 to i_2 and increases the equilibrium quantity of loanable funds from L_1 to L_2. As a result, saving and investment both increase.

121

Figure 5

The Effect of a Budget Deficit on the Market for Loanable Funds

When the government begins running a budget deficit, the supply curve for loanable funds shifts to the left. The equilibrium interest rate increases from i_1 to i_2, and the equilibrium quantity of loanable funds falls from L_1 to L_2. As a result, saving and investment both decline.

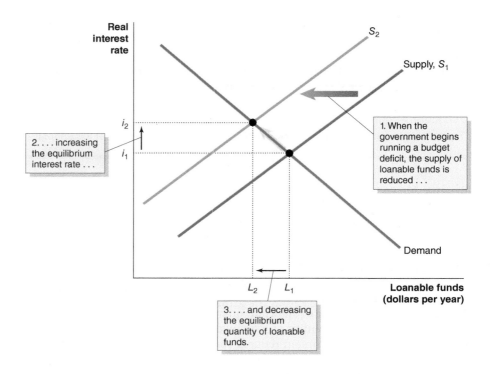

2. . . . increasing the equilibrium interest rate . . .

1. When the government begins running a budget deficit, the supply of loanable funds is reduced . . .

3. . . . and decreasing the equilibrium quantity of loanable funds.

Crowding out A decline in private expenditures as a result of an increase in government purchases.

We can also use the market for loanable funds to examine the effect of a government budget deficit. Putting aside the effects of foreign saving, recall that if the government begins running a budget deficit, it reduces the total amount of saving in the economy. Suppose the government increases spending, which results in a budget deficit. We illustrate the effects of the budget deficit in Figure 5 by shifting the supply curve for loanable funds to the left. In the new equilibrium, the interest rate is higher, and the equilibrium quantity of loanable funds is lower. Running a deficit has reduced the level of total saving in the economy and, by increasing the interest rate, has also reduced the level of investment spending by firms. By borrowing to finance its budget deficit, the government will have *crowded out* some firms that would otherwise have been able to borrow to finance investment. **Crowding out** refers to a decline in investment spending as a result of an increase in government purchases. In Figure 5, the decline in investment spending due to crowding out is shown by the movement from L_1 to L_2 on the demand for loanable funds curve. Lower investment spending means that the capital stock and the quantity of capital per hour worked will not increase as much.

A government budget surplus has the opposite effect of a deficit: A budget surplus increases the total amount of saving in the economy, shifting the supply curve for loanable funds to the right. In the new equilibrium, the interest rate will be lower, and the quantity of loanable funds will be higher. We can conclude that a budget surplus increases the level of saving and investment.

In practice, however, the effect of government budget deficits and surpluses on the equilibrium interest rate is relatively small. (This finding reflects in part the importance of global saving in determining the interest rate.) For example, one study found that increasing government borrowing by an amount equal to 1 percent of GDP would increase the equilibrium real interest rate by only about 0.003 percentage point. However, this small effect on interest rates does not imply that we can ignore the effect of deficits on economic growth. Paying off government debt in the future may require higher taxes, which can depress economic growth. In 2013, many economists and policymakers were concerned that the large deficits projected for future years might be an obstacle to growth.

In addition to budget deficits, other government policies can affect the supply of loanable funds. The federal government gives special tax incentives for saving. For example, 401(k) retirement accounts allow individuals to delay paying taxes on income put into these accounts until they actually retire. The delay in paying taxes increases the after-tax return to saving, so this policy encourages individuals to save.

Solved Problem 2

How Would a Consumption Tax Affect Saving, Investment, the Interest Rate, and Economic Growth?

Some economists and policymakers have suggested that the federal government shift from relying on an income tax to relying on a *consumption tax*. Under the income tax, households pay taxes on all income earned. Under a consumption tax, households pay taxes only on the income they spend.

Households would pay taxes on saved income only if they spent the money at a later time. Use the market for loanable funds model to analyze the effect on saving, investment, the interest rate, and economic growth of switching from an income tax to a consumption tax.

Solving the Problem

Step 1: **Review the chapter material.** This problem is about applying the market for loanable funds model, so you may want to review the section "Explaining Movements in Saving, Investment, and Interest Rates."

Step 2: **Explain the effect of switching from an income tax to a consumption tax.** Households are interested in the return they receive from saving after they have paid their taxes. For example, consider someone who puts his savings in a certificate of deposit at an interest rate of 4 percent and whose tax rate is 25 percent. Under an income tax, this person's after-tax return to saving is 3 percent $[= 4 - (4 \times 0.25)]$. Under a consumption tax, income that is saved is not taxed, so the return rises to 4 percent. We can conclude that moving from an income tax to a consumption tax would increase the return to saving, causing the supply of loanable funds to increase.

Step 3: **Draw a graph of the market for loanable funds to illustrate your answer.** The supply curve for loanable funds will shift to the right as the after-tax return to saving increases under the consumption tax. The equilibrium interest rate will fall, and the levels of saving and investment will both increase. Because investment increases, the capital stock and the quantity of capital per hour worked will grow, and the rate of economic growth should increase. Note that the size of the fall in the interest rate and the size of the increase in loanable funds shown in the following graph are larger than the effects that most economists expect would actually result from the replacement of the income tax with a consumption tax.

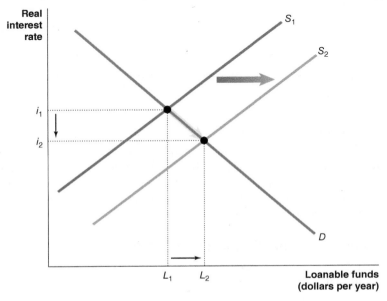

Your Turn: For more practice, do related problem 2.17 at the end of this chapter.

Table 1

Summary of Loanable Funds Model

An increase in ...	will shift the ...	causing ...	Graph of the effect on equilibrium in the loanable funds market
the government's budget deficit	supply of loanable funds curve to the left	the real interest rate to increase and investment to decrease.	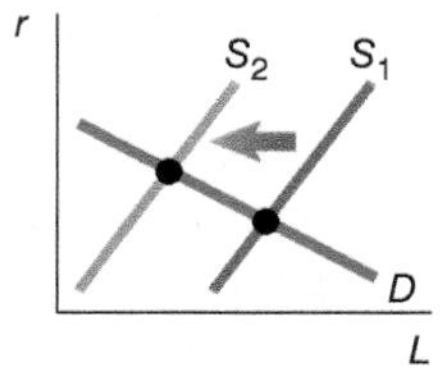
the desire of households to consume today	supply of loanable funds curve to the left	the real interest rate to increase and investment to decrease.	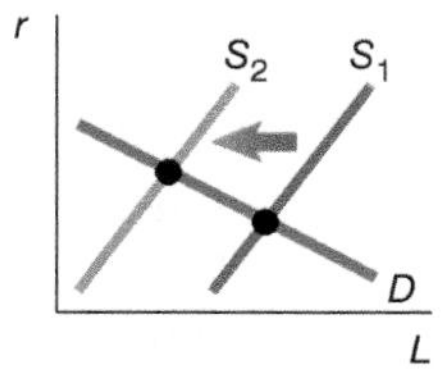
tax benefits for saving, such as 401(k) retirement accounts, which increase the incentive to save	supply of loanable funds curve to the right	the real interest rate to decrease and investment to increase.	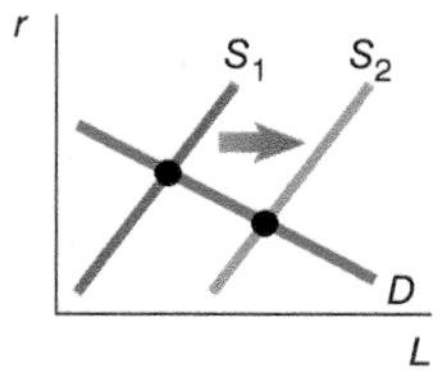
expected future profits	demand for loanable funds curve to the right	the real interest rate and the level of investment to increase.	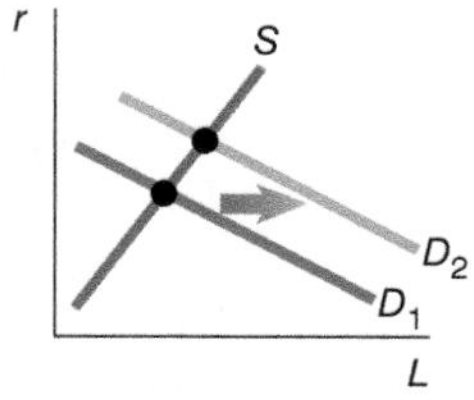
corporate taxes	demand for loanable funds curve to the left	the real interest rate and the level of investment to decrease.	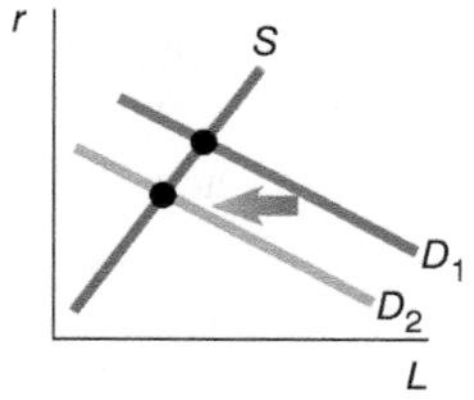

Table 1 summarizes the key factors that cause shifts in the demand and supply curves for loanable funds.

3 LEARNING OBJECTIVE

Explain what happens during the business cycle.

The Business Cycle

Figure 1 illustrates the tremendous increase during the past century in the standard of living of the average American. But close inspection of the figure reveals that real GDP per capita did not increase every year during this time. For example, during the first half of the 1930s, real GDP per capita *fell* for several years in a row. What accounts for these fluctuations in the long-run upward trend?

Some Basic Business Cycle Definitions

The fluctuations in real GDP *per capita* shown in Figure 1 reflect underlying fluctuations in real GDP. Since at least the early nineteenth century, the U.S. economy has experienced business cycles that consist of alternating periods of expanding and contracting economic activity. Because real GDP is our best measure of economic activity, the business cycle is usually illustrated using movements in real GDP.

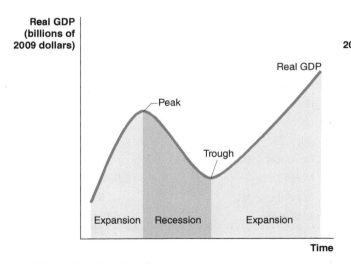

(a) An idealized business cycle

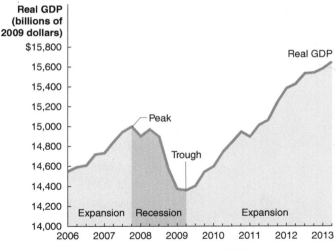

(b) Movements in real GDP, 2006–2013

Figure 6 **The Business Cycle**

Panel (a) shows an idealized business cycle, with real GDP increasing smoothly in an expansion to a business cycle peak and then decreasing smoothly in a recession to a business cycle trough, which is followed by another expansion. The periods of expansion are shown in green, and the period of recession is shown in red. Panel (b) shows the actual movements in real GDP from 2006 to 2013. The recession that began following the business cycle peak in December 2007 was the longest and the most severe since the Great Depression of the 1930s.

During the *expansion phase* of the business cycle, production, employment, and income are increasing. The period of expansion ends with a *business cycle peak.* Following the business cycle peak, production, employment, and income decline as the economy enters the *recession phase* of the cycle. The recession comes to an end with a *business cycle trough*, after which another period of expansion begins. Figure 6 illustrates the phases of the business cycle. Panel (a) shows an idealized business cycle, with real GDP increasing smoothly in an expansion to a business cycle peak and then decreasing smoothly in a recession to a business cycle trough, which is followed by another expansion. Panel (b) shows the somewhat messier reality of an actual business cycle by plotting fluctuations in real GDP during the period from 2006 to 2013. The figure shows that the expansion that began in 2001 continued until a business cycle peak was reached in December 2007. The following recession was the longest and the most severe since the Great Depression of the 1930s. The severity of the recession led some economists to refer to it as the "Great Recession." A business cycle trough was reached in June 2009, when the next expansion began. Although real GDP grew following the business cycle trough, the growth was slower than is typical at the beginning of a business cycle expansion.

How Do We Know When the Economy Is in a Recession?

The federal government produces many statistics that make it possible to monitor the economy. But the federal government does not officially decide when a recession begins or when it ends. Instead, most economists and policymakers accept the decisions of the Business Cycle Dating Committee of the National Bureau of Economic Research (NBER), a private research group located in Cambridge, Massachusetts. Although writers for newspapers and magazines often define a recession as two consecutive quarters of declining real GDP, the NBER has a broader definition: "A recession is a significant decline in activity spread across the economy, lasting more than a few months, visible in industrial production, employment, real income, and wholesale–retail trade."

The NBER is fairly slow in announcing business cycle dates because it takes time to gather and analyze economic statistics. Typically, the NBER will announce that the economy is in a recession only well after the recession has begun. For instance, it did

Table 2

The U.S. Business Cycle

Peak	Trough	Length of Recession
July 1953	May 1954	10 months
August 1957	April 1958	8 months
April 1960	February 1961	10 months
December 1969	November 1970	11 months
November 1973	March 1975	16 months
January 1980	July 1980	6 months
July 1981	November 1982	16 months
July 1990	March 1991	8 months
March 2001	November 2001	8 months
December 2007	June 2009	18 months

Source: National Bureau of Economic Research.

not announce that a recession had begun in December 2007 until 11 months later, at the end of November 2008. Table 2 lists the business cycle peaks and troughs identified by the NBER for the years since 1950. The length of each recession is the number of months from each peak to the following trough.

Making the Connection	**Can a Recession Be a Good Time for a Business to Expand?**

During a recession, business managers have to quickly make many decisions, such as whether to reduce production, cut prices, close stores or other facilities, or lay off workers. In addition to making decisions aimed at dealing with the immediate effects of the recession, managers have to consider how to prepare for the expansion that will follow the recession. Managers know that every recession, even one as severe as the recession of 2007–2009, will be followed by an expansion during which demand for their products is likely to increase. But it can be difficult to commit resources to future expansion when current conditions are bleak and when the end of the recession is difficult to predict.

The payoff to preparing for future growth can be very large, however. For example, at the end of World War II in 1945, many economists and business managers expected that the U.S. economy would enter a severe recession. Sears and Montgomery Ward were the two largest department store chains in the country. Robert Wood, CEO of Sears, expected continuing prosperity and moved to open new stores across the country. Sewell Avery, CEO of Montgomery Ward, expected falling incomes and rising unemployment and refused to authorize any new stores and closed a number of existing ones. As a result, when strong economic growth occurred during the late 1940s, Sears rapidly gained market share at Montgomery Ward's expense.

Following the September 11, 2001, terrorist attacks in the United States, the managers of many hotels expected a prolonged period of reduced travel. They responded by laying off workers and postponing or canceling new construction. Isadore Sharp, the chairman and CEO of Four Seasons Hotels, decided that although the recession would severely hurt the hotel industry, the effects would be short-lived. He decided to finish construction of 18 hotels and begin construction of 10 more. By his own account: "We maintained or enhanced our market share in most regions, contrary to the predictions of various industry experts." In a letter to his shareholders in March 2002, he wrote: "We are well positioned for the economic recovery expected later this year."

During the severe recession of 2007–2009, managers had similar decisions to make. Based in Greensboro, North Carolina, VF Corporation is the largest apparel maker in the world. Among its brands are North Face, Timberland, and Wrangler.

Businesses such as VF viewed the recession of 2007–2009 as an opportunity to expand operations.

While many firms, such as J.Crew, Anne Klein, and Liz Claiborne, were closing stores or postponing opening new ones, Eric Wiseman, CEO of VF, pushed ahead, opening 89 stores in 2008 and 70 in 2009. One retail analyst was quoted as saying: "Unfortunately, many companies pull in the reins in a downturn, but these are often the best opportunities to grow." Similarly, Intel, the computer chip manufacturer, decided in early 2009 to proceed with a $7 billion expansion of its factories in the United States, while many rival firms were reducing their spending on new factories as computer sales declined. Paul Otellini, CEO of Intel, was quoted as saying: "I thought it was important for a company like Intel to stand up and say we have confidence." Heavy equipment manufacturer Caterpillar, Inc., announced that it would build several new facilities and expand some existing ones "to meet the expected increase in customer demand."

By 2013, the recovery from the 2007–2009 recession was well under way, although much slower than a typical recovery. VF's decision to expand appeared to have been a good one as sales and profits continued to increase. The company continued to open new stores and forecast that its sales would increase 60 percent between 2013 and 2017. The verdict for Caterpillar and Intel was more mixed. Although both firms remained profitable, Intel was suffering more than expected from a worldwide decline in computer sales as more consumers began using tablets. Caterpillar, whose sales have become increasingly dependent on demand in foreign countries, was suffering from a slowdown in growth in China and other countries. As a result, sales of its mining equipment, in particular, had been hurt.

Over the long run, though, for most firms, betting on the future of the U.S. economy has paid off.

Sources: Andria Cheng, "VF Lays Out Ambitious Growth Plan," *Wall Street Journal*, June 11, 2013; Robert Sobel, *When Giants Stumble*, Paramus, NJ: Prentice Hall, 1999; Isadore Sharp, *Four Seasons: The Story of a Business Philosophy*, New York: Portfolio, 2009; Bob Tita, "Caterpillar to Expand Kansas Plant," *Wall Street Journal*, August 18, 2011; Rachel Dodes, "VF Dresses Up Its Operations, Bucking Recession," *Wall Street Journal*, March 31, 2009; and Don Clark, "Intel to Spend Heavily on U.S. Plants," *Wall Street Journal*, February 10, 2009.

Your Turn: Test your understanding by doing related problem 3.6 at the end of this chapter.

What Happens during the Business Cycle?

Each business cycle is different. The lengths of the expansion and recession phases and which sectors of the economy are most affected are rarely the same in any two cycles. But most business cycles share certain characteristics, which we will discuss in this section. As the economy nears the end of an expansion, interest rates are usually rising, and the wages of workers are usually increasing faster than prices. As a result of rising interest rates and wages, the profits of firms will be falling. Typically, toward the end of an expansion, both households and firms will have substantially increased their debts. These debts are the result of the borrowing that firms and households undertake to help finance their spending during the expansion. Rising debts can eventually lead households and firms to reduce their spending.

A recession will often begin with a decline in spending by firms on capital goods, such as machinery, equipment, new factories, and new office buildings, or by households on new houses and consumer durables, such as furniture and automobiles. As spending declines, firms selling capital goods and consumer durables will find their sales declining. As sales decline, firms cut back on production and begin to lay off workers. Rising unemployment and falling profits reduce income, which leads to further declines in spending.

As the recession continues, economic conditions eventually begin to improve. The declines in spending finally come to an end; households and firms begin to reduce their debts, thereby increasing their ability to spend; and interest rates decline, making it more likely that households and firms will borrow to finance new spending. Firms begin to increase their spending on capital goods as they anticipate the need for additional production during the next expansion. Increased spending by households on new houses and consumer durables and by businesses on capital goods will finally bring the recession to an end and begin the next expansion.

The Effect of the Business Cycle on Whirlpool

Durables are goods that are expected to last for three or more years. Consumer durables include furniture, appliances, and automobiles, and producer durables include machine tools, electric generators, and commercial airplanes. *Nondurables* are goods that are expected to last for fewer than three years. Consumer nondurables include goods such as food and clothing. Durables are affected more by the business cycle than are nondurables. During a recession, workers reduce spending if they lose their jobs, fear losing their jobs, or suffer wage cuts. Because people can often continue using their existing furniture, appliances, or automobiles, they are more likely to postpone spending on durables than spending on nondurables. Similarly, when firms experience declining sales and profits during a recession, they often cut back on purchases of producer durables.

We mentioned in our discussion of Whirlpool at the beginning of this chapter that the firm's sales are significantly affected by the business cycle. Panel (a) of Figure 7 shows movements in real GDP for each quarter from the beginning of 1998 through the beginning of 2013. We can see both the upward trend in real GDP over time and the effects of the recessions of 2001 and 2007–2009. Data for Whirlpool are not available separately, but panel (b) shows movements in the real value of manufacturers' sales of household appliances during the same years. The effects of the recessions on Whirlpool and other appliance manufacturers are typically more dramatic than the effects on the economy as a whole. Sales of household appliances are heavily affected by the housing market. When homebuilders construct

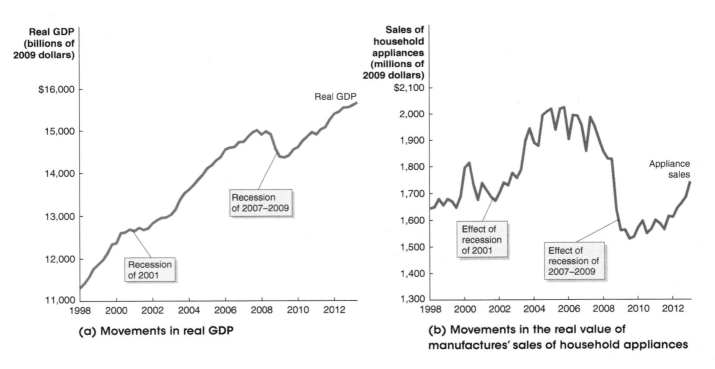

(a) Movements in real GDP

(b) Movements in the real value of manufactures' sales of household appliances

Figure 7   The Effect of the Business Cycle on Whirlpool

Panel (a) shows movements in real GDP for each quarter from the beginning of 1998 through the beginning of 2013. Panel (b) shows movements in the real value of manufacturers' sales of household appliances for the same years. In panel (b), the effects of the recessions on the sales of Whirlpool and other appliance manufacturers are more dramatic than the effects on the economy as a whole.

Note: Sales of household appliances are manufacturers' shipments of household appliances deflated by the BEA price index for furnishings and durable household equipment.
Sources: U.S. Bureau of Economic Analysis; and Federal Reserve Bank of St. Louis.

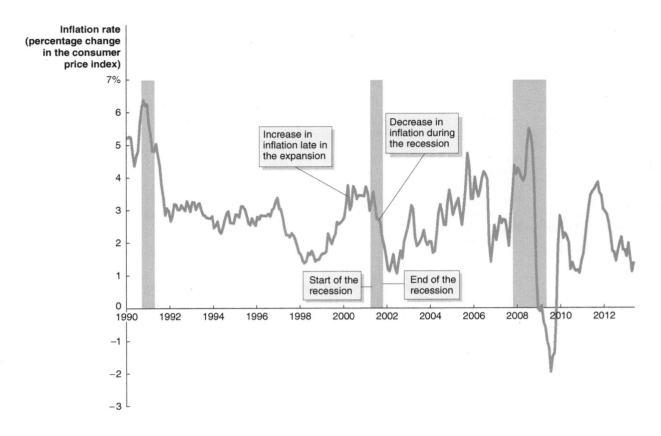

Figure 8 The Effect of Recessions on the Inflation Rate

Toward the end of a typical expansion, the inflation rate begins to rise. Recessions, marked by the shaded vertical bars, cause the inflation rate to fall. By the end of a recession, the inflation rate is significantly below what it had been at the beginning of the recession.

Note: The points on the figure represent the annual inflation rate measured by the percentage change in the consumer price index from the same month during the previous year.
Source: U.S. Bureau of Labor Statistics.

a new house, they typically furnish it with a new refrigerator, dishwasher, stove, and other appliances. People moving into a new home often buy washers, dryers, or other appliances. People buying an existing home also often buy new appliances. As panel (b) shows, sales of household appliances declined by 8 percent during the 2001 recession—when the housing market suffered only a mild decline—but declined by 23 percent during the 2007–2009 recession—when the housing market crashed. As of mid-2013, appliance sales remained far below their 2007 peak.

The Effect of the Business Cycle on the Inflation Rate The *price level* measures the average prices of goods and services in the economy, and the *inflation rate* is the percentage increase in the price level from one year to the next. An important fact about the business cycle is that the inflation rate usually increases during economic expansions—particularly near the end of an expansion—and the inflation rate usually decreases during recessions. Figure 8 illustrates this pattern for the three recessions since the late 1980s.

In every recession since 1950, the inflation rate has been lower during the 12 months after the recession ends than it was during the 12 months before the recession began. The average decline in the inflation rate has been about 2.5 percentage points. This result is not surprising. During a business cycle expansion, spending by businesses and households is strong, and producers of goods and services find it easier to raise prices. As spending declines during a recession, firms have a more difficult time selling their goods and services and are likely to increase prices less than they otherwise might have.

Don't Let This Happen to You

Don't Confuse the Price Level and the Inflation Rate

Do you agree with the following statement: "The consumer price index is a widely used measure of the inflation rate"? This statement may sound plausible, but it is incorrect. The consumer price index (CPI) tells us what a typical urban family of four pays for the goods and services they purchase relative to a base year, but values for the CPI do not directly measure the inflation rate. We can measure the inflation rate as the *percentage change* in the CPI from one year to the next. In macroeconomics, it is important not to confuse the level of a variable with the change in the variable. To give another example, real GDP does not measure economic growth. Economic growth is measured by the percentage change in real GDP from one year to the next.

Your Turn: Test your understanding by doing related problem 3.7 at the end of this chapter.

The Effect of the Business Cycle on the Unemployment Rate Recessions cause the inflation rate to fall, but they cause the unemployment rate to increase. As firms see their sales decline, they begin to reduce production and lay off workers. Figure 9 illustrates this pattern for the three recessions since the late 1980s. Notice in the figure that the unemployment rate continued to rise even after the recessions of 1990–1991, 2001, and 2007–2009 had ended. This lag in the unemployment rate, which is typical, is due to two factors. First, even though employment begins to increase as a recession ends, it may be increasing more slowly than the increase in the labor force resulting from population growth. If employment increases slowly enough relative to the growth in the labor force, it is possible for the unemployment rate to rise. Second, some

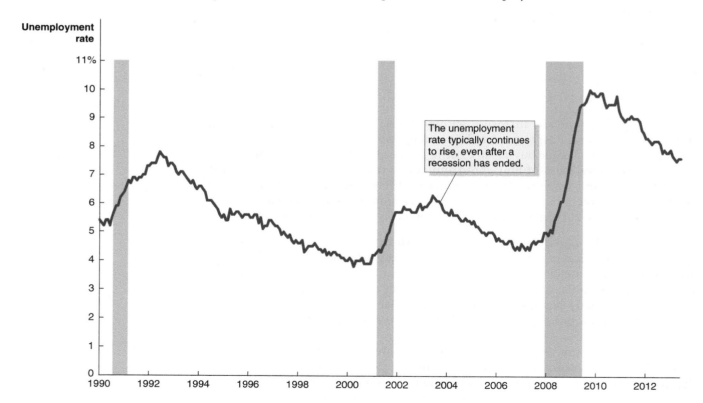

Figure 9 **How Recessions Affect the Unemployment Rate**

Unemployment rises during recessions and falls during expansions. The reluctance of firms to hire new employees during the early stages of a recovery means that the unemployment rate usually continues to rise even after the recession has ended.
Source: U.S. Bureau of Labor Statistics.

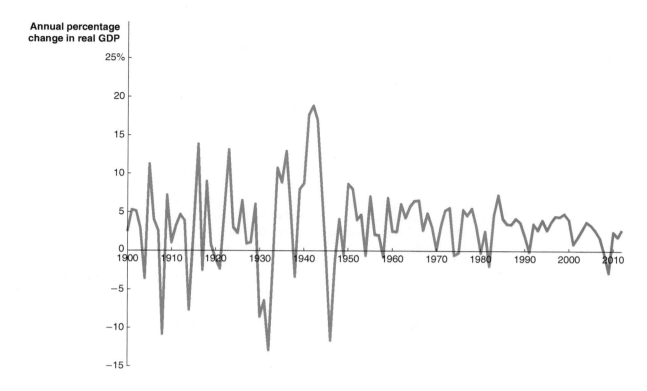

Figure 10 Fluctuations in Real GDP, 1900–2012

Fluctuations in real GDP were greater before 1950 than they have been since 1950.
Sources: Samuel H. Williamson, "What Was the U.S. GDP Then?" MeasuringWorth, August 2013; and U.S. Bureau of Economic Analysis.

firms continue to operate well below their capacity even after a recession has ended and sales have begun to increase. As a result, at first, firms may not hire back all the workers they have laid off and may even continue for a while to lay off more workers.

During the recessions since 1950, the unemployment rate has risen on average by about 1.2 percentage points during the 12 months after a recession has begun. So, on average, more than 1 million more workers have been unemployed during the 12 months after a recession has begun than during the previous 12 months.

Is the "Great Moderation" Over? Figure 10, which shows the year-to-year percentage changes in real GDP since 1900, illustrates a striking change in fluctuations in real GDP beginning around 1950. Before 1950, real GDP went through much greater year-to-year fluctuations than it has since that time. Fluctuations since the mid-1980s have been particularly mild. By the early twenty-first century, some economists had begun referring to the absence of severe recessions in the United States as the "Great Moderation." However, economists began questioning this view with the recession that began in December 2007. This recession was the longest and the most severe since the Great Depression of the 1930s and has been called the Great Contraction. The percentage decline in real GDP during 2009 was the largest since 1932. Economists and policymakers remain unsure whether the Great Moderation will return even though several years have passed since the end of the Great Contraction.

The unusual severity of the 2007–2009 recession can be seen by comparing its length to the lengths of other recent recessions. Table 3 shows that in the late nineteenth century, the average length of recessions was the same as the average length of expansions. During the first half of the twentieth century, the average length of expansions decreased slightly, and the average length of recessions decreased significantly. As a result, expansions were about six months longer than recessions during these years. The most striking change came after 1950, when the length of expansions greatly increased and the length of recessions decreased. After 1950, expansions were more than five times as long as recessions. In other words, in the late nineteenth

Table 3

Until 2007, the Business Cycle Had Become Milder

Period	Average Length of Expansions	Average Length of Recessions
1870–1900	26 months	26 months
1900–1950	25 months	19 months
1950–2009	61 months	11 months

century, the U.S. economy spent as much time in recession as it did in expansion. After 1950, the U.S. economy experienced long expansions interrupted by relatively short recessions.

The recession of 2007–2009 is an exception to this experience of relatively short, mild recessions. The recession lasted 18 months, the longest of the post-1950 period. Does the length and depth of the 2007–2009 recession indicate that the United States is returning to an era of severe fluctuations in real GDP? A full answer to this question will not be possible for at least several years. But in the next section, we provide some perspective on the question by considering why the period from 1950 to 2007 was one of relative macroeconomic stability.

Will the U.S. Economy Return to Stability?

Shorter recessions, longer expansions, and less severe fluctuations in real GDP have resulted in a significant improvement in the economic well-being of Americans. Economists have offered several explanations for why the U.S. economy experienced a period of relative stability from 1950 to 2007:

- *The increasing importance of services and the declining importance of goods.* As services such as medical care or investment advice have become a much larger fraction of GDP, there has been a corresponding relative decline in the production of goods. For example, at one time, manufacturing production accounted for about 40 percent of GDP, but in 2013, it accounted for less than 12 percent. Manufacturing production, particularly production of durable goods such as automobiles, fluctuates more than the production of services because during a recession households will cut back more on purchases of durables than they will on purchases of services.

- *The establishment of unemployment insurance and other government transfer programs that provide funds to the unemployed.* Before the 1930s, programs such as unemployment insurance, which provides government payments to workers who lose their jobs, and Social Security, which provides government payments to retired and disabled workers, did not exist. These and other government programs make it possible for workers who lose their jobs during recessions to have higher incomes and, therefore, to spend more than they would otherwise. This additional spending may have helped to shorten recessions.

- *Active federal government policies to stabilize the economy.* Before the Great Depression of the 1930s, the federal government did not attempt to end recessions or prolong expansions. Because the Great Depression was so severe, with the unemployment rate rising to more than 20 percent of the labor force and real GDP declining by almost 30 percent, public opinion began favoring government attempts to stabilize the economy. In the years since World War II, the federal government has actively used macroeconomic policy measures to try to end recessions and prolong expansions. Many economists believe that these government policies have played a key role in stabilizing the economy. Other economists, however, argue that active government policy has had little effect. The debate over the role of macroeconomic policy became particularly intense during and after the 2007–2009 recession.

- *The increased stability of the financial system.* The severity of the Great Depression of the 1930s was caused in part by instability in the financial system. More than 5,000 banks failed between 1929 and 1933, reducing the savings of many households and making it difficult for households and firms to obtain the credit needed to maintain their spending. In addition, a decline of more than 80 percent in stock prices greatly reduced the wealth of many households and made it difficult for firms to raise funds by selling stock. Most economists believe that the return of financial instability during the 2007–2009 recession is a key reason the recession was so severe. If the United States is to return to macroeconomic stability, stability will first have to return to the financial system.

Continued

Economics in Your Life

Do You Help the Economy More if You Spend or if You Save?

At the beginning of this chapter, we posed a question: Which of your two roommates is right—the one who argues that you would help the economy more by saving your tax refund check, or the one who argues that you should spend it? In this chapter, we have seen that consumption spending promotes the production of more consumption goods and services—such as jeans and haircuts—and fewer investment goods and services—such as physical capital and research and development. Saving (and, therefore, not consuming) is necessary to fund investment expenditure. So, saving your refund check will help the economy over the long run. But if the economy is in a recession, spending your refund check will spur more production of consumption goods. In a sense, then, both of your roommates are correct: Spending your check will help stimulate the economy during a recession, while saving it will help the economy grow over the long run.

Conclusion

The U.S. economy remains a remarkable engine for improving the well-being of Americans. The standard of living of Americans today is much higher than it was 100 years ago. But households and firms are still subject to the ups and downs of the business cycle. Ever-increasing long-run prosperity is achieved in the context of short-run instability is a basic fact of macroeconomics.

Visit MyEconLab for a news article and analysis related to the concepts in this chapter.

Chapter Summary and Problems

Key Terms

Business cycle	Financial intermediaries	Labor productivity	Market for loanable funds
Capital	Financial markets	Long-run economic growth	Potential GDP
Crowding out	Financial system		

Long-Run Economic Growth

LEARNING OBJECTIVE: Discuss the importance of long-run economic growth.

Summary

The U.S. economy has experienced both *long-run economic growth* and the *business cycle*. The **business cycle** refers to alternating periods of economic expansion and economic recession. **Long-run economic growth** is the process by which rising productivity increases the standard of living of the typical person. Because of economic growth, the typical American today can buy almost eight times as much as the typical American of 1900. Long-run growth is measured by increases in real GDP per capita. Increases in real GDP per capita depend on increases in labor productivity. **Labor productivity** is the quantity of goods and services that can be produced by one worker or by one hour of work. Economists believe two key factors determine labor productivity: the quantity of capital per hour worked and the level of technology. **Capital** refers to manufactured goods that are used to produce other goods and services. *Human capital* is the accumulated knowledge and skills workers acquire from education, training, or their life experiences. Economic growth occurs if the quantity of capital per hour worked increases and if technological change occurs. Economists often discuss economic growth in terms of growth in **potential GDP**, which is the level of GDP attained when all firms are producing at capacity.

Visit **www.myeconlab.com** to complete these exercises online and get instant feedback.

Review Questions

1.1 By how much did real GDP per capita increase in the United States between 1900 and 2012? Discuss whether the increase in real GDP per capita is likely to be greater or smaller than the true increase in living standards.

1.2 What is the rule of 70? If real GDP per capita grows at a rate of 5 percent per year, how many years will it take to double?

1.3 What two key factors cause labor productivity to increase over time?

1.4 What is potential GDP? Does potential GDP remain constant over time?

Problems and Applications

1.5 Briefly discuss whether you would rather live in the United States of 1900 with an income of $1,000,000 per year or the United States of 2014 with an income of $50,000 per year. Assume that the incomes for both years are measured in 2014 dollars.

1.6 Based on what you read about economic growth in this chapter, elaborate on the importance of growth in GDP, particularly real GDP per capita, to the quality of life of a country's citizens.

1.7 **[Related to** Making the Connection: **The Connection Between Economic Prosperity and Health]** Think about the relationship between economic prosperity and life expectancy. What implications does this relationship have for the size of the health care sector of the economy? In particular, is this sector of the U.S. economy likely to expand or contract in coming years?

1.8 Use the table to answer the following questions.

Year	Real GDP (Billions of 2009 Dollars)
1990	$8,945
1991	8,939
1992	9,257
1993	9,511
1994	9,895

a. Calculate the growth rate of real GDP for each year from 1991 to 1994.

b. Calculate the average annual growth rate of real GDP for the period from 1991 to 1994.

1.9 As discussed in this chapter, real GDP per capita in the United States grew from about $6,000 in 1900 to about $49,200 in 2012, which represents an annual growth rate of 1.9 percent. If the U.S. economy continues to grow at this rate, how many years will it take for real GDP per capita to double? If government economic policies meant to stimulate economic growth result in the annual growth rate increasing to 2.2 percent, how many years will it take for real GDP per capita to double?

1.10 A few years ago, Russian Prime Minister Vladimir Putin called for a doubling of labor productivity over the next decade. An article on the Web site *Russia Beyond the Headlines* states that: "Russian productivity is a third of that in the United States."

a. What factors would cause Russian labor productivity to be a third of U.S. labor productivity?

b. The article notes that one cause of low Russian productivity is "just bad management." Why might Russian businesses suffer from bad management?

Source: "Putin Calls for Doubling Labor Productivity in the Next Decade," *Russia Beyond the Headlines*, rbth.ru, April 29, 2011.

1.11 **[Related to** Solved Problem 1**]** An article in the *Economist* magazine compares Panama to Singapore. It quotes Panama's president as saying: "We copy a lot from Singapore and we need to copy more." The article observes that: "Panama is not even one-fifth as rich as its Asian model on a per-person basis. But Singapore would envy its growth: from 2005 to 2010 its economy expanded by more than 8% a year, the fastest rate in the Americas." Judging from the experience of Singapore, if Panama is to maintain these high growth rates, what needs to be true about the sources of Panama's growth?

Source: "A Singapore for Central America?" *Economist*, July 14, 2011.

1.12 A newspaper article on labor productivity in the United States observes that "the best measure of productivity is probably output per hour, not output per person." Briefly explain whether you agree.

Source: David Leonhardt, "Even More Productive than Americans," *New York Times*, January 26, 2011.

1.13 **[Related to** Making the Connection: **Can India Sustain Its rapid Growth?]** Amartya Sen, a professor of economics at Harvard University and a Nobel Laureate, has argued: "For India to match China in its range of manufacturing capacity . . . it needs a better-educated and healthier labor force at all levels of society." What role do education and health care play in economic growth? How has India been able to experience rapid economic growth since 1991 despite poor education and health care systems?

Source: Amartya Sen, "Why India Trails China," *New York Times*, June 19, 2013.

1.14 **[Related to** Making the Connection: **Can India Sustain Its rapid Growth?]** According to an article on India in the *Economist*: "When the government announced its package of measures last September (2012), optimists hoped it was a moment to rival 1991." The article further states: "It is now clear that deep reforms are not going to happen in the near future, reflecting . . . a tricky political climate."

a. Why is 1991 an important date in the history of India's economy?

b. Why does India have a "tricky political climate"?

c. The article also states that "the hope is that India's politicians will finally be more serious about fighting graft and enacting reform." What is graft? While businesspeople might be annoyed to pay bribes, why would graft affect economic growth in India?

Source: "India's Economy: Start Me Up," *Economist*, June 29, 2013.

2	**Saving, Investment, and the Financial System**

LEARNING OBJECTIVE: Discuss the role of the financial system in facilitating long-run economic growth.

Summary

Financial markets and financial intermediaries together comprise the **financial system**. A well-functioning financial system is an important determinant of economic growth. Firms acquire funds from households, either directly through financial markets—such as the stock and bond markets—or indirectly through financial intermediaries—such as banks. The funds available to firms come from *saving*. There are two categories of saving in the economy: *private saving* by households and *public saving* by the government. The value of total saving in the economy is always equal to the value of total investment spending. In the model of the **market for loanable funds**, the interaction of borrowers and lenders determines the market interest rate and the quantity of loanable funds exchanged.

Visit **www.myeconlab.com** to complete these exercises online and get instant feedback.

Review Questions

2.1 Why is a country's financial system important for long-run economic growth?

2.2 How does the financial system—both financial markets and financial intermediaries—provide risk sharing, liquidity, and information to savers and borrowers?

2.3 Briefly explain why the total value of saving in the economy must equal the total value of investment.

2.4 What are loanable funds? Why do businesses demand loanable funds? Why do households supply loanable funds?

Problems and Applications

2.5 Suppose you can receive an interest rate of 3 percent on a certificate of deposit at a bank that is charging borrowers 7 percent on new car loans. Why might you be unwilling to loan money directly to someone who wants to borrow from you to buy a new car, even if that person offers to pay you an interest rate higher than 3 percent?

2.6 An International Monetary Fund Factsheet makes the following observation regarding sound financial systems: "A country's financial system . . . provide[s] a framework . . . [for] supporting economic growth." Do you agree with this observation? Briefly explain.

Source: "Financial System Soundness," *International Monetary Fund Factsheet*, March 2013.

2.7 Consider the following data for a closed economy:

$$Y = \$11 \text{ trillion}$$
$$C = \$8 \text{ trillion}$$
$$I = \$2 \text{ trillion}$$
$$TR = \$1 \text{ trillion}$$
$$T = \$3 \text{ trillion}$$

Use these data to calculate the following:
a. Private saving
b. Public saving
c. Government purchases
d. The government budget deficit or budget surplus

2.8 Consider the following data for a closed economy:

$$Y = \$12 \text{ trillion}$$
$$C = \$8 \text{ trillion}$$
$$G = \$2 \text{ trillion}$$
$$S_{\text{Public}} = -\$0.5 \text{ trillion}$$
$$T = \$2 \text{ trillion}$$

Use these data to calculate the following:
a. Private saving
b. Investment spending
c. Transfer payments
d. The government budget deficit or budget surplus

2.9 In problem 2.8, suppose that government purchases increase from $2 trillion to $2.5 trillion. If the values for Y and C are unchanged, what must happen to the values of S and I? Briefly explain.

2.10 Match each of the following scenarios with the appropriate graph of the market for loanable funds.
a. An increase in the real interest rate results in only a small increase in private saving by households.
b. A decrease in the real interest rate results in a substantial increase in spending on investment projects by businesses.
c. The federal government eliminates 401(k) retirement accounts
d. The federal government reduces the tax on corporate profits (assume no change in the federal budget deficit or budget surplus)

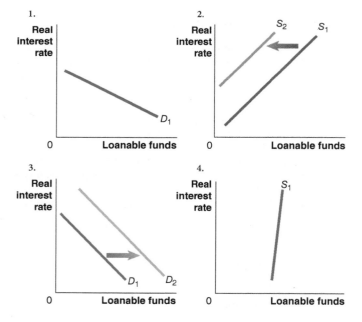

2.11 Use the following graph to answer the questions:
a. Does the shift from S_1 to S_2 represent an increase or a decrease in the supply of loanable funds?
b. With the shift in supply, what happens to the equilibrium quantity of loanable funds?

c. With the change in the equilibrium quantity of loanable funds, what happens to the quantity of saving? What happens to the quantity of investment?

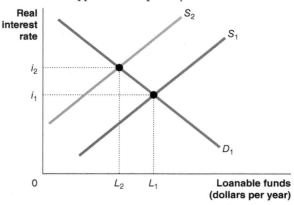

2.12 Use the following graph to answer the questions:

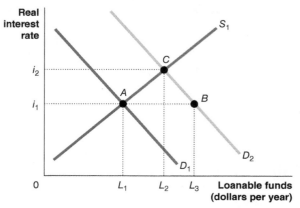

a. With the shift in the demand curve for loanable funds, what happens to the equilibrium real interest rate and the equilibrium quantity of loanable funds?
b. How can the equilibrium quantity of loanable funds increase when the real interest rate increases? Doesn't the quantity of loanable funds demanded decrease when the interest rate increases?
c. How much would the quantity of loanable funds demanded have increased if the interest rate had remained at i_1?
d. How much does the quantity of loanable funds supplied increase with the increase in the interest rate from i_1 to i_2?

2.13 Suppose that the economy is currently in a recession but economic forecasts indicate that the economy will soon enter an expansion. What is the likely effect of the expansion on the expected profitability of new investment in plant and equipment? In the market for loanable funds, draw a graph and explain the effect of the forecast of an economic expansion, assuming that borrowers and lenders believe the forecast is accurate. What happens to the equilibrium real interest rate and the quantity of loanable funds? What happens to the level of saving and investment?

2.14 Firms care about their after-tax rate of return on investment projects. In the market for loanable funds, draw a graph and explain the effect of an increase in taxes on business profits. (For simplicity, assume no change in the federal budget deficit or budget surplus.) What happens to the equilibrium real interest rate and the quantity of loanable funds? What will be the effect on the level of investment by firms and the economy's capital stock in the future?

2.15 The federal government in the United States has been running large budget deficits.

   a. Use a market for loanable funds graph to illustrate the effect of the federal budget deficits. What happens to the equilibrium real interest rate and the quantity of loanable funds? What happens to the level of saving and investment?

   b. Now suppose that households believe that deficits will be financed by higher taxes in the near future, and households increase their saving in anticipation of paying those higher taxes. Briefly explain how your analysis in part (a) will be affected.

2.16 **[Related to** Making the Connection: **Ebenezer Scrooge: Accidental Promoter of Economic Growth?]** This feature claims that Ebenezer Scrooge promoted economic growth more when he was a miser and saved most of his income than when he reformed and began spending freely. Suppose,

though, that most of his spending after he reformed involved buying food for the Cratchits and other poor families. Many economists believe that there is a close connection between how much very poor people eat and how much they are able to work and how productive they are while working. Does this fact affect the conclusion about whether the pre-reform or post-reform Scrooge had a more positive impact on economic growth? Briefly explain.

2.17 **[Related to** Solved Problem 2**]** Savers are taxed on the nominal interest payments they receive rather than the real interest payments. Suppose the federal government shifts from taxing nominal interest payments to taxing only real interest payments. (That is, savers will be allowed to subtract the inflation rate from the nominal interest rate they receive and only pay taxes on the resulting real interest rate.) Use a market for loanable funds graph to analyze the effects of this change in tax policy. What happens to the equilibrium real interest rate and the equilibrium quantity of loanable funds? What happens to the level of saving and investment?

 ## The Business Cycle

LEARNING OBJECTIVE: Explain what happens during the business cycle.

Summary

During the expansion phase of the business cycle, production, employment, and income are increasing. The period of expansion ends with a business cycle peak. Following the business cycle peak, production, employment, and income decline during the recession phase of the cycle. The recession comes to an end with a business cycle trough, after which another period of expansion begins. The inflation rate usually rises near the end of a business cycle expansion and then falls during a recession. The unemployment rate declines during the later part of an expansion and increases during a recession. The unemployment rate often continues to increase even after an expansion has begun. Until the severe recession of 2007–2009, recessions had been milder and the economy had been more stable in the period since 1950. Economists debate whether the economy will return to the stability it experienced during the period of the "Great Moderation."

Visit **www.myeconlab.com** to complete these exercises online and get instant feedback.

Review Questions

3.1 What are the names of the following events that occur during a business cycle?

   a. The high point of economic activity

   b. The low point of economic activity

   c. The period between the high point of economic activity and the following low point

   d. The period between the low point of economic activity and the following high point

3.2 Briefly describe the effect of the business cycle on the inflation rate and the unemployment rate. Why might the unemployment rate continue to rise during the early stages of an expansion?

3.3 Briefly compare the severity of recessions before and after 1950. What explanations have economists offered for the period of relative macroeconomic stability from 1950 to 2007?

Problems and Applications

3.4 **[Related to the** Chapter Opener**]** Briefly explain whether production of each of the following goods is likely to fluctuate more or less than real GDP does during the business cycle:

   a. Ford F-150 trucks

   b. McDonald's Big Macs

   c. Whirlpool washing machines

   d. Huggies diapers

   e. Boeing passenger aircraft

3.5 The National Bureau of Economic Research, a private group, is responsible for declaring when recessions begin and end. Can you think of reasons the Bureau of Economic Analysis, part of the federal government, might not want to take on this responsibility?

3.6 **[Related to** Making the Connection: **Can a Recession Be a Good Time for a Business to Expand?]** As we have seen, some firms prosper by expanding during recessions. What risks do firms take when they pursue this strategy? Are there circumstances in particular industries under which a more cautious approach might be advisable? Briefly explain.

3.7 **[Related to the** Don't Let This Happen to You**]** "Real GDP in 2012 was $15.5 trillion. This value is a large number. Therefore, economic growth must have been high during 2012." Briefly explain whether you agree with this statement.

3.8 **[Related to the** Chapter Opener**]** In 2012, Jeff Fettig, CEO of Whirlpool, based an optimistic forecast of his company's sales on forecasts of increasing sales of new homes in the United States. Explain why changes in the demand for housing affect Whirlpool's sales.

Source: James R. Hagerty, "Whirlpool Expects Lift from Housing Upturn," *Wall Street Journal*, July 24, 2012.

3.9 Imagine that you own a business and that during the next recession, you lay off 10 percent of your workforce. When an economic expansion begins and your sales begin to increase, why might you not immediately start rehiring workers?

3.10 An article in the *Economist* refers to "The Great Delusion of a Great Moderation." What is the Great Moderation? Why might some people consider the Great Moderation to have been a delusion?

Source: "Lending a Hand," *Economist*, September 10, 2011.

Real-Time-Data Exercises

D1 **[Analyzing real GDP over the business cycle]** Go to the Web site of the Federal Reserve Bank of St. Louis (FRED) (research.stlouisfed.org/fred2/).

   a. Find the values for the most recent quarter for the following three variables: (1) Nominal Gross Domestic Product (GDP), (2) Real Gross Domestic Product (GDPC1), and (2) Real Potential Gross Domestic Product (GDPPOT).

   b. Using the data from part (a), calculate the GDP Price Deflator for the most recent quarter.

   c. Calculate for this quarter the percentage difference between real GDP and potential GDP.

   d. Using Figure 2, describe the relationship between real GDP and potential GDP over the past 10 years.

D2 **[Analyzing saving and investment]** Go to the Web site of the Federal Reserve Bank of St. Louis (FRED) (research.stlouisfed.org/fred2/).

   a. Find the most recent values and the values from the same quarter three years earlier for Gross Private Saving (GPSAVE) and Gross Government Saving (GGSAVE).

   b. Using the values found in part (a), calculate the value of total saving in the economy for these two periods.

   c. Draw a graph to show the loanable funds market in equilibrium. Explain which curve represents total saving.

   d. On the graph you drew in part (c), show the effect on the loanable funds market from the change you calculated in part (b) for total saving between the two periods.

D3 **[Analyzing saving and investment]** Go to the Web site of the Federal Reserve Bank of St. Louis (FRED) (research.stlouisfed.org/fred2/).

   a. Find the most recent value and the value from the same quarter four years earlier for Gross Government Saving (GGSAVE).

   b. Total saving in the economy is composed of private saving and government saving. What does government saving represent?

   c. Using the values found in part (a), explain whether the government budget in each of the two periods is balanced, in a surplus, or in a deficit. From the first period to the most recent period, has government saving increased, decreased, or remained constant?

   d. Draw a graph showing the loanable funds market in equilibrium. Use the graph to show the effect of the change in government saving that you calculated in part (c) on the loanable funds market. (Assume that the level of private saving is unchanged.) Explain what will happen to the level of investment in the economy.

Glossary

Business cycle Alternating periods of economic expansion and economic recession.

Capital Manufactured goods that are used to produce other goods and services.

Crowding out A decline in private expenditures as a result of an increase in government purchases.

Financial intermediaries Firms, such as banks, mutual funds, pension funds, and insurance companies, that borrow funds from savers and lend them to borrowers.

Financial markets Markets where financial securities, such as stocks and bonds, are bought and sold.

Financial system The system of financial markets and financial intermediaries through which firms acquire funds from households.

Labor productivity The quantity of goods and services that can be produced by one worker or by one hour of work.

Long-run economic growth The process by which rising productivity increases the average standard of living.

Market for loanable funds The interaction of borrowers and lenders that determines the market interest rate and the quantity of loanable funds exchanged.

Potential GDP The level of real GDP attained when all firms are producing at capacity.

Credits

Credits are listed in the order of appearance.

Photo

Daniel Acker/Bloomberg/Getty Images; Everett Collection; Bloomberg/Getty Images

Text

Richard Sylla, "Financial Systems and Economic Modernization," *Journal of Economic History*, Vol. 62. No. 2, June 2002, pp. 279–292.

Long-Run Economic Growth: Sources and Policies

Long-Run Economic Growth: Sources and Policies

Chapter Outline and Learning Objectives

Can China Save General Motors?

The General Motors Company (GM) was founded in 1908. Under the leadership of Alfred P. Sloan, GM's chief executive officer from 1923 to 1946, the company became the world's largest seller of automobiles. In the 1980s, GM's sales began a long decline because the firm had difficulty competing with rival firms offering smaller, more fuel-efficient cars. GM was hit particularly hard by the severe recession of 2007–2009, and the company filed for bankruptcy in June 2009.

With $50 billion in aid from the federal government a smaller, restructured GM emerged later that year with a new focus on increasing sales in foreign markets. By 2013, GM was selling more cars in China than in the United States and the company announced plans to invest another $11 billion to increase production capacity in China. Some industry observers even joked that General Motors should be renamed "China Motors."

From the time the Communist Party seized control of China in 1949 until the late 1970s, China was a *centrally planned economy* in which the government controlled production of goods and services. The country experienced very little economic growth during those years. China moved away from a centrally planned economy in 1978. Real GDP per capita grew at a rate of 6.5 percent per year between 1979 and 1995, and at the white-hot rate of more than 9 percent per year between 1996 and 2012. These rapid growth rates have transformed the Chinese economy: Real GDP per capita today is more than 10 times higher than it was 50 years ago. China's economic growth has presented GM and other firms with the opportunity to profit from its rapidly expanding consumer market.

But China is not a democracy and the Chinese government has failed to fully establish the rule of law, particularly with respect to consistently enforcing property rights. For example, GM has been unwilling to bring its latest technology for building electric and hybrid cars to China for fear that its intellectual property will be stolen. Failing to establish the rule of law is a problem for the long-term prospects of the Chinese economy because without the rule of law, entrepreneurs cannot fulfill their role in the market system of bringing together the factors of production—labor, capital, and natural resources—to produce goods and services.

Sources: Colum Murphy, "GM to Build Cadillac Plant in China," *Wall Street Journal*, May 7, 2013; Gordon G. Chang, "General Motors Is Riding High in China—For Now," *Forbes*, August 19, 2012; "Alfred P. Sloan Jr. Dead at 90; G.M. Leader and Philanthropist," *New York Times*, February 18, 1966; and The World Bank.

Economics in Your Life

Would You Be Better Off without China?

Suppose that you could choose to live and work in a world with the Chinese economy growing very rapidly or in a world with the Chinese economy as it was before 1978—very poor and growing slowly. Which world would you choose to live in? How does the current high-growth, high-export Chinese economy affect you as a consumer? How does it affect you as someone about to start a career? As you read the chapter, try to answer these questions. You can check your answers against those we provide at the end of this chapter.

Economic growth is not inevitable. For most of human history, no sustained increases in output per capita occurred, and, in the words of the philosopher Thomas Hobbes, the lives of most people were "poor, nasty, brutish, and short." Sustained economic growth first began with the Industrial Revolution in England in the late eighteenth century. From there, economic growth spread to the United States, Canada, and the countries of Western Europe. Following World War II, rapid economic growth also began in Japan and, eventually, in several other Asian countries, but the economies of many other countries stagnated, leaving their people mired in poverty.

Real GDP per capita is the best measure of a country's standard of living because it represents the ability of the average person to buy goods and services. Economic growth occurs when real GDP per capita increases. Why have countries such as the United States and the United Kingdom, which had high standards of living at the beginning of the twentieth century, continued to grow rapidly? Why have countries such as Argentina, which at one time had relatively high standards of living, failed to keep pace? Why was the Soviet Union unable to sustain the rapid growth rates of its early years? Why are some countries that were very poor at the beginning of the twentieth century still very poor? And why have some countries, such as South Korea and Japan, that once were very poor now become much richer? What explains China's very rapid recent growth rates? In this chapter, we will develop a *model of economic growth* that helps us answer these important questions.

1 LEARNING OBJECTIVE

Define economic growth, calculate economic growth rates, and describe global trends in economic growth.

Economic Growth over Time and around the World

You live in a world that is very different from the world when your grandparents were young. You can listen to music on an iPhone that fits in your pocket; your grandparents played vinyl records on large stereo systems. You can send a text message to someone in another city, state, or country; your grandparents mailed letters that took days or weeks to arrive. More importantly, you have access to health care and medicines that have prolonged life and improved its quality. In many poorer countries, however, people endure grinding poverty and have only the bare necessities of life, just as their great-grandparents did.

The difference between you and people in poor countries is that you live in a country that has experienced substantial economic growth. A growing economy produces both increasing quantities of goods and services and better goods and services. It is only through economic growth that living standards can increase, but through most of human history, no economic growth took place. Even today, billions of people are living in countries where economic growth is extremely slow.

Economic Growth from 1,000,000 B.C. to the Present

In 1,000,000 B.C., our ancestors survived by hunting animals and gathering edible plants. Farming was many years in the future, and production was limited to food, clothing, shelter, and simple tools. Bradford DeLong, an economist at the University of California, Berkeley, estimates that in those primitive circumstances, GDP per capita was about $145 per year in 2012 dollars, which was the minimum amount necessary to sustain life. DeLong estimates that real GDP per capita worldwide was still $145 in the year 1300 A.D. In other words, no sustained economic growth occurred between 1,000,000 B.C. and 1300 A.D. A peasant toiling on a farm in France in the year 1300 was no better off than his ancestors thousands of years before. In fact, for most of human existence, the typical person had only the bare minimum of food, clothing, and shelter necessary to sustain life. Few people survived beyond age 40, and most people suffered from debilitating illnesses.

Industrial Revolution The application of mechanical power to the production of goods, beginning in England around 1750.

Sustained economic growth did not begin until the **Industrial Revolution**, which started in England around the year 1750. The production of cotton cloth in factories using machinery powered by steam engines marked the beginning of the Industrial Revolution. Before that time, production of goods had relied almost exclusively on human or animal power. The use of mechanical power spread to the production of many other goods, greatly increasing the quantity of goods each worker could produce. First England and then other countries, such as the United States, France, and Germany, experienced *long-run economic growth*, with sustained increases in real GDP per capita that eventually raised living standards in those countries to the high levels of today.

Making the Connection | Why Did the Industrial Revolution Begin in England?

The Industrial Revolution was a key turning point in human history. Before the Industrial Revolution, economic growth was slow and halting. After the Industrial Revolution, economic growth became rapid and sustained in a number of countries. Although historians and economists agree on the importance of the Industrial Revolution, they have not reached a consensus on why it happened in the time and place that it did. Why the eighteenth century and not the sixteenth century or the twenty-first century? Why England and not China or India or Africa or Japan?

There is always a temptation to read history backward. We know when and where the Industrial Revolution occurred; therefore, it had to happen where it did and when it did. But what was so special about England in the eighteenth century? Nobel Laureate Douglass North of Washington University in St. Louis has argued that institutions in England differed significantly from those in other countries in ways that greatly aided economic growth. North believes that the Glorious Revolution of 1688 was a key turning point. After that date, the British Parliament, rather than the king, controlled the government. The British court system also became independent of the king. As a result, the British government was credible when it committed to upholding private property rights, protecting wealth, and eliminating arbitrary increases in taxes. These institutional changes gave entrepreneurs the incentive to make the investments necessary to use the important technological developments of the second half of the eighteenth century—particularly the spinning jenny and the water frame, which were used in the production of cotton textiles, and the steam engine, which was used in mining and in the manufacture of textiles and other products. Without the institutional changes, entrepreneurs would have been reluctant to risk their property or their wealth by starting new businesses.

Although not all economists agree with North's specific argument about the origins of the Industrial Revolution, we will see that most economists accept the idea that economic growth is not likely to occur unless a country's government provides the type of institutional framework North describes.

The British government's guarantee of property rights set the stage for the Industrial Revolution.

Sources: Douglass C. North, *Understanding the Process of Economic Change*, Princeton, NJ: Princeton University Press, 2005; and Douglass C. North and Barry R. Weingast, "Constitutions and Commitment: The Evolution of Institutions Governing Public Choice in Seventeenth-Century England," *Journal of Economic History*, Vol. 49, No. 4, December 1989, pp. 803–832.

Your Turn: Test your understanding by doing related problem 1.3 at the end of this chapter.

Figure 1 shows how growth rates of real GDP per capita for the entire world have changed over long periods. Prior to 1300 A.D., there were no sustained increases in real GDP per capita. Over the next 500 years, to 1800, there was very slow growth. Significant growth began in the nineteenth century, as a result of the Industrial Revolution. A further acceleration in growth occurred during the twentieth century, as the average growth rate increased from 1.3 percent per year to 2.3 percent per year.

Small Differences in Growth Rates Are Important

The difference between 1.3 percent and 2.3 percent may seem trivial, but over long periods, small differences in growth rates can have a large effect. Suppose you have $100 in a savings account earning an interest rate of 1.3 percent, which means you

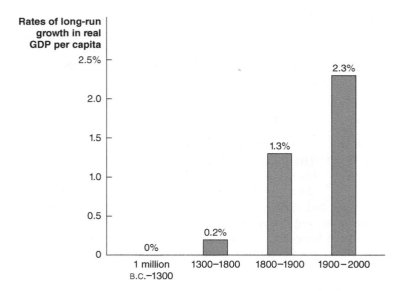

Figure 1

Average Annual Growth Rates for the World Economy

World economic growth was essentially zero in the years before 1300, and it was very slow—an average of only 0.2 percent per year—between 1300 and 1800. The Industrial Revolution made possible the sustained increases in real GDP per capita that have allowed some countries to attain high standards of living.

Source: J. Bradford DeLong, "Estimating World GDP, One Million B.C.–Present," Working paper, University of California, Berkeley.

will receive an interest payment of $1.30 this year. If the interest rate on the account is 2.3 percent, you will earn $2.30. The difference of an extra $1.00 interest payment seems insignificant. But if you leave the interest as well as the original $100 in your account for another year, the difference becomes greater because now the higher interest rate is applied to a larger amount—$102.30—and the lower interest rate is applied to a smaller amount—$101.30. This process, known as *compounding*, magnifies even small differences in interest rates over long periods of time. Over a period of 50 years, your $100 would grow to $312 at an interest rate of 2.3 percent but to only $191 at an interest rate of 1.3 percent.

The principle of compounding applies to economic growth rates as well as to interest rates. For example, in 1950, real GDP per capita in Argentina was $5,474 (measured in 2005 dollars), which was larger than Italy's real GDP per capita of $5,361. Over the next 60 years, the economic growth rate in Italy averaged 2.7 percent per year, while in Argentina, the growth rate was only 1.5 percent per year. Although this difference in growth rates of only 1.2 percentage points may seem small, in 2012, real GDP per capita in Italy had risen to $27,316, while real GDP per capita in Argentina was only $14,003. In other words, because of a relatively small difference in the growth rates of the two economies, the standard of living of a typical person in Italy went from being below that of a typical person in Argentina to being much higher. Here is the key point to keep in mind: *In the long run, small differences in economic growth rates result in big differences in living standards.*

Why Do Growth Rates Matter?

Why should anyone care about growth rates? Growth rates matter because an economy that grows too slowly fails to raise living standards. In some countries in Africa and Asia, very little economic growth has occurred in the past 50 years, so many people remain in severe poverty. In high-income countries, only 4 out of every 1,000 babies die before they are one year old. In the poorest countries, more than 100 out of every 1,000 babies die before they are one year old, and millions of children die annually from diseases that could be avoided by having access to clean water or that could be cured by using medicines that cost only a few dollars.

Although their problems are less dramatic, countries that experience slow growth have also missed opportunities to improve the lives of their citizens. For example, the failure of Argentina to grow as rapidly as other countries that had similar levels of GDP per capita in 1950 has left many of its people in poverty. Life expectancy in Argentina is lower than in the United States and other high-income countries, and nearly twice as many babies in Argentina die before the age of one.

Don't Let This Happen to You

Don't Confuse the Average Annual Percentage Change with the Total Percentage Change

When economists talk about growth rates over a period of more than one year, the numbers are always *average annual percentage changes* and *not* total percentage changes. For example, in the United States, real GDP per capita was $14,384 in 1950 and $49,226 in 2012. The percentage change in real GDP per capita between these two years is:

$$\left(\frac{\$49{,}226 - \$14{,}384}{\$14{,}384}\right) \times 100 = 242\%.$$

However, this is *not* the growth rate between the two years. The growth rate between these two years is the rate at which $14,384 in 1950 would have to grow on average *each year* to end up as $49,226 in 2012, which is 2.0 percent.

Your Turn: Test your understanding by doing related problem 1.6 at the end of this chapter.

"The Rich Get Richer and ..."

We can divide the world's economies into two groups: the *high-income countries*, sometimes also referred to as the *industrial countries* or the *developed countries*, and the poorer countries, or *developing countries*. The high-income countries include Australia, Canada, Japan, New Zealand, the United States, and the countries of Western Europe. The developing countries include most of the countries of Africa, Asia, and Latin America. In the 1980s and 1990s, a small group of countries, mostly East Asian countries such as Singapore, South Korea, and Taiwan, experienced high rates of growth and are sometimes referred to as the *newly industrializing countries*. Figure 2 shows the levels of GDP

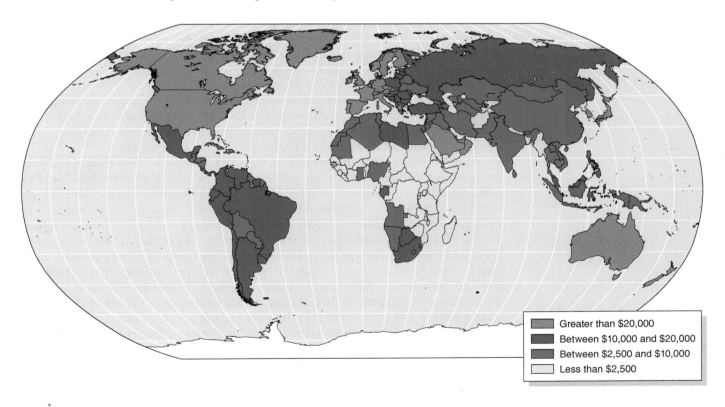

Greater than $20,000
Between $10,000 and $20,000
Between $2,500 and $10,000
Less than $2,500

Figure 2 GDP per Capita, 2012

GDP per capita is measured in U.S. dollars, corrected for differences across countries in the cost of living.

per capita around the world in 2012. GDP is measured in U.S. dollars, corrected for differences across countries in the cost of living. In 2012, GDP per capita ranged from a high of $103,900 in the Persian Gulf country of Qatar to a low of $400 in the Democratic Republic of the Congo. To understand why the gap between rich and poor countries exists, we need to look at what causes economies to grow.

Making
the
Connection

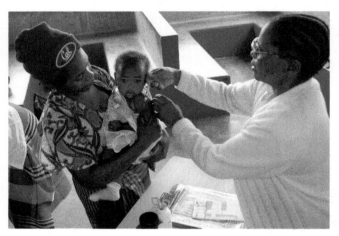

In sub-Saharan Africa and other parts of the world, increases in technology and knowledge are leading to improvements in health care and the standard of living.

Is Income All That Matters?

The more income you have, the more goods and services you can buy. When people are surviving on very low incomes of $2 per day or less, their ability to buy even minimal amounts of food, clothing, and housing is limited. So, most economists argue that unless the incomes of the very poor increase significantly, they will be unable to attain a higher standard of living. In some countries—primarily those colored yellow in Figure 2—the growth in average income has been very slow, or even negative, over a period of decades. Most economists and policymakers have concluded that the standard of living in these countries has been largely unchanged for many years.

Some economists argue, though, that if we look beyond income to other measures of the standard of living, we can see that even the poorest countries have made significant progress in recent decades. For example, Charles Kenny, an economist with the Center for Global Development, argues that "those countries with the lowest quality of life are making the fastest progress in improving it—across a range of measures including health, education, and civil and political liberties." For example, between 1960 and 2010, deaths among children declined, often by more than 50 percent, in nearly all countries, including most of those with the lowest incomes. Even in sub-Saharan Africa, where growth in incomes has been very slow, the percentage of children dying before age five has decreased by more than 30 percent over the past 50 years. Similarly, the percentage of people able to read and write has more than doubled in sub-Saharan Africa since 1970. Many more people now live in democracies where basic civil rights are respected than at any other time in world history. Although some countries, such as Somalia, the Democratic Republic of the Congo, and Afghanistan, have suffered from civil wars, political instability has decreased in many countries in recent years, which has reduced the likelihood of dying from violence.

What explains these improvements in health, education, democracy, and political stability? William Easterly, an economist at New York University, has found that although, at any given time, countries that have a higher income also have a higher standard of living, over time, increases in income *within a particular country* are typically not the main cause of improvements in a country's standard of living in terms of health, education, individual rights, political stability, and similar factors. Kenny's argument and Easterly's finding are connected: Some increases in living standards do not require significant increases in income. The key factors in raising living standards in low-income countries have been increases in technology and knowledge—such as the development of inexpensive vaccines that reduce epidemics or the use of mosquito-resistant netting that reduces the prevalence of malaria—that are inexpensive enough to be widely available. Changes in attitudes, such as placing a greater value on education, particularly for girls, or increasing support for political freedoms, have also played a role in improving conditions in low-income countries.

There are limits, of course, to how much living standards can increase if incomes stagnate. Ultimately, much higher rates of economic growth will be necessary for low-income countries to significantly close the gap in living standards with high-income countries.

Sources: Charles Kenny, *Getting Better*, New York: Basic Books, 2011; Ursula Casabonne and Charles Kenny, "The Best Things in Life Are (Nearly) Free: Technology, Knowledge, and Global Health," *World Development*, Vol. 40, No. 1, January 2012, pp. 21–35; and William Easterly, "Life during Growth," *Journal of Economic Growth*, Vol. 4, No. 3, September 1999, pp. 239–276.

Your Turn: Test your understanding by doing related problems 1.7 and 1.8 at the end of this chapter.

What Determines How Fast Economies Grow?

2 LEARNING OBJECTIVE

Use the economic growth model to explain why growth rates differ across countries.

To explain changes in economic growth rates over time within countries and differences in growth rates among countries, we need to develop an *economic growth model*. An **economic growth model** explains growth rates in real GDP per capita over the long run. An average person can buy more goods and services only if the average worker produces more goods and services. **Labor productivity** is the quantity of goods and services that can be produced by one worker or by one hour of work. Because of the importance of labor productivity in explaining economic growth, the economic growth model focuses on the causes of long-run increases in labor productivity.

How can a country's workers become more productive? Economists believe two key factors determine labor productivity: the quantity of capital per hour worked and the level of technology. Therefore, to explain changes in real GDP per capita, the economic growth model focuses on technological change and changes over time in the quantity of capital available to workers. **Technological change** is a change in the quantity of output firms can produce using a given quantity of inputs.

There are three main sources of technological change:

- *Better machinery and equipment.* Beginning with the steam engine during the Industrial Revolution, the invention of new machinery has been an important source of rising labor productivity. Today, continuing improvements in computers, factory machine tools, electric generators, and many other machines contribute to increases in labor productivity.

- *Increases in human capital.* Capital refers to *physical capital*, including computers, factory buildings, machine tools, warehouses, and trucks. The more physical capital workers have available, the more output they can produce. **Human capital** is the accumulated knowledge and skills that workers acquire from education and training or from their life experiences. As workers increase their human capital through education or on-the-job training, their productivity also increases. The more educated workers are, the greater is their human capital.

- *Better means of organizing and managing production.* Labor productivity increases if managers can do a better job of organizing production. For example, the *just-in-time system*, first developed by Toyota Motor Corporation, involves assembling goods from parts that arrive at the factory at exactly the time they are needed. With this system, firms need fewer workers to store and keep track of parts in the factory, so the quantity of goods produced per hour worked increases.

Note that technological change is *not* the same thing as more physical capital. New capital can *embody* technological change, as when a faster computer chip is embodied in a new computer. But simply adding more capital that is the same as existing capital is not technological change. To summarize, we can say that a country's standard of living will be higher the more capital workers have available on their jobs, the better the capital, the more human capital workers have, and the better the job managers do in organizing production.

The Per-Worker Production Function

The economic growth model explains increases in real GDP per capita over time as resulting from increases in just two factors: the quantity of capital available to workers and technological change. Often when analyzing economic growth, we look at increases in real GDP *per hour worked* and increases in capital *per hour worked*. We

Economic growth model A model that explains growth rates in real GDP per capita over the long run.

Labor productivity The quantity of goods and services that can be produced by one worker or by one hour of work.

Technological change A change in the quantity of output a firm can produce using a given quantity of inputs.

Human capital The accumulated knowledge and skills that workers acquire from education and training or from their life experiences.

Figure 3

The Per-Worker Production Function

The per-worker production function shows the relationship between capital per hour worked and real GDP per hour worked, holding technology constant. Increases in capital per hour worked increase output per hour worked but at a diminishing rate. For example, an increase in capital per hour worked from $75 to $100 increases real GDP per hour worked from $48 to $53. An increase in capital per hour worked from $100 to $125 increases real GDP per hour worked by a smaller amount from $53 to $57. Each additional $25 increase in capital per hour worked results in a progressively smaller increase in output per hour worked.

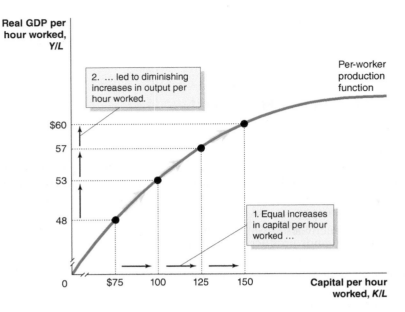

Per-worker production function The relationship between real GDP per hour worked and capital per hour worked, holding the level of technology constant.

use measures of GDP per hour and capital per hour rather than per person, so we can analyze changes in the underlying ability of an economy to produce more goods with a given amount of labor without having to worry about changes in the fraction of the population working or in the length of the workday. We can illustrate the economic growth model using the **per-worker production function**, which is the relationship between real GDP per hour worked and capital per hour worked, *holding the level of technology constant*. For simplicity, from now on we will shorten "per-worker production function" to just "production function." Figure 3 shows the production function as a graph. In the figure, we measure capital per hour worked along the horizontal axis and real GDP per hour worked along the vertical axis. Letting K stand for capital, L stand for labor, and Y stand for real GDP, real GDP per hour worked is Y/L, and capital per hour worked is K/L. The curve represents the production function. Notice that we do not explicitly show technological change in the figure. We assume that as we move along the production function, the level of technology remains constant. As we will see, we can illustrate technological change using this graph by *shifting up* the curve representing the production function.

The figure shows that increases in the quantity of capital per hour worked result in movements up along the production function, increasing the quantity of output each worker produces. When *we hold technology constant*, however, equal increases in the amount of capital per hour worked lead to *diminishing* increases in output per hour worked. For example, increasing capital per hour worked from $75 to $100 increases real GDP per hour worked from $48 to $53, an increase of $5. Another $25 increase in capital per hour worked, from $100 to $125, increases real GDP per hour worked from $53 to $57, an increase of only $4. Each additional $25 increase in capital per hour worked results in progressively smaller increases in real GDP per hour worked. In fact, at very high levels of capital per hour worked, further increases in capital per hour worked will not result in any increase in real GDP per hour worked. This effect results from the *law of diminishing returns*, which states that as we add more of one input—in this case, capital—to a fixed quantity of another input—in this case, labor—output increases by smaller additional amounts.

Why are there diminishing returns to capital? Consider a simple example in which you own a copy store. At first you have 10 employees but only 1 copy machine, so each of your workers is able to produce relatively few copies per day. When you buy a second copy machine, your employees will be able to produce more copies. Adding additional copy machines will continue to increase your output—but by increasingly smaller amounts. For example, adding a twentieth copy machine to the 19 you already have will not increase the copies each worker is able to make by nearly as much as adding a second copy machine did. Eventually, adding additional copying machines will not increase your output at all.

Which Is More Important for Economic Growth: More Capital or Technological Change?

Technological change helps economies avoid diminishing returns to capital. Let's consider two simple examples of the effects of technological change. First, suppose you have 10 copy machines in your copy store. Each copy machine can produce 10 copies per minute. You don't believe that adding an eleventh machine identical to the 10 you already have will significantly increase the number of copies your employees can produce in a day. Then you find out that a new copy machine has become available that produces 20 copies per minute. If you replace your existing machines with the new machines, the productivity of your workers will increase. The replacement of existing capital with more productive capital is an example of technological change.

Or suppose you realize that the layout of your store could be improved. Maybe the paper for the machines is on shelves at the back of the store, which requires your workers to spend time walking back and forth whenever the machines run out of paper. By placing the paper closer to the copy machines, you can improve the productivity of your workers. Reorganizing how production takes place so as to increase output is also an example of technological change.

Technological Change: The Key to Sustaining Economic Growth

Figure 4 shows the effect of technological change on the production function. Technological change shifts up the production function and allows an economy to produce more real GDP per hour worked with the same quantity of capital per hour worked. For example, if the current level of technology puts the economy on Production function$_1$, then when capital per hour worked is $150, real GDP per hour worked is $60. Technological change that shifts the economy to Production function$_2$ makes it possible to produce $65 in goods and services per hour worked with the same level of capital per hour worked. Further increases in technology that shift the economy to

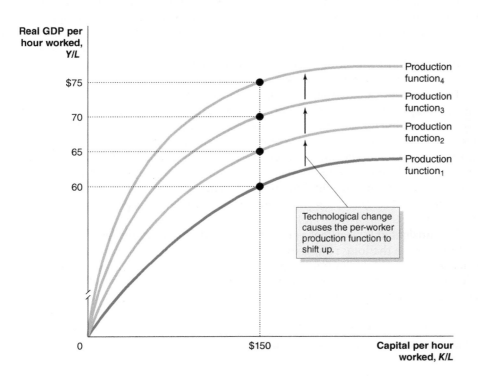

Figure 4

Technological Change Increases Output per Hour Worked

Technological change shifts up the production function and allows more output per hour worked with the same amount of capital per hour worked. For example, along Production function$_1$ with $150 in capital per hour worked, the economy can produce $60 in real GDP per hour worked. However, an increase in technology that shifts the economy to Production function$_2$ makes it possible to produce $65 in real GDP per hour worked with the same level of capital per hour worked.

higher production functions result in further increases in real GDP per hour worked. Because of diminishing returns to capital, continuing increases in real GDP per hour worked can be sustained only if there is technological change. Remember that a country will experience increases in its standard of living only if it experiences increases in real GDP per hour worked. Therefore, we can draw the following important conclusion: *In the long run, a country will experience an increasing standard of living only if it experiences continuing technological change.*

Making the Connection

What Explains the Economic Failure of the Soviet Union?

The economic growth model can help explain one of the most striking events of the twentieth century: the economic collapse of the Soviet Union. The Soviet Union was formed from the old Russian Empire following the Communist revolution of 1917. Under Communism, the Soviet Union was a centrally planned economy where the government owned nearly every business and made all production and pricing decisions. In 1960, Nikita Khrushchev, the leader of the Soviet Union, addressed the United Nations in New York City. He declared to the United States and the other democracies: "We will bury you. Your grandchildren will live under Communism."

The fall of the Berlin Wall in 1989 symbolized the failure of Communism.

Many people at the time took Khrushchev's boast seriously. Capital per hour worked grew rapidly in the Soviet Union from 1950 through the 1980s. At first, these increases in capital per hour worked also produced rapid increases in real GDP per hour worked. Rapid increases in real GDP per hour worked during the 1950s caused some economists in the United States to predict incorrectly that the Soviet Union would someday surpass the United States economically. In fact, diminishing returns to capital meant that the additional factories the Soviet Union was building resulted in smaller and smaller increases in real GDP per hour worked.

The Soviet Union did experience some technological change—but at a rate much slower than in the United States and other high-income countries. Why did the Soviet Union fail the crucial requirement for growth: implementing new technologies? The key reason is that in a centrally planned economy, the people managing most businesses are government employees and not entrepreneurs or independent businesspeople, as is the case in market economies. Soviet managers had little incentive to adopt new ways of doing things. Their pay depended on producing the quantity of output specified in the government's economic plan, not on discovering new, better, and lower-cost ways to produce goods. In addition, these managers did not have to worry about competition from either domestic or foreign firms.

Entrepreneurs and managers of firms in the United States, by contrast, are under intense competitive pressure from other firms. They must constantly search for better ways of producing the goods and services they sell. Developing and using new technologies is an important way to gain a competitive edge and earn higher profits. The drive for profit provides an incentive for technological change that centrally planned economies are unable to duplicate. In market economies, entrepreneurs and managers who have their own money on the line make decisions about which investments to make and which technologies to adopt. Nothing concentrates the mind like having your own funds at risk.

In hindsight, it is clear that a centrally planned economy, such as the Soviet Union's, could not, over the long run, grow faster than a market economy. The Soviet Union collapsed in 1991, and contemporary Russia now has a more market-oriented system, although the government continues to play a much larger role in the economy than does the government in the United States.

Your Turn: Test your understanding by doing related problem 2.7 at the end of this chapter.

Solved Problem 2

**Using the Economic Growth Model to Analyze
the Failure of the Soviet Economy**

Use the economic growth model and the information in the *Making the Connection*: What Explains the Economic Failure of the Soviet Union? to analyze the economic problems the Soviet Union encountered.

Solving the Problem

Step 1: **Review the chapter material.** This problem is about using the economic growth model to explain the failure of the Soviet economy, so you may want to review the *Making the Connection*: What Explains the Economic Failure of the Soviet Union?.

Step 2: **Draw a graph like Figure 3 to illustrate the economic problems of the Soviet Union.** For simplicity, assume that the Soviet Union experienced no technological change.

The Soviet Union experienced rapid increases in capital per hour worked from 1950 through the 1980s, but its failure to implement new technology meant that output per hour worked grew at a slower and slower rate.

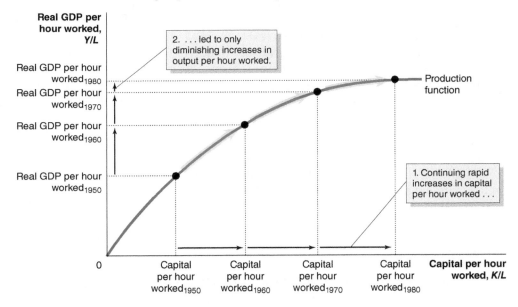

Extra Credit: The Soviet Union hoped to raise the standard of living of its citizens above that enjoyed in the United States and other high-income countries. Its strategy was to make continuous increases in the quantity of capital available to its workers. The economic growth model helps us understand the flaws in this policy for achieving economic growth.

Your Turn: For more practice, do related problems 2.8, 2.9, and 2.10 at the end of this chapter.

New Growth Theory

The economic growth model we have been using was first developed in the 1950s by Nobel Laureate Robert Solow of MIT. According to this model, productivity growth is the key factor in explaining long-run growth in real GDP per capita. In recent years, some economists have become dissatisfied with this model because it does not explain

New growth theory A model of long-run economic growth that emphasizes that technological change is influenced by economic incentives and so is determined by the working of the market system.

the factors that determine productivity growth. Paul Romer, of New York University, developed the **new growth theory** to provide a better explanation of the sources of technological change. Romer argues that the rate of technological change is influenced by how individuals and firms respond to economic incentives. Earlier accounts of economic growth did not explain technological change or attributed it to factors such as chance scientific discoveries.

Romer argues that the accumulation of *knowledge capital* is a key determinant of economic growth. Firms add to an economy's stock of knowledge capital when they engage in research and development or otherwise contribute to technological change. We have seen that accumulation of physical capital is subject to diminishing returns: Increases in capital per hour worked lead to increases in real GDP per hour worked but at a decreasing rate. Romer argues that the same is true of knowledge capital *at the firm level*. As firms add to their stock of knowledge capital, they increase their output but at a decreasing rate. At the level of the entire economy, however, Romer argues that knowledge capital is subject to *increasing returns*. Increasing returns can exist because knowledge, once discovered, becomes available to everyone. The use of physical capital, such as a computer or machine tool, is *rival* because if one firm uses it, other firms cannot, and it is *excludable* because the firm that owns the capital can keep other firms from using it. The use of knowledge capital, such as the chemical formula for a drug that cures cancer, is nonrival, however, because one firm's using that knowledge does not prevent another firm from using it. Knowledge capital is also nonexcludable because once something like a chemical formula becomes known, it becomes widely available for other firms to use (unless, as we discuss shortly, the government gives the firm that invents a new product the legal right to its exclusive use).

Because knowledge capital is nonrival and nonexcludable, firms can *free ride* on the research and development of other firms. Firms free ride when they benefit from the results of research and development they did not pay for. For example, transistor technology was first developed at Western Electric's Bell Laboratories in the 1950s and served as the basic technology of the information revolution. Bell Laboratories, however, received only a tiny fraction of the immense profits that were eventually made by all the firms that used this technology. Romer points out that firms are unlikely to invest in research and development up to the point where the marginal cost of the research equals the marginal return from the knowledge gained because *other* firms gain much of the marginal return. Therefore, there is likely to be an inefficiently small amount of research and development, slowing the accumulation of knowledge capital and economic growth.

Government policy can help increase the accumulation of knowledge capital in three ways:

Patent The exclusive right to produce a product for a period of 20 years from the date the patent is applied for.

- *Protecting intellectual property with patents and copyrights.* Governments can increase the incentive to engage in research and development by giving firms the exclusive rights to their discoveries for a period of years. The U.S. government grants patents to companies that develop new products or new ways of making existing products. A **patent** gives a firm the exclusive legal right to a new product for a period of 20 years from the date the patent is filed with the government. For example, a pharmaceutical firm that develops a drug that cures cancer can secure a patent on the drug, keeping other firms from manufacturing the drug without permission. The profits earned during the period the patent is in force provide firms with an incentive for undertaking research and development. The patent system has drawbacks, however. In filing for a patent, a firm must disclose information about the product or process. This information enters the public record and may help competing firms develop products or processes that are similar but that do not infringe on the patent. To avoid this problem, a firm may try to keep the results of its research a *trade secret*, without patenting it. (A famous example of a trade secret is the formula for Coca-Cola.) Tension also arises between the government's objectives of providing patent protection that gives firms the incentive to engage in research and development and making sure that the knowledge gained through the research is widely available, which increases the positive effect of the knowledge on the economy. Economists debate the features of an ideal patent system.

- *Subsidizing research and development.* The government can use subsidies to increase the quantity of research and development that takes place. In the United States, the federal government conducts some research directly. For example, the National Institutes of Health conducts medical research. The forerunner of the Internet was the Advanced Research Project Agency Network (ARPANET), which was developed by the U.S. Department of Defense to improve communication among defense researchers around the country. The government also subsidizes research by providing grants to researchers in universities through the National Science Foundation and other agencies. Finally, the government provides tax benefits to firms that invest in research and development.

- *Subsidizing education.* People with technical training carry out research and development. If firms are unable to capture all the profits from research and development, they will pay lower wages and salaries to technical workers. These lower wages and salaries reduce the incentive to workers to receive this training. If the government subsidizes education, it can increase the number of workers who have technical training. In the United States, the government subsidizes education by directly providing free education from grades kindergarten through 12 and by providing support for public colleges and universities. The government also provides student loans at reduced interest rates.

These government policies can bring the accumulation of knowledge capital closer to the optimal level.

Joseph Schumpeter and Creative Destruction

The new growth theory has revived interest in the ideas of Joseph Schumpeter. Born in Austria in 1883, Schumpeter served briefly as that country's finance minister. In 1932, he became an economics professor at Harvard University. Schumpeter developed a model of growth that emphasized his view that new products unleash a "gale of creative destruction" that drives older products—and, often, the firms that produced them—out of the market. According to Schumpeter, the key to rising living standards is not small changes to existing products but, rather, new products that meet consumer wants in qualitatively better ways. For example, in the early twentieth century, the automobile displaced the horse-drawn carriage by meeting consumer demand for personal transportation in a way that was qualitatively better. In the early twenty-first century, the DVD and the DVD player displaced the VHS tape and the VCR by better meeting consumer demand for watching films at home. Downloading or streaming movies from the Internet may be in the process of displacing the DVD just as the DVD displaced the VHS tape.

To Schumpeter, the entrepreneur is central to economic growth: "The function of entrepreneurs is to reform or revolutionize the pattern of production by exploiting an invention or, more generally, an untried technological possibility for producing new commodities or producing an old one in a new way."

The profits an entrepreneur hopes to earn provide the incentive for bringing together the factors of production—labor, capital, and natural resources—to start new firms and introduce new goods and services. Successful entrepreneurs can use their profits to finance the development of new products and are better able to attract funds from investors.

Economic Growth in the United States

3 LEARNING OBJECTIVE

Discuss fluctuations in productivity growth in the United States.

The economic growth model can help us understand the record of growth in the United States. Figure 5 shows average annual growth rates in real GDP per hour worked since 1800. As the United States experienced the Industrial Revolution during the nineteenth century, U.S. firms increased the quantities of capital per hour worked.

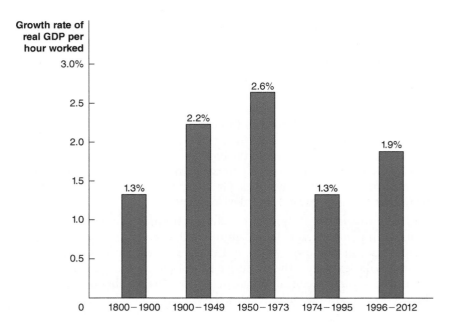

Figure 5

Average Annual Growth Rates in Real GDP per Hour Worked in the United States

The growth rate in the United States increased from 1800 through the mid-1970s. Then, for more than 20 years, growth slowed before increasing again in the mid-1990s. *Note:* The values for 1800–1900 are real GDP per worker. The values for 1900–2012 are real GDP per hour worked; for the period 1900–1969 they are the authors' calculations, based on the methods used in Neville Francis and Valerie A. Ramey, "The Source of Historical Economic Fluctuations: An Analysis Using Long-Run Restrictions," in Jeffrey Frankel, Richard Clarida, and Francesco Giavazzi, eds., *International Seminar in Macroeconomics*, Chicago: University of Chicago Press, 2005; the authors thank Neville Francis for kindly providing data through 2004; for 1969–2012, the data are from the U.S. Bureau of Labor Statistics.

New technologies such as the steam engine, the railroad, and the telegraph also became available. Together, these factors resulted in an average annual growth rate of real GDP per worker of 1.3 percent from 1800 to 1900. Real GDP *per capita* grew at a slower rate of 1.1 percent during this period. At this growth rate, real GDP per capita would double about every 63 years, which means that living standards were growing steadily but relatively slowly.

By the twentieth century, technological change had been institutionalized. Many large corporations began to set up research and development facilities to improve the quality of their products and the efficiency with which they produced them. Universities also began to conduct research that had business applications. After World War II, many corporations began to provide significant funds to universities to help pay for research. In 1950, the federal government created the National Science Foundation, whose main goal is to support university researchers. The accelerating rate of technological change led to more rapid growth rates.

Economic Growth in the United States since 1950

Continuing technological change allowed the U.S. economy to avoid the diminishing returns to capital that stifled growth in the Soviet economy. In fact, until the 1970s, the growth rate of the U.S. economy accelerated over time. As Figure 5 shows, growth in the first half of the twentieth century was faster than growth during the nineteenth century, and growth in the immediate post–World War II period from 1950 to 1973 was faster yet. Then the unexpected happened: For more than 20 years, from 1974 to 1995, the growth rate of real GDP per hour worked slowed. The growth rate during these years was more than 1 percentage point per year lower than during the 1950–1973 period. Beginning in the mid-1990s, the growth rate picked up again, although it remained below the levels that prevailed during most of the twentieth century.

What Caused the Productivity Slowdown of 1974–1995?

Several explanations have been offered for the productivity slowdown of the mid-1970s to mid-1990s, but none is completely satisfying. Some economists argue that productivity really didn't slow down; it only *appears* to have slowed down because of problems in measuring productivity accurately. After 1970, services—such as haircuts and financial advice—became a larger fraction of GDP, and goods—such as automobiles and hamburgers—became a smaller fraction. It is more difficult to measure increases in the output of services than to measure increases in the output of goods. For example, before banks began using automated teller machines (ATMs) in the 1980s, you could withdraw money only by going to a bank before closing time—which was usually 3:00 P.M. Once ATMs became available, you could withdraw money at any time of the day or night at a variety of locations. This increased convenience from ATMs does not show up in GDP. If it did, measured output per hour worked would have grown more rapidly.

There may also be a measurement problem in accounting for improvements in the environment and in health and safety. During these years, new laws required firms to spend billions of dollars reducing pollution, improving workplace safety, and redesigning products to improve their safety. This spending did not result in additional output that would be included in GDP—although it may have increased overall well-being. If these increases in well-being had been included in GDP, measured output per hour worked would have grown more rapidly.

Some economists argue that deterioration in the U.S. educational system may have contributed to the slowdown in growth from the mid-1970s to mid-1990s. Scores on some standardized tests began to decline in the 1970s, which may indicate that workers entering the labor force were less well educated and less productive than in earlier decades. Another possibility is that the skills required to perform many jobs increased during the 1970s and 1980s, while the preparation that workers had received in school did not keep pace.

The United States was not alone in experiencing the slowdown in productivity. All the high-income countries experienced a slowdown in growth between the mid-1970s and the mid-1990s. Because all the high-income economies began producing more services and fewer goods and enacted stricter environmental regulations at about the same time, explanations of the productivity slowdown that emphasize measurement problems become more plausible. In the end, though, economists are still debating why the productivity slowdown took place.

Is the United States Headed for Another Productivity Slowdown?

Productivity growth, as measured by changes in real GDP per hour worked, increased between 1996 and 2012 compared to the previous 20-year period, while remaining well below the levels attained during most of the twentieth century. Some economists believe that the development of a "new economy" based on *information technology* (*IT*) caused the higher productivity growth that began in the mid-1990s. As computers became less expensive and faster, they made it possible for people and organizations to communicate and process data more efficiently. Today, a single laptop computer has more computing power than all the mainframe computers NASA used to control the *Apollo* spacecrafts that landed on the moon in the late 1960s and early 1970s.

Faster data processing has had a major effect on nearly every firm. Business record keeping, once done laboriously by hand, is now done more quickly and accurately by computers. During the 1990s, firms used the Internet to market and sell products. Smartphones, laptop computers, and wireless Internet access allow people to work at home and while traveling. These developments in IT have significantly increased labor productivity.

Despite the wonders of IT, growth in productivity was still slow compared with the pre-1974 period. And productivity growth from 2006 to 2012 fell to an average of 1.2%—the same level as during the period of slow growth from the mid-1970s to the mid-1990s. Is IT no longer a productivity booster, or are the data not capturing some of IT's benefits? What insight do the answers to these questions give us about how rapid growth will be in the coming decades?

Some economists argue that measured growth rates in recent years have understated the actual growth of the economy. These economists believe that developments in IT have improved the delivery of services to both consumers and firms in ways that the

GDP statistics fail to capture. For instance, finding detailed driving directions is much easier using Mapquest or a similar app than was possible before smartphones were developed. Similarly, a store manager can quickly check on available warehouse inventory using a dedicated smartphone or tablet app.

Economists who are optimistic about the effects of IT on the economy are usually also optimistic about future growth rates. David Byrne of the Federal Reserve Board, Stephen Oliner of the American Enterprise Institute, and Daniel Sichel of Wellesley College argue that at the heart of the IT revolution is "the ability to harness ever-greater computing power that comes in progressively smaller and less expensive packages." They believe that continuing advances in semiconductor technology—which underlie progress in IT—will result in gains in labor productivity. The gains will come from higher productivity in the IT sector itself and in other sectors of the economy as the result of progress made possible by advances in IT. For example, ever more rapid and inexpensive computing lowers the cost and speeds the adoption of existing products, such as 3-D printers, and helps innovators develop new products, which, in turn, raise productivity growth above its current levels. Byrne, Oliner, and Sichel forecast an increase in productivity growth to an annual rate of 1.8 percent. James Kahn of Yeshiva University and Robert Rich of the Federal Reserve Bank of New York, using a different method, have also estimated an increase in annual productivity growth to 1.8 percent. While this rate is below the pre-1974 rate, it is well above the low rate of 2006–2012.

Some economists are skeptical, however, that the U.S. economy can return to even these growth rates. These economists also doubt that the unmeasured benefits of the IT revolution are any greater than the unmeasured benefits of earlier innovations, including, even, television. Robert J. Gordon of Northwestern University has argued that productivity increases from the IT revolution were much smaller than increases resulting from earlier innovations, such as the railroad, electrification of homes and businesses, petroleum refining, and the automobile. Moreover, Gordon and some other economists argue that most of the gains from the IT revolution occurred in the 1990s, as a result of the development of the World Wide Web, Windows 95, and computerized inventory control systems. These innovations raised labor productivity because they changed how businesses operated. By the early 2000s, the IT revolution was having a greater effect on consumer products, such as smartphones and tablets, than on labor productivity. Gordon identifies other factors, such as an aging population, declining educational achievement, and the consequences of increased regulations and higher taxes, that will lead to lower productivity growth rates. Gordon forecasts an extended period of productivity growth rates of 0.5 percent or less.

The debate over future productivity growth is an important one. If the optimistic forecasts of productivity growth are correct, then in 30 years real GDP per hour worked will be nearly 50 percent higher than if the pessimistic forecasts are correct. Such a large difference in the standard of living will have an enormous effect on nearly every aspect of American life, including the extent of poverty, the ability of individuals and the government to finance increasing medical costs, and the ability of the country to deal with the effects of the aging of the population.

4 LEARNING OBJECTIVE

Explain economic catch-up and discuss why many poor countries have not experienced rapid economic growth.

Why Isn't the Whole World Rich?

The economic growth model tells us that economies grow when the quantity of capital per hour worked increases and when technological change occurs. This model seems to provide a good blueprint for developing countries to become rich: (1) Increase the quantity of capital per hour worked and (2) use the best available technology. There are economic incentives for both of these things to happen in poor countries. The profitability of using additional capital or better technology is generally greater in a developing country than in a high-income country. For example, replacing an existing computer with a new, faster computer will generally have a relatively small payoff for a firm in the United States. In contrast, installing a new computer in a Zambian firm where records have been kept by hand is likely to have an enormous payoff.

This observation leads to an important conclusion: *The economic growth model predicts that poor countries will grow faster than rich countries.* If this prediction is correct, we should observe poor countries catching up to rich countries in levels of GDP per capita (or income per capita). Has this **catch-up**—or *convergence*—actually occurred? Here we come to a paradox: If we look only at the countries that currently have high incomes, we see that the lower-income countries have been catching up to the higher-income countries, but the developing countries as a group have not been catching up to the high-income countries as a group.

Catch-Up: Sometimes but Not Always

We can construct a graph that makes it easier to see whether catch-up is happening. In Figure 6, the horizontal axis shows the initial level of real GDP per capita, and the vertical axis shows the rate at which real GDP per capita is growing. We can then plot points on the graph for rich and poor countries. Each point represents the combination of a country's initial level of real GDP per capita and its growth rate over the following years. The catch-up line in the figure shows the situation where the catch-up prediction holds exactly: Low-income countries should be on the upper-left section of the line because they would have low initial levels of real GDP per capita but fast growth rates. High-income countries should be in the lower-right section of the line because they would have high initial levels of real GDP per capita but slow growth rates. When we plot the actual observations for each country, the closer the points for each country are to the line, the more accurate the catch-up prediction is.

Catch-Up among the High-Income Countries If we look at only the countries that currently have high incomes, we can see the catch-up predicted by the economic growth model. Figure 7 shows that the high-income countries that had the lowest incomes in 1960, such as Taiwan, Korea, and Singapore, grew the fastest between 1960 and 2010. Countries that had the highest incomes in 1960, such as Switzerland and the United States, grew the slowest.

Are the Developing Countries Catching Up to the High-Income Countries? If we expand our analysis to include every country for which statistics are available, it becomes more difficult to find the catch-up predicted by the economic growth model. Figure 8 does not show a consistent relationship between the level of real GDP in 1960 and growth from 1960 to 2010. Some countries that had low levels of real GDP per capita in 1960, such as Niger and the Democratic Republic of the Congo, actually

Catch-up The prediction that the level of GDP per capita (or income per capita) in poor countries will grow faster than in rich countries.

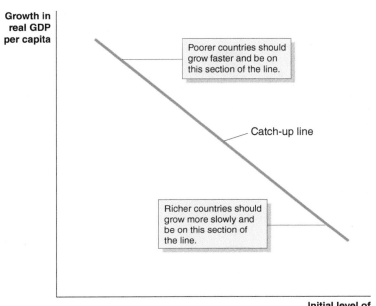

Growth in real GDP per capita

Poorer countries should grow faster and be on this section of the line.

Catch-up line

Richer countries should grow more slowly and be on this section of the line.

Initial level of real GDP per capita

Figure 6

The Catch-up Predicted by the Economic Growth Model

According to the economic growth model, countries that start with lower levels of real GDP per capita should grow faster (points near the upper-left section of the line) than countries that start with higher levels of real GDP per capita (points near the lower-right section of the line).

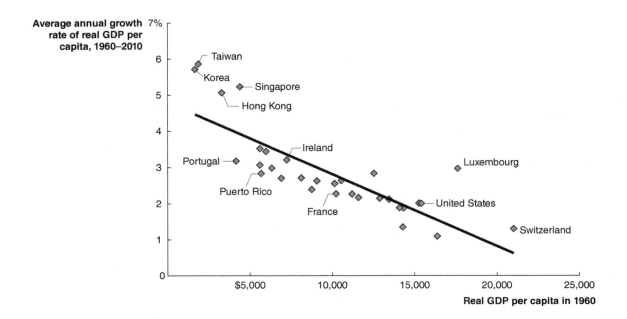

Figure 7 There Has Been Catch-Up among High-Income Countries

If we look only at countries that currently have high incomes, we see that countries such as Taiwan, Korea, and Singapore that had the lowest incomes in 1960 grew the fastest between 1960 and 2010. Countries such as Switzerland and the United States that had the highest incomes in 1960 grew the slowest.

Note: Data are real GDP per capita in 2005 dollars. Each point in the figure represents one high-income country.
Authors' calculations from data in Alan Heston, Robert Summers, and Bettina Aten, *Penn World Table Version 7.1*, Center for International Comparisons of Production, Income and Prices at the University of Pennsylvania, November 2012.

experienced *negative* economic growth: They had *lower* levels of real GDP per capita in 2010 than in 1960. Other countries that started with low levels of real GDP per capita, such as Malaysia and China and grew rapidly. Some middle-income countries in 1960, such as Venezuela, hardly grew between 1960 and 2010, while others, such as Ireland, experienced significant growth.

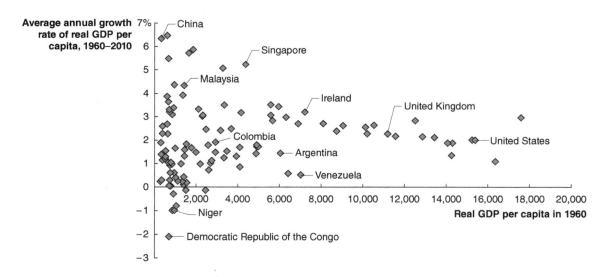

Figure 8 Most of the World Hasn't Been Catching Up

If we look at all countries for which statistics are available, we do not see the catch-up predicted by the economic growth model. Some countries that had low levels of real GDP per capita in 1960, such as Niger and the Democratic Republic of the Congo, actually experienced *negative* economic growth. Other countries that started with low levels of real GDP per capita, such as Malaysia and China, grew rapidly. Some middle-income countries in 1960, such as Venezuela, hardly grew

between 1960 and 2010, while others, such as Ireland, experienced significant growth.

Note: Data are real GDP per capita. Each point in the figure represents one country.
Authors' calculations from data in Alan Heston, Robert Summers, and Bettina Aten, *Penn World Table Version 7.1*, Center for International Comparisons of Production, Income and Prices at the University of Pennsylvania, November 2012.

Solved Problem 4

The Economic Growth Model's Prediction of Catch-Up

The economic growth model makes predictions about an economy's initial level of real GDP per capita relative to other economies and how fast the economy will grow in the future.

a. Consider the statistics in the following table:

Country	Real GDP per Capita in 1960 (2005 dollars)	Annual Growth in Real GDP per Capita, 1960–2010
Taiwan	$1,861	5.86%
Panama	2,120	3.32
Brazil	2,483	2.45
Algeria	4,105	0.85
Venezuela	7,015	0.52

Are these statistics consistent with the economic growth model? Briefly explain.

b. Now consider the statistics in the following table:

Country	Real GDP per Capita in 1960 (2005 dollars)	Annual Growth in Real GDP per Capita, 1960–2010
Japan	$5,586	3.52%
Belgium	10,132	2.54
United Kingdom	11,204	2.26
New Zealand	14,263	1.34

Are these statistics consistent with the economic growth model? Briefly explain.

c. Construct a new table that lists all nine countries, from the lowest real GDP per capita in 1960 to the highest, along with their growth rates. Are the statistics in your new table consistent with the economic growth model?

Solving the Problem

Step 1: **Review the chapter material.** This problem is about catch-up in the economic growth model, so you may want to review the section "Why Isn't the Whole World Rich?"

Step 2: **Explain whether the statistics in the table in part (a) are consistent with the economic growth model.** These statistics are consistent with the economic growth model. The countries with the lowest levels of real GDP per capita in 1960 had the fastest growth rates between 1960 and 2010, and the countries with the highest levels of real GDP per capita had the slowest growth rates.

Step 3: **Explain whether the statistics in the table in part (b) are consistent with the economic growth model.** These statistics are also consistent with the economic growth model. Once again, the countries with the lowest levels of real GDP per capita in 1960 had the fastest growth rates between 1960 and 2010, and the countries with the highest levels of real GDP per capita had the slowest growth rates.

Step 4: **Construct a table that includes all nine countries from the tables in parts (a) and (b) and discuss the results.**

Country	Real GDP per Capita in 1960 (2005 dollars)	Annual Growth in Real GDP per Capita, 1960–2010
Taiwan	$1,861	5.86%
Panama	2,120	3.32
Brazil	2,483	2.45
Algeria	4,105	0.85
Japan	5,586	3.52
Venezuela	7,015	0.52
Belgium	10,132	2.54
United Kingdom	11,204	2.26
New Zealand	14,263	1.34

The statistics in the new table are *not* consistent with the predictions of the economic growth model. For example, New Zealand and the United Kingdom had higher levels of real GDP per capita in 1960 than did Algeria and Venezuela. The economic growth model predicts that New Zealand and the United Kingdom should, therefore, have grown more slowly than Algeria and Venezuela. The data in the table show, however, that New Zealand and the United Kingdom grew faster. Similarly, Belgium grew faster than Brazil, even though its real GDP per capita was already much higher than Brazil's in 1960.

Extra Credit: The statistics in these tables confirm what we saw in Figures 7 and 8: There has been catch-up among the high-income countries, but there has not been catch-up if we include in the analysis all the countries of the world.

Your Turn: For more practice, do problems 4.5 and 4.6 at the end of this chapter.

Why Haven't Most Western European Countries, Canada, and Japan Caught Up to the United States?

Figure 7 indicates that there has been catch-up among the high-income countries over the past 50 years. If we look at the catch-up of other high-income countries to the United States during the most recent period, we discover a surprising fact: Over the past 20 years, other high-income countries have actually fallen further behind the United States rather than catching up to it. Figure 9 shows real GDP per capita in Canada, Japan, and the five largest economies in Western Europe relative to real GDP per capita in the United States. The blue bars show real GDP per capita in 1990 relative to the United States, and the red bars show real GDP per capita in 2012 relative to the United States. In each case, relative levels of real GDP per capita were lower in 2012 than they were in 1990. Each of these countries experienced significant catch-up to the United States between 1960 and 1990, but they have experienced no catch-up since 1990.

Why have other high-income countries had trouble completely closing the gap in real GDP per capita with the United States? Many economists believe there are two main explanations: the greater flexibility of U.S. labor markets and the greater efficiency of the U.S. financial system. U.S. labor markets are more flexible than labor markets in other countries for several reasons. In many European countries, government regulations make it difficult for firms to fire workers and thereby make firms reluctant to hire workers in the first place. As a result, many younger workers have difficulty finding jobs, and once a job is found, a worker tends to remain in it even if his or her skills and preferences are not a good match for the characteristics of the job. In the United States, by contrast, government regulations are less restrictive, workers have an easier time finding jobs, and workers change jobs fairly frequently. This high rate of job mobility ensures a better match between workers' skills and preferences and the characteristics of jobs, which increases labor productivity. Many European countries also have restrictive

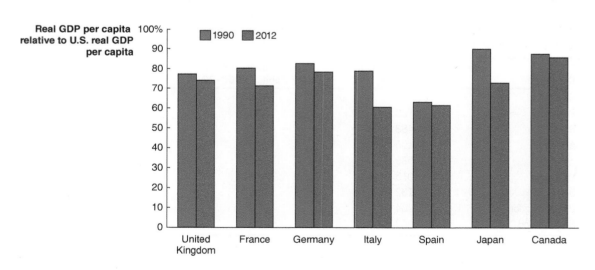

Figure 9 **Other High-Income Countries Have Stopped Catching Up to the United States**

The blue bars show real GDP per capita in 1990 relative to the United States, and the red bars show real GDP per capita in 2012 relative to the United States. In each case, relative levels of real GDP per capita are lower in 2012 than they were in 1990, which means that these countries have ceased catching up to the United States.

Sources: Authors' calculations from data in Alan Heston, Robert Summers, and Bettina Aten, *Penn World Table Version 7.1*, Center for International Comparisons of Production, Income and Prices at the University of Pennsylvania, November 2012; and Organization for Economic Cooperation and Development, OECD stat.extracts.

work rules that limit the flexibility of firms to implement new technologies. These rules restrict the tasks firms can ask workers to perform and the number of hours they work. The rules reduce the ability of firms to use new technologies that may require workers to learn new skills, perform new tasks, or work during the night or early mornings.

Workers in the United States tend to enter the labor force earlier, retire later, and experience fewer long spells of unemployment than do workers in Europe. Unemployed workers in the United States typically receive smaller government payments for a shorter period of time than do unemployed workers in Canada and most of the countries of Western Europe. Because the opportunity cost of being unemployed is lower in those countries, the unemployment rate tends to be higher, and the fraction of the labor force that is unemployed for more than one year also tends to be higher. Studies have shown that workers who are employed for longer periods tend to have greater skills, greater productivity, and higher wages. Many economists believe that the design of the U.S. unemployment insurance program has contributed to the greater flexibility of U.S. labor markets and to higher rates of growth in labor productivity and real GDP per capita.

As we have seen, technological change is essential for rapid productivity growth. To obtain the funds needed to implement new technologies, firms turn to the financial system. It is important that funds for investment be not only available but also allocated efficiently. Large corporations can raise funds by selling stocks and bonds in financial markets. U.S. corporations benefit from the efficiency of U.S. financial markets. The level of legal protection of investors is relatively high in U.S. financial markets, which encourages both U.S. and foreign investors to buy stocks and bonds issued by U.S. firms. The volume of trading in U.S. financial markets also ensures that investors will be able to quickly sell the stocks and bonds they buy. This *liquidity* serves to attract investors to U.S. markets.

Smaller firms that are unable to issue stocks and bonds often obtain funding from banks. Entrepreneurs founding new firms—"start-ups"—particularly firms that are based on new technologies, generally find that investors are unwilling to buy their stocks and bonds because the firms lack records of profitability. Banks are also reluctant to lend to new firms founded to introduce new and unfamiliar technologies. In the United States, some technology start-ups obtain funds from *venture capital firms*, which raise funds from institutional investors, such as pension funds, and from wealthy individuals. The owners of venture capital firms closely examine the business plans of start-up firms, looking for those that appear most likely to succeed. In exchange for providing funding, a venture capital firm often becomes part owner of the start-up and may even play a role in managing the firm. A successful venture capital firm is able to attract investors who would not otherwise be willing to provide funds to start-ups because the investors would lack enough information on the start-up. A number of well-known U.S. high-technology firms, such as Google, relied on venture capital firms to fund their early expansion. The ability of venture capital firms to finance technology-driven start-up firms may be giving the United States an advantage in bringing new products and new processes to market.

The U.S. financial system suffered severe problems between 2007 and 2009. But, over the long run, it has succeeded in efficiently allocating investment funds.

Why Don't More Low-Income Countries Experience Rapid Growth?

The economic growth model predicts that the countries that were very poor in 1960 should have grown rapidly over the next 50 years. As we have just seen, some did, but many did not. Why are many low-income countries growing so slowly? There is no single answer, but most economists point to four key factors:

- Failure to enforce the rule of law
- Wars and revolutions
- Poor public education and health
- Low rates of saving and investment

Failure to Enforce the Rule of Law In the years since 1960, increasing numbers of developing countries, including China, have abandoned centrally planned economies in favor of more market-oriented economies. For entrepreneurs in a market economy to

Property rights The rights individuals or firms have to the exclusive use of their property, including the right to buy or sell it.

Rule of law The ability of a government to enforce the laws of the country, particularly with respect to protecting private property and enforcing contracts.

succeed, however, the government must guarantee private **property rights** and enforce contracts. Unless entrepreneurs feel secure in their property, they will not risk starting a business. Business owners also have difficulty being successful unless they can use an independent court system to enforce contracts. The **rule of law** refers to the ability of a government to enforce the laws of the country, particularly with respect to protecting private property and enforcing contracts. The failure of many developing countries to guarantee private property rights and to enforce contracts has hindered their economic growth.

Consider, for example, the production of shoes. Suppose the owner of a shoe factory signs a contract with a leather tannery to deliver a specific quantity of leather on a particular date for a particular price. On the basis of this contract, the owner of the shoe factory signs a contract to deliver a specific quantity of shoes to a shoe wholesaler. This contract states the quantity of shoes to be delivered, the quality of the shoes, the delivery date, and the price. The owner of the leather tannery uses the contract with the shoe factory to enter into a contract with cattle ranchers for the delivery of hides. The shoe wholesaler enters into contracts to deliver shoes to retail stores, where they are sold to consumers. For the flow of goods from cattle ranchers to shoe customers to operate efficiently, each business must carry out the terms of the contract it has signed. In developed countries, such as the United States, businesses know that if they fail to carry out a contract, they may be sued in court and forced to compensate the other party for any economic damages.

Many developing countries do not have functioning, independent court systems. Even if a court system does exist, a case may not be heard for many years. In some countries, bribery of judges and political favoritism in court rulings are common. If firms cannot enforce contracts through the court system, they may insist on carrying out only face-to-face cash transactions. For example, the shoe manufacturer will wait until the leather producer brings the hides to the factory and will then buy the hides for cash. The wholesaler will wait until the shoes have been produced before making plans for sales to retail stores. Production still takes place, but it is carried out more slowly and inefficiently. With slow and inefficient production, firms have difficulty finding investors willing to provide them with the funds they need to expand.

Making the Connection	**What Do Parking Tickets in New York City Tell Us about Poverty in the Developing World?**

In many developing countries, government officials insist on receiving bribes to process most transactions. For example, someone may need to pay an official before being allowed to open a shoe store or to purchase farmland. This corruption represents a breakdown in the rule of law. Generally, the more corrupt a country's government, the lower the country's growth rate. Economists at the World Bank have developed an index that ranks the countries of the world from most corrupt to least corrupt. The following figure compares GDP per capita in the 20 most corrupt and the 20 least corrupt countries. GDP per capita is more than 10 times higher in the least corrupt countries than in the most corrupt countries.

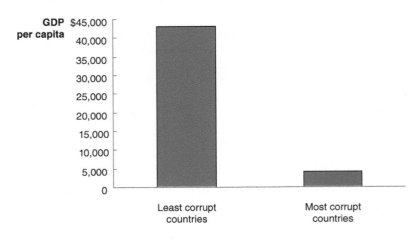

But does corruption cause countries to be poor, or does a country's being poor lead to its being corrupt? Some economists have made the controversial argument that corruption may be the result of culture. If a culture of corruption exists in a country, then the country may have great difficulty establishing an honest government that is willing to enforce the rule of law. Economists Raymond Fisman of the Columbia Business School and Edward Miguel of the University of California, Berkeley, came up with an ingenious method of testing whether a culture of corruption exists in some countries. Every country in the world sends delegates to the United Nations in New York City. Under international law, these delegates cannot be prosecuted for violating U.S. laws, including parking regulations. So, a delegate to the United Nations can double park or park next to a fire hydrant and ignore any parking ticket he or she would receive.

Fisman and Miguel argue that if a culture of corruption exists in some countries, the delegates from these countries will be more likely to ignore parking tickets than will the delegates from countries without a culture of corruption. Fisman and Miguel gathered statistics on the number of parking violations per delegate and compared the statistics to the World Bank's index of corruption. They found that as the level of corruption in a country increases, so does the number of parking violations by the country's United Nations delegates. For example, the following figure shows that the 15 percent of countries that are most corrupt had more than 10 times as many parking violations as the 15 percent of countries that are least corrupt.

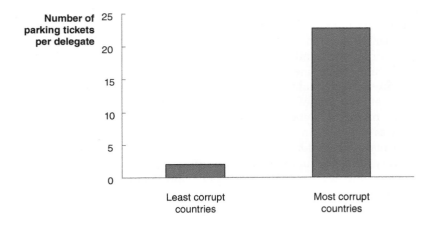

Of course, ignoring parking regulations is a relatively minor form of corruption. But if Fisman and Miguel are correct, and a culture of corruption has taken hold in some developing countries, then it may be difficult to reform their governments enough to establish the rule of law.

Sources: Raymond Fisman and Edward Miguel, *Economic Gangsters*, Princeton, NJ: Princeton University Press, 2008, Chapter 4; World Bank, *Worldwide Governance Indicators*, September 14, 2012; and *The World Factbook* 2013–14. Washington, DC: Central Intelligence Agency, 2013.

Your Turn: Test your understanding by doing related problem 4.9 at the end of this chapter.

Wars and Revolutions Many of the countries that were very poor in 1960 have experienced extended periods of war or violent changes of government during the years since. These wars have made it impossible for countries such as Afghanistan, Angola, Ethiopia, the Central African Republic, and the Democratic Republic of the Congo to accumulate capital or adopt new technologies. In fact, conducting any kind of business has been very difficult. Ending war has a positive effect on growth, as shown by the case of Mozambique, which suffered through almost two decades of civil war and declining real GDP per capita. With the end of civil war, Mozambique experienced a strong annual growth rate of 5 percent in real GDP per capita from 1990 to 2012.

Poor Public Education and Health We have seen that human capital is one of the determinants of labor productivity. Many low-income countries have weak public school systems, so many workers are unable to read and write. Few workers acquire the skills necessary to use the latest technology.

People in many low-income countries suffer from diseases that are either nonexistent or treated readily in high-income countries. For example, few people in developed countries suffer from malaria, but about 1 million Africans die from it each year. Treatments for AIDS have greatly reduced deaths from this disease in the United States and Europe. But millions of people in low-income countries continue to die from AIDS. These countries often lack the resources, and their governments are often too ineffective, to provide even routine medical care, such as childhood vaccinations.

People who are sick work less and are less productive when they do work. Poor nutrition or exposure to certain diseases in childhood can leave people permanently weakened and can affect their intelligence as adults. Poor health has a significant negative effect on the human capital of workers in developing countries.

Low Rates of Saving and Investment To invest in factories, machinery, and computers, firms need funds. Some of the funds can come from the owners of the firm and from their friends and families, but firms in high-income countries raise most of their funds from bank loans and selling stocks and bonds in financial markets. In most developing countries, stock and bond markets do not exist, and often the banking system is very weak. In high-income countries, the funds that banks lend to businesses come from the savings of households. In high-income countries, many households are able to save a significant fraction of their income. In developing countries, many households barely survive on their incomes and, therefore, have little or no savings.

The low saving rates in developing countries can contribute to a *vicious cycle of poverty*. Because households have low incomes, they save very little. Because households save very little, few funds are available for firms to borrow. Lacking funds, firms do not invest in the new factories, machinery, and equipment needed for economic growth. Because the economy does not grow, household incomes remain low, as do their savings, and so on.

The Benefits of Globalization

Foreign direct investment (FDI) The purchase or building by a corporation of a facility in a foreign country.

Foreign portfolio investment The purchase by an individual or a firm of stocks or bonds issued in another country.

One way for a developing country to break out of the vicious cycle of low saving and investment and low growth is through foreign investment. **Foreign direct investment (FDI)** occurs when corporations build or purchase facilities in foreign countries. **Foreign portfolio investment** occurs when an individual or a firm buys stocks or bonds issued in another country. Foreign direct investment and foreign portfolio investment can give a low-income country access to technology and funds that otherwise would not be available. Until fairly recently, many developing countries were reluctant to take advantage of this opportunity.

From the 1940s through the 1970s, many developing countries closed themselves off from the global economy. They did this for several reasons. During the 1930s and early 1940s, the global trading and financial system collapsed as a result of the Great Depression and World War II. Developing countries that relied on exporting to the high-income countries were hurt economically. Also, many countries in Africa and Asia achieved independence from the colonial powers of Europe during the 1950s and 1960s and were afraid of being dominated by them economically. As a result, many developing countries imposed high tariffs on foreign imports and strongly discouraged or even prohibited foreign investment. These policies made it difficult to break out of the vicious cycle of poverty.

The policies of erecting high tariff barriers and avoiding foreign investment failed to produce much growth, so by the 1980s, many developing countries began to change policies. The result was **globalization**, which refers to the process of countries becoming more open to foreign trade and investment. Developing countries that are more globalized have grown faster than developing countries that are less globalized. Globalization has benefited developing countries by making it easier for them to obtain technology and investment funds.

Globalization The process of countries becoming more open to foreign trade and investment.

Growth Policies

What can governments do to promote long-run economic growth? We have seen that even small differences in growth rates compounded over the years can lead to major differences in standards of living. Therefore, there is potentially a very high payoff to government policies that increase growth rates. We have already discussed some of these policies in this chapter. In this section, we explore additional policies.

5 LEARNING OBJECTIVE

Discuss government policies that foster economic growth.

Enhancing Property Rights and the Rule of Law

A market system cannot work well unless property rights are enforced. Entrepreneurs are unlikely to risk their own funds, and investors are unlikely to lend their funds to entrepreneurs, unless property is safe from being arbitrarily seized. We have seen that in many developing countries, the rule of law and property rights are undermined by government *corruption*. In some developing countries, it is impossible for an entrepreneur to obtain a permit to start a business without paying bribes, often to several different government officials. Is it possible for a country to reform a corrupt government bureaucracy?

Although today the United States ranks among the least corrupt countries, recent research by economists Edward Glaeser and Claudia Goldin of Harvard University has shown that in the late nineteenth and early twentieth centuries, corruption was a significant problem in the United States. The fact that political reform movements and crusading newspapers helped to reduce corruption in the United States to relatively low levels by the 1920s provides some hope for reform movements that aim to reduce corruption in developing countries today.

Property rights are unlikely to be secure in countries that are afflicted by wars and civil strife. For a number of countries, increased political stability is a necessary prerequisite to economic growth.

Making the Connection	**Will China's Standard of Living Ever Exceed That of the United States?**

In 2012, GDP per capita in the United States was more than five times higher than GDP per capita in China. However, the growth rate of real GDP per capita in the United States has averaged only 1.7 percent per year since 1980, compared to China's average growth rate of 8.9 percent per year over the same time period. If these growth rates were to continue, China's standard of living would exceed the U.S. standard of living in the year 2037. For China to maintain its high rates of growth in real GDP per capita, however, it would have to maintain high rates of productivity growth, which is unlikely for several reasons. First, the United States invests more in activities, such as research and development, that result in new technologies and increases in productivity. Although China has been successful in adopting existing technologies developed in the United States and other countries, it has been much less successful in developing new technologies. Second, a good part of China's growth is due to the transition from a centrally planned economy to a market economy, so China's growth rate is likely to decrease as the transition is completed. Third, China's economic growth has depended on moving workers from agriculture, where their productivity was low, to manufacturing jobs in the city, where their productivity is much higher. The large supply of low-wage agricultural workers

Some economists argue that China may have overinvested in physical capital, such as bullet trains.

helped to keep manufacturing wages low and provided China with a cost advantage in manufacturing goods compared with the United States and other high-income countries. China has exhausted much of its supply of low-wage agricultural workers, so manufacturing wages have begun to rise, eroding China's cost advantage.

Another looming problem is demographic. Because of China's low birthrate, the country will soon experience a decline in its labor force. Over the next two decades, the population of men and women between 15 and 29 years will fall by roughly 100 million, or about 30 percent. China will also experience a large increase in older workers, a group that will on average be less productive and less healthy than younger workers. Given current trends, the U.S. Census Bureau projects fewer people under age 50 in China in 2030 than today, including fewer people in their twenties and early thirties and many more people in their sixties and older. China still has potential sources for enhancing productivity, including the wider application of technology and the movement of workers into high-productivity industries, such as the manufacture of automobiles and household appliances, provided domestic demand increases rapidly. These factors can fuel future growth, but at some point, China's demographic problems could slow growth.

Perhaps most troubling for China is the fact that the country remains autocratic, with the Communist Party refusing to allow meaningful elections and continuing to limit freedom of expression. The government has yet to establish secure property rights and the rule of law. Some observers believe that the lack of political freedom in China may ultimately lead to civil unrest, which could slow growth rates. Whether or not civil unrest eventually develops, the lack of democracy in China may already be resulting in problems that could slow growth in the near future. Large, state-owned firms, controlled by Communist Party members, continue to receive government subsidies. The result is that these firms, which typically have low productivity and are not globally competitive, receive funds that otherwise would have allowed high-productivity firms to expand.

Nouriel Roubini, an economist at New York University, argues that China's Communist Party may be repeating some of the mistakes the Soviet Communist Party committed decades ago. He argues that by employing policies that have resulted in investment being 50 percent of GDP, the government may have boosted short-term growth at the expense of the health of the economy in the long term. He notes:

> China is rife with overinvestment in physical capital, infrastructure, and property. To a visitor, this is evident in sleek but empty airports and bullet trains... highways to nowhere, thousands of colossal new central and provincial government buildings, ghost towns, and brand-new aluminum smelters kept closed to prevent global prices from plunging.

Growth in China is already giving signs of slowing. It appeared likely that growth in 2013 would be the lowest China has experienced since 1990.

China has been engaged in an economic experiment: Can a country maintain high rates of economic growth in the long run while denying its citizens basic political rights?

Sources: Pranab Bardhan, "The Slowing of Two Economic Giants," *New York Times*, July 14, 2013; Alex Frangos and Eric Bellman, "China Slump Ripples Globally," *Wall Street Journal*, July 15, 2013; Nicholas Eberstadt, "The Demographic Future," *Foreign Affairs*, Vol. 89, No. 6, November/December 2010, pp. 54–64; and Nouriel Roubini, "Beijing's Empty Bullet Trains," *Slate*, April 14, 2011.

Your Turn: Test your understanding by doing related problem 5.4 at the end of this chapter.

Improving Health and Education

Recently, many economists have become convinced that poor health is a major impediment to growth in some countries. The research of the late Nobel Laureate Robert Fogel emphasizes the important interaction between health and economic growth. As people's health improves and they become stronger and less susceptible to diseases, they also become more productive. Recent initiatives in developing countries to increase vaccinations against infectious diseases, to improve access to treated water, and to improve sanitation have begun to reduce rates of illness and death.

We discussed earlier in this chapter Paul Romer's argument that there are increasing returns to knowledge capital. Nobel Laureate Robert Lucas of the University of Chicago similarly argues that there are increasing returns to *human* capital. Lucas argues that productivity increases as the total stock of human capital increases but that these productivity increases are not completely captured by individuals as they decide how much education to purchase. Therefore, the market may produce an inefficiently low level of education and training unless the government subsidizes education. Some researchers have been unable to find evidence of increasing returns to human capital, but many economists believe that government subsidies for education have played an important role in promoting economic growth.

The rising incomes that result from economic growth can help developing countries deal with the *brain drain*, which refers to highly educated and successful individuals leaving developing countries for high-income countries. This migration occurs when successful individuals believe that economic opportunities are very limited in the domestic economy. Rapid economic growth in India and China in recent years has resulted in more entrepreneurs, engineers, and scientists deciding to remain in those countries rather than leave for the United States or other high-income countries.

Policies That Promote Technological Change

One of the lessons from the economic growth model is that technological change is more important than increases in capital in explaining long-run growth. Government policies that facilitate access to technology are crucial for low-income countries. The easiest way for developing countries to gain access to technology is through foreign direct investment, where foreign firms are allowed to build new facilities or to buy domestic firms. Recent economic growth in India has been greatly aided by the Indian government's relaxation of regulations on foreign investment. Relaxing these regulations made it possible for India to gain access to the technology of Dell, Microsoft, and other multinational corporations.

In high-income countries, government policies can aid the growth of technology by subsidizing research and development. As we noted previously, in the United States, the federal government conducts some research and development on its own and also provides grants to researchers in universities. Tax breaks to firms undertaking research and development also facilitate technological change.

Policies That Promote Saving and Investment

Firms turn to the loanable funds market to finance expansion and research and development. Policies that increase the incentives to save and invest will increase the equilibrium level of loanable funds and may increase the level of real GDP per capita. For instance, governments can use tax incentives to increase saving. In the United States, many workers are able to save for retirement by placing funds in 401(k) or 403(b) plans or in Individual Retirement Accounts (IRAs). Income placed in these accounts is not taxed until it is withdrawn during retirement. Because the funds are allowed to accumulate tax free, the return is increased, which raises the incentive to save.

Governments also increase incentives for firms to engage in investment in physical capital by using *investment tax credits*. Investment tax credits allow firms to deduct from their taxes some fraction of the funds they have spent on investment. Reductions in the taxes firms pay on their profits also increase the after-tax return on investments.

Is Economic Growth Good or Bad?

Although we didn't state so explicitly, in this chapter we have assumed that economic growth is desirable and that governments should undertake policies that will increase growth rates. It seems undeniable that increasing the growth rates of very low-income countries would help relieve the daily suffering that many people in those countries endure. But some people are unconvinced that, at least in the high-income countries, further economic growth is desirable.

The arguments against further economic growth reflect concern about the effects of growth on the environment or concern about the effects of the globalization process that has accompanied economic growth. In 1973, the Club of Rome published a controversial book titled *The Limits to Growth*, which predicted that economic growth would likely grind to a halt in the United States and other high-income countries because of increasing pollution and the depletion of natural resources, such as oil. Although these dire predictions have not yet come to pass, many people remain concerned that economic growth may be contributing to global warming, deforestation, and other environmental problems.

Some people believe that globalization has undermined the distinctive cultures of many countries, as imports of food, clothing, movies, and other goods have displaced domestically produced goods. Allowing foreign direct investment is an important way in which low-income countries can gain access to the latest technology. Some people, however, believe multinational firms behave unethically in low-income countries because they claim the firms pay very low wages and fail to follow the same safety and environmental regulations the firms are required to follow in high-income countries.

As with many other normative questions, economic analysis can contribute to the ongoing political debate over the consequences of economic growth, but it cannot settle the issue.

Continued

Economics in Your Life

Would You Be Better Off without China?

At the beginning of the chapter, we asked you to imagine that you could choose to live and work in a world with the Chinese economy growing very rapidly or in a world with the Chinese economy as it was before 1978—very poor and growing slowly. Which world would you choose to live in? How does the current high-growth, high-export Chinese economy affect you as a consumer? How does it affect you as someone about to start a career?

It's impossible to walk into most stores in the United States without seeing products imported from China. Many of these products were at one time made in the United States. Imports from China replace domestically produced goods when the imports are either priced lower or have higher quality than the domestic goods they replace. Therefore, the rapid economic growth that has enabled Chinese firms to be competitive with firms in the United States has benefited you as a consumer: You have lower-priced goods and better goods available for purchase than you would if China had remained very poor. As you begin your career, there are some U.S. industries that, because of competition from Chinese firms, will have fewer jobs to offer. But, as we saw when discussing international trade, expanding trade changes the types of products each country makes, and, therefore, the types of jobs available, but it does not affect the total number of jobs. So, the economic rise of China will affect the mix of jobs available to you in the United States but will not make finding a job any more difficult.

Conclusion

For much of human history, most people have had to struggle to survive. Even today, more than half of the world's population lives in extreme poverty. The differences in living standards among countries today are a result of many decades of sharply different rates of economic growth. According to the economic growth model, increases in the quantity of capital per hour worked and increases in technology determine the growth in real GDP per hour worked and a country's standard of living. The keys to higher living standards seem straightforward: Establish the rule of law, provide basic education and health care for the population, increase the amount of capital per hour worked, adopt the best technology, and participate in the global economy. However, for many countries, these policies have proved very difficult to implement.

Visit MyEconLab for a news article and analysis related to the concepts in this chapter.

Chapter Summary and Problems

Key Terms

Catch-up

Economic growth model

Foreign direct investment (FDI)

Foreign portfolio investment

Globalization

Human capital

Industrial Revolution

Labor productivity

New growth theory

Patent

Per-worker production function

Property rights

Rule of law

Technological change

 1 ## Economic Growth over Time and around the World

LEARNING OBJECTIVE: Define economic growth, calculate economic growth rates, and describe global trends in economic growth.

Summary

For most of history, the average person survived with barely enough food. Living standards began to rise significantly only after the start of the **Industrial Revolution** in England in the 1700s, with the application of mechanical power to the production of goods. The best measure of a country's standard of living is its level of real GDP per capita. Economic growth occurs when real GDP per capita increases, thereby increasing the country's standard of living.

Visit **www.myeconlab.com** to complete these exercises online and get instant feedback.

Review Questions

1.1 Why does a country's economic growth rate matter?

1.2 Explain the difference between the total percentage increase in real GDP between 2003 and 2013 and the average annual growth rate in real GDP between the same years.

Problems and Applications

1.3 **[Related to** Making the Connection: **Why Did the Industrial Revolution Begin in England?]** Economists Carol Shiue and Wolfgang Keller of the University of Colorado published a study of "market efficiency" in the eighteenth century in England, other European countries, and China. If the markets in a country are efficient, a product should have the same price wherever in the country it is sold, allowing for the effect of transportation costs. If prices are not the same in two areas within a country, it is possible to make profits by buying the product where its price is low and reselling it where its price is high. This trading will drive prices to equality. Trade is most likely to occur, however, if entrepreneurs feel confident that their gains will not be seized by the government and that contracts to buy and sell can be enforced in the courts. Therefore, in the eighteenth century, the more efficient a country's markets, the more its institutions favored long-run growth. Shiue and Keller found that in 1770, the efficiency of markets in England was significantly greater than the efficiency of markets elsewhere in Europe and in China. How does this finding relate to

Douglass North's argument concerning why the Industrial Revolution occurred in England?

Source: Carol H. Shiue and Wolfgang Keller, "Markets in China and Europe on the Eve of the Industrial Revolution," *American Economic Review*, Vol. 97, No. 4, September 2007, pp. 1189–1216.

1.4 Use the data on real GDP in this table to answer the following questions. The values are measured in each country's domestic currency.

Country	2009	2010	2011	2012
Brazil	1,034	1,112	1,142	1,152
Mexico	8,378	8,823	9,168	9,530
Thailand	4,263	4,596	4,600	4,896

a. Which country experienced the highest rate of economic growth during 2010 (that is, for which country did real GDP increase the most from 2009 to 2010)?

b. Which country experienced the highest average annual growth rate between 2010 and 2012?

c. Does it matter for your answers to parts (a) and (b) that each country's real GDP is measured in a different currency? Briefly explain.

Source: International Monetary Fund, *World Economic Outlook Database*, April 2013.

1.5 Andover Bank and Lowell Bank each sell one-year certificates of deposit (CDs). The interest rates on these CDs are given in the following table for a three-year period:

Bank	2014	2015	2016
Andover Bank	5%	5%	5%
Lowell Bank	2%	6%	7%

Suppose you deposit $1,000 in a CD in each bank at the beginning of 2014. At the end of 2014, you take your $1,000 and any interest earned and invest it in a CD for the following year. You do this again at the end of 2015. At the end of 2016, will you have earned more on your Andover Bank CDs or on your Lowell Bank CDs? Briefly explain.

1.6 **[Related to the** Don't Let This Happen to You**]** Use the data for the United States in this table to answer the following questions:

Year	Real GDP per Capita (2009 prices)
2008	$48,708
2009	46,927
2010	47,710
2011	48,239
2012	49,226

a. What was the percentage change in real GDP per capita between 2008 and 2012?

b. What was the average annual growth rate in real GDP per capita between 2008 and 2012? (*Hint:* The average annual growth rate for relatively short periods can be approximated by averaging the growth rates for each year during the period.)

1.7 **[Related to the** Making the Connection**: Is Income All That Matters?]** In his book *The White Man's Burden*, William Easterly reports:

> A vaccination campaign in southern Africa virtually eliminated measles as a killer of children. Routine childhood immunization combined with measles vaccination in seven southern Africa nations starting in 1996 virtually eliminated measles in those countries by 2000. A national campaign in Egypt to make parents aware of the use of oral rehydration therapy from 1982 to 1989 cut childhood deaths from diarrhea by 82 percent over that period.

a. Is it likely that real GDP per capita increased significantly in southern Africa and Egypt as a result of the near elimination of measles and the large decrease in childhood deaths from diarrhea? If these events did not increase real GDP per capita, is it still possible that they increased the standard of living in southern Africa and Egypt? Briefly explain.

b. Which seems more achievable for a developing country: the elimination of measles and childhood deaths from diarrhea or sustained increases in real GDP per capita? Briefly explain.

Source: William Easterly, *The White Man's Burden: Why the West's Efforts to Aid the Rest Have Done So Much Ill and So Little Good*, New York: The Penguin Press, 2006, p. 241.

1.8 **[Related to** Making the Connection**: Is Income All That Matters?]** Economist Charles Kenny of the Center for Global Development has argued:

> The process technologies—institutions like laws and inventory management systems—that appear central to raising incomes per capita flow less like water and more like bricks. But ideas and inventions—the importance of [education] and vaccines for DPT—really might flow more easily across borders and over distances.

If Kenny is correct, what are the implications of these facts for the ability of low-income countries to rapidly increase their rates of growth of real GDP per capita in the decades ahead? What are the implications for the ability of these countries to increase their standards of living? Briefly explain.

Source: Charles Kenny, *Getting Better*, New York: Basic Books, 2011, p. 117.

What Determines How Fast Economies Grow?

LEARNING OBJECTIVE: Use the economic growth model to explain why growth rates differ across countries.

Summary

An **economic growth model** explains changes in real GDP per capita in the long run. **Labor productivity** is the quantity of goods and services that can be produced by one worker or by one hour of work. Economic growth depends on increases in labor productivity. Labor productivity will increase if there is an increase in the amount of *capital* available to each worker or if there is an improvement in *technology*. **Technological change** is a change in the ability of a firm to produce a given level of output with a given quantity of inputs. There are three main sources of technological change: better machinery and equipment, increases in human capital, and better means of organizing and managing production. **Human capital** is the accumulated knowledge and skills that workers acquire from education and training or from their life experiences. We can say that an economy will have a higher standard of living the more capital it has per hour worked, the more human capital its workers have, the better its capital, and the better the job its business managers do in organizing production.

The **per-worker production function** shows the relationship between capital per hour worked and output per hour worked,

holding technology constant. *Diminishing returns to capital* means that increases in the quantity of capital per hour worked will result in diminishing increases in output per hour worked. Technological change shifts up the per-worker production function, resulting in more output per hour worked at every level of capital per hour worked. The economic growth model stresses the importance of changes in capital per hour worked and technological change in explaining growth in output per hour worked. **New growth theory** is a model of long-run economic growth that emphasizes that technological change is influenced by how individuals and firms respond to economic incentives.

One way governments can promote technological change is by granting **patents**, which are exclusive rights to a product for a period of 20 years from the date the patent is filed with the government. To Joseph Schumpeter, the entrepreneur is central to the "creative destruction" by which the standard of living increases as qualitatively better products replace existing products.

Visit **www.myeconlab.com** to complete these exercises online and get instant feedback.

Review Questions

2.1 Using the per-worker production function graph from Figures 3 and 4, show the effect on real GDP per hour worked of an increase in capital per hour worked, holding technology constant. Now, again using the per-worker production function graph, show the effect on real GDP per hour worked of an increase in technology, holding constant the quantity of capital per hour worked.

2.2 What are the consequences for growth of diminishing returns to capital? How are some economies able to maintain high growth rates despite diminishing returns to capital?

2.3 What is the *new growth theory*? How does the new growth theory differ from the growth theory developed by Robert Solow?

2.4 Why are firms likely to underinvest in research and development? Briefly discuss three ways in which government policy can increase the accumulation of knowledge capital.

2.5 Why does knowledge capital experience increasing returns at the economy level while physical capital experiences decreasing returns?

Problems and Applications

2.6 Which of the following will result in a movement along China's per-worker production function, and which will result in a shift of China's per-worker production function? Briefly explain.
  a. Capital per hour worked increases from 200 yuan per hour worked to 250 yuan per hour worked.
  b. The Chinese government doubles its spending on support for university research.
  c. A reform of the Chinese school system results in more highly trained Chinese workers.

2.7 **[Related to** Making the Connection: **What Explains the Economic Failure of the Soviet Union?]** The *Making the Connection: What Explains the Economic Failure of the Soviet Union?* argues that a key difference between market economies and centrally planned economies, like that of the former Soviet Union, is as follows:

> In market economies, decisions about which investments to make and which technologies to adopt are made by entrepreneurs and managers with their own money on the line. In the Soviet system, these decisions were usually made by salaried bureaucrats trying to fulfill a plan formulated in Moscow.

But in large corporations, investment decisions are often made by salaried managers who do not have their own money on the line. These managers are spending the money of the firm's shareholders rather than their own money. Why, then, do the investment decisions of salaried managers in the United States tend to be better for the long-term growth of the economy than were the decisions of salaried bureaucrats in the Soviet Union?

2.8 **[Related to** Solved Problem 2**]** Use the following graph to answer the questions. In each case, briefly explain your answer.

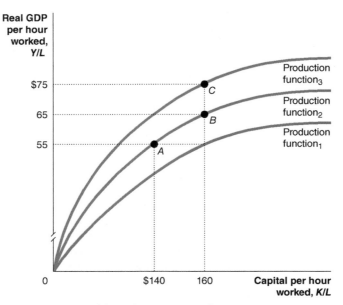

a. True or false: The movement from point *A* to point *B* shows the effects of technological change.
b. True or false: The economy can move from point *B* to point *C* only if there are no diminishing returns to capital.
c. True or false: To move from point *A* to point *C*, the economy must increase the amount of capital per hour worked *and* experience technological change.

2.9 **[Related to** Solved Problem 2**]** If the per-worker production function were shaped as shown in the following graph, what would be the implications for economic growth of a country that was accumulating increasing quantities of capital per hour worked? Briefly explain.

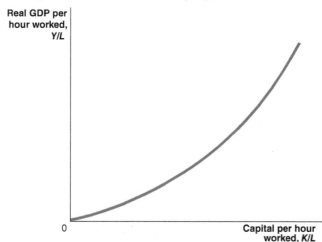

2.10 **[Related to** Solved Problem 2**]** Shortly before the fall of the Soviet Union, the economist Gur Ofer of Hebrew University of Jerusalem wrote: "The most outstanding characteristic of Soviet growth strategy is its consistent policy of very high rates of investment, leading to a rapid growth rate of [the] capital stock." Explain why this economic growth strategy turned out to be a very poor one.
Source: Gur Ofer, "Soviet Economic Growth, 1928–1985," *Journal of Economic Literature*, Vol. 25, No. 4, December 1987, p. 1,784.

2.11 Why is the role of entrepreneurs much more important in the new growth theory than in the traditional economic growth model?

Economic Growth in the United States

LEARNING OBJECTIVE: Discuss fluctuations in productivity growth in the United States.

Summary

Productivity in the United States grew rapidly from the end of World War II until the mid-1970s. Growth then slowed down for 20 years before increasing again after 1995. Economists continue to debate the reasons for the slowdown of growth from the mid-1970s to mid-1990s. Because Western Europe and Japan experienced a productivity slowdown at the same time as the United States, explanations that focus on factors affecting only the United States are unlikely to be correct. Some economists argue that the development of a "new economy" based on information technology caused the higher productivity growth that began in the mid-1990s. Economists debate whether the U.S. economy may be facing another period of lower productivity growth.

Visit **www.myeconlab.com** to complete these exercises online and get instant feedback.

Review Questions

3.1 Describe the record of productivity growth in the United States from 1800 to the present. What explains the slowdown in productivity growth from the mid-1970s to the mid-1990s? Why did productivity growth increase beginning in 1996?

3.2 Briefly describe the debate among economists over how high U.S. productivity growth rates are likely to be in the future.

Problems and Applications

3.3 Figure 5 shows growth rates in real GDP per hour worked in the United States for various periods from 1800 onward. How might the growth rates in the figure be different if they were calculated for real GDP *per capita* instead of per hour worked? (*Hint:* How do you think the number of hours worked per person has changed in the United States since 1800?)

3.4 An article in the *Wall Street Journal* observes: "For 2008, productivity grew an astounding 2.8% from 2007 even as the economy suffered through its worst recession in decades." How is it possible for labor productivity—output per hour worked—to increase if output—real GDP—is falling?

Source: Brian Blackstone, "Productivity Proves Resilient," *Wall Street Journal*, April 29, 2009.

3.5 Economist Robert Gordon of Northwestern University has argued:

> My interpretation of the [information] revolution is that it is increasingly burdened by diminishing returns. The push to ever smaller devices runs up against the fixed size of the human finger that must enter information on the device. Most of the innovations since 2000 have been directed to consumer enjoyment rather than business productivity, including video games, DVD players, and iPods. iPhones are nice, but the ability to reschedule business meetings and look up corporate documents while on the road already existed by 2003.

If Gordon's observations about the information revolution are correct, what are the implications for future labor productivity growth rates in the United States?

Source: Robert J. Gordon, "Revisiting U.S. Productivity Growth over the Past Century with a View of the Future," National Bureau of Economic Research Working Paper 15834, March 2010.

Why Isn't the Whole World Rich?

LEARNING OBJECTIVE: Explain economic catch-up and discuss why many poor countries have not experienced rapid economic growth.

Summary

The economic growth model predicts that poor countries will grow faster than rich countries, resulting in **catch-up**. In recent decades, some poor countries have grown faster than rich countries, but many have not. Some poor countries have not experience rapid growth for four main reasons: wars and revolutions, poor public education and health, failure to enforce the rule of law, and low rates of saving and investment. The **rule of law** refers to the ability of a government to enforce the laws of the country, particularly with respect to protecting private property and enforcing contracts. **Globalization** has aided countries that have opened their economies to foreign trade and investment. **Foreign direct investment (FDI)** is the purchase or building by a corporation of a facility in a foreign country. **Foreign portfolio investment** is the purchase by an individual or firm of stocks or bonds issued in another country.

Visit **www.myeconlab.com** to complete these exercises online and get instant feedback.

Review Questions

4.1 Why does the economic growth model predict that poor countries should catch up to rich countries in income per capita? Have poor countries been catching up to rich countries?

4.2 In what ways does the United States have greater flexibility in its labor markets and greater efficiency in its financial system than other higher-income countries such as those in Europe? How might this greater flexibility in labor markets and greater efficiency in financial markets lead to higher growth rates in real GDP per capita?

4.3 What are the main reasons many poor countries have experienced slow growth?

4.4 What does *globalization* mean? How have developing countries benefited from globalization?

Problems and Applications

4.5 [**Related to** Solved Problem 4] Briefly explain whether the statistics in the following table are consistent with the economic growth model's predictions of catch-up.

Country	Real GDP per Capita in 1960 (2005 dollars)	Growth in Real GDP per Capita, 1960–2010
China	$331	6.33%
Uganda	657	1.04
Madagascar	1,051	–0.80
Ireland	7,223	3.20
United States	15,398	2.00

Source: Authors' calculations from data in Alan Heston, Robert Summers, and Bettina Aten, *Penn World Table Version 7.1*, Center for International Comparisons of Production, Income and Prices at the University of Pennsylvania, November 2012.

4.6 [**Related to** Solved Problem 4] In the following figure, each dot represents a particular country's initial level of real GDP per capita and its growth rate of real GDP per capita.

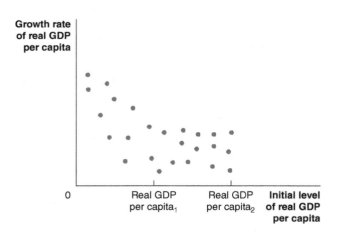

a. For the range of initial GDP per capita from 0 to Real GDP per capita$_2$, does the figure support the economic growth model's prediction of catch-up? Briefly explain.

b. For the range of initial GDP per capita from 0 to Real GDP per capita$_1$, does the figure support the catch-up prediction? Briefly explain.

c. For the range from initial Real GDP per capita$_1$ to Real GDP per capita$_2$, does the figure support the catch-up prediction? Briefly explain.

4.7 Refer to Figures 7–9. The lines in the following three graphs show the average relationship between the initial level of real GDP per capita and the growth rate of real GDP per capita for three groups of countries over a given time period. Match each group of countries with the graph that best depicts the relationship between the initial level of real GDP per capita and the growth rate of real GDP per capita for that group.

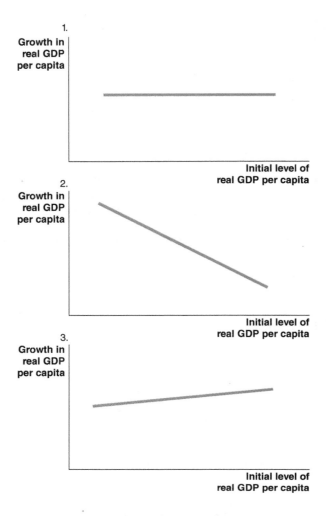

a. All countries for which statistics are available, 1960–2010

b. United States, Western Europe, Canada, and Japan, 1990–2012

c. Current high income countries, 1960–2010

4.8 An opinion column in the *Economist* argued: "Globalisation, far from being the greatest cause of poverty, is its only feasible cure." What does globalization have to do with reducing poverty?

Source: Clive Crook, "Globalisation and Its Critics," *Economist*, September 27, 2001.

4.9 [**Related to** Making the Connection: **What Do Parking Tickets in New York City Tell Us About Poverty in the Developing World?**] The relationship that Raymond Fisman and Edward Miguel found between the extent of corruption in a country and the number of parking violations committed by the country's United Nations delegates in New York isn't perfect. For example, "Ecuador and Colombia both have perfectly clean parking slates, despite the experts' view of them as fairly corrupt places." Does this observation invalidate Fisman and Miguel's conclusions about whether the parking violations data provide evidence in favor of there being a culture of corruption in some countries? Briefly explain.

Source: Raymond Fisman and Edward Miguel, *Economic Gangsters*, Princeton, NJ: Princeton University Press, 2009, p. 89.

4.10 In a speech, President Barack Obama made the following observations: "I know that for many, the face of globalization is contradictory …. Trade can bring new wealth and opportunities, but also huge disruptions and change in communities." How does trade bring "new wealth and opportunities"? How does trade bring "huge disruptions and change"?

Source: "Obama's Speech in Cairo," *Wall Street Journal*, June 4, 2009.

4.11 A columnist in the *New York Times* observes that, "many analysts agree that economic reform, of which integration into the global economy was a key element, has lifted millions of people out of poverty in India." What does "integration into the global economy" mean? How might integration into the global economy reduce poverty in India?

Source: Vivek Dehejia, "Has Globalization Helped India's Poor?" *New York Times*, October 7, 2011.

4.12 The Roman Empire lasted from 27 B.C. to 476 A.D. The empire was wealthy enough to build such monuments as the Roman Coliseum. Roman engineering skill was at a level high enough that aqueducts built during the empire to carry water long distances remained in use for hundreds of years. Yet, although the empire experienced some periods of growth in real GDP per capita, these periods did not last and there is little evidence that growth would have been sustained even if the empire had survived. Why didn't the Roman Empire experience sustained economic growth? What would the world be like today if it had? (Note: There are no definite answers to these questions; they are intended to get you to think about the preconditions for economic growth. Looking beyond this problem, if you are interested in the macroeconomics of the Roman economy, see Peter Temin, *The Roman Market Economy*, Princeton: Princeton University Press, 2013, Chapters 9–11.)

---

5 | Growth Policies

LEARNING OBJECTIVE: Discuss government policies that foster economic growth.

Summary

Governments can attempt to increase economic growth through policies that enhance property rights and the rule of law, improve health and education, subsidize research and development, and provide incentives for savings and investment. Whether continued economic growth is desirable is a normative question that cannot be settled by economic analysis.

Visit **www.myeconlab.com** to complete these exercises online and get instant feedback.

Review Questions

5.1 Briefly describe three government policies that can increase economic growth.

5.2 Can economic analysis arrive at the conclusion that economic growth will always improve economic well-being? Briefly explain.

Problems and Applications

5.3 **[Related to the** Chapter Opener**]** By 2012, General Motors (GM) had established 12 joint ventures and employed more than 55,000 workers in China. In 2013, GM announced that it would invest an additional $11 billion to increase production of its vehicles in China. Why would GM choose to invest in China rather than to export vehicles to China from the United States?

Source: Colum Murphy, "GM to Build Cadillac Plant in China," *Wall Street Journal*, May 7, 2013.

5.4 **[Related to** Making the Connection: **Will China's Standard of Living Ever Exceed That of the United States?]** In China, why may a lower birthrate lead to slower growth in real GDP per capita? Why might high levels of spending on investment in China lead to high rates of growth in the short run, but not in the long run?

5.5 Pranab Bardhan, an economist at the University of California, Berkeley, argues: "China may be close to exhausting the possibilities of technological catch-up with the West, particularly in manufacturing."
  a. What does Bardhan mean by "technological catch-up"?
  b. If Bardhan is correct, what problems might the Chinese economy encounter in the future?
  c. Briefly discuss the similarities and differences between the Chinese economy today and the Soviet economy in the 1980s.

Source: Pranab Bardhan, "The Slowing of Two Economic Giants," *New York Times*, July 14, 2013.

5.6 Briefly explain which of the following policies are likely to increase the rate of economic growth in the United States.
  a. Congress passes an investment tax credit, which reduces a firm's taxes if it installs new machinery and equipment.
  b. Congress passes a law that allows taxpayers to reduce their income taxes by the amount of state sales taxes they pay.
  c. Congress provides more funds for low-interest loans to college students.

5.7 Economist George Ayittey, in an interview on PBS about economic development in Africa, stated that of the 54 African countries, only 8 had a free press. For Africa's economic development, Ayittey argued strongly for the establishment of a free press. Why would a free press be vital for the enhancement of property rights and the rule of law? How could a free press help reduce corruption?

Source: George Ayittey, *Border Jumpers*, Anchor Interview Transcript, WideAngle, PBS.org, July 24, 2005.

5.8 More people in high-income countries than in low-income countries tend to believe that rapid rates of economic growth are not desirable. Does the concept of a "normal good" provide insight into why some people in high-income countries might be more concerned with certain consequences of rapid economic growth than are people in low-income countries?

Real-Time-Data Exercises

D1 **[Analyzing labor productivity]** Using data from the St. Louis Federal Reserve (FRED) (research.stlouisfed.org/fred2/), analyze the relationship between labor productivity in the manufacturing sector and in the non-farm business sector as a whole.

    a. Download data since 1987 on output per hour of all persons in the manufacturing sector (OPHMFG) and in the non-farm business sector (OPHNFB).

    b. Which has increased more since 1987, labor productivity in manufacturing or in the non-farm business sector?

    c. The manufacturing sector has been shrinking relative to the size of the economy in the United States and other advanced economies. What do your results imply about future labor productivity growth in advanced economies?

D2 **[Comparing labor productivity across countries]** Using data from the St. Louis Federal Reserve (FRED) (research.stlouisfed.org/fred2/), analyze differences in labor productivity among China, India, and the United States.

    a. From 1952 to the present, chart the following series on the same graph: real GDP per worker for China (RG-DPL2CNA627NUPN), real GDP per worker for India

(RGDPLWINA627NUPN), and real GDP per worker for the United States (RGDPLWUSA627NUPN). To chart the series on the same graph follow these steps: (1) On the page for real GDP per worker for China, click on the "Edit graph" link under the graph; (2) on the bottom of the next page, click on the "Add Data Series" link; (3) search for the other two series and click on them to add them to your graph.

    b. Calculate the relative productivity of workers in China and the United States by dividing U.S. labor productivity by China's labor productivity. Describe the change in this measure of relative productivity since 1952.

    c. Repeat part (b) for the United States and India.

D3 **[The U.S. economy in a world context]** The U.S. Central Intelligence Agency's World Factbook (www.cia.gov/library/publications/the-world-factbook/index.html) offers many comparative tables of world data. Go to this site and find the following:

    a. The countries with the highest and lowest real GDPs

    b. The countries with the highest and lowest per capita real GDPs, adjusted for purchasing power

    c. The countries with the most equal and least equal income distributions

    d. The countries with the highest and lowest real GDP growth rates

    e. The rank of the United States in these categories

Glossary

Catch-up The prediction that the level of GDP per capita (or income per capita) in poor countries will grow faster than in rich countries.

Economic growth model A model that explains growth rates in real GDP per capita over the long run.

Foreign direct investment (FDI) The purchase or building by a corporation of a facility in a foreign country.

Foreign portfolio investment The purchase by an individual or a firm of stocks or bonds issued in another country.

Globalization The process of countries becoming more open to foreign trade and investment.

Human capital The accumulated knowledge and skills that workers acquire from formal training and education or from life experiences.

Industrial Revolution The application of mechanical power to the production of goods, beginning in England around 1750.

Labor productivity The quantity of goods and services that can be produced by one worker or by one hour of work.

New growth theory A model of long-run economic growth that emphasizes that technological change is influenced by economic incentives and so is determined by the working of the market system.

Patent The exclusive right to a product for a period of 20 years from the date the patent is filed with the government.

Per-worker production function The relationship between real GDP per hour worked and capital per hour worked, holding the level of technology constant.

Property rights The rights individuals or firms have to the exclusive use of their property, including the right to buy or sell it.

Rule of law The ability of a government to enforce the laws of the country, particularly with respect to protecting private property and enforcing contracts.

Technological change A change in the ability of a firm to produce a given level of output with a given quantity of inputs.

Credits

Credits are listed in the order of appearance.

Photo

Gao yuwen-Imaginechina/AP Images; Franck Iren/Alamy; Grant Neuenburg/Reuters/Corbis; Lionel Cionneau/AP Images; Claro Cortes IV/Reuters/Corbis

Text

Socialism, and Democracy, New York: Harper, 1962 (originally published 1942), p. 132. ; David M Byrne, Stephen D Oliner, and Daniel E. Sichel, "Is the Information Technology Revolution Over?" Finance and Economics Discussion Series, Federal Reserve Board, March 2013; James Kahn and Robert Rich, "The Productivity Slowdown Reaffirmed," Federal Reserve Bank of New York, September 28, 2011; Robert J. Gordon, "Is U.S. Economic Growth Over? Innovation Confronts Six Headwinds," NBER Working Paper 18315, August 2012; Edward Glaeser and Claudia Goldin, eds., *Corruption and Reform: Lessons from America's History*, Chicago, IL: University of Chicago Press, 2006.

Aggregate Demand and Aggregate Supply Analysis

From Chapter 13 of *Macroeconomics*, Fifth Edition. R. Glenn Hubbard and Anthony Patrick O'Brien. Copyright © 2015 by Pearson Education, Inc.

Aggregate Demand and Aggregate Supply Analysis

Chapter Outline and Learning Objectives

The Fortunes of FedEx Follow the Business Cycle

FedEx is the world's largest shipper of packages by air. The value of packages handled by FedEx is about 4 percent of U.S. gross domestic product (GDP) and 1.5 percent of global GDP. Some Wall Street analysts use a "FedEx indicator" to gauge the state of the economy because FedEx's business rises and falls along with GDP.

Fred Smith came up with the idea for the company in 1965 in an undergraduate term paper. He proposed an entirely new system of delivering packages: One firm would control shipping freight, from pickup to delivery. The firm would operate its own planes on a "hub-and-spoke" system: Packages would be collected and flown to a central hub, where they would be sorted and then flown to their destination for final delivery by truck.

Despite FedEx's tremendous success over the past 50 years, the company's business is dependent on the ups and downs of the business cycle. For example, as the U.S. economy entered a recession in December 2007, firms and households cut back on shipping packages. In the first quarter of 2008, FedEx reported its first loss after 11 straight years of profits. As the 2007–2009 recession dragged on, FedEx announced layoffs for some employees and pay cuts for most other employees. By September 2009, economic conditions had begun to improve, and so had the company's profits. The economic recovery from the recession, however, was slower than most economists and FedEx had expected. Many of FedEx's customers began shipping by cheaper ocean freight, which reduced demand for FedEx's air cargo services. As one newspaper article put it: "The slow boat to China is what gives FedEx Corp. executives nightmares."

As of July 2013, Gene Huang, FedEx's chief economist, was predicting continued slow growth in U.S. and world GDP through the end of the year with faster growth in 2014. Without faster growth in GDP, FedEx would not be able to hit its long-run goals for increases in revenue and profits.

To understand how the business cycle affects FedEx and other firms, we need to explore the effects that recessions and expansions have on production, employment, and prices.

Sources: Spencer Jakab, "FedEx Down, Not Out, on Express Slump," *Wall Street Journal*, June 18, 2012; Bob Sechler, "FedEx Boosts Outlook," *Wall Street Journal*, September 11, 2009; "Economic Update," July 1, 2013, investors.fedex.com/phoenix.zhtml?c=73289&p=irol-economicupdate; and Hal Weiztman, "FedEx to Cut Costs by $1 Bn," *Financial Times*, March 19, 2009.

Economics in Your Life

Is an Employer Likely to Cut Your Pay during a Recession?

Suppose that you have worked as a barista for a local coffeehouse for two years. From on-the-job training and experience, you have honed your coffee-making skills and mastered the perfect latte. Then the economy moves into a recession, and sales at the coffeehouse decline. Is the owner of the coffeehouse likely to cut the prices of lattes and other drinks? Suppose the owner asks to meet with you to discuss your wages for next year. Is the owner likely to cut your pay? As you read this chapter, try to answer these questions. You can check your answers against those we provide at the end of this chapter.

e have seen that the U.S. economy has experienced a long-run upward trend in real GDP. This upward trend has resulted in the standard of living in the United States being much higher today than it was 100 years ago. In the short run, however, real GDP fluctuates around this long-run upward trend because of the business cycle. Fluctuations in GDP lead to fluctuations in employment. These fluctuations in real GDP and employment are the most visible and dramatic part of the business cycle. During recessions, we are more likely to see factories close, small businesses declare bankruptcy, and workers lose their jobs. During expansions, we are more likely to see new businesses open and new jobs created. In addition to these changes in output and employment, the business cycle causes changes in wages and prices. Some firms react to a decline in sales by cutting back on production, but they may also cut the prices they charge and the wages they pay. Other firms respond to a recession by raising prices and workers' wages by less than they otherwise would have.

In this chapter, we expand our story of the business cycle by developing the aggregate demand and aggregate supply model. This model will help us analyze the effects of recessions and expansions on production, employment, and prices.

Aggregate Demand

Identify the determinants of aggregate demand and distinguish between a movement along the aggregate demand curve and a shift of the curve.

Aggregate demand and aggregate supply model A model that explains short-run fluctuations in real GDP and the price level.

Aggregate demand (AD) curve A curve that shows the relationship between the price level and the quantity of real GDP demanded by households, firms, and the government.

Short-run aggregate supply (SRAS) curve A curve that shows the relationship in the short run between the price level and the quantity of real GDP supplied by firms.

To understand what happens during the business cycle, we need an explanation of why real GDP, the unemployment rate, and the inflation rate fluctuate. Fluctuations in the unemployment rate are caused mainly by fluctuations in real GDP. In this chapter, we use the **aggregate demand and aggregate supply model** to explain short-run fluctuations in real GDP and the price level. As Figure 1 shows, real GDP and the price level in this model are determined in the short run by the intersection of the *aggregate demand curve* and the *aggregate supply curve*. Fluctuations in real GDP and the price level are caused by shifts in the aggregate demand curve or in the aggregate supply curve.

The **aggregate demand (AD) curve** shows the relationship between the price level and the quantity of real GDP demanded by households, firms, and the government. The **short-run aggregate supply (SRAS) curve** shows the relationship in the short run between the price level and the quantity of real GDP supplied by firms. The aggregate demand and short-run aggregate supply curves in Figure 1 look similar to the individual market demand and supply curves. However, because these curves apply to the whole economy, rather than to just a single market, the aggregate demand and aggregate supply model is very different from the model of demand and supply in individual markets. Because we are dealing with the economy as a whole, we need *macroeconomic* explanations of why the aggregate demand curve is

Figure 1

Aggregate Demand and Aggregate Supply

In the short run, real GDP and the price level are determined by the intersection of the aggregate demand curve and the short-run aggregate supply curve. In the figure, real GDP is measured on the horizontal axis, and the price level is measured on the vertical axis by the GDP deflator. In this example, the equilibrium real GDP is $17.0 trillion, and the equilibrium price level is 110.

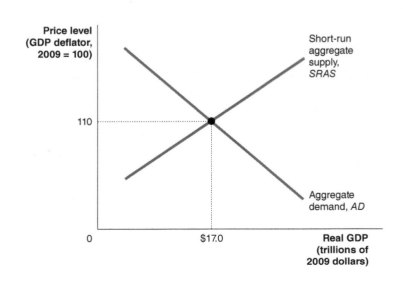

downward sloping, why the short-run aggregate supply curve is upward sloping, and why the curves shift. We begin by explaining why the aggregate demand curve is downward sloping.

Why Is the Aggregate Demand Curve Downward Sloping?

GDP has four components: consumption (C), investment (I), government purchases (G), and net exports (NX). If we let Y stand for GDP, we have the following relationship:

$$Y = C + I + G + NX.$$

The aggregate demand curve is downward sloping because a fall in the price level increases the quantity of real GDP demanded. To understand why, we need to look at how changes in the price level affect each component of aggregate demand. We begin with the assumption that government purchases are determined by the policy decisions of lawmakers and are not affected by changes in the price level. We can then consider the effect of changes in the price level on the three other components: consumption, investment, and net exports.

The Wealth Effect: How a Change in the Price Level Affects Consumption Current income is the most important variable determining consumption by households. As income rises, consumption will rise, and as income falls, consumption will fall. But consumption also depends on household wealth, which is the difference between the value of a household's assets and the value of its debts. Consider two households, both with incomes of $80,000 per year. The first household has wealth of $5 million, and the second household has wealth of $50,000. The first household is likely to spend more of its income than the second household. So, as total household wealth rises, consumption will rise. Some household wealth is held in cash or other *nominal assets* that lose value as the price level rises and gain value as the price level falls. For instance, if you have $10,000 in cash, a 10 percent increase in the price level will reduce the purchasing power of that cash by 10 percent. When the price level rises, the *real value* of household wealth declines, and so will consumption, thereby reducing the demand for goods and services. When the price level falls, the real value of household wealth rises, and so will consumption and the demand for goods and services. The effect of the price level on consumption is called the *wealth effect*, and it is one reason the aggregate demand curve is downward sloping.

The Interest-Rate Effect: How a Change in the Price Level Affects Investment When prices rise, households and firms need more money to finance buying and selling. Therefore, when the price level rises, households and firms will try to increase the amount of money they hold by withdrawing funds from banks, borrowing from banks, or selling financial assets, such as bonds. These actions tend to drive up the interest rate banks charge on loans and the interest rate on bonds. A higher interest rate raises the cost of borrowing for firms and households. As a result, firms will borrow less to build new factories or install new machinery and equipment, and households will borrow less to buy new houses. To a smaller extent, consumption will also fall as households borrow less to finance spending on automobiles, furniture, and other durable goods. Because a higher price level increases the interest rate and reduces investment spending, it also reduces the quantity of goods and services demanded. A lower price level will decrease the interest rate and increase investment spending, thereby increasing the quantity of goods and services demanded. The effect of the price level on investment is known as the *interest-rate effect*, and it is a second reason the aggregate demand curve is downward sloping.

rising prices → withdrawing/borrowing from banks → intrest goes up → firms borrow less

The International-Trade Effect: How a Change in the Price Level Affects Net Exports *Net exports* equal spending by foreign households and firms on goods and services produced in the United States minus spending by U.S. households and

US price level ↑ means exports become more expensive → some consumers will buy else where

firms on goods and services produced in other countries. If the price level in the United States rises relative to the price levels in other countries, U.S. exports will become relatively more expensive, and foreign imports will become relatively less expensive. Some consumers in foreign countries will shift from buying U.S. products to buying domestic products, and some U.S. consumers will also shift from buying U.S. products to buying imported products. U.S. exports will fall and U.S. imports will rise, causing net exports to fall, thereby reducing the quantity of goods and services demanded. A lower price level in the United States relative to other countries has the reverse effect, causing net exports to rise, thereby increasing the quantity of goods and services demanded. The effect of the price level on net exports is known as the *international-trade effect*, and it is a third reason the aggregate demand curve is downward sloping.

Shifts of the Aggregate Demand Curve versus Movements along It

An important point to remember is that the aggregate demand curve tells us the relationship between the price level and the quantity of real GDP demanded, *holding everything else constant*. If the price level changes but other variables that affect the willingness of households, firms, and the government to spend are unchanged, the result is a movement up or down a stationary aggregate demand curve. If any variable other than the price level changes, the aggregate demand curve will shift. For example, if government purchases increase and the price level remains unchanged, the aggregate demand curve will shift to the right at every price level. Or, if firms become pessimistic about the future profitability of investment and cut back spending on factories and machinery, the aggregate demand curve will shift to the left.

The Variables That Shift the Aggregate Demand Curve

The variables that cause the aggregate demand curve to shift fall into three categories:

- Changes in government policies
- Changes in the expectations of households and firms
- Changes in foreign variables

Monetary policy The actions the Federal Reserve takes to manage the money supply and interest rates to achieve macroeconomic policy objectives.

Changes in Government Policies The federal government uses monetary policy and fiscal policy to shift the aggregate demand curve. **Monetary policy** involves actions the Federal Reserve—the nation's central bank—takes to manage the money supply and interest rates and to ensure the flow of funds from lenders to borrowers. The Federal Reserve takes these actions to achieve macroeconomic policy objectives, such as high employment, price stability, high rates of economic growth, and stability of the financial system. For example, the Federal Reserve can lower the cost to firms and households of borrowing by taking actions that reduce interest rates. Lower borrowing costs increase consumption and investment spending, which shifts the aggregate demand curve to the right. Higher interest rates shift the aggregate demand curve to the left. **Fiscal policy** involves changes in federal taxes and purchases that are intended to achieve macroeconomic policy objectives. Because government purchases are one component of aggregate demand, an increase in government purchases shifts the aggregate demand curve to the right, and a decrease in government purchases shifts the aggregate demand curve to the left. An increase in personal income taxes reduces the amount of spendable income available to households, which reduces consumption spending and shifts the aggregate demand curve to the left. Lower personal income taxes shift the aggregate demand curve to the right. Increases in business taxes reduce the profitability of investment spending and shift the aggregate demand curve to the left. Decreases in business taxes shift the aggregate demand curve to the right.

Fiscal policy Changes in federal taxes and purchases that are intended to achieve macroeconomic policy objectives.

Changes in the Expectations of Households and Firms If households become more optimistic about their future incomes, they are likely to increase their current

Don't Let This Happen to You

Understand Why the Aggregate Demand Curve Is Downward Sloping

The aggregate demand curve and the demand curve for a single product are both downward sloping—but for different reasons. When we draw a demand curve for a single product, such as apples, we know that it will slope downward because as the price of apples rises, apples become more expensive relative to other products—such as oranges—and consumers will buy fewer apples and more of the other products. In other words, consumers substitute other products for apples. When the overall price level rises, the prices of all domestically produced goods and services are rising, so consumers

have no other domestic products to which they can switch. The aggregate demand curve slopes downward for the reasons stated under "Why Is the Aggregate Demand Curve Downward Sloping?": A higher price level reduces the real value of household wealth (which decreases consumption), raises interest rates (which decreases investment and consumption), and makes U.S. exports more expensive and foreign imports less expensive (which decreases net exports).

Your Turn: Test your understanding by doing related problem 1.7 at the end of this chapter.

---

consumption. This increased consumption will shift the aggregate demand curve to the right. If households become more pessimistic about their future incomes, the aggregate demand curve will shift to the left. Similarly, if firms become more optimistic about the future profitability of investment spending, the aggregate demand curve will shift to the right. If firms become more pessimistic, the aggregate demand curve will shift to the left.

Changes in Foreign Variables If firms and households in other countries buy fewer U.S. goods or if firms and households in the United States buy more foreign goods, net exports will fall, and the aggregate demand curve will shift to the left. When real GDP increases, so does the income available for consumers to spend. If real GDP in the United States increases faster than real GDP in other countries, U.S. imports will increase faster than U.S. exports, and net exports will fall. Net exports will also fall if the *exchange rate* between the dollar and foreign currencies rises because the price in foreign currency of U.S. products sold in other countries will rise, and the dollar price of foreign products sold in the United States will fall. For example, if the current exchange rate between the dollar and the euro is $1 = €1, then a $20 Blu-ray disc exported from the United States to France will cost €20 in France, and a €50 bottle of French wine will cost $50 in the United States. But if the exchange rate rises to $1 = €1.50, the disc's price will rise to €30 in France, causing its sales to decline, and the price of the French wine will fall to $33.33 per bottle in the United States, causing its sales to increase. U.S. exports will fall, U.S. imports will rise, and the aggregate demand curve will shift to the left.

An increase in net exports at every price level will shift the aggregate demand curve to the right. Net exports will increase if real GDP grows more slowly in the United States than in other countries or if the value of the dollar falls against other currencies. A change in net exports that results from a change in the price level in the United States will result in a movement along the aggregate demand curve, *not* a shift of the aggregate demand curve.

Solved Problem 1

Movements along the Aggregate Demand Curve versus Shifts of the Aggregate Demand Curve

Suppose the current price level is 105, and the current level of real GDP is $17.2 trillion. Illustrate each of the following situations on a graph.

a. The price level rises to 110, while all other variables remain constant.

b. Firms become pessimistic and reduce their investment. Assume that the price level remains constant.

Solving the Problem

Step 1: **Review the chapter material.** This problem is about understanding the difference between movements along an aggregate demand curve and shifts of an aggregate demand curve, so you may want to review the section "Shifts of the Aggregate Demand Curve versus Movements along It."

Step 2: **To answer part (a), draw a graph that shows a movement along the aggregate demand curve.** Because there will be a movement along the aggregate demand curve but no shift of the aggregate demand curve, your graph should look like this:

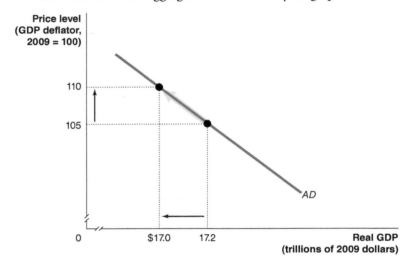

We don't have enough information to be certain what the new level of real GDP demanded will be. We only know that it will be less than the initial level of $17.2 trillion; the graph shows the value as $17.0 trillion.

Step 3: **To answer part (b), draw a graph that shows a shift of the aggregate demand curve.** We know that the aggregate demand curve will shift to the left, but we don't have enough information to know how far to the left it will shift. Let's assume that the shift is $300 billion (or $0.3 trillion). In that case, your graph should look like this:

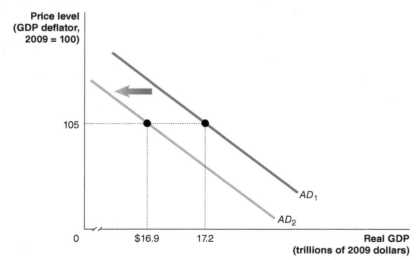

The graph shows a parallel shift in the aggregate demand curve so that at every price level, the quantity of real GDP demanded declines by $300 billion. For example, at a price level of 105, the quantity of real GDP demanded declines from $17.2 to $16.9 trillion.

Your Turn: For more practice, do related problems 1.8 at the end of this chapter.

Table 1 summarizes the most important variables that cause the aggregate demand curve to shift. The table shows the shift in the aggregate demand curve that results from an increase in each of the variables. A *decrease* in these variables would cause the aggregate demand curve to shift in the opposite direction.

Table 1

Variables That Shift the Aggregate Demand Curve

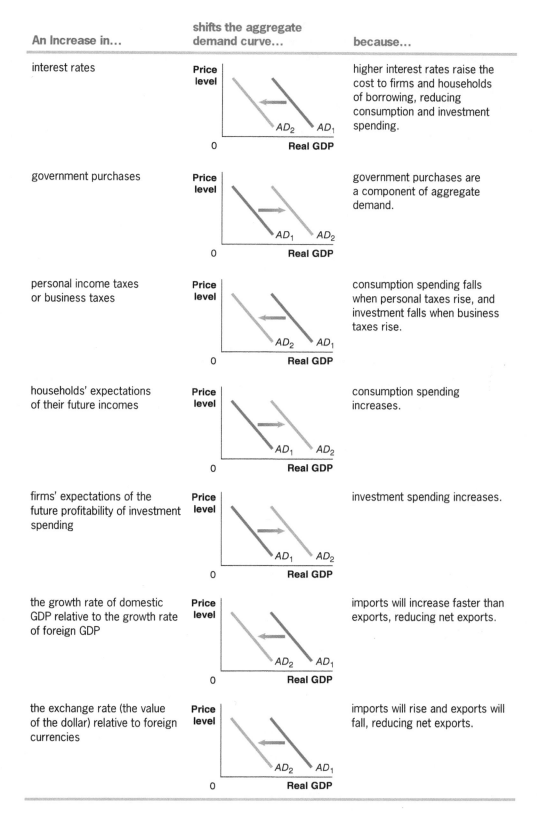

An Increase in...	shifts the aggregate demand curve...	because...
interest rates	Price level / AD₂ ← AD₁ / Real GDP	higher interest rates raise the cost to firms and households of borrowing, reducing consumption and investment spending.
government purchases	Price level / AD₁ → AD₂ / Real GDP	government purchases are a component of aggregate demand.
personal income taxes or business taxes	Price level / AD₂ ← AD₁ / Real GDP	consumption spending falls when personal taxes rise, and investment falls when business taxes rise.
households' expectations of their future incomes	Price level / AD₁ → AD₂ / Real GDP	consumption spending increases.
firms' expectations of the future profitability of investment spending	Price level / AD₁ → AD₂ / Real GDP	investment spending increases.
the growth rate of domestic GDP relative to the growth rate of foreign GDP	Price level / AD₂ ← AD₁ / Real GDP	imports will increase faster than exports, reducing net exports.
the exchange rate (the value of the dollar) relative to foreign currencies	Price level / AD₂ ← AD₁ / Real GDP	imports will rise and exports will fall, reducing net exports.

<table>
<tr><td>Making
the
Connection</td><td>**Which Components of Aggregate Demand Changed the Most during the 2007–2009 Recession?**</td></tr>
</table>

The recession of 2007–2009 was the longest and most severe since the Great Depression of the 1930s. We can gain some insight into the reasons for the length and severity of the 2007–2009 recession by looking at changes over time in the components of aggregate demand. In the following graphs, we show changes in three components of aggregate demand that showed the largest movements between the first quarter of 2005 and the second quarter of 2013: consumption, spending on residential construction, and net exports. The shaded areas represent the 2007–2009 recession. We know that potential GDP, or the level of GDP when all firms are producing at capacity, grows over time. So, economists are often interested in measuring changes in the components of aggregate demand *relative to potential GDP*, which is what we have done in these graphs.

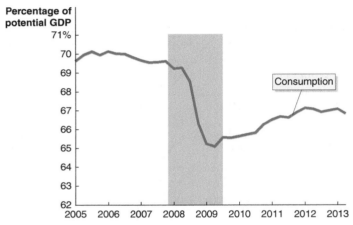

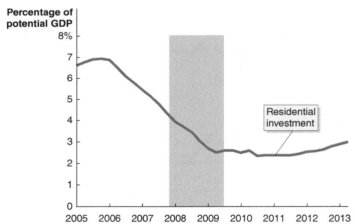

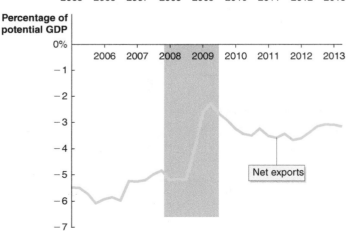

The graphs illustrate a number of facts about the 2007–2009 recession:

- In the two years before the beginning of the recession, spending on residential construction had already declined significantly relative to potential GDP.

- For the first two years following the end of the recession, spending on residential construction did not increase relative to potential GDP. Beginning in late 2011, spending on residential construction began to increase slowly, but in mid-2013, it was still far below its 2005–2006 levels.

- Consumption, which usually remains relatively stable during a recession, declined significantly relative to potential GDP during the recession and remained low four years after the recession had ended.

- Net exports increased during the recession. (Because net exports was negative throughout this period, it increased by becoming a smaller negative number.)

Although not shown in the graphs, business fixed investment and changes in business inventories—the nonresidential construction components of investment spending—actually rose relative to potential GDP during the recession. Government purchases remained fairly stable relative to potential GDP during the recession, before declining from late 2010 through mid-2013. Federal government purchases surged during the recession but declined in later years as temporary spending programs intended to fight the recession ended and Congress and the president cut spending further to address concerns over the federal budget deficit.

We can briefly account for the four facts listed above. The housing sector underwent a boom from 2002 to 2005, with rapid increases in both housing prices and spending on new housing. But the housing boom turned into a housing bust beginning in 2006, which explains the sharp decline in spending on residential construction. The continued low levels of spending on residential construction help explain why the recession was the longest since the Great Depression and why the economic expansion that began in June 2009 was relatively weak.

High levels of unemployment reduced household incomes and led to declines in consumption spending. In addition, many households increased their saving and paid off debts, further reducing consumption spending. The continuing low levels of consumption spending also contributed to the severity of the recession and the weakness of the following expansion. Finally, efforts by the Federal Reserve to reduce interest rates helped to lower the value of the U.S. dollar, thereby reducing the prices of U.S. exports and increasing the prices of foreign imports. The result was an increase in net exports.

Sources: U.S. Bureau of Economic Analysis; Congressional Budget Office; and S. Mitra Kalita, "Housing's Job Engine Falters," *Wall Street Journal*, October 5, 2011.

Your Turn: Test your understanding by doing related problem 1.9 at the end of this chapter.

Aggregate Supply

2 LEARNING OBJECTIVE

Identify the determinants of aggregate supply and distinguish between a movement along the short-run aggregate supply curve and a shift of the curve.

Having discussed aggregate demand, we now turn to aggregate supply, which shows the effect of changes in the price level on the quantity of goods and services that firms are willing and able to supply. Because the effect of changes in the price level on aggregate supply is very different in the short run from what it is in the long run, we use two aggregate supply curves: one for the short run and one for the long run. We start by considering the *long-run aggregate supply curve*.

The Long-Run Aggregate Supply Curve

In the long run, the level of real GDP is determined by the number of workers, the *capital stock*—including factories, office buildings, and machinery and equipment—and the available technology. Because changes in the price level do not affect the number of workers, the capital stock, or technology, *in the long run, changes in the price level do not affect the level of real GDP*. Remember that the level of real GDP in the

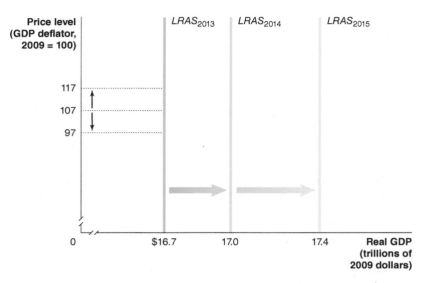

Figure 2

The Long-Run Aggregate Supply Curve

Changes in the price level do not affect the level of aggregate supply in the long run. Therefore, the long-run aggregate supply (*LRAS*) curve is a vertical line at the potential level of real GDP. For instance, the price level was 107 in 2013, and potential GDP was $16.7 trillion. If the price level had been 117, or if it had been 97, long-run aggregate supply would still have been a constant $16.7 trillion. Each year, the long-run aggregate supply curve shifts to the right, as the number of workers in the economy increases, more machinery and equipment are accumulated, and technological change occurs.

Long-run aggregate supply (*LRAS*) curve A curve that shows the relationship in the long run between the price level and the quantity of real GDP supplied.

long run is called *potential GDP*, or *full-employment GDP*. At potential GDP, firms will operate at their normal level of capacity, and everyone who wants a job will have one, except the structurally and frictionally unemployed. There is no reason for this normal level of capacity to change just because the price level has changed. The **long-run aggregate supply (*LRAS*) curve** shows the relationship in the long run between the price level and the quantity of real GDP supplied. As Figure 2 shows, in 2013, the price level was 107, and potential GDP was $16.7 trillion. If the price level had been 117, or if it had been 97, long-run aggregate supply would still have been a constant $16.7 trillion. Therefore, the *LRAS* curve is a vertical line.

Figure 2 also shows that the long-run aggregate supply curve shifts to the right each year. This shift occurs because potential GDP increases each year, as the number of workers in the economy increases, the economy accumulates more machinery and equipment, and technological change occurs. Figure 2 shows potential GDP increasing from $16.7 trillion in 2013 to $17.0 trillion in 2014 and to $17.4 trillion in 2015.

The Short-Run Aggregate Supply Curve

While the *LRAS* curve is vertical, the *SRAS* curve is upward sloping because, over the short run, as the price level increases, the quantity of goods and services firms are willing to supply will increase. The main reason firms behave this way is that, *as prices of final goods and services rise, prices of inputs—such as the wages of workers or the price of natural resources—rise more slowly.* Profits rise when the prices of goods and services firms sell rise more rapidly than the prices they pay for inputs. Therefore, a higher price level leads to higher profits and increases the willingness of firms to supply more goods and services. A secondary reason the *SRAS* curve slopes upward is that, as the price level rises or falls, some firms are slow to adjust their prices. A firm that is slow to raise its prices when the price level is increasing may find its sales increasing and, therefore, will increase production. A firm that is slow to reduce its prices when the price level is decreasing may find its sales falling and, therefore, will decrease production.

Why do some firms adjust prices more slowly than others, and why might the wages of workers and the prices of other inputs change more slowly than the prices of final goods and services? Most economists believe the explanation is that *some firms and workers fail to accurately predict changes in the price level.* If firms and workers could predict the future price level exactly, the short-run aggregate supply curve would be the same as the long-run aggregate supply curve.

But how does the failure of workers and firms to predict the price level accurately result in an upward-sloping *SRAS* curve? Economists are not in complete agreement on this point, but we can briefly discuss the three most common explanations:

1. Contracts make some wages and prices "sticky."
2. Firms are often slow to adjust wages.
3. Menu costs make some prices sticky.

Contracts Make Some Wages and Prices "Sticky" Prices or wages are said to be "sticky" when they do not respond quickly to changes in demand or supply. Contracts can make wages or prices sticky. For example, suppose United Parcel Service (UPS) negotiates a three-year contract with the Independent Pilots Association, the union for the pilots who fly the company's cargo planes, during a time when the economy is in recession and the volume of packages being shipped is falling. Suppose that after the union signs the contract, the economy begins to expand rapidly, and the volume of packages shipped increases, so that UPS can raise the rates it charges. UPS will find that shipping more packages will be profitable because the prices it charges are rising, while the wages it pays its pilots are fixed by contract. Or a steel mill might have signed a multiyear contract to buy coal, which is used in making steel, at a time when the demand for steel was stagnant. If steel demand and steel prices begin to rise rapidly, producing additional steel will be profitable because coal prices will remain fixed by contract. In both of these cases, rising prices lead to higher output. If these examples are representative of enough firms in the economy, a rising price level should lead to a greater quantity of goods and services supplied. In other words, the short-run aggregate supply curve will be upward sloping.

Notice, though, that if the pilots at UPS or the managers of the coal companies had accurately predicted what would happen to prices, this prediction would have been reflected in the contracts, and UPS and the steel mill would not have earned greater profits when prices rose. In that case, rising prices would not have led to higher output.

Firms Are Often Slow to Adjust Wages We just noted that the wages of many union workers remain fixed by contract for several years. Many nonunion workers have their wages or salaries adjusted only once a year. Suppose you accept a job at a management consulting firm in June, at a salary of $45,000 per year. The firm probably will not adjust your salary until the following June, even if the prices it can charge for its services later in the year are higher or lower than the firm had expected them to be when they hired you. If firms are slow to adjust wages, a rise in the price level will increase the profitability of hiring more workers and producing more output. A fall in the price level will decrease the profitability of hiring more workers and producing more output. Once again, we have an explanation for why the short-run aggregate supply curve slopes upward.

It is worth noting that firms are often slower to *cut* wages than to increase them. Cutting wages can have a negative effect on the morale and productivity of workers and can also cause some of a firm's best workers to quit and look for jobs elsewhere.

Making the Connection	**How Sticky Are Wages?**

We can assume that if the demand curve or supply curve for a product shifted, the price would adjust quickly from the old equilibrium to the new equilibrium. As we have just discussed, though, many economists argue that at least some wages and prices are sticky and do *not* adjust quickly to changes in demand or supply. Other economists argue that stickiness in wages and prices is not widespread enough to be important in macroeconomic analysis. In other words, these economists believe that the aggregate supply curve may be vertical in the short run, as well as in the long run.

Recently, a number of economists have looked closely at the evidence for wage stickiness. Each month, the Bureau of Labor Statistics (BLS) collects data on average hourly earnings for all workers and for various subcategories of workers, such as workers in manufacturing. These data are not the best way to measure wage stickiness, though, because each of the BLS categories contains many workers. As a result, the average hourly earnings data the BLS reports represent the average change in wages but do not show how many workers received wage increases, wage decreases, or unchanged wages or how large those changes may have been. To better understand how frequently employers change wages, economists have looked instead at data on individual workers.

Separate studies of data on individual workers have arrived at similar results. One important result from these studies is that during a recession, firms are much more likely to reduce wages offered to newly hired workers than to reduce wages paid to current workers in the same job. This result is consistent with the finding in a number of studies that firms are reluctant to cut the wages they pay current workers. For example, Mary C. Daly, Bart Hobijn, and Timothy Ni of the Federal Reserve Bank of San Francisco have shown that rather than cut wages during a recession, many firms reduce the raises they give workers, with more workers having their wages frozen, sometimes for long periods. The nominal wage is the number of dollars a firm pays a worker, while the real wage is the nominal wage divided by a price index. If a firm freezes a worker's nominal wage, the worker's real wage will gradually decline over time because of inflation. Most workers appear to be less upset if their real wage falls because of inflation than if it falls because of a cut in their nominal wage.

Daly, Hobijn, and Ni have used census data on individual workers to calculate the percentage of workers who each month were paid the same wage as they received in the same month during the previous year. The following figure shows these data for the years from 1996 through 2012. (The shaded areas are periods of recession.) Note that the percentage of workers with unchanged wages increases dramatically during recessions and the following months as the unemployment rate rises. Other researchers using data for other countries have also found that firms are reluctant to cut nominal wages during recessions but instead freeze workers' nominal wages and allow inflation to gradually reduce real wages.

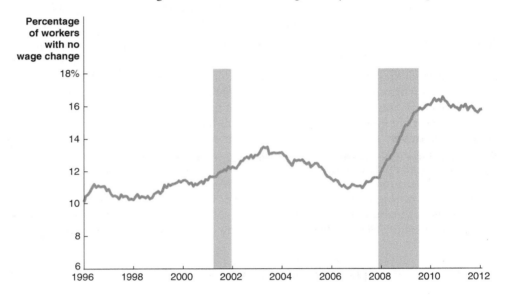

During recessions, why do firms often freeze nominal wages—frequently for extended periods—while at the same time laying off workers? Many economists believe that the main reason is that wage cuts upset workers. As a consequence, worker productivity may fall and some workers may quit to find new jobs, either immediately or once the economy improves and the unemployment rate falls. As Truman Bewley, an economist at Yale, puts it, "The advantage of layoffs over pay reductions was that they 'get misery out of the door.' "

Sources: Mary C. Daly, Bart Hobijn, and Timothy Ni, "The Path of Wage Growth and Unemployment," *Federal Reserve Bank of San Francisco Economic Letter*, July 15, 2013; Floyd Norris, "Median Pay in U.S. Is Stagnant, but Low-Paid Workers Lose," *New York Times*, April 26, 2013; Anabela Carneiro, Paulo Guimarães, and Pedro Portugal, "Real Wages and the Business Cycle: Worker, Firm, and Job Title Heterogeneity," *American Economic Review: Macroeconomics*, Vol. 4, No. 2, April 2012, pp. 133–152; Hervé Le Bihan, Jérémi Montornès, and Thomas Heckel, "Sticky Wage: Evidence from Quarterly Microeconomic Data," *American Economic Review: Macroeconomics*, Vol. 4, No. 3, July 2012, pp. 1–32; Alessando Barattieri, Susanto Basu, and Peter Gottschalk, "Some Evidence on the Importance of Sticky Wages," National Bureau of Economic Research Working Paper 16130, June 2010; and William T. Dickens et al., "How Wages Change: Micro Evidence from the International Wage Flexibility Project," *Journal of Economic Perspectives*, Vol. 21, No. 2, Spring 2007, pp. 195–214.

Your Turn: Test your understanding by doing related problem 2.13 at the end of this chapter.

Menu Costs Make Some Prices Sticky Firms base their prices today partly on what they expect future prices to be. For instance, if you own a restaurant, you will have to decide what prices to have printed on your menu. Similarly, many firms print catalogs that list the prices of their products. If demand for their products is higher or lower than the firms had expected, they may want to charge prices that are different from the ones printed in their menus or catalogs. Changing prices would be costly, however, because it would involve printing new menus or catalogs. The costs to firms of changing prices are called **menu costs**. To see why menu costs can lead to an upward-sloping short-run aggregate supply curve, consider the effect of an unexpected increase in the price level. In this case, firms will want to increase the prices they charge. Some firms, however, may not be willing to increase prices because of menu costs. Because their prices are now lower relative to competitors, these firms will find their sales increasing, which will cause them to increase output. Once again, a higher price level leads to a larger quantity of goods and services supplied.

Menu costs The costs to firms of changing prices.

Shifts of the Short-Run Aggregate Supply Curve versus Movements along It

Keep in mind the difference between a shift in a curve and a movement along a curve. The short-run aggregate supply curve tells us the short-run relationship between the price level and the quantity of goods and services firms are willing to supply, *holding constant all other variables that affect the willingness of firms to supply goods and services.* If the price level changes but other variables are unchanged, the economy will move up or down a stationary aggregate supply curve. If any variable other than the price level changes, the aggregate supply curve will shift.

Variables That Shift the Short-Run Aggregate Supply Curve

We now briefly discuss the five most important variables that cause the short-run aggregate supply curve to shift.

Increases in the Labor Force and in the Capital Stock A firm will supply more output at every price if it has more workers and more physical capital. The same is true of the economy as a whole. So, as the labor force and the capital stock grow, firms will supply more output at every price level, and the short-run aggregate supply curve will shift to the right. In Japan, the population is aging, and the labor force is decreasing. Holding other variables constant, this decrease in the labor force causes the short-run aggregate supply curve in Japan to shift to the left.

Technological Change As positive technological change takes place, the productivity of workers and machinery increases, which means firms can produce more goods and services with the same amount of labor and machinery. This increase in productivity reduces the firms' costs of production and allows them to produce more output at every price level. As a result, the short-run aggregate supply curve shifts to the right.

Expected Changes in the Future Price Level If workers and firms believe that the price level is going to increase by 3 percent during the next year, they will try to adjust their wages and prices accordingly. For instance, if a labor union believes there will be 3 percent inflation next year, it knows that wages must rise 3 percent to preserve the purchasing power of those wages. Similar adjustments by other workers and firms will result in costs increasing throughout the economy by 3 percent. The result, shown in Figure 3, is that the short-run aggregate supply curve will shift to the left, so that any level of real GDP is now associated with a price level that is 3 percent higher. In general, *if workers and firms expect the price level to increase by a certain percentage, the* SRAS *curve will shift by an equivalent amount*, holding constant all other variables that affect the SRAS curve.

Adjustments of Workers and Firms to Errors in Past Expectations about the Price Level Workers and firms sometimes make incorrect predictions about the price level. As time passes, they will attempt to compensate for these errors. Suppose

Figure 3

How Expectations of the Future Price Level Affect the Short-Run Aggregate Supply Curve

The *SRAS* curve shifts to reflect worker and firm expectations of future prices.

1. If workers and firms expect that the price level will rise by 3 percent, from 110.0 to 113.3, they will adjust their wages and prices by that amount.

2. Holding constant all other variables that affect aggregate supply, the short-run aggregate supply curve will shift to the left.

If workers and firms expect that the price level will be lower in the future, the short-run aggregate supply curve will shift to the right.

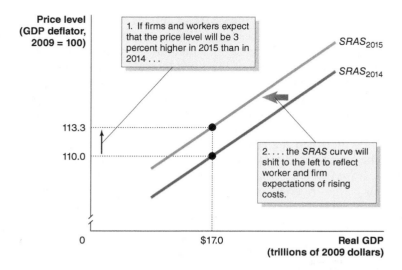

> 1. If firms and workers expect that the price level will be 3 percent higher in 2015 than in 2014 . . .

> 2. . . . the *SRAS* curve will shift to the left to reflect worker and firm expectations of rising costs.

Supply shock An unexpected event that causes the short-run aggregate supply curve to shift.

that the Independent Pilots Association signs a contract with UPS that provides for only small wage increases because the company and the union both expect only small increases in the price level. If increases in the price level turn out to be unexpectedly large, the union will take this into account when negotiating the next contract. The higher wages UPS pilots receive under the new contract will increase the company's costs and result in its needing to receive higher prices to produce the same level of output. If workers and firms across the economy are adjusting to the price level being higher than expected, the *SRAS* curve will shift to the left. If they are adjusting to the price level being lower than expected, the *SRAS* curve will shift to the right.

Unexpected Changes in the Price of an Important Natural Resource An unexpected event that causes the short-run aggregate supply curve to shift is called a **supply shock**. Supply shocks are often caused by unexpected increases or decreases in the prices of important natural resources that cause firms' costs to be different from what they had expected. Oil prices can be particularly volatile. Some firms use oil in the production process. Other firms use products, such as plastics, that are made from oil. If oil prices rise unexpectedly, the costs of production will rise for these firms. Some utilities also burn oil to generate electricity, so electricity prices will rise. Rising oil prices lead to rising gasoline prices, which raise transportation costs for many firms. Because firms face rising costs, they will supply the same level of output only if they receive higher prices, and the short-run aggregate supply curve will shift to the left.

Because the U.S. economy has experienced at least some inflation every year since the 1930s, workers and firms always expect next year's price level to be higher than this year's price level. Holding everything else constant, expectations of a higher price level will cause the *SRAS* curve to shift to the left. But everything else is not constant because every year, the U.S. labor force and the U.S. capital stock expand, and changes in technology occur, which cause the *SRAS* curve to shift to the right. Whether in any particular year the *SRAS* curve shifts to the left or to the right depends on how large an effect these variables have during that year.

Table 2 summarizes the most important variables that cause the *SRAS* curve to shift. The table shows the shift in the *SRAS* curve that results from an *increase* in each of the variables. A *decrease* in these variables would cause the *SRAS* curve to shift in the opposite direction.

3 LEARNING OBJECTIVE

Use the aggregate demand and aggregate supply model to illustrate the difference between short-run and long-run macroeconomic equilibrium.

Macroeconomic Equilibrium in the Long Run and the Short Run

Now that we have discussed the components of the aggregate demand and aggregate supply model, we can use it to analyze changes in real GDP and the price level. In Figure 4, we bring the aggregate demand curve, the short-run aggregate supply curve, and the long-run aggregate supply curve together in one graph, to show the *long-run*

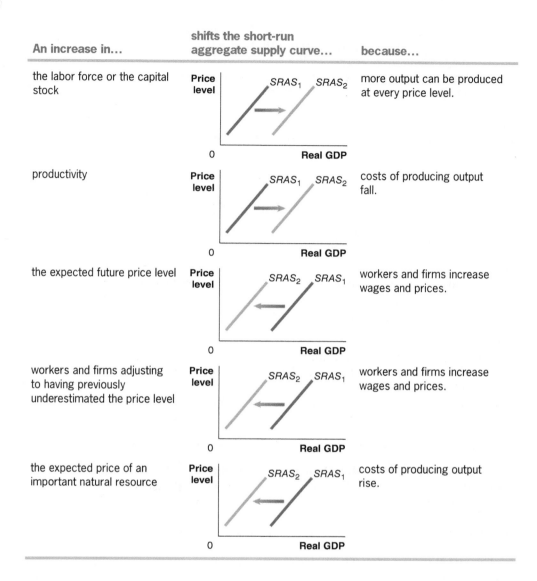

An increase in...	shifts the short-run aggregate supply curve...	because...
the labor force or the capital stock		more output can be produced at every price level.
productivity		costs of producing output fall.
the expected future price level		workers and firms increase wages and prices.
workers and firms adjusting to having previously underestimated the price level		workers and firms increase wages and prices.
the expected price of an important natural resource		costs of producing output rise.

Table 2

Variables That Shift the Short-Run Aggregate Supply Curve

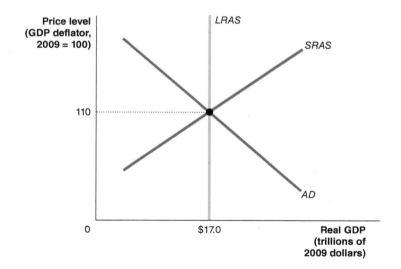

Figure 4

Long-Run Macroeconomic Equilibrium

In long-run macroeconomic equilibrium, the *AD* and *SRAS* curves intersect at a point on the *LRAS* curve. In this case, equilibrium occurs at real GDP of $17.0 trillion and a price level of 110.

macroeconomic equilibrium for the economy. In the figure, equilibrium occurs at real GDP of $17.0 trillion and a price level of 110. Notice that in long-run equilibrium, the short-run aggregate supply curve and the aggregate demand curve intersect at a point on the long-run aggregate supply curve. Because equilibrium occurs at a point along the long-run aggregate supply curve, we know the economy is at potential GDP: Firms will be operating at their normal level of capacity, and everyone who wants a job will have one, except the structurally and frictionally unemployed. We know, however, that the economy is often not in long-run macroeconomic equilibrium. In the following section, we discuss the economic forces that can push the economy away from long-run equilibrium.

Recessions, Expansions, and Supply Shocks

Because the full analysis of the aggregate demand and aggregate supply model can be complicated, we begin with a simplified case, using two assumptions:

1. The economy has not been experiencing any inflation. The price level is currently 110, and workers and firms expect it to remain at 110 in the future.

2. The economy is not experiencing any long-run growth. Potential GDP is $17.0 trillion and will remain at that level in the future.

These assumptions are simplifications because in reality, the U.S. economy has experienced at least some inflation every year since the 1930s, and potential GDP also increases every year. However, the assumptions allow us to understand more easily the key ideas of the aggregate demand and aggregate supply model. In this section, we examine the short-run and long-run effects of recessions, expansions, and supply shocks.

Recession

The Short-Run Effect of a Decline in Aggregate Demand Suppose that rising interest rates cause firms to reduce spending on factories and equipment and cause households to reduce spending on new homes. The decline in investment that results will shift the aggregate demand curve to the left, from AD_1 to AD_2, as shown in Figure 5. The economy moves from point A to a new *short-run macroeconomic equilibrium*, where the AD_2 curve intersects the $SRAS_1$ curve at point B. In the new short-run equilibrium, real GDP has declined from $17.0 trillion to $16.8 trillion and is below its potential level. This lower level of GDP will result in declining profitability for many firms and layoffs for some workers: The economy will be in recession.

Adjustment Back to Potential GDP in the Long Run We know that a recession will eventually end because there are forces at work that push the economy back to potential GDP in the long run. Figure 5 shows how the economy moves from recession back to potential GDP. The shift from AD_1 to AD_2 initially leads to a short-run equilibrium, with the price level having fallen from 110 to 108 (point B). Workers and firms will begin to adjust to the price level being lower than they had expected it to be. Workers will be willing to accept lower wages—because each dollar of wages is able to buy more goods and services—and firms will be willing to accept lower prices. In addition, the unemployment resulting from the recession will make workers more willing to accept lower wages, and the decline in demand will make firms more willing to accept lower prices. As a result, the $SRAS$ curve will shift to the right, from $SRAS_1$ to $SRAS_2$. At this point, the economy will be back in long-run equilibrium (point C). The shift from $SRAS_1$ to $SRAS_2$ will not happen instantly. It may take the economy several years to return to potential GDP. The important conclusion is that a decline in aggregate demand causes a recession in the short run, but in the long run it causes only a decline in the price level.

Economists refer to the process of adjustment back to potential GDP just described as an *automatic mechanism* because it occurs without any actions by the government. An alternative to waiting for the automatic mechanism to end a recession

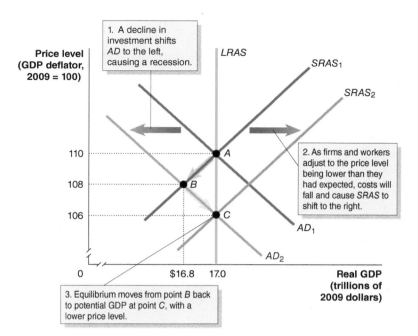

1. A decline in investment shifts AD to the left, causing a recession.

2. As firms and workers adjust to the price level being lower than they had expected, costs will fall and cause SRAS to shift to the right.

3. Equilibrium moves from point B back to potential GDP at point C, with a lower price level.

Figure 5

The Short-Run and Long-Run Effects of a Decrease in Aggregate Demand

In the short run, a decrease in aggregate demand causes a recession. In the long run, it causes only a decline in the price level.

is for the government to use monetary and fiscal policy to shift the AD curve to the right and restore potential GDP more quickly. Economists debate whether it is better to wait for the automatic mechanism to end recessions or whether it is better to use monetary policy and fiscal policy.

Making the Connection | Does It Matter What Causes a Decline in Aggregate Demand?

We have seen that GDP has four components and that a decrease in any of them can cause the aggregate demand curve to shift to the left, bringing on a recession. In practice, most recessions in the United States since World War II have begun with a decline in residential construction. Edward Leamer of the University of California, Los Angeles has gone so far as to argue that "housing *is* the business cycle," meaning that declines in residential construction are the most important reason for the declines in aggregate demand that lead to recessions. The shaded periods in the following graph represent recessions. The graph shows that spending on residential construction has declined prior to every recession since 1955.

The collapse in spending on housing added to the severity of the 2007–2009 recession.

The following graph shows again a fact that we noted earlier in this chapter: The decline in residential construction during the 2007–2009 recession was particularly severe. Spending on residential construction declined by almost 60 percent from the fourth quarter of 2005 to the second quarter of 2010. Largely because of these problems in the housing sector, the decline in real GDP during the recession of 2007–2009 was larger than during any other recession since the Great Depression of the 1930s.

What causes declines in spending on residential construction, and why was the decline that preceded the 2007–2009 recession so severe? Late in a business cycle expansion, the inflation rate and interest rates start to increase. Higher interest rates often result from monetary policy actions as the Federal Reserve tries to slow down the economy and reduce the rate of inflation. Higher interest rates reduce consumer demand for new houses by increasing the cost of loans.

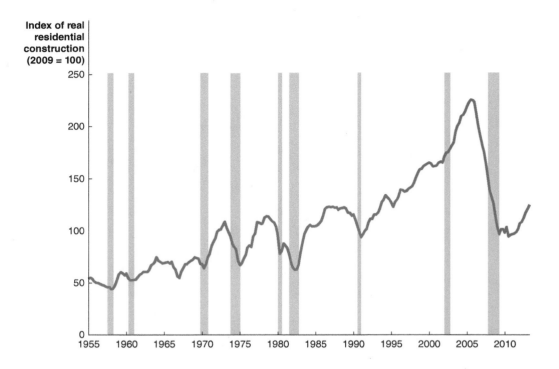

But the collapse in residential construction prior to and during the recession of 2007–2009 was due more to the deflating of the "housing bubble" of 2002–2005 and to the financial crisis that began in 2007 than to higher interest rates. We will discuss both the housing bubble and the financial crisis later in this chapter. At this point, we can note that research by Carmen M. Reinhart and Kenneth S. Rogoff of Harvard University shows that declines in aggregate demand that result from financial crises tend to be larger and more long lasting than declines due to other factors. So, the experience of 2007–2009 indicates that, in fact, the source of the decline in aggregate demand can be important in determining the severity of a recession.

Sources: Edward E. Leamer, "Housing Is the Business Cycle," in *Housing, Housing Finance, and Monetary Policy*, Federal Reserve Bank of Kansas City, August 2007; Carmen M. Reinhart and Kenneth S. Rogoff, "The Aftermath of Financial Crises," *American Economic Review*, Vol. 99, No. 2, May 2009, pp. 466–472; and U.S. Bureau of Economic Analysis.

Your Turn: Test your understanding by doing related problem 3.7 at the end of this chapter.

Expansion

The Short-Run Effect of an Increase in Aggregate Demand Suppose that instead of becoming pessimistic, many firms become optimistic about the future profitability of new investment, as happened during the information technology and telecommunications booms of the late 1990s. The resulting increase in investment will shift the *AD* curve to the right, as shown in Figure 6. Equilibrium moves from point *A* to point *B*. Real GDP rises from $17.0 trillion to $17.3 trillion, and the price level rises from 110 to 113. Real GDP will be above potential GDP: Firms are operating beyond their normal level of capacity, and some workers who would ordinarily be structurally or frictionally unemployed or who would not be in the labor force are employed.

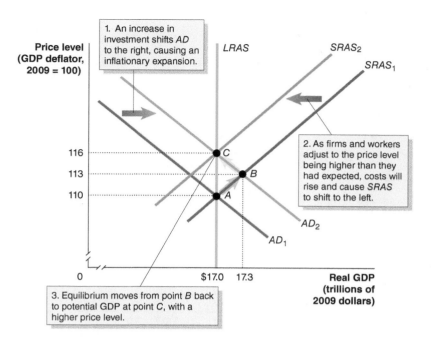

Figure 6

The Short-Run and Long-Run Effects of an Increase in Aggregate Demand

In the short run, an increase in aggregate demand causes an increase in real GDP. In the long run, it causes only an increase in the price level.

Adjustment Back to Potential GDP in the Long Run

Just as an automatic mechanism brings the economy back to potential GDP from a recession, an automatic mechanism brings the economy back from a short-run equilibrium beyond potential GDP. Figure 6 illustrates this mechanism. The shift from AD_1 to AD_2 initially leads to a short-run equilibrium, with the price level rising from 110 to 113 (point B). Workers and firms will begin to adjust to the price level being higher than they had expected. Workers will push for higher wages—because each dollar of wages is able to buy fewer goods and services—and firms will charge higher prices. In addition, the low levels of unemployment resulting from the expansion will make it easier for workers to negotiate for higher wages, and the increase in demand will make it easier for firms to receive higher prices. As a result, the SRAS curve will shift to the left, from $SRAS_1$ to $SRAS_2$. At this point, the economy will be back in long-run equilibrium. Once again, the shift from $SRAS_1$ to $SRAS_2$ will not happen instantly. The process of returning to potential GDP may stretch out for more than a year.

Supply Shock

The Short-Run Effect of a Supply Shock Suppose oil prices increase substantially. This supply shock will increase many firms' costs and cause the SRAS curve to shift to the left, as shown in panel (a) of Figure 7. Notice that the price level is higher in the new short-run equilibrium (112 rather than 110), but real GDP is lower ($16.7 trillion rather than $17.0 trillion). This unpleasant combination of inflation and recession is called **stagflation**.

Stagflation A combination of inflation and recession, usually resulting from a supply shock.

Adjustment Back to Potential GDP in the Long Run The recession caused by a supply shock increases unemployment and reduces output. Workers will eventually be willing to accept lower wages and firms will be willing to accept lower prices. In panel (b) of Figure 7, the short-run aggregate supply curve shifts from $SRAS_2$ to $SRAS_1$, moving equilibrium from point B back to point A. Real GDP is back to potential GDP at the original price level. It may take several years for this process to be completed. An alternative would be to use monetary and fiscal policy to shift the aggregate demand curve to the right. Using policy in this way would bring real GDP back to potential GDP more quickly but would result in a permanently higher price level.

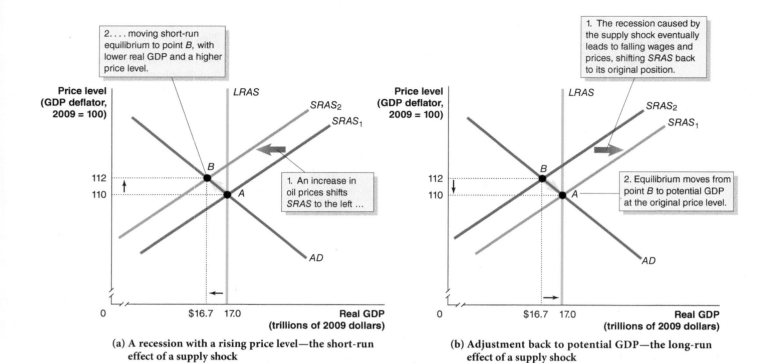

(a) A recession with a rising price level—the short-run effect of a supply shock

(b) Adjustment back to potential GDP—the long-run effect of a supply shock

Figure 7 The Short-Run and Long-Run Effects of a Supply Shock

Panel (a) shows that a supply shock, such as a large increase in oil prices, will cause a recession and a higher price level in the short run. The recession caused by the supply shock increases unemployment and reduces output.

Panel (b) shows that rising unemployment and falling output result in workers being willing to accept lower wages and firms being willing to accept lower prices. The short-run aggregate supply curve shifts from $SRAS_2$ to $SRAS_1$. Equilibrium moves from point B back to potential GDP and the original price level at point A.

In 2011, Alan Krueger, who was then the chair of the Council of Economic Advisers in the Obama administration, provided an estimate of how long the economy would take to return to potential GDP.

Making the Connection

How Long Does It Take to Return to Potential GDP? Economic Forecasts Following the Recession of 2007–2009

Making accurate macroeconomic forecasts is difficult. As we have seen, many factors can cause aggregate demand or aggregate supply to shift. Because it is challenging to predict how much aggregate demand and aggregate supply will shift, economists often have difficulty predicting the beginning and end of a recession. The Federal Reserve, foreign central banks, other government agencies, large banks, forecasting firms, and academic economists use a variety of forecasting models to predict changes in GDP. Most forecasting models consist of equations that represent the macroeconomic relationships—such as the relationship between disposable income and consumption spending—that underlie the aggregate demand and aggregate supply model. After economists have statistically estimated the equations using economic data, they can use the models to forecast values for GDP and the price level.

Most economists agree that an automatic mechanism brings the economy back to potential GDP in the long run. But how long is the long run? When the recession of 2007–2009 ended in June 2009, real GDP was far from potential GDP. Even two years later, in mid-2011, real GDP remained more than 7 percent below potential GDP. How long would it take for real GDP to finally return to potential GDP from that point? The following figure shows the Congressional Budget Office's (CBO) estimates of potential GDP along with three forecasts of real GDP made in 2011 by the following:

- Economists on the president's staff at the White House
- Officials at the Federal Reserve
- Economists at the CBO

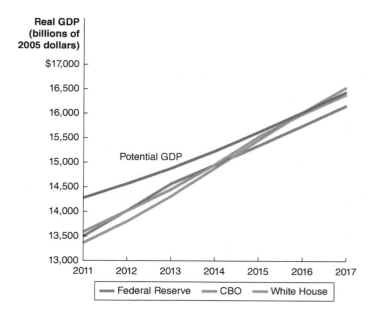

The forecasts of the White House and the CBO agreed that real GDP would not return to potential GDP until 2016. The projections of the Federal Reserve were even more pessimistic, with real GDP remaining below potential GDP in 2017. These forecasts indicate how severe the 2007–2009 recession was because real GDP was not expected to return to potential GDP until seven years after the end of the recession. Prior to the 2007–2009 recession, the recession of 1981–1982 had been the most severe since the Great Depression. Yet it took less than three years after the end of that recession for real GDP to return to potential GDP.

How accurate were these forecasts? Pessimistic as they seem, in mid-2013 they appear to have been too *optimistic*. Economists refer to the percentage difference between real GDP and potential GDP as the *output gap*. The table shows the 2011 forecasts of the output gap and the actual output gap as of the end of June 2013.

2011 Estimates of 2013 Output Gap			Actual Output Gap
White House	CBO	Federal Reserve	
3.8%	2.7%	2.1%	5.4%

The actual output gap was about twice as large as the CBO or the Fed had forecast and nearly 45 percent larger than the White House had forecast.

Note: The Federal Reserve's forecast uses averages of the forecasts of the individual members of the Federal Open Market Committee.

Sources: Board of Governors of the Federal Reserve System, "Economic Projections of Federal Reserve Board Members and Federal Reserve Bank Presidents, April 2011," April 27, 2011; Congressional Budget Office, "Data Underlying Selected Economic Figures, Real Gross Domestic Product, 1980–2021," January 27, 2011; and Office of Management and Budget, "Budget of the U.S. Government, Fiscal Year 2012, Mid-Session Review," September 1, 2011.

Your Turn: Test your understanding by doing related problem 3.10 at the end of this chapter.

4 LEARNING OBJECTIVE

Use the dynamic aggregate demand and aggregate supply model to analyze macroeconomic conditions.

A Dynamic Aggregate Demand and Aggregate Supply Model*

The basic aggregate demand and aggregate supply model used so far in this chapter provides important insights into how short-run macroeconomic equilibrium is determined. Unfortunately, the model also provides some misleading results. For instance, it incorrectly predicts that a recession caused by the aggregate demand curve shifting to the left will result in a lower price level, which has not happened for an entire year since the 1930s. The difficulty with the basic model arises because we assumed: (1) The economy does not experience continuing inflation, and (2) the economy does not experience long-run growth. We can develop a more useful aggregate demand and aggregate supply model by dropping these assumptions. The result will be a model that takes into account that the economy is not *static*, with an unchanging level of potential GDP and no continuing inflation, but *dynamic*, with potential GDP that grows over time and inflation that continues every year. We can create a *dynamic aggregate demand and aggregate supply model* by making changes to the basic model that incorporate the following important macroeconomic facts:

- Potential GDP increases continually, shifting the long-run aggregate supply curve to the right.

- During most years, the aggregate demand curve shifts to the right.

- Except during periods when workers and firms expect high rates of inflation, the short-run aggregate supply curve shifts to the right.

Figure 8 illustrates how incorporating these macroeconomic facts changes the basic aggregate demand and aggregate supply model. We start with $SRAS_1$ and AD_1 intersecting at point A, at a price level of 110 and real GDP of $17.0 trillion. Because this intersection occurs at a point on $LRAS_1$, we know the economy is in long-run equilibrium. We show the long-run aggregate supply curve shifting to the right, from $LRAS_1$ to $LRAS_2$, because during the year, potential GDP increases as the U.S. labor force and the U.S. capital stock increase and technological progress occurs. The short-run aggregate supply curve shifts from $SRAS_1$ to $SRAS_2$ because the same variables that cause the long-run aggregate supply curve to shift to the right will also increase the quantity of goods and services that firms are willing to supply in the short run. Finally, the aggregate demand curve shifts to the right, from AD_1 to AD_2. The aggregate demand curve shifts for several reasons: As the population grows and incomes rise, consumption will increase over time. As the economy grows, firms will expand capacity, and new firms will be formed, increasing investment. An expanding population and an expanding economy require increased government services, such as more police officers and teachers, so government purchases will increase.

The new equilibrium in Figure 8 occurs at point B, where AD_2 intersects $SRAS_2$ on $LRAS_2$. In the new equilibrium, the price level remains at 110, while real GDP increases to $17.4 trillion. Notice that there has been no inflation because the price level is unchanged, at 110. There has been no inflation because aggregate demand and aggregate supply shifted to the right by exactly as much as long-run aggregate supply. In fact, though, we wouldn't expect that all three curves will typically shift by the same amount. For instance, the $SRAS$ curve is also affected by workers' and firms' expectations of future changes in the price level and by supply shocks. These variables can partially or completely offset the normal tendency of the $SRAS$ curve to shift to the right over the course of a year. We also know that changes in the expenditures of consumers, firms, and the government may result in the AD curve shifting to the right by more or less than the $SRAS$ and $LRAS$ curves. In fact, as we will see shortly, *changes in the price level and in real GDP in the short run are determined by how much the* SRAS *and* AD *curves shift.*

*This section may be omitted without loss of continuity.

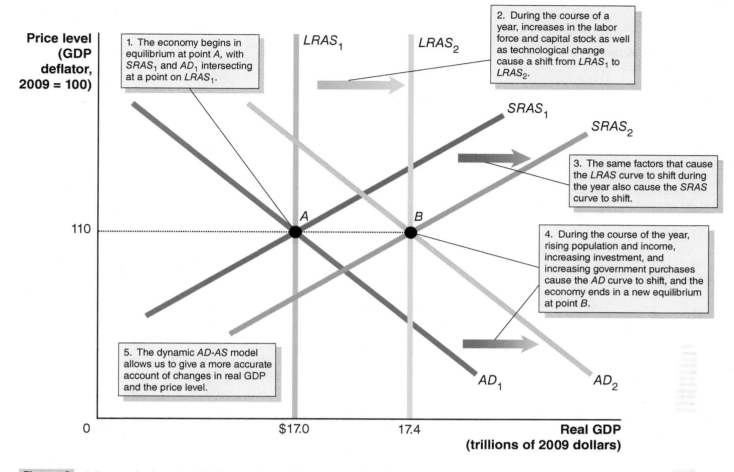

Price level (GDP deflator, 2009 = 100)

1. The economy begins in equilibrium at point *A*, with *SRAS₁* and *AD₁* intersecting at a point on *LRAS₁*.

2. During the course of a year, increases in the labor force and capital stock as well as technological change cause a shift from *LRAS₁* to *LRAS₂*.

3. The same factors that cause the *LRAS* curve to shift during the year also cause the *SRAS* curve to shift.

4. During the course of the year, rising population and income, increasing investment, and increasing government purchases cause the *AD* curve to shift, and the economy ends in a new equilibrium at point *B*.

5. The dynamic *AD-AS* model allows us to give a more accurate account of changes in real GDP and the price level.

LRAS₁   *LRAS₂*   *SRAS₁*   *SRAS₂*   *AD₁*   *AD₂*

110

0   $17.0   17.4   **Real GDP (trillions of 2009 dollars)**

Figure 8   **A Dynamic Aggregate Demand and Aggregate Supply Model**

We start with the basic aggregate demand and aggregate supply model. In the dynamic model, increases in the labor force and capital stock as well as technological change cause long-run aggregate supply to shift over the course of a year, from *LRAS₁* to *LRAS₂*. Typically, these same factors cause short-run aggregate supply to shift from *SRAS₁* to *SRAS₂*. Aggregate demand will shift from *AD₁* to *AD₂* if, as is usually the case, spending by consumers, firms, and the government increases during the year.

What Is the Usual Cause of Inflation?

The dynamic aggregate demand and aggregate supply model provides a more accurate explanation of the source of most inflation. If total spending in the economy grows faster than total production, prices rise. Figure 9 illustrates this point by showing that if the *AD* curve shifts to the right by more than the *LRAS* curve, inflation results because equilibrium occurs at a higher price level, point *B*. In the new equilibrium, the *SRAS* curve has shifted to the right by less than the *LRAS* curve because the anticipated increase in prices offsets some of the effect of the technological change and increases in the labor force and capital stock that occur during the year. Although inflation generally results from total spending growing faster than total production, a shift to the left of the short-run aggregate supply curve can also cause an increase in the price level, as we saw earlier in discussing supply shocks.

As we saw in Figure 8, if aggregate demand increases by the same amount as short-run and long-run aggregate supply, the price level will not change. In this case, the economy experiences economic growth without inflation.

The Recession of 2007–2009

We can use the dynamic aggregate demand and aggregate supply model to analyze the recession of 2007–2009. The recession began in December 2007, with the end of the

Figure 9

Using Dynamic Aggregate Demand and Aggregate Supply to Understand Inflation

The most common cause of inflation is total spending increasing faster than total production.

1. The economy begins at point *A*, with real GDP of $17.0 trillion and a price level of 110. An increase in full-employment real GDP from $17.0 trillion to $17.4 trillion causes long-run aggregate supply to shift from *LRAS*₁ to *LRAS*₂. Aggregate demand shifts from *AD*₁ to *AD*₂.

2. Because *AD* shifts to the right by more than the *LRAS* curve, the price level in the new equilibrium rises from 110 to 114.

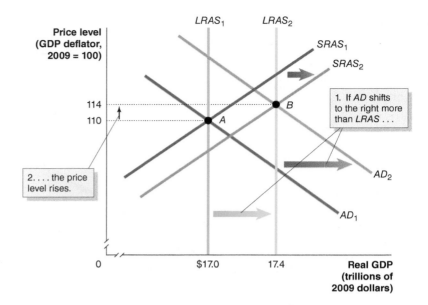

economic expansion that started in November 2001. Several factors combined to cause the recession:

- *The end of the housing bubble.* The figure in the *Making the Connection: Does It Matter What Causes a Decline in Aggregate Demand?* shows that spending on residential construction increased rapidly from 2002 to 2005, before declining more than 60 percent between the end of 2005 and the beginning of 2010. The increase in spending on housing was partly the result of actions the Federal Reserve had taken to lower interest rates during and after the recession of 2001. As interest rates on mortgage loans declined, more consumers began to buy new homes. But by 2005 it was clear that a speculative bubble was partly responsible for the rapidly rising prices of both newly built and existing homes. A bubble occurs when people become less concerned with the underlying value of an asset—either a physical asset, such as a house, or a financial asset, such as a stock—and focus instead on expectations of the price of the asset increasing. In some areas of the country, such as California, Arizona, and Florida, many homes were purchased by investors who intended to resell them for higher prices than they paid for them and did not intend to live in them. Some popular television programs explored ways that people could "flip" houses by buying and quickly reselling them. Speculative bubbles eventually end, and the housing bubble started to deflate in 2006. Both new home sales and housing prices began to decline. The growth of aggregate demand slowed as spending on residential construction—a component of investment spending—fell.

- *The financial crisis.* Problems in the housing market were bad news for workers and firms involved with residential construction. In addition, falling housing prices led to an increased number of borrowers defaulting on their mortgage loans. These defaults caused banks and some other financial institutions to suffer heavy losses. Beginning in the spring of 2008, the U.S. Department of the Treasury and the Federal Reserve intervened to save several large financial institutions from bankruptcy. For now we can note that the financial crisis led to a *credit crunch* that made it difficult for many households and firms to obtain the loans they needed to finance their spending. This drying up of credit contributed to declines in consumption spending and investment spending.

- *The rapid increase in oil prices during 2008.* Oil prices, which had been as low as $34 per barrel in 2004, had risen to $140 per barrel by mid-2008. The increase in the price of oil appeared to be caused by increased demand in rapidly growing economies, particularly India and China, and by the difficulty in developing new supplies of oil in the short run. With the deepening of the recession, worldwide demand for oil declined, and oil prices fell to about $40 per barrel in early 2009. As we have seen in this chapter, rising oil prices can result in a *supply shock* that causes the short-run aggregate supply curve to shift to the left, increasing the severity of the recession.

Figure 10 illustrates the beginning of the recession by showing the economy's short-run macroeconomic equilibrium in 2007 and 2008. In the figure, short-run equilibrium for 2007 occurs where AD_{2007} intersects $SRAS_{2007}$ at real GDP of $14.88 trillion and a price level of 97.3. Real GDP in 2007 was above potential GDP of $14.84 trillion, shown by $LRAS_{2007}$. During 2008, aggregate demand shifted to the right, from AD_{2007} to AD_{2008}. Aggregate demand increased by less than potential GDP because of the negative effects of the bursting of the housing bubble and the financial crisis on consumption spending and investment spending. The supply shock from higher oil prices caused short-run aggregate supply to shift to the left, from $SRAS_{2007}$ to $SRAS_{2008}$. Short-run equilibrium for 2008 occurred at real GDP of $14.83 trillion and a price level of 99.2. A large gap opened between short-run equilibrium real GDP and potential GDP. Not surprisingly, unemployment rose from 4.6 percent in 2007 to 5.8 percent in 2008. The price level increased only from 97.3 to 99.2, so the inflation rate was a low 2.0 percent.

The recession persisted into 2009, as potential GDP increased to $15.53 trillion, while real GDP fell to $14.42 trillion. (The situation in 2009 is not shown in Figure 10.) The increased gap between real GDP and potential GDP caused the unemployment rate to soar to 9.3 percent—the highest unemployment rate since the recession of 1981–1982 and the second highest since the Great Depression of the 1930s. Although the recession ended in June 2009, real GDP grew only slowly during 2010 and 2011, leaving the unemployment rate above 8.5 percent.

The severity of the recession of 2007–2009 resulted in some of the most dramatic changes in government economic policy since the Great Depression.

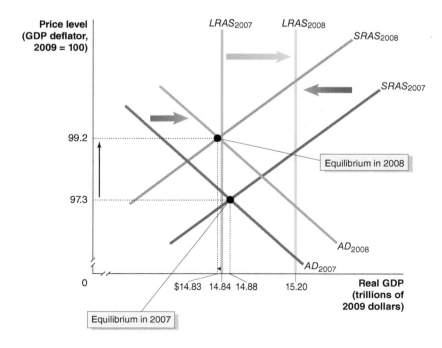

Figure 10

The Beginning of the Recession of 2007–2009

Between 2007 and 2008, the *AD* curve shifted to the right, but not by nearly enough to offset the shift to the right of the *LRAS* curve, which represented the increase in potential GDP from $14.84 trillion to $15.20 trillion. Because of a sharp increase in oil prices, short-run aggregate supply shifted to the left, from $SRAS_{2007}$ to $SRAS_{2008}$. Real GDP decreased from $14.88 trillion in 2007 to $14.83 trillion in 2008, which was far below the potential GDP, shown by $LRAS_{2008}$. Because the increase in aggregate demand was small, the price level increased only from 97.3 in 2007 to 99.2 in 2008, so the inflation rate for 2008 was only 2.0 percent.

Solved Problem 4

Showing the Oil Shock of 1974–1975 on a Dynamic Aggregate Demand and Aggregate Supply Graph

The 1974–1975 recession clearly illustrates how a supply shock affects the economy. Following the Arab–Israeli War of 1973, the Organization of the Petroleum Exporting Countries (OPEC) took actions that increased the price of a barrel of oil from less than $3 to more than $10. Use this information and the statistics in the following table to draw a dynamic aggregate demand and aggregate supply graph showing macroeconomic equilibrium for 1974 and 1975. Assume that the aggregate demand curve did not shift between 1974 and 1975. Provide a brief explanation of your graph.

	Actual Real GDP	Potential GDP	Price Level
1974	$5.39 trillion	$5.42 trillion	28.7
1975	$5.38 trillion	$5.61 trillion	31.4

Sources: U.S. Bureau of Economic Analysis; and Federal Reserve Bank of St. Louis.

Solving the Problem

Step 1: **Review the chapter material.** This problem is about applying the dynamic aggregate demand and aggregate supply model, so you may want to review the section "A Dynamic Aggregate Demand and Aggregate Supply Model."

Step 2: **Use the information in the table to draw the graph.** You need to draw five curves: SRAS and LRAS for both 1974 and 1975 and AD, which is the same for both years. You know that the two LRAS curves will be vertical lines at the values given for potential GDP in the table. Because of the large supply shock, you know that the SRAS curve shifted to the left. The problem says to assume that the AD curve did not shift. Your graph should look like this one:

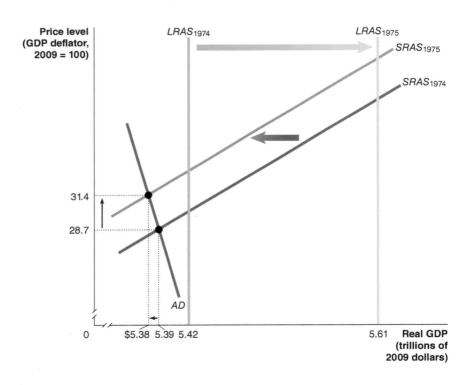

Step 3: **Explain your graph.** $LRAS_{1974}$ and $LRAS_{1975}$ are at the levels of potential GDP for each year. Macroeconomic equilibrium for 1974 occurs where the AD curve intersects the $SRAS_{1974}$ curve, with real GDP of $5.39 trillion and a price level of 28.7. Macroeconomic equilibrium for 1975 occurs where the AD curve intersects the $SRAS_{1975}$ curve, with real GDP of $5.38 trillion and a price level of 31.4.

Extra Credit: As a result of the supply shock, equilibrium real GDP moved from being just below potential GDP in 1974 (the recession actually began right at the end of 1973) to well below potential GDP in 1975. With real GDP in 1975 about 4.1 percent below its potential level, the unemployment rate soared from 5.6 percent in 1974 to 8.5 percent in 1975.

Your Turn: For more practice, do related problems 4.5 and 4.6 at the end of this chapter.

Continued

Economics in Your Life

Is an Employer Likely to Cut Your Pay during a Recession?

At the beginning of this chapter, we asked you to consider whether during a recession your employer is likely to reduce your pay and cut the prices of the products he or she sells. We have seen that even during a recession, the price level rarely falls. In fact, in the United States, the GDP deflator has not fallen for an entire year since the 1930s. Although some firms reduced prices during the recession of 2007–2009, most firms did not. So, the owner of the coffeehouse where you work will probably not cut the price of lattes unless sales have declined drastically. We also saw that most firms are more reluctant to cut wages than to increase them because wage cuts can have a negative effect on worker morale and productivity. Because the recession of 2007–2009 was particularly severe, some firms did cut wages. But given that you are a highly skilled barista, your employer is unlikely to cut your wages for fear that you might quit and work for a competitor.

Conclusion

This chapter showed that we need a different model to explain the behavior of the whole economy. We saw that the macroeconomic model of aggregate demand and aggregate supply explains fluctuations in real GDP and the price level.

Fluctuations in real GDP, employment, and the price level have led the federal government to implement macroeconomic policies.

Visit MyEconLab for a news article and analysis related to the concepts in this chapter.

Chapter Summary and Problems

Key Terms

Aggregate demand (*AD*) curve

Aggregate demand and aggregate supply model

Fiscal policy

Long-run aggregate supply (*LRAS*) curve

Menu costs

Monetary policy

Short-run aggregate supply (*SRAS*) curve

Stagflation

Supply shock

 1 **Aggregate Demand**

LEARNING OBJECTIVE: Identify the determinants of aggregate demand and distinguish between a movement along the aggregate demand curve and a shift of the curve.

Summary

The **aggregate demand and aggregate supply model** enables us to explain short-run fluctuations in real GDP and the price level. The **aggregate demand curve** shows the relationship between the price level and the level of planned aggregate expenditures by households, firms, and the government. The **short-run aggregate supply curve** shows the relationship in the short run between the price level and the quantity of real GDP supplied by firms. The **long-run aggregate supply curve** shows the relationship in the long run between the price level and the quantity of real GDP supplied. The four components of aggregate demand are consumption (*C*), investment (*I*), government purchases (*G*), and net exports (*NX*). The aggregate demand curve is downward sloping because a decline in the price level causes consumption, investment, and net exports to increase. If the price level changes but all else remains constant, the result is a movement up or down a stationary aggregate demand curve. If any variable other than the price level changes, the aggregate demand curve will shift. The variables that cause the aggregate demand curve to shift are divided into three categories: changes in government policies, changes in the expectations of households and firms, and changes in foreign variables. For example, **monetary policy** involves the actions the Federal Reserve takes to manage the money supply and interest rates to pursue macroeconomic policy objectives. When the Federal Reserve takes actions to change interest rates, consumption and investment spending will change, shifting the aggregate demand curve. **Fiscal policy** involves changes in the federal government's taxes and purchases that are intended to achieve macroeconomic policy objectives. Changes in federal taxes and purchases shift the aggregate demand curve.

Visit **www.myeconlab.com** to complete these exercises online and get instant feedback.

Review Questions

1 What relationship does the aggregate demand curve show? What relationship does the aggregate supply curve show?

2 Explain the three reasons the aggregate demand curve slopes downward.

3 What are the differences between the *AD* curve and the demand curve for an individual product, such as apples?

4 What variables cause the *AD* curve to shift? For each variable, identify whether an increase in that variable will cause the *AD* curve to shift to the right or to the left, and indicate which component(s) of GDP—consumption, investment, government purchases, or net exports—will change.

Problems and Applications

5 Explain how each of the following events would affect the aggregate demand curve.
   a. An increase in the price level
   b. An increase in government purchases
   c. Higher state income taxes
   d. Higher interest rates
   e. Faster income growth in other countries
   f. A higher exchange rate between the dollar and foreign currencies

6 Consider the two aggregate demand curves in the following graph. What would cause a movement from point *A* to point *B* on *AD*$_1$? What would cause a movement from point *A* to point *C*?

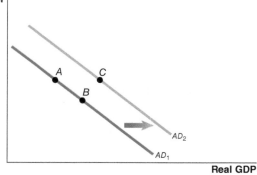

7 **[Related to the** Don't Let This Happen to You**]** An economics student makes the following statement: "It's easy to understand why the aggregate demand curve is downward sloping: When the price level increases, consumers substitute into less expensive products, thereby decreasing total spending in the economy." Briefly explain whether you agree.

8 **[Related to** Solved Problem 1**]** Explain whether each of the following will cause a shift of the *AD* curve or a movement along the *AD* curve.
  a. Firms become more optimistic and increase their spending on machinery and equipment.
  b. The federal government increases taxes in an attempt to reduce a budget deficit.
  c. The U.S. economy experiences 4 percent inflation.

9 **[Related to** Making the Connection: **Which Components of Aggregate Demand Changed the Most during the 2007–2009 Recession?]** If real GDP in the United States declined by more during the 2007–2009 recession than did real GDP in Canada, China, and other trading partners of the United States, would the effect be to increase or decrease U.S. net exports? Briefly explain.

2 Aggregate Supply

LEARNING OBJECTIVE: Identify the determinants of aggregate supply and distinguish between a movement along the short-run aggregate supply curve and a shift of the curve.

Summary

The **long-run aggregate supply curve** is a vertical line because in the long run, real GDP is always at its potential level and is unaffected by the price level. The short-run aggregate supply curve slopes upward because workers and firms fail to predict accurately the future price level. The three main explanations of why this failure results in an upward-sloping aggregate supply curve are that: (1) contracts make wages and prices "sticky," (2) businesses often adjust wages slowly, and (3) menu costs make some prices sticky. **Menu costs** are the costs to firms of changing prices. If the price level changes but all else remains constant, the result is a movement up or down a stationary aggregate supply curve. If any other variable that affects the willingness of firms to supply goods and services changes, the aggregate supply curve will shift. The aggregate supply curve shifts as a result of increases in the labor force and capital stock, technological change, expected increases or decreases in the future price level, adjustments of workers and firms to errors in past expectations about the price level, and unexpected increases or decreases in the price of an important raw material. A **supply shock** is an unexpected event that causes the short-run aggregate supply curve to shift.

Visit **www.myeconlab.com** to complete these exercises online and get instant feedback.

Review Questions

1 Explain why the long-run aggregate supply curve is vertical.
2 What variables cause the long-run aggregate supply curve to shift? For each variable, identify whether an increase in that variable will cause the long-run aggregate supply curve to shift to the right or to the left.
3 Why does the short-run aggregate supply curve slope upward?
4 What variables cause the short-run aggregate supply curve to shift? For each variable, identify whether an increase in that variable will cause the short-run aggregate supply curve to shift to the right or to the left.

Problems and Applications

5 Explain how each of the following events would affect the long-run aggregate supply curve.
  a. A higher price level
  b. An increase in the labor force
  c. An increase in the quantity of capital goods
  d. Technological change

6 A student was asked to draw an aggregate demand and aggregate supply graph to illustrate the effect of an increase in aggregate supply. The student drew the following graph:

The student explains the graph as follows:

An increase in aggregate supply causes a shift from $SRAS_1$ to $SRAS_2$. Because this shift in the aggregate supply curve results in a lower price level, consumption, investment, and net exports will increase. This change causes the aggregate demand curve to shift to the right, from AD_1 to AD_2. We know that real GDP will increase, but we can't be sure whether the price level will rise or fall because that depends on whether the aggregate supply curve or the aggregate demand curve has shifted farther to the right. I assume that aggregate supply shifts out farther than aggregate demand, so I show the final price level, P_3, as being lower than the initial price level, P_1.

Explain whether you agree with the student's analysis. Be careful to explain exactly what—if anything—you find wrong with this analysis.

7 Consider the short-run aggregate supply curves in the following graph. What would cause a movement from point A to point B on SRAS₁? What would cause a movement from point A to point C?

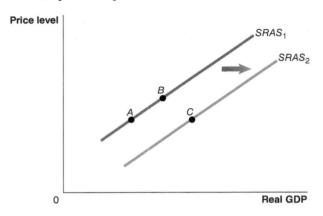

8 An article in the *Economist* magazine noted that "the economy's potential to supply goods and services [is] determined by such things as the labour force and capital stock, as well as inflation expectations." Do you agree with this list of the determinants of potential GDP? Briefly explain.

Source: "Money's Muddled Message," *Economist*, May 19, 2009.

9 Explain how each of the following events would affect the short-run aggregate supply curve.
a. An increase in the price level
b. An increase in what the price level is expected to be in the future
c. A price level that is currently higher than expected
d. An unexpected increase in the price of an important raw material
e. An increase in the labor force participation rate

10 Consider the variables that shift long-run aggregate supply and the variables that shift short-run aggregate supply. Match each of the following scenarios with one of the three graphs of long-run aggregate supply and short-run aggregate supply.

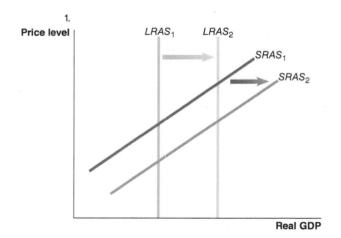

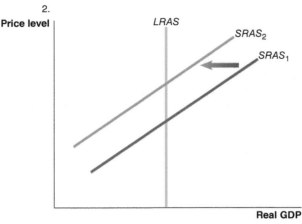

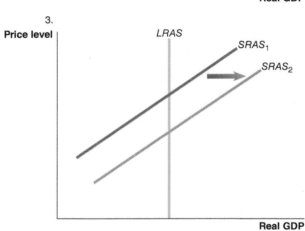

a. A decrease in the expected future price level
b. Workers and firms adjust to having previously underestimated the price level
c. A positive technological change occurs

11 Suppose that workers and firms could always predict next year's price level with perfect accuracy. Briefly explain whether in these circumstances the SRAS curve would still slope upward.

12 Workers and firms often enter into contracts that fix prices or wages, sometimes for years at a time. If the price level turns out to be higher or lower than was expected when the contract was signed, one party to the contract will lose out. Briefly explain why, despite knowing this, workers and firms still sign long-term contracts.

13 **[Related to** Making the Connection: **How Sticky Are Wages?]** Economists Mary Daly, Bart Hobijn, and Timothy Ni of the Federal Reserve Bank of San Francisco argue that "employers hesitate to reduce wages and workers are reluctant to accept wage cuts, even during recessions." If a firm faces declining sales during a recession, why might the firm's managers decide to lay off some workers and freeze the wages of other workers rather than to cut workers' nominal wages?

Source: Mary C. Daly, Bart Hobijn, and Timothy Ni, "The Path of Wage Growth and Unemployment," *Federal Reserve Bank of San Francisco Economic Letter*, July 15, 2013.

14 What are menu costs? How has the widespread use of computers and the Internet affected menu costs? If menu costs were eliminated, would the short-run aggregate supply curve be a vertical line? Briefly explain.

Macroeconomic Equilibrium in the Long Run and the Short Run

LEARNING OBJECTIVE: Use the aggregate demand and aggregate supply model to illustrate the difference between short-run and long-run macroeconomic equilibrium.

Summary

In long-run macroeconomic equilibrium, the aggregate demand and short-run aggregate supply curves intersect at a point *on* the long-run aggregate supply curve. In short-run macroeconomic equilibrium, the aggregate demand and short-run aggregate supply curves often intersect at a point *off* the long-run aggregate supply curve. An automatic mechanism drives the economy to long-run equilibrium. If short-run equilibrium occurs at a point below potential GDP, wages and prices will fall, and the short-run aggregate supply curve will shift to the right until potential GDP is restored. If short-run equilibrium occurs at a point beyond potential GDP, wages and prices will rise, and the short-run aggregate supply curve will shift to the left until potential GDP is restored. Real GDP can be temporarily above or below its potential level, either because of shifts in the short-run aggregate demand curve or because supply shocks lead to shifts in the short-run aggregate supply curve. **Stagflation** is a combination of inflation and recession, usually resulting from a supply shock.

Visit **www.myeconlab.com** to complete these exercises online and get instant feedback.

Review Questions

1 Describe the relationship of the *AD*, *SRAS*, and *LRAS* curves when the economy is in long-run macroeconomic equilibrium.
2 Why might a supply shock lead to stagflation?
3 According to an article in the *Economist*, "Four main types of spending drive GDP...." What are the four main types of spending and in what sense do they "drive" GDP?
   Source: "Double-Dip Trouble," *Economist*, April 28, 2012.

4 Why are the long-run effects of an increase in aggregate demand on price and output different from the short-run effects?

Problems and Applications

5 Draw a basic aggregate demand and aggregate supply graph (with *LRAS* constant) that shows the economy in long-run equilibrium.
   a. Assume that there is a large increase in demand for U.S. exports. Show the resulting short-run equilibrium on your graph. In this short-run equilibrium, is the unemployment rate likely to be higher or lower than it was before the increase in exports? Briefly explain. Explain how the economy adjusts back to long-run equilibrium. When the economy has adjusted back to long-run equilibrium, how have the values of each of the following changed relative to what they were before the increase in exports:
      i. Real GDP
      ii. The price level
      iii. The unemployment rate
   b. Assume that there is an unexpected increase in the price of oil. Show the resulting short-run equilibrium on your graph. Explain how the economy adjusts back to long-run equilibrium. In this short-run equilibrium, is the unemployment rate likely to be higher or lower

than it was before the unexpected increase in the price of oil? Briefly explain. When the economy has adjusted back to long-run equilibrium, how have the values of each of the following changed relative to what they were before the unexpected increase in the price of oil:
      i. Real GDP
      ii. The price level
      iii. The unemployment rate

6 List four variables that would cause a decrease in real GDP (possibly resulting in a recession). Indicate whether changes in each variable increase or decrease aggregate demand or short-run aggregate supply. Next, list four variables that would cause an increase in the price level (short-run inflation). Indicate whether changes in the variable increase or decrease aggregate demand or short-run aggregate supply.

7 **[Related to** Making the Connection**: Does It Matter What Causes a Decline in Aggregate Demand?]** Edward Leamer of the University of California, Los Angeles, has argued that "housing *is* the business cycle." Why would spending on housing be likely to fluctuate more than spending by households on consumer durables, such as automobiles or furniture, or spending by firms on plant and equipment?
   Source: Edward E. Leamer, "Housing Is the Business Cycle," in *Housing, Housing Finance, and Monetary Policy*, Federal Reserve Bank of Kansas City, August 2007.

8 Consider the data in the following table for 1969 and 1970 (where the values for real GDP and potential GDP are in 2009 dollars):

Year	Actual Real GDP	Potential GDP	Unemployment Rate
1969	$4.71 trillion	$4.63 trillion	3.5%
1970	$4.72 trillion	$4.80 trillion	4.9%

   Sources: U.S. Bureau of Labor Statistics; and Federal Reserve Bank of St. Louis.

   a. In 1969, actual real GDP was greater than potential GDP. Briefly explain how this is possible.
   b. Even though real GDP in 1970 was slightly greater than real GDP in 1969, the unemployment rate increased substantially from 1969 to 1970. Why did this increase in unemployment occur?
   c. Was the inflation rate in 1970 likely to have been higher or lower than the inflation rate in 1969? Does your answer depend on whether the recession that began in December 1969 was caused by a change in a component of aggregate demand or by a supply shock?
9 Use the graph to answer the following questions:
   a. Which of the points *A*, *B*, *C*, or *D* can represent a long-run equilibrium?
   b. Suppose that initially the economy is at point *A*. If aggregate demand increases from AD_1 to AD_2, which point represents short-run equilibrium? Which point represents the eventual long-run equilibrium? Briefly

explain how the economy adjusts from the short-run equilibrium to the long-run equilibrium.

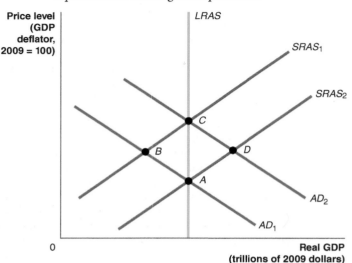

10 **[Related to** Making the Connection**: How Long Does It Take to Return to Potential GDP?]** In early 2009, Christina Romer, who was then the chair of the Council of Economic Advisers, and Jared Bernstein, who was then an economic adviser to Vice President Joseph Biden, forecast how long they expected it would take for real GDP to return to potential GDP, assuming that Congress passed fiscal policy legislation proposed by President Obama:

> It should be understood that all of the estimates presented in this memo are subject to significant margins of error. There is the obvious uncertainty that comes from modeling a hypothetical package rather than the final legislation passed by the Congress. But there is the more fundamental uncertainty that comes with any estimate of the effects of a program. Our estimates of economic relationships ... are derived from historical experience and so will not apply exactly in any given episode. Furthermore, the uncertainty is surely higher than normal now because the current recession is unusual both in its fundamental causes and its severity.

Why would the causes of a recession and its severity affect the accuracy of forecasts of when the economy would return to potential GDP?

Source: Christina Romer and Jared Bernstein, *The Job Impact of the American Recovery and Reinvestment Plan*, January 9, 2009, p. 2.

11 The following graphs show either aggregate demand or short-run aggregate supply shifting to the right or to the left.
   a. Match the following scenarios to the appropriate graph.
      i.   An increase in the expected price level
      ii. An increase in households' expectations of their future income
      iii. A decrease in the price of an important natural resource
      iv. A decrease in firms' expectations of the future profitability of investment spending
   b. Match one or more of the four graphs to each of the following scenarios:
      i.   The economy experiences a recession
      ii. The economy experiences short-term inflation
      iii. The economy experiences stagflation

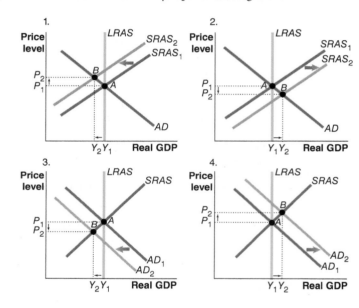

4

A Dynamic Aggregate Demand and Aggregate Supply Model

LEARNING OBJECTIVE: Use the dynamic aggregate demand and aggregate supply model to analyze macroeconomic conditions.

Summary

To make the aggregate demand and aggregate supply model more realistic, we need to make it *dynamic* by incorporating three facts that were left out of the basic model: (1) Potential GDP increases continually, shifting the long-run aggregate supply curve to the right; (2) during most years, aggregate demand shifts to the right; and (3) except during periods when workers and firms expect high rates of inflation, the aggregate supply curve shifts to the right. The dynamic aggregate demand and aggregate supply model allows us to analyze macroeconomic conditions, including the beginning of the 2007–2009 recession.

Review Questions

1 What are the key differences between the basic aggregate demand and aggregate supply model and the dynamic aggregate demand and aggregate supply model?

2 In the dynamic aggregate demand and aggregate supply model, what is the result of aggregate demand increasing more than potential GDP increases? What is the result of aggregate demand increasing less than potential GDP increases?

3 Briefly discuss the factors that caused the recession of 2007–2009.

Visit **www.myeconlab.com** to complete these exercises online and get instant feedback.

214

Problems and Applications

4 Draw a dynamic aggregate demand and aggregate supply graph showing the economy moving from potential GDP in 2015 to potential GDP in 2016, with no inflation. Your graph should contain the *AD*, *SRAS*, and *LRAS* curves for both 2015 and 2016 and should indicate the short-run macroeconomic equilibrium for each year and the directions in which the curves have shifted. Identify what must happen to have growth during 2016 without inflation.

5 **[Related to** Solved Problem 4**]** Consider the information in the following table for the first two years of the Great Depression (where the values for real GDP and potential GDP are in 2009 dollars):

Year	Actual Real GDP	Potential GDP	Price Level
1929	$1,005.6 billion	$1,006.3 billion	10.6
1930	$965.8 billion	$1,094.1 billion	10.2

Sources: U.S. Bureau of Labor Statistics; and Federal Reserve Bank of St. Louis.

a. The table shows that something happened during 1929–1930 that has not happened during the recessions of the past 50 years. What is it?

b. Draw a dynamic aggregate demand and aggregate supply graph to illustrate what happened during these years. Your graph should contain the *AD*, *SRAS*, and *LRAS* curves for both 1929 and 1930 and should indicate the short-run macroeconomic equilibrium for each year and the directions in which the curves shifted.

6 **[Related to** Solved Problem 4**]** Look at the table in *Solved Problem 4*. The price level for 1974 is given as 28.7, and the price level for 1975 is given as 31.4. The values for the price level are well below 100. Does this indicate that inflation must have been low during these years? Briefly explain.

7 In the following graph, suppose that the economy moves from point *A* in year 1 to point *B* in year 2. Using the graph, briefly explain your answer to each of the questions.

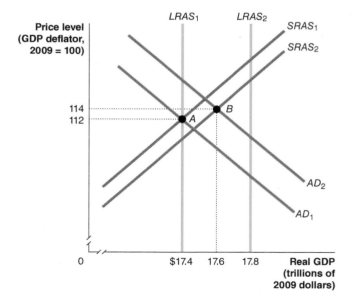

a. What is the growth rate in potential GDP from year 1 to year 2?

b. Is the unemployment rate in year 2 higher or lower than in year 1?

c. What is the inflation rate in year 2?

d. What is the growth rate of real GDP in year 2?

8 Explain whether you agree with the following statement:

The dynamic aggregate demand and aggregate supply model predicts that a recession caused by a decline in *AD* will cause the inflation rate to fall. I know that the 2007–2009 recession was caused by a fall in *AD*, but the inflation rate was not lower as a result of the recession. The prices of most products were definitely higher in 2008 than they were in 2007, so the inflation rate could not have fallen.

9 In a speech in late 2011, President Barack Obama argued that: "Probably the single greatest cause of the financial crisis and this brutal recession has been the housing bubble that burst four years ago." What did the president mean by the "housing bubble"? How can a housing bubble bring on a recession?

Source: Laura Meckler, "Obama Says Plan Will Cut Mortgage Payments for Millions," *Wall Street Journal*, October 24, 2011.

10 **[Related to the** Chapter Opener**]** According to an article in the *Wall Street Journal* about FedEx: "The world's largest air-cargo shipper by revenue and its rivals have been wrestling with a shift by clients toward cheaper and slower delivery services, such as ocean freight." What are the implications of this information for the usefulness of the "FedEx indicator" discussed in the chapter opener?

Source: Bob Sechler, "FedEx Earnings: Hurt by Restructuring Charges," *Wall Street Journal*, June 19, 2013.

Real-Time Data Exercises

D1 **[Showing movements in equilibrium real GDP and the price level]** Go to the Web site of the Federal Reserve Bank of St. Louis (FRED) (research.stlouisfed.org/fred2/) and find data on real GDP (GDPCA) and the GDP price deflator (USAGDPDEFAISMEI) for 1960, 1973, 1975, and 2007.

a. In an *AD–AS* graph, using the actual values for real GDP and the GDP price deflator, show equilibrium for 1960 and for 2007. Assume that the economy was at equilibrium at potential GDP in both years. From 1960 to 2007, what happened to long-run aggregate supply? Given the change in the GDP implicit price deflator, did aggregate demand grow more or less than long-run aggregate supply?

b. In an *AD–AS* graph, using the actual values for real GDP and the GDP price deflator, show equilibrium for 1973 and for 1975. Assume that the economy was in equilibrium at potential GDP in 1973 but in only a short-run equilibrium in 1975. Given the changes in real GDP and the GDP implicit price deflator, briefly explain what happened to short-run aggregate supply from 1973 to 1975.

D2 **[The effects of a positive supply shock]** Using data from the St. Louis Federal Reserve (research.stlouisfed.org/fred2/) FRED database, examine the experience of the U.S. economy during the 1990s. The U.S. economy experienced a positive supply shock with the spread of information communication technology and the Internet after 1995.

    a. Download monthly data on the Personal Consumption Expenditure price index (PCEPI) from 1981 to the present. Calculate the inflation rate from 1982 to 2007 as the percentage change in the Personal Consumption Expenditure price index from the same month in the previous year.

    b. Calculate the average inflation rate from 1982 through 1994 and the average inflation rate from 1995 through 2007.

    c. Are your calculations consistent with a positive supply shock after 1994? Briefly explain.

D3 **[Comparing business cycles across countries]** During the 2007–2009 period, the economies of the United Kingdom and the United States experienced similar problems. High oil prices and a housing bubble affected both economies. The financial crisis in the United States also affected investment in the United Kingdom, both by limiting credit and by increasing risk premiums. Using data from the St. Louis Federal Reserve (research.stlouisfed.org/fred2/) FRED database, examine the behavior of the U.K. economy since 2007.

    a. Download quarterly data for real GDP (GBRRGDPQDSNAQ) and the GDP deflator (GBRGDPDEFQISMEI) for the United Kingdom from 2006 to the present. Calculate the growth rate of real GDP as the percentage change from the same quarter in the previous year and calculate the inflation rate as the percentage change in the GDP deflator from the same quarter in the previous year. Download data on the unemployment rate (GBRURHARMMDSMEI) for the same time period. For the frequency of the unemployment rate data, select quarterly, to match the frequency of the real GDP and GDP deflator data.

    b. Download the three data series from 2007 to the present in the same graph. How similar do the data indicate that the experience of the United Kingdom was during these years compared with the experience of the United States?

Appendix

Macroeconomic Schools of Thought

LEARNING OBJECTIVE

Understand macroeconomic schools of thought.

Macroeconomics became a separate field of economics in 1936, with the publication of John Maynard Keynes's book *The General Theory of Employment, Interest, and Money.* Keynes, an economist at the University of Cambridge in England, was attempting to explain the devastating Great Depression of the 1930s. Real GDP in the United States declined more than 25 percent between 1929 and 1933 and did not return to its potential level until the United States entered World War II in 1941. The unemployment rate soared above 20 percent by 1933 and did not return to its 1929 level until 1942. Keynes developed a version of the aggregate demand and aggregate supply model to explain these facts. The widespread acceptance during the 1930s and 1940s of Keynes's model became known as the **Keynesian revolution**.

Keynesian revolution The name given to the widespread acceptance during the 1930s and 1940s of John Maynard Keynes's macroeconomic model.

In fact, using the aggregate demand and aggregate supply model remains the most widely accepted approach to analyzing macroeconomic issues. Because the model has been modified significantly from Keynes's day, many economists who use the model today refer to themselves as *new Keynesians*. The new Keynesians emphasize the importance of the stickiness of wages and prices in explaining fluctuations in real GDP. A significant number of economists, however, dispute whether using the aggregate demand and aggregate supply model, as we have discussed it in this chapter, is the best way to analyze macroeconomic issues. These alternative *schools of thought* use models that differ significantly from the standard aggregate demand and aggregate supply model. We can briefly consider four major alternative models:

1. The monetarist model
2. The new classical model
3. The real business cycle model
4. The Austrian model

The Monetarist Model

The monetarist model—also known as the neo-quantity theory of money model—was developed beginning in the 1940s by Milton Friedman, an economist at the University of Chicago who was awarded the Nobel Prize in Economics in 1976. Friedman argued that the Keynesian approach overstates the amount of macroeconomic instability in the economy. In particular, he argued that the economy will ordinarily be at potential GDP. In the book *A Monetary History of the United States: 1867–1960*, written with Anna Jacobson Schwartz, Friedman argued that most fluctuations in real output were caused by fluctuations in the money supply rather than by fluctuations in consumption spending or investment spending. Friedman and Schwartz argued that the severity of the Great Depression was caused by the Federal Reserve allowing the quantity of money in the economy to fall by more than 25 percent between 1929 and 1933.

In the United States, the Federal Reserve is responsible for managing the quantity of money. The Federal Reserve has typically focused more on controlling interest rates than on controlling the money supply. Friedman argued that the Federal Reserve should change its practices and adopt a **monetary growth rule**, which is a plan for increasing the quantity of money at a fixed rate. He believed that adopting a monetary growth rule would reduce fluctuations in real GDP, employment, and inflation.

Monetary growth rule A plan for increasing the quantity of money at a fixed rate that does not respond to changes in economic conditions.

Friedman's ideas, which are referred to as **monetarism**, attracted significant support during the 1970s and early 1980s, when the U.S. economy experienced high rates of unemployment and inflation. The support for monetarism declined during the late 1980s and 1990s, when the unemployment and inflation rates were relatively low.

Monetarism The macroeconomic theories of Milton Friedman and his followers, particularly the idea that the quantity of money should be increased at a constant rate.

The New Classical Model

The new classical model was developed in the mid-1970s by a group of economists including Nobel Laureate Robert Lucas of the University of Chicago, Nobel Laureate Thomas Sargent of New York University, and Robert Barro of Harvard University. Some of the views held by the new classical macroeconomists are similar to those held by economists before the Great Depression. Keynes referred to the economists before the Great Depression as *classical economists*. Like the classical economists, the new classical macroeconomists believe that the economy normally will be at potential GDP. They also believe that wages and prices adjust quickly to changes in demand and supply. Put another way, they believe the stickiness in wages and prices emphasized by the new Keynesians is unimportant.

Lucas argues that workers and firms have *rational expectations*, meaning that they form their expectations of the future values of economic variables, such as the inflation rate, by making use of all available information, including information on changes in the quantity of money and other factors that might affect aggregate demand. Fluctuations in output and employment occur if households and firms form incorrect expectations of the inflation rate. If the actual inflation rate is lower than the expected inflation rate, the actual real wage will be higher than the expected real wage. Higher real wages will lead to a recession because firms will hire fewer workers and cut back on production. As workers and firms adjust their expectations to the lower inflation rate, the real wage will decline, and employment and production will expand, bringing the economy out of recession. The ideas of Lucas and his followers are referred to as the **new classical macroeconomics**. Supporters of the new classical model agree with supporters of the monetarist model that the Federal Reserve should adopt a monetary growth rule. They argue that a monetary growth rule will make it easier for workers and firms to accurately forecast the price level, thereby reducing fluctuations in real GDP.

New classical macroeconomics The macroeconomic theories of Robert Lucas and others, particularly the idea that workers and firms have rational expectations.

The Real Business Cycle Model

In the 1980s, some economists, including Nobel Laureates Finn Kydland of the University of California, Santa Barbara, and Edward Prescott of Arizona State University, argued that Lucas was correct in assuming that workers and firms formed their expectations rationally and that wages and prices adjust quickly to supply and demand but was wrong about the source of fluctuations in real GDP. But they argued that fluctuations in real GDP are caused by temporary shocks to productivity and not by inaccurate forecasts of the price level. These shocks can be negative, such as a decline in the availability of oil or other raw materials, or positive, such as technological change that makes it possible to produce more output with the same quantity of inputs.

According to this school of thought, shifts in the aggregate demand curve have no effect on real GDP because the short-run aggregate supply curve is vertical. (Other schools of thought believe that the short-run aggregate supply curve is upward sloping and that only the *long-run* aggregate supply curve is vertical.) Fluctuations in real GDP occur when a negative productivity shock causes the short-run aggregate supply curve to shift to the left—reducing real GDP—or a positive productivity shock causes the short-run aggregate supply curve to shift to the right—increasing real GDP. Because this model focuses on "real" factors—productivity shocks—rather than changes in the quantity of money to explain fluctuations in real GDP, it is known as the **real business cycle model**.

Real business cycle model A macroeconomic model that focuses on real, rather than monetary, causes of the business cycle.

The Austrian Model

The *Austrian school* of economics began in the late nineteenth century with the writings of Carl Menger, an economist at the University of Vienna. Important later contributors to this school of thought were Ludwig von Mises, who spent the later years of his career at New York University, and Friedrich von Hayek, who spent most of his career at the London School of Economics. The Austrian school is best known for arguing the superiority of the market system over government economic planning. Hayek, in particular, emphasized that only the price system operating through markets could make use of the dispersed information available to households and firms to bring about an efficient allocation of resources.

During the 1930s, Hayek developed a theory of the business cycle that emphasized the problems arising from central banks forcing interest rates to very low levels. Low interest rates cause businesses to spend more on factories, machinery, office buildings, and other types of capital. Initially, the surge in investment spending will produce an economic expansion, but the additional capital goods eventually produce more output than firms can sell for a profit. Businesses suffer losses, reduce output, and lay off workers, resulting in a recession. The lower the central bank drives interest rates, the greater the increase in investment spending, the larger the economic expansion, and the deeper the eventual recession.

For a time in the early 1930s, Hayek's theory of the business cycle attracted significant interest from economists, particularly in the United Kingdom. After the publication of Keynes's *General Theory* in 1936, interest in Hayek's theory declined and today only a relatively few economists belong to the Austrian school. In the past few years, however, Austrian economists have argued that the events of the 2007–2009 recession fit their model well: The Federal Reserve lowered interest rates to fight the 2001 recession, and the low interest rates sparked a surge in capital spending—in this case, spending on houses rather than on factories or office buildings. Eventually, the excessive investment in housing ended with a housing bust and a severe recession.

Making the Connection	## Karl Marx: Capitalism's Severest Critic

The schools of macroeconomic thought we have discussed in this appendix are considered part of mainstream economic theory because of their acceptance of the market system as the best means of raising living standards in the long run. One quite influential critic of mainstream economic theory was Karl Marx. Marx was born in Trier, Germany, in 1818. After graduating from the University of Berlin in 1841, he began a career as a political journalist and agitator. His political activities caused him to be expelled first from Germany and then from France and Belgium. In 1849, he moved to London, where he spent the remainder of his life.

In 1867, Marx published the first volume of his greatest work, *Das Kapital*. Marx read closely the most prominent mainstream economists, including Adam Smith, David Ricardo, and John Stuart Mill. But Marx believed that he understood how market systems would evolve in the long run much better than those earlier authors. He argued that the market system would eventually be replaced by a Communist economy, in which the workers would control production. He believed in the *labor theory of value*, which attributed all of the value of a good or service to the labor embodied in it. According to Marx, the owners of businesses—capitalists—did not earn profits by contributing anything of value to the production of goods or services. Instead, they earned profits because their "monopoly of the means of production"—their ownership of factories and machinery—allowed them to exploit workers by paying them wages that were much lower than the value of workers' contribution to production.

Marx argued that the wages of workers would be driven to levels that allowed only bare survival. He also argued that small firms would eventually be driven out of business by larger firms, forcing owners of small firms into the working class. Control of production would ultimately be concentrated in the hands of a few firms, which would have difficulty selling the goods they produced to the impoverished masses. A final economic crisis would lead the working classes to rise up, seize control of the economy, and

Karl Marx predicted that a final economic crisis would lead to the collapse of the market system.

establish Communism. Marx died in 1883, without having provided a detailed explanation of how the Communist economy would operate.

Marx had relatively little influence on mainstream thinking in the United States, but several political parties in Europe were guided by his ideas. In 1917, the Bolshevik party seized control of Russia and established the Soviet Union, the first Communist state. Although the Soviet Union was a vicious dictatorship under Vladimir Lenin and his successor, Joseph Stalin, its prestige rose when it avoided the macroeconomic difficulties that plagued the market economies during the 1930s. By the late 1940s, Communist parties had also come to power in China and the countries of Eastern Europe. Poor economic performance contributed to the eventual collapse of the Soviet Union and its replacement by a market system, although one with significant government intervention in the economy. The Communist Party remains in power in China, but the economy is evolving toward a market system. Today, only North Korea and Cuba have economies that claim to be based on the ideas of Karl Marx.

Key Terms

Keynesian revolution	Monetary growth rule	Real business cycle model
Monetarism	New classical macroeconomics	

Glossary

Aggregate demand (*AD*) curve A curve that shows the relationship between the price level and the quantity of real GDP demanded by households, firms, and the government.

Aggregate demand and aggregate supply model A model that explains short-run fluctuations in real GDP and the price level.

Fiscal policy Changes in federal taxes and purchases that are intended to achieve macroeconomic policy objectives.

Keynesian revolution The name given to the widespread acceptance during the 1930s and 1940s of John Maynard Keynes's macroeconomic model.

Long-run aggregate supply (*LRAS*) curve A curve that shows the relationship in the long run between the price level and the quantity of real GDP supplied.

Menu costs The costs to firms of changing prices.

Monetarism The macroeconomic theories of Milton Friedman and his followers, particularly the idea that the quantity of money should be increased at a constant rate.

Monetary growth rule A plan for increasing the quantity of money at a fixed rate that does not respond to changes in economic conditions.

Monetary policy The actions the Federal Reserve takes to manage the money supply and interest rates to pursue macroeconomic policy objectives.

New classical macroeconomics The macroeconomic theories of Robert Lucas and others, particularly the idea that workers and firms have rational expectations.

Real business cycle model A macroeconomic model that focuses on real rather than monetary, causes of the business cycle.

Short-run aggregate supply (*SRAS*) curve A curve that shows the relationship in the short run between the price level and the quantity of real GDP supplied by firms.

Stagflation A combination of inflation and recession, usually resulting from a supply shock.

Supply shock An unexpected event that causes the short-run aggregate supply curve to shift.

Credits

Credits are listed in the order of appearance.

Photo

Money, Banks, and the Federal Reserve System

From Chapter 14 of *Macroeconomics*, Fifth Edition. R. Glenn Hubbard and Anthony Patrick O'Brien. Copyright © 2015 by Pearson Education, Inc.
All rights reserved.

Money, Banks, and the Federal Reserve System

Chapter Outline and Learning Objectives

Washing Dollar Bills to Save the Economy of Zimbabwe

The OK Mart is a supermarket in Hare, the capital of Zimbabwe. In 2008, the OK Mart, like other stores in Zimbabwe, had few goods to sell and few customers with money to buy those goods. A single bottle of Coca-Cola sold for 15 billion Zimbabwean dollars! Zimbabwe was suffering the effects of an inflation rate so high that it is called a *hyperinflation*. The country's hyperinflation was of epic proportions, perhaps the worst in world history. When the currency was first introduced in 1980, 1 Zimbabwean dollar was worth 1.47 U.S. dollars. By the end of 2008, the exchange rate was 1 U.S. dollar to 2 *billion* Zimbabwean dollars, and prices for some large transactions in Zimbabwe were calculated in quadrillions (15 zeros) and quintillions (18 zeros).

The OK Mart is part of the OK Zimbabwe supermarket chain. During the hyperinflation, the chain could not obtain the U.S. dollars it needed to import goods from foreign suppliers who refused to accept Zimbabwean dollars. Local banks were no help because, as one banker put it: "We had no customers, no deposits, a bucket load of expenses and zero revenue."

By 2013, the OK Mart had well-stocked shelves and many customers. The revival of the Zimbabwean economy was made possible by the government taking the drastic step of making the U.S. dollar the country's official currency. Using U.S. dollars for buying and selling ended the hyperinflation but caused another problem—a shortage of dollars. The shortage was so bad that Zimbabweans would carefully hand-wash U.S. dollars to keep them in use as long as possible. The shortage of U.S. coins meant that many stores priced goods only in round dollar amounts—such as $1 for a loaf of bread—or gave change in bags of peanuts or candy.

What made the Zimbabwean dollar almost worthless? The government of Zimbabwe had decided to pay for all of its expenses by printing more and more money. The faster the government printed money, the faster prices rose. Eventually, both foreigners and local residents refused to accept the Zimbabwean dollar in exchange for goods and services.

In this chapter, we will study banks, the money supply, and the link between changes in the money supply and the inflation rate. We will also discuss the operations of the Federal Reserve, which is the central bank of the United States.

Sources: "In Dollars They Trust," *Economist*, April 27, 2013; "The Hottest Frontier," *Economist*, April 6, 2013; and Patrick McGroarty and Farai Mutsaka, "Hanging on to Dollars in Zimbabwe," *Wall Street Journal*, March 26, 2012.

Economics in Your Life

What If Money Became Increasingly Valuable?

Most people are used to the fact that as prices rise each year, the purchasing power of money falls. You will be able to buy fewer goods and services with $1,000 one year from now, and you will be able to buy even fewer goods and services the year after that. In fact, with an inflation rate of just 3 percent, in 25 years, $1,000 will buy only what $475 can buy today. Suppose that you could live in an economy where the purchasing power of money *rose* each year? What would be the advantages and disadvantages of living in such an economy? As you read this chapter, try to answer these questions. You can check your answers against those we provide at the end of this chapter.

I n this chapter, we will explore the role of money in the economy. We will see how the banking system creates money and what policy tools the Federal Reserve uses to manage the quantity of money in the United States. We will also examine the recent crisis in the banking system. At the end of this chapter, we will explore the link between changes in the quantity of money and changes in the price level. What you learn in this chapter will serve as an important foundation for understanding monetary policy and fiscal policy.

1 LEARNING OBJECTIVE

Define money and discuss the four functions of money.

Money Assets that people are generally willing to accept in exchange for goods and services or for payment of debts.

Asset Anything of value owned by a person or a firm.

Commodity money A good used as money that also has value independent of its use as money.

What Is Money, and Why Do We Need It?

Could an economy function without money? We know the answer to this question is "yes" because there are many historical examples of economies in which people traded goods for other goods rather than using money. For example, on the American frontier during colonial times very little money was available, so a farmer might have traded a plow for a cow. Most economies, though, use money. What is money? The economic definition of **money** is any asset that people are generally willing to accept in exchange for goods and services or for payment of debts. An **asset** is anything of value owned by a person or a firm. There are many possible kinds of money: In West Africa, at one time, cowrie shells served as money. During World War II, prisoners of war used cigarettes as money.

Barter and the Invention of Money

To understand the importance of money, let's consider further the situation in economies that do not use money. Economies where goods and services are traded directly for other goods and services are called *barter economies*. Barter economies have a major shortcoming. To illustrate this shortcoming, consider a farmer on the American frontier in colonial days. Suppose the farmer needed a cow and proposed trading a spare plow to a neighbor for one of the neighbor's cows. If the neighbor did not want the plow, the trade would not happen. For a barter trade to take place between two people, each person must want what the other one has. Economists refer to this requirement as a *double coincidence of wants*. The farmer who wants the cow might eventually be able to obtain one if he first trades with some other neighbor for something the neighbor with the cow wants. However, it may take several trades before the farmer is ultimately able to trade for what the neighbor with the cow wants. Locating several trading partners and making several intermediate trades can take considerable time and energy.

To avoid the problems with barter, societies have an incentive to identify a product that most people will accept in exchange for what they have to trade. For example, in colonial times, animal skins were very useful in making clothing. The first governor of Tennessee actually received a salary of 1,000 deerskins per year, and the state's secretary of the Treasury received 450 otter skins per year. A good used as money that also has value independent of its use as money is called a **commodity money**. Historically, once a good became widely accepted as money, people who did not have an immediate use for it would be willing to accept it. A colonial farmer—or the governor of Tennessee— might not want a deerskin, but as long as he knew he could use the deerskin to buy other goods and services, he would be willing to accept it in exchange for what he had to sell.

Trading goods and services is much easier when money becomes available. People only need to sell what they have for money and then use the money to buy what they want. If the colonial family could find someone to buy their plow, they could use the money to buy the cow they wanted. The family with the cow would accept the money because they knew they could use it to buy what they wanted. When money is available, families are more likely to specialize and less likely to produce everything or nearly everything they need themselves.

Most people in modern economies are highly specialized. They do only one thing—work as a nurse, an accountant, or an engineer—and use the money they earn to buy everything else they need. People become much more productive by specializing because they can pursue their *comparative advantage*. The high income levels in modern economies are based on the specialization that money makes possible. We can now answer the question, "Why do we need money?" *By making exchange easier, money allows people to specialize and become more productive.*

The Functions of Money

Anything used as money—whether a deerskin, a cowrie seashell, cigarettes, or a dollar bill—must serve four key functions in the economy:

1. It must act as a medium of exchange.

2. It must serve as a unit of account.

3. It must serve as a store of value.

4. It must offer a standard of deferred payment.

Medium of Exchange Money serves as a medium of exchange when sellers are willing to accept it in exchange for goods or services. When the local supermarket accepts your $5 bill in exchange for bread and milk, the $5 bill is serving as a medium of exchange. With a medium of exchange, people can sell goods and services for money and use the money to buy what they want. An economy is more efficient when people accept a single good as a medium of exchange.

Unit of Account In a barter system, each good has many prices. A cow may be worth 2 plows, 20 bushels of wheat, or 6 axes. Once a single good is used as money, each good has a single price rather than many prices. This function of money gives buyers and sellers a *unit of account*, a way of measuring value in the economy in terms of money. Because the U.S. economy uses dollars as money, each good has a price in terms of dollars.

Store of Value Money allows people to easily store value: If you do not use all your dollars to buy goods and services today, you can hold the rest to use in the future. Money is not the only store of value, however. Any asset—shares of Facebook stock, Treasury bonds, real estate, or Renoir paintings, for example—represents a store of value. Financial assets, such as stocks and bonds, offer an important benefit relative to holding money because they pay a higher rate of interest or may increase in value in the future. Other assets also have advantages relative to money because they provide services. A house, for example, offers you a place to sleep.

Why, then, do people hold any money? The answer has to do with *liquidity*, or the ease with which people can convert an asset into the medium of exchange. Because money is the medium of exchange, it is the most liquid asset. If you want to buy something and you need to sell an asset to do so, you are likely to incur a cost. For example, if you want to buy a car and need to sell bonds or stocks to do so, you will need to pay a commission to your broker. To avoid such costs, people are willing to hold some of their wealth in the form of money, even though other assets offer a greater return as a store of value.

Standard of Deferred Payment Money is useful because it can serve as a standard of deferred payment in borrowing and lending. It can facilitate exchange at a *given point in time* by providing a medium of exchange and unit of account. Money can facilitate exchange *over time* by providing a store of value and a standard of deferred payment. For example, a computer manufacturer may buy hard drives from another firm in exchange for the promise of making payment in 60 days.

How important is it that money be a reliable store of value and standard of deferred payment? People care about how much food, clothing, and other goods and services their dollars will buy. The value of money depends on its *purchasing power*, which refers to its ability to buy goods and services. Inflation causes a decline in purchasing power because with rising prices, a given amount of money can purchase fewer goods and services. When inflation reaches the levels seen in Zimbabwe, money is no longer a reliable store of value or standard of deferred payment.

What Can Serve as Money?

Having a medium of exchange helps to make transactions easier, allowing the economy to work more efficiently. The next logical question is: What can serve as money? That is, which assets should be used as the medium of exchange? We saw earlier that an asset must, at a minimum, be generally accepted as payment to serve as money. In practical terms, however, it must be even more.

Five criteria make a good suitable for use as a medium of exchange:

1. The good must be *acceptable* to (that is, usable by) most people.
2. It should be of *standardized quality* so that any two units are identical.
3. It should be *durable* so that value is not lost by spoilage.
4. It should be *valuable* relative to its weight so that amounts large enough to be useful in trade can be easily transported.
5. It should be *divisible* so that it can be used in purchases of both low-priced and high-priced goods.

Dollar bills meet all these criteria. What determines the acceptability of dollar bills as a medium of exchange? Basically, it is through self-fulfilling expectations: You value something as money only if you believe that others will accept it from you as payment. A society's willingness to use paper dollars as money makes them an acceptable medium of exchange.

Commodity Money Commodity money has value independent of its use as money. Gold, for example, was a common form of money in the nineteenth century because it was a medium of exchange, a unit of account, a store of value, and a standard of deferred payment. But commodity money has a significant problem: Its value depends on its purity. Therefore, someone who wanted to cheat could mix impure metals with a precious metal. Another problem with using gold as money was that the money supply was difficult to control because it depended partly on unpredictable discoveries of new gold fields.

Fiat Money It can be inefficient for an economy to rely on only gold or other precious metals for its money supply. What if you had to transport bars of gold to settle your transactions? Not only would doing so be difficult and costly, but you would run the risk of being robbed. To get around this problem, private institutions or governments began to store gold and issue paper certificates that could be redeemed for gold. In modern economies, paper currency is generally issued by a *central bank*, which is an agency of the government that regulates the money supply. The **Federal Reserve** is the central bank of the United States. Today, no government in the world issues paper currency that can be redeemed for gold. Paper currency has no value unless it is used as money, and it is therefore not a commodity money. Instead, paper currency is a **fiat money**, which has no value except as money. If paper currency has no value except as money, why do consumers and firms use it?

If you look at the top of a U.S. dollar bill, you will see the words "Federal Reserve Note" because it is issued by the Federal Reserve. Because U.S. dollars are fiat money, the Federal Reserve is not required to give you gold or silver for your dollar bills. Federal Reserve currency is *legal tender* in the United States, which means the federal government requires that it be accepted in payment of debts and requires that cash or checks denominated in dollars be used in payment of taxes. Despite being legal tender, dollar bills would not be a good medium of exchange and could not serve as money if people didn't usually accept them. The key to this acceptance is that *households and firms have confidence that if they accept paper dollars in exchange for goods and services, the dollars will not lose much value during the time they hold them.* Without this confidence, dollar bills would not serve as a medium of exchange.

Federal Reserve The central bank of the United States.

Fiat money Money, such as paper currency, that is authorized by a central bank or governmental body and that does not have to be exchanged by the central bank for gold or some other commodity money.

Making the Connection

Apple Didn't Want My Cash!

If Federal Reserve Notes are legal tender, doesn't that mean that everyone in the United States, including every business, has to accept paper money? The answer to this question is "no," as a woman in California found out when she went to an Apple store in Palo Alto and tried to buy an iPad using $600 in currency. The store refused to sell her the iPad for cash. At that time, the iPad had just been released, and Apple did not want to sell large numbers to people who were buying them to resell on eBay, Craigslist, or elsewhere. So, a customer wanting to buy an iPad had to pay with either a credit card or a debit card, which would make it easier for Apple to keep track of anyone attempting to buy more than the limit of two per customer.

Because Federal Reserve Notes are legal tender, creditors must accept them in payment of debts, and the government will accept them in payment of taxes. However, as this incident demonstrates, firms do not have to accept cash as payment for goods and services. As the U.S. Treasury Department explains on its Web site:

The law doesn't require Apple to accept paper money from these customers.

There is … no Federal statute mandating that a private business, a person or an organization must accept currency or coins as payment for goods and/or services…. For example, a bus line may prohibit payment of fares in pennies or dollar bills. In addition, movie theaters, convenience stores and gas stations may refuse to accept large denomination currency (usually notes above $20) as a matter of policy.

The woman who tried to buy an iPad for cash was disabled and on a limited income, so the incident led to negative publicity for Apple. As a result, Apple decided to lift its ban on paying for iPads with cash, provided that the customer was willing to set up an Apple account at the time of purchase. In addition, Apple presented a free iPad to the customer who was originally turned down when she tried to pay with cash.

Sources: Michael Winter, "Apple Ends No-Cash Policy and California Woman Gets Free iPad," www.usatoday.com, May 20, 2010; and U.S. Treasury, "FAQs: Currency," www.treasury.gov/resource-center/faqs/Currency/Pages/edu_faq_currency_index2.aspx.

Your Turn: Test your understanding by doing related problem 1.9 at the end of this chapter.

How Is Money Measured in the United States Today?

2 LEARNING OBJECTIVE

Discuss the definitions of the money supply used in the United States today.

People are interested in the money supply because, as we will see, changes in the money supply can affect other economic variables, including employment, gross domestic product (GDP), and inflation. If the only function of money was to serve as a medium of exchange, then a narrow definition of the money supply should include only currency, checking account deposits, and traveler's checks because households and firms can easily use these assets to buy goods and services. A broader definition of the money supply would include other assets that can be used as a medium of exchange even though they are not as liquid as currency or checking account deposits. For example, you can withdraw cash from your savings account at a bank.

Congress gave the Federal Reserve the responsibility of regulating the money supply and the task of determining how to measure it. The Federal Reserve's measures of the money supply have changed several times over the decades. Currently, the Federal Reserve publishes data on two measures of the money supply: *M1* and *M2*. These measures are sometimes called *monetary aggregates*. Understanding these two measures of the money supply is important, so we devote the following sections to discussing them.

M1: A Narrow Definition of the Money Supply

Figure 1 illustrates the definitions of the money supply. The narrow definition of the money supply, **M1**, includes the following:

M1 The narrow definition of the money supply: the sum of currency in circulation, checking account deposits in banks, and holdings of traveler's checks.

1. *Currency*, which is all the paper money and coins held by households and firms (not including currency held by banks)

2. The value of all checking account deposits in banks

3. The value of traveler's checks (Because this last category is so small—typically less than $4 billion—relative to the other two categories, we will ignore it in our discussion of the money supply.)

Although currency has almost as large a value as checking account deposits, checking account deposits are used much more often than currency to make payments. More than 80 percent of all expenditures on goods and services are made with checks rather than with currency. In fact, the total amount of currency in circulation—$1.1 trillion in July 2013—is a misleading number. This amount is more than $3,500 per person—adult or child—in the United States. If this sounds like an unrealistically large amount of currency to be held per person, it is. Economists estimate that more than 60 percent of U.S. currency is actually outside the borders of the United States. In 2013, more than three-quarters of U.S. paper currency was in denominations of $100 or larger—too large to be used for routine buying and selling within the United States.

Who holds these dollars outside the United States? Foreign banks and foreign governments hold some U.S. currency, but most is held by households and firms in countries where there is not much confidence in the local currency or where the underground economy is large. When inflation rates are very high, many households and firms do not want to hold their domestic currency because it is losing its value too rapidly. The value of the U.S. dollar will be much more stable than their domestic currency. If enough people are willing to accept dollars as well as—or instead of—domestic currency, dollars become a second currency for the country. As we saw in the

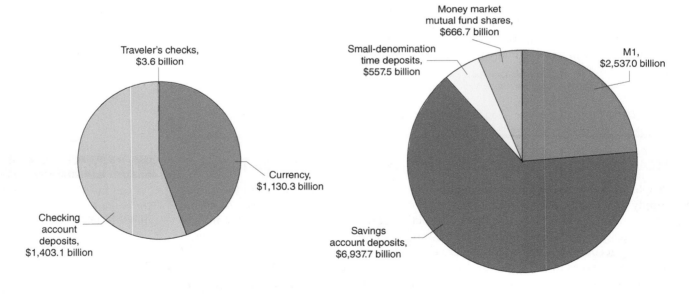

(a) M1 = $2,537.0 billion

(b) M2 = $10,698.9 billion

Figure 1 Measuring the Money Supply, July 2013

The Federal Reserve uses two different measures of the money supply: M1 and M2. Panel (a) shows the assets in M1. Panel (b) shows M2, which includes the assets in M1, as well as money market mutual fund shares, small-denomination time deposits, and savings account deposits.

Source: Board of Governors of the Federal Reserve System, "Federal Reserve Statistical Release, H.6," July 25, 2013.

chapter opener, when inflation soared in Zimbabwe, the government adopted the U.S. dollar as the country's official currency.

M2: A Broad Definition of Money

Before 1980, U.S. law prohibited banks from paying interest on checking account deposits. Households and firms held checking account deposits primarily to buy goods and services. M1 was, therefore, very close to the function of money as a medium of exchange. Almost all currency, checking account deposits, and traveler's checks were held with the intention of buying and selling, not with the intention of storing value. In 1980, the law was changed to allow banks to pay interest on certain types of checking accounts. This change reduced the difference between checking accounts and savings accounts, although people are still not allowed to write checks against their savings account balances.

After 1980, economists began to pay closer attention to a broader definition of the money supply, **M2**. As panel (b) of Figure 1 shows, M2 includes everything that is in M1, plus savings account deposits, small-denomination time deposits—such as certificates of deposit (CDs)—balances in money market deposit accounts in banks, and noninstitutional money market fund shares. Small-denomination time deposits are similar to savings accounts, but the deposits are for a fixed period of time—usually from six months to several years—and withdrawals before that time are subject to a penalty. Mutual fund companies sell shares to investors and use the funds raised to buy financial assets such as stocks and bonds. Some of these mutual funds, such as Vanguard's Treasury Money Market Fund or Fidelity's Cash Reserves Fund, are called *money market mutual funds* because they invest in very short-term bonds, such as U.S. Treasury bills. The balances individual investors hold in these funds are included in M2. Each week, the Federal Reserve publishes statistics on M1 and M2. In the discussion that follows, we will use the M1 definition of the money supply because it corresponds most closely to money as a medium of exchange.

> **M2** A broader definition of the money supply: It includes M1 plus savings account deposits, small-denomination time deposits, balances in money market deposit accounts in banks, and noninstitutional money market fund shares.

There are two key points to keep in mind about the money supply:

1. The narrowest definition of the money supply consists of *both* currency and checking account deposits.

2. Because balances in checking account deposits are included in the money supply, banks play an important role in the way the money supply increases and decreases. We will discuss this second point further in the next section.

Don't Let This Happen to You

Don't Confuse Money with Income or Wealth

According to *Forbes*, in 2013, Bill Gates's wealth of $67 billion made him the second-richest person in the world. He also has a very large income, but how much money does he have? Your *wealth* is equal to the value of your assets minus the value of any debts you have. Your *income* is equal to your earnings during the year. Bill Gates's earnings as chairman of Microsoft and from his investments are very large. But his *money* is just equal to what he has in currency and checking accounts. Only a small proportion of Gates's $67 billion in wealth is likely to be in currency or checking accounts. Most of his wealth is invested in stocks and bonds and other financial assets that are not included in the definition of money.

In everyday conversation, we often describe someone who is wealthy or who has a high income as "having a lot of money." But when economists use the word *money*, they are usually referring to currency plus checking account deposits. It is important to keep straight the differences between wealth, income, and money.

Just as money and income are not the same for a person, they are not the same for the whole economy. National income in the United States was equal to $14.0 trillion in 2012. The money supply in 2012 was $2.3 trillion (using the M1 measure). There is no reason why national income in a country should be equal to the country's money supply, nor will an increase in a country's money supply necessarily increase the country's national income.

Source: "The World's Billionaires," *Forbes*, March 4, 2013.

Your Turn: Test your understanding by doing related problems 2.5 and 2.6 at the end of this chapter.

Solved Problem 2

The Definitions of M1 and M2

Suppose you decide to withdraw $2,000 from your checking account and use the money to buy a bank certificate of deposit (CD). Briefly explain how this action will affect M1 and M2.

Solving the Problem

Step 1: **Review the chapter material.** This problem is about the definitions of the money supply, so you may want to review the section "How Is Money Measured in the United States Today?"

Step 2: **Use the definitions of M1 and M2 to answer the problem.** Funds in checking accounts are included in both M1 and M2. Funds in CDs are included only in M2. It is tempting to answer this problem by saying that shifting $2,000 from a checking account to a CD reduces M1 by $2,000 and increases M2 by $2,000, but the $2,000 in your checking account was already counted in M2. So, the correct answer is that your action reduces M1 by $2,000 but leaves M2 unchanged.

Your Turn: For more practice, do related problems 2.7 and 2.8 at the end of this chapter.

What about Credit Cards and Debit Cards?

Many people buy goods and services with credit cards, yet credit cards are not included in definitions of the money supply. The reason is that when you buy something with a credit card, you are in effect taking out a loan from the bank that issued the credit card. The transaction is complete only when you pay your credit card bill at the end of the month—often with a check or an electronic transfer from your checking account. In contrast, with a debit card, the funds to make the purchase are taken directly from your checking account. In either case, the cards themselves do not represent money.

<table>
<tr><td>Making
the
Connection</td><td>

Are Bitcoins Money?

Typically, when we think of "money," we think of currency issued by a government. But we have just seen that currency represents only a small part of the money supply of the United

</td></tr>
</table>

States, whether measured as M1 or M2. The non-currency components of M1 or M2, although not issued by the government, are familiar financial assets such as checking or savings accounts. Some households and firms have shifted away from M1 or M2 to finance their buying and selling of goods and services and are instead using e-money, or digital funds. The best-known form of e-money is PayPal, which is owned by eBay, the online auction site. An individual or a firm can set up a PayPal account by transferring funds from a checking account or credit card. As long as a seller is willing to accept funds from a buyer's PayPal (or other e-money) account, e-money functions like conventional government-issued money.

Recently, journalists, economists, and policymakers have been debating the merits of Bitcoin, a new form of e-money. Unlike PayPal and other similar services for transferring money electronically, Bitcoin is not owned by a firm but is instead the product of a decentralized system of linked computers. Bitcoin was founded in 2009 by "Satoshi Nakamoto," which is likely an assumed name taken by Bitcoin's founder or founders. Bitcoins are produced by people performing the complicated calculations necessary to ensure that online purchases made with Bitcoins are legitimate—that is, that someone doesn't try to spend the same Bitcoin multiple times. People who successfully complete these calculations are awarded a fixed amount of Bitcoins—typically 25. This process of

Bitcoin "mining" will continue until a maximum of 21 million Bitcoins are produced; a total expected to be reached in 2030.

People can buy and sell Bitcoins in exchange for dollars and other currencies on Web sites, such as Mt. Gox, which is based in Tokyo. You can buy Bitcoins and store them in a "digital wallet" on a smartphone. You can then buy something in a store that accepts Bitcoins by scanning a bar code with your phone. A number of Web sites, such as BitPay, which is based in Atlanta, allow merchants to process purchases made with Bitcoins in a way similar to how they process credit card payments.

Why would buyers and sellers prefer to use Bitcoins rather than cash or a credit card? The popularity of Bitcoins with some buyers may be due to its being a new and fashionable way to make purchases and because of the convenience of using a smartphone to make a purchase. In addition, some people are afraid that because central banks in most countries greatly increased the money supply during and after the recession of 2007–2009, the result will eventually be high rates of inflation. These people hope that because the total amount of Bitcoins is limited, inflation will not undermine their value. Finally, when you buy something with a credit card, the credit card company has a permanent record of your transaction. Bitcoin transactions are more private because no such record of your transaction exists. Some retailers prefer Bitcoins to credit card purchases because the retailers pay only about 1 percent of the sale in processing costs, as opposed to about 3 percent for a credit card purchase. In addition, a Bitcoin sale is final, just as if the purchase was made with cash, unlike credit card sales, where the buyer can dispute the purchase even months after it was made.

Policymakers are concerned about Bitcoins and other virtual money. For example, the U.S. Department of the Treasury monitors attempts at "money laundering," which refers to actions by criminals and terrorists to disguise movements of cash. Congress requires all banks in the United States to report cash transactions of $10,000 or more, and other governments have similar requirements. But the exchanges where virtual currencies are traded have been largely exempt from such rules. In June 2013, though, Mt. Gox agreed to follow U.S. money laundering rules. Some policymakers are also concerned that investors on exchanges might manipulate the prices of Bitcoins and other virtual currencies. The value of Bitcoins in exchange for dollars rose from $5 per Bitcoin in June 2012 to $266 per Bitcoin in April 2013, before falling to $94 per Bitcoin in July 2013. Whether these swings in value represented underlying movements in demand and supply for Bitcoins or manipulation of their values was not clear.

Should the Federal Reserve include Bitcoins and other virtual currencies in its measures of the money supply? So far, the volume of transactions in these currencies has been small, which makes the question of little practical importance. At this point, the Federal Reserve treats virtual currencies as being the equivalent of credit or debit cards, rather than currency or checking account balances, and does not include them in M1 or M2.

Sources: Sarah E. Needleman, "More Small Businesses Embrace Bitcoin," *Wall Street Journal*, June 26, 2013; Lingling Wei, "Fed Studying Risk at Online Payment Providers," *Wall Street Journal*, June 3, 2013; "Bits and Bob," *Economist*, June 13, 2011; and "How Does Bitcoin Work?" *Economist*, April 11, 2013.

Your Turn: Test your understanding by doing related problem 2.11 at the end of this chapter.

Bitcoins are created by computer calculations, not by central banks.

How Do Banks Create Money?

3 LEARNING OBJECTIVE

Explain how banks create money.

We have seen that the most important component of the money supply is checking accounts in banks. To understand the role money plays in the economy, we need to look more closely at how banks operate. Banks are profit-making private businesses, just like department stores and supermarkets. Some banks are quite small, with just a few branches, and do business in a limited area. Others are among the largest corporations in the United States, with thousands of branches spread across many states. Banks play an important role in the economy by accepting deposits and making loans. By taking these actions, banks fulfill a key function in the *money supply process* by which central banks control the money supply.

Bank Balance Sheets

To understand how banks create money, we need to briefly examine a typical bank balance sheet. On a balance sheet, a firm's assets are listed on the left, and its liabilities and stockholders' equity are listed on the right. Assets are the value of anything owned by the firm, liabilities are the value of anything the firm owes, and stockholders' equity is the difference between the total value of assets and the total value of liabilities. Stockholders' equity represents the value of the firm if it were closed, all its assets were sold, and all its liabilities were paid off. A corporation's stockholders' equity is also called its *net worth*. A bank's shareholders' equity or net worth is also called its *capital*.

Figure 2 shows a typical balance sheet for a large bank. The key assets on a bank's balance sheet are its *reserves*, loans, and holdings of securities, such as U.S. Treasury bills. **Reserves** are deposits that a bank has retained rather than loaned out or invested. Banks keep reserves either physically within the bank, as *vault cash*, or on deposit with the Federal Reserve. Banks are required by law to keep as reserves 10 percent of their checking account deposits above a threshold level, which in 2013 was $79.5 million. These reserves are called **required reserves**. The minimum fraction of deposits that banks are required to keep as reserves is called the **required reserve ratio**. We can abbreviate the required reserve ratio as *RR*. Any reserves that banks hold over the legal requirement are called **excess reserves**. The balance sheet in Figure 2 shows that loans are a typical bank's largest asset.

Banks make *consumer loans* to households and *commercial loans* to businesses. A loan is an asset to a bank because it represents a promise by the person taking out the loan to make certain specified payments to the bank. A bank's reserves and its holdings of securities are also assets because they are things of value the bank owns.

Deposits are a typical bank's largest liability. Deposits include checking accounts, savings accounts, and CDs. Deposits are liabilities to banks because they are owed to the households or firms that have deposited the funds. If you deposit $100 in your checking account, the bank owes you the $100, and you can ask for it back at any time. So, your checking account is an asset to you, and it is a liability to the bank. Banks also borrow short term from other banks and from the Federal Reserve and borrow long term by selling bonds to investors. These *borrowings* are also liabilities.

Using T-Accounts to Show How a Bank Can Create Money

It is easier to show how banks create money by using a T-account than by using a balance sheet. A T-account is a stripped-down version of a balance sheet that shows only how a transaction *changes* a bank's balance sheet. Suppose you deposit $1,000 in

Reserves Deposits that a bank keeps as cash in its vault or on deposit with the Federal Reserve.

Required reserves Reserves that a bank is legally required to hold, based on its checking account deposits.

Required reserve ratio The minimum fraction of deposits banks are required by law to keep as reserves.

Excess reserves Reserves that banks hold over the legal requirement.

Figure 2

Balance Sheet of a Typical Large Bank

The items on a bank's balance sheet of greatest economic importance are its reserves, loans, and deposits. Notice that the difference between the value of this bank's total assets and its total liabilities is equal to its stockholders' equity. As a consequence, the left side of the balance sheet always equals the right side.

Note: Some entries have been combined to simplify the balance sheet.

Assets (in billions)		Liabilities and Stockholders' Equity (in billions)	
Reserves	$135	Deposits	$1,000
Loans	900	Short-term borrowing	400
Securities	700	Long-term debt	360
Buildings and equipment	15	Other liabilities	275
Other assets	550	Total liabilities	$2,035
		Stockholders' equity	265
Total assets	$2,300	Total liabilities and stockholders' equity	$2,300

currency into an account at Bank of America. This transaction raises the total deposits at Bank of America by $1,000 and also raises its reserves by $1,000. We show this result on the following T-account:

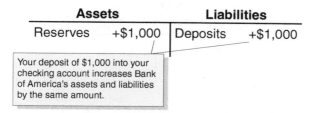

Assets		Liabilities	
Reserves	+$1,000	Deposits	+$1,000

Your deposit of $1,000 into your checking account increases Bank of America's assets and liabilities by the same amount.

Remember that because the total value of all the entries on the right side of a balance sheet must always be equal to the total value of all the entries on the left side of a balance sheet, any transaction that increases (or decreases) one side of the balance sheet must also increase (or decrease) the other side of the balance sheet. In this case, the T-account shows that we increased both sides of the balance sheet by $1,000.

Initially, this transaction does not increase the money supply. The currency component of the money supply declines by $1,000 because the $1,000 you deposited is no longer in circulation and, therefore, is not counted in the money supply. But the decrease in currency is offset by a $1,000 increase in the checking account deposit component of the money supply.

This initial change is not the end of the story, however. Banks are required to keep 10 percent of deposits as reserves. Because the Federal Reserve pays banks only a low rate of interest on their reserves, banks have an incentive to loan out or buy securities with the other 90 percent. Suppose, for simplicity, that initially Bank of America holds no excess reserves. In that case, Bank of America can keep $100 of your deposit as required reserves and loan out the other $900, which represents its excess reserves. Assume Bank of America loans out the $900 to someone to buy a very inexpensive used car. Bank of America could give the $900 to the borrower in currency, but usually banks make loans by increasing the borrower's checking account. We can show this transaction with another T-account:

Assets		Liabilities	
Reserves	+$1,000	Deposits	+$1,000
Loans	+$900	Deposits	+$900

1. By loaning out $900 in excess reserves . . .

2. . . . Bank of America has increased the money supply by $900.

Notice that *by making this $900 loan, Bank of America has increased the money supply by $900.* The initial $1,000 in currency you deposited into your checking account has been turned into $1,900 in checking account deposits—a net increase in the money supply of $900.

But the story does not end here. The person who took out the $900 loan did so to buy a used car. To keep things simple, let's suppose he buys the car for exactly $900 and pays by writing a check on his account at Bank of America. The seller of the used car will now deposit the check in her bank. That bank may also be a branch of Bank of America, but in most cities, there are many banks, so let's assume that the seller of the car has her account at a branch of PNC Bank. Once she deposits the check, PNC Bank will send it to Bank of America to *clear* the check and collect the $900. We show the result in the following T-accounts:

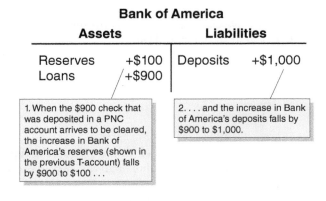

Bank of America

Assets		Liabilities	
Reserves	+$100	Deposits	+$1,000
Loans	+$900		

1. When the $900 check that was deposited in a PNC account arrives to be cleared, the increase in Bank of America's reserves (shown in the previous T-account) falls by $900 to $100 . . .

2. . . . and the increase in Bank of America's deposits falls by $900 to $1,000.

PNC Bank

Assets		Liabilities	
Reserves	+$900	Deposits	+$900

After the check drawn on the account at Bank of America clears, PNC's reserves and deposits both increase by $900.

After the car buyer's check clears, Bank of America has lost $900 in deposits—the amount loaned to the car buyer—and $900 in reserves—the amount it had to pay PNC when PNC sent Bank of America the car buyer's check. PNC has an increase in checking account deposits of $900—the deposit of the car seller—and an increase in reserves of $900—the amount it received from Bank of America.

PNC has 100 percent reserves against this new $900 deposit, but it needs only 10 percent reserves. The bank has an incentive to keep $90 as reserves and to loan out the other $810, which are excess reserves. If PNC does this, we can show the change in its balance sheet by using another T-account:

PNC Bank

Assets		Liabilities	
Reserves	+$900	Deposits	+$900
Loans	+$810	Deposits	+$810

By making an $810 loan, PNC has increased both its loans and its deposits by $810.

In loaning out the $810 in excess reserves, PNC creates a new checking account deposit of $810. The initial deposit of $1,000 in currency into Bank of America has now resulted in the creation of $1,000 + $900 + $810 = $2,710 in checking account deposits. The money supply has increased by $2,710 − $1,000 = $1,710.

The process is still not finished. The person who borrows the $810 will spend it by writing a check against his account. Whoever receives the $810 will deposit it in her bank, which could be a Bank of America branch or a PNC branch or a branch of some other bank. That new bank—if it's not PNC—will send the check to PNC and will receive $810 in new reserves. That new bank will have an incentive to loan out 90 percent of these reserves—keeping 10 percent to meet the legal requirement—and the process will go on. At each stage, the additional loans being made and the additional deposits being created are shrinking by 10 percent, as each bank has to keep that amount as required reserves. We can use a table to show the total increase in checking account deposits started by your initial deposit of $1,000. The dots in the table represent additional rounds in the money supply process:

Bank	Increase in Checking Account Deposits
Bank of America	$1,000
PNC	+ 900 (= 0.9 × $1,000)
Third Bank	+ 810 (= 0.9 × $900)
Fourth Bank	+ 729 (= 0.9 × $810)
•	+ •
•	+ •
•	+ •
Total change in checking account deposits	= $10,000

The Simple Deposit Multiplier

Your initial deposit of $1,000 increased the reserves of the banking system by $1,000 and led to a total increase in checking account deposits of $10,000. The ratio of the amount of deposits created by banks to the amount of new reserves is called the **simple deposit multiplier**. In this case, the simple deposit multiplier is equal to $10,000/$1,000 = 10. Why 10? How do we know that your initial $1,000 deposit ultimately leads to a total increase in deposits of $10,000?

Simple deposit multiplier The ratio of the amount of deposits created by banks to the amount of new reserves.

There are two ways to answer this question. First, each bank in the money supply process is keeping reserves equal to 10 percent of its deposits. For the banking system as a whole, the total increase in reserves is $1,000—the amount of your original currency deposit. Therefore, the system as a whole will end up with $10,000 in deposits because $1,000 is 10 percent of $10,000.

A second way to answer the question is by deriving an expression for the simple deposit multiplier. The total increase in deposits equals:

$$\$1,000 + [0.9 \times \$1,000] + [(0.9 \times 0.9) \times \$1,000] + [(0.9 \times 0.9 \times 0.9) \times \$1,000] + \ldots$$

or

$$\$1,000 + [0.9 \times \$1,000] + [0.9^2 \times \$1,000] + [0.9^3 \times \$1,000] + \ldots$$

or

$$\$1,000 \times (1 + 0.9 + 0.9^2 + 0.9^3 + \ldots).$$

The rules of algebra tell us that an expression like the one in the parentheses sums to:

$$\frac{1}{1 - 0.9}.$$

Simplifying further, we have:

$$\frac{1}{0.10} = 10.$$

So,

$$\text{Total increase in deposits} = \$1,000 \times 10 = \$10,000.$$

Don't Let This Happen to You

Don't Confuse Assets and Liabilities

Consider the following reasoning: "How can checking account deposits be a liability to a bank? After all, they are something of value that is in the bank. Therefore, checking account deposits should be counted as a bank *asset* rather than as a bank liability."

This statement is incorrect. The balance in a checking account represents something the bank *owes* to the owner of the account. Therefore, it is a liability to the bank, although it is an asset to the owner of the account. Similarly, your car loan is a liability to you—because it is a debt you owe to the bank—but it is an asset to the bank.

Your Turn: Test your understanding by doing related problem 3.11 at the end of this chapter.

Note that 10 is equal to 1 divided by the required reserve ratio, *RR*, which in this case is 10 percent, or 0.10. So, we have another way of expressing the simple deposit multiplier:

$$\text{Simple deposit multiplier} = \frac{1}{RR}.$$

This formula makes it clear that the higher the required reserve ratio, the smaller the simple deposit multiplier. With a required reserve ratio of 10 percent, the simple deposit multiplier is 10. If the required reserve ratio were 20 percent, the simple deposit multiplier would fall to 1/0.20, or 5.

We can use this formula to calculate the total increase in checking account deposits from an increase in bank reserves due to, for instance, currency being deposited in a bank:

$$\text{Change in checking account deposits} = \text{Change in bank reserves} \times \frac{1}{RR}.$$

For example, if $100,000 in currency is deposited in a bank and the required reserve ratio is 10 percent, then

$$\text{Change in checking account deposits} = \$100,000 \times \frac{1}{0.10}$$
$$= \$100,000 \times 10 = \$1,000,000.$$

Solved Problem 3

Showing How Banks Create Money

Suppose you deposit $5,000 in currency into your checking account at a branch of PNC Bank, which we will assume has no excess reserves at the time you make your deposit. Also assume that the required reserve ratio is 0.10.

a. Use a T-account to show the initial effect of this transaction on PNC's balance sheet.

b. Suppose that PNC makes the maximum loan it can from the funds you deposited. Use a T-account to show the initial effect on PNC's balance sheet from granting the loan. Also include in this T-account the transaction from part (a).

c. Now suppose that whoever took out the loan in part (b) writes a check for this amount and that the person receiving the check deposits it in Bank of America. Show the effect of these transactions on the balance sheets of PNC Bank and Bank of America *after the check has cleared*. On the T-account for PNC Bank, include the transactions from parts (a) and (b).

d. What is the maximum increase in checking account deposits that can result from your $5,000 deposit? What is the maximum increase in the money supply that can result from your deposit? Explain.

Solving the Problem

Step 1: **Review the chapter material.** This problem is about how banks create checking account deposits, so you may want to review the section "Using T-Accounts to Show How a Bank Can Create Money."

Step 2: **Answer part (a) by using a T-account to show the effect of the deposit.** Keeping in mind that T-accounts show only the changes in a balance sheet that result from the relevant transaction and that assets are on the left side of the account and liabilities are on the right side, we have:

PNC Bank

Assets		Liabilities	
Reserves	+$5,000	Deposits	+$5,000

Because the bank now has your $5,000 in currency in its vault, its reserves (and, therefore, its assets) have risen by $5,000. This transaction also increases your checking account balance by $5,000. Because the bank owes you this money, the bank's liabilities have also risen by $5,000.

Step 3: **Answer part (b) by using a T-account to show the effect of the loan.** The problem tells you to assume that PNC Bank currently has no excess reserves and that the required reserve ratio is 10 percent. This requirement means that if the bank's checking account deposits go up by $5,000, the bank must keep $500 as reserves and can loan out the remaining $4,500. Remembering that new loans usually take the form of setting up, or increasing, a checking account for the borrower, we have:

PNC Bank

Assets		Liabilities	
Reserves	+$5,000	Deposits	+$5,000
Loans	+$4,500	Deposits	+$4,500

The first line of the T-account shows the transaction from part (a). The second line shows that PNC has loaned out $4,500 by increasing the checking account of the borrower by $4,500. The loan is an asset to PNC because it represents the borrower's promise to make certain payments spelled out in the loan agreement.

Step 4: **Answer part (c) by using T-accounts for PNC and Bank of America to show the effect of the check clearing.** We now show the effect of the borrower having spent the $4,500 he received as a loan from PNC. The person who received the $4,500 check deposits it in her account at Bank of America. We need two T-accounts to show this activity:

PNC Bank

Assets		Liabilities	
Reserves	+$500	Deposits	+$5,000
Loans	+$4,500		

Bank of America

Assets		Liabilities	
Reserves	+$4,500	Deposits	+$4,500

Look first at the T-account for PNC. Once Bank of America sends the check written by the borrower to PNC, PNC loses $4,500 in reserves, and Bank of America gains $4,500 in reserves. The $4,500 is also deducted from the account of the borrower. PNC is now satisfied with the result. It received a $5,000 deposit in currency from you. When that money was sitting in the bank vault, it wasn't earning any interest for PNC. Now $4,500 of the $5,000 has been loaned out and is earning interest. These interest payments allow PNC to cover its costs, which it has to do to remain in business.

Bank of America now has an increase in deposits of $4,500, resulting from the check being deposited, and an increase in reserves of $4,500. Bank of America is in the same situation as PNC was in part (a): It has excess reserves as a result of this transaction and a strong incentive to lend them out.

Step 5: **Answer part (d) by using the simple deposit multiplier formula to calculate the maximum increase in checking account deposits and the maximum increase in the money supply.** The simple deposit multiplier expression is (remember that RR is the required reserve ratio):

$$\text{Change in checking account deposits} = \text{Change in bank reserves} \times \frac{1}{RR}.$$

In this case, bank reserves rose by $5,000 as a result of your initial deposit, and the required reserve ratio is 0.10, so:

$$\text{Change in checking account deposits} = \$5,000 \times \frac{1}{0.10}$$
$$= \$5,000 \times 10 = \$50,000.$$

Because checking account deposits are part of the money supply, it is tempting to say that the money supply has also increased by $50,000. Remember, though, that your $5,000 in currency was counted as part of the money supply while you had it, but it is not counted when it is sitting in a bank vault. Therefore:

$$\text{Increase in checking account deposits} - \text{Decline in currency in}$$
$$\text{circulation} = \text{Change in the money supply.}$$

Or,

$$\$50,000 - \$5,000 = \$45,000.$$

Your Turn: For more practice, do related problem 3.12 at the end of the chapter.

The Simple Deposit Multiplier versus the Real-World Deposit Multiplier

The story we have just told of the money supply process has been simplified in two ways. First, we assumed that banks do not keep any excess reserves. That is, we assumed that when you deposited $1,000 in currency into your checking account at Bank of America, it loaned out $900, keeping only the $100 in required reserves. In fact, banks often keep some excess reserves to guard against the possibility that many depositors may simultaneously make withdrawals from their accounts. Since the financial crisis that began in 2007, banks have kept substantial excess reserves. The more excess reserves banks keep, the smaller the deposit multiplier. Imagine an extreme case in which Bank of America kept your entire $1,000 as reserves, loaning out none of it. In this case, the process we described earlier—loans leading to the creation of new deposits, leading to the making of additional loans, and so on—will not take place. The $1,000 increase in reserves will lead to just a $1,000 increase in deposits, and the deposit multiplier will be $1,000/$1,000 = 1$, not 10.

Second, we assumed that the whole amount of every check is deposited in a bank; no one takes any of it out as currency. In reality, households and firms keep roughly constant the amount of currency they hold relative to the value of their checking account balances. So, we would expect to see people increasing the amount of currency they hold as the balances in their checking accounts rise. Once again, think of the extreme case. Suppose that when Bank of America makes the initial $900 loan to the borrower who wants to buy a used car, the seller of the car cashes the check instead of depositing it. In that case, PNC does not receive any new reserves and does not make any new loans. Once again, the $1,000 increase in your checking account at Bank of America is the only increase in deposits, and the deposit multiplier is 1.

The effect of these two factors is to reduce the real-world deposit multiplier to about 1.6 during normal times. So, a $1 increase in the reserves of the banking system typically results in about a $1.60 increase in deposits. Following the financial crisis of 2007–2009, the surge in bank holdings of excess reserves reduced the multiplier to less than 1.

Although the story of the deposit multiplier can be complicated, the key point to bear in mind is that the most important part of the money supply is the checking account balance component. When banks make loans, they increase checking account balances, and the money supply expands. Banks make new loans whenever they gain reserves. The whole process can also work in reverse: If banks lose reserves, they reduce their outstanding loans and deposits, and the money supply contracts.

We can summarize these important conclusions:

1. When banks gain reserves, they make new loans, and the money supply expands.
2. When banks lose reserves, they reduce their loans, and the money supply contracts.

The Federal Reserve System

4 LEARNING OBJECTIVE

Discuss the three policy tools the Federal Reserve uses to manage the money supply.

Many people are surprised to learn that banks do not keep locked away in their vaults all the funds that are deposited in checking accounts. The United States, like nearly all other countries, has a **fractional reserve banking system**, which means that banks keep less than 100 percent of deposits as reserves. When people deposit money in a bank, the bank loans most of the money to someone else. What happens if depositors want their money back? Depositors withdrawing money would seem to be a problem because banks have loaned out most of the money and can't easily get it back.

In practice, withdrawals are usually not a problem for banks. On a typical day, about as much money is deposited as is withdrawn. If a small amount more is withdrawn than deposited, banks can cover the difference from their excess reserves or by borrowing from other banks. Sometimes depositors lose confidence in a bank when they question the value of the bank's underlying assets, particularly its loans. Often, the reason for a loss of confidence is bad news about the bank, whether true or false. When many depositors simultaneously decide to withdraw their money from a bank, there is a **bank run**. If many banks experience runs at the same time, the result is a **bank panic**. It is possible for one bank to handle a run by borrowing from other banks, but if many banks simultaneously experience runs, the banking system may be in trouble.

A central bank, like the Federal Reserve in the United States, can help stop a bank panic by acting as a *lender of last resort*. In acting as a lender of last resort, a central bank makes loans to banks that cannot borrow funds elsewhere. The banks can use these loans to pay off depositors. When the panic ends and the depositors put their money back in their accounts, the banks can repay the loans to the central bank.

Fractional reserve banking system A banking system in which banks keep less than 100 percent of deposits as reserves.

Bank run A situation in which many depositors simultaneously decide to withdraw money from a bank.

Bank panic A situation in which many banks experience runs at the same time.

The Establishment of the Federal Reserve System

Bank panics lead to severe disruptions in business activity because households and firms have trouble gaining access to their accounts and may be unable to borrow money. Not surprisingly, in the United States, each bank panic in the late nineteenth and early twentieth centuries was accompanied by a recession. With the intention of putting an end to bank panics, in 1913, Congress passed the Federal Reserve Act, setting up the Federal Reserve System—often referred to as "the Fed." The system began operation in 1914, with the authority to make loans to banks. The loans the Fed makes to banks are called

Discount loans Loans the Federal Reserve makes to banks.

Discount rate The interest rate the Federal Reserve charges on discount loans.

discount loans, and the interest rate it charges on the loans is called the **discount rate**. When a bank receives a loan from the Fed, its reserves increase by the amount of the loan.

The Fed's first test as a lender of last resort came in the early years of the Great Depression of the 1930s, when many banks were hit by bank runs as depositors pulled funds out of checking and savings accounts. Although the Fed had been established to act as a lender of last resort, Fed officials declined to make loans to many banks because the officials were worried that banks experiencing runs had made bad loans and other investments. The Fed believed that making loans to banks that were in financial trouble because of bad investments might reduce the incentive bank managers had to be careful in their investment decisions. Partly due to the Fed's unwillingness to act as a lender of last resort, more than 5,000 banks failed during the early 1930s. Today, many economists are critical of the Fed's decisions in the early 1930s because they believe these decisions increased the severity of the Great Depression. In 1934, Congress established the Federal Deposit Insurance Corporation (FDIC) to insure deposits in most banks up to a limit, which is currently $250,000 per deposit. Deposit insurance has greatly reduced bank runs because it has reassured all but the largest depositors that their deposits are safe, even if their bank goes out of business. During the financial crisis of 2007–2009, some banks experienced runs when depositors with funds exceeding the deposit insurance limit feared that they would suffer losses if their banks failed.

In setting up the Federal Reserve System, Congress divided the country into 12 Federal Reserve districts, as shown in Figure 3. Each district has its own Federal Reserve Bank,

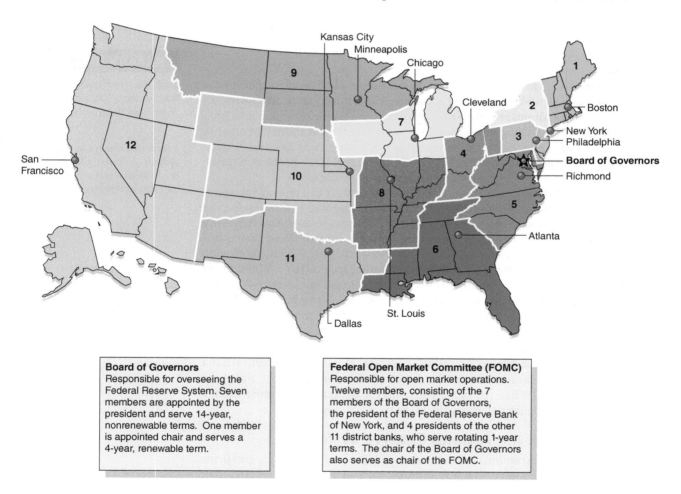

Board of Governors
Responsible for overseeing the Federal Reserve System. Seven members are appointed by the president and serve 14-year, nonrenewable terms. One member is appointed chair and serves a 4-year, renewable term.

Federal Open Market Committee (FOMC)
Responsible for open market operations. Twelve members, consisting of the 7 members of the Board of Governors, the president of the Federal Reserve Bank of New York, and 4 presidents of the other 11 district banks, who serve rotating 1-year terms. The chair of the Board of Governors also serves as chair of the FOMC.

Figure 3 **The Federal Reserve System**

The United States is divided into 12 Federal Reserve districts, each of which has a Federal Reserve Bank. The real power within the Federal Reserve System, however, lies in Washington, DC, with the Board of Governors, which consists of 7 members appointed by the president. The 12-member Federal Open Market Committee carries out monetary policy.
Source: Board of Governors of the Federal Reserve System.

which provides services to banks in that district. The real power of the Fed, however, lies in Washington, DC, with the Board of Governors. The seven members of the Board of Governors are appointed by the president of the United States to 14-year, nonrenewable terms. One member of the Board of Governors is appointed chair and serves a 4-year, renewable term. In addition to acting as a lender of last resort to banks, the Fed acts as a bankers' bank, providing services such as check clearing to banks, and has the responsibility of managing the U.S. money supply.

How the Federal Reserve Manages the Money Supply

Although Congress established the Fed primarily to stop bank panics by acting as a lender of last resort, today the Fed is also responsible for managing the money supply. Managing the money supply is part of **monetary policy**, which the Fed undertakes to pursue macroeconomic policy objectives. To manage the money supply, the Fed uses three *monetary policy tools*:

Monetary policy The actions the Federal Reserve takes to manage the money supply and interest rates to pursue macroeconomic policy objectives.

1. Open market operations
2. Discount policy
3. Reserve requirements

Remember that the most important component of the money supply is checking account deposits. Not surprisingly, all three of the Fed's policy tools are aimed at affecting the reserves of banks as a means of changing the volume of checking account deposits.

Open Market Operations Eight times per year, the **Federal Open Market Committee (FOMC)** meets in Washington, DC, to discuss monetary policy. The committee has 12 voting members: the 7 members of the Federal Reserve's Board of Governors, the president of the Federal Reserve Bank of New York, and 4 presidents from the other 11 Federal Reserve Banks. These 4 presidents serve one-year rotating terms as voting members of the FOMC. All 12 Federal Reserve Bank presidents attend meetings and participate in discussions. The chair of the Board of Governors also serves as the chair of the FOMC.

Federal Open Market Committee (FOMC) The Federal Reserve committee responsible for open market operations and managing the money supply in the United States.

The U.S. Treasury borrows money by selling bills, notes, and bonds. Remember that the *maturity* of a financial asset is the period of time until the purchaser receives payment of the face value or principal. Usually, bonds have face values of $1,000. Treasury bills have maturities of 1 year or less, Treasury notes have maturities of 2 years to 10 years, and Treasury bonds have maturities of 30 years. To control the size of the money supply, the Fed buys and sells Treasury securities in a process called **open market operations**. To increase the money supply, the FOMC directs the *trading desk*, located at the Federal Reserve Bank of New York, to carry out an *open market purchase* by buying U.S. Treasury securities—most frequently bills, but sometimes notes or bonds—from banks. The Fed pays for the Treasury bills by depositing the funds in the reserve accounts banks maintain with the Fed.

Open market operations The buying and selling of Treasury securities by the Federal Reserve in order to control the money supply.

Suppose that the Fed engages in an open market purchase of $10 million. We can illustrate the results with two T-accounts: one for the Fed and one for the banking system. The banking system's T-account is based on the banking system's balance sheet, which simply adds together all the assets and liabilities of all the commercial banks in the United States. As a result of the open market purchase, the banking system's holdings of Treasury bills fall by $10 million and its reserves increase by $10 million:

Banking System

Assets		Liabilities
Treasury bills	−$10 million	
Reserves	+$10 million	

The Fed's holdings of Treasury bills increase by $10 million, and the value of the banking system's reserve balances—which are a liability to the Fed—also increase by $10 million:

Federal Reserve

Assets		Liabilities	
Treasury bills	+$10 million	Reserves	+$10 million

This increase in reserves starts the process of expanding loans and checking account deposits that increases the money supply. To decrease the money supply, the FOMC directs the trading desk to carry out an *open market sale* by selling Treasury securities. When the buyers of the Treasury securities pay for them with checks, the banking system's reserves fall. This decrease in reserves starts a contraction of loans and checking account deposits that reduces the money supply.

There are three reasons the Fed conducts monetary policy principally through open market operations. First, because the Fed initiates open market operations, it completely controls their volume allowing it to make both large and small open market operations. Second, open market operations are easily reversible. If the Fed believes that previous open market purchases have caused the money supply to increase too rapidly, it can engage in open market sales. Third, the Fed can implement its open market operations quickly, with no administrative delay or required changes in regulations. Many other central banks, including the European Central Bank and the Bank of Japan, also use open market operations to conduct monetary policy.

The Federal Reserve is responsible for putting the paper currency of the United States into circulation. Recall that if you look at the top of a dollar bill, you see the words "Federal Reserve Note." When the Fed takes actions to increase the money supply, commentators sometimes say that it is "printing more money." The main way the Fed increases the money supply, however, is not by printing more currency but by buying Treasury securities. Similarly, to reduce the money supply, the Fed does not set fire to stacks of paper currency. Instead, it sells Treasury securities.

Discount Policy As we have seen, when a bank borrows money from the Fed by taking out a discount loan, the interest rate the bank pays is called the discount rate. By lowering the discount rate, the Fed can encourage banks to take additional loans and thereby increase their reserves. With more reserves, banks will make more loans to households and firms, which will increase checking account deposits and the money supply. Raising the discount rate will have the reverse effect.

Reserve Requirements When the Fed reduces the required reserve ratio, it converts required reserves into excess reserves. For example, suppose a bank has $100 million in checking account deposits, and the required reserve ratio is 10 percent. The bank will be required to hold $10 million as reserves. If the Fed reduces the required reserve ratio to 8 percent, the bank will need to hold only $8 million as reserves. The Fed can thereby convert $2 million worth of reserves from required reserves to excess reserves. This $2 million is then available for the bank to lend out. If the Fed *raises* the required reserve ratio from 10 percent to 12 percent, it will have the reverse effect.

The Fed changes reserve requirements much more rarely than it conducts open market operations or changes the discount rate. Because changes in reserve require-ments cause significant alterations in banks' holdings of loans and securities, frequent changes would be disruptive. Also, because the Fed pays banks only a low interest rate on reserves, the use of reserve requirements to manage the money supply effectively places a tax on banks' deposit-taking and lending activities, which can be costly for the economy.

The "Shadow Banking System" and the Financial Crisis of 2007-2009

The banks we have been discussing in this chapter are *commercial banks*, whose most important economic role is to accept funds from depositors and lend those funds to borrowers. Large firms can sell stocks and bonds on financial markets, but investors are typically unwilling to buy stocks and bonds from small and medium-sized firms because they lack sufficient information on the financial health of smaller firms. So, smaller firms—and households—have traditionally relied on bank loans for their credit needs. In the past 25 years, however, two important developments have occurred in the financial system: (1) Banks have begun to resell many of their loans rather than keeping them until borrowers pay them off, and (2) financial firms other than commercial banks have become important sources of credit to businesses.

Securitization Comes to Banking Traditionally, when a bank made a *residential mortgage loan* to a household to buy a home or made a commercial loan to a business, the bank would keep the loan and collect the payments until the borrower paid off the loan. A financial asset—such as a loan or a stock or a bond—is considered a **security** if it can be bought and sold in a *financial market* as, for instance, shares of stock issued by the Coca-Cola Company can be bought and sold on the New York Stock Exchange. When a financial asset is first sold, the sale takes place in the *primary market*. If an investor resells the asset, the sale takes place in the *secondary market*. Prior to 1970, most loans were not securities because they could not be resold—there was no secondary market for them. First, residential mortgages and then other loans, including car loans and commercial loans, began to be *securitized*. The process of **securitization** involves creating a secondary market in which loans that have been bundled together can be bought and sold in financial markets, just as corporate or government bonds are. Figure 4 outlines the securitization process.

Security A financial asset—such as a stock or a bond—that can be bought and sold in a financial market.

The Shadow Banking System In addition to the changes resulting from securitization, the financial system was transformed in the 1990s and 2000s by the increasing importance of *nonbank financial firms*. Investment banks, such as Goldman Sachs and Morgan Stanley, differ from commercial banks in that they do not accept deposits, and they rarely lend directly to households. Instead, investment banks traditionally

Securitization The process of transforming loans or other financial assets into securities.

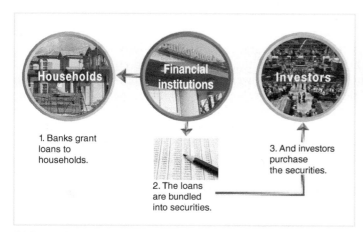

1. Banks grant loans to households.

2. The loans are bundled into securities.

3. And investors purchase the securities.

(a) Securitizing a loan

1. Banks collect loan payments from households.

2. Banks receive a fee for processing the payments.

3. Banks send payments to investors in the securities.

(b) The flow of payments on a securitized loan

Figure 4 **The Process of Securitization**

Panel (a) shows how in the securitization process banks grant loans to households and bundle the loans into securities that are then sold to investors.

Panel (b) shows that banks collect payments on the original loans and, after taking a fee, send the payments to the investors who bought the securities.

concentrated on providing advice to firms issuing stocks and bonds or considering mergers with other firms. In the late 1990s, investment banks expanded their buying of mortgages, bundling large numbers of them together as bonds known as *mortgage-backed securities*, and reselling them to investors. Mortgage-backed securities proved very popular with investors because they often paid higher interest rates than other securities that seemed to have comparable default risk.

Money market mutual funds have also increased their importance in the financial system over time. These funds sell shares to investors and use the money to buy short-term securities such as Treasury bills and commercial paper issued by corporations. Commercial paper represents short-term borrowing corporations use to fund their day-to-day operations. Many corporations that previously met such needs by borrowing from banks began instead to sell commercial paper to money market mutual funds.

Hedge funds raise money from wealthy investors and use sophisticated investment strategies that often involve significant risk. By the mid-2000s, hedge funds had become an important source of demand for securitized loans and an important source of loans to other financial firms.

In 2008, Timothy Geithner, who became Treasury secretary in the Obama administration, used the term the *shadow banking system* to refer to investment banks, money market mutual funds, hedge funds, and other nonbank financial firms engaged in similar activities. By raising money from investors and lending it directly or indirectly to firms and households, these firms were carrying out a function that at one time was almost exclusively the domain of commercial banks.

The Financial Crisis of 2007–2009 The firms in the shadow banking system differed from commercial banks in two important ways: First, the government agencies—including the Federal Reserve—that regulated the commercial banking system did not regulate these firms. Second, these firms were more highly *leveraged*—that is, they relied more heavily on borrowed money to finance their operations—than were commercial banks. If a firm uses a small amount of its own money and a lot of borrowed money to make an investment, both the firm's potential profits and its potential losses are increased. Suppose a firm invests $100 of its own money. If the investment earns a return of $3, the firm has earned 3 percent ($3/$100) on its funds. But if the firm's investment consists of $10 of its own money and $90 it has borrowed, a profit of $3 becomes a return of 30 percent ($3/$10) on the firm's $10 investment. If the investment loses $2, however, the firm's return is −20 percent (−$2/$10). Leveraged investments have a potential for both large gains and large losses.

As mentioned earlier, commercial banks rarely experienced runs after Congress established federal deposit insurance in the 1930s. However, beginning in 2007, firms in the shadow banking system were vulnerable to runs. The underlying cause of the financial crisis of 2007–2009 was problems in the U.S. housing market. As housing prices began to fall, a significant number of borrowers defaulted on their mortgages, which caused mortgage-backed securities to lose value. Financial firms, including both commercial banks and many firms in the shadow banking system, that had invested in these securities suffered losses. The more leveraged the firm, the larger the losses. Although deposit insurance helped commercial banks avoid runs, investment banks and other financial firms that had borrowed short term and invested the funds long term were in trouble. As lenders refused to renew their short-term loans, many of these firms had to sell their holdings of securities in an attempt to raise cash. But as the prices of the securities continued to fall, the losses to these firms increased.

In the spring of 2008, the investment bank Bear Stearns was saved from bankruptcy only when the Federal Reserve arranged for it to be acquired by JPMorgan Chase. In the fall of 2008, the Federal Reserve and the U.S. Treasury decided not to take action to save the investment bank Lehman Brothers, which failed. The failure of Lehman Brothers reverberated throughout the financial system, setting off a panic. The process of securitization—apart from government-guaranteed residential mortgages—ground to a halt. The well-publicized difficulties of a money market mutual fund that had suffered losses on loans to Lehman Brothers led to a wave of withdrawals from these funds. In turn, the funds were no longer able to fulfill their role as buyers of corporate commercial paper. As banks and other financial firms sold assets and cut back on lending to shore up their financial positions, the flow of funds from savers to borrowers was disrupted. The resulting *credit crunch* significantly worsened the recession that had begun in December 2007.

The Fed's Response The Fed, in combination with the U.S. Treasury, took vigorous action to deal with the financial crisis. We can mention several particularly important policy actions. First, in the fall of 2008, under the Troubled Asset Relief Program (TARP), the Fed and Treasury began attempting to stabilize the commercial banking system by providing funds to banks in exchange for stock. Taking partial ownership of private commercial banks was an unprecedented move by the federal government. The Fed also modified its discount policy by setting up several new "lending facilities." These lending facilities made it possible for the Fed to grant discount loans to financial firms—such as investment banks—that had not previously been eligible. In addition, the Fed addressed problems in the commercial paper market by directly buying commercial paper for the first time since the 1930s.

Although the recession continued into 2009, the extraordinary actions of the Treasury and Fed stabilized the financial system. Still, even by late 2013, the flow of funds from savers to borrowers had not yet returned to normal levels, and economists and policymakers were debating the wisdom of some of the Fed's actions.

The Quantity Theory of Money

5 LEARNING OBJECTIVE

Explain the quantity theory of money and use it to explain how high rates of inflation occur.

People have been aware of the connection between increases in the money supply and inflation for centuries. In the sixteenth century, the Spanish conquered Mexico and Peru and shipped large quantities of gold and silver from those countries back to Spain. The gold and silver were minted into coins and spent across Europe to further the political ambitions of the Spanish kings. Prices in Europe rose steadily during these years, and many observers discussed the relationship between this inflation and the flow of gold and silver into Europe from the Americas.

Connecting Money and Prices: The Quantity Equation

In the early twentieth century, Irving Fisher, an economist at Yale University, formalized the connection between money and prices by using the *quantity equation*:

$$M \times V = P \times Y.$$

The quantity equation states that the money supply (M) multiplied by the *velocity of money* (V) equals the price level (P) multiplied by real output (Y). Fisher defined the **velocity of money**, often called simply "velocity," as the average number of times each dollar of the money supply is used to purchase goods and services included in GDP. Rewriting the original equation by dividing both sides by M, we have the equation for velocity:

$$V = \frac{P \times Y}{M}.$$

Velocity of money The average number of times each dollar in the money supply is used to purchase goods and services included in GDP.

If we use M1 to measure the money supply, the GDP price deflator to measure the price level, and real GDP to measure real output, the value for velocity for 2012 was:

$$V = \frac{1.05 \times \$15{,}471 \text{ billion}}{\$2{,}309 \text{ billion}} = 7.0.$$

This result tells us that, during 2012, each dollar of M1 was on average spent seven times on goods or services included in GDP.

Quantity theory of money A theory about the connection between money and prices that assumes that the velocity of money is constant.

Because velocity is defined to be equal to $(P \times Y)/M$, we know that the quantity equation must always hold true: The left side of the equation *must* be equal to the right side. A theory is a statement about the world that might possibly be false. Therefore, the quantity equation is not a theory. Irving Fisher turned the quantity equation into the **quantity theory of money** by arguing that velocity was constant. He argued that the average number of times a dollar is spent depends on how often people get paid, how often they do their grocery shopping, how often businesses mail bills, and other factors that do not change very often. Because this assertion may be true or false, the quantity theory of money is, in fact, a theory.

The Quantity Theory Explanation of Inflation

The quantity equation gives us a way of showing the relationship between changes in the money supply and changes in the price level, or inflation. To see this relationship more clearly, we can use a handy mathematical rule that states that an equation where variables are multiplied together is equal to an equation where the *growth rates* of these variables are *added* together. So, we can transform the quantity equation from

$$M \times V = P \times Y$$

to

Growth rate of the money supply + Growth rate of velocity =
Growth rate of the price level (or the inflation rate) + Growth rate of real output.

This way of writing the quantity equation is more useful for investigating the effect of changes in the money supply on the inflation rate. Remember that the growth rate for any variable is the percentage change in the variable from one year to the next. The growth rate of the price level is the inflation rate, so we can rewrite the quantity equation to help understand the factors that determine inflation:

Inflation rate = Growth rate of the money supply +
Growth rate of velocity − Growth rate of real output.

If Irving Fisher was correct that velocity is constant, then the growth rate of velocity will be zero. That is, if velocity is, say, always equal to seven, then its percentage change from one year to the next will always be zero. This assumption allows us to rewrite the equation one last time:

Inflation rate = Growth rate of the money supply − Growth rate of real output.

This equation leads to the following predictions:

1. If the money supply grows at a faster rate than real GDP, there will be inflation.
2. If the money supply grows at a slower rate than real GDP, there will be deflation. (Recall that *deflation* is a decline in the price level.)
3. If the money supply grows at the same rate as real GDP, the price level will be stable, and there will be neither inflation nor deflation.

It turns out that Irving Fisher was wrong in asserting that the velocity of money is constant. From year to year, there can be significant fluctuations in velocity. As a result, the predictions of inflation based on the quantity theory of money do not hold every year, but most economists agree that the quantity theory provides useful insight into the long-run relationship between the money supply and inflation: *In the long run, inflation results from the money supply growing at a faster rate than real GDP.*

How Accurate Are Forecasts of Inflation Based on the Quantity Theory?

Note that the accuracy of the quantity theory depends on whether the key assumption that velocity is constant is correct. If velocity is not constant, there may not be a tight link between increases in the money supply and increases in the price level. For example, an increase in the quantity of money might be offset by a decline in velocity, leaving the price level unaffected. Because velocity can move erratically in the short run, we would not expect the quantity equation to provide good forecasts of inflation in the short run. Over the long run, however, there is a strong link between changes in the money supply and inflation. Panel (a) of Figure 5 shows by decade the relationship in the United States between the growth of the M2 measure of the money supply and the inflation rate. (We use M2 here because data on M2 are available for a longer period of time than are data for M1.) Because of variations in the rate of growth of real GDP and in velocity, there is not an exact relationship between the growth rate of M2 and the inflation rate. But there is a clear pattern that decades with higher growth rates in the money supply were also decades with higher inflation rates. In other words, most of the variation in inflation rates across decades can be explained by variation in the rates of growth of the money supply.

Panel (b) provides further evidence consistent with the quantity theory by looking at rates of growth of the money supply and rates of inflation across 56 countries for the years 1995–2011. Although there is not an exact relationship between rates of growth of the money supply and rates of inflation across countries, panel (b) shows that countries where the money supply grew rapidly tended to have high inflation rates, while countries where the money supply grew more slowly tended to have much lower inflation rates. Not included in panel (b) are data for Zimbabwe, which we mentioned at the beginning of the chapter. Over this period, the money supply in Zimbabwe grew in some years by more than 7,500 percent. The result was an accelerating rate of inflation that eventually reached 15 billion percent during 2008. Zimbabwe was suffering from *hyperinflation*—that is, a rate of inflation that exceeds 50 percent per month.

High Rates of Inflation

The quantity theory can help us to understand the reasons for very high rates of inflation. Hyperinflation is caused by central banks increasing the money supply at a rate far in excess of the growth rate of real GDP. A high rate of inflation causes money to lose its value so rapidly that households and firms avoid holding it. If, as happened in

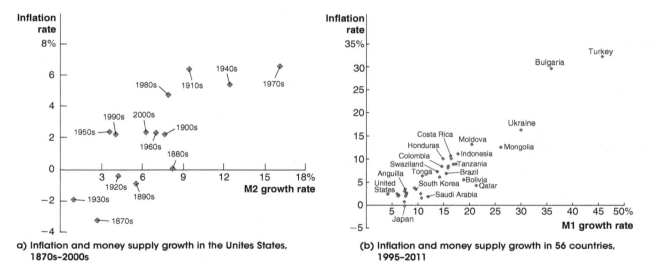

a) Inflation and money supply growth in the Unites States, 1870s-2000s

(b) Inflation and money supply growth in 56 countries, 1995-2011

Figure 5   The Relationship between Money Growth and Inflation over Time and around the World

Panel (a) shows that, by and large, the rate of inflation in the United States has been highest during the decades in which the money supply has increased most rapidly, and the rate of inflation has been lowest during the decades in which the money supply has increased least rapidly. Panel (b) shows the relationship between money supply growth and inflation for 56 countries between 1995 and 2011. There is not an exact relationship between money supply growth and inflation, but countries such as Bulgaria, Turkey, and Ukraine that had high rates of money supply growth had high inflation rates, and countries

such as the United States and Japan had low rates of money supply growth and low inflation rates.

Sources: Panel (a): For the 1870s to the 1960s, Milton Friedman and Anna J. Schwartz, *Monetary Trends in the United States and United Kingdom: Their Relation to Income, Prices, and Interest Rates, 1867–1975*, Chicago: University of Chicago Press, 1982, Table 4.8; and for the 1970s to the 2000s, Federal Reserve Board of Governors and U.S. Bureau of Economic Analysis; Panel (b): International Monetary Fund, *International Monetary Statistics*.

Zimbabwe, the inflation rate becomes high enough, people stop using paper currency, so it no longer serves the important functions of money discussed earlier in this chapter. Economies suffering from high inflation usually also suffer from very slow growth, if not severe recession.

Given the dire consequences that follow from high inflation, why do governments cause it by expanding the money supply so rapidly? The main reason is that governments often want to spend more than they are able to raise through taxes. Developed countries, such as the United States, can usually bridge gaps between spending and taxes by borrowing through selling bonds to the public. Developing countries, such as Zimbabwe, often have difficulty selling bonds because investors are skeptical of their ability to pay back the money. If they are unable to sell bonds to the public, governments in developing countries will force their central banks to purchase them. As we discussed previously, when a central bank buys government bonds, the money supply will increase. In the United States, the Federal Reserve always buys Treasury securities from banks, never directly from the U.S. Treasury. This procedure helps ensure that the Treasury only issues bonds in amounts that private investors—rather than the central bank—are willing to buy.

Making the Connection | The German Hyperinflation of the Early 1920s

When Germany lost World War I, a revolution broke out that overthrew Kaiser Wilhelm II and installed a new government known as the Weimar Republic. In the peace treaty of 1919, the Allies—the United States, Great Britain, France, and Italy—imposed payments called *reparations* on the new German government. The reparations were meant as compensation to the Allies for the damage Germany had caused during the war. It was very difficult for the German government to use tax revenue to cover both its normal spending and the reparations.

The German government decided to pay for the difference between its spending and its tax revenues by selling bonds to the central bank, the Reichsbank. After a few years, the German government fell far behind in its reparations payments. In January 1923, the French government sent troops into the German industrial area known as the Ruhr to try to collect the payments directly. German workers in the Ruhr went on strike, and the German government decided to support them by paying their salaries. The government raised the funds by selling bonds to the Reichsbank, thereby increasing the money supply.

During the hyperinflation of the 1920s, people in Germany used paper currency to light their stoves.

The inflationary increase in the money supply was very large: The total number of marks—the German currency—in circulation rose from 115 million in January 1922 to 1.3 billion in January 1923 and then to 497 billion *billion*, or 497,000,000,000,000,000,000, in December 1923. Just as the quantity theory predicts, the result was a staggeringly high rate of inflation. The German price index that stood at 100 in 1914 and 1,440 in January 1922 had risen to 126,160,000,000,000 in December 1923. The German mark became worthless. The German government ended the hyperinflation by (1) negotiating a new agreement with the Allies that reduced its reparations payments, (2) reducing other government expenditures and raising taxes to balance its budget, and (3) replacing the existing mark with a new mark. Each new mark was worth 1 trillion old marks. The German central bank was also limited to issuing a total of 3.2 billion new marks.

These steps were enough to bring the hyperinflation to an end—but not before the savings of anyone holding the old marks had been wiped out. Most middle-income Germans were extremely resentful of this outcome. Many historians believe that the hyperinflation greatly reduced the allegiance of many Germans to the Weimar Republic and may have helped pave the way for Adolph Hitler and the Nazis to seize power 10 years later.

Sources: Thomas Sargent, "The End of Four Big Hyperinflations," *Rational Expectations and Inflation*, New York: Harper & Row, 1986; and John Parke Young, *European Currency and Finance*, Washington, DC: Government Printing Office, 1925.

Your Turn: Test your understanding by doing related problem 5.10 at the end of this chapter.

Economics in Your Life

What If Money Became Increasingly Valuable?

At the beginning of this chapter, we asked you to consider whether you would like to live in an economy in which the purchasing power of money rises every year. The first thing to consider when thinking about the advantages and disadvantages of this situation is that the only way for the purchasing power of money to increase is for the price level to fall; in other words, *deflation* must occur. Because the price level in the United States hasn't fallen for an entire year since the 1930s, most people alive today have experienced only rising price levels—and declining purchasing power of money. Would replacing rising prices with falling prices necessarily be a good thing? It might be tempting to say "yes," because if you have a job, your salary will buy more goods and services each year. But in fact, just as a rising price level results in most wages and salaries rising each year, a falling price level is likely to mean falling wages and salaries each year. So, it is likely that, on average, people would not see the purchasing power of their incomes increase, even if the purchasing power of any currency they hold would increase. There can also be a significant downside to deflation, particularly if the transition from inflation to deflation happens suddenly. The real interest rate is equal to the nominal interest rate minus the inflation rate. If an economy experiences deflation, then the real interest rate will be greater than the nominal interest rate. A rising real interest rate can be bad news for anyone who has borrowed, including homeowners who may have substantial mortgage loans. So, you are probably better off living in an economy experiencing mild inflation than one experiencing deflation.

Conclusion

Money plays a key role in the functioning of an economy by facilitating trade in goods and services and by making specialization possible. Without specialization, no advanced economy can prosper. Households and firms, banks, and the central bank (the Federal Reserve in the United States) are participants in the process of creating the money supply.

Visit MyEconLab for a news article and analysis related to the concepts of this chapter.

Chapter Summary and Problems

Key Terms

Asset	Federal Open Market Committee (FOMC)	M2	Reserves
Bank panic		Monetary policy	Securitization
Bank run	Federal Reserve	Money	Security
Commodity money	Fiat money	Open market operations	Simple deposit multiplier
Discount loans	Fractional reserve banking system	Quantity theory of money	Velocity of money
Discount rate	M1	Required reserve ratio	
Excess reserves		Required reserves	

What Is Money, and Why Do We Need It?

LEARNING OBJECTIVE: Define money and discuss the four functions of money.

Summary

A *barter economy* is an economy that does not use money and in which people trade goods and services directly for other goods and services. Barter trade occurs only if there is a *double coincidence of wants*, where both parties to the trade want what the other one has. Because barter is inefficient, there is strong incentive to use **money**, which is any **asset** that people are generally willing to accept in exchange for goods or services or in payment of debts. An *asset* is anything of value owned by a person or a firm. A **commodity money** is a good used as money that also has value independent of its use as money. Money has four functions: It is a medium of exchange, a unit of account, a store of value, and a standard of deferred payment. The *gold standard* was a monetary system under which the government produced gold coins and paper currency that were convertible into gold. The gold standard collapsed in the early 1930s. Today, no government in the world issues paper currency that can be redeemed for gold. Instead, paper currency is **fiat money**, which has no value except as money.

Visit **www.myeconlab.com** to complete these exercises online and get instant feedback.

Review Questions

1.1 A baseball fan with a Mike Trout baseball card wants to trade it for a Miguel Cabrera baseball card, but everyone the fan knows who has a Cabrera card doesn't want a Trout card. What do economists call the problem this fan is having?

1.2 What is the difference between commodity money and fiat money?

1.3 What are the four functions of money? Can something be considered money if it does not fulfill all four functions?

1.4 Why do businesses accept paper currency when they know that, unlike a gold coin, the paper the currency is printed on is worth very little?

Problems and Applications

1.5 The English economist William Stanley Jevons described a world tour during the 1880s by a French singer, Mademoiselle Zélie. One stop on the tour was a theater in the Society Islands, part of French Polynesia in the South Pacific. She performed for her usual fee, which was one-third of the receipts. This turned out to be 3 pigs, 23 turkeys, 44 chickens, 5,000 coconuts, and "considerable quantities of bananas, lemons, and oranges." She estimated that all of this would have had a value in France of 4,000 francs. According to Jevons, "as Mademoiselle could not consume any considerable portion of the receipts herself, it became necessary in the meantime to feed the pigs and poultry with the fruit." Do the goods Mademoiselle Zélie received as payment fulfill the four functions of money described in this chapter? Briefly explain.

Source: W. Stanley Jevons, *Money and the Mechanism of Exchange*, New York: D. Appleton and Company, 1889, pp. 1–2.

1.6 **[Related to the** Chapter Opener**]** An article in the *New York Times* provides the following description of a hospital in Zimbabwe: "People lined up on the veranda of the American mission hospital here from miles around to barter for doctor visits and medicines, clutching scrawny chickens, squirming goats and buckets of maize." Why wouldn't the people buying medical services at this hospital use money to pay for the medical services they are buying? What problems might this method of payment cause for the hospital?

Source: Celia W. Dugger, "Zimbabwe Health Care, Paid with Peanuts," *New York Times*, December 18, 2011.

1.7 In the late 1940s, the Communists under Mao Zedong were defeating the government of China in a civil war. The paper currency issued by the Chinese government was losing much of its value, and most businesses refused to accept it. At the same time, there was a paper shortage in Japan. During these years, Japan was still under military occupation by the United States, following its defeat in World War II. Some of the U.S. troops in Japan realized that they could use dollars to buy up vast amounts of paper currency in China, ship it to Japan to be recycled into paper, and make a substantial profit. Under these circumstances, was the Chinese paper currency a commodity money or a fiat money? Briefly explain.

1.8 According to Peter Heather, a historian at King's College London, during the Roman Empire, the German tribes east of the Rhine River (the area the Romans called Germania) produced no coins of their own but used Roman coins instead:

> Although no coinage was produced in Germania, Roman coins were in plentiful circulation and could easily have provided a medium of exchange (already in the first century, Tacitus tells us, Germani of the Rhine region were using good-quality Roman silver coins for this purpose).

a. What is a medium of exchange?

b. What does the author mean when he writes that Roman coins could have provided the German tribes with a medium of exchange?

c. Why would any member of a German tribe have been willing to accept a Roman coin from another member of the tribe in exchange for goods or services when the tribes were not part of the Roman Empire and were not governed by Roman law?

Source: Peter Heather, *The Fall of the Roman Empire: A New History of Rome and the Barbarians*, New York: Oxford University Press, 2006, p. 89.

1.9 **[Related to** Making the Connection: **Apple Didn't Want My Cash!]** Suppose that Congress passes a new law that requires all firms to accept paper currency in exchange for whatever they are selling. Briefly discuss who would gain and who would lose from this legislation.

1.10 On January 1, 2002, Germany officially adopted the euro as its currency, and the deutsche mark stopped being legal tender. According to an article in the *Wall Street Journal*, even 10 years later many Germans continued using the deutsche mark, and many stores in Germany continued to accept it. Briefly explain how it is possible for people to continue to use a currency when the government that issued it has replaced it with another currency.

Source: Vanessa Fuhrmans, "Who Needs the Euro When You Can Pay with Deutsche Marks?" *Wall Street Journal*, July 18, 2012.

---

2 | How Is Money Measured in the United States Today?

LEARNING OBJECTIVE: Discuss the definitions of the money supply used in the United States today.

Summary

The narrowest definition of the money supply in the United States today is **M1**, which includes currency, checking account balances, and traveler's checks. A broader definition of the money supply is **M2**, which includes everything that is in M1, plus savings accounts, small-denomination time deposits (such as certificates of deposit [CDs]), money market deposit accounts in banks, and noninstitutional money market fund shares.

Visit **www.myeconlab.com** to complete these exercises online and get instant feedback.

Review Questions

2.1 What is the main difference between the M1 and M2 definitions of the money supply?

2.2 Why does the Federal Reserve use two definitions of the money supply rather than one?

2.3 Distinguish among money, income, and wealth. Which one of the three does the central bank of a country control?

Problems and Applications

2.4 Briefly explain whether each of the following is counted in M1.
   a. The coins in your pocket
   b. The funds in your checking account
   c. The funds in your savings account
   d. The traveler's checks that you have left over from a trip
   e. Your Citibank Platinum MasterCard

2.5 **[Related to** Don't Let This Happen to You: **Don't Confuse Money with Income or Wealth]** Briefly explain whether you agree with the following statement: "I recently read that more than half of the money the government prints is actually held by people in foreign countries. If that's true, then the United States is less than half as wealthy as government statistics indicate."

2.6 **[Related to** Don't Let This Happen to You: **Don't Confuse Money with Income or Wealth]** A newspaper article contains the statement: "Income is only one way of measuring wealth." Do you agree that income is a way of measuring wealth?

Source: Sam Roberts, "As the Data Show, There's a Reason the Wall Street Protesters Chose New York," *New York Times*, October 25, 2011.

2.7 **[Related to** Solved Problem 2**]** Suppose you have $200 in currency in a shoebox in your closet. One day, you decide to deposit the money in a checking account. Briefly explain how this will affect M1 and M2.

2.8 **[Related to** Solved Problem 2**]** Suppose you decide to withdraw $100 in currency from your checking account. What is the effect on M1? Ignore any actions the bank may take as a result of your having withdrawn the $100.

2.9 The paper currency of the United States is technically called "Federal Reserve Notes." The following excerpt is from the Federal Reserve Act: "Federal Reserve Notes … shall be redeemed in lawful money on demand at the Treasury Department of the United States, in the city of Washington, District of Columbia, or at any Federal Reserve bank." If you took a $20 bill to the Treasury Department or a Federal Reserve Bank, with what type of "lawful money" is the government likely to redeem it?

2.10 Friedrich Schneider, an economist at the Johannes Kepler University of Linz in Austria, made the following observation about China: "The average Chinese trusts neither the Chinese banks nor the Communist Party."
   a. If Schneider is correct, how might businesses and consumers prefer to carry out transactions?
   b. The Chinese government has refused to print currency in denominations higher than the 100-renminbi note, which is the equivalent of about $16. The United States prints $100 bills and all other countries print currency in denominations that are at least that high. Given your answer to part (a), why might the Chinese government be reluctant to print currency in high denominations?

Source: David Barboza, "Chinese Way of Doing Business: In Cash We Trust," *New York Times*, April 30, 2013.

2.11 [Related to Making the Connection**: Are Bitcoins Money?]** According to an article in the *Economist* magazine, Senator Charles Schumer of New York claimed that Bitcoin is "just what drug dealers have been waiting for." Why might drug dealers find using a virtual currency like Bitcoin to be appealing?

Source: "Bits and Bob," *Economist*, June 13, 2013.

2.12 The U.S. penny is made primarily of zinc. There have been several times in recent years when zinc prices have been high and it has cost the U.S. Treasury more than one cent

to manufacture a penny. There are currently about 1.4 billion pennies in circulation. Economist François Velde of the Federal Reserve Bank of Chicago has proposed making the current penny worth 5 cents. If the U.S. Treasury adopted Velde's proposal, what would be the effect on the value of M1? Is this change likely to have much effect on the economy? (*Hint:* According to the information given in this chapter, what is the current value of M1?)

Source: Austan Goolsbee, "Now That a Penny Isn't Worth Much, It's Time to Make It Worth 5 Cents," *New York Times*, February 1, 2007.

How Do Banks Create Money?

LEARNING OBJECTIVE: Explain how banks create money.

Summary

On a bank's balance sheet, *reserves* and loans are assets, and deposits are liabilities. **Reserves** are deposits that the bank has retained rather than loaned out or invested. **Required reserves** are reserves that banks are legally required to hold. The fraction of deposits that banks are required to keep as reserves is called the **required reserve ratio**. Any reserves banks hold over the legal requirement are called **excess reserves**. When a bank accepts a deposit, it keeps only a fraction of the funds as reserves and loans out the remainder. In making a loan, a bank increases the checking account balance of the borrower. When the borrower uses a check to buy something with the funds the bank has loaned, the seller deposits the check in his or her bank. The seller's bank keeps part of the deposit as reserves and loans out the remainder. This process continues until no banks have excess reserves. In this way, the process of banks making new loans increases the volume of checking account balances and the money supply. This money creation process can be illustrated with T-accounts, which are stripped-down versions of balance sheets that show only how a transaction changes a bank's balance sheet. The **simple deposit multiplier** is the ratio of the change in deposits to the change in reserves. An expression for the simple deposit multiplier is $1/RR$.

Visit **www.myeconlab.com** to complete these exercises online and get instant feedback.

Review Questions

3.1 What are the largest asset and the largest liability of a typical bank?

3.2 Suppose you decide to withdraw $100 in cash from your checking account. Draw a T-account showing the effect of this transaction on your bank's balance sheet.

3.3 What does it mean to say that banks "create money"?

3.4 Give the formula for the simple deposit multiplier. If the required reserve ratio is 20 percent, what is the maximum increase in checking account deposits that will result from an increase in bank reserves of $20,000?

3.5 What causes the real-world money multiplier to be smaller than the simple deposit multiplier?

Problems and Applications

3.6 An article on how the Zimbabwean economy had recovered after the end of the hyperinflation notes the following fact as being important: "Bank deposits increased by 31% last year, to $4.4 billion." Why would an increase in bank deposits be considered important in explaining growth in a developing country such as Zimbabwe?

Source: "In Dollars They Trust," *Economist*, April 27, 2013.

3.7 The following is from an article on community banks: "Their commercial-lending businesses, funded by their stable deposit bases, make them steady earners." What is commercial lending? In what sense are loans "funded" by deposits?

Source: Karen Richardson, "Clean Books Bolster Traditional Lenders," *Wall Street Journal*, April 30, 2007.

3.8 In a newspaper column, author Delia Ephron described a conversation with a friend who had a large balance on her credit card with an interest rate of 18 percent per year. The friend was worried about paying off the debt. Ephron was earning only 0.4 percent interest on her bank certificate of deposit (CD). She considered withdrawing the money from her CD and loaning it to her friend so her friend could pay off her credit card balance: "So I was thinking that all of us earning 0.4 percent could instead loan money to our friends at 0.5 percent. ... [M]y friend would get out of debt [and] I would earn $5 a month instead of $4." Why don't more people use their savings to make loans rather than keeping the funds in bank accounts that earn very low rates of interest?

Source: Delia Ephron, "Banks Taketh, but Don't Giveth," *New York Times*, January 27, 2012.

3.9 Suppose that Deja owns a McDonald's franchise. She decides to move her restaurant's checking account to Wells Fargo, which causes the changes shown on the following T-account. If the required reserve ratio is 0.10, or 10 percent, and Wells Fargo currently has no excess reserves, what is the maximum loan Wells Fargo can make as result of this transaction?

Wells Fargo

Assets		Liabilities	
Reserves	+$100,000	Deposits	+$100,000

3.10 Consider the following simplified balance sheet for a bank:

Assets		Liabilities	
Reserves	$10,000	Deposits	$70,000
Loans	$66,000	Stockholders' equity	$6,000

    a. If the required reserve ratio is 0.10, or 10 percent, how much in excess reserves does the bank hold?

    b. What is the maximum amount by which the bank can expand its loans?

    c. If the bank makes the loans in part (b), show the *immediate* effect on the bank's balance sheet.

3.11 **[Related to** Don't Let This Happen to You**: Don't Confuse Assets and Liabilities]** Briefly explain whether you agree with the following statement: "Assets are things of value that people own. Liabilities are debts. Therefore, a bank will always consider a checking account deposit to be an asset and a car loan to be a liability."

3.12 **[Related to** Solved Problem 3**]** Suppose you deposit $2,000 in currency into your checking account at a branch of Bank of America, which we will assume has no excess reserves at the time you make your deposit. Also assume that the required reserve ratio is 0.20, or 20 percent.

    a. Use a T-account to show the initial effect of this transaction on Bank of America's balance sheet.

    b. Suppose that Bank of America makes the maximum loan it can from the funds you deposited. Using a T-account, show the initial effect of granting the loan on Bank of America's balance sheet. Also include on this T-account the transaction from part (a).

    c. Now suppose that whoever took out the loan in part (b) writes a check for this amount and that the person receiving the check deposits it in a branch of Citibank. Show the effect of these transactions on the balance sheets of Bank of America and Citibank *after the check has been cleared.* (On the T-account for Bank of America, include the transactions from parts (a) and (b).)

    d. What is the maximum increase in checking account deposits that can result from your $2,000 deposit? What is the maximum increase in the money supply? Briefly explain.

---

4 | The Federal Reserve System

LEARNING OBJECTIVE: Discuss the three policy tools the Federal Reserve uses to manage the money supply.

Summary

The United States has a **fractional reserve banking system** in which banks keep less than 100 percent of deposits as reserves. In a **bank run**, many depositors decide simultaneously to withdraw money from a bank. In a **bank panic**, many banks experience runs at the same time. The **Federal Reserve System** ("the Fed") is the central bank of the United States. It was originally established in 1913 to stop bank panics. The recession of 2007–2009 put renewed emphasis on the Fed's goal of financial market stability. **Monetary policy** refers to the actions the Federal Reserve takes to manage the money supply and interest rates to pursue macroeconomic policy objectives. The Fed's three monetary policy tools are open market operations, discount policy, and reserve requirements. **Open market operations** are the buying and selling of Treasury securities by the Federal Reserve. The loans the Fed makes to banks are called **discount loans**, and the interest rate the Fed charges on discount loans is the **discount rate**. The **Federal Open Market Committee (FOMC)** meets in Washington, DC, eight times per year to discuss monetary policy. In the past 20 years, a "shadow banking system" has developed. During the financial crisis of 2007–2009, the existence of the shadow banking system complicated the Fed's policy response. A **security** is a financial asset—such as a stock or a bond—that can be bought and sold in a financial market. The process of **securitization** involves creating a secondary market in which loans that have been bundled together can be bought and sold in financial markets just as corporate or government bonds are.

Visit **www.myeconlab.com** to complete these exercises online and get instant feedback.

Review Questions

4.1 Why did Congress decide to establish the Federal Reserve System in 1913?

4.2 What policy tools does the Fed use to control the money supply? Which tool is the most important?

4.3 Why does an open market purchase of Treasury securities by the Federal Reserve increase bank reserves? Why does an open market sale of Treasury securities by the Federal Reserve decrease bank reserves?

4.4 What is the "shadow banking system"? Why were the financial firms of the shadow banking system more vulnerable than commercial banks to bank runs?

Problems and Applications

4.5 The text explains that the United States has a "fractional reserve banking system." Why do most depositors seem to be unworried that banks loan out most of the deposits they receive?

4.6 Suppose that you are a bank manager, and the Federal Reserve raises the required reserve ratio from 10 percent to 12 percent. What actions would you need to take? How would your actions and those of other bank managers end up affecting the money supply?

4.7 Suppose that the Federal Reserve makes a $10 million discount loan to First National Bank (FNB) by increasing FNB's account at the Fed.

    a. Use a T-account to show the effect of this transaction on FNB's balance sheet. Remember that the funds a bank has on deposit at the Fed count as part of its reserves.

b. Assume that before receiving the discount loan, FNB has no excess reserves. What is the maximum amount of this $10 million that FNB can lend out?

c. What is the maximum total increase in the money supply that can result from the Fed's discount loan? Assume that the required reserve ratio is 10 percent.

4.8 Suppose that the Federal Reserve engages in an open market sale of $25 million in U.S. Treasury bills to banks. In the T-accounts for the Fed and for the banking system shown here, fill in the missing information.

Federal Reserve

Assets	Liabilities	
_____	−$25 million	Reserves −$25 million

Banking System

Assets	Liabilities
Treasury bills +$25 million	
_____ −$25 million	

4.9 In a speech delivered in June 2008, Timothy Geithner, then president of the Federal Reserve Bank of New York and later U.S. Treasury secretary, said:

> The structure of the financial system changed fundamentally during the boom.... [The] non-bank financial system grew to be very large....

> [The] institutions in this parallel financial system [are] vulnerable to a classic type of run, but without the protections such as deposit insurance that the banking system has in place to reduce such risks.

a. What did Geithner mean by the "nonbank financial system"?

b. What is a "classic type of run," and why were institutions in the nonbank financial system vulnerable to it?

c. Why would deposit insurance provide the banking system with protection against runs?

Source: Timothy F. Geithner, "Reducing Systemic Risk in a Dynamic Financial System," Remarks at the Economics Club of New York, June 9, 2008.

4.10 When the Federal Reserve steps in as the lender of last resort to prevent a bank panic, does this constitute a "bail out of the banks"? Briefly explain.

4.11 An article on Bloomberg.com reported in 2012 that the People's Bank of China "cut the amount of cash that banks must set aside as reserves for the third time in six months, pumping money into the financial system to support lending after data showed a slowdown in growth is deepening." What monetary policy tool did the People's Bank of China use to "cut the amount of cash that banks must set aside as reserves." How would this action "pump money into the financial system to support lending"?

Source: "China Lowers Banks' Reserve Requirements to Support Growth," Bloomberg.com, May 12, 2012.

  The Quantity Theory of Money

LEARNING OBJECTIVE: Explain the quantity theory of money and use it to explain how high rates of inflation occur.

Summary

The *quantity equation*, which relates the money supply to the price level, is $M \times V = P \times Y$, where M is the money supply, V is the *velocity of money*, P is the price level, and Y is real output. The **velocity of money** is the average number of times each dollar in the money supply is spent during the year. Economist Irving Fisher developed the **quantity theory of money**, which assumes that the velocity of money is constant. If the quantity theory of money is correct, the inflation rate should equal the rate of growth of the money supply minus the rate of growth of real output. Although the quantity theory of money is not literally correct because the velocity of money is not constant, it is true that in the long run, inflation results from the money supply growing faster than real GDP. When governments attempt to raise revenue by selling large quantities of bonds to the central bank, the money supply will increase rapidly, resulting in high rates of inflation.

Visit **www.myeconlab.com** to complete these exercises online and get instant feedback.

Review Questions

5.1 What is the quantity theory of money? What explanation does the quantity theory provide for inflation?

5.2 Is the quantity theory of money better able to explain the inflation rate in the long run or in the short run? Briefly explain.

5.3 What is hyperinflation? Why do governments sometimes allow it to occur?

Problems and Applications

5.4 If the money supply is growing at a rate of 6 percent per year, real GDP is growing at a rate of 3 percent per year, and velocity is constant, what will the inflation rate be? If velocity is increasing 1 percent per year instead of remaining constant, what will the inflation rate be?

5.5 According to the quantity theory of money, if velocity does not change, when the money supply of a country increases, will nominal GDP increase? Will real GDP increase? Briefly explain.

5.6 Suppose that during one period, the velocity of money is constant, and during another period, it undergoes large fluctuations. During which period will the quantity theory of money be more useful in explaining changes in the inflation rate? Briefly explain.

5.7 In an article in the *American Free Press*, Professor Peter Spencer of York University in England is quoted as saying: "This printing of money 'will keep the [deflation] wolf from the door.'" In the same article, Ambrose Evans-Pritchard, a writer for the London-based newspaper *The Telegraph*, is quoted as saying: "Deflation has ... insidious traits. It causes shoppers to hold back. Once this psychology gains a grip, it can gradually set off a self-feeding spiral that is hard to stop."

a. What is price deflation?

b. What does Professor Spencer mean by the statement, "This printing of money 'will keep the [deflation] wolf from the door'"?

c. Why would deflation cause "shoppers to hold back," and what does Evans-Pritchard mean when he says: "Once this psychology gains a grip, it can gradually set off a self-feeding spiral that is hard to stop"?

Source: Doug French, "We Should Celebrate Price Deflation," *American Free Press*, November 17, 2008.

5.8 During the Civil War, the Confederate States of America printed large amounts of its own currency—Confederate dollars—to fund the war. By the end of the war, the Confederate government had printed nearly 1.5 billion paper dollars. How would such a large quantity of Confederate dollars have affected the value of the Confederate currency? With the war drawing to an end, would Southerners have been as willing to use and accept Confederate dollars? How else could they have bought and sold goods?

Source: Federal Reserve Bank of Richmond, "Textual Transcript of Confederate Currency."

5.9 [Related to the Chapter Opener**]** An article in the *Economist* described the difference between the rate of inflation in Zimbabwe before and after the government abandoned its own currency and made the U.S. dollar its official currency in 2009:

> Zimbabwe's dollar had been too liberally printed: a swollen stock of local banknotes was chasing a diminished supply of goods. Now the American banknotes the economy relies on have to be begged, borrowed or earned. Even so, the monetary system works surprisingly well. A scarcity of greenbacks keeps inflation in the low single digits.

Briefly describe whether Zimbabwe's recent inflation history can be explained using the quantity theory of money.
Source: "In Dollars They Trust," *Economist*, April 27, 2013.

5.10 [Related to Making the Connection**: The German Hyperinflation of the Early 1920s]** During the German hyperinflation of the 1920s, many households and firms in Germany were hurt economically. Do you think any groups in Germany benefited from the hyperinflation? Briefly explain.

Real-Time-Data Exercises

D1 [The components of M1] Go to the Web site of the Federal Reserve Bank of St. Louis (FRED) (research.stlouisfed.org/fred2/) and find the most recent values for the following four variables: (1) M1 Money Stock (M1), (2) the Currency Component of M1 (CURRENCY), (3) Total Checkable Deposits (TCD), and (4) Travelers Checks Outstanding (WTCSL). Which of the components of M1 is the largest? Which is the smallest?

D2 [Calculating M1 from data on M2] Go to the Web site of the Federal Reserve Bank of St. Louis (FRED) (research.stlouisfed.org/fred2/) and find the most recent values for the following four variables(1) the M2 Money Stock (M2), (2) the Total Savings Deposits at all Depository Institutions (SAVINGS), (3) Retail Money Funds (WRMFSL), and (4) Small Time Deposits - Total (WSMTIME).
a. Using these data, calculate the value of M1.
b. What are Retail Money Funds? What percentage of M2 are they?

c. If households were to shift funds from savings accounts to checking accounts, what would happen to the values of M1 and M2?

D3 [The relationship between M1 and M2] Go to the Web site of the Federal Reserve Bank of St. Louis (FRED) (research.stlouisfed.org/fred2/) and find the most recent monthly values and values from the same month 5 years and 10 years earlier for the M1 Money Stock (M1SL) and the M2 Money Stock (M2SL).
a. Using these data, calculate M1 as a proportion of M2 for each of the years.
b. Explain whether this proportion has increased, decreased, or remained the same over time. Can you think of an explanation for any changes you observe?

D4 [The equation of exchange] Go to the Web site of the Federal Reserve Bank of St. Louis (FRED) (research.stlouisfed.org/fred2/) and find the most recent values and values for the same quarter in 1985 for the following three variables: (1) nominal Gross Domestic Product (GDP), (2) the Velocity of M1 Money Stock (M1V), and (3) the Velocity of M2 Money Stock (M2V).
a. Using these data, calculate M1 and M2 for both periods.
b. Describe how M1 velocity and M2 velocity differ in the two quarters.

D5 [Applying the equation of exchange] Go to the Web site of the Federal Reserve Bank of St. Louis (research.stlouisfed.org/fred2/) and find the most recent values and values from the same quarter 10 years earlier for the following three variables: (1) Real Gross Domestic Product (GDPC1), (2) the GDP Price Deflator (GDPDEF), and (3) the M2 Money Stock (M2SL).
a. Using these data, calculate the average annual rate of change in both real GDP and M2 over this 10-year period.
b. If we assume that velocity was constant during this period, what was the average annual inflation rate?
c. Using the GDP Price Deflator data, calculate the average annual inflation rate over this 10-year period.
d. Use your answers to parts (b) and (c) to discuss what must have happened to velocity during this period.

D6 [Applying the equation of exchange] Go to the Web site of the Federal Reserve Bank of St. Louis (FRED) (research.stlouisfed.org/fred2/) and find the most recent value for Real Gross Domestic Product (GDPC1) and the value from the same quarter eight years in the future for Real Potential Gross Domestic Product (GDPPOT).
a. Using these data, calculate the average annual rate of growth in real GDP over this eight-year period assuming that real GDP equals potential GDP in the quarter that is eight years in the future.
b. If the velocity of money is constant during this eight-year period, what will the growth rate of M1 have to be if the annual inflation rate averages 2 percent? Briefly explain.
c. Suppose that M1 grows at this rate, but the actual inflation over this period averages more than 2 percent. What can be concluded about velocity during this period?

Glossary

Asset Anything of value owned by a person or a firm.

Bank panic A situation in which many banks experience runs at the same time.

Bank run A situation in which many depositors simultaneously decide to withdraw money from a bank.

Commodity money A good used as money that also has value independent of its use as money.

Discount loans Loans the Federal Reserve makes to banks.

Discount rate The interest rate the Federal Reserve charges on discount loans.

Excess reserves Reserves that banks hold over the legal requirement.

Federal Open Market Committee (FOMC) The Federal Reserve committee responsible for open market operations and managing the money supply in the United States.

Federal Reserve The central bank of the United States.

Fiat money Money, such as paper currency, that is authorized by a central bank or governmental body and that does not have to be exchanged by the central bank for gold or some other commodity money.

Fractional reserve banking system A banking system in which banks keep less than 100 percent of deposits as reserves.

M1 The narrow definition of the money supply: the sum of currency in circulation, checking account deposits in banks, and holdings of traveler's checks.

M2 A broader definition of the money supply: It includes M1 plus savings account deposits, small-denomination time deposits, balances in money market deposit accounts in banks, and noninstitutional money market fund shares.

Monetary policy The actions the Federal Reserve takes to manage the money supply and interest rates to pursue macroeconomic policy objectives.

Money Assets that people are generally willing to accept in exchange for goods and services or for payment of debts.

Open market operations The buying and selling of Treasury securities by the Federal Reserve in order to control the money supply.

Quantity theory of money A theory about the connection between money and prices that assumes that the velocity of money is constant.

Required reserve ratio The minimum fraction of deposits banks are required by law to keep as reserves.

Required reserves Reserves that a bank is legally required to hold, based on its checking account deposits.

Reserves Deposits that a bank keeps as cash in its vault or on deposit with the Federal Reserve.

Securitization The process of transforming loans or other financial assets into securities.

Security A financial asset—such as a stock or a bond—that can be bought and sold in a financial market.

Simple deposit multiplier The ratio of the amount of deposits created by banks to the amount of new reserves.

Velocity of money The average number of times each dollar in the money supply is used to purchase goods and services included in GDP.

Credits

Credits are listed in the order of appearance.

Photo

Tsvangirayi Mukwazhi/AP Images; Stephen Lam/Reuters; Bloomberg/Getty Images; Lynne Sladky/AP Images; Ezio Petersen/UPI/Landov; Eightfish/Alamy; Dietmar Plewka/imagebroker/Alamy; Bettmann/Corbis

Monetary Policy

From Chapter 15 of *Macroeconomics*, Fifth Edition. R. Glenn Hubbard and Anthony Patrick O'Brien. Copyright © 2015 by Pearson Education, Inc. All rights reserved.

Monetary Policy

Chapter Outline and Learning Objectives

Why Do Businesses Care What the Federal Reserve Does?

In June 2013, President Barack Obama was scheduled to make an important speech in Berlin, Germany. According to the *Wall Street Journal*, however: "Financial markets (even in Europe), business executives and economists will be paying more attention to the Washington headquarters of the Federal Reserve." A policy meeting that day at the Federal Reserve's headquarters in Washington, DC, would be followed by a statement on monetary policy and a news conference by then Federal Reserve Chairman Ben Bernanke. What Bernanke said at the news conference disappointed investors because it indicated that the Fed might not be acting as aggressively to expand employment and GDP. As a result, the Dow Jones Industrial Average fell by more than 200 points and interest rates on Treasury bonds increased.

Do these events indicate that the Fed chair is more important to the U.S. economy than the president of the United States? Does monetary policy matter for businesses? Most economists would answer "yes" to both questions. The president can take actions that affect the economy. But he needs the approval of Congress before he can enact most polices. In contrast, the structure of the Fed gives the chair substantial control over monetary policy. As a result, the Fed chair can often have greater influence over the economy than can the president.

Many businesses pay close attention to the Fed's actions for two reasons. First, when the Fed acts to change interest rates, it directly affects some businesses—particularly homebuilders and car dealers—that sell durable goods. Second, other businesses will be affected indirectly because changes in interest rates cause changes in aggregate demand. Recessions often begin after the Federal Reserve increases interest rates to reduce the inflation rate by slowing the growth in aggregate demand. In particular, higher interest rates increase the cost of buying houses, reducing demand for them. Not surprisingly, homebuilders watch the Fed carefully for signs of whether interest rates are likely to rise or fall.

Hovnanian Enterprises is a homebuilder headquartered in Red Bank, New Jersey. Like most other homebuilders, it benefited from the Fed's policy of low interests during the mid-2000s. But during and immediately after the recession of 2007–2009, Hovnanian along with nearly all homebuilders suffered sharp declines in sales. In 2013, policymakers at the Fed were still struggling to help the economy recover fully from the recession.

In this chapter, we will study the Federal Reserve and how monetary policy affects GDP, employment, and inflation.

Sources: David Wessel, "The Pressure Is on Bernanke," *Wall Street Journal*, June 19, 2013; Jon Hilsenrath and Victoria McGrane, "Federal Reserve Eyes End of Bond Buying, Spooking Markets," *Wall Street Journal*, June 19, 2013; and "Hovnanian Posts Its First Profit in 2 Years," Reuters, June 6, 2012.

Economics in Your Life

Should You Buy a House during a Recession?

If you are like most college students, buying a house is one of the furthest things from your mind. But think ahead a few years to when you might be married and maybe even (gasp!) have children. You decide to leave behind years of renting apartments and buy a house, but then you read a *Wall Street Journal* article that states that a majority of economists predict a recession is likely to begin soon. What should you do? Would it be a good time or a bad time to buy a house? As you read this chapter, try to answer these questions. You can check your answers against those we provide at the end of this chapter.

B anks play an important role in providing credit to households and firms and in creating the money supply. Congress established the Federal Reserve to stabilize the financial system and that the Fed is responsible for managing the money supply. In this chapter, we will discuss the Fed's main policy goals. We will also explore how the Federal Reserve decides which *monetary policy* actions to take to achieve its goals.

1 LEARNING OBJECTIVE

Define monetary policy and describe the Federal Reserve's monetary policy goals.

Monetary policy The actions the Federal Reserve takes to manage the money supply and interest rates to achieve macroeconomic policy goals.

What Is Monetary Policy?

In 1913, Congress passed the Federal Reserve Act, creating the Federal Reserve System (the Fed). The main responsibility of the Fed was to make discount loans to banks to prevent the bank panics. As a result of the Great Depression of the 1930s, Congress amended the Federal Reserve Act to give the Federal Reserve's Board of Governors broader responsibility to act "so as to promote effectively the goals of maximum employment, stable prices, and moderate long-term interest rates."

Since World War II, the Federal Reserve has carried out an active *monetary policy*. **Monetary policy** refers to the actions the Fed takes to manage the money supply and interest rates to achieve its macroeconomic policy goals.

The Goals of Monetary Policy

The Fed has four main *monetary policy goals* that are intended to promote a well-functioning economy:

1. Price stability
2. High employment
3. Stability of financial markets and institutions
4. Economic growth

We briefly consider each of these goals.

Price Stability Rising prices erode the value of money as a medium of exchange and a store of value. Especially after inflation rose dramatically and unexpectedly during the 1970s, policymakers in most industrial countries have had price stability as a policy goal. Figure 1 shows that from the early 1950s until 1968, the inflation rate in the United States remained below 4 percent per year. Inflation was above 4 percent for most of the 1970s. In early 1979, the inflation rate increased to more than 10 percent, where it remained until late 1981, when it began to rapidly fall back to the 4 percent

Figure 1

The Inflation Rate, January 1952–June 2013

For most of the 1950s and 1960s, the inflation rate in the United States was 4 percent or less. During the 1970s, the inflation rate increased, peaking during 1979–1981, when it averaged more than 10 percent. After 1992, the inflation rate was usually less than 4 percent, until increases in oil prices pushed it above 5 percent during summer 2008. The effects of the recession caused several months of deflation—a falling price level—during early 2009.

Note: The inflation rate is measured as the percentage change in the consumer price index from the same month in the previous year.

Source: Federal Reserve Bank of St. Louis.

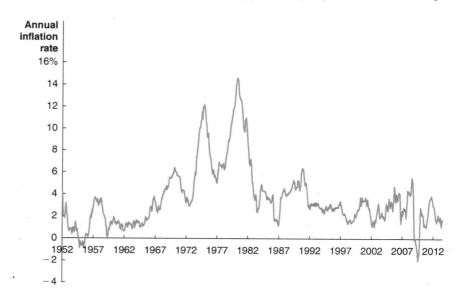

range. After 1992, the inflation rate was usually below 4 percent, until rapid increases in gasoline prices helped push it above 5 percent in the summer of 2008. The effects of the 2007–2009 recession caused several months of deflation—a falling price level—during early 2009.

The inflation rates during the years 1979–1981 were the highest the United States has ever experienced during peacetime. When Paul Volcker became chairman of the Federal Reserve's Board of Governors in August 1979, he made fighting inflation his top policy goal. Later Fed chairs continued to focus on inflation, arguing that if inflation is low over the long run, the Fed will have the flexibility it needs to increase aggregate demand to fight recessions. Although the severity of the 2007–2009 recession led the Fed to adopt extraordinary policy measures that we will discuss later in this chapter, price stability remains a key policy goal of the Fed.

High Employment In addition to price stability, high employment (or a low rate of unemployment) is an important monetary policy goal. Unemployed workers and underused factories and office buildings reduce GDP below its potential level. Unemployment causes financial distress and decreases the self-esteem of workers who lack jobs. The goal of high employment extends beyond the Fed to other branches of the federal government. At the end of World War II, Congress passed the Employment Act of 1946, which stated that it was the "responsibility of the Federal Government … to foster and promote … conditions under which there will be afforded useful employment, for those able, willing, and seeking to work, and to promote maximum employment, production, and purchasing power." Because price stability and high employment are explicitly mentioned in the Employment Act, it is sometimes said that the Fed has a *dual mandate* to attain these two goals.

Stability of Financial Markets and Institutions Firms need access to funds to design, develop, produce, and market their products. Savers look to financial investments to increase the value of their savings as they prepare to buy homes, pay for the educations of their children, and provide for their retirement. The Fed promotes the stability of financial markets and institutions so that an efficient flow of funds from savers to borrowers will occur. The financial crisis of 2007–2009 brought the issue of stability in financial markets to the forefront.

The financial crisis was similar to the banking crises that led Congress to create the Federal Reserve System in 1913. A key difference is that while earlier banking crises affected commercial banks, the events of 2007–2009 also affected investment banks and other financial firms in the *shadow banking system*. Investment banks, money market mutual funds, and other financial firms can be subject to *liquidity problems* because they often borrow short term—sometimes as short as overnight—and invest the funds in long-term securities. Just as commercial banks can experience crises if depositors begin to withdraw funds, investment banks and other financial firms can experience crises if investors stop providing them with short-term loans. In 2008, the Fed took several steps to ease the liquidity problems of these financial firms because the Fed believed these problems were increasing the severity of the recession. Later in this chapter, we will discuss in more detail the new policies the Fed enacted to help deal with the financial crisis.

Economic Growth Economic growth is important to raising living standards. Policymakers aim to encourage *stable* economic growth, which allows households and firms to plan accurately and encourages firms to engage in the investment that is needed to sustain growth. Policy can spur economic growth by providing incentives for saving to ensure a large pool of investment funds, as well as by providing direct incentives for business investment. Congress and the president, however, may be better able to increase saving and investment than is the Fed. For example, Congress and the president can change the tax laws to increase the return to saving and investing. In fact, some economists question whether the Fed can play a role in promoting economic growth beyond attempting to meet its goals of price stability, high employment, and financial stability.

In the next section, we will look at how the Fed attempts to achieve its monetary policy goals. Although the Fed has multiple monetary policy goals, during most periods, its most important goals have been price stability and high employment. The turmoil in financial markets that began in 2007 led the Fed to put new emphasis on the goal of financial market stability.　MyEconLab Concept Check

2 LEARNING OBJECTIVE

Describe the Federal Reserve's monetary policy targets and explain how expansionary and contractionary monetary policies affect the interest rate.

The Money Market and the Fed's Choice of Monetary Policy Targets

The Fed uses its policy tools to achieve its monetary policy goals. The Fed's policy tools are open market operations, discount policy, and reserve requirements. At times, the Fed encounters conflicts among its policy goals. For example, as we will discuss later in this chapter, the Fed can raise interest rates to reduce the inflation rate. But higher interest rates typically reduce household and firm spending, which may result in slower growth and higher unemployment. So, a policy that is intended to achieve one monetary policy goal, such as reducing inflation, may make it more difficult to achieve another policy goal, such as high employment.

Monetary Policy Targets

The Fed tries to keep both the unemployment and inflation rates low, but it can't affect either of these economic variables directly. The Fed cannot tell firms how many people to employ or what prices to charge for their products. Instead, the Fed uses variables, called *monetary policy targets*, that it can affect directly and that, in turn, affect variables, such as real GDP, employment, and the price level, that are closely related to the Fed's policy goals. The two main monetary policy targets are the money supply and the interest rate. As we will see, the Fed typically uses the interest rate as its policy target.

Bear in mind that while the Fed has typically used the money supply and the interest rate as its targets, these targets were not central to the Fed's policy decisions during the recession of 2007–2009. As we will discuss later in this chapter, because U.S. financial markets suffered a degree of disruption not seen since the Great Depression of the 1930s, the Fed was forced to develop new policy tools. However, it is still important to have a good grasp of how the Fed carries out policy during normal times.

The Demand for Money

The Fed's two monetary policy targets are related. To understand this relationship, we first need to examine the *money market*, which brings together the demand and supply for money. Figure 2 shows the demand curve for money. The interest rate is on the vertical axis, and the quantity of money is on the horizontal axis. Here we are using the M1 definition of money, which equals currency plus checking account deposits. Notice that the demand curve for money is downward sloping.

To understand why the demand curve for money is downward sloping, consider that households and firms have a choice between holding money and holding other financial assets, such as U.S. Treasury bills. Money has one particularly desirable characteristic: You can use it to buy goods, services, or financial assets. Money also has one undesirable characteristic: It earns either a zero interest rate or a very low interest rate. The currency in your wallet earns no interest, and the money in your checking account earns either no interest or very little interest. Alternatives to money, such as U.S. Treasury bills, pay interest but have to be sold if you want to use the funds to buy something. When interest rates rise on financial assets such as U.S. Treasury bills, the amount of interest that households and firms lose by holding money increases. When interest rates fall, the amount of interest households and firms lose by holding money decreases. Remember that *opportunity cost* is what you have to forgo to engage in an activity. The interest rate is the opportunity cost of holding money.

We now have an explanation for why the demand curve for money slopes downward: When interest rates on Treasury bills and other financial assets are low, the opportunity

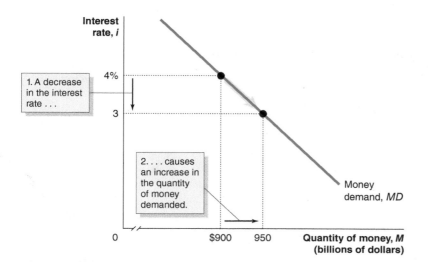

1. A decrease in the interest rate . . .

2. . . . causes an increase in the quantity of money demanded.

Money demand, *MD*

Figure 2

The Demand for Money

The money demand curve slopes downward because a lower interest rate causes households and firms to switch from financial assets such as U.S. Treasury bills to money. All other things being equal, a fall in the interest rate from 4 percent to 3 percent will increase the quantity of money demanded from $900 billion to $950 billion. An increase in the interest rate will decrease the quantity of money demanded.

cost of holding money is low, so the quantity of money demanded by households and firms will be high; when interest rates are high, the opportunity cost of holding money will be high, so the quantity of money demanded will be low. In Figure 2, a decrease in the interest rate from 4 percent to 3 percent causes the quantity of money demanded by households and firms to rise from $900 billion to $950 billion.

Shifts in the Money Demand Curve

We know that the demand curve for a good is drawn holding constant all variables, other than the price, that affect the willingness of consumers to buy the good. Changes in variables other than the price cause the demand curve to shift. Similarly, the demand curve for money is drawn holding constant all variables, other than the interest rate, that affect the willingness of households and firms to hold money. Changes in variables other than the interest rate cause the demand curve to shift. The two most important variables that cause the money demand curve to shift are real GDP and the price level.

An increase in real GDP means that the amount of buying and selling of goods and services will increase. This additional buying and selling increases the demand for money as a medium of exchange, so the quantity of money households and firms want to hold increases at each interest rate, shifting the money demand curve to the right. A decrease in real GDP decreases the quantity of money demanded at each interest rate, shifting the money demand curve to the left. A higher price level increases the quantity of money required for a given amount of buying and selling. Eighty years ago, for example, when the price level was much lower and someone could purchase a new car for $500 and a salary of $30 per week was typical for someone in the middle class, the quantity of money demanded by households and firms was much lower than today, even adjusting for the effect of the lower real GDP and smaller population of those years. An increase in the price level increases the quantity of money demanded at each interest rate, shifting the money demand curve to the right. A decrease in the price level decreases the quantity of money demanded at each interest rate, shifting the money demand curve to the left. Figure 3 illustrates shifts in the money demand curve.

How the Fed Manages the Money Supply: A Quick Review

Having discussed money demand, we now turn to money supply. We know how the Federal Reserve manages the money supply. Eight times per year, the Federal Open Market Committee (FOMC) meets in Washington, DC. If the FOMC decides to increase the money supply, it orders the trading desk at the Federal Reserve Bank of New York to purchase U.S. Treasury securities. The sellers of these Treasury securities deposit the funds they receive from the Fed in banks, which increases bank reserves. Typically, banks loan out most of these reserves, which creates new checking account

Figure 3

Shifts in the Money Demand Curve

Changes in real GDP or the price level cause the money demand curve to shift. An increase in real GDP or an increase in the price level will cause the money demand curve to shift from MD_1 to MD_2. A decrease in real GDP or a decrease in the price level will cause the money demand curve to shift from MD_1 to MD_3.

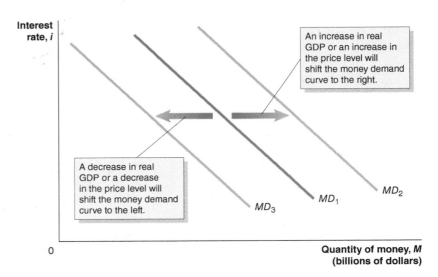

deposits and expands the money supply. If the FOMC decides to decrease the money supply, it orders the trading desk to sell Treasury securities, which decreases bank reserves and contracts the money supply.

Equilibrium in the Money Market

In Figure 4, we include both the money demand and money supply curves. We can use this figure to see how the Fed affects both the money supply and the interest rate. For simplicity, we assume that the Federal Reserve is able to completely control the money supply. With this assumption, the money supply curve is a vertical line, and changes in the interest rate have no effect on the quantity of money supplied. Just as with other markets, equilibrium in the *money market* occurs where the money demand curve crosses the money supply curve. If the Fed increases the money supply, the money supply curve will shift to the right, and the equilibrium interest rate will fall. In Figure 4, when the Fed increases the money supply from $900 billion to $950 billion, the money supply curve shifts from MS_1 to MS_2, and the equilibrium interest rate falls from 4 percent to 3 percent.

In the money market, the adjustment from one equilibrium to another equilibrium is a little different from the adjustment in the market for a good. In Figure 4, the money market is initially in equilibrium, with an interest rate of 4 percent and a money supply of $900 billion. When the Fed increases the money supply by $50 billion,

Figure 4

The Effect on the Interest Rate When the Fed Increases the Money Supply

When the Fed increases the money supply, households and firms will initially hold more money than they want, relative to other financial assets. Households and firms use the money they don't want to hold to buy Treasury bills and make deposits in interest-paying bank accounts. This increase in demand allows banks and sellers of Treasury bills and similar securities to offer lower interest rates. Eventually, interest rates will fall enough that households and firms will be willing to hold the additional money the Fed has created. In the figure, an increase in the money supply from $900 billion to $950 billion causes the money supply curve to shift to the right, from MS_1 to MS_2, and causes the equilibrium interest rate to fall from 4 percent to 3 percent.

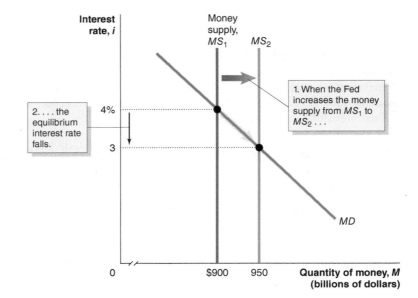

```
              Bistro 1908
        James Madison Univer
299 Miranda
-------------------------------

2213
          OCT24'17 10:08AM
-------------------------------

    7
  1 TABLE NUMBER              0.00
  1 DD The Farmer            7.00
     DD Fruit
     DD Juice
     Food&Bev Sales           7.00
     Total Paid           7.00
     Trans: 417999120
     Meal Plan #: 3
     Code: 00
     Meal Plan                7.00  X
----299 Closed OCT24 10:08AM----
        Enjoy Your Meal

FL _ 1
```

households and firms have more money than they want to hold at an interest rate of 4 percent. What do households and firms do with the extra $50 billion? They are most likely to use the money to buy short-term financial assets, such as Treasury bills, or to deposit the money in interest-paying bank accounts, such as certificates of deposit. This increase in demand for interest-paying bank accounts and short-term financial assets allows banks to offer lower interest rates on certificates of deposit, and it allows sellers of Treasury bills and similar assets to also offer lower interest rates. As the interest rates on certificates of deposit, Treasury bills, and other short-term assets fall, the opportunity cost of holding money also falls. The result is a movement down the money demand curve. Eventually the interest rate falls enough that households and firms are willing to hold the additional $50 billion worth of money the Fed has created, and the money market will be back in equilibrium. To summarize: *When the Fed increases the money supply, the short-term interest rate must fall until it reaches a level at which households and firms are willing to hold the additional money.*

Figure 5 shows what happens when the Fed decreases the money supply. The money market is initially in equilibrium, at an interest rate of 4 percent and a money supply of $900 billion. If the Fed decreases the money supply to $850 billion, households and firms will be holding less money than they would like, relative to other financial assets, at an interest rate of 4 percent. To increase their money holdings, they will sell Treasury bills and other short-term financial assets and withdraw funds from certificates of deposit and other interest-paying bank accounts. Banks will have to offer higher interest rates to retain depositors, and sellers of Treasury bills and similar securities will have to offer higher interest rates to find buyers. Rising short-term interest rates increase the opportunity cost of holding money, causing a movement up the money demand curve. Equilibrium is restored at an interest rate of 5 percent.

A Tale of Two Interest Rates

In the loanable funds model of the interest rate, the equilibrium interest rate is determined by the demand and supply for loanable funds. We need two models of the interest rate because the loanable funds model is concerned with the *long-term real rate of interest*, and the money market model is concerned with the *short-term nominal rate of interest*. The long-term real rate of interest is the interest rate that is most relevant when savers consider purchasing a long-term financial investment such as a corporate bond. It is also the rate of interest that is most relevant to firms that are borrowing to finance long-term

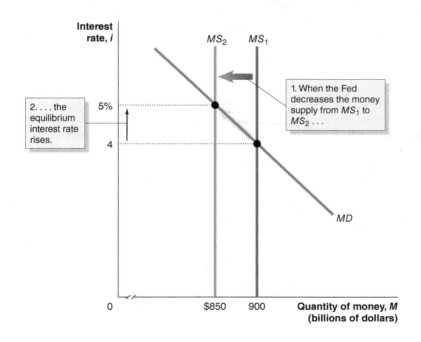

Figure 5

The Effect on the Interest Rate When the Fed Decreases the Money Supply

When the Fed decreases the money supply, households and firms will initially hold less money than they want, relative to other financial assets. Households and firms will sell Treasury bills and other financial assets and withdraw money from interest-paying bank accounts. These actions will increase interest rates. Interest rates will rise to the point at which households and firms will be willing to hold the smaller amount of money that results from the Fed's actions. In the figure, a reduction in the money supply from $900 billion to $850 billion causes the money supply curve to shift to the left, from MS_1 to MS_2, and causes the equilibrium interest rate to rise from 4 percent to 5 percent.

investment projects such as new factories or office buildings, or to households that are taking out mortgage loans to buy new homes.

When conducting monetary policy, however, the focus is the short-term nominal interest rate because it is the interest rate most affected by increases and decreases in the money supply. Often—but not always—there is a close connection between movements in the short-term nominal interest rate and movements in the long-term real interest rate. So, when the Fed takes actions to increase the short-term nominal interest rate, usually the long-term real interest rate also increases. In other words, as we will discuss in the next section, when the interest rate on Treasury bills rises, the real interest rate on mortgage loans usually also rises, although sometimes only after a delay.

Choosing a Monetary Policy Target

As we have seen, the Fed uses monetary policy targets to affect economic variables, such as real GDP or the price level, that are closely related to the Fed's policy goals. The Fed can use either the money supply or the interest rate as its monetary policy target. As Figure 5 shows, the Fed is capable of affecting both. The Fed has generally focused on the interest rate rather than on the money supply. In 1980, Congress began allowing banks to pay interest on checking accounts. At the same time, money market mutual funds were becoming more popular with small savers as a way to earn higher interest rates than banks offered. As a result of these developments, some economists argued that the Fed should focus less on M1 than on M2. They argued that the relationship between M2 and inflation and changes in GDP was more stable than the relationship between M1 and these variables. But even the relationship between M2 and other key economic variables broke down in the early 1990s. In July 1993, then Fed Chairman Alan Greenspan informed the U.S. Congress that the Fed would cease using M1 or M2 targets to guide the conduct of monetary policy. The Fed has correspondingly increased its reliance on interest rate targets.

There are many different interest rates in the economy. For purposes of monetary policy, the Fed has targeted the interest rate known as the *federal funds rate*. In the next section, we will discuss the federal funds rate before examining how targeting the interest rate can help the Fed achieve its monetary policy goals.

The Importance of the Federal Funds Rate

Recall that every bank must keep 10 percent of its checking account deposits above a certain threshold amount as reserves, either as currency held in the bank or as deposits with the Fed. The Fed pays banks a low interest rate on their reserve deposits, so banks normally have an incentive to invest reserves above the 10 percent minimum. As the financial crisis that began in 2007 deepened during 2008, bank reserves soared as banks attempted to meet an increase in deposit withdrawals and as they became reluctant to lend to any borrowers except those with the most flawless credit histories. Banks continued to hold large reserve deposits for several years following the end of the financial crisis. These conditions were very unusual, however. In normal times, banks keep few excess reserves, and when they need additional reserves, they borrow in the *federal funds market* from banks that have reserves available. The **federal funds rate** is the interest rate banks charge each other on loans in the federal funds market. The loans are usually very short term, often just overnight.

Federal funds rate The interest rate banks charge each other for overnight loans.

Despite the name, the Fed does not actually set the federal funds rate. Instead, the rate is determined by the demand and supply for reserves. Because the Fed can increase and decrease the supply of bank reserves through open market operations, it can set a *target* for the federal funds rate and usually come very close to hitting it. The FOMC announces a target for the federal funds rate after each meeting. In Figure 6, the orange line shows the Fed's targets for the federal funds rate since 2000. The jagged green line represents the actual federal funds rate on a weekly basis. The figure shows the rapid declines in the target for the federal funds rate beginning in September 2007, as the Fed responded to the start of the financial crisis. In December 2008, the Fed announced a

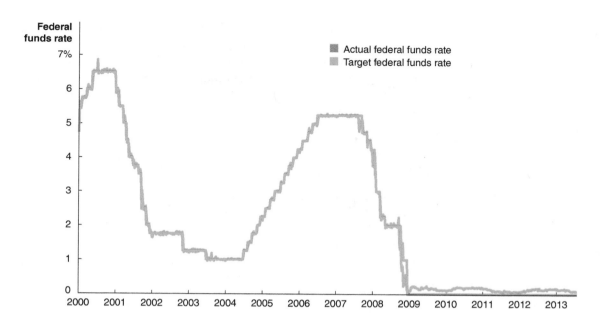

Figure 6 Federal Funds Rate Targeting, January 2000–July 2013

The Fed does not set the federal funds rate. However, the Fed's ability to increase or decrease bank reserves quickly through open market operations keeps the actual federal funds rate close to the Fed's target rate. The orange line is the Fed's target for the federal funds rate, and the jagged green line represents the actual value for the federal funds rate on a weekly basis.

Note: The federal funds target for the period after December 2008 was 0 to 0.25 percent.
Source: Board of Governors of the Federal Reserve System.

range of 0 to 0.25 percent as its target. The actual federal funds rate fluctuated between 0.06 and 0.23 percent. These very low federal funds rates reflect the severity of the financial crisis.

Because only banks can borrow or lend in the federal funds market, the federal funds rate is not directly relevant for households and firms. However, changes in the federal funds rate usually result in changes in interest rates on both short-term financial assets, such as Treasury bills, and long-term financial assets, such as corporate bonds and mortgages. A change in the federal funds rate has a greater effect on short-term interest rates than on long-term interest rates, and its effect on long-term interest rates may occur only after a lag in time. Although a majority of economists support the Fed's choice of the interest rate as its monetary policy target, some economists believe the Fed should concentrate on the money supply instead. We will discuss the views of these economists later in this chapter.

Monetary Policy and Economic Activity

Remember that the Fed uses the federal funds rate as a monetary policy target because it controls this interest rate through open market operations and because it believes that changes in the federal funds rate will ultimately affect economic variables that are related to its monetary policy goals. It is important to consider again the distinction between the nominal interest rate and the real interest rate. We calculate the real interest rate by subtracting the inflation rate from the nominal interest rate. Ultimately, the ability of the Fed to use monetary policy to affect economic variables such as real GDP depends on its ability to affect long-term real interest rates, such as the real interest rates on mortgages and corporate bonds. Because the federal funds rate is a short-term nominal interest rate, the Fed sometimes has difficulty affecting long-term real interest rates. Nevertheless, for purposes of the following discussion, we will assume that the Fed is able to use open market operations to affect long-term real interest rates.

3 LEARNING OBJECTIVE

Use aggregate demand and aggregate supply graphs to show the effects of monetary policy on real GDP and the price level.

How Interest Rates Affect Aggregate Demand

Changes in interest rates affect *aggregate demand*, which is the total level of spending in the economy. Aggregate demand has four components: consumption, investment, government purchases, and net exports. Changes in interest rates will not affect government purchases, but they will affect the other three components of aggregate demand in the following ways:

- *Consumption.* Many households finance purchases of consumer durables, such as automobiles and furniture, by borrowing. Lower interest payments on loans increase household spending on consumer durables. Higher interest rates reduce household spending on consumer durables. Lower interest rates also reduce the return to saving, leading households to save less and spend more. Higher interest rates increase the return to saving, leading households to save more and spend less.

- *Investment.* Firms finance most of their spending on machinery, equipment, and factories out of their profits or by borrowing. Firms borrow either in financial markets by issuing corporate bonds or by obtaining loans from banks. Higher interest rates on corporate bonds or on bank loans make it more expensive for firms to borrow, so they will undertake fewer investment projects. Lower interest rates make it less expensive for firms to borrow, so they will undertake more investment projects. Lower interest rates can also increase investment through their effect on stock prices. As interest rates decline, stocks become a more attractive investment relative to bonds. The increase in demand for stocks raises their prices. By issuing additional shares of stock, firms can acquire the funds they need to buy new factories and equipment, thereby increasing investment.

  Spending by households on new homes is also part of investment. When interest rates on mortgage loans rise, the cost of buying new homes rises, and fewer new homes will be purchased. When interest rates on mortgage loans fall, more new homes will be purchased.

- *Net exports.* Recall that net exports are equal to spending by foreign households and firms on goods and services produced in the United States minus spending by U.S. households and firms on goods and services produced in other countries. The value of net exports depends partly on the exchange rate between the U.S. dollar and foreign currencies. When the value of the dollar rises, households and firms in other countries will pay more for goods and services produced in the United States, but U.S. households and firms will pay less for goods and services produced in other countries. As a result, the United States will export less and import more, so net exports will fall. When the value of the dollar falls, net exports will rise. If interest rates in the United States rise relative to interest rates in other countries, investing in U.S. financial assets will become more desirable, causing foreign investors to increase their demand for dollars, which will increase the value of the dollar. As the value of the dollar increases, net exports will fall. If interest rates in the United States decline relative to interest rates in other countries, the value of the dollar will fall, and net exports will rise.

The Effects of Monetary Policy on Real GDP and the Price Level

In the basic version of the aggregate demand and aggregate supply model to explain fluctuations in real GDP and the price level, we assume that there is no economic growth, so the long-run aggregate supply curve does not shift. In panel (a) of Figure 7, we assume that short-run equilibrium is at point A, where the aggregate demand (AD_1) curve intersects the short-run aggregate supply ($SRAS$) curve. Real GDP is below potential GDP, as shown by the $LRAS$ curve, so the economy is in a recession, with some firms operating below normal capacity and some

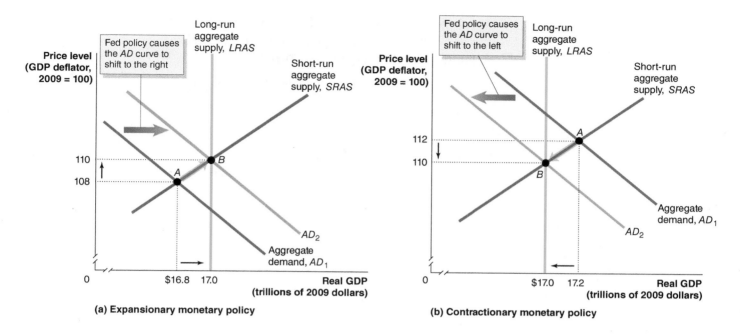

Figure 7 Monetary Policy

In panel (a), short-run equilibrium is at point A, with real GDP of $16.8 trillion and a price level of 108. An expansionary monetary policy causes aggregate demand to shift to the right, from AD_1 to AD_2, increasing real GDP from $16.8 trillion to $17.0 trillion and the price level from 108 to 110 (point B). With real GDP back at its potential level, the Fed can meet its goal of high employment.

In panel (b), short-run equilibrium is at point A, with real GDP at $17.2 trillion and the price level at 112. Because real GDP is greater than potential GDP, the economy experiences rising wages and prices. A contractionary monetary policy causes aggregate demand to shift to the left, from AD_1 to AD_2, causing real GDP to decrease from $17.2 trillion to $17.0 trillion and the price level to decrease from 112 to 110 (point B). With real GDP back at its potential level, the Fed can meet its goal of price stability.

workers having been laid off. To reach its goal of high employment, the Fed carries out an **expansionary monetary policy** by increasing the money supply and decreasing interest rates. Lower interest rates cause an increase in consumption, investment, and net exports, which shifts the aggregate demand curve to the right, from AD_1 to AD_2. Real GDP increases from $16.8 trillion to potential GDP of $17.0 trillion, and the price level rises from 108 to 110 (point B). The policy successfully returns real GDP to its potential level. Rising production leads to increasing employment, allowing the Fed to achieve its goal of high employment.

In panel (b) of Figure 7, short-run equilibrium is at point A, with real GDP of $17.2 trillion, which is above potential GDP of $17.0 trillion. With some firms producing beyond their normal capacity and the unemployment rate being very low, wages and prices are increasing. To reach its goal of price stability, the Fed needs to carry out a **contractionary monetary policy** by decreasing the money supply and increasing interest rates. Higher interest rates cause a decrease in consumption, investment, and net exports, which shifts the aggregate demand curve from AD_1 to AD_2. Real GDP decreases from $17.2 trillion to $17.0 trillion, and the price level falls from 112 to 110 (point B). Why would the Fed want to intentionally cause real GDP to decline? Because in the long run, real GDP cannot continue to remain above potential GDP. Attempting to keep real GDP above potential GDP would result in rising inflation. As aggregate demand declines and real GDP returns to its potential level, upward pressure on wages and prices will be reduced, allowing the Fed to achieve its goal of price stability.

We can conclude that the Fed can use monetary policy to affect the price level and, in the short run, the level of real GDP, allowing it to attain its policy goals of high employment and price stability.

Expansionary monetary policy The Federal Reserve's policy of decreasing interest rates to increase real GDP.

Contractionary monetary policy The Federal Reserve's policy of increasing interest rates to reduce inflation.

<table>
<tr><td>Making
the
Connection</td><td>**Too Low for Zero: The Fed Tries
Quantitative Easing and
Operation Twist**</td></tr>
</table>

Figure 6 shows that in December 2008, the Fed pushed the target for the federal funds rate to nearly zero and kept it there through 2013. Because the 2007–2009 recession was so severe, even this very low rate did little to stimulate the economy. To lower the federal funds rate, the Fed buys Treasury bills through open market purchases, which increases bank reserves. Banks then lend out these reserves to households and firm. As the following graph shows, however, in late 2008, many banks began piling up excess reserves rather than lending the funds out. Total bank reserves had been less than $50 billion in August 2008, but as the financial crisis became more severe, excess reserves soared to more than $900 billion by May 2009.

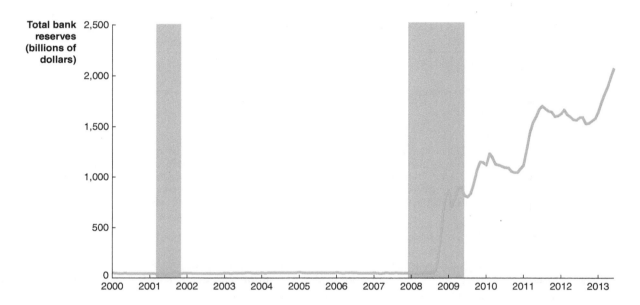

The increase in bank reserves was partly due to the Fed having received authorization from Congress in October 2008 to start paying interest of 0.25 percent on bank reserves held as deposits at the Fed. Primarily, though, the increase in reserves occurred because banks were reluctant to make loans at low interest rates to households and firms whose financial positions had been damaged by the recession. Some economists argued that the Fed was facing a situation known as a *liquidity trap*, in which short-term interest rates are pushed to zero, leaving the central bank unable to lower them further. Liquidity traps may also have occurred in the United States during the 1930s and in Japan during the 1990s.

Not being able to push the target for the federal funds rate below zero was a problem for the Fed. Glenn Rudebusch, an economist at the Federal Reserve Bank of San Francisco, calculated that given how high the unemployment rate was, the appropriate target for the federal funds rate was –5 percent. Because the federal funds rate cannot be negative, the Fed turned to other policies. In particular, the Fed decided to embark on a policy of *quantitative easing*, which involves buying securities beyond the short-term Treasury securities that are usually involved in open market operations. The Fed began purchasing 10-year Treasury notes to keep their interest rates from rising. Interest rates on home mortgage loans typically move closely with interest rates on 10-year Treasury notes. The Fed also purchased certain *mortgage-backed securities*. The Fed's objective was to keep interest rates on mortgages low and to keep funds flowing into the mortgage market to help stimulate demand for housing.

The Fed's first round of quantitative easing began in November 2008 and ended in June 2010. With the economy recovering only slowly, in November 2010, the Fed announced a second round of quantitative easing (dubbed QE2). With QE2, the Fed bought an additional $600 billion in long-term Treasury securities through June 2011. In September 2011, with the economic recovery remaining weak, the Fed announced a new program under which it would purchase $400 billion in long-term Treasury securities while selling an equal amount of short-term Treasury securities. This program, which some people in financial markets called *Operation Twist*, had the same objective as quantitative easing: to reduce interest rates on long-term Treasury securities to increase aggregate demand. In September 2012, the Fed announced a third round of quantitative easing (QE3), with additional purchases of mortgage-backed securities and long-term Treasury securities. The Fed pledged to continue QE3 until growth in real GDP and employment returned to more normal levels. Economists remain divided over whether the rounds of quantitative easing had significantly expanded the growth of employment and output in the U.S. economy.

Later in this chapter, we will consider other new programs the Fed put in place to deal with the recession of 2007–2009 and the slow recovery that followed, as its traditional focus on lowering the federal funds rate to stimulate the economy proved ineffective.

Sources: Glenn Rudebusch, "The Fed's Monetary Policy Response to the Current Crisis," FRBSF Economic Letter, May 22, 2009; and Federal Reserve Bank of St. Louis.

Your Turn: Test your understanding by doing related problems 3.9 and 3.10 at the end of this chapter.

Can the Fed Eliminate Recessions?

Panel (a) of Figure 7 shows a completely successful expansionary monetary policy that shifts the *AD* curve to bring real GDP back to potential GDP. In fact, however, this ideal is very difficult for the Fed to achieve, as the length and severity of the 2007–2009 recession illustrates. In practice, the best the Fed can do is keep recessions shorter and milder than they would otherwise be.

If the Fed is to be successful in offsetting the effects of the business cycle, it needs to quickly recognize the need for a change in monetary policy. If the Fed is late in recognizing that a recession has begun or that the inflation rate is increasing, it may not be able to implement a new policy quickly enough to do much good. There is typically a lag, or delay, between a policy change and its effect on real GDP, employment, inflation, and other economic variables. Nobel Laureate Milton Friedman famously described the lags for monetary policy as "long and variable," which means that it can take months or years for changes in monetary policy to affect real GDP and inflation and that the lags vary based on economic circumstances. Once the Fed reduces the target federal funds rate, it takes time for the interest rates that affect firm and household behavior to also decline. Then it takes time for firms to identify newly profitable investment projects, obtain loans from banks or arrange to sell bonds, and start spending the borrowed funds. Similarly, it takes time for families to respond to lower mortgage interest rates by buying houses. As a result, the full effect of a change in monetary policy is typically spread out over several years.

Implementing a policy too late may actually destabilize the economy. To see why, consider Figure 8. The straight line represents the long-run growth trend in real GDP in the United States. On average, real GDP grows about 3 percent per year. The actual path of real GDP differs from the underlying trend because of the business cycle, which is shown by the red curved line. The actual business cycle is more irregular than the stylized cycle shown here.

Suppose that a recession begins in August 2016. Because it takes months for economic statistics to be gathered by the Commerce Department, the Census Bureau, the Bureau of Labor Statistics, and the Fed itself, there is a lag before the Fed recognizes that a recession has begun. Finally, in June 2017, the FOMC concludes that the economy is in recession and begins an expansionary monetary policy. As it turns out, June 2017 is actually the trough of the recession, meaning that the recession has already ended, and an expansion has begun. In these circumstances, the Fed's expansionary policy is not needed to end the recession. The increase in aggregate demand caused by the Fed's lowering interest rates is likely to push the economy beyond potential GDP and cause a

The Effect of a Poorly Timed Monetary Policy on the Economy

The upward-sloping straight line represents the long-run growth trend in real GDP. The curved red line represents the path real GDP takes because of the business cycle. If the Fed is too late in implementing a change in monetary policy, real GDP will follow the curved blue line. The Fed's expansionary monetary policy results in too great an increase in aggregate demand during the next expansion, which causes an increase in the inflation rate.

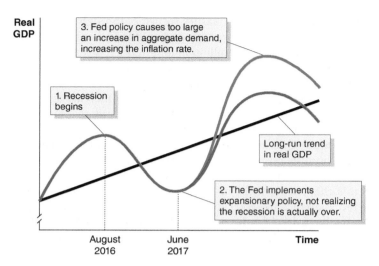

significant acceleration in inflation. Real GDP ends up following the path indicated by the blue curved line. The Fed has inadvertently engaged in a *procyclical policy*, which increases the severity of the business cycle, as opposed to a *countercyclical policy*, which is meant to reduce the severity of the business cycle, and which is what the Fed intends to use. The typical recession since 1950 has lasted less than one year, which increases the likelihood that the Fed may accidentally engage in a procyclical policy. Making this mistake is, of course, less likely in a long and severe recession such as the recession of 2007–2009.

Fed Forecasts

Because it can take a long time for a change in monetary policy to affect real GDP, the Fed tries to set policy according to what it forecasts the state of the economy will be in the future, when the policy change actually affects the economy. For example, when the Fed cut its federal funds rate target by 0.5 percent on October 8, 2008, the lag associated with monetary policy meant that the full effect of the rate cut on real GDP was spread out over several years. In making that cut, the Fed was thinking about the economy's future performance.

For the Fed to succeed in reducing the severity of business cycles, it must often act before a recession or an acceleration of inflation shows up in the economic data. So, good policy requires good economic forecasts based on models that describe accurately how the economy functions. Unfortunately, economic forecasts and models can be unreliable because changes in aggregate demand and short-run aggregate supply can be unpredictable. For example, the forecasts of most economists at the end of 2006 and the beginning of 2007 did not anticipate the severity of the recession that began in December 2007. Only after financial market conditions began to deteriorate rapidly did economists significantly reduce their forecasts of GDP growth in 2008 and 2009.

Table 1 summarizes the Fed's estimates for the growth rate of real GDP for 2007 and 2008 in its Monetary Policy Report to Congress. To keep a recession from

Fed Forecasts of Real GDP Growth during 2007 and 2008

Date Forecast Was Made	Forecast Growth Rate		Actual Growth Rate	
	For 2007	For 2008	2007	2008
February 2006	3% to 4%	No forecast	1.8%	−0.3%
May 2006	2.5% to 3.25%	No forecast		
February 2007	2.25% to 3.25%	2.5% to 3.25%		
July 2007	No forecast	2.5% to 3.0%		

Sources: Board of Governors of the Federal Reserve System, *Monetary Policy Report to the Congress*, various dates; and U.S. Bureau of Economic Analysis.

starting in 2007, the Fed would have had to change policy before 2007. However, in February 2006, the Fed expected the economy to grow by 3 percent to 4 percent in 2007, so it had little reason to change policy. Similarly, the Fed could have changed policy in an attempt to keep the economy growing in 2008, but it would have had to change policy before 2008, and as late as July 2007, the Fed still expected the economy to grow by 2.5 percent to 3.0 percent in 2008. In fact, real GDP increased by only 1.8 percent in 2007 and declined by 0.3 percent in 2008. We can conclude that, although the Fed could have taken actions that would have at least greatly reduced the severity of the 2007–2009 recession, it could not prevent the recession because it did not see the recession coming.

Making the Connection	### Trying to Hit a Moving Target: Making Policy with "Real-Time Data"

The Fed relies on macroeconomic data to formulate monetary policy. One key piece of economic data is GDP, which is calculated quarterly by the Bureau of Economic Analysis (BEA). Unfortunately for Fed policymakers, the GDP data the BEA provides are frequently revised, and the revisions can be large enough that the actual state of the economy can be different from what it at first appeared to be.

The BEA's *advance estimate* of a quarter's GDP is not released until about a month after the quarter has ended. This delay can be a problem for policymakers because it means that they will not receive an estimate of GDP for the period from January through March, for instance, until the end of April. Presenting even more difficulty is the fact that the advance estimate will be subject to a number of revisions. The second estimate of a quarter's GDP is released about two months after the end of the quarter. The third estimate is released about three months after the end of the quarter. Although the BEA used to refer to the third estimate as the "final estimate," in fact, it continues to revise its estimates through the years. The BEA releases its first annual, second annual, and third annual estimates one, two, and three years after the third estimate. Nor is that the end because benchmark revisions occur in later years.

Why so many estimates? Because GDP is such a comprehensive measure of output in the economy, it is very time-consuming to collect the necessary data. To provide the advance estimate, the BEA relies on surveys conducted by the Commerce Department of retail sales and manufacturing shipments, as well as data from trade organizations, estimates of government spending, and so on. As time passes, these organizations gather additional data, and the BEA is able to refine its estimates.

Do these revisions to the GDP estimates matter? Sometimes they do, as the following example indicates. At the beginning of 2001, some economists believed that the U.S. economy might be headed for recession. The dot-com stock market bubble had burst the previous spring, wiping out trillions of dollars in stockholder wealth. Overbuilding of fiber-optic cable networks and other information technology also weighed on the economy. The advance estimate of the first quarter's GDP, though, showed a reasonably healthy increase in real GDP of 2.0 percent at an annual rate. It seemed as if there was nothing for government policymakers to be worried about. But as the following graph shows, that estimate of 2.0 percent real GDP growth was revised a number of times over the years, mostly downward. Currently, BEA data indicate that real GDP actually declined by 1.1 percent at an annual rate during the first quarter of 2001. This swing of more than 3 percentage points is a large difference, which changes the picture of what happened during the first quarter of 2001 from one of an economy experiencing moderate growth to one of an economy suffering a significant decline. The National Bureau of Economic Research dates the recession of 2001 as having begun in March, but some economists believe it actually began at the end of 2000. The current BEA estimates of GDP provide some support for this view.

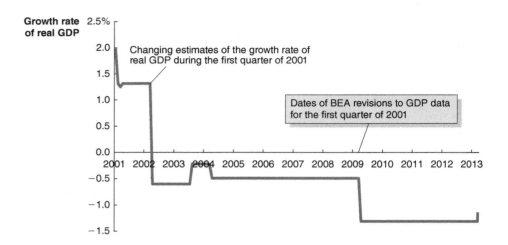

This example shows that in addition to the other problems the Federal Reserve encounters in successfully conducting monetary policy, it must make decisions using data that may be subject to substantial revisions.

Sources: Federal Reserve Bank of Philadelphia, "Historical Data Files for the Real-Time Data Set," August 15, 2013; and Bruce T. Grimm and Teresa Weadock, "Gross Domestic Product: Revisions and Source Data," *Survey of Current Business*, Vol. 86, No. 2, February 2006, pp. 11–15.

Your Turn: Test your understanding by doing related problems 3.11 and 3.12 at the end of this chapter.

A Summary of How Monetary Policy Works

Table 2 compares the steps involved in expansionary and contractionary monetary policies. We need to note an important qualification to this summary. At every point, we should add the phrase "relative to what would have happened without the policy." The table isolates the effect of monetary policy, *holding constant all other factors affecting the variables involved*. In other words, we are invoking the *ceteris paribus* condition. This point is important because a contractionary monetary policy, for example, does not cause the price level to fall; instead, a contractionary monetary policy causes the price level *to rise by less than it would have without the policy*. One final note on terminology: An expansionary monetary policy is sometimes called a *loose* policy, or an *easy* policy. A contractionary monetary policy is sometimes called a *tight* policy.

Table 2 **Expansionary and Contractionary Monetary Policies**

| FOMC orders an expansionary policy | → | The money supply increases and interest rates fall | → | Investment, consumption, and net exports all increase | → | The *AD* curve shifts to the right | → | Real GDP and the price level rise |

(a) An expansionary policy

| FOMC orders a contractionary policy | → | The money supply decreases and interest rates rise | → | Investment, consumption, and net exports all decrease | → | The *AD* curve shifts to the left | → | Real GDP and the price level fall |

(b) A contractionary policy

Don't Let This Happen to You

Remember That with Monetary Policy, It's the Interest Rates—Not the Money—That Counts

It is tempting to think of monetary policy as working like this: If the Fed wants more spending in the economy, it increases the money supply, and people spend more because they now have more money. If the Fed wants less spending in the economy, it decreases the money supply, and people spend less because they now have less money. In fact, that is *not* how monetary policy works. Remember the important difference between money and income: The Fed increases the money supply by buying Treasury bills. The sellers of the Treasury bills have just exchanged one asset—Treasury bills—for another asset—a check from the Fed; the sellers have *not* increased their income. Even though the money supply is now larger, no one's income has increased, so no one's spending should be affected.

It is only when this increase in the money supply results in lower interest rates that spending is affected. When interest rates are lower, households are more likely to buy new homes and automobiles, and businesses are more likely to buy new factories and computers. Lower interest rates also lead to a lower value of the dollar, which lowers the prices of exports and raises the prices of imports, thereby increasing net exports. It isn't the increase in the money supply that has brought about this additional spending, *it's the lower interest rates*. To understand how monetary policy works, and to interpret news reports about the Fed's actions, remember that it is the change in interest rates, not the change in the money supply, that is most important.

Your Turn: Test your understanding by doing related problem 3.13 at the end of this chapter.

Monetary Policy in the Dynamic Aggregate Demand and Aggregate Supply Model*

4 LEARNING OBJECTIVE

Use the dynamic aggregate demand and aggregate supply model to analyze monetary policy.

The overview of monetary policy we just finished contains a key idea: The Fed can use monetary policy to affect aggregate demand, thereby changing the price level and the level of real GDP. The discussion of monetary policy illustrated by Figure 7 is simplified, however, because it ignores two important facts about the economy: (1) The economy experiences continuing inflation, with the price level rising every year, and (2) the economy experiences long-run growth, with the *LRAS* curve shifting to the right every year. We develop a *dynamic aggregate demand and aggregate supply model* that takes into account these two facts. In this section, we use the dynamic model to gain a more complete understanding of monetary policy. Let's briefly review the dynamic model. Recall that over time, the U.S. labor force and the U.S. capital stock will increase. Technological change will also occur. The result will be an increase in potential GDP, which we show by the long-run aggregate supply curve shifting to the right. These factors will also result in firms supplying more goods and services at any given price level in the short run, which we show by the short-run aggregate supply curve shifting to the right. During most years, the aggregate demand curve will also shift to the right, indicating that aggregate expenditure will be higher at every price level. There are several reasons aggregate expenditure usually increases: As population grows and incomes rise, consumption will increase over time. Also, as the economy grows, firms expand capacity, and new firms are established, increasing investment spending. Finally, an expanding population and an expanding economy require increased government services, such as more police officers and teachers, so government purchases will expand.

The Effects of Monetary Policy on Real GDP and the Price Level: A More Complete Account

During certain periods, *AD* does not increase enough during the year to keep real GDP at potential GDP. This slow growth in aggregate demand may be due to households and firms becoming pessimistic about the future state of the economy, leading

---

*This section may be omitted without loss of continuity.

them to cut back their spending on consumer durables, houses, and factories. The collapse of the housing bubble and the resulting financial crisis had a negative effect on aggregate demand during the 2007–2009 recession. Other possibilities exist as well: The federal government might decide to balance the budget by cutting back its purchases and raising taxes, or recessions in other countries might cause a decline in U.S. exports. In the hypothetical situation shown in Figure 9, in the first year, equilibrium is at point A, with potential GDP of $17.0 trillion and a price level of 110. In the second year, $LRAS$ increases to $17.4 trillion, but AD increases only to $AD_{2(without policy)}$, which is not enough to keep real GDP at potential GDP. If the Fed does not intervene, the new short-run equilibrium will occur at $17.3 trillion (point B). The $100 billion gap between this level of real GDP and potential GDP at $LRAS_2$ means that some firms are operating at less than their normal capacity. Incomes and profits will fall, firms will begin to lay off workers, and the unemployment rate will rise.

Economists at the Federal Reserve closely monitor the economy and continually update forecasts of future levels of real GDP and prices. When these economists anticipate that aggregate demand is not growing fast enough to allow the economy to remain at full employment, they present their findings to the FOMC, which decides whether circumstances require a change in monetary policy. For example, suppose that the FOMC meets and considers a forecast from the staff indicating that during the following year, a gap of $100 billion will open between equilibrium real GDP and potential GDP. In other words, the macroeconomic equilibrium illustrated by point B in Figure 9 will occur. The FOMC may then decide to carry out an expansionary monetary policy to lower interest rates to stimulate aggregate demand. The figure shows the results of a successful attempt to do this: AD has shifted to the right, and equilibrium occurs at potential GDP (point C). The Fed will have successfully headed off the falling incomes and rising unemployment that otherwise would have occurred. Bear in mind that we are illustrating a perfectly executed monetary policy that keeps the economy at potential GDP, which is difficult to achieve in practice for reasons discussed in the previous section.

Notice in Figure 9 that the expansionary monetary policy caused the inflation rate to be higher than it would have been. Without the expansionary policy, the price level would have risen from 110 to 112, so the inflation rate for the year would have been

Figure 9

An Expansionary Monetary Policy

Initially, equilibrium is at point A, with real GDP of $17.0 trillion and a price level of 110. Without monetary policy, aggregate demand will shift from AD_1 to $AD_{2(without policy)}$, which is not enough to keep the economy at full employment because long-run aggregate supply has shifted from $LRAS_1$ to $LRAS_2$. Short-run equilibrium is at point B, with real GDP of $17.3 trillion and a price level of 112. By lowering interest rates, the Fed increases investment, consumption, and net exports sufficiently to shift aggregate demand to $AD_{2(with policy)}$. Equilibrium will be at point C, with real GDP of $17.4 trillion, which is its full employment level, and a price level of 113. The price level is higher than it would have been if the Fed had not acted to increase spending in the economy.

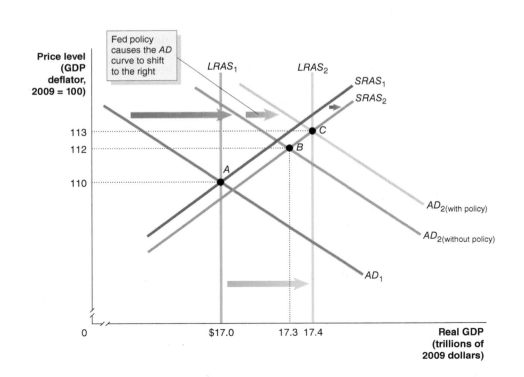

1.8 percent. By shifting the aggregate demand curve, the expansionary policy caused the price level to increase from 112 to 113, raising the inflation rate from 1.8 percent to 2.7 percent.

Using Monetary Policy to Fight Inflation

In addition to using an expansionary monetary policy to reduce the severity of recessions, the Fed can use a contractionary monetary policy to keep aggregate demand from expanding so rapidly that the inflation rate begins to increase. Figure 10 shows the situation during 2005 and 2006, when the Fed faced this possibility. During 2005, real GDP was equal to potential GDP, but Fed Chair Alan Greenspan and other members of the FOMC were concerned that the continuing boom in the housing market might lead aggregate demand to increase so rapidly that the inflation rate would begin to accelerate. The Fed had been gradually increasing the target for the federal funds rate since mid-2004.

When Ben Bernanke was appointed Fed chair in early 2006, he advocated continued increases in the target for the federal funds rate to slow the growth in aggregate demand. By June 2006, the target for the federal funds rate had been raised to 5.25 percent, from the low rate of 1 percent that had prevailed from June 2003 to May 2004. The FOMC issues a statement after each meeting that summarizes the committee's views on the current state of the economy and gives some indication of how monetary policy might change in the near future. After its meeting on June 29, 2006, the FOMC included the following remarks in its statement:

> The Federal Open Market Committee decided today to raise its target for the federal funds rate . . . to 5-1/4 percent. Recent indicators suggest that economic growth is moderating from its quite strong pace earlier this year, partly reflecting a gradual cooling of the housing market and the lagged effects of increases in . . . interest rates. . . . Although the moderation in the growth of aggregate demand should help to limit inflation pressures over time, the Committee judges that some inflation risks remain.

The committee kept the target for the federal funds rate constant at 5.25 percent until September 2007, when concern about difficulties in financial markets led it to cut the target to 4.75 percent. Although it is impossible to know exactly what would have happened during 2006 without the Fed's policy change, Figure 10 presents a

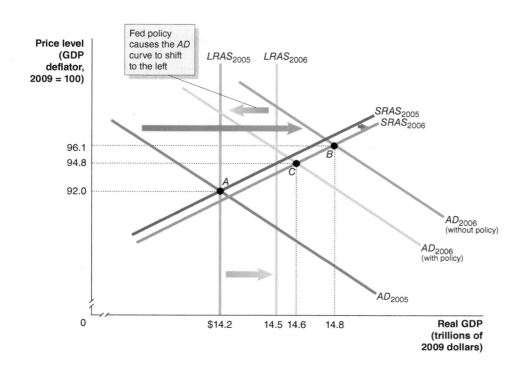

Figure 10

A Contractionary Monetary Policy in 2006

In 2005, equilibrium is at point *A*, with real GDP equal to potential GDP of $14.2 trillion and a price level of 92.0. From 2005 to 2006, potential GDP increased from $14.2 trillion to $14.5 trillion, as long-run aggregate supply increased from $LRAS_{2005}$ to $LRAS_{2006}$. The Fed raised interest rates because it believed the housing boom was causing aggregate demand to increase too rapidly. Without the increase in interest rates, aggregate demand would have shifted from AD_{2005} to $AD_{2006(without policy)}$, and the new short-run equilibrium would have occurred at point *B*. Real GDP would have been $14.8 trillion—$300 billion greater than potential GDP—and the price level would have been 96.1. The increase in interest rates resulted in aggregate demand increasing only to $AD_{2006(with policy)}$. Equilibrium occurred at point *C*, with real GDP of $14.6 trillion being only $100 billion greater than potential GDP and the price level rising only to 94.8.

plausible scenario. The figure shows that without the Fed's actions to increase interest rates, aggregate demand would have shifted farther to the right, and equilibrium would have occurred at a level of real GDP that was further beyond the potential level. The price level would have risen from 92.0 in 2005 to 96.1 in 2006, meaning that the inflation rate would have been 4.5 percent. Because the Fed kept aggregate demand from increasing as much as it otherwise would have, short-run equilibrium occurred closer to potential GDP, and the price level in 2006 rose to only 94.8, keeping the inflation rate at 3.0 percent.

Solved Problem 4

The Effects of Monetary Policy

The hypothetical information in the following table shows what the values for real GDP and the price level will be in 2017 if the Fed does *not* use monetary policy:

Year	Potential GDP	Real GDP	Price Level
2016	$17.7 trillion	$17.7 trillion	114
2017	18.1 trillion	17.9 trillion	116

a. If the Fed wants to keep real GDP at its potential level in 2017, should it use an expansionary policy or a contractionary policy? Should the trading desk buy Treasury bills or sell them?

b. Suppose the Fed's policy is successful in keeping real GDP at its potential level in 2017. State whether each of the following will be higher or lower than if the Fed had taken no action:
   i.   Real GDP
   ii. Potential GDP
   iii. The inflation rate
   iv. The unemployment rate

c. Draw an aggregate demand and aggregate supply graph to illustrate your answer. Be sure that your graph contains *LRAS* curves for 2016 and 2017; *SRAS* curves for 2016 and 2017; *AD* curves for 2016 and for 2017, with and without monetary policy action; and equilibrium real GDP and the price level in 2017, with and without policy.

Solving the Problem

Step 1: **Review the chapter material.** This problem is about the effects of monetary policy on real GDP and the price level, so you may want to review the section "The Effects of Monetary Policy on Real GDP and the Price Level: A More Complete Account."

Step 2: **Answer the questions in part (a) by explaining how the Fed can keep real GDP at its potential level.** The information in the table tells us that without monetary policy, the economy will be below potential GDP in 2017. To keep real GDP at its potential level, the Fed must undertake an expansionary policy. To carry out an expansionary policy, the trading desk needs to buy Treasury bills. Buying Treasury bills will increase reserves in the banking system. Banks will increase their loans, which will increase the money supply and lower the interest rate.

Step 3: **Answer part (b) by explaining the effect of the Fed's policy.** If the Fed's policy is successful, real GDP in 2017 will increase from $17.9 trillion, as given in the table, to its potential level of $18.1 trillion. Potential GDP is not affected by monetary policy, so its value will not change. Because the level of real GDP will be higher, the unemployment rate will be lower than it would have been without policy. The expansionary monetary policy shifts the *AD* curve to the right, so short-run equilibrium will move up the short-run aggregate supply (*SRAS*) curve, and the price level will be higher.

Step 4: **Answer part (c) by drawing the graph.** Your graph should look similar to Figure 9.

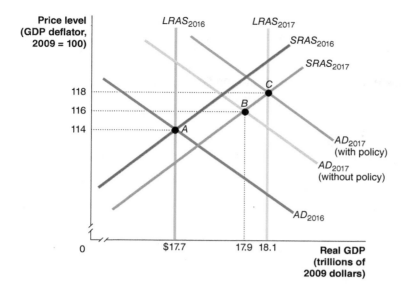

Equilibrium in 2016 is at point *A*, with the *AD* and *SRAS* curves intersecting along the *LRAS* curve. Real GDP is at its potential level of $17.7 trillion, and the price level is 114. Without monetary policy, the *AD* curve shifts to $AD_{2017(\text{without policy})}$, and short-run equilibrium is at point *B*. Because potential GDP has increased from $17.1 trillion to $18.1 trillion, real GDP of $17.9 trillion is below the potential level. The price level has increased from 114 to 116. With policy, the *AD* curve shifts to $AD_{2017(\text{with policy})}$, and equilibrium is at point *C*. Real GDP is at its potential level of $18.1 trillion. We don't have enough information to be sure of the new equilibrium price level. We do know that it will be higher than 116. The graph shows the price level rising to 118. Therefore, without the Fed's expansionary policy, the inflation rate in 2017 would have been about 1.8 percent. With policy, it will be about 3.5 percent.

Extra Credit: Bear in mind that in reality, the Fed is unable to use monetary policy to keep real GDP exactly at its potential level, as this problem suggests.

Your Turn: For more practice, do related problems 4.4 and 4.5 at the end of this chapter.

A Closer Look at the Fed's Setting of Monetary Policy Targets

5 LEARNING OBJECTIVE

Discuss the Fed's setting of monetary policy targets.

We have seen that in carrying out monetary policy, the Fed changes its target for the federal funds rate depending on the state of the economy. During times when the economy is not experiencing a financial crisis, is using the federal funds rate as a target the best way to conduct monetary policy? If the Fed targets the federal funds rate, how should it decide what the target level should be? In this section, we consider these important issues concerning the Fed's targeting policy.

Should the Fed Target the Money Supply?

Some economists have argued that rather than use an interest rate as its monetary policy target, the Fed should use the money supply. Many of the economists who make this argument belong to a school of thought known as *monetarism*. The leader of the monetarist school was Milton Friedman, who was skeptical that the Fed would be able to correctly time changes in monetary policy.

Friedman and his followers favored replacing *monetary policy* with a *monetary growth rule*. Ordinarily, we expect monetary policy to respond to changing economic conditions: When the economy is in recession, the Fed reduces interest rates, and when inflation is increasing, the Fed raises interest rates. A monetary growth rule, in contrast, is a plan for increasing the money supply at a constant rate that does not change in response to economic conditions. Friedman and his followers proposed a monetary growth rule of increasing the money supply every year at a rate equal to the long-run annual growth rate of real GDP, which is about 3 percent. If the Fed adopted this monetary growth rule, it would stick to it through changing economic conditions.

But what happens under a monetary growth rule if the economy moves into recession? Shouldn't the Fed abandon the rule to drive down interest rates? Friedman argued that the Fed should stick to the rule even during recessions because he believed active monetary policy destabilizes the economy by increasing the number of recessions and their severity. By keeping the money supply growing at a constant rate, Friedman argued, the Fed would greatly increase economic stability.

During the 1970s some economists and politicians pressured the Federal Reserve to adopt a monetary growth rule. Most of that pressure has disappeared in recent years because the fairly close relationship between movements in the money supply and movements in real GDP and the price level that existed before 1980 has become much weaker. Since 1980, the growth rate of M1 has been unstable. In some years, M1 has grown more than 10 percent, while in other years, it has actually fallen. Yet despite these wide fluctuations in the growth of M1, growth in real GDP has been fairly stable, and inflation has remained low during most years.

Why Doesn't the Fed Target Both the Money Supply and the Interest Rate?

Most economists believe that the interest rate is the best monetary policy target. But as we have just seen, other economists believe the Fed should target the money supply. Why doesn't the Fed satisfy both groups by targeting both the money supply and the interest rate? The simple answer is that the Fed can't target both at the same time. To see why, look at Figure 11, which shows the money market.

Remember that the Fed controls the money supply, but it does not control money demand. Money demand is determined by decisions of households and firms as they weigh the trade-off between the convenience of money and its low interest rate compared with other financial assets. Suppose the Fed is targeting the interest rate and decides, given conditions in the economy, that the interest rate should be 5 percent. Or, suppose the Fed is targeting the money supply and decides that the money supply

Figure 11

The Fed Can't Target Both the Money Supply and the Interest Rate

The Fed is forced to choose between using either the interest rate or the money supply as its monetary policy target. In this figure, the Fed can set a target of $900 billion for the money supply or a target of 5 percent for the interest rate, but the Fed can't hit both targets because it can achieve only combinations of the interest rate and the money supply that represent equilibrium in the money market.

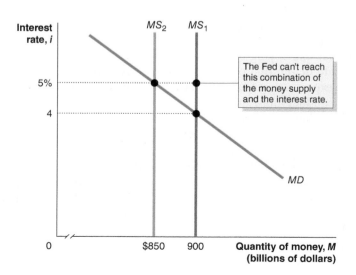

should be $900 billion. Figure 11 shows that the Fed can bring about an interest rate of 5 percent or a money supply of $900 billion, but it can't bring about both. The point representing an interest rate of 5 percent and a money supply of $900 billion is not on the money demand curve, so it can't represent an equilibrium in the money market. Only combinations of the interest rate and the money supply that represent equilibrium in the money market are possible.

The Fed has to choose between targeting an interest rate and targeting the money supply. For most of the period since World War II, the Fed has chosen the federal funds rate as its target.

The Taylor Rule

How does the Fed choose a target for the federal funds rate? The discussions at the meetings of the FOMC can be complex, and they take into account many economic variables. John Taylor of Stanford University has analyzed Fed decision making and developed the **Taylor rule** to explain federal funds rate targeting. The Taylor rule begins with an estimate of the value of the equilibrium real federal funds rate, which is the federal funds rate—adjusted for inflation—that would be consistent with real GDP being equal to potential GDP in the long run. According to the Taylor rule, the Fed should set the target for the federal funds rate so that it is equal to the sum of the inflation rate, the equilibrium real federal funds rate, and two additional terms. The first of these additional terms is the *inflation gap*—the difference between current inflation and a target rate; the second is the *output gap*—the percentage difference between real GDP and potential GDP. The inflation gap and output gap are each given "weights" that reflect their influence on the federal funds target rate. With weights of 1/2 for both gaps, we have the following Taylor rule:

Taylor rule A rule developed by John Taylor that links the Fed's target for the federal funds rate to economic variables.

Federal funds target rate = Current inflation rate + Equilibrium real federal funds rate + [(1/2) × Inflation gap] + [(1/2) × Output gap].

The Taylor rule includes expressions for the inflation gap and the output gap because the Fed is concerned about both inflation and fluctuations in real GDP. Taylor demonstrated that if the equilibrium real federal funds rate is 2 percent and the target rate of inflation is 2 percent, the preceding expression does a good job of explaining changes in the Fed's target for the federal funds rate during most years. Consider an example in which the current inflation rate is 1 percent, and real GDP is 1 percent below potential GDP. In that case, the inflation gap equals 1 percent − 2 percent = −1 percent and the output gap is also −1 percent. Inserting these values in the Taylor rule, we can calculate the predicted value for the federal funds target rate:

Federal funds target rate = 1% + 2% + [(1/2) × −1%] + [(1/2) × −1%] = 2%.

The Taylor rule accurately predicted changes in the federal funds target during the period of Alan Greenspan's leadership of the Federal Reserve from 1987 to 2006. For the period of the late 1970s and early 1980s, when Paul Volcker was chairman of the Federal Reserve, the Taylor rule predicts a federal funds rate target *lower* than the actual target the Fed used. In other words, Chairman Volcker kept the federal funds rate at an unusually high level to bring down the very high inflation rates of the late 1970s and early 1980s. In contrast, using data from the chairmanship of Arthur Burns from 1970 to 1978, the Taylor rule predicts a federal funds rate target *higher* than the actual target. Chairman Burns kept the federal funds rate at an unusually low level during these years, which helps to explain why the inflation rate grew worse. During the mid-2000s, the actual federal funds rate was also lower than the predicted federal funds rate. Some economists, including Taylor, argue that these low targets for the federal funds rate contributed to the excessive increase in spending on housing that we will discuss in the next section.

Although the Taylor rule does not account for changes in the target inflation rate or the equilibrium interest rate, many economists view the rule as a convenient tool for analyzing the federal funds target.

Inflation Targeting

In the years before the financial crisis, many economists and central bankers expressed strong interest in using inflation targeting as a framework for carrying out monetary policy. With **inflation targeting**, a central bank publicly sets an explicit target for the inflation rate over a period of time, and the government and the public then judge the performance of the central bank on the basis of its success in hitting the target.

Inflation targeting has been adopted by the central banks of New Zealand (1989), Canada (1991), the United Kingdom (1992), Finland (1993), Sweden (1993), and Spain (1994), and by the European Central Bank. Inflation targeting has also been used in some newly industrializing countries, such as Chile, South Korea, Mexico, and South Africa, as well as in some transition economies in Eastern Europe, such as the Czech Republic, Hungary, and Poland. After many years of not having an explicit inflation target, the Fed announced in 2012 that it would attempt to maintain an average inflation rate of 2 percent per year.

With inflation targeting, the Fed can still respond to periods of recession or other economic problems without following an inflexible rule. Nevertheless, an inflation target allows monetary policy to focus on inflation and inflation forecasts, except during times of severe recession. Arguments supporting the Fed using an explicit inflation target focus on the following points. First, announcing explicit targets for inflation draws the public's attention to what the Fed can actually achieve in practice. Most economists believe that over the long run, monetary policy has a greater effect on inflation than on the growth of real GDP. Second, announcing an inflation target provides an anchor for inflationary expectations. If households, firms, and participants in financial markets believe that the Fed will hit an annual inflation target of 2 percent, then they will expect that if inflation were temporarily lower or higher, it will eventually return to the target rate. Third, inflation targets promote accountability for the Fed by providing a yardstick against which its performance can be measured.

Some economists and policymakers were critical of the Fed's decision to adopt an explicit inflation target. Opponents make several arguments. First, rigid numerical targets for inflation diminish the flexibility of monetary policy to address other policy goals. Second, because monetary policy affects inflation with a lag, inflation targeting requires that the Fed use forecasts of future inflation, which may turn out to be inaccurate. Third, holding the Fed accountable only for a goal of low inflation may make it more difficult for elected officials to monitor the Fed's support for good economic policy overall. Finally, inflation targets may increase uncertainty over whether the Fed will take prompt action to return the economy to full employment following a recession.

Economists and policymakers continue to debate whether inflation targets improve economic policy.

Inflation targeting A framework for conducting monetary policy that involves the central bank announcing its target level of inflation.

| Making the Connection | How Does the Fed Measure Inflation? |

How Does the Fed Measure Inflation?

To attain its goal of price stability, the Fed has to consider carefully the best way to measure the inflation rate. The consumer price index (CPI) is the most widely used measure of inflation. But the CPI suffers from biases that cause it to overstate the true underlying rate of inflation. An alternative measure of changes in consumer prices can be constructed from the data gathered to calculate GDP. The GDP deflator is a broad measure of the price level that includes the price of every good or service that is in GDP. Changes in the GDP deflator are not a good measure of inflation experienced by the typical consumer, worker, or firm, however, because the deflator includes prices of goods, such as industrial equipment, that are not widely purchased. The *personal consumption expenditures price index (PCE)* is a measure of the price level that is similar to the GDP deflator, except it includes only the prices of goods from the consumption category of GDP.

In 2000, the Fed announced that it would rely more on the PCE than on the CPI in tracking inflation because the PCE has these advantages over the CPI:

1. The PCE is a so-called chain-type price index, as opposed to the market-basket approach used in constructing the CPI. Because consumers shift the mix of products they buy each year, the market-basket approach causes the CPI to overstate actual inflation. A chain-type price index allows the mix of products to change each year.

2. The PCE includes the prices of more goods and services than the CPI, so it is a broader measure of inflation.

3. Past values of the PCE can be revised as better ways of computing price indexes are developed and as new data become available. These revisions allow the Fed to better track historical trends in the inflation rate.

The Fed excludes food and energy prices from its main measure of inflation.

In 2004, the Fed announced that it would begin to rely on a subcategory of the PCE index: the so-called core PCE index, which excludes food and energy prices. Prices of food and energy tend to fluctuate for reasons that may not be related to the causes of general inflation and that cannot easily be controlled by monetary policy. Oil prices, in particular, have moved dramatically up and down in recent years. Therefore, a price index that includes food and energy prices may not give a clear view of underlying trends in inflation. The following graph shows movements in the CPI, the PCE, and the core PCE from January 1999 through June 2013. Although the three measures of inflation move roughly together, the core PCE has been more stable than the other two. Note in particular that in early 2009, when the CPI and the PCE were indicating that the economy was experiencing deflation, the core PCE was still showing inflation rates above 1 percent.

If you want to know what the Fed thinks the current inflation rate is, look at data on the core PCE. The Bureau of Economic Analysis publishes these data monthly.

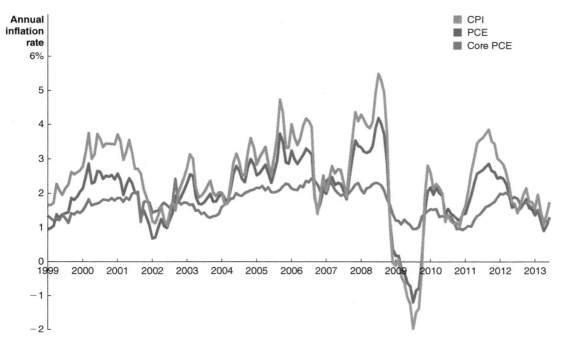

Source: Federal Reserve Bank of St. Louis.

Your Turn: Test your understanding by doing related problem 5.8 at the end of this chapter.

6 LEARNING OBJECTIVE

Discuss the policies the Federal Reserve used during the 2007–2009 recession.

Fed Policies during the 2007–2009 Recession

As we have seen, the Fed's traditional response to a recession is to lower the target for the federal funds rate. The severity of the recession of 2007–2009, particularly the problems in financial markets during those years, complicated the Fed's job. By December 2008, the Fed had effectively lowered the target for the federal funds rate to zero, but the zero interest rate alone did not result in a sufficient increase in aggregate demand to end the recession. In this section, we will discuss some of the additional policy measures the Fed took during the 2007–2009 recession. Some of these measures were used for the first time in the Fed's history.

The Inflation and Deflation of the Housing Market Bubble

To understand the 2007–2009 recession and the financial crisis that accompanied it, we need to start by considering the housing market. As we mentioned in the chapter opener, the Fed lowered the target for the federal funds rate during the 2001 recession to stimulate demand for housing. The policy was successful, and most builders, such as Hovnanian Enterprises, experienced several years of high demand. By 2005, however, many economists argued that a "bubble" had formed in the housing market. The price of any asset reflects the returns the owner of the asset expects to receive. For example, the price of a share of stock reflects the profitability of the firm issuing the stock because the owner of a share of stock has a claim on the firm's profits.

Many economists believe, however, that sometimes a *stock market bubble* can form when the prices of stocks rise above levels that can be justified by the profitability of the firms issuing the stocks. Stock market bubbles end when enough investors decide stocks are overvalued and begin to sell. Why would an investor be willing to pay more for stocks than would be justified by their underlying value? There are two main explanations: The investor may be caught up in the enthusiasm of the moment and, by failing to gather sufficient information, may overestimate the true value of the stocks, or the investor may expect to profit from buying stocks at inflated prices if the investor can sell them at even higher prices before the bubble bursts.

The price of a house should reflect the value of the housing services it provides. We can use the rents charged for comparable houses in an area to measure the value of housing services. We would expect, then, that housing prices and rents would increase at roughly the same rate. If prices of single-family homes rise significantly relative to rents for single-family homes, it is likely that the housing market is experiencing a bubble. As Figure 12 shows, housing prices and housing rents generally increase at about the same rate, but between January 2000 and May 2006, housing prices more than doubled, while rents increased by less than 25 percent. This divergence between housing prices and rents is evidence of a bubble. In addition, in some cities, there was an increase in the number of buyers who did not intend to live in the houses they purchased but were using them as investments. Like stock investors during a stock market bubble, these housing investors were expecting to make a profit by selling houses at higher prices than they had paid for them, and they were not concerned about whether the prices of the houses were above the value of the housing services provided.

During 2006 and 2007, the air was rapidly escaping from the housing bubble. Figure 13 shows new home sales for each month from January 2000 through June 2013. New home sales rose by 60 percent between January 2000 and July 2005 and then fell by 80 percent between July 2005 and May 2010. Sales then began to gradually increase but were still at low levels well into 2013. Sales of existing homes followed a similar pattern. Prices of new and existing homes in most markets also began to decline beginning in 2006, and the inventory of unsold homes offered for sale soared. Some homebuyers began having trouble making their loan payments. When lenders foreclosed on some of these loans, the lenders sold the homes, causing housing prices to decline further. *Subprime loans* are loans granted to borrowers with flawed credit histories. Some mortgage lenders that had concentrated on making subprime loans suffered heavy losses and went out of business, and most banks and other lenders tightened the requirements for borrowers. This *credit crunch* made it more difficult for potential homebuyers to obtain mortgages, further depressing the market.

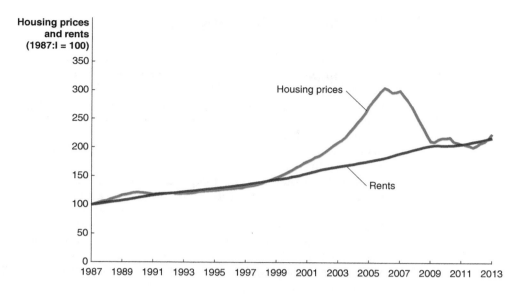

Figure 12 **Housing Prices and Housing Rents**

Typically, housing prices increase at about the same rate as housing rents. But during the housing bubble, housing prices increased far more than did rents.

Note: For both series, the values for the first quarter of 1987 (1987:I) are set equal to 100. **Source:** Federal Reserve Bank of St. Louis.

The decline in the housing market affected other markets as well. For example, with home prices falling, consumption spending on furniture, appliances, and home improvements declined because many households found it more difficult to borrow against the value of their homes.

Was the housing bubble the result of overly optimistic expectations by homebuyers and builders who believed that new residential construction and housing prices would continue to rise at rapid rates indefinitely? While overly optimistic expectations may have played some role in the housing bubble, many economists believe that changes in the market for mortgages may have played a bigger role.

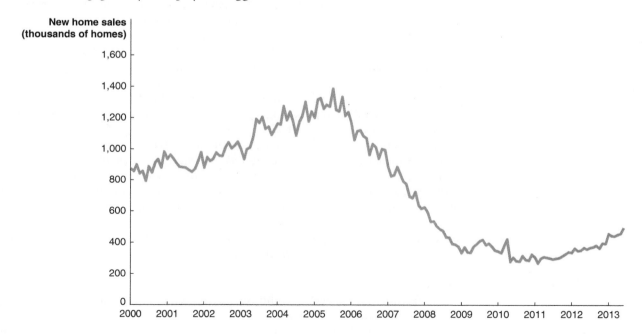

Figure 13 **The Housing Bubble**

Sales of new homes in the United States went on a roller-coaster ride, rising by 60 percent between January 2000 and July 2005, before falling by 80 percent between July 2005 and May 2010.

Note: The data are seasonally adjusted at an annual rate. **Source:** U.S. Bureau of the Census.

The Changing Mortgage Market

Until the 1970s, the commercial banks and savings and loans that granted mortgages kept the loans until the borrowers paid them off. A financial asset such as a mortgage is a security only if it can be resold in a secondary market. Many members of Congress believed that home ownership could be increased by creating a secondary market in mortgages. If banks and savings and loans could resell mortgages, then, in effect, individual investors would be able to provide funds for mortgages. The process would work like this: If a bank or savings and loan granted a mortgage and then resold the mortgage to an investor, the bank could use the funds received from the investor to grant another mortgage. In this way, banks and savings and loans could grant more mortgage loans because they would no longer depend only on deposits for the funds needed to make the loans. One barrier to creating a secondary market in mortgages was that most investors were unwilling to buy mortgages because they were afraid of losing money if the borrower stopped making payments, or *defaulted*, on the loan.

To reassure investors, Congress used two *government-sponsored enterprises (GSEs)*: the Federal National Mortgage Association ("Fannie Mae") and the Federal Home Loan Mortgage Corporation ("Freddie Mac"). These two institutions stand between investors and banks that grant mortgages. Fannie Mae and Freddie Mac sell bonds to investors and use the funds to purchase mortgages from banks. By the 1990s, a large secondary market existed in mortgages, with funds flowing from investors through Fannie Mae and Freddie Mac to banks and, ultimately, to individuals and families borrowing money to buy houses.

The Role of Investment Banks

By the 2000s, further changes had taken place in the mortgage market. First, investment banks became significant participants in the secondary market for mortgages. Investment banks, such as Goldman Sachs and Morgan Stanley, differ from commercial banks in that they do not take in deposits and rarely lend directly to households. Instead, investment banks concentrate on providing advice to firms issuing stocks and bonds or considering mergers with other firms. Investment banks began buying mortgages, bundling large numbers of them together as bonds called *mortgage-backed securities*, and reselling them to investors. Mortgage-backed securities proved very popular with investors because they often paid higher interest rates than other securities that investors believed had comparable default risk.

Second, by the height of the housing bubble in 2005 and early 2006, lenders had greatly loosened the standards for obtaining a mortgage loan. Traditionally, only borrowers with good credit histories and who were willing to make a down payment equal to at least 20 percent of the value of the house they were buying would be able to receive a mortgage. By 2005, however, lenders were issuing many mortgages to subprime borrowers with flawed credit histories. In addition, "Alt-A" borrowers who stated—but did not document—their incomes and borrowers who made very small down payments found it easier to get loans. Lenders also created new types of *adjustable-rate mortgages* that allowed borrowers to pay a very low interest rate for the first few years of the mortgage and then pay a higher rate in later years. The chance that the borrowers using these nontraditional mortgages would default was higher than for borrowers using traditional mortgages. Why would borrowers take out mortgages if it might be difficult for them to make the payments, and why would lenders grant these mortgages? Both borrowers and lenders were anticipating that housing prices would continue to rise, which would reduce the chance that borrowers would default on the mortgages and would also make it easier for borrowers to convert to more traditional mortgages in the future.

Unfortunately, the decline in housing prices led to rising defaults among subprime and Alt-A borrowers, borrowers with adjustable-rate mortgages, and borrowers who had made only small down payments. When borrowers began defaulting on mortgages, the value of many mortgage-backed securities declined sharply. Investors feared that if they purchased these securities, they would not receive the promised payments because the payments on the securities depended on borrowers making their mortgage payments, which an increasing number were failing to do. Many commercial and investment banks owned these mortgage-backed securities, so the decline in the value of the securities caused these banks to suffer heavy losses. By mid-2007, the decline in the value of mortgage-backed securities and the large losses suffered by commercial and investment banks began to cause turmoil in the financial system. Many investors refused to buy mortgage-backed securities, and some investors would buy only bonds issued by the U.S. Treasury.

<table>
<tr><td>Making
the
Connection</td><td>

The Wonderful World of Leverage

Traditionally, most people taking out a mortgage made a down payment equal to 20 percent of the price of the house and borrowed the remaining 80 percent. During the housing boom, however, many people purchased houses with down payments</td></tr>
</table>

of 5 percent or less. These borrowers were highly *leveraged*, which means that their investment in their house was made mostly with borrowed money.

To see how leverage works in the housing market, consider the following example: Suppose you buy a $200,000 house on January 1, 2016. On January 1, 2017, the price of the house—if you decide to sell it—has risen to $220,000. What return have you earned on your investment in the house? The answer depends on how much you invested when you bought the house. For example, if you paid $200,000 in cash for the house, your return on that $200,000 investment is the $20,000 increase in the price of the house divided by your $200,000 investment, or 10 percent. Suppose that rather than paying cash, you made a down payment of 20 percent, or $40,000, and borrowed the rest by taking out a mortgage loan of $160,000. Now the return on your investment in the house is the $20,000 increase in the price of the house divided by your $40,000 investment, or 50 percent. If the down payment is less than 20 percent, your return on investment will be higher. The second column in the following table shows how the return on your investment increases as your down payment decreases:

Making a very small down payment on a home mortgage leaves a buyer vulnerable to falling house prices.

Down Payment	Return on your investment as a result of . . .	
	a 10 percent increase in the price of your house.	a 10 percent decrease in the price of your house.
100%	10%	−10%
20	50	−50
10	100	−100
5	200	−200

An investment financed at least partly by borrowing is called a *leveraged investment*. As this example shows, the larger the fraction of an investment financed by borrowing, the greater the degree of leverage in the investment, and the greater the potential return. But as the third column in the table shows, the reverse is also true: The greater the leverage, the greater the potential loss. To see why, suppose once again that you buy a house for $200,000, except that in this case, after one year the price of the house falls to $180,000. If you paid $200,000 in cash for the house—so your leverage was zero—the $20,000 decline in the price of the house represents a loss of 10 percent of your investment. But if you made a down payment of only $10,000 and borrowed the remaining $190,000, then the $20,000 decline in the price of the house represents a loss of 200 percent of your investment. In fact, the house is now worth $10,000 less than the amount of your mortgage loan. The *equity* in your house is the difference between the market price of the house and the amount you owe on a loan. If the amount you owe is greater than the price of the house, you have *negative equity*. A homeowner who has negative equity is also said to be "upside down" on his or her mortgage.

When the housing bubble burst and housing prices started to fall, many people found that they had negative equity. In that situation, some people defaulted on their loans, sometimes by simply moving out and abandoning their homes. Leverage had contributed to the housing boom and bust and the severity of the 2007–2009 recession.

Your Turn: Test your understanding by doing related problem 6.9 at the end of this chapter.

The Fed and the Treasury Department Respond

Because the problems in financial markets resulting from the bursting of the housing bubble were so severe, the Fed entered into an unusual partnership with the U.S. Treasury Department to develop suitable policies. Fed Chairman Ben Bernanke and U.S. Treasury Secretaries Henry Paulson (in the Bush administration) and Timothy Geithner (in the Obama administration) responded to the crisis by intervening in financial markets in unprecedented ways.

Initial Fed and Treasury Actions The financial crisis significantly worsened following the bankruptcy of the investment bank Lehman Brothers on September 15, 2008. So it is useful to look at the actions taken by the Fed and the Treasury before and after that date. First, although the Fed traditionally made loans only to commercial banks, in March 2008, it announced it would temporarily make discount loans to *primary dealers*—firms that participate in regular open market transactions with the Fed. This change was intended to provide short-term funds to these dealers, some of which are investment banks. Second, also in March, the Fed announced that it would loan up to $200 billion of Treasury securities in exchange for mortgage-backed securities. This temporary program made it possible for primary dealers that owned mortgage-backed securities that were difficult or impossible to sell to have access to Treasury securities that they could use as collateral for short-term loans. Third, also in March, the Fed and the Treasury helped JPMorgan Chase acquire the investment bank Bear Stearns, which was on the edge of failing. The Fed agreed that if JPMorgan Chase would acquire Bear Stearns, the Fed would guarantee any losses JPMorgan Chase suffered on Bear Stearns's holdings of mortgage-backed securities, up to a limit of $29 billion. The Fed and the Treasury were convinced that the failure of Bear Stearns had the potential of causing a financial panic, as many investors and financial firms would have stopped making short-term loans to other investment banks. Finally, in early September, the Treasury moved to have the federal government take control of Fannie Mae and Freddie Mac. Although Fannie Mae and Freddie Mac had been sponsored by the federal government, they were actually private businesses whose stock was bought and sold on the New York Stock Exchange. Under the Treasury's plan, Fannie Mae and Freddie Mac were each provided with up to $100 billion in exchange for 80 percent ownership of the firms. The firms were placed under the supervision of the Federal Housing Finance Agency. The Treasury believed that the bankruptcy of Fannie Mae and Freddie Mac would have caused a collapse in confidence in mortgage-backed securities, further devastating the already weak housing market.

Responses to the Failure of Lehman Brothers Some economists and policymakers criticized the decision by the Fed and the Treasury to help arrange the sale of Bear Stearns to JPMorgan Chase. Their main concern was with the *moral hazard problem*, which is the possibility that managers of financial firms such as Bear Stearns might make riskier investments if they believe that the federal government will save them from bankruptcy. The Treasury and the Fed acted to save Bear Stearns because they believed that the failure of a large financial firm could have wider economic repercussions. When a financial firm sells off its holdings of bonds and other assets, it causes their prices to fall, which in turn can undermine the financial position of other firms that also own these assets. In September 2008, when the investment bank Lehman Brothers was near bankruptcy, the Fed and the Treasury had to weigh the moral hazard problem against the possibility that the failure of Lehman Brothers would lead to further declines in asset prices and endanger the financial positions of other firms.

The Fed and the Treasury decided to allow Lehman Brothers to go bankrupt, which it did on September 15. The adverse reaction in financial markets was stronger than the Fed and the Treasury had expected, which led them to reverse course two days later, when the Fed agreed to provide an $85 billion loan to the American International Group (AIG)—the largest insurance company in the United States—in exchange for an 80 percent ownership stake, effectively giving the federal government control of the company. One important result of the failure of Lehman Brothers was the heavy losses suffered by Reserve Primary Fund, a money market mutual fund that had made short-term loans to Lehman Brothers. The problems at Reserve led many investors to withdraw their funds from it and other money market funds. These withdrawals reduced the ability of the money market funds to purchase commercial paper from corporations. Because in recent years corporations had become dependent on selling commercial paper to finance their operations, the Treasury and the Fed moved to stabilize this market and ensure that the flow of funds from investors to corporations continued. The Treasury announced a plan to temporarily provide insurance for deposits in money market mutual funds, similar to the existing insurance on bank deposits. The Fed announced that for a limited time it would lend directly to corporations by purchasing three-month commercial paper issued by nonfinancial corporations.

Finally, in October 2008, Congress passed the *Troubled Asset Relief Program (TARP)*, under which the Treasury attempted to stabilize the commercial banking system by providing funds to banks in exchange for stock. Taking partial ownership positions in private commercial banks was an unprecedented action for the federal government.

Many of the Treasury and the Fed's new approaches to policy were controversial because they involved partial government ownership of financial firms, implicit guarantees to large financial firms that they would not be allowed to go bankrupt, and unprecedented intervention in financial markets. Although the approaches were new, they were intended to achieve the traditional macroeconomic policy goals of high employment, price stability, and stability of financial markets. What remains to be seen is whether these new approaches represent a permanent increase in federal government involvement in U.S. financial markets or whether policy will eventually return to more traditional approaches.

Continued

Economics in Your Life

Should You Buy a House during a Recession?

At the beginning of this chapter, we asked whether it is a good idea to buy a house during a recession. Buying a house is the largest purchase you are likely to make in your lifetime, so you need to carefully consider a number of factors, including the price of the house relative to other comparable houses in the neighborhood; whether house prices in the neighborhood have been rising or falling; and the location of the house relative to stores, work, and good schools. Also important is the interest rate you will have to pay on the mortgage loan you would need in order to buy the house. As we have seen in this chapter, during a recession the Fed often takes actions to lower interest rates. So, mortgage rates are typically lower during a recession than at other times. You may want to take advantage of low interest rates to buy a house during a recession. But recessions are also times of rising unemployment and you would not want to make a commitment to borrow a lot of money for 15 or more years if you were in danger of losing your job. We can conclude that if your job seems secure, buying a house during a recession may be a good idea.

Conclusion

Monetary policy is one way governments pursue goals for inflation, employment, and financial stability. The chairman of the Federal Reserve may have a greater ability than the president of the United States to affect the U.S. economy. Congress and the president, however, also use their power over spending and taxes to try to stabilize the economy. Visit MyEconLab for a news article and analysis related to the concepts of this chapter.

Chapter Summary and Problems

Key Terms

Contractionary monetary policy

Expansionary monetary policy

Federal funds rate

Inflation targeting

Monetary policy

Taylor rule

What Is Monetary Policy?

LEARNING OBJECTIVE: Define monetary policy and describe the Federal Reserve's monetary policy goals.

Summary

Monetary policy is the actions the Fed takes to manage the money supply and interest rates to achieve its macroeconomic policy goals. The Fed has four *monetary policy goals* that are intended to promote a well-functioning economy: price stability, high employment, stability of financial markets and institutions, and economic growth.

Visit **www.myeconlab.com** to complete these exercises online and get instant feedback.

Review Questions

1.1 When Congress established the Federal Reserve in 1913, what was its main responsibility? When did Congress broaden the Fed's responsibilities?
1.2 What are the Fed's four monetary policy goals?
1.3 In what sense does the Fed have a "dual mandate"?
1.4 How can investment banks be subject to liquidity problems?

Problems and Applications

1.5 What is a bank panic? Why are policymakers more concerned about bank failures than failures of restaurants or clothing stores?
1.6 Why is price stability one of the Fed's monetary policy goals? What problems can high inflation rates cause for the economy?
1.7 A former Federal Reserve official argued that at the Fed, "the objectives of price stability and low long-term interest rates are essentially the same objective." Briefly explain his reasoning.

   Source: William Poole, "Understanding the Fed," *Federal Reserve Bank of St. Louis Review*, Vol. 89, No. 1, January/February 2007, p. 4.

1.8 Stock prices rose rapidly in 2005, as did housing prices in many parts of the country. By 2008, both stock prices and housing prices were declining sharply. Some economists have argued that rapid increases and decreases in the prices of assets such as shares of stock or houses can damage the economy. Currently, stabilizing asset prices is not one of the Federal Reserve's policy goals. In what ways would a goal of stabilizing asset prices be different from the four goals of the Fed? Do you believe that stabilizing asset prices should be added to the list of the Fed's policy goals? Briefly explain.

The Money Market and the Fed's Choice of Monetary Policy Targets

LEARNING OBJECTIVE: Describe the Federal Reserve's monetary policy targets and explain how expansionary and contractionary monetary policies affect the interest rate.

Summary

The Fed's *monetary policy targets* are economic variables that it can affect directly and that in turn affect variables such as real GDP and the price level that are closely related to the Fed's policy goals. The two main monetary policy targets are the money supply and the interest rate. The Fed has most often chosen to use the interest rate as its monetary policy target. The Federal Open Market Committee announces a target for the **federal funds rate** after each meeting. The federal funds rate is the interest rate banks charge each other for overnight loans. To lower the interest rate, the Fed increases the money supply. To raise the interest rate, the Fed decreases the money supply. In a graphical analysis of the money market, when the money supply curve shifts to the right, the result is a movement down the money demand curve and a new equilibrium at a lower interest rate. When the money supply curve shifts to the left, the result is a movement up the money demand curve and a new equilibrium at a higher interest rate.

Visit **www.myeconlab.com** to complete these exercises online and get instant feedback.

Review Questions

2.1 What is a monetary policy target? Why does the Fed use policy targets?
2.2 What do economists mean by the *demand for money*? What is the advantage of holding money? What is the disadvantage? Why does an increase in the interest rate decrease the quantity of money demanded?

2.3 Draw a demand and supply graph showing equilibrium in the money market. Suppose the Fed wants to lower the equilibrium interest rate. Show on the graph how the Fed would accomplish this objective.

2.4 What is the federal funds rate? What role does it play in monetary policy?

Problems and Applications

2.5 In the following graph of the money market, what could cause the money supply curve to shift from MS_1 to MS_2? What could cause the money demand curve to shift from MD_1 to MD_2?

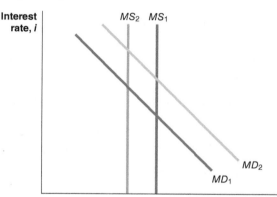

2.6 In 2013, one article in the *Wall Street Journal* noted that: "The Fed's Board of Governors kept the discount rate unchanged at 0.75%," while another article predicted that: "The Fed can be expected to state again that the target rate won't change until mid-2015."
   a. What is the name of the Fed's "target rate"?
   b. Briefly explain who borrows money and who lends money at this "target interest rate."

c. What is the discount rate, and how is it different from the "target rate"?
Sources: Michael J. Casey, "Let's Get This Over and Done With, Fed," *Wall Street Journal*, June 19, 2013; and Sarah Portlock and Eric Morath, "Some Fed Officials See 'Diminished' Downside Risks," *Wall Street Journal*, February 26, 2013.

2.7 If the Federal Reserve purchases $100 million worth of U.S. Treasury bills from banks, predict what will happen to the money supply. Explain your reasoning.

2.8 In response to problems in financial markets and a slowing economy, the Federal Open Market Committee (FOMC) began lowering its target for the federal funds rate from 5.25 percent in September 2007. Over the next year, the FOMC cut its federal funds rate target in a series of steps. Economist Price Fishback of the University of Arizona observed: "The Fed has been pouring more money into the banking system by cutting the target federal funds rate to 0 to 0.25 percent in December 2008." What is the relationship between the federal funds rate falling and the money supply increasing? How does lowering the target for the federal funds rate "pour money" into the banking system?
Source: Price Fishback, "The Financial Meltdown Now and Then," freakonomics.com, May 12, 2009.

2.9 An article in the *New York Times* in 1993 stated the following about Fed Chairman Alan Greenspan's decision to no longer announce targets for the money supply: "Since the late 1970's, the Federal Reserve has made many of its most important decisions by setting a specific target for growth in the money supply ... and often adjusted interest rates to meet them." If the Fed would no longer have a specific target for the money supply, what was it targeting? Why did the Fed give up targeting the money supply?
Source: Steven Greenhouse, "Fed Abandons Policy Tied to Money Supply," *New York Times*, July 23, 1993.

 Monetary Policy and Economic Activity

LEARNING OBJECTIVE: Use aggregate demand and aggregate supply graphs to show the effects of monetary policy on real GDP and the price level.

Summary

An **expansionary monetary policy** lowers interest rates to increase consumption, investment, and net exports. This increase in aggregate demand increases real GDP and the price level. An expansionary monetary policy can help the Fed achieve its goal of high employment. A **contractionary monetary policy** raises interest rates to decrease consumption, investment, and net exports. This decrease in aggregate demand reduces both real GDP and the inflation rate below what they would be in the absence of policy. A contractionary monetary policy can help the Fed achieve its goal of price stability.

Visit **www.myeconlab.com** to complete these exercises online and get instant feedback.

Review Questions

3.1 How does an increase in interest rates affect aggregate demand? Briefly discuss how the increase affects each component of aggregate demand.

3.2 If the Fed believes the economy is headed for a recession, what actions should it take? If the Fed believes the inflation rate is about to sharply increase, what actions should it take?

3.3 Describe quantitative easing and Operation Twist and the Fed's objective in using them.

Problems and Applications

3.4 A student says the following: "I understand why the Fed uses expansionary policy, but I don't understand why it would ever use contractionary policy. Why would the government ever want the economy to contract?" Briefly answer the student's question.

3.5 In explaining why monetary policy did not pull Japan out of a recession in the early 2000s, an official at the Bank of Japan was quoted as saying that despite "major increases in the money supply," the money "stay[ed] in banks." Explain what the official meant by saying that the money stayed in banks. Why would that be a problem? Where does the money go if an expansionary monetary policy is successful?

Source: James Brooke, "Critics Say Koizumi's Economic Medicine Is a Weak Tea," *New York Times*, February 27, 2002.

3.6 According to an article in the *Economist* magazine, in 2013 the Japanese economy was experiencing falling prices "on everything from chocolate bars to salad."
   a. What is the term for a *falling price level*?
   b. The article also stated that Japanese Prime Minister Shinzo Abe was pressuring the Bank of Japan, the Japanese central bank, to take steps to hit an inflation target of 2 percent. Why would the Japanese government consider a falling price level to be undesirable? What steps could the Bank of Japan take to increase the price level?

Source: "Waging a New War," *Economist*, March 9, 2013.

3.7 William McChesney Martin, who was Federal Reserve chairman from 1951 to 1970, was once quoted as saying, "The role of the Federal Reserve is to remove the punchbowl just as the party gets going." What did he mean?

3.8 Former president Ronald Reagan once stated that inflation "has one cause and one cause alone: government spending more than government takes in." Briefly explain whether you agree.

Source: Edward Nelson, "Budget Deficits and Interest Rates," *Monetary Trends*, Federal Reserve Bank of St. Louis, March 2004.

3.9 **[Related to** Making the Connection: **Too Low for Zero]** John Maynard Keynes is said to have remarked that using an expansionary monetary policy to pull an economy out of a deep recession can be like "pushing on a string." Briefly explain what Keynes is likely to have meant.

3.10 **[Related to** Making the Connection: **Too Low for Zero]** An article in the *Wall Street Journal* notes that before the financial crisis of 2007–2009, the Fed "managed just one short-term interest rate and expected that to be enough to meet its goals for inflation and unemployment."
   a. What short-term interest rate is the article referring to? How would the Fed expect controlling that one interest rate would allow it to meet its goals for inflation and unemployment?
   b. The article also notes that after the financial crisis, "the Fed is working through a broader spectrum of interest rates." What does "a broader spectrum of interest rates" mean? How is the Fed able to affect a broader spectrum of interest rates?

Source: Jon Hilsenrath, "Easy-Money Era a Long Game for Fed," *Wall Street Journal*, March 17, 2013.

3.11 **[Related to** Making the Connection: **Trying to Hit a Moving Target]** An article in *Bloomberg BusinessWeek* in 2013 reported that Fed Chairman Ben Bernanke testified to Congress that: "If we see continued improvement and we have confidence that that is going to be sustained, then we could—in the next few meetings—we could take a step down in our pace of purchases." According to the article, Bernanke also told Congress that " 'premature tightening' could 'carry a substantial risk of slowing or ending the economic recovery.' "
   a. What purchases is Fed Chairman Bernanke referring to?
   b. Why might a "premature tightening" of the "pace of purchases" slow down the economic recovery?

Source: Nick Summers, "Confusion about the Fed Slowing Its $85 Billion in Monthly Bond Buying Is Roiling the Markets," *Bloomberg BusinessWeek*, June 10–16, 2013.

3.12 **[Related to** Making the Connection: **Trying to Hit a Moving Target]** The following is from a Federal Reserve publication:

> In practice, monetary policymakers do not have up-to-the-minute, reliable information about the state of the economy and prices. Information is limited because of lags in the publication of data. Also, policymakers have less-than-perfect understanding of the way the economy works, including the knowledge of when and to what extent policy actions will affect aggregate demand. The operation of the economy changes over time, and with it the response of the economy to policy measures. These limitations add to uncertainties in the policy process and make determining the appropriate setting of monetary policy . . . more difficult.

If the Fed itself admits that there are many obstacles in the way of effective monetary policy, why does it still engage in active monetary policy rather than use a monetary growth rule, as suggested by Milton Friedman and his followers?

Source: Board of Governors of the Federal Reserve System, *The Federal Reserve System: Purposes and Functions*, Washington, DC, 1994.

3.13 **[Related to the** Don't Let This Happen to You**]** Briefly explain whether you agree with the following statement: "The Fed has an easy job. Say it wants to increase real GDP by $200 billion. All it has to do is increase the money supply by that amount."

3.14 **[Related to the** Chapter Opener**]** An article in the *Wall Street Journal* referred to the chair of the Fed as "the nation's top economic position." Do you agree with this assessment? Briefly explain.

Source: Jon Hilsenrath, "Summers Hedges His Doubts on Fed's Bond Buying," *Wall Street Journal*, July 31, 2013.

4 Monetary Policy in the Dynamic Aggregate Demand and Aggregate Supply Model

LEARNING OBJECTIVE: Use the dynamic aggregate demand and aggregate supply model to analyze monetary policy.

Summary

We can use the *dynamic aggregate demand and aggregate supply model* to look more closely at expansionary and contractionary monetary policies. The dynamic aggregate demand and aggregate supply model takes into account that: (1) the economy experiences continuing inflation, with the price level rising every year, and (2) the economy experiences long-run growth, with the *LRAS* curve shifting to the right every year. In the dynamic model, an expansionary monetary policy tries to ensure that the aggregate demand curve will shift far enough to the right to bring about macroeconomic equilibrium with real GDP equal to potential GDP. A contractionary monetary policy attempts to offset movements in aggregate demand that would cause macroeconomic equilibrium to occur at a level of real GDP that is greater than potential GDP.

Visit **www.myeconlab.com** to complete these exercises online and get instant feedback.

Review Questions

4.1 What are the key differences between how we illustrate an expansionary monetary policy in the basic aggregate demand and aggregate supply model and in the dynamic aggregate demand and aggregate supply model?

4.2 What are the key differences between how we illustrate a contractionary monetary policy in the basic aggregate demand and aggregate supply model and in the dynamic aggregate demand and aggregate supply model?

Problems and Applications

4.3 Explain whether you agree with this argument:

If the Fed actually ever carried out a contractionary monetary policy, the price level would fall. Because the price level has not fallen in the United States over an entire year since the 1930s, we can conclude that the Fed has not carried out a contractionary policy since the 1930s.

4.4 **[Related to** Solved Problem 4**]** Use the graph to answer the following questions.
  a. If the Fed does not take any policy action, what will be the level of real GDP and the price level in 2017?
  b. If the Fed wants to keep real GDP at its potential level in 2017, should it use an expansionary policy or a contractionary policy? Should the trading desk be buying Treasury bills or selling them?
  c. If the Fed takes no policy action, what will be the inflation rate in 2017? If the Fed uses monetary policy to keep real GDP at its full-employment level, what will be the inflation rate in 2017?

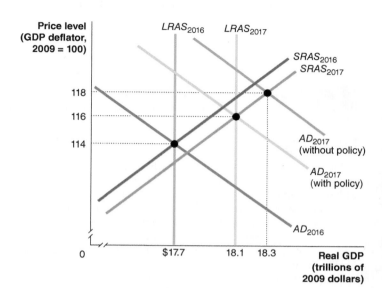

4.5 **[Related to** Solved Problem 4**]** The hypothetical information in the following table shows what the situation will be in 2017 if the Fed does *not* use monetary policy.

Year	Potential GDP	Real GDP	Price Level
2016	$17.7 trillion	$17.7 trillion	110.0
2017	18.1 trillion	18.3 trillion	115.5

  a. If the Fed wants to keep real GDP at its potential level in 2017, should it use an expansionary policy or a contractionary policy? Should the trading desk be buying T-bills or selling them?
  b. If the Fed's policy is successful in keeping real GDP at its potential level in 2017, state whether each of the following will be higher, lower, or the same as it would have been if the Fed had taken no action:
    i.   Real GDP
    ii. Potential GDP
    iii. The inflation rate
    iv. The unemployment rate
  c. Draw an aggregate demand and aggregate supply graph to illustrate the effects of the Fed's policy. Be sure that your graph contains *LRAS* curves for 2016 and 2017; *SRAS* curves for 2016 and 2017; *AD* curves for 2016 and 2017, with and without monetary policy action; and equilibrium real GDP and the price level in 2017, with and without policy.

4.6 According to an online article, the Reserve Bank of India lowered its key policy interest rate in early 2013 "to help support an economy set to post its slowest annual growth rate in a decade." The article notes that the central bank lists constraints to further interest rate cuts including the "risk that inflation could flare again."

a. Use the dynamic aggregate demand and aggregate supply model to show where the Reserve Bank of India expected the country's economy to be in 2013 without the interest rate cut, and indicate what the central bank is trying to achieve with the interest rate cut. Assume, for simplicity, that real GDP in India in 2012 equaled potential GDP.

b. Why might the Reserve Bank of India be afraid that additional interest rate cuts would cause inflation to increase?

Source: "India's Central Bank Lowers Interest Rate," GulfNews.com, January 29, 2013.

 5

A Closer Look at the Fed's Setting of Monetary Policy Targets

LEARNING OBJECTIVE: Discuss the Fed's setting of monetary policy targets.

Summary

Some economists have argued that the Fed should use the money supply, rather than an interest rate, as its monetary policy target. Milton Friedman and other monetarists argued that the Fed should adopt a monetary growth rule of increasing the money supply every year at a fixed rate. Support for this proposal declined after 1980 because the relationship between movements in the money supply and movements in real GDP and the price level weakened. John Taylor analyzed the factors involved in Fed decision making and developed the **Taylor rule** for federal funds targeting. The Taylor rule links the Fed's target for the federal funds rate to economic variables. Over the past decade, many economists and central bankers have expressed significant interest in using **inflation targeting**, under which monetary policy is conducted to commit the central bank to achieving a publicly announced inflation target. In 2012, the Fed joined a number of foreign central banks in adopting inflation targeting. The Fed's performance in the 1980s, 1990s, and early 2000s generally received high marks from economists.

Visit **www.myeconlab.com** to complete these exercises online and get instant feedback.

Review Questions

5.1 What is a *monetary rule*, as opposed to a *monetary policy*? What monetary rule would Milton Friedman have liked the Fed to follow? Why has support for a monetary rule of the kind Friedman advocated declined since 1980?

5.2 For more than 20 years, the Fed has used the federal funds rate as its monetary policy target. Why doesn't the Fed target the money supply at the same time?

5.3 What is the Taylor rule? What is its purpose?

Problems and Applications

5.4 Suppose that the equilibrium real federal funds rate is 2 percent and the target rate of inflation is 2 percent. Use the following information and the Taylor rule to calculate the federal funds rate target:

Current inflation rate = 4 percent
Potential GDP = $17.0 trillion
Real GDP = $17.17 trillion

5.5 In 2013, John Taylor wrote: "I realize that there are differences of opinion about what is the best rule to guide policy and that some at the Fed (including Janet Yellen) now prefer a rule with a higher coefficient [on the output gap]."

a. If Fed policy were guided by a Taylor rule with a coefficient of 1, rather than 0.5, on the output gap, would the federal funds rate be higher or lower during a recession? Briefly explain.

b. Why might economists and policymakers disagree over the best rule to guide monetary policy?

Source: John Taylor, "Cross Checking 'Checking in on the Taylor Rule,'" www.economicsone.com, July 16, 2013.

5.6 Glenn Rudebusch, an economist at the Federal Reserve Bank of San Francisco, argues that if the Fed had followed the Taylor rule during the recession of 2007–2009, then by the end of 2009 the target for the federal funds rate would have been −5 percent. Provide values for the Taylor rule equation given under "The Taylor Rule" that would result in a negative target for the federal funds rate. Is it possible for the federal funds rate to be negative?

Source: Glenn Rudebusch, "The Fed's Monetary Policy Response to the Current Crisis," *FRBSF Economic Letter*, May 22, 2009.

5.7 While serving as the president of the Federal Reserve Bank of St. Louis, William Poole stated: "Although my own preference is for zero inflation properly managed, I believe that a central bank consensus on some other numerical goal of reasonably low inflation is more important than the exact number." Briefly explain why the economy might benefit from an explicit inflation target even if the target chosen is not a zero rate of inflation.

Source: William Poole, "Understanding the Fed," *Federal Reserve Bank of St. Louis Review*, Vol. 89, No. 1, January/February 2007, p. 4.

5.8 **[Related to** Making the Connection: **How Does the Fed Measure Inflation?]** If the core PCE price index is a better measure of the inflation rate than is the CPI, why is the CPI more widely used? In particular, can you think of reasons the federal government uses the CPI when deciding how much to increase Social Security payments to retired workers to keep the purchasing power of the payments from declining?

6 Fed Policies during the 2007–2009 Recession

LEARNING OBJECTIVE: Discuss the policies the Federal Reserve used during the 2007–2009 recession.

Summary

A housing bubble that began to deflate in 2006 helped cause the recession of 2007–2009 and an accompanying financial crisis. In response, the Federal Reserve instituted a variety of policy actions. In a series of steps, it cut the target for the federal funds rate from 5.25 percent in September 2007 to effectively zero in December 2008. The decline in the housing market caused wider problems in the financial system, as defaults on home mortgages rose and the value of mortgage-backed securities declined. The Fed and the U.S. Treasury Department implemented a series of new policies to provide liquidity and restore confidence. The Fed expanded the types of firms eligible for discount loans and began lending directly to corporations by purchasing commercial paper. Under the *Troubled Asset Relief Program*, the Treasury provided financial support to banks and other financial firms in exchange for part ownership. The Treasury also moved to have the federal government take control of Fannie Mae and Freddie Mac, government-sponsored firms that play a key role in the mortgage market. The failure of the investment bank Lehman Brothers in September 2008 led to a deepening of the financial crisis and provided the motivation for some of the new policies. Ultimately, the new policies stabilized the financial system, but their long-term effects remain the subject of debate.

Visit **www.myeconlab.com** to complete these exercises online and get instant feedback.

Review Questions

6.1 What is a mortgage? What were the important developments in the mortgage market during the years after 1970?

6.2 Beginning in 2008, the Federal Reserve and the U.S. Treasury Department responded to the financial crisis by intervening in financial markets in unprecedented ways. Briefly summarize the actions of the Fed and the Treasury.

Problems and Applications

6.3 **[Related to the** Chapter Opener**]** A newspaper article in the fall of 2007 stated that: "The luxury-home builder Hovnanian Enterprises reported its fourth consecutive quarterly loss on Thursday, citing continuing problems of credit availability and high inventory." Why was Hovnanian suffering losses? What does the article mean by "credit availability"? How would problems of credit availability affect a homebuilder such as Hovnanian Enterprises?

Source: "New Loss for Home Builder," Associated Press, September 7, 2007.

6.4 **[Related to the** Chapter Opener**]** At the beginning of 2005, Robert Toll, CEO of Toll Brothers, argued that the United States was not experiencing a housing bubble. Instead, he argued that higher house prices reflected restrictions imposed by local governments on building new

houses. He believed that the restrictions resulted from "NIMBY"—"Not in My Back Yard"—politics. Many existing homeowners are reluctant to see nearby farms and undeveloped land turned into new housing developments. As a result, according to Toll, "Towns don't want anything built." Why would the factors Robert Toll mentioned cause housing prices to rise? Would it be possible to decide whether these factors or a bubble was the cause of rising housing prices?

Source: Shawn Tully, "Toll Brothers: The New King of the Real Estate Boom," *Fortune*, April 5, 2005.

6.5 An article in a Federal Reserve publication observes that "20 or 30 years ago, local financial institutions were the only option for some borrowers. Today, borrowers have access to national (and even international) sources of mortgage finance." What caused this change in the sources of mortgage finance? What would be the likely consequence of this change for the interest rates borrowers have to pay on mortgages? Briefly explain.

Source: Daniel J. McDonald and Daniel L. Thornton, "A Primer on the Mortgage Market and Mortgage Finance," *Federal Reserve Bank of St. Louis Review*, January/February 2008.

6.6 In late 2012, the U.S. Treasury sold the last of the stock it purchased in the insurance company AIG. The Treasury earned a profit on the $22.7 billion it had invested in AIG in 2008. An article in *Wall Street Journal* noted that: "This step in AIG's turnaround, which essentially closes the book on one of the most controversial bailouts of the financial crisis, seemed nearly unattainable in 2008, when the insurer's imminent collapse sent shockwaves through the global economy."

a. Why did the federal government bail out AIG?

b. Why was the government bailout controversial?

c. Does the fact the federal government earned a profit on its investment in AIG mean that economists and policymakers who opposed the bailout were necessarily wrong? Briefly explain.

Source: Jeffrey Sparshott and Erik Holm, "End of a Bailout: U.S. Sells Last AIG Shares," *Wall Street Journal*, December 11, 2012.

6.7 Recall that *securitization* is the process of turning a loan, such as a mortgage, into a bond that can be bought and sold in secondary markets. An article in the *Economist* notes:

> That securitization caused more subprime mortgages to be written is not in doubt. By offering access to a much deeper pool of capital, securitization helped to bring down the cost of mortgages and made home-ownership more affordable for borrowers with poor credit histories.

What is a "subprime mortgage"? What is a "deeper pool of capital"? Why would securitization give mortgage borrowers access to a deeper pool of capital? Would a subprime borrower be likely to pay a higher or a lower interest rate than a borrower with a better credit history? Under what circumstances might a lender prefer to loan money to a borrower with a poor credit history rather than to a borrower with a good credit history? Briefly explain.

Source: "Ruptured Credit," *Economist*, May 15, 2008.

6.8 In the fall of 2011, investors began to fear that some European governments, particularly Greece and Italy, might default on the bonds they had issued, making the prices of the bonds fall sharply. Many European banks owned these bonds, and some investors worried that these banks might also be in financial trouble. An article in the *Economist* referred to the "prospect of another Lehman moment." The article noted that: "Governments are once again having to step in to support their banks." What did the article mean by another "Lehman moment"? Why might European governments have felt the need to support their banks to avoid another Lehman moment?

Source: "Here We Go Again," *Economist*, October 8, 2011.

6.9 **[Related to** Making the Connection: **The Wonderful World of Leverage]** Suppose you buy a house for $150,000. One year later, the market price of the house has risen to $165,000. What is the return on your investment in the house if you made a down payment of 20 percent and took out a mortgage loan for the other 80 percent? What if you made a down payment of 5 percent and borrowed the other 95 percent? Be sure to show your calculations in your answer.

Real-Time Data Exercises

D1 **[Following news of FOMC meetings]** Go to www.federalreserve.gov, the Web site for the Federal Reserve Board of Governors, and read the most recent Federal Open Market Committee (FOMC) press release. At the Web site, select "Monetary Policy" at the top of the screen and then select "Federal Open Market Committee" on the far left of the screen. Select "Meeting Calendars, Statement, and Minutes." Finally, scroll down and select Statement for the date of the most recent FOMC meeting. Answer the following questions on the basis of the FOMC press release.

   a. Did the FOMC change the target for the federal funds rate? If so, what was the change?

   b. On balance, in its statement does the FOMC appear to be more concerned about slow economic growth or high inflation?

   c. Did the FOMC change the interest rate paid on bank reserves?

   d. Did the Fed announce any other monetary policy actions?

D2 **[Movements in the federal funds rate relative to the target]** Go to the Web site of the Federal Reserve Bank of St. Louis (FRED) (research.stlouisfed.org/fred2) and download and graph the data series for the effective federal funds rate (DFF), the upper limit of the target range for the federal funds rate (DFEDTARU), and the lower limit for the target range (DFEDTARL). Plot on the same graph values for all three data series from December 16, 2008 to the most recent day available. Over this period, has the Fed been able to keep the effective federal funds rate within the target range? Briefly explain.

D3 **[Comparing different measures of the inflation rate]** Go to the Web site of the Federal Reserve Bank of St. Louis (FRED) (research.stlouisfed.org/fred2/) and find the most recent values and values from the same month one year before for the following three measures of the price level: (1) the Consumer Price Index for All Urban Consumers: All Items (CPIAUCSL), (2) the Personal Consumption Expenditures: Chain-type Price Index (PCEPI), and (3) the Personal consumption expenditures excluding food and energy (chain-type price index) (DPCCRG3A086NBEA).

   a. Using these data, calculate the inflation rate over this year as measured by each of the three price indexes.

   b. Which of the three measures of inflation was highest during this year? Which measure was lowest? Why do the measures of inflation differ?

Glossary

Contractionary monetary policy The Federal Reserve's policy of increasing interest rates to reduce inflation.

Expansionary monetary policy The Federal Reserve's policy of decreasing interest rates to increase real GDP.

Federal funds rate The interest rate banks charge each other for overnight loans.

Inflation targeting A framework for conducting monetary policy that involves the central bank announcing its target level of inflation.

Monetary policy The actions the Federal Reserve takes to manage the money supply and interest rates to pursue macroeconomic policy objectives.

Taylor rule A rule developed by John Taylor that links the Fed's target for the federal funds rate to economic variables.

Credits

Credits are listed in the order of appearance.

Photo

Reed Saxon/AP Images; Iofoto/Shutterstock; Rebecca Cook/Reuters/Corbis

Fiscal Policy

From Chapter 16 of *Macroeconomics*, Fifth Edition. R. Glenn Hubbard and Anthony Patrick O'Brien. Copyright © 2015 by Pearson Education, Inc. All rights reserved.

Fiscal Policy

Chapter Outline and Learning Objectives

Does Government Spending Create Jobs?

Tutor-Saliba was founded in Southern California in 1949 and is today one of the largest heavy construction firms in the United States. In the fall of 2013, Tutor-Saliba's work on the Caldecott Tunnel in Northern California was nearing completion. The project expanded the tunnel through the Berkeley Hills from six lanes to eight in order to ease congestion between the cities of Orinda and Oakland.

Part of the funding for the project came from the American Recovery and Reinvestment Act (ARRA, often referred to as the "stimulus bill"), which President Barack Obama and Congress had enacted in early 2009, in an attempt to increase aggregate demand during the recession of 2007–2009. Without this funding, the state of California would not have gone ahead with the project. The ARRA is an example of *discretionary fiscal policy* aimed at increasing real GDP and employment. To carry out the Caldecott Tunnel project, Tutor-Saliba hired an additional 106 workers. A spokesperson for the state agency in charge of the project argued that the increased employment effects from the project were even larger: "There is a ripple effect. There's truckers and equipment builders, and the deli in Orinda has never been as busy before."

The project to expand the Caldecott Tunnel is an example of increased government spending resulting in increased employment. Or is it? A majority of economists agree that a temporary increase in government spending can lead to increased employment during a recession. But some economists argue that fiscal policy actions like ARRA shift employment from one group of workers to another but do not increase *total* employment. The argument over the effect of government spending on employment continued years after the end of the recession of 2007–2009.

When the federal government spends more than it collects in taxes, the result is a federal budget deficit. Following the recession, the federal government ran the largest peacetime deficits in history. At the end of 2012, Congress and President Obama enacted cuts in federal spending and increases in taxes to try to reduce the budget deficit. A further series of automatic spending cuts, called "the sequester," took effect in March 2013. Some economists and policymakers were critical of these spending cuts and tax increases, arguing that they would slow the growth of employment at a time when the unemployment rate was still well above 7 percent.

In this chapter, we will examine discretionary fiscal policy, the federal budget deficit, and the debate over their effects.

Sources: Metropolitan Transit Commission, "Fans Installed in Caldecott Fourth Bore as Project Nears Completion," June 26, 2013, http://www.mtc.ca.gov/news/current_topics/6-13/caldecott.htm; Zusha Elinson, "Caldecott Tunnel Edges Forward, Tribute to Stimulus Bill," *New York Times*, September 10, 2011; and Catherine Rampell, "Yes, the Sequester Is Affecting the Job Market," *New York Times*, July 5, 2013.

Economics in Your Life

What Would You Do with an Extra $500?

Suppose that the federal government announces that it will immediately mail you, and everyone else in the economy, a $500 tax rebate. In addition, you expect that in future years your taxes will also decrease by $500. How will you respond to this increase in your disposable income? What effect will this tax rebate likely have on equilibrium real GDP in the short run? As you read this chapter, try to answer these questions. You can check your answers against those we provide at the end of this chapter.

I n this chapter, we will explore how the government uses *fiscal policy*, which involves changes in taxes and government purchases, to achieve macroeconomic policy goals. In the short run, the price level and the levels of real GDP and total employment in the economy depend on aggregate demand and short-run aggregate supply. The government can affect the levels of both aggregate demand and aggregate supply through fiscal policy. We will explore how Congress and the president decide which fiscal policy actions to take to achieve their goals. We will also discuss the debates among economists and policymakers over the effectiveness of fiscal policy.

1 LEARNING OBJECTIVE

Define fiscal policy.

Fiscal policy Changes in federal taxes and purchases that are intended to achieve macroeconomic policy goals.

What Is Fiscal Policy?

Since the end of World War II, the federal government has been committed under the Employment Act of 1946 to intervening in the economy "to promote maximum employment, production, and purchasing power." The Federal Reserve's Federal Open Market Committee meets eight times per year to decide whether to change monetary policy. Less frequently, Congress and the president also make changes in taxes and government purchases to achieve macroeconomic policy goals, such as high employment, price stability, and high rates of economic growth. Changes in federal taxes and purchases that are intended to achieve macroeconomic policy goals are called **fiscal policy**.

What Fiscal Policy Is and What It Isn't

In the United States, federal, state, and local governments all have responsibility for taxing and spending. Economists typically use the term *fiscal policy* to refer only to the actions of the federal government. State and local governments sometimes change their taxing and spending policies to aid their local economies, but these are not fiscal policy actions because they are not intended to affect the national economy. The federal government makes many decisions about taxes and spending, but not all of these decisions are fiscal policy actions because they are not intended to achieve macroeconomic policy goals. For example, a decision to cut the taxes of people who buy hybrid cars is an environmental policy action, not a fiscal policy action. Similarly, the spending increases to fund the war on terrorism and the wars in Iraq and Afghanistan were part of defense and homeland security policy, not fiscal policy.

Automatic Stabilizers versus Discretionary Fiscal Policy

Automatic stabilizers Government spending and taxes that automatically increase or decrease along with the business cycle.

There is an important distinction between *automatic stabilizers* and *discretionary fiscal policy*. Government spending and taxes that automatically increase or decrease along with the business cycle are called **automatic stabilizers**. The word *automatic* in this case refers to the fact that changes in these types of spending and taxes happen without actions by the government. For example, when the economy is expanding and employment is increasing, government spending on unemployment insurance payments to workers who have lost their jobs will automatically decrease. During a recession, as employment declines, this type of spending will automatically increase. Similarly, when the economy is expanding and incomes are rising, the amount the government collects in taxes will increase as people pay additional taxes on their higher incomes. When the economy is in a recession, the amount the government collects in taxes will fall.

With discretionary fiscal policy, the government takes actions to change spending or taxes. The tax cuts and spending increases in the ARRA that Congress and the president enacted in 2009 are an example of a discretionary fiscal policy action.

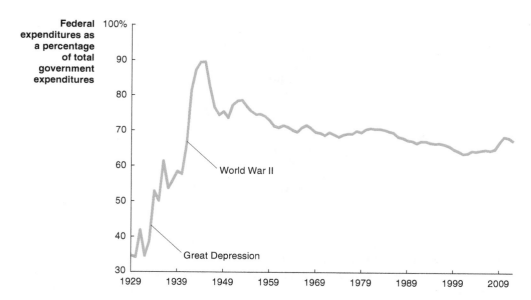

Figure 1

The Federal Government's Share of Total Government Expenditures, 1929–2012

Until the Great Depression of the 1930s, the majority of government spending in the United States occurred at the state and local levels. Since World War II, the federal government's share of total government expenditures has been between two-thirds and three-quarters.

Source: U.S. Bureau of Economic Analysis.

An Overview of Government Spending and Taxes

To provide a context for discussing fiscal policy, it is important to understand the big picture of government taxing and spending. Before the Great Depression of the 1930s, the majority of government spending took place at the state and local levels. As Figure 1 shows, the size of the federal government expanded significantly during the crisis of the Great Depression. Since World War II, the federal government's share of total government expenditures has been between two-thirds and three-quarters.

Economists often measure government spending relative to the size of the economy by calculating government spending as a percentage of GDP. There is a difference between federal government *purchases* and federal government *expenditures*. When the federal government purchases an aircraft carrier or the services of an FBI agent, it receives a good or service in return. Federal government expenditures include purchases plus federal government spending—such as Social Security payments—that does not involve a purchase. As Figure 2 shows, federal government *purchases* as a percentage of GDP have actually been falling since the end of the Korean War in the early 1950s. Total federal *expenditures* as a percentage of GDP rose from 1950 to the early 1990s and then fell from 1992 to 2001, before rising again. The decline in expenditures between 1992 and 2001 was partly the result of the end of the Cold War between the Soviet Union and the United States, which allowed for a substantial reduction in defense spending. Real federal government spending on national defense declined

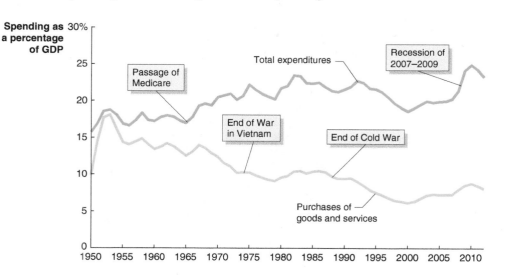

Figure 2

Federal Purchases and Federal Expenditures as a Percentage of GDP, 1950–2012

As a fraction of GDP, the federal government's *purchases* of goods and services have been declining since the Korean War in the early 1950s. Total *expenditures* by the federal government—including transfer payments—as a fraction of GDP slowly rose from 1950 through the early 1990s and fell from 1992 to 2001, before rising again. The recession of 2007–2009 and the slow recovery that followed led to a surge in federal government expenditures, causing them to rise to their highest level as a percentage of GDP since World War II.

Source: U.S. Bureau of Economic Analysis.

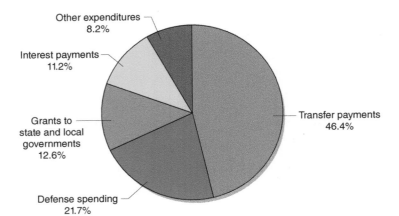

Figure 3

Federal Government Expenditures, 2012

Federal government *purchases* can be divided into defense spending—which makes up 21.7 percent of the federal budget—and spending on everything else the federal government does—from paying the salaries of FBI agents, to operating the national parks, to supporting scientific research—which makes up 8.2 percent of the budget. In addition to purchases, there are three other categories of federal government *expenditures*: interest on the national debt, grants to state and local governments, and transfer payments. Transfer payments rose from 25 percent of federal government expenditures in the 1960s to 46.4 percent in 2012.

Source: U.S. Bureau of Economic Analysis.

by almost 25 percent between 1990 and 1998, before rising by more than 60 percent between 1998 and 2010 in response to the war on terrorism and the wars in Iraq and Afghanistan. The recession of 2007–2009 and the slow recovery that followed led to a surge in federal government expenditures, causing them to rise to their highest level as a percentage of GDP since World War II.

In addition to purchases, there are three other categories of federal government expenditures: *interest on the national debt, grants to state and local governments*, and *transfer payments*. Interest on the national debt represents payments to holders of the bonds the federal government has issued to borrow money. Grants to state and local governments are payments made by the federal government to support government activity at the state and local levels. For example, to help reduce crime, Congress implemented a program of grants to local governments to hire more police officers. The largest and fastest-growing category of federal expenditures is transfer payments. Some of these programs, such as Social Security and unemployment insurance, began in the 1930s. Others, such as Medicare, which finances health care for the elderly, or the food stamp (Supplemental Nutrition Assistance Program) and Temporary Assistance for Needy Families programs, which are intended to aid the poor, began in the 1960s or later.

Figure 3 shows that in 2012, transfer payments were 46.4 percent of federal government expenditures. In the 1960s, transfer payments were only 25 percent of federal government expenditures. As the U.S. population ages and medical costs continue to increase, federal government spending on the Social Security and Medicare programs will continue to rise, causing transfer payments to consume an increasing share of federal expenditures. Figure 3 shows that spending on most of the federal government's day-to-day activities—including running federal agencies such as the Environmental Protection Agency, the Federal Bureau of Investigation, the National Park Service, and the Immigration and Naturalization Service—makes up only 8.2 percent of federal government expenditures.

Figure 4 shows that in 2012, the federal government raised 42.7 percent of its revenue from individual income taxes. Payroll taxes to fund the Social Security and

Figure 4

Federal Government Revenue, 2012

In 2012, individual income taxes raised 42.7 percent of the federal government's revenues. Corporate income taxes raised 13.9 percent of revenue. Payroll taxes to fund the Social Security and Medicare programs raised 35.0 percent of revenue. The remaining 8.5 percent of revenues were raised from excise taxes, tariffs on imports, and other sources.

Source: U.S. Bureau of Economic Analysis.

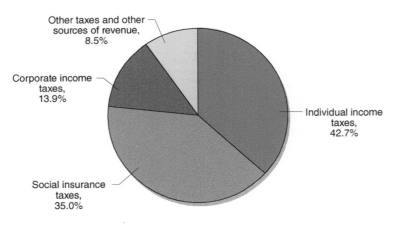

Medicare programs raised 35 percent of federal revenues. This percentage was smaller than usual because of a temporary cut in payroll taxes intended to increase consumer spending as the economy recovered slowly from the 2007–2009 recession. This temporary tax cut expired at the end of 2012. The tax on corporate profits raised 13.9 percent of federal revenues. The remaining 8.5 percent of federal revenues were raised from excise taxes on certain products, such as cigarettes and gasoline, from tariffs on goods imported from other countries, and from other sources, such as payments by companies that cut timber on federal lands.

Making the Connection	**Is Spending on Social Security and Medicare a Fiscal Time Bomb?**

Social Security, established in 1935 to provide payments to retired workers, began as a "pay-as-you-go" system, meaning that payments to current retirees were made with taxes collected from current workers. In the early years of the program, many workers were paying into the system, and there were relatively few retirees. For example, in 1940, more than 35 million workers were paying into the system, and only 222,000 people were receiving benefits—a ratio of more than 150 workers to each retiree. In those early years, most retirees received far more in benefits than they had paid in taxes. For example, the first beneficiary was a legal secretary named Ida May Fuller. She worked for three years after the program began and paid total taxes of only $24.75. During her retirement, she collected $22,888.92 in benefits.

The Social Security and Medicare programs have been very successful in reducing poverty among older Americans, but in recent years, the ability of the federal government to finance current promises has been called into doubt. After World War II, the United States experienced a "baby boom," as birthrates rose and remained high through the early 1960s. Falling birthrates after 1965 have caused long-run problems for the Social Security system because the number of workers per retiree has continually declined. Currently, there are only about three workers per retiree, and that ratio is expected to decline to two workers per retiree by 2035. Congress has attempted to deal with this problem by raising the age to receive full benefits from 65 to 67 and by increasing payroll taxes. Social Security and Medicare are financed from a payroll tax on individuals' wages and self-employment income. Workers and firms are each liable for half the tax. In 1940, the payroll tax rate was 2 percent; in 2013, it was 15.3 percent. Beginning in 2013, individuals earning more than $200,000 in either wages or self-employment income have paid two additional Medicare taxes: an additional 0.9 percent tax on their wages and an additional 3.8 percent tax on their investment income.

Under the Medicare program, which was established in 1965, the federal government provides health care coverage to people age 65 and over. The long-term financial situation for Medicare is an even greater cause for concern than is Social Security. As Americans live longer and as new—and expensive—medical procedures are developed, the projected expenditures under the Medicare program will eventually far outstrip projected tax revenues. The federal government also faces increasing expenditures under the Medicaid program, which is administered by state governments and provides health care coverage to low-income people. In 2013, federal spending on Social Security, Medicare, and Medicaid equaled 9.9 percent of GDP. Spending on these three programs was less than 3 percent of GDP in 1962. The Congressional Budget Office (CBO) forecasts that federal spending on these three programs will rise to 14.4 percent of GDP in 2030, 17.5 percent by 2050, and 23.4 percent by 2087. The graph on the next page illustrates these forecasts. Over the past 40 years, the federal government has spent an average of about 21.5 percent of GDP on *all programs* combined—from buying aircraft carriers to paying the salaries of FBI agents to making Social Security and Medicare payments. So, if current trends continue, the federal government will eventually be spending, as a fraction of GDP, more on these three programs than it currently does on all programs combined.

The Board of Trustees of the Social Security System forecasts that through 2090, the gap between the benefits projected to be paid under the Social Security and Medicare programs and projected tax revenues is a staggering $58 *trillion*, or more than three times the value of GDP in 2013. If current projections are accurate, policymakers are faced with the choice of significantly restraining spending on these programs, greatly increasing taxes on households and firms, or implementing some combination of spending restraints and tax increases. The alternatives are all unpleasant. A report from the CBO concluded: "Even if taxation reached levels that were unprecedented in the United States, current spending policies could become financially unsustainable."

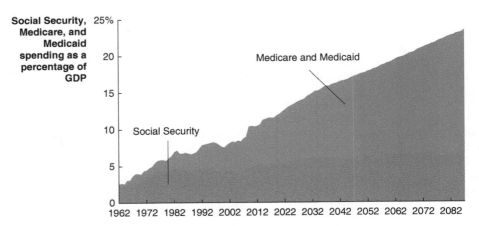

Note: The area labeled "Medicare and Medicaid" also includes federal spending on the Children's Health Insurance Program (CHIP) and federal subsidies to health care exchanges.

A lively political debate has taken place over the future of the Social Security and Medicare programs. Some policymakers have proposed increasing taxes to fund future benefit payments. The tax increases needed, however, could be as much as 50 percent higher than current rates, and tax increases of that magnitude could discourage work effort, entrepreneurship, and investment, thereby slowing economic growth. There have also been proposals to slow the rate of growth of future benefits, while guaranteeing benefits to current recipients. While this strategy would avoid the need to raise taxes significantly, it would also require younger workers to save more for their retirements. Some economists and policymakers have argued for slower benefit growth for higher-income workers while leaving future benefits unchanged for lower-income workers. Whatever changes are ultimately made in the Medicare and Social Security programs, the outcome of this policy debate will have important effects on the futures of today's college students.

Sources: Congressional Budget Office, *Supplemental Data for CBO's 2012 Long-Term Budget Outlook*, October 2012; Congressional Budget Office, *Baseline Projections of Mandatory Outlays*, January 2013; The Board of Trustees, Federal Old-Age and Survivors Insurance and Federal Disability Insurance Trust Funds, "The 2013 Annual Report of the Board of Trustees of the Federal Old-Age and Survivors Insurance and Disability Insurance Trust Funds," May 31, 2013; and the Social Security Administration Web site (www.ssa.gov).

Your Turn: Test your understanding by doing related problem 1.7 at the end of this chapter.

2 LEARNING OBJECTIVE

Explain how fiscal policy affects aggregate demand and how the government can use fiscal policy to stabilize the economy.

The Effects of Fiscal Policy on Real GDP and the Price Level

The federal government uses macroeconomic policies to offset the effects of the business cycle on the economy. The Federal Reserve carries out monetary policy through changes in interest rates and the money supply. Congress and the president carry out fiscal policy through changes in government purchases and taxes. Because changes in government purchases and taxes lead to changes in aggregate demand, they can affect the level of real GDP, employment, and the price level. When the economy is in a recession, *increases* in government purchases or *decreases* in taxes will increase aggregate demand. The inflation rate may increase when real GDP is beyond potential GDP. Decreasing government purchases or raising taxes can slow the growth of aggregate demand and reduce the inflation rate.

Expansionary and Contractionary Fiscal Policy

Expansionary fiscal policy involves increasing government purchases or decreasing taxes. An increase in government purchases will increase aggregate demand directly because government purchases are a component of aggregate demand. A cut in taxes has an indirect effect on aggregate demand. The income households have available to spend after they have paid their taxes is called *disposable income*. Cutting the individual income tax will increase household disposable income and consumption spending. Cutting taxes on business income can increase aggregate demand by increasing business investment.

Figure 5 shows the results of an expansionary fiscal policy, using the basic aggregate demand and aggregate supply model. In this model, there is no economic growth, so the long-run aggregate supply (*LRAS*) curve does not shift. The goal of both expansionary monetary policy and expansionary fiscal policy is to increase aggregate demand relative to what it would have been without the policy.

In panel (a) of Figure 5, we assume short-run equilibrium occurs at point *A*, where the aggregate demand (*AD*₁) curve intersects the short-run aggregate supply (*SRAS*) curve. Real GDP is below potential GDP, so the economy is in a recession, with some firms operating below normal capacity and some workers having been laid off. To bring real GDP back to potential GDP, Congress and the president increase government purchases or cut taxes, which will shift the aggregate demand curve to the right, from *AD*₁ to *AD*₂. Real GDP increases from \$17.2 trillion to potential GDP of \$17.4 trillion, and the price level rises from 108 to 110 (point *B*). The policy has successfully returned real GDP to its potential level. Rising production will lead to increasing employment, reducing the unemployment rate.

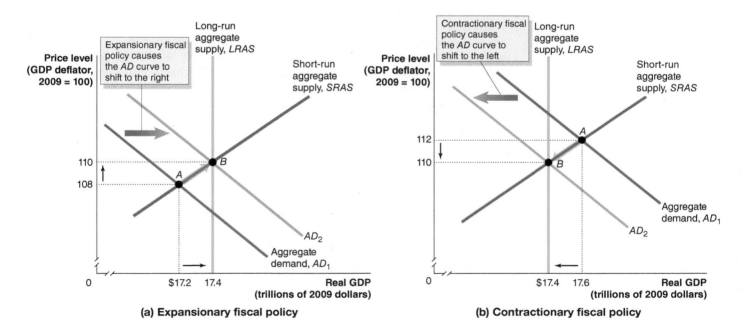

Figure 5 **Fiscal Policy**

In panel (a), short-run equilibrium is at point *A*, with real GDP of \$17.2 trillion and a price level of 108. Real GDP is below potential GDP, so the economy is in a recession. An expansionary fiscal policy will cause aggregate demand to shift to the right, from *AD*₁ to *AD*₂, increasing real GDP from \$17.2 trillion to \$17.4 trillion and the price level from 108 to 110 (point *B*).

In panel (b), the economy begins at point *A*, with real GDP at \$17.6 trillion and the price level at 112. Because real GDP is greater than potential GDP, the economy will experience rising wages and prices. A contractionary fiscal policy will cause aggregate demand to shift to the left, from *AD*₁ to *AD*₂, decreasing real GDP from \$17.6 trillion to \$17.4 trillion and the price level from 112 to 110 (point *B*).

Don't Let This Happen to You

Don't Confuse Fiscal Policy and Monetary Policy

If you keep in mind the definitions of *money*, *income*, and *spending*, the difference between monetary policy and fiscal policy will be clearer. Students often make these two related mistakes: (1) They think of monetary policy as the Federal Reserve fighting recessions by increasing the money supply so people will have more money to spend; and (2) they think of fiscal policy as Congress and the president fighting recessions by spending more money. In this view, the only difference between fiscal policy and monetary policy is the source of the money.

To understand what's wrong with the descriptions of fiscal policy and monetary policy just given, first remember that the problem during a recession is not that there is too little *money*—currency plus checking account deposits—but too little *spending*. There may be too little spending for a number of reasons. For example, households may cut back on their spending on cars and houses because they are pessimistic about the future. Firms may reduce their spending because they have lowered their estimates of the future profitability of new machinery and

factories. Or major trading partners of the United States—such as Japan and Canada—may be suffering from recessions, which cause households and firms in those countries to reduce their spending on U.S. products.

The purpose of expansionary monetary policy is to lower interest rates, which in turn increases aggregate demand. When interest rates fall, households and firms are willing to borrow more to buy cars, houses, and factories. The purpose of expansionary fiscal policy is to increase aggregate demand either by having the government directly increase its own purchases or by cutting taxes to increase household disposable income and, therefore, consumption spending.

Just as increasing or decreasing the money supply does not have a direct effect on government spending or taxes, increasing or decreasing government spending or taxes does not have a direct effect on the money supply. Fiscal policy and monetary policy have the same goals, but they attempt to reach those goals in different ways.

Your Turn: Test your understanding by doing related problem 2.6 at the end of this chapter.

Contractionary fiscal policy involves decreasing government purchases or increasing taxes. Policymakers use contractionary fiscal policy to reduce increases in aggregate demand that seem likely to lead to inflation. In panel (b) of Figure 5, short-run equilibrium occurs at point *A*, with real GDP of $17.6 trillion, which is above potential GDP of $17.4 trillion. With some firms producing beyond their normal capacity and the unemployment rate very low, wages and prices will be increasing. To bring real GDP back to potential GDP, Congress and the president decrease government purchases or increase taxes, which will shift the aggregate demand curve to the left, from AD_1 to AD_2. Real GDP falls from $17.6 trillion to $17.4 trillion, and the price level falls from 112 to 110 (point *B*).

We can conclude that Congress and the president can attempt to stabilize the economy by using fiscal policy to affect the price level and the level of real GDP. Of course, in practice it is extremely difficult for Congress and the president to use fiscal policy to eliminate the effects of the business cycle and keep real GDP always equal to potential GDP.

A Summary of How Fiscal Policy Affects Aggregate Demand

Table 1 summarizes how fiscal policy affects aggregate demand. Just as we did with monetary policy, we must add a very important qualification to this summary of fiscal policy: The table isolates the effect of fiscal policy *by holding constant monetary policy*

Table 1	Problem	Type of Policy Required	Actions by Congress and the President	Result
Countercyclical Fiscal Policy	Recession	Expansionary	Increase government purchases or cut taxes	Real GDP and the price level rise.
	Rising inflation	Contractionary	Decrease government purchases or raise taxes	Real GDP and the price level fall.

and all other factors affecting the variables involved. This point is important because, for example, in the actual economy a contractionary fiscal policy does not cause the price level to fall. A contractionary fiscal policy causes the price level *to rise by less than it would have without the policy.*

Fiscal Policy in the Dynamic Aggregate Demand and Aggregate Supply Model*

The overview of fiscal policy we just finished contains a key idea: Congress and the president can use fiscal policy to affect aggregate demand, thereby changing the price level and the level of real GDP. The discussion of expansionary and contractionary fiscal policy illustrated by Figure 5 is simplified, however, because it ignores two important facts about the economy: (1) The economy experiences continuing inflation, with the price level rising every year, and (2) the economy experiences long-run growth, with the *LRAS* curve shifting to the right every year. In this section, we use the *dynamic aggregate demand and aggregate supply model* to gain a more complete understanding of fiscal policy.

To briefly review the dynamic model, over time, potential GDP increases, which we show by shifting the *LRAS* curve to the right. The factors that cause the *LRAS* curve to shift also cause firms to supply more goods and services at any given price level in the short run, which we show by shifting the *SRAS* curve to the right. Finally, during most years, the aggregate demand curve also shifts to the right, indicating that aggregate expenditure is higher at every price level.

Figure 6 shows the results of an expansionary fiscal policy using the dynamic aggregate demand and aggregate supply model. The goal of both expansionary monetary policy and expansionary fiscal policy is to increase aggregate demand relative to what it would have been without the policy.

In the hypothetical situation shown in Figure 6, equilibrium is initially at point A, with real GDP equal to potential GDP of $17.0 trillion and the price level equal to 110. In the second year, *LRAS* increases to $17.4 trillion, but aggregate demand increases only from AD_1 to $AD_{2(\text{without policy})}$, which is not enough to keep real GDP equal to

3 LEARNING OBJECTIVE

Use the dynamic aggregate demand and aggregate supply model to analyze fiscal policy.

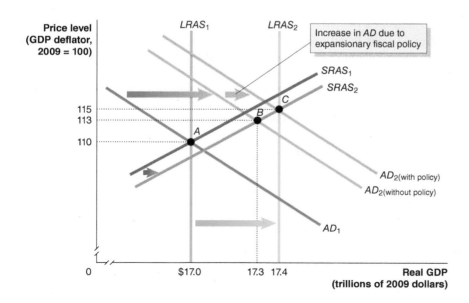

Figure 6

An Expansionary Fiscal Policy in the Dynamic Model

Equilibrium is initially at point A, with real GDP equal to potential GDP of $17.0 trillion and the price level equal to 110. Without an expansionary policy, aggregate demand will shift from AD_1 to $AD_{2(\text{without policy})}$, which is not enough to keep real GDP equal to potential GDP because long-run aggregate supply has shifted from $LRAS_1$ to $LRAS_2$. The new short-run equilibrium is at point B, with real GDP of $17.3 trillion and a price level of 113. Increasing government purchases or cutting taxes will shift aggregate demand to $AD_{2(\text{with policy})}$. Equilibrium will be at point C, with real GDP of $17.4 trillion, which is its potential level, and a price level of 115. The price level is higher than it would have been without an expansionary fiscal policy.

*This section may be omitted without loss of continuity.

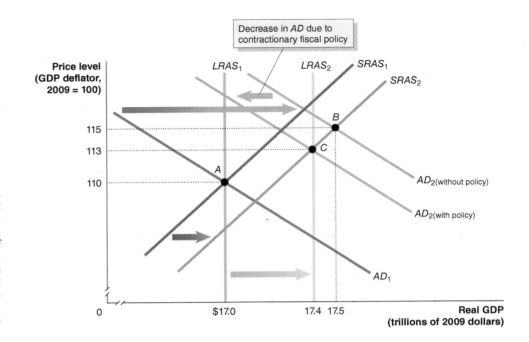

Figure 7

A Contractionary Fiscal Policy in the Dynamic Model

Equilibrium is initially at point *A*, with real GDP equal to potential GDP of $17.0 trillion and the price level equal to 110. Without a contractionary policy, aggregate demand will shift from AD_1 to $AD_{2(\text{without policy})}$, which results in a short-run equilibrium at point *B*, with real GDP of $17.5 trillion, which is greater than potential GDP, and a price level of 115. Decreasing government purchases or increasing taxes can shift aggregate demand to $AD_{2(\text{with policy})}$. Equilibrium will be at point *C*, with real GDP of $17.4 trillion, which is its potential level, and a price level of 113. The inflation rate will be 2.7 percent, as opposed to the 4.5 percent it would have been without the contractionary fiscal policy.

potential GDP. Let's assume that the Fed does not react to the situation with an expansionary monetary policy. In that case, short-run equilibrium will occur at point *B* with real GDP of $17.3 trillion and a price level of 113. The $100 billion gap between real GDP and potential GDP means that some firms are operating at less than their full capacity. Incomes and profits will be falling, firms will begin to lay off workers, and the unemployment rate will increase.

Increasing government purchases or cutting taxes can shift aggregate demand to $AD_{2(\text{with policy})}$. Equilibrium will be at point *C*, with real GDP of $17.4 trillion, which is its potential level, and a price level of 115. The price level is higher than it would have been without an expansionary fiscal policy.

Contractionary fiscal policy involves decreasing government purchases or increasing taxes. Policymakers use contractionary fiscal policy to reduce increases in aggregate demand that seem likely to lead to inflation. In Figure 7, equilibrium is initially at point *A*, with real GDP equal to potential GDP of $17.0 trillion and the price level equal to 110. Once again, *LRAS* increases to $17.4 trillion in the second year. In this scenario, the shift in aggregate demand to $AD_{2(\text{without policy})}$ results in a short-run macroeconomic equilibrium at point *B*, with real GDP of $17.5 trillion, which is greater than potential GDP. If we assume that the Fed does not respond to the situation with a contractionary monetary policy, the economy will experience a rising inflation rate. Decreasing government purchases or increasing taxes can keep real GDP from moving beyond its potential level. The result, shown in Figure 7, is that in the new equilibrium at point *C*, the inflation rate is 2.7 percent rather than 4.5 percent.

4 LEARNING OBJECTIVE

Explain how the government purchases and tax multipliers work.

The Government Purchases and Tax Multipliers

We saw in the chapter opener that Congress and the president authorized spending to widen the Caldecott Tunnel in Northern California in an attempt to increase aggregate demand during the recession of 2007–2009. Suppose that Congress and the president decide to spend $100 billion on expanding the Caldecott Tunnel and similar projects. (The total increase in federal spending under the American Recovery and Reinvestment Act (ARRA) was actually about $500 billion, including the $180 million spent to widen the Caldecott Tunnel.) How much will equilibrium real GDP increase as a result of this increase in government purchases? We might expect by more than $100 billion because the initial increase in aggregate demand should lead to additional increases in income and spending. For example, to expand the Caldecott Tunnel, the California state government hired Tutor-Saliba, a private construction firm. Tutor-Saliba and the subcontractors it used hired workers for the project. The firms that carried out the many other projects authorized under the ARRA also hired new workers. Workers who were formerly unemployed are likely to increase their spending on cars, furniture, appliances, and other products. Sellers of these products will increase their production and hire more workers, and so on. At each step, real GDP and income will rise, thereby increasing consumption spending and aggregate demand. These additional waves of hiring are what the spokesperson for the state agency in charge of the Caldecott Tunnel project referred to in the chapter opener as a "ripple effect" from the project.

Economists call the initial increase in government purchases as *autonomous* because it is a result of a decision by the government and is not directly caused by changes in the level of real GDP. The increases in consumption spending that result from the initial autonomous increase in government purchases are *induced* because they are caused by the initial increase in autonomous spending. Economists call the series of induced increases in consumption spending that results from an initial increase in autonomous expenditures the **multiplier effect**.

Figure 8 illustrates how an increase in government purchases affects the aggregate demand curve. The initial increase causes the aggregate demand curve to shift to the right because total spending in the economy is now higher at every price level. The shift to the right from AD_1 to the dashed AD curve represents the effect of the initial increase of $100 billion in government purchases. Because this initial increase in government purchases raises incomes and leads to further increases in consumption spending, the aggregate demand curve will ultimately shift from AD_1 all the way to AD_2.

To better understand the multiplier effect, let's start with a simplified analysis in which we assume that the price level is constant. In other words, initially we will ignore the effect of an upward-sloping *SRAS* curve. Figure 9 shows how spending and real GDP increase over a number of periods, beginning with the initial increase in government purchases in the first period, which raises real GDP and total income in the economy by $100 billion. How much additional consumption spending will result from $100 billion in additional income? We know that in addition to increasing their consumption spending on domestically produced goods, households will save some of the increase in income, use some to pay income taxes, and use some to purchase imported goods, which will have no direct effect on spending and production in the U.S. economy. In Figure 9, we assume that in the second period, households

Multiplier effect The series of induced increases in consumption spending that results from an initial increase in autonomous expenditures.

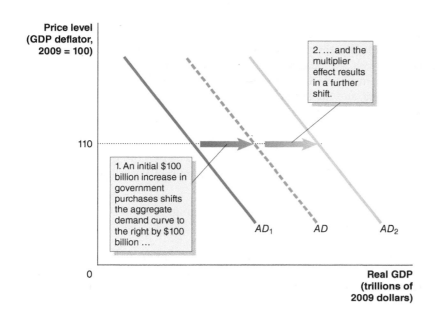

1. An initial $100 billion increase in government purchases shifts the aggregate demand curve to the right by $100 billion ...

2. ... and the multiplier effect results in a further shift.

Figure 8

The Multiplier Effect and Aggregate Demand

An initial increase in government purchases of $100 billion causes the aggregate demand curve to shift to the right, from AD_1 to the dashed AD curve, and represents the effect of the initial increase of $100 billion in government purchases. Because this initial increase raises incomes and leads to further increases in consumption spending, the aggregate demand curve will ultimately shift further to the right, to AD_2.

Period	Additional Spending This Period	Cumulative Increase in Spending and Real GDP
1	$100 billion in government purchases	$100 billion
2	$50 billion in consumption spending	$150 billion
3	$25 billion in consumption spending	$175 billion
4	$12.5 billion in consumption spending	$187.5 billion
⋮	⋮	⋮
n	0	$200 billion

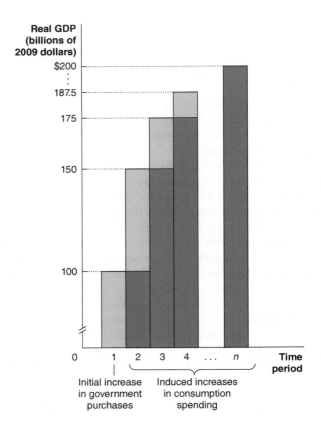

Figure 9 **The Multiplier Effect of an Increase in Government Purchases**

Following an initial increase in government purchases, spending and real GDP increase over a number of periods due to the multiplier effect. The new spending and increased real GDP in each period is shown in orange, and the level of spending from the previous period is shown in blue. The sum of the blue and orange areas represents the cumulative increase in spending and real GDP. In total, equilibrium real GDP will increase by $200 billion as a result of an initial increase of $100 billion in government purchases.

increase their consumption spending by half the increase in income from the first period—or by $50 billion. This spending in the second period will, in turn, increase real GDP and income by an additional $50 billion. In the third period, consumption spending will increase by $25 billion, or half the $50 billion increase in income from the second period.

The multiplier effect will continue through a number of periods, with the additional consumption spending in each period being half of the income increase from the previous period. Eventually, the process will be complete, although we cannot say precisely how many periods it will take, so we simply label the final period n rather than give it a specific number. In Figure 9, the new spending and increased real GDP in each period is shown in orange, and the level of spending from the previous period is shown in blue. The sum of the blue and orange areas represents the cumulative increase in spending and real GDP.

How large will the total increase in equilibrium real GDP be as a result of the initial increase of $100 billion in government purchases? The ratio of the change in equilibrium real GDP to the initial change in government purchases is called the *government purchases multiplier*:

$$\text{Government purchases multiplier} = \frac{\text{Change in equilibrium real GDP}}{\text{Change in government purchases}}.$$

If, for example, the government purchases multiplier has a value of 2, an increase in government purchases of $100 billion should increase equilibrium real GDP by $2 \times \$100$ billion = $200 billion. We show this result in Figure 9 by having the cumulative increase in real GDP equal $200 billion.

Tax cuts also have a multiplier effect because they increase the disposable income of households. When household disposable income rises, so will consumption spending. These increases in consumption spending will set off further increases in real GDP and income, just as increases in government purchases do. Suppose we consider a change in taxes of a specific amount—say, a tax cut of $100 billion—with the tax *rate* remaining unchanged. The expression for this tax multiplier is:

$$\text{Tax multiplier} = \frac{\text{Change in equilibrium real GDP}}{\text{Change in taxes}}.$$

The tax multiplier is a negative number because changes in taxes and changes in real GDP move in opposite directions: An increase in taxes reduces disposable income, consumption, and real GDP, and a decrease in taxes raises disposable income, consumption, and real GDP. For example, if the tax multiplier is −1.6, a $100 billion *cut* in taxes will increase real GDP by −1.6 × (−$100 billion) = $160 billion. We would expect the tax multiplier to be smaller in absolute value than the government purchases multiplier. To see why, think about the difference between a $100 billion increase in government purchases and a $100 billion decrease in taxes. The whole of the $100 billion in government purchases results in an increase in aggregate demand. But households will save rather than spend some portion of a $100 billion decrease in taxes, and they will spend some portion on imported goods. The fraction of the tax cut that households save or spend on imports will not increase aggregate demand. Therefore, the first period of the multiplier process will involve a smaller increase in aggregate demand than occurs when there is an increase in government purchases, and the total increase in equilibrium real GDP will be smaller.

The Effect of Changes in the Tax Rate

A change in the tax *rate* has a more complicated effect on equilibrium real GDP than does a tax cut of a fixed amount. To begin with, the value of the tax rate affects the size of the multiplier effect. The higher the tax rate, the smaller the multiplier effect. To see why, think about the size of the additional spending increases that take place in each period following an increase in government purchases. The higher the tax rate, the smaller the amount of any increase in income that households have available to spend, which reduces the size of the multiplier effect. So, a cut in the tax rate affects equilibrium real GDP through two channels: (1) A cut in the tax rate increases the disposable income of households, which leads them to increase their consumption spending, and (2) a cut in the tax rate increases the size of the multiplier effect.

Taking into Account the Effects of Aggregate Supply

To this point, as we discussed the multiplier effect, we assumed that the price level was constant. We know, though, that because the *SRAS* curve is upward sloping, when the *AD* curve shifts to the right, the price level will rise. As a result of the rise in the price level, equilibrium real GDP will not increase by the full amount that the multiplier effect indicates. Figure 10 illustrates how an upward-sloping *SRAS* curve affects the size of the multiplier. To keep the graph relatively simple, we assume that the *SRAS* and *LRAS* curves do not shift. Short-run equilibrium is initially at point *A*, with real GDP below its potential level. An increase in government purchases shifts the aggregate demand curve from AD_1 to the dashed *AD* curve. Just as in Figure 8, the multiplier effect causes a further shift in the aggregate demand curve to AD_2. If the price level remained constant, real GDP would increase from $16.0 trillion at point *A* to $17.2 trillion at point *B*. However, because the *SRAS* curve is upward sloping, the price level rises from 110 to 113, reducing the total quantity of goods and services demanded in the economy. The new equilibrium occurs at point *C*, with real GDP having risen to $17.0 trillion, or by $200 billion less than if the price level had remained unchanged. We can conclude that the actual change in real GDP resulting from an increase in government purchases or a cut in taxes will be less than that indicated by the simple multiplier effect with a constant price level.

Figure 10

The Multiplier Effect and Aggregate Supply

Short-run equilibrium is initially at point A. An increase in government purchases causes the aggregate demand curve to shift to the right, from AD_1 to the dashed AD curve. The multiplier effect results in the aggregate demand curve shifting further to the right, to AD_2 (point B). Because of the upward-sloping supply curve, the shift in aggregate demand results in a higher price level. In the new equilibrium at point C, both real GDP and the price level have increased. The increase in real GDP is less than that indicated by the multiplier effect with a constant price level.

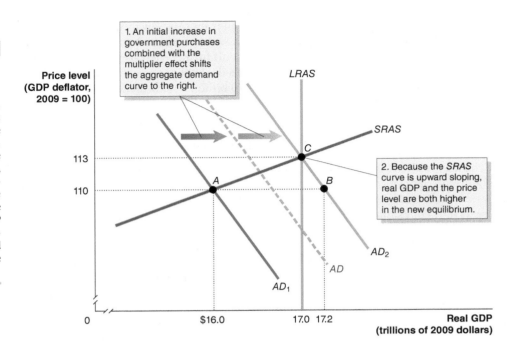

The Multipliers Work in Both Directions

Increases in government purchases and cuts in taxes have a positive multiplier effect on equilibrium real GDP. Decreases in government purchases and increases in taxes also have a multiplier effect on equilibrium real GDP, but in this case, the effect is negative. An increase in taxes will reduce household disposable income and consumption. As households buy fewer cars, furniture, refrigerators, and other products, the firms that sell these products will cut back on production and begin laying off workers. Falling incomes will lead to further reductions in consumption. A reduction in government spending on defense would set off a similar process of decreases in real GDP and income. The reduction would affect defense contractors first because they sell directly to the government, and then it would spread to other firms.

We look more closely at the government purchases multiplier and the tax multiplier in the appendix to this chapter.

Solved Problem 4

Fiscal Policy Multipliers

Briefly explain whether you agree with the following statement: "Real GDP is currently $17.2 trillion, and potential GDP is $17.4 trillion. If Congress and the president would increase government purchases by $200 billion or cut taxes by $200 billion, the economy could be brought to equilibrium at potential GDP."

Solving the Problem

Step 1: Review the chapter material. This problem is about the multiplier process, so you may want to review the section "The Government Purchases and Tax Multipliers."

Step 2: Explain how the necessary increase in purchases or cut in taxes is less than $200 billion because of the multiplier effect. The statement is incorrect because it does not consider the multiplier effect. Because of the multiplier effect, an increase in government purchases or a decrease in taxes of less than $200 billion is necessary to increase equilibrium real GDP by $200 billion. For instance, assume that the government purchases multiplier is 2 and the tax multiplier is −1.6. We can then calculate the necessary increase in government purchases as follows:

$$\text{Government purchases multiplier} = \frac{\text{Change in equilibrium real GDP}}{\text{Change in government purchases}}$$

$$2 = \frac{\$200 \text{ billion}}{\text{Change in government purchases}}$$

$$\text{Change in government purchases} = \frac{\$200 \text{ billion}}{2} = \$100 \text{ billion}.$$

And the necessary change in taxes:

$$\text{Tax multiplier} = \frac{\text{Change in equilibrium real GDP}}{\text{Change in taxes}}$$

$$-1.6 = \frac{\$200 \text{ billion}}{\text{Change in taxes}}$$

$$\text{Change in taxes} = \frac{\$200 \text{ billion}}{-1.6} = -\$125 \text{ billion}.$$

Your Turn: For more practice, do related problems 4.6 and 4.7 at the end of this chapter.

The Limits of Using Fiscal Policy to Stabilize the Economy

5 LEARNING OBJECTIVE

Discuss the difficulties that can arise in implementing fiscal policy.

Poorly timed fiscal policy, like poorly timed monetary policy, can do more harm than good. It takes time for policymakers to collect statistics and identify changes in the economy. If the government decides to increase spending or cut taxes to fight a recession that is about to end, the effect may be to increase the inflation rate. Similarly, cutting spending or raising taxes to slow down an economy that has actually already moved into a recession can increase the length and depth of the recession.

Getting the timing right can be more difficult with fiscal policy than with monetary policy for two main reasons. Control over monetary policy is concentrated in the hands of the Federal Open Market Committee, which can change monetary policy at any of its meetings. By contrast, the president and a majority of the 535 members of Congress have to agree on changes in fiscal policy. The delays caused by the legislative process can be very long. For example, in 1962, President John F. Kennedy concluded that the U.S. economy was operating below potential GDP and proposed a tax cut to stimulate aggregate demand. Congress eventually agreed to the tax cut—but not until 1964. The events of 2001 and 2009 show, though, that it is sometimes possible to authorize changes in fiscal policy relatively quickly. When George W. Bush came into office in January 2001, the economy was on the verge of a recession, and he immediately proposed a tax cut. Congress passed the tax cut, and the president signed it into law in early June 2001. Similarly, Barack Obama proposed a stimulus package as soon as he came into office in January 2009, and Congress had passed the proposal by February.

Even after a change in fiscal policy has been approved, it takes time to implement it. Suppose Congress and the president agree to increase aggregate demand by spending $30 billion more on constructing subway systems in several cities. It will probably take at least several months to prepare detailed plans for the construction. Local governments will then ask for bids from private construction companies. Once the winning bidders have been selected, they will usually need several months to begin the project. Only then will significant amounts of spending actually take place. This delay may push the spending beyond the end of the recession that the spending was intended to fight. Delays of this type are less of a concern during long and severe recessions, such as that of 2007–2009.

Does Government Spending Reduce Private Spending?

In addition to the timing issue, using increases in government purchases to increase aggregate demand presents another potential problem. We have been assuming that when the federal government increases its purchases by $30 billion, the multiplier effect will cause the increase in aggregate demand to be greater than $30 billion. However, the size of the multiplier effect may be limited if the increase in government purchases causes one of the nongovernment, or private, components of aggregate expenditures—consumption, investment, or net exports—to fall. A decline in private expenditures as a result of an increase in government purchases is called **crowding out**.

Crowding out A decline in private expenditures as a result of an increase in government purchases.

Crowding Out in the Short Run

Consider the case of a temporary increase in government purchases. Suppose the federal government decides to fight a recession by spending $30 billion more this year on subway construction. When the $30 billion has been spent, the program will end, and government purchases will drop back to their previous level. As the spending takes place, income and real GDP will increase. These increases in income and real GDP will cause households and firms to increase their demand for currency and checking account balances to accommodate the increased buying and selling. Figure 11 shows the result, using the money market graph.

At higher levels of real GDP and income, households and firms demand more money at every interest rate. When the demand for money increases, the equilibrium interest rate will rise. Higher interest rates will result in a decline in each component of private expenditures. Consumption spending and investment spending will decline because households will borrow less to buy houses, cars, furniture, and appliances, and firms will borrow less to buy factories, computers, and machine tools. Net exports will also decline because higher interest rates in the United States will attract foreign investors. German, Japanese, and Canadian investors will want to exchange the currencies of their countries for U.S. dollars to invest in U.S. Treasury bills and other U.S. financial assets. This increased demand for U.S. dollars will cause an increase in the exchange rate between the dollar and other currencies. When the dollar increases in value, the prices

Figure 11

An Expansionary Fiscal Policy Increases Interest Rates

An increase in government purchases will increase the demand for money from Money demand$_1$ to Money demand$_2$ as real GDP and income rise. With the supply of money constant, at $950 billion, the result is an increase in the equilibrium interest rate from 3 percent to 5 percent, which crowds out some consumption, investment, and net exports.

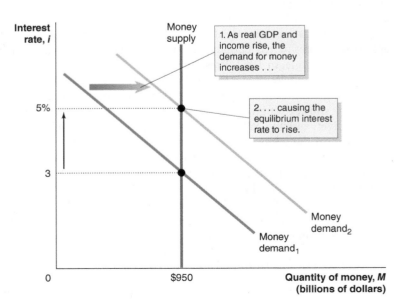

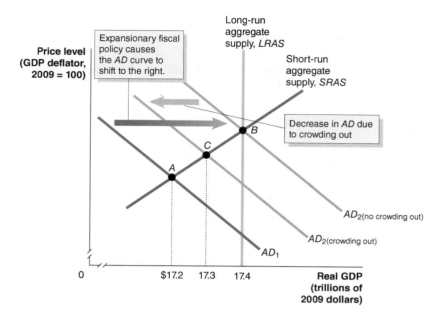

of U.S. products in foreign countries rise—causing a reduction in U.S. exports—and the prices of foreign products in the United States fall—causing an increase in U.S. imports. Falling exports and rising imports mean that net exports are falling.

The greater the sensitivity of consumption, investment, and net exports to changes in interest rates, the more crowding out will occur. In a deep recession, many firms may be pessimistic about the future and have so much excess capacity that investment spending will fall to very low levels and will be unlikely to fall much further, even if interest rates rise. In this case, crowding out is unlikely to be a problem. If the economy is close to potential GDP, however, and firms are optimistic about the future, an increase in interest rates may result in a significant decline in investment spending.

Figure 12 shows that crowding out may reduce the effectiveness of an expansionary fiscal policy. Short-run equilibrium is initially at point *A*, with real GDP at $17.2 trillion. Real GDP is below potential GDP, so the economy is in a recession. Suppose that Congress and the president decide to increase government purchases to increase real GDP to potential GDP. In the absence of crowding out, the increase in government purchases will shift the aggregate demand curve to $AD_{2(\text{no crowding out})}$ and equilibrium will be at point *B*, with real GDP equal to potential GDP of $17.4 trillion. But the higher interest rate resulting from the increased government purchases will reduce consumption, investment, and net exports, causing the aggregate demand curve to shift back to $AD_{2(\text{crowding out})}$. The result is a new short-run equilibrium at point *C*, with real GDP of $17.3 trillion, which is $100 billion short of potential GDP. (Note that the price level increase shown in Figure 10 also contributes to reducing the effect of an increase in government purchases on equilibrium real GDP.)

Crowding Out in the Long Run

Most economists agree that in the short run, an increase in government purchases results in partial, but not complete, crowding out. What is the long-run effect of a *permanent* increase in government spending? In this case, most economists agree that the result is complete crowding out. In the long run, the decline in investment, consumption, and net exports exactly offsets the increase in government purchases, and aggregate demand remains unchanged. *In the long run, real GDP returns to potential GDP.* Suppose that real GDP currently equals potential GDP and that government spending is 35 percent of GDP. In that case, private expenditures—the sum of consumption, investment, and net exports—will make up the other 65 percent of GDP. If government spending is increased permanently to 37 percent of GDP, in the long run, private expenditures must fall to 63 percent of GDP. There has been complete crowding out: Private expenditures have fallen by the same amount that government spending has increased. If government spending is taking a larger share of GDP, then private spending must take a smaller share.

An expansionary fiscal policy does not have to cause complete crowding out in the short run. If real GDP is below potential GDP, it is possible for both government purchases and private expenditures to increase. But in the long run, any permanent increase in government spending must come at the expense of private expenditures. Keep in mind, however, that it may take several—possibly many—years to arrive at this long-run outcome.

Fiscal Policy in Action: Did the Stimulus Package of 2009 Succeed?

As we have seen, Congress and the president can increase government purchases and cut taxes to increase aggregate demand either to avoid a recession or to shorten the length or severity of a recession that is already under way. The recession of 2007–2009 occurred during the end of the presidency of George W. Bush and the beginning of the presidency of Barack Obama. Both presidents used fiscal policy to fight the recession.

In early 2008, economists advising President Bush believed that the housing crisis, the resulting credit crunch, and rising oil prices were pushing the economy into a recession. (As we now know, a recession had actually already begun in December 2007.) These economists proposed cutting taxes to increase household disposable income, which would increase consumption spending and aggregate demand. Congress enacted a tax cut that took the form of *rebates* of taxes households had already paid. Rebate checks totaling $95 billion were sent to taxpayers between April and July 2008.

How effective were the rebates in increasing consumption spending? While economists are still studying the issue, economic analysis can give us some insight. Many economists believe that consumers base their spending on their *permanent income* rather than just on their *current income*. A consumer's permanent income reflects the consumer's expected future income. By basing spending on permanent income, a consumer can smooth out consumption over a period of years. For example, a medical student may have very low current income but a high expected future income. The student may borrow against this high expected future income rather than having to consume at a very low level in the present. Some people, however, have difficulty borrowing against their future income because banks or other lenders may not be convinced that a borrower's future income will be significantly higher than his or her current income. One-time tax rebates, such as the one in 2008, increase consumers' current income but not their permanent income. Only a permanent decrease in taxes increases consumers' permanent income. Therefore, a tax rebate is likely to increase consumption spending less than would a permanent tax cut.

Some estimates of the effect of the 2008 tax rebate, including studies by Christian Broda of the University of Chicago and Jonathan Parker of Northwestern University, and by economists at the Congressional Budget Office, indicate that taxpayers spent between 33 and 40 percent of the rebates they received. Taxpayers who have difficulty borrowing against their future income increased their consumption the most. The 2008 tax rebates totaled $95 billion, so consumers may have increased their spending by about $35 billion.

American Recovery and Reinvestment Act of 2009 Although the tax rebates helped to increase aggregate demand, the recession worsened in September 2008, following the bankruptcy of the Lehman Brothers investment bank and the deepening of the financial crisis. President Obama took office in January 2009, pledging to pursue an expansionary fiscal policy. Congress responded in February by passing the American Recovery and Reinvestment Act of 2009, a $840 billion package of spending increases and tax cuts that was by far the largest fiscal policy action in U.S. history. The "stimulus package," as it came to be known, is difficult to summarize, but Figure 13 provides some highlights.

About two-thirds of the stimulus package took the form of increases in government expenditures, and one-third took the form of tax cuts. Panel (a) shows the major categories of spending increases. The largest category—health care, social services, and

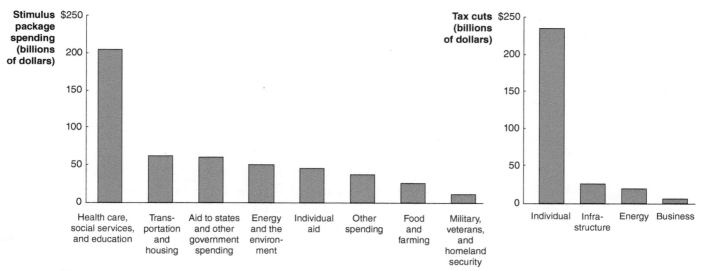

Figure 13   The 2009 Stimulus Package

Congress and President Obama intended the spending increases and tax cuts in the stimulus package to increase aggregate demand and help pull the economy out of the 2007–2009 recession. Panel (a) shows how the increases in spending were distributed, and panel (b) shows how the tax cuts were distributed.

Source: Congressional Budget Office.

education—included funds for biomedical research and grants to state governments to help fund Medicare spending, as well as funds for many other programs. The energy category included funds for research into alternative energy sources as well as modernization of the electric grid. Transportation and housing included substantial spending on infrastructure projects, such as repairing and expanding highways, bridges, and airports. Individual aid included spending on extended unemployment insurance payments. Panel (b) shows the major categories of tax cuts. The largest category was individual tax cuts, which included a $400 reduction in payroll taxes for workers earning up to $75,000 per year and a tax credit of up to $2,500 for tuition and other college expenses.

Congress and the president intended the changes to federal expenditures and taxes from the stimulus package to be temporary. Figure 14 shows the effect of the stimulus package on federal government expenditures and revenue over time. Panel (a) shows that the effect on federal government expenditures was greatest during 2010 and declined sharply during 2011. Panel (b) shows that the effect on federal government revenue was greatest during 2010 and had declined to almost zero by early 2011.

How Can We Measure the Effectiveness of the Stimulus Package?   At the time the stimulus package was passed, economists working for the administration estimated that the increase in aggregate demand resulting from the package would increase real GDP by 3.5 percent by the end of 2010 and increase employment by 3.5 million. In fact, between the beginning of 2009 and the end of 2010, real GDP increased by 4.0 percent, while employment declined by 3.3 million. Do these results indicate that the stimulus package was successful in increasing GDP, but not employment? We have to be careful in drawing that conclusion. To judge the effectiveness of the stimulus package, we have to measure its effects on real GDP and employment, *holding constant all other factors affecting real GDP and employment*. In other words, the actual movements in real GDP and employment are a mixture of the effects of the stimulus package and the effects of other factors, such as the Federal Reserve's monetary policy and the typical changes in real GDP and employment during a business cycle that occur independently of government policy. Isolating the effects of the stimulus package from the effects of these other factors is very difficult and explains why economists differ in their views on the effectiveness of the stimulus package.

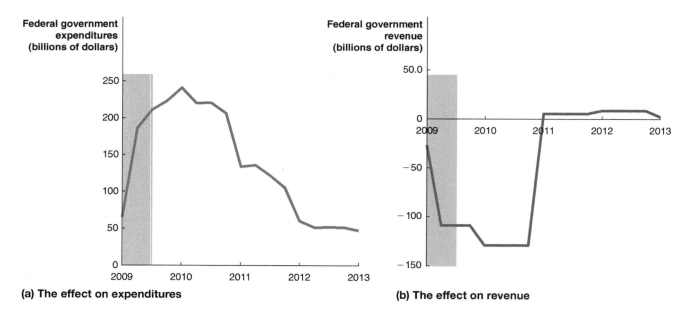

(a) The effect on expenditures

(b) The effect on revenue

Figure 14 The Effect of the Stimulus Package on Federal Expenditures and Revenue

Congress and President Obama intended the spending increases and tax cuts in the stimulus package to be temporary. Panel (a) shows the effect of the stimulus package on federal expenditures was greatest during 2010 and declined in the following years. Panel (b) shows that the effect on federal government revenue was greatest during 2010 and had declined to almost zero by early 2011.

Source: Federal Reserve Bank of St. Louis.

Table 2 shows estimates from economists at the CBO of the effectiveness of the stimulus package. The CBO is a nonpartisan organization, and many economists believe its estimates are reasonable. But because the estimates depend on particular assumptions about the size of the government purchases and tax multipliers, some economists believe that the CBO estimates are too high, while other economists believe the estimates are too low. To reflect the uncertainty in its calculation, the CBO provides a range of estimates. For example, in the absence of the stimulus package, the CBO estimates that in 2010 between 0.9 million and 4.7 million *fewer* people would have been employed than actually were and the unemployment rate would have been between 0.4 percent and 1.8 percent *higher* than it actually was. By 2013, the effects of the stimulus package were small, because several years had passed since most of the temporary spending increases and tax cuts had ended and because the economy had gradually moved back toward potential GDP.

If the CBO's estimates of the effects of the stimulus package are accurate, then this fiscal policy action reduced the severity of the recession of 2007–2009 and its aftermath. However, relative to the severity of the recession, the effect of the package was comparatively small. For example, in 2010, the unemployment rate was 9.6 percent, which was far above the unemployment rate of 4.6 percent in 2007. According to the CBO, without the stimulus package, the unemployment rate would have been somewhere between 10.0 percent and 11.4 percent. So, the stimulus package reduced the increase in the unemployment rate that might otherwise have occurred, but did not come close to bringing the economy back to full employment.

Table 2

CBO Estimates of the Effects of the Stimulus Package

Year	Change in Real GDP	Change in the Unemployment Rate	Change in Employment (millions of people)
2009	0.4% to 1.8%	−0.1% to −0.5%	0.3 to 1.3
2010	0.7% to 4.1%	−0.4% to −1.8%	0.9 to 4.7
2011	0.4% to 2.3%	−0.2% to −1.4%	0.6 to 3.6
2012	0.1% to 0.8%	−0.1% to −0.6%	0.2 to 1.3
2013	0.1% to 0.4%	0% to −0.3%	0.1 to 0.5

Source: Congressional Budget Office, "Estimated Impact of the American Recovery and Reinvestment Act on Employment and Economic Output from October 2012 through December 2012," February 2013.

Making the Connection

Why Was the Recession of 2007–2009 So Severe?

Even a stimulus package with $840 billion in increased government spending and tax cuts left the economy with real GDP far from potential GDP and the unemployment rate well above normal levels. Why was the recession of 2007–2009 so severe? The recession was accompanied by a financial crisis. The U.S. economy had not experienced a significant financial crisis since the Great Depression of the 1930s. Both the Great Depression and the recession of 2007–2009 were severe. Do recessions accompanied by financial crises tend to be more severe than recessions that do not involve financial crises?

The financial crisis made the recession of 2007–2009 more severe and long-lasting than many other recessions.

In an attempt to answer this question, Carmen Reinhart and Kenneth Rogoff of Harvard University have gathered data on recessions and financial crises in a number of countries. The following table shows the average change in key economic variables during the period following a financial crisis for a number of countries, including the United States during the Great Depression and European and Asian countries in the post–World War II era. The table shows that for these countries, on average, the recessions following financial crises were quite severe. Unemployment rates increased by 7 percentage points—for example, from 5 percent to 12 percent—and continued increasing for nearly five years after a crisis had begun. Real GDP per capita also declined sharply, and the average length of a recession following a financial crisis has been nearly two years. Adjusted for inflation, stock prices declined by more than half, and housing prices declined by more than one third. Government debt soared by 86 percent. The increased government debt was partly the result of increased government spending, including spending to bail out failed financial institutions. But most of the increased debt was the result of government budget deficits resulting from sharp declines in tax revenues as incomes, and profits fell as a result of the recession. (We discuss government budget deficits and government debt in the next section.)

Economic Variable	Average Change	Average Duration of Change	Number of Countries
Unemployment rate	+7 percentage points	4.8 years	14
Real GDP per capita	−9.3%	1.9 years	14
Real stock prices	−55.9%	3.4 years	22
Real house prices	−35.5%	6 years	21
Real government debt	+86%	3 years	13

The following table shows some key indicators for the 2007–2009 U.S. recession compared with other U.S. recessions of the post–World War II period:

	Duration	Decline in Real GDP	Peak Unemployment Rate
Average for postwar recessions	10.4 months	−1.7%	7.6%
Recession of 2007–2009	18 months	−4.1%	10.0%

Consistent with Reinhart and Rogoff's findings that recessions following financial panics tend to be unusually severe, the 2007–2009 recession was the worst in the United States since the Great Depression of the 1930s. The recession lasted nearly twice as long as the average of earlier postwar recessions, GDP declined by more than twice the average, and the peak unemployment rate was about one-third higher than the average.

Because most economists and policymakers did not see the financial crisis coming, they also failed to anticipate the severity of the 2007–2009 recession.

Note: In the second table, the duration of recessions is based on National Bureau of Economic Research business cycle dates, the decline in real GDP is measured as the simple percentage change from the quarter of the cyclical peak to the quarter of the cyclical trough, and the peak unemployment rate is the highest unemployment rate in any month following the cyclical peak.

Sources: The first table is adapted from data in Carmen M. Reinhart and Kenneth S. Rogoff, *This Time Is Different: Eight Centuries of Financial Folly*, Princeton, NJ: Princeton University Press, 2009, Figures 14.1–14.5; and the second table uses data from the U.S. Bureau of Economic Analysis and National Bureau of Economic Research.

Your Turn: Test your understanding by doing related problem 5.6 at the end of this chapter.

The Size of the Multiplier: A Key to Estimating the Effects of Fiscal Policy

In preparing the values shown in Table 2, the CBO relied on estimates of the government purchases and tax multipliers. Economists have been debating the size of these multipliers for many years. When British economist John Maynard Keynes and his followers first developed the idea of spending and tax multipliers in the 1930s, they argued that the government purchases multiplier might be as large as 10. In that case, a $1 billion increase in government purchases would increase real GDP by $10 billion. Later research by economists indicated that the government purchases multiplier was much smaller, perhaps less than 2.

Estimating an exact number for the multiplier is difficult because over time, several factors can cause the aggregate demand and short-run aggregate supply curves to shift, leading to a change in equilibrium real GDP. It can be challenging to isolate the effect of an increase in government purchases on equilibrium GDP. Before the stimulus package was proposed to Congress in 2009, economists in the Obama administration estimated the package's effect on GDP by using an average of multiplier estimates from the Federal Reserve and from a private macroeconomic forecasting firm. Their estimate that the government purchases multiplier was 1.57 means that a $1 billion increase in government purchases would increase equilibrium real GDP by $1.57 billion.

Because of the difficulty of estimating the size of the multiplier, some economists argue that the value economists in the Obama administration used was too high, while others argued that it was too low. Robert Barro of Harvard University maintains that increases in government spending during wartime are so large relative to other changes in aggregate demand that data from periods of war are best suited to estimating the size of the multiplier. Using such data, Barro estimated that the government purchases multiplier is only 0.8. Lawrence Christiano, Martin Eichenbaum, and Sergio Rebelo of Northwestern University argued, on the other hand, that the multiplier is likely to be larger when, as during 2009, short-term interest rates are near zero. They estimated that for these periods, the government purchases multiplier could be as large as 3.7.

As Table 3 shows, economists' estimates of the size of the multiplier vary widely. The uncertainty about the size of the multiplier indicates the difficulty that economists have in arriving at a firm estimate of the effects of fiscal policy.

6 LEARNING OBJECTIVE

Define federal budget deficit and federal government debt, and explain how the federal budget can serve as an automatic stabilizer.

Budget deficit The situation in which the government's expenditures are greater than its tax revenue.

Budget surplus The situation in which the government's expenditures are less than its tax revenue.

Deficits, Surpluses, and Federal Government Debt

The federal government's budget shows the relationship between its expenditures and its tax revenue. If the federal government's expenditures are greater than its tax revenue, a **budget deficit** results. If the federal government's expenditures are less than its tax revenue, a **budget surplus** results. As with many other macroeconomic variables, it is useful to consider the size of the surplus or deficit relative to the size of the overall economy. Figure 15 shows that, as a percentage of GDP, the largest deficits of the twentieth century came during World Wars I and II. During major wars, higher taxes only partially offset massive increases in government expenditures, leaving large budget deficits. Figure 15 also shows that during recessions government spending increases and tax revenues fall, increasing the budget deficit. In 1970, the federal government entered a long period of continuous budget deficits. From 1970 through 1997, the federal government's budget was in deficit every year. From 1998 through 2001, there were four years

Table 3 Estimates of the Size of the Multiplier

Economist Making the Estimate	Type of Multiplier	Size of Multiplier
Congressional Budget Office	Government purchases	0.5–2.5
Lawrence Christiano, Martin Eichenbaum, and Sergio Rebelo	Government purchases	1.05 (when short-term interest rates are not zero); 3.7 (when short-term interest rates are expected to be zero for at least five quarters)
Tommaso Monacelli, Roberto Perotti, and Antonella Trigari, Universita Bocconi	Government purchases	1.2 (after one year) and 1.5 (after two years)
Ethan Ilzetzki, London School of Economics, Enrique G. Mendoza, and Carlos A. Vegh, University of Maryland	Government purchases	0.8
Valerie Ramey, University of California, San Diego	Military expenditure	0.6–1.1
Robert J. Barro, Harvard University, and Charles J. Redlick, Bain Capital, LLC	Military expenditure	0.4–0.5 (after one year) and 0.6–0.7 (after two years)
John Cogan and John Taylor, Stanford University, and Tobias Cwik and Volker Wieland, Gothe University	A permanent increase in government expenditures	0.4
Christina Romer, University of California, Berkeley, and Jared Bernstein, chief economist and economic policy adviser to Vice President Joseph Biden	A permanent increase in government expenditures	1.6
Christina Romer (prior to serving as chair of the Council of Economic Advisers) and David Romer, University of California, Berkeley	Tax	2–3
Congressional Budget Office	Tax	0.3–1.5 (two-year tax cut for lower- and middle-income people); 0.1–0.6 (one-year tax cut for higher-income people)
Robert J. Barro, Harvard University, and Charles J. Redlick, Bain Capital, LLC	Tax	1.1

Note: The sources of these estimates are given on the.

of budget surpluses. The recessions of 2001 and 2007–2009, tax cuts, and increased government spending on homeland security and the wars in Iraq and Afghanistan helped keep the budget in deficit in the years after 2001.

Figure 15 also shows the effects on the federal budget deficit of the Obama administration's $840 billion stimulus package and the severity of the 2007–2009 recession.

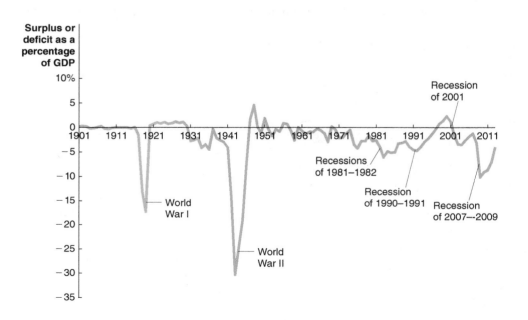

Figure 15

The Federal Budget Deficit, 1901–2013

During wars, government spending increases far more than tax revenues, increasing the budget deficit. The budget deficit also increases during recessions, as government spending increases and tax revenues fall.

Note: The value for 2013 is an estimate prepared by the Congressional Budget Office in May 2013.

Sources: *Budget of the United States Government, Fiscal Year 2003, Historical Tables,* Washington, DC: U.S. Government Printing Office, 2002; U.S. Bureau of Economic Analysis; and Congressional Budget Office.

From 2009 through 2011, the federal budget deficit was greater than 8 percent of GDP, which was the first time the deficit had been this large except during major wars in the history of the country. The economic recovery combined with tax increases and reductions in federal spending lowered the deficit to 4 percent of GDP in 2013.

How the Federal Budget Can Serve as an Automatic Stabilizer

Discretionary fiscal policy can increase the federal budget deficit during recessions by increasing spending or cutting taxes to increase aggregate demand. For example, as we have just seen, the Obama administration's spending increases and tax cuts significantly increased the federal budget deficit during 2009 and 2010. In many milder recessions, though, no significant fiscal policy actions are taken. In fact, most of the increase in the federal budget deficit during a typical recession takes place without Congress and the president taking any action, but is instead due to the effects of the *automatic stabilizers* we mentioned earlier in this chapter.

Deficits occur automatically during recessions for two reasons: First, during a recession, wages and profits fall, causing government tax revenues to fall. Second, the government automatically increases its spending on transfer payments when the economy moves into a recession. The federal government's contributions to the unemployment insurance program will increase as unemployment rises. Spending will also increase on programs to aid low-income people, such as the food stamp, Temporary Assistance for Needy Families, and Medicaid programs. These spending increases take place without Congress and the president taking any action. Existing laws already specify who is eligible for unemployment insurance and these other programs. As the number of eligible persons increases during a recession, so does government spending on these programs.

Because budget deficits automatically increase during recessions and decrease during expansions, economists often look at the *cyclically adjusted budget deficit or surplus*, which can provide a more accurate measure of the effects on the economy of the government's spending and tax policies than can the actual budget deficit or surplus. The **cyclically adjusted budget deficit or surplus** measures what the deficit or surplus would be if real GDP were at potential GDP. For example, in 2013, the CBO projected that the deficit in 2014 would be about 3.5 percent of GDP. The CBO estimated that if real GDP were at its potential level, the deficit would be about 1.0 percent of GDP, with the remaining 2.5 percent representing the effects of automatic stabilizers on the deficit. When the federal government runs an expansionary fiscal policy, the result is a cyclically adjusted budget deficit. When the federal government runs a contractionary fiscal policy, the result is a cyclically adjusted budget surplus.

Cyclically adjusted budget deficit or surplus The deficit or surplus in the federal government's budget if the economy were at potential GDP.

Automatic budget surpluses and deficits can help to stabilize the economy. When the economy moves into a recession, wages and profits fall, reducing the taxes that households and firms owe the government. In effect, households and firms have received an automatic tax cut that keeps their spending higher than it otherwise would have been. In a recession, workers who have been laid off receive unemployment insurance payments, and households whose incomes have fallen below a certain level become eligible for food stamps and other government transfer programs. By receiving this extra income, households are able to spend more than they otherwise would have spent. The extra spending helps reduce the length and severity of the recession. Many economists argue that the lack of an unemployment insurance system and other government transfer programs contributed to the severity of the Great Depression. During the Great Depression, workers who lost their jobs saw their wage income fall to zero and had to rely on their savings, what they could borrow, or what they received from private charities. As a result, many unemployed workers cut back drastically on their spending, which made the downturn worse.

When GDP increases above its potential level, households and firms have to pay more taxes to the federal government, and the federal government makes fewer transfer payments. Higher taxes and lower transfer payments cause total spending to rise by less than it otherwise would have, which helps reduce the chance that the economy will experience higher inflation.

Making the Connection

Did Fiscal Policy Fail during the Great Depression?

Modern macroeconomic analysis began during the 1930s, with the publication of *The General Theory of Employment, Interest, and Money* by John Maynard Keynes. One conclusion many economists drew from Keynes's book was that an expansionary fiscal policy would be necessary to pull the United States out of the Great Depression. When Franklin D. Roosevelt became president in 1933, federal government expenditures increased as part of his New Deal program, and there was a federal budget deficit during each remaining year of the decade, except for 1937. The U.S. economy recovered very slowly, however, and did not reach potential GDP again until the outbreak of World War II in 1941.

Although government spending increased during the Great Depression, the cyclically adjusted budget was in surplus most years.

Some economists and policymakers at the time argued that because the economy recovered slowly despite increases in government spending, fiscal policy had been ineffective. During the debate over President Obama's stimulus package, the argument that fiscal policy had failed during the New Deal was raised again. Economic historians have noted, however, that despite the increases in government spending, Congress and the president had not, in fact, implemented an expansionary fiscal policy during the 1930s. In separate studies, economists E. Cary Brown of MIT and Larry Peppers of Washington and Lee University argued that there was a cyclically adjusted budget deficit during only one year of the 1930s, and that one deficit was small. The following table provides data supporting their arguments. (All variables in the table are nominal rather than real.) The second column shows federal government expenditures increasing from 1933 to 1936, falling in 1937, and then increasing in 1938 and 1939. The third column shows a similar pattern, with the federal budget being in deficit each year after 1933 except for 1937. The fourth column, however, shows that in each year after 1933, the federal government ran a cyclically adjusted budget *surplus*. Because the level of income was so low and the unemployment rate was so high during these years, tax collections were far below what they would have been if the economy had been at potential GDP. As the fifth column shows, in 1933 and again from 1937 to 1939, the cyclically adjusted surpluses were large relative to GDP.

Year	Federal Government Expenditures (billions of dollars)	Actual Federal Budget Deficit or Surplus (billions of dollars)	Cyclically Adjusted Budget Deficit or Surplus (billions of dollars)	Cyclically Adjusted Budget Deficit or Surplus as a Percentage of GDP
1929	$2.6	$1.0	$1.24	1.20%
1930	2.7	0.2	0.81	0.89
1931	4.0	−2.1	−0.41	−0.54
1932	3.0	−1.3	0.50	0.85
1933	3.4	−0.9	1.06	1.88
1934	5.5	−2.2	0.09	0.14
1935	5.6	−1.9	0.54	0.74
1936	7.8	−3.2	0.47	0.56
1937	6.4	0.2	2.55	2.77
1938	7.3	−1.3	2.47	2.87
1939	8.4	−2.1	2.00	2.17

Although President Roosevelt proposed many new government spending programs, he had also promised during the 1932 presidential election campaign to balance the federal budget. He achieved a balanced budget only in 1937, but his reluctance to allow the actual budget deficit to grow too large helps explain why the cyclically adjusted budget remained in surplus. Many economists today would agree with E. Cary Brown's conclusion: "Fiscal policy, then, seems to have been an unsuccessful recovery device in the 'thirties—not because it did not work, but because it was not tried."

Sources: E. Cary Brown, "Fiscal Policy in the 'Thirties: A Reappraisal," *American Economic Review*, Vol. 46, No. 5, December 1956, pp. 857–879; and Larry Peppers, "Full Employment Surplus Analysis and Structural Changes," *Explorations in Economic History*, Vol. 10, Winter 1973, pp. 197–210; and U.S. Bureau of Economic Analysis.

Your Turn: Test your understanding by doing related problem 6.6 at the end of this chapter.

Solved Problem 6

The Effect of Economic Fluctuations on the Budget Deficit

The federal government's budget deficit was $379.5 billion in 2004 and $283.0 billion in 2005. A student comments: "The government must have acted during 2005 to raise taxes or cut spending or both." Do you agree? Briefly explain.

Solving the Problem

Step 1: **Review the chapter material.** This problem is about the federal budget as an automatic stabilizer, so you may want to review the section "How the Federal Budget Can Serve as an Automatic Stabilizer." is

Step 2: **Explain how changes in the budget deficit can occur without Congress and the president acting.** If Congress and the president take action to raise taxes or cut spending, the federal budget deficit will decline. But the deficit will also decline automatically when GDP increases, even if the government takes no action. When GDP increases, rising household incomes and firm profits result in higher tax revenues. Increasing GDP also usually means falling unemployment, which reduces government spending on unemployment insurance and other transfer payments. So, you should disagree with the comment. A falling deficit does not mean that the government *must* have acted to raise taxes or cut spending.

Extra Credit: Although you don't have to know it to answer the question, GDP did increase from $12.3 trillion in 2004 to $13.1 trillion in 2005.

MyEconLab Study Plan   **Your Turn:** For more practice, do related problem 6.8 at the end of this chapter.

Should the Federal Budget Always Be Balanced?

Although many economists believe that it is a good idea for the federal government to have a balanced budget when real GDP is at potential GDP, few economists believe that the federal government should attempt to balance its budget every year. To see why economists take this view, consider what the federal government would have to do to keep the budget balanced during a recession, when the budget automatically moves into deficit. To bring the budget back into balance, the government would have to raise taxes or cut spending, but these actions would reduce aggregate demand, thereby making the recession worse. Similarly, when GDP increases above its potential level, the budget automatically moves into surplus. To eliminate this surplus, the government would have to cut taxes or increase government spending. But these actions would increase aggregate demand, thereby pushing GDP further beyond potential GDP and increasing the risk of higher inflation. To balance the budget every year, the government might have to take actions that would destabilize the economy.

Some economists argue that the federal government should normally run a deficit, even at potential GDP. When the federal budget is in deficit, the U.S. Treasury sells bonds to investors to raise the funds necessary to pay the government's bills. Borrowing to pay the bills is a bad policy for a household, a firm, or the government when the bills are for current expenses, but it is not a bad policy if the bills are for long-lived capital goods. For instance, most families pay for a new home by taking out a 15- to 30-year mortgage. Because houses last many years, it makes sense to pay for a house out of the income the family makes over a long period of time rather than out of the income they receive in the year they bought the house. Businesses often borrow the funds to buy machinery, equipment, and factories by selling 30-year corporate bonds. Because these capital goods generate profits for the businesses over many years, it makes sense to pay for them over a period of years as well. By similar reasoning, when the federal government contributes to the building of a new highway, bridge, or subway, it may want to borrow funds by selling Treasury bonds. The alternative is to pay for these long-lived capital goods out of the tax revenues received in the year the goods were purchased. But that means that the taxpayers in that year have to bear the whole burden of paying for the projects, even though taxpayers for many years in the future will be enjoying the benefits.

The Federal Government Debt

Every time the federal government runs a budget deficit, the Treasury must borrow funds from investors by selling Treasury securities. For simplicity, we will refer to all Treasury securities as "bonds." When the federal government runs a budget surplus, the Treasury pays off some existing bonds. Figure 15 shows that there are many more years of federal budget deficits than years of federal budget surpluses. As a result, the total number of Treasury bonds outstanding has grown over the years. The total value of U.S. Treasury bonds outstanding is called the *federal government debt* or, sometimes, the *national debt*. Each year the federal budget is in deficit, the federal government debt grows. Each year the federal budget is in surplus, the debt shrinks.

Figure 16 shows federal government debt as a percentage of GDP in the years since 1901. The ratio of debt to GDP increased during World Wars I and II and the Great Depression, reflecting the large government budget deficits of those years. After the end of World War II, GDP grew faster than the debt until the early 1980s, which caused the ratio of debt to GDP to fall. The large budget deficits of the 1980s and early 1990s sent the debt-to-GDP ratio climbing. The budget surpluses of 1998 to 2001 caused the debt-to-GDP ratio to fall, but it rose again with the return of deficits beginning in 2002. The large deficits beginning in 2008 caused the ratio to spike up to its highest level since 1947.

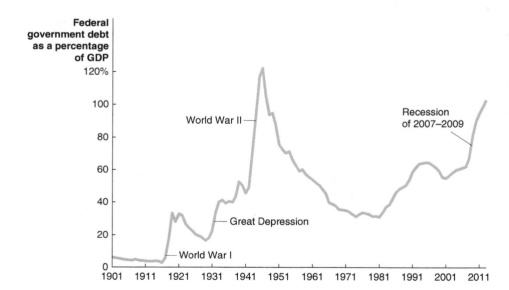

Figure 16

The Federal Government Debt, 1901–2013

The federal government debt increases whenever the federal government runs a budget deficit. The large deficits incurred during World Wars I and II, the Great Depression, and the 1980s and early 1990s increased the ratio of debt to GDP. The large deficits after 2008 caused the ratio to spike up to its highest level since 1947.
Note: The value for 2013 is an estimate prepared by the Congressional Budget Office in May 2013.
Sources: U.S. Bureau of the Census, *Historical Statistics of the United States, Colonial Times to 1970*, Washington, DC: U.S. Government Printing Office, 1975; Budget of the United States Government, Fiscal Year 2003, Historical Printing Office, 2002; Federal Reserve Bank of St. Louis; and Congressional Budget Office.

Is Government Debt a Problem?

Debt can be a problem for a government for the same reasons it can be a problem for a household or a business. If a family has difficulty making the monthly mortgage payment, it will have to cut back spending on other goods and services. If the family is unable to make the payments, it will have to *default* on the loan and will probably lose its house. The federal government is not in danger of defaulting on its debt. Ultimately, the government can raise the funds it needs through taxes to make the interest payments on the debt. If the debt becomes very large relative to the economy, however, the government may have to raise taxes to high levels or cut back on other types of spending to make the interest payments on the debt. Interest payments are currently about 11 percent of total federal expenditures. At this level, tax increases or significant cutbacks in other types of federal spending are not required.

In the long run, a debt that increases in size relative to GDP, as happened after 2008, can pose a problem. As we discussed previously, crowding out of investment spending may occur if an increasing debt drives up interest rates. Lower investment spending means a lower capital stock in the long run and a reduced capacity of the economy to produce goods and services. This effect is somewhat offset if some of the government debt was incurred to finance improvements in *infrastructure*, such as bridges, highways, and ports; to finance education; or to finance research and development. Improvements in infrastructure, a better-educated labor force, and additional research and development can add to the productive capacity of the economy.

The Effects of Fiscal Policy in the Long Run

Some fiscal policy actions are intended to meet the short-run goal of stabilizing the economy. Other fiscal policy actions are intended to have long-run effects by expanding the productive capacity of the economy and increasing the rate of economic growth. Because these policy actions primarily affect aggregate supply rather than aggregate demand, they are sometimes called *supply-side economics*. Most fiscal policy actions that attempt to increase aggregate supply do so by changing taxes to increase the incentives to work, save, invest, and start a business.

The Long-Run Effects of Tax Policy

Tax wedge The difference between the pretax and posttax return to an economic activity.

The difference between the pretax and posttax return to an economic activity is called the **tax wedge**. It is determined by the *marginal tax rate*, which is the fraction of each additional dollar of income that must be paid in taxes. For example, the U.S. federal income tax has several tax brackets, which are the income ranges within which a tax rate applies. In 2013, for a single taxpayer, the tax rate was 10 percent on the first $8,925 earned during a year. The tax rate rose for higher income brackets, until it reached 39.6 percent on income earned above $400,000. Suppose you are paid a wage of $20 per hour. If your marginal income tax rate is 25 percent, then your after-tax wage is $15, and the tax wedge is $5. Increasing the price of a good or service increases the quantity supplied. So, we would expect that reducing the tax wedge by cutting the marginal tax rate on income would result in a larger quantity of labor supplied because the after-tax wage would be higher. Similarly, a reduction in the income tax rate would increase the after-tax return to saving, causing an increase in the supply of loanable funds, a lower equilibrium interest rate, and an increase in investment spending. In general, economists believe that the smaller the tax wedge for any economic activity—such as working, saving, investing, or starting a business—the more of that economic activity that will occur. When workers, savers, investors, or entrepreneurs change their actions as a result of a tax change, economists say that there has been a *behavioral response* to the tax change.

We can look briefly at the effects on aggregate supply of cutting each of the following taxes:

- ***Individual income tax.*** As we have seen, reducing the marginal tax rates on individual income will reduce the tax wedge workers face, thereby increasing the quantity of labor supplied. Many small businesses are *sole proprietorships*, whose profits are taxed at the individual income tax rates. Therefore, cutting the individual income tax rates also raises the return to entrepreneurship, encouraging the opening of new businesses. Most households are taxed on their returns from saving at the individual income tax rates. Reducing marginal income tax rates, therefore, also increases the return to saving.

- **Corporate income tax.** The federal government taxes the profits corporations earn under the corporate income tax. In 2013, most corporations faced a marginal corporate tax rate of 35 percent. Cutting the marginal corporate income tax rate would encourage investment spending by increasing the return corporations receive from new investments in equipment, factories, and office buildings. Because innovations are often embodied in new investment goods, cutting the corporate income tax can potentially increase the pace of technological change.

- **Taxes on dividends and capital gains.** Corporations distribute some of their profits to shareholders in the form of payments known as *dividends*. Shareholders also may benefit from higher corporate profits by receiving *capital gains*. A capital gain is the increase in the price of an asset, such as a share of stock. Rising profits usually result in rising stock prices and capital gains to shareholders. Individuals pay taxes on both dividends and capital gains (although the tax on capital gains can be postponed if the stock is not sold). As a result, the same earnings are, in effect, taxed twice: once when a corporation pays the corporate income tax on its profits and a second time when individual investors receive the profits in the form of dividends or capital gains. Economists debate the costs and benefits of a separate tax on corporate profits. With the corporate income tax remaining in place, one way to reduce the "double taxation" problem is to reduce the tax rates on dividends and capital gains. These rates were reduced in 2003 before being increased in 2013. Generally, the marginal tax rates on dividends and capital gains are still below the top marginal tax rate on individual income. Lowering the tax rates on dividends and capital gains increases the supply of loanable funds from households to firms, increasing saving and investment and lowering the equilibrium real interest rate.

Tax Simplification

In addition to the potential gains from cutting individual taxes, there are also gains from tax simplification. The complexity of the tax code, which is 3,000 pages long, has created a whole industry of tax preparation services, such as H&R Block. The Internal Revenue Service estimates that taxpayers spend more than 6.4 billion hours each year filling out their tax forms, or about 45 hours per tax return. Households and firms have to deal with more than 480 tax forms to file their federal taxes. It is not surprising that there are more H&R Block offices around the country than Starbucks coffeehouses.

If the tax code were greatly simplified, the economic resources currently used by the tax preparation industry would be available to produce other goods and services. In addition to wasting resources, the complexity of the tax code may also distort the decisions households and firms make. For example, the tax rate on dividends has clearly affected whether corporations pay dividends. When Congress passed a reduction in the tax on dividends in 2003, many firms—including Microsoft—began paying dividends for the first time. A simplified tax code would increase economic efficiency by reducing the number of decisions households and firms make solely to reduce their tax payments.

The Economic Effect of Tax Reform

We can analyze the economic effects of tax reduction and simplification by using the aggregate demand and aggregate supply model. Figure 17 shows that without tax changes, the long-run aggregate supply curve will shift from $LRAS_1$ to $LRAS_2$. This shift represents the increases in the labor force and the capital stock and the technological change that would occur even without tax reduction and simplification. To focus on the effect of tax changes on aggregate supply, we will ignore any shifts in the short-run aggregate supply curve, and we will assume that the aggregate demand curve remains unchanged, at AD_1. In this case, equilibrium moves from point A to point B, with real GDP increasing from Y_1 to Y_2 and the price level decreasing from P_1 to P_2.

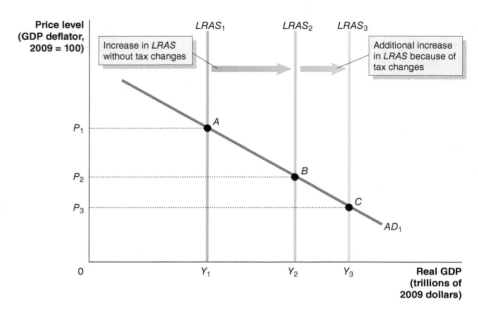

Figure 17

**The Supply-Side Effects
of a Tax Change**

The initial equilibrium is at point *A*. With
no tax change, the long-run aggregate supply curve shifts to the right, from *LRAS*₁ to
*LRAS*₂. Equilibrium moves to point *B*, with
the price level falling from *P*₁ to *P*₂ and real
GDP increasing from *Y*₁ to *Y*₂. With tax reductions and simplifications, the long-run
aggregate supply curve shifts further to the
right, to *LRAS*₃, and equilibrium moves to
point *C*, with the price level falling to *P*₃ and
real GDP increasing to *Y*₂.

If tax reduction and simplification are effective, the economy will experience increases in labor supply, saving, investment, and the formation of new firms. Economic
efficiency will also be improved. Together these factors will result in an increase in the
quantity of real GDP supplied at every price level. We show the effects of the tax changes
in Figure 17 by a shift in the long-run aggregate supply curve to $LRAS_3$. With aggregate
demand remaining unchanged, equilibrium moves from point A to point C (rather than
to point B, which is the equilibrium without tax changes), with real GDP increasing
from Y_1 to Y_3 and the price level decreasing from P_1 to P_3. Notice that compared with
the equilibrium without tax changes (point B), the equilibrium with tax changes (point
C) occurs at a lower price level and a higher level of real GDP. We can conclude that the
tax changes have benefited the economy by increasing output and employment while at
the same time reducing the price level.

Clearly, our analysis is unrealistic because we have ignored the changes that will
occur in aggregate demand and short-run aggregate supply. How would a more realistic
analysis differ from the simplified one in Figure 17? The change in real GDP would be
the same because in the long run, real GDP is equal to its potential level, which is represented by the *long-run aggregate supply* curve. The outcome for the price level would
be different, however, because we would expect both the aggregate demand curve and
the short-run aggregate supply curve to shift to the right. The likeliest outcome is that
the price level would end up higher in the new equilibrium than in the original equilibrium. However, because the position of the long-run aggregate supply curve is further
to the right as a result of the tax changes, the increase in the price level will be smaller;
that is, the price level at point C is likely to be lower than P_2, even if it is higher than P_3,
although—as we will discuss in the next section—not all economists would agree. We
can conclude that a successful policy of tax reductions and simplifications will benefit
the economy by increasing output and employment and, at the same time, may result in
smaller increases in the price level.

How Large Are Supply-Side Effects?

Most economists would agree that there are supply-side effects to reducing taxes: Decreasing marginal income tax rates will increase the quantity of labor supplied, cutting
the corporate income tax will increase investment spending, and so on. The magnitude
of the effects is the subject of considerable debate, however. For example, some economists argue that the increase in the quantity of labor supplied following a tax cut will
be limited because many people work a number of hours set by their employers and
lack the opportunity to work additional hours. Similarly, some economists believe that
tax changes have only a small effect on saving and investment. In this view, saving and
investment are affected much more by changes in income or changes in expectations

of the future profitability of new investment due to technological change or improving macroeconomic conditions than they are by changes in taxes.

Economists who are skeptical of the magnitude of supply-side effects believe that tax cuts have their greatest effect on aggregate demand rather than on aggregate supply. In their view, focusing on the effect of tax cuts on aggregate demand, while ignoring any effect on aggregate supply, yields accurate forecasts of future movements in real GDP and the price level, which indicates that the supply-side effects must be small. If tax changes have only small effects on aggregate supply, they are unlikely to reduce the size of price increases to the extent shown in Figure 17.

Ultimately, the debate over the size of the supply-side effects of tax policy can be resolved only through careful study of the effects of differences in tax rates on labor supply and on saving and investment decisions. Some recent studies have arrived at conflicting conclusions, however. For example, a study by Nobel Laureate Edward Prescott of Arizona State University concludes that the differences between the United States and Europe with respect to the average number of hours worked per week and the average number of weeks worked per year are due to differences in tax rates. The lower marginal tax rates in the United States compared with Europe increase the return to working for U.S. workers and result in a larger quantity of labor supplied. But another study by Alberto Alesina and Edward Glaeser of Harvard University and Bruce Sacerdote of Dartmouth College argues that the more restrictive labor market regulations in Europe explain the shorter work weeks and longer vacations of European workers and that differences in tax rates have only a small effect.

As in other areas of economics, differences among economists in their estimates of the supply-side effects of tax changes may narrow over time as they conduct more studies.

Continued

Economics in Your Life

What Would You Do with an Extra $500?

At the beginning of the chapter, we asked how you would respond to a $500 tax rebate and what effect this tax rebate would likely have on equilibrium real GDP in the short run. This chapter has shown that tax cuts increase disposable income and, therefore, consumption spending. So, you will likely respond to a permanent $500 increase in your disposable income by increasing your spending. How much your spending increases depends in part on your overall financial situation. As mentioned in the chapter, people who are able to borrow usually try to smooth out their spending over time and don't increase spending much in response to a one-time increase in their income. But if you are a student struggling to get by on a low income and you are unable to borrow against the higher income you expect to earn in the future, you may well spend most of the rebate. This chapter has also shown that tax cuts have a multiplier effect on the economy. That is, an increase in consumption spending sets off further increases in real GDP and income. So, if the economy is not already at potential GDP, this tax rebate will likely increase equilibrium real GDP in the short run.

Conclusion

In this chapter, we have seen how the federal government uses changes in government purchases and taxes to achieve its economic policy goals. We have seen that economists debate the effectiveness of discretionary fiscal policy actions intended to stabilize the economy. Congress and the president share responsibility for economic policy with the Federal Reserve.

Visit MyEconLab for a news article and analysis related to the concepts in this chapter.

Chapter Summary and Problems

Key Terms

Automatic stabilizers

Budget deficit

Budget surplus

Crowding out

Cyclically adjusted budget
deficit or surplus

Fiscal policy

Multiplier effect

Tax wedge

 What Is Fiscal Policy?

LEARNING OBJECTIVE: Define fiscal policy.

Summary

Fiscal policy involves changes in federal taxes and purchases that are intended to achieve macroeconomic policy goals. **Automatic stabilizers** are government spending and taxes that automatically increase or decrease along with the business cycle. Since World War II, the federal government's share of total government expenditures has been between two-thirds and three-quarters. Federal government *expenditures* as a percentage of GDP rose from 1950 to the early 1990s and fell between 1992 and 2001, before rising again. Federal government *purchases* have declined as a percentage of GDP since the end of the Korean War in the early 1950s. The largest component of federal expenditures is transfer payments. The largest sources of federal government revenue are individual income taxes, followed by social insurance taxes, which are used to fund the Social Security and Medicare systems.

Visit **www.myeconlab.com** to complete these exercises online and get instant feedback.

Review Questions

1.1 What is fiscal policy? Who is responsible for fiscal policy?

1.2 What is the difference between fiscal policy and monetary policy?

1.3 What is the difference between federal purchases and federal expenditures? Are federal purchases higher today as a percentage of GDP than they were in 1960? Are federal expenditures as a percentage of GDP higher?

Problems and Applications

1.4 In 2009, Congress and the president enacted "cash for clunkers" legislation that paid up to $4,500 to people buying new cars if they traded in an older, low-gas-mileage car. Was this legislation an example of fiscal policy? Does your answer depend on what goals Congress and the president had in mind when they enacted the legislation?

Source: Justin Lahart, "Trade-in Program Tunes Up Economic Engine," *Wall Street Journal*, August 4, 2009.

1.5 Briefly explain whether each of the following is an example of (1) a discretionary fiscal policy, (2) an automatic stabilizer, or (3) not a fiscal policy.

  a. The federal government increases spending on rebuilding the New Jersey shore following a hurricane.

  b. The Federal Reserve sells Treasury securities.

  c. The total the federal government pays out for unemployment insurance decreases during an expansion.

  d. The revenue the federal government collects from the individual income tax declines during a recession.

  e. The federal government changes the required gasoline mileage for new cars.

  f. Congress and the president enact a temporary cut in payroll taxes.

1.6 Based on the discussion in this chapter, which source of government revenue shown in Figure 4 do you think is likely to increase the most in the future? Briefly explain.

1.7 **[Related to the** Making the Connection**: Is Spending on Social Security and Medicare a Fiscal Time Bomb?]** According to a Congressional Budget Office (CBO) report:

> CBO projects that the population age 65 or older will increase by 87 percent between now and 2037, compared with an increase of just 12 percent over that period in the number of people ages 20 to 64. . . . CBO . . . estimates that, unless changes are made to Social Security, spending for the program will rise from 5.0 percent of GDP today to 6.2 percent by 2037.

Why is the over-65 population increasing so much more rapidly than other age groups? Is there a connection between the increases in the over-65 population and the projected increases in federal spending on Social Security as a percentage of GDP? Briefly explain.

Source: Congressional Budget Office, *The 2012 Long-Term Budget Outlook*, June 2012, p. 65.

2 The Effects of Fiscal Policy on Real GDP and the Price Level

LEARNING OBJECTIVE: Explain how fiscal policy affects aggregate demand and how the government can use fiscal policy to stabilize the economy.

Summary

To fight recessions, Congress and the president can increase government purchases or cut taxes. This expansionary policy increases aggregate demand, raising the level of real GDP and the price level. To fight rising inflation, Congress and the president can decrease government purchases or raise taxes. This contractionary policy reduces aggregate demand relative to what it would otherwise be, thereby reducing the inflation rate.

Visit www.myeconlab.com to complete these exercises online and get instant feedback.

Review Questions

2.1 What is an expansionary fiscal policy? What is a contractionary fiscal policy?

2.2 If Congress and the president decide that an expansionary fiscal policy is necessary, what changes should they make in government spending or taxes? What changes should they make if they decide that a contractionary fiscal policy is necessary?

Problems and Applications

2.3 Briefly explain whether you agree with the following statements: "An expansionary fiscal policy involves an increase in government purchases or an increase in taxes. A contractionary fiscal policy involves a decrease in government purchases or a decrease in taxes."

2.4 Identify each of the following as (1) part of an expansionary fiscal policy, (2) part of a contractionary fiscal policy, or (3) not part of fiscal policy.
   a. The corporate income tax rate is increased.
   b. Defense spending is increased.

   c. The Federal Reserve lowers the target for the federal funds rate.
   d. Families are allowed to deduct all their expenses for day care from their federal income taxes.
   e. The individual income tax rate is decreased.

2.5. Use an aggregate demand and aggregate supply graph to illustrate the situation where equilibrium initially occurs with real GDP equal to potential GDP, and then the aggregate demand curve shifts to the left. What actions can Congress and the president take to move real GDP back to potential GDP? Show the results of these actions on your graph.

2.6. **[Related to the** Don't Let This Happen to You**]** Is it possible for Congress and the president to carry out an expansionary fiscal policy if the money supply does not increase? Briefly explain.

2.7 A political commentator argues: "Congress and the president are more likely to enact an expansionary fiscal policy than a contractionary fiscal policy because expansionary policies are popular and contractionary policies are unpopular." Briefly explain whether you agree.

2.8 **[Related to the** Chapter Opener**]** We saw in the chapter opener that during 2013, Congress and President Obama were unable to reach an agreement to avoid the sequester, which involved a series of automatic cuts in federal government purchases. In testifying before Congress, then Federal Reserve Chairman Ben Bernanke said that the sequester "could create a significant headwind for the economic recovery."
   a. What did Bernanke mean by a "headwind"?
   b. Why would the sequester create a headwind for the economic recovery?

   Source: Binyamin Appelbaum, "Austerity Kills Government Jobs as Cuts to Budgets Loom," *New York Times*, February 26, 2013.

3 Fiscal Policy in the Dynamic Aggregate Demand and Aggregate Supply Model

LEARNING OBJECTIVE: Use the dynamic aggregate demand and aggregate supply model to analyze fiscal policy.

Summary

We can use the *dynamic aggregate demand and aggregate supply model* to look more closely at expansionary and contractionary fiscal policies. This model takes into account that: (1) The economy experiences continuing inflation, with the price level rising every year, and (2) the economy experiences long-run growth, with the *LRAS* curve shifting to the right every year. In the dynamic model, an expansionary fiscal policy tries to ensure that the aggregate demand curve will shift far enough to the right to bring about macroeconomic equilibrium with real GDP equal to potential GDP. A contractionary fiscal policy attempts to offset movements in aggregate demand that would cause macroeconomic equilibrium to occur at a level of real GDP that is greater than potential GDP.

Visit www.myeconlab.com to complete these exercises online and get instant feedback.

Review Questions

3.1 What are the key differences between how we illustrate an expansionary fiscal policy in the basic aggregate demand and aggregate supply model and in the dynamic aggregate demand and aggregate supply model?

3.2 What are the key differences between how we illustrate a contractionary fiscal policy in the basic aggregate demand and aggregate supply model and in the dynamic aggregate demand and aggregate supply model?

Problems and Applications

3.3 An article in the *Economist* states that the value of potential GDP "is almost impossible to pin down in real time since the economy's equilibrium long-run stock of capital and labour are so difficult to estimate with precision. . . ."

    a. What does the article mean by "real time"?

    b. What does the difficulty in estimating the "long-run stock of capital and labor" have to do with the difficulty of estimating the value of potential GDP in real time?

    c. Does the difficulty of estimating potential GDP matter for policymakers? Briefly explain.

    Source: "Remembering When the Future Kept Getting Bigger," *Economist*, May 24, 2012.

3.4 Use the graph to answer the following questions.

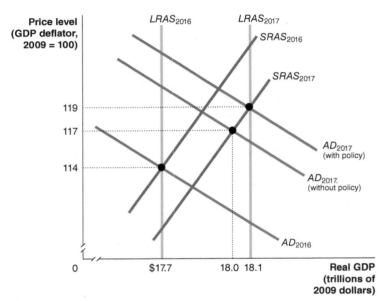

    a. If the government takes no policy actions, what will be the values of real GDP and the price level in 2017?

    b. What actions can the government take to bring real GDP to its potential level in 2017?

    c. If the government takes no policy actions, what will the inflation rate be in 2017? If the government uses fiscal policy to keep real GDP at its potential level, what will the inflation rate be in 2017?

3.5 The hypothetical information in the following table shows what the situation will be in 2017 if Congress and the President do *not* use fiscal policy:

Year	Potential GDP	Real GDP	Price Level
2016	$17.8 trillion	$17.8 trillion	113.7
2017	$18.2 trillion	$17.8 trillion	115.9

    a. If Congress and the president want to keep real GDP at its potential level in 2017, should they use an expansionary policy or a contractionary policy? In your answer, be sure to explain whether Congress and the president should increase or decrease government purchases and taxes.

    b. If Congress and the president are successful in keeping real GDP at its potential level in 2017, state whether each of the following will be higher, lower, or the same as it would have been if they had taken no action:

      i. Real GDP

      ii. Potential GDP

      iii. The inflation rate

      iv. The unemployment rate

    c. Draw an aggregate demand and aggregate supply graph to illustrate your answer. Be sure that your graph contains *LRAS* curves for 2016 and 2017; *SRAS* curves for 2016 and 2017; *AD* curves for 2016 and 2017, with and without fiscal policy action; and equilibrium real GDP and the price level in 2017, with and without fiscal policy.

3.6 Use a dynamic aggregate demand and aggregate supply graph to illustrate the change in macroeconomic equilibrium from 2017 to 2018, assuming that the economy experiences deflation during 2018. In order for deflation to take place in 2018, does the economy also have to be experiencing a recession? Briefly explain.

---

4 | ## The Government Purchases and Tax Multipliers

LEARNING OBJECTIVE: Explain how the government purchases and tax multipliers work.

Summary

Because of the **multiplier effect**, an increase in government purchases or a cut in taxes will have a multiplied effect on equilibrium real GDP. The *government purchases multiplier* is equal to the change in equilibrium real GDP divided by the change in government purchases. The *tax multiplier* is equal to the change in equilibrium real GDP divided by the change in taxes. Increases in government purchases and cuts in taxes have a positive multiplier effect on equilibrium real GDP. Decreases in government purchases and increases in taxes have a negative multiplier effect on equilibrium real GDP.

Review Questions

4.1 Why can a $1 increase in government purchases lead to more than a $1 increase in income and spending?

4.2 Define the *government purchases multiplier* and the *tax multiplier*.

4.3 Why does a higher income tax rate reduce the multiplier effect?

Problems and Applications

4.4 **[Related to the** Chapter Opener**]** Why would the Caldecott Tunnel in Northern California and similar construction projects elsewhere in the country be expected to help the economy in the short run? A spokesperson for the California state agency in charge of

Visit **www.myeconlab.com** to complete these exercises online and get instant feedback.

336

the project mentioned that the Caldecott Tunnel project would have a "ripple effect" on employment. What does the spokesperson mean by a ripple effect?

4.5 In *The General Theory of Employment, Interest, and Money*, John Maynard Keynes wrote:

> If the Treasury were to fill old bottles with banknotes, bury them at suitable depths in disused coal mines which are then filled up to the surface with town rubbish, and leave it to private enterprise . . . to dig the notes up again . . . there need be no more unemployment and, with the help of the repercussions, the real income of the community ... would probably become a good deal greater than it is.

Which important macroeconomic effect is Keynes discussing here? What does he mean by "repercussions"? Why does he appear unconcerned about whether government spending is wasteful?

4.6 **[Related to** Solved Problem 4**]** Suppose that real GDP is currently $17.1 trillion, potential GDP is $17.4 trillion, the government purchases multiplier is 2, and the tax multiplier is −1.6.

    a. Holding other factors constant, by how much will government purchases need to be increased to bring the economy to equilibrium at potential GDP?

    b. Holding other factors constant, by how much will taxes have to be cut to bring the economy to equilibrium at potential GDP?

    c. Construct an example of a *combination* of increased government spending and tax cuts that will bring the economy to equilibrium at potential GDP.

4.7 **[Related to** Solved Problem 4**]** Briefly explain whether you agree with the following statement:

> Real GDP is currently $17.7 trillion, and potential GDP is $17.4 trillion. If Congress and the president would decrease government purchases by $300 billion or increase taxes by $300 billion, the economy could be brought to equilibrium at potential GDP.

4.8 A Federal Reserve publication discusses an estimate of the tax multiplier that gives it a value of 1.2 after one year and 2.8 after two years. Briefly explain why the tax multiplier might have a larger value after two years than after one year.

Source: Sylvain Leduc, "Fighting Downturns with Fiscal Policy," Federal Reserve Bank of San Francisco *Economic Letter*, June 19, 2009.

4.9 If the short-run aggregate supply (*SRAS*) curve were a horizontal line at the current price level, what would be the effect on the size of the government purchases and tax multipliers? Briefly explain.

---

5 | The Limits of Using Fiscal Policy to Stabilize the Economy

LEARNING OBJECTIVE: Discuss the difficulties that can arise in implementing fiscal policy.

Summary

Poorly timed fiscal policy can do more harm than good. Getting the timing right with fiscal policy can be difficult because for a president to obtain approval from Congress for a new fiscal policy can be a very long process and because it can take months for an increase in authorized spending to actually take place. Because an increase in government purchases may lead to a higher interest rate, it may result in a decline in consumption, investment, and net exports. A decline in private expenditures as a result of an increase in government purchases is called **crowding out**. Crowding out may cause an expansionary fiscal policy to fail to meet its goal of keeping real GDP at potential GDP.

Visit **www.myeconlab.com** to complete these exercises online and get instant feedback.

Review Questions

5.1 Which can be changed more quickly: monetary policy or fiscal policy? Briefly explain.

5.2 What is meant by "crowding out"? Explain the difference between crowding out in the short run and in the long run.

Problems and Applications

5.3 Some economists argue that because increases in government spending crowd out private spending, increased government spending will reduce the long-run growth rate of real GDP.

    a. Is this outcome most likely to occur if the private spending being crowded out is consumption spending, investment spending, or net exports? Briefly explain.

    b. In terms of its effect on the long-run growth rate of real GDP, would it matter if the additional government spending involves (i) increased spending on highways and bridges or (ii) increased spending on national parks? Briefly explain.

5.4 An article in the *Economist* argued that "heavy public debt risks more than just crowding out private investment. It can, in the extreme, bring on insolvency." What does the article mean by "heavy public debts"? How might heavy public debts lead to insolvency?

Source: "Running Out of Road," *Economist*, June 16, 2011.

5.5 We saw that in calculating the stimulus package's effect on real GDP, economists in the Obama administration estimated that the government purchases multiplier has a value of 1.57. John F. Cogan, Tobias Cwik, John B. Taylor, and Volker Wieland argue that the value is only 0.4.

    a. Briefly explain how the government purchases multiplier can have a value of less than 1.

    b. Why does an estimate of the size of the multiplier matter in evaluating the effects of an expansionary fiscal policy?

Source: John Cogan, Tobias Cwik, John Taylor, and Volker Wieland, "New Keynesian versus Old Keynesian Government Spending Multipliers," *Journal of Economic Dynamics and Control*, Vol. 34, No. 3, March 2010, pp. 281–295.

5.6 **[Related to the** Making the Connection: **Why Was the Recession of 2007–2009 So Severe?]** Why would a recession accompanied by a financial crisis be more severe than a recession that did not involve a financial crisis? Were the large budget deficits in 2009 and 2010 primarily the result of the stimulus package of 2009? Briefly explain.

5.7 Suppose that at the same time Congress and the president pursue an expansionary fiscal policy, the Federal Reserve pursues an expansionary monetary policy. How might an expansionary monetary policy affect the extent of crowding out in the short run?

 ## 6 Deficits, Surpluses, and Federal Government Debt

LEARNING OBJECTIVE: Define federal budget deficit and federal government debt, and explain how the federal budget can serve as an automatic stabilizer.

Summary

A **budget deficit** occurs when the federal government's expenditures are greater than its tax revenues. A **budget surplus** occurs when the federal government's expenditures are less than its tax revenues. A budget deficit automatically increases during recessions and decreases during expansions. The automatic movements in the federal budget help to stabilize the economy by cushioning the fall in spending during recessions and restraining the increase in spending during expansions. The **cyclically adjusted budget deficit or surplus** measures what the deficit or surplus would be if the economy were at potential GDP. The federal government debt (or national debt) is the value of outstanding bonds issued by the U.S. Treasury. The national debt is a problem if interest payments on it require taxes to be raised substantially or require other federal expenditures to be cut.

Visit **www.myeconlab.com** to complete these exercises online and get instant feedback.

Review Questions

6.1 In what ways does the federal budget serve as an automatic stabilizer for the economy?

6.2 What is the cyclically adjusted budget deficit or surplus? Suppose that real GDP is currently at potential GDP, and the federal budget is balanced. If the economy moves into a recession, what will happen to the federal budget?

6.3 Why do few economists believe it would be a good idea to balance the federal budget every year?

6.4 What is the difference between the federal budget deficit and federal government debt?

Problems and Applications

6.5 In a column in the *Financial Times*, the prime minister and the finance minister of the Netherlands argue that the European Union, an organization of 28 countries in Europe, should appoint "a commissioner for budgetary discipline." They believe that: "The new commissioner should be given clear powers to set requirements for the budgetary policy of countries that run excessive deficits." What is an "excessive" budget deficit? Does judging whether a deficit is excessive depend in part on whether the country is in a recession? How can budgetary policies be used to reduce a budget deficit?

Source: Mark Rutte and Jan Kees de Jager, "Expulsion from the Eurozone Has to Be the Final Penalty," *Financial Times*, September 7, 2011.

6.6 **[Related to the** Making the Connection: **Did Fiscal Policy Fail during the Great Depression?]** The following is from a message by President Hoover to Congress, dated May 5, 1932:

I need not recount that the revenues of the Government as estimated for the next fiscal year show a decrease of about $1,700,000,000 below the fiscal year 1929, and inexorably require a broader basis of taxation and a drastic reduction of expenditures in order to balance the Budget. Nothing is more necessary at this time than balancing the Budget.

Do you think President Hoover was correct in saying that, in 1932, nothing was more necessary than balancing the federal government's budget? Explain.

6.7 In February 2013, the Congressional Budget Office (CBO) forecast that the federal budget deficit for fiscal year 2013 would be approximately $850 billion. In May 2013, the CBO revised down its forecast of the budget deficit to $642 billion. The CBO stated that a major reason for the downward revision was "factors related mainly to the strengthening economy."

a. Why would a "strengthening economy" lead to a downward revision of the projected budget deficit?

b. Suppose that Congress and the president were committed to balancing the budget each year. Does what happened during 2013 provide any insight into difficulties they might run into in trying to balance the budget every year?

Source: Susan Davis, "CBO Drops 2013 Deficit Estimate to $642 Billion," usatoday.com, May 15, 2013.

6.8 **[Related to** Solved Problem 6**]** The federal government's budget surplus was $236.2 billion in 2000 and $128.2 billion in 2001. What does this information tell us about fiscal policy actions that Congress and the president took during those years?

6.9 An editorial in the *Wall Street Journal* states: "We don't put much stock in future budget forecasts because they depend on so many variables." What variables would a forecast of future federal budget deficits depend on? Why do these variables make future budget deficits difficult to predict?

Source: "Fiscal Revelation," *Wall Street Journal*, February 6, 2007.

6.10 In 2013, Japan's government debt was approaching 250 percent of GDP, more than twice as high as in the United States. An article in the *Economist* noted that "the sheer size of the debt weighs ever more heavily." What would government debt be weighing heavily on?

Source: "Don't Mention the Debt," *Economist*, May 4, 2013.

6.11 A political columnist wrote the following:

Today … the main purpose [of government's issuing bonds] is to let craven politicians launch projects they know the public, at the moment, would rather not fully finance. The tab for these projects will not come due, probably, until after the politicians have long since departed for greener (excuse the expression) pastures.

Do you agree with this commentator's explanation for why some government spending is financed through tax receipts and other government spending is financed through borrowing, by issuing bonds? Briefly explain.

Source: Paul Carpenter, "The Bond Issue Won't Be Repaid by Park Tolls," (Allentown, PA) *Morning Call*, May 26, 2002.

7 | The Effects of Fiscal Policy in the Long Run

LEARNING OBJECTIVE: Discuss the effects of fiscal policy in the long run.

Summary

Some fiscal policy actions are intended to have long-run effects by expanding the productive capacity of the economy and increasing the rate of economic growth. Because these policy actions primarily affect aggregate supply rather than aggregate demand, they are sometimes called *supply-side economics*. The difference between the pretax and posttax return to an economic activity is called the **tax wedge**. Economists believe that the smaller the tax wedge for any economic activity—such as working, saving, investing, or starting a business—the more of that economic activity will occur. Economists debate the size of the supply-side effects of tax changes.

Visit **www.myeconlab.com** to complete these exercises online and get instant feedback.

Review Questions

7.1 What is meant by "supply-side economics"?

7.2 What is the "tax wedge"?

Problems and Applications

7.3 It seems that both households and businesses would benefit if the federal income tax were simpler and tax forms were easier to fill out. Why then have the tax laws become increasingly complicated?

7.4 Some economists and policymakers have argued in favor of a "flat tax." A flat tax would replace the current individual income tax system, with its many tax brackets, exemptions, and deductions, with a new system containing a single tax rate and few, or perhaps no, deductions and exemptions. Suppose a political candidate hired you to develop two arguments in favor of a flat tax. What two arguments would you advance? Alternatively, if you were hired to develop two arguments against a flat tax, what two arguments would you advance?

7.5 Suppose that an increase in marginal tax rates on individual income affects both aggregate demand and aggregate supply. Briefly describe the effect of the tax increase on equilibrium real GDP and the equilibrium price level. Will the changes in equilibrium real GDP and the price level be larger or smaller than they would be if the tax increase affected only aggregate demand? Briefly explain.

7.6 Writing in the *Wall Street Journal*, Martin Feldstein, an economist at Harvard University, argues that "behavioral responses" of taxpayers to the cuts in marginal tax rates enacted in 1986 resulted in "an enormous rise in the taxes paid, particularly by those who experienced the greatest reductions in marginal tax rates." How is it possible for cuts in marginal tax rates to result in an increase in total taxes collected? What does Feldstein mean by a "behavioral response" to tax cuts?

Source: Martin Feldstein, "The Tax Reform Evidence from 1986," *Wall Street Journal*, October 24, 2011.

Real-Time Data Exercises

D1 **[Comparing macroeconomic conditions in different countries.]** The International Monetary Fund (IMF) publishes *The World Economic Outlook*. Go to www.imf.org and look at the most recent version available. The IMF measures the output gap as the difference between real GDP and potential GDP as a percentage of potential GDP. A negative value for the output gap means that real GDP is below potential GDP. Look at the data on the output gap for Japan, the United Kingdom, and the United States for 2013 to 2018 (the values for the later years will be forecasts).

   a. Which country had the largest output gap (in absolute value) in 2013? Which country had the smallest output gap?

   b. Discuss what fiscal policies the governments of these countries could use to bring the output gaps to zero.

   c. Describe at least two problems that these countries would have in implementing your suggested policies.

D2 **[Comparing the actual and cyclically adjusted budget deficits in the United States.]** The Congressional Budget Office (CBO) provides data on the actual and cyclically adjusted budget deficits. You can find data for the years 1961–2012 using this link: www.cbo.gov/publication/43999. Once on that page, click on the link on the left "Tables to Accompany the 2013 Automatic Stabilizers Report" and download the Excel file.

   a. The budget deficit or surplus is called "Deficit or Surplus with Automatic Stabilizers" and the cyclically adjusted deficit or surplus is called "Deficit or Surplus without Automatic Stabilizers." Briefly explain why the CBO uses these labels.

   b. Graph the budget deficit or surplus and the cyclically adjusted deficit or surplus for these years.

   c. Calculate the average surplus or deficit and the average cyclically adjusted surplus or deficit for these years. Which was larger? Briefly explain your result.

D3 **[Comparing budget deficits in different countries.]** The International Monetary Fund (IMF) publishes *The World Economic Outlook*. Go to www.imf.org and find the IMF data for the cyclically adjusted budget deficit (which the IMF calls "General Government Structural Balance") for Brazil, China, France, and Germany from 2000 to 2018 (the values for the later years will be forecasts). Use the series for the cyclically adjusted budget deficit that is measured as a percentage of potential GDP.

   a. Download the data and plot it in a graph. Which country relied the most on discretionary fiscal policy in response to the financial crisis of 2008 and 2009? Briefly explain how you are able to tell.

   b. From 2013 to 2018, which of these four countries is expected to have the most expansionary fiscal policy? Briefly explain.

Appendix

A Closer Look at the Multiplier

In this chapter, we saw that changes in government purchases and changes in taxes have a multiplied effect on equilibrium real GDP. In this appendix, we will build a simple economic model of the multiplier effect. When economists forecast the effect of a change in spending or taxes, they often rely on *econometric models*. These are economic models written in the form of equations, where each equation has been statistically estimated.

An Expression for Equilibrium Real GDP

We can write a set of equations that includes the key macroeconomic relationships we have studied in this chapter. It is important to note that in this model, we will be assuming that the price level is constant. We know that this assumption is unrealistic because an upward-sloping *SRAS* curve means that when the aggregate demand curve shifts, the price level will change. Nevertheless, our model will be approximately correct when changes in the price level are small. It also serves as an introduction to more complicated models that take into account changes in the price level. For simplicity, we start with three assumptions: (1) that taxes, *T*, do not depend on the level of real GDP, *Y*; (2) that there are no government transfer payments to households; and (3) that we have a closed economy, with no imports or exports. The numbers (with the exception of the *MPC*) represent billions of dollars:

(1) $C = 1{,}000 + 0.75(Y - T)$	Consumption function
(2) $I = 1{,}500$	Planned investment function
(3) $G = 1{,}500$	Government purchases function
(4) $T = 1{,}000$	Tax function
(5) $Y = C + I + G$	Equilibrium condition

The first equation is the consumption function. The marginal propensity to consume, or *MPC*, is 0.75, and 1,000 is the level of autonomous consumption, which is the level of consumption that does not depend on income. We assume that consumption depends on disposable income, which is $Y - T$. The functions for planned investment spending, government spending, and taxes are very simple because we have assumed that these variables are not affected by GDP and, therefore, are constant. Economists who use this type of model to forecast GDP would, of course, use more realistic planned investment, government purchases, and tax functions.

Equation (5)—the equilibrium condition—states that equilibrium GDP equals the sum of consumption, planned investment spending, and government purchases. To calculate a value for equilibrium real GDP, we need to substitute equations (1) through (4) into equation (5). This substitution gives us the following:

$$Y = 1{,}000 + 0.75(Y - 1{,}000) + 1{,}500 + 1{,}500$$
$$= 1{,}000 + 0.75Y - 750 + 1{,}500 + 1{,}500.$$

We need to solve this equation for *Y* to find equilibrium GDP. The first step is to subtract $0.75Y$ from both sides of the equation:

$$Y - 0.75Y = 1{,}000 - 750 + 1{,}500 + 1{,}500.$$

Then, we solve for Y:

$$0.25Y = 3,250,$$

or

$$Y = \frac{3,250}{0.25} = 13,000.$$

To make this result more general, we can replace particular values with general values represented by letters:

$C = \overline{C} + MPC(Y - T)$	Consumption function
$I = \overline{I}$	Planned investment function
$G = \overline{G}$	Government purchases function
$T = \overline{T}$	Tax function
$Y = C + I + G$	Equilibrium condition

The letters with bars above them represent fixed, or *autonomous*, values that do not depend on the values of other variables. So, $\overline{C}$ represents autonomous consumption, which had a value of 1,000 in our original example. Now, solving for equilibrium, we get:

$$Y = \overline{C} + MPC(Y - \overline{T}) + \overline{I} + \overline{G}$$

or

$$Y - MPC(Y) = \overline{C} - (MPC \times \overline{T}) + \overline{I} + \overline{G}$$

or

$$Y(1 - MPC) = \overline{C} - (MPC \times \overline{T}) + \overline{I} + \overline{G}$$

or

$$Y = \frac{\overline{C} - (MPC \times \overline{T}) + \overline{I} + \overline{G}}{1 - MPC}.$$

A Formula for the Government Purchases Multiplier

To find a formula for the government purchases multiplier, we need to rewrite the last equation for changes in each variable rather than levels. Letting Δ stand for the change in a variable, we have

$$\Delta Y = \frac{\Delta \overline{C} - (MPC \times \Delta \overline{T}) + \Delta \overline{I} + \Delta \overline{G}}{1 - MPC}.$$

We can find a formula for the government purchases multiplier, which is the ratio of the change in equilibrium real GDP to the change in government purchases. If we hold constant changes in autonomous consumption spending, planned investment spending, and taxes, then from the previous equation we have the following:

$$\Delta Y = \frac{\Delta G}{1 - MPC}.$$

So, we have:

$$\text{Government purchases multiplier} = \frac{\Delta Y}{\Delta G} = \frac{1}{1 - MPC}.$$

For an MPC of 0.75, the government purchases multiplier will be:

$$\frac{1}{1 - 0.75} = 4.$$

A government purchases multiplier of 4 means that an increase in government spending of $10 billion will increase equilibrium real GDP by $4 \times \$10$ billion $= \$40$ billion.

A Formula for the Tax Multiplier

We can also find a formula for the tax multiplier. We start again with this equation:

$$\Delta Y = \frac{\Delta \overline{C} - (MPC \times \Delta \overline{T}) + \Delta \overline{I} + \Delta \overline{G}}{1 - MPC}.$$

Now we hold constant the values of autonomous consumption spending, planned investment spending, and government purchases, but we allow the value of taxes to change:

$$\Delta Y = \frac{-MPC \times \Delta T}{1 - MPC}.$$

So, we have:

$$\text{The tax multiplier} = \frac{\Delta Y}{\Delta T} = \frac{-MPC}{1 - MPC}.$$

For an MPC of 0.75, the tax multiplier will be:

$$\frac{-0.75}{1 - 0.75} = -3.$$

The tax multiplier is a negative number because an increase in taxes causes a decrease in equilibrium real GDP, and a decrease in taxes causes an increase in equilibrium real GDP. A tax multiplier of -3 means that a decrease in taxes of \$10 billion will increase equilibrium real GDP by $-3 \times -\$10$ billion = \$30 billion. Earlier in this chapter, we discussed the economic reasons for the tax multiplier being smaller than the government spending multiplier.

The "Balanced Budget" Multiplier

What will be the effect of equal increases (or decreases) in government purchases and taxes on equilibrium real GDP? At first, it might appear that the tax increase would exactly offset the government purchases increase, leaving real GDP unchanged. But we have just seen that the government purchases multiplier is larger (in absolute value) than the tax multiplier. We can use our formulas for the government purchases multiplier and the tax multiplier to calculate the net effect of increasing government purchases by \$10 billion at the same time that taxes are increased by \$10 billion:

Increase in real GDP from the increase in government purchases

$$= \$10 \text{ billion} \times \frac{1}{1 - MPC}.$$

Decrease in real GDP from the increase in taxes $= \$10 \text{ billion} \times \frac{-MPC}{1 - MPC}.$

So, the combined effect equals:

$$\$10 \text{ billion} \times \left[\left(\frac{1}{1 - MPC} \right) + \left(\frac{-MPC}{1 - MPC} \right) \right],$$

or

$$\$10 \text{ billion} \times \left(\frac{1 - MPC}{1 - MPC} \right) = \$10 \text{ billion}.$$

The balanced budget multiplier is, therefore, equal to $(1 - MPC)/(1 - MPC)$, or 1. Equal dollar increases and decreases in government purchases and in taxes lead to the same dollar increase in real GDP in the short run.

The Effects of Changes in Tax Rates on the Multiplier

We now consider the effect of a change in the tax *rate*, as opposed to a change in a fixed amount of taxes. Changing the tax rate actually changes the value of the multiplier.

To see this, suppose that the tax rate is 20 percent, or 0.2. In that case, an increase in household income of $10 billion will increase *disposable income* by only $8 billion [or 10 billion $\times$ $(1 - 0.2)$]. In general, an increase in income can be multiplied by $(1 - t)$ to find the increase in disposable income, where t is the tax rate. So, we can rewrite the consumption function as:

$$C = \overline{C} + MPC(1 - t)Y.$$

We can use this expression for the consumption function to find an expression for the government purchases multiplier, using the same method we used previously:

$$\text{Government purchases multiplier} = \frac{\Delta Y}{\Delta G} = \frac{1}{1 - MPC(1 - t)}.$$

We can see the effect of changing the tax rate on the size of the multiplier by trying some values. First, assume that $MPC = 0.75$ and $t = 0.2$. Then:

$$\text{Government purchases multiplier} = \frac{\Delta Y}{\Delta G} = \frac{1}{1 - 0.75(1 - 0.2)} = \frac{1}{1 - 0.6} = 2.5.$$

This value is smaller than the multiplier of 4 that we calculated by assuming that there was only a fixed amount of taxes (which is the same as assuming that the marginal tax *rate* was zero). This multiplier is smaller because spending in each period is now reduced by the amount of taxes households must pay on any additional income they earn. We can calculate the multiplier for an MPC of 0.75 and a lower tax rate of 0.1:

$$\text{Government purchases multiplier} = \frac{\Delta Y}{\Delta G} = \frac{1}{1 - 0.75(1 - 0.1)} = \frac{1}{1 - 0.675} = 3.1.$$

Cutting the tax rate from 20 percent to 10 percent increased the value of the multiplier from 2.5 to 3.1.

The Multiplier in an Open Economy

Up to now, we have assumed that the economy is closed, with no imports or exports. We can consider the case of an open economy by including net exports in our analysis. Net exports equal exports minus imports. Exports are determined primarily by factors—such as the exchange value of the dollar and the levels of real GDP in other countries—that we do not include in our model. So, we will assume that exports are fixed, or autonomous:

$$\text{Exports} = \overline{\text{Exports}}.$$

Imports will increase as real GDP increases because households will spend some portion of an increase in income on imports. We can define the *marginal propensity to import (MPI)* as the fraction of an increase in income that is spent on imports. So, our expression for imports is

$$\text{Imports} = MPI \times Y.$$

We can substitute our expressions for exports and imports into the expression we derived earlier for equilibrium real GDP:

$$Y = \overline{C} + MPC(1 - t)Y + \overline{I} + \overline{G} + [\overline{\text{Exports}} - (MPI \times Y)],$$

where the expression $[\overline{\text{Exports}} - (MPI \times Y)]$ represents net exports. We can now find an expression for the government purchases multiplier by using the same method we used previously:

$$\text{Government purchases multiplier} = \frac{\Delta Y}{\Delta G} = \frac{1}{1 - [MPC(1 - t) - MPI]}.$$

We can see the effect of changing the value of the marginal propensity to import on the size of the multiplier by trying some values of key variables. First, assume that $MPC = 0.75$, $t = 0.2$, and $MPI = 0.1$. Then:

$$\text{Government purchases multiplier} = \frac{\Delta Y}{\Delta G} = \frac{1}{1 - (0.75(1 - 0.2) - 0.1)} = \frac{1}{1 - 0.5}$$
$$= 2.$$

This value is smaller than the multiplier of 2.5 that we calculated by assuming that there were no exports or imports (which is the same as assuming that the marginal propensity to import was zero). This multiplier is smaller because spending in each period is now reduced by the amount of imports households buy with any additional income they earn. We can calculate the multiplier with $MPC = 0.75$, $t = 0.2$, and a higher MPI of 0.2:

$$\text{Government purchases multiplier} = \frac{\Delta Y}{\Delta G} = \frac{1}{1 - (0.75(1 - 0.2) - 0.2)} = \frac{1}{1 - 0.4}$$
$$= 1.7.$$

Increasing the marginal propensity to import from 0.1 to 0.2 decreases the value of the multiplier from 2 to 1.7. We can conclude that countries with a higher marginal propensity to import will have smaller multipliers than countries with a lower marginal propensity to import.

Bear in mind that the multiplier is a short-run effect that assumes that real GDP is less than potential GDP. In the long run, real GDP equals potential GDP, so an increase in government purchases causes a decline in the nongovernment components of real GDP but leaves the level of real GDP unchanged.

The analysis in this appendix is simplified compared to what would be carried out by an economist forecasting the effects of changes in government purchases or changes in taxes on equilibrium real GDP in the short run. In particular, our assumption that the price level is constant is unrealistic. However, looking more closely at the determinants of the multiplier has helped us see more clearly some important macroeconomic relationships.

A Closer Look at the Multiplier

LEARNING OBJECTIVE: Apply the multiplier formula.

Visit www.myeconlab.com to complete these exercises online and get instant feedback.

Problem and Applications

A.1 Assuming a fixed amount of taxes and a closed economy, calculate the value of the government purchases multiplier, the tax multiplier, and the balanced budget multiplier if the marginal propensity to consume equals 0.6.

A.2 Calculate the value of the government purchases multiplier if the marginal propensity to consume equals 0.8, the tax rate equals 0.25, and the marginal propensity to import equals 0.2.

A.3 Use a graph to show the change in the aggregate demand curve resulting from an increase in government purchases if the government purchases multiplier equals 2. On the same graph, show the change in the aggregate demand curve resulting from an increase in government purchases if the government purchases multiplier equals 4.

A.4 Using your understanding of multipliers, explain why an increase in the tax rate would decrease the size of the government purchases multiplier. Similarly, explain why a decrease in the marginal propensity to import would increase the size of the government purchases multiplier.

A.5 In 2012, the ratio of imports to GDP was 14 percent in Japan and 83 percent in Belgium. On the basis of this information, can you draw any conclusions about the relative sizes of the government purchases multiplier in each country?

Glossary

Automatic stabilizers Government spending and taxes that automatically increase or decrease along with the business cycle.

Budget deficit The situation in which the government's expenditures are greater than its tax revenue.

Budget surplus The situation in which the government's expenditures are less than its tax revenue.

Cyclically adjusted budget deficit or surplus The deficit or surplus in the federal government's budget if the economy were at potential GDP.

Fiscal policy Changes in federal taxes and purchases that are intended to achieve macroeconomic policy objectives.

Multiplier effect The process by which an increase in autonomous expenditure leads to a larger increase in real GDP.

Tax wedge The difference between the pretax and posttax return to an economic activity.

Credits

Credits are listed in the order of appearance.

Photo

Macroeconomics in an Open Economy

Macroeconomics in an Open Economy

Chapter Outline and Learning Objectives

A Strong Dollar Hurts McDonald's Profits

The McDonald's Big Mac is one of the most widely available products in the world. McDonald's has 32,000 restaurants in 118 countries, serving 60 million customers per day. Although McDonald's owns some of its restaurants, many are franchises. A franchise is a business with the legal right to sell a good or a service in a particular area. When a firm uses franchises, local entrepreneurs are able to buy and run the stores in their area. Because of its success, McDonald's has come close to saturation in its home market, with relatively few good locations for opening new restaurants still available.

With expansion in the U.S. market limited, McDonald's has grown in recent years mostly by expanding in foreign markets. Less than one-third of its sales come from the United States; 40 percent come from Europe; about one-quarter from the Middle East, Asia, and Africa; and the rest from Canada and Latin America. Because McDonald's has restaurants in so many countries, it receives revenue in many different currencies. As a result, the company's profits are affected by fluctuations in the value of the dollar in exchange for other currencies. In some years, converting revenue from foreign currencies yields more dollars than in other years. For example, in 2012, McDonald's global profits increased by 6.3 percent from the previous year when measured in local currencies—pounds in Great Britain, euros in France, yen in Japan. But when measured in terms of dollars, the company's profits fell by 0.7 percent. Why the discrepancy? The value of the dollar had increased relative to most other currencies. So, converting pounds, euros, and yen into dollars yielded fewer dollars for McDonald's.

What explains fluctuations in the exchange rate between the dollar and other currencies? In this chapter, we will look more closely at how exchange rates are determined and at other important issues involving the international financial system.

Sources: Julie Jargon, "McDonald's Earnings: Fast-Food Chain Sees Challenging Year," *Wall Street Journal*, July 22, 2013; and McDonald's, *2012 Annual Report*.

Economics in Your Life

The South Korean Central Bank and Your Car Loan

Suppose that you are shopping for a new car, which you plan to finance with a loan from a local bank. While reading a *Wall Street Journal* story on your smartphone one morning, you see this headline: "The Bank of Korea, South Korea's central bank, announces it will sell its large holdings of U.S. Treasury bonds." Will the Bank of Korea's decision to sell its U.S. Treasury bonds affect the interest rate you pay on your car loan? As you read this chapter, try to answer this question. You can check your answer against the one we provide at the end of this chapter.

W e know the basics of international trade. In this chapter, we look more closely at the linkages among countries at the macroeconomic level. Countries are linked by trade in goods and services and by flows of financial investment. We will see how policymakers in all countries take these linkages into account when conducting monetary policy and fiscal policy.

Open economy An economy that has interactions in trade or finance with other countries.

Closed economy An economy that has no interactions in trade or finance with other countries.

Balance of payments The record of a country's trade with other countries in goods, services, and assets.

Current account The part of the balance of payments that records a country's net exports, net income on investments, and net transfers.

Balance of trade The difference between the value of the goods a country exports and the value of the goods a country imports.

The Balance of Payments: Linking the United States to the International Economy

Today, consumers, firms, and investors routinely interact with consumers, firms, and investors in other economies. A consumer in France may use computer software produced in the United States, watch a television made in South Korea, and wear a sweater made in Italy. A firm in the United States may sell its products in dozens of countries around the world. An investor in London may sell a U.S. Treasury bill to an investor in Mexico City. Nearly all economies are **open economies** and have extensive interactions in trade or finance with other countries. Open economies interact by trading goods and services and by making investments in each other's economies. A **closed economy** has no interactions in trade or finance with other countries. No economy today is completely closed, although a few countries, such as North Korea, have very limited economic interactions with other countries.

A good way to understand the interactions between one economy and other economies is through the **balance of payments**, which is a record of a country's trade with other countries in goods, services, and assets. Just as the U.S. Bureau of Economic Analysis is responsible for collecting data on the gross domestic product (GDP), it is also responsible for collecting data on the balance of payments. Table 1 shows the balance of payments for the United States in 2012. Notice that the table contains three "accounts": the *current account*, the *financial account*, and the *capital account*.

The Current Account

The **current account** records *current*, or short-term, flows of funds into and out of a country. The current account for the United States includes exports and imports of goods and services (the difference between exports and imports of goods and services is called *net exports*); income received by U.S. residents from investments in other countries; income paid on investments in the United States owned by residents of other countries (the difference between investment income received and investment income paid is called *net income on investments*); and the difference between transfers made to residents of other countries and transfers received by U.S. residents from other countries (called *net transfers*). If you make a donation to a charity caring for orphans in Afghanistan, it would be included in net transfers. Any payments received by U.S. residents are positive numbers in the current account, and any payments made by U.S. residents are negative numbers in the current account.

The Balance of Trade Part of the current account is the **balance of trade**, which is the difference between the value of the goods a country exports and the value of the goods a country imports. The balance of trade is the largest item in the current account and is often a topic that politicians and the media discuss. If a country exports more goods than it imports, it has a *trade surplus*. If a country exports less than it imports, it has a *trade deficit*. In 2012, the United States had a trade deficit of $742 billion. In the same year, Japan had a trade deficit of $87 billion, and China had a trade surplus of $231 billion. Figure 1 shows imports and exports of goods between the United States and its trading partners and between Japan and its trading partners. The data show that the United States ran a trade deficit in 2012 with all its major trading partners and with every region of the world except for Latin America. Japan ran trade surpluses with the United States and Asia (except China), and it ran trade deficits with the other regions. (Note that exports from the United States to

Current Account

Exports of goods	$1,561	
Imports of goods	−2,303	
Balance of trade		−742
Exports of services	649	
Imports of services	−443	
Balance of services		207
Income received on investments	776	
Income payments on investments	−552	
Net income on investments		224
Net transfers		−130
Balance on current account		**−440**

Financial Account

Increase in foreign holdings of assets in the United States	544	
Increase in U.S. holdings of assets in foreign countries	−105	
Balance on financial account		**439**

Balance on Capital Account	**7**
Statistical discrepancy	**−6**
Balance of payments	**0**

Table 1

The Balance of Payments, 2012 (billions of dollars)

The sum of the balance of trade and the balance of services equals net exports.

Note: Subtotals may not sum to totals because of rounding.
Source: U.S. Bureau of Economic Analysis, "U.S. International Transactions," June 14, 2013.

Japan in panel (a) of Figure 1 should equal imports by Japan from the United States in panel (b). These two numbers are different because international trade statistics are not measured exactly.)

Net Exports Equals the Sum of the Balance of Trade and the Balance of Services We know that *net exports* is a component of aggregate expenditure. Net exports is not explicitly shown in Table 1, but we can calculate it by adding the balance of trade and the balance of services. The *balance of services* is the difference between the value of the services a country exports and the value of the services a country imports. Notice that, technically, net exports is *not* equal to the current account balance because this account also includes net income on investments and net transfers. Because these other two items are relatively small, it is often a convenient simplification to think of net exports as being equal to the current account balance.

The Financial Account

The **financial account** records purchases of assets a country has made abroad and foreign purchases of assets in the country. The financial account records long-term flows of funds into and out of a country. There is a *capital outflow* from the United States when an investor in the United States buys a bond issued by a foreign company or government or when a U.S. firm builds a factory in another country. There is a *capital inflow* into the United States when a foreign investor buys a bond issued by a U.S. firm or by the government or when a foreign firm builds a factory in the United States. Notice that we are

Financial account The part of the balance of payments that records purchases of assets a country has made abroad and foreign purchases of assets in the country.

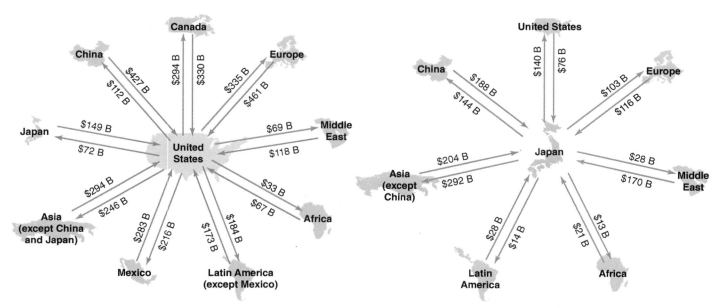

(a) Trade flows for the United States (in billions of dollars)

(b) Trade flows for Japan (in billions of dollars)

Figure 1 **Trade Flows for the United States and Japan, 2012**

Panel (a) shows that in 2012, the United States ran a trade deficit with all its major trading partners and with every region of the world except for Latin America. Panel (b) shows that Japan ran trade deficits with China, Latin America, Europe, Africa, and the Middle East, and ran trade surpluses with the United States and Asia. In each panel, the green arrows represent exports from the United States or Japan, and the red arrows represent imports.

Note: Japanese data are converted from yen to dollars at the average 2012 exchange rate of 79.8 yen per dollar.

Sources: U.S. Bureau of Economic Analysis, "U.S. International Transactions," June 14, 2013; and Japanese Ministry of Finance, *Trade Statistics of Japan.*

---

using the word *capital* here to apply not just to physical assets, such as factories, but also to financial assets, such as shares of stock. When firms build or buy facilities in foreign countries, they are engaging in *foreign direct investment*. When investors buy stock or bonds issued in another country, they are engaging in *foreign portfolio investment*.

Another way of thinking of the balance on the financial account is as a measure of *net capital flows*, or the difference between capital inflows and capital outflows. (Here we are omitting a few transactions included in the capital account, as discussed in the next section.) A concept closely related to net capital flows is **net foreign investment**, which is equal to capital outflows minus capital inflows. Net capital flows and net foreign investment are always equal but have opposite signs: When net capital flows are positive, net foreign investment is negative, and when net capital flows are negative, net foreign investment is positive. Net foreign investment is also equal to net foreign direct investment plus net foreign portfolio investment. Later in this chapter, we will use the relationship between the balance on the financial account and net foreign investment to understand an important aspect of the international economic system.

The Capital Account

A third, less important, part of the balance of payments is called the *capital account*. The **capital account** records relatively minor transactions, such as migrants' transfers—which consist of goods and financial assets people take with them when they leave or enter a country—and sales and purchases of nonproduced, nonfinancial assets. A nonproduced, nonfinancial asset is a copyright, patent, trademark, or right to natural resources. The definitions of the financial account and the capital account are often misunderstood because the capital account prior to 1999 recorded all the transactions included now in both the financial account and the capital account. In other words, capital account transactions went from being a very important part of the balance of

Net foreign investment The difference between capital outflows from a country and capital inflows, also equal to net foreign direct investment plus net foreign portfolio investment.

Capital account The part of the balance of payments that records relatively minor transactions, such as migrants' transfers and sales and purchases of nonproduced, nonfinancial assets.

payments to being a relatively unimportant part. Because the balance on what is now called the capital account is so small—only $7 billion in 2012—for simplicity we will ignore it in the remainder of this chapter.

Why Is the Balance of Payments Always Zero?

The sum of the current account balance, the financial account balance, and the capital account balance equals the balance of payments. Table 1 shows that the balance of payments for the United States in 2012 was zero. It's not just by chance that this balance was zero; *the balance of payments is always zero*. Notice that the current account balance in 2012 was –$440 billion. The balance on the financial account (which has the opposite sign to the balance on the current account) was $439 billion. To make the balance on the current account equal to the balance on the financial account, the balance of payments includes an entry called the *statistical discrepancy*. (Remember that we are ignoring the balance on the capital account. If we included it, we would say that the statistical discrepancy takes on a value equal to the difference between the current account balance and the sum of the balance on the financial account and the balance on the capital account.)

Why does the U.S. Department of Commerce include the statistical discrepancy entry to force the balance of payments to equal zero? If the sum of the current account balance and the financial account balance does not equal zero, some imports or exports of goods and services or some capital inflows or capital outflows were not measured accurately.

To better understand why the balance of payments must equal zero every year, consider the following: In 2012, the United States spent $440 billion more on goods, services, and other items in the current account than it received. What happened to that $440 billion? We know that every dollar of that $440 billion was used by foreign individuals or firms to invest in the United States or was added to foreign holdings of dollars. We know this because logically there is nowhere else for the dollars to go: If the dollars weren't spent on U.S. goods and services—and we know they weren't because in that case they would have shown up in the current account—they must have been spent on investments in the United States or not spent at all. Dollars that aren't spent are added to foreign holdings of dollars. Changes in foreign holdings of dollars are called

Don't Let This Happen to You

Don't Confuse the Balance of Trade, the Current Account Balance, and the Balance of Payments

The terminology of international economics can be tricky. Remember that the *balance of trade* includes only trade in goods; it does not include services. This observation is important because the United States, for example, usually imports more *goods* than it exports, but it usually exports more *services* than it imports. As a result, the U.S. trade deficit is almost always larger than the current account deficit. The *current account balance* includes the balance of trade, the balance of services, net investment income, and net transfers. Net investment income and net transfers are much smaller than the balance of trade and the balance of services.

Even though the *balance of payments* is equal to the sum of the current account balance and the financial account balance—and must equal zero—you may sometimes see references to a balance of payments "surplus" or

"deficit." These references have two explanations. The first is that the person making the reference has confused the balance of payments with either the balance of trade or the current account balance. This is a very common mistake. The second explanation is that the person is not including official reserve transactions in the financial account. If we separate changes in U.S. holdings of foreign currencies and changes in foreign holdings of U.S. dollars from other financial account entries, the current account balance and the financial account balance do not have to sum to zero, and there can be a balance of payments surplus or deficit. This may sound complicated—and it is! But don't worry. How official reserve transactions are accounted for is not crucial to understanding the basic ideas behind the balance of payments.

Your Turn: Test your understanding by doing related problem 1.6 at the end of this chapter.

official reserve transactions. Foreign investment in the United States and additions to foreign holdings of dollars both show up as positive entries in the U.S. financial account. Therefore, a current account deficit must be exactly offset by a financial account surplus, leaving the balance of payments equal to zero. Similarly, a country that runs a current account surplus, such as China, must run a financial account deficit of exactly the same size. If a country's current account surplus is not exactly equal to its financial account deficit, or if a country's current account deficit is not exactly equal to its financial account surplus, some transactions must not have been accounted for. The statistical discrepancy is included in the balance of payments to compensate for these uncounted transactions.

Solved Problem 1

Understanding the Arithmetic of the Balance of Payments

Test your understanding of the relationship between the current account and the financial account by evaluating the following assertion by a political commentator:

> The industrial countries are committing economic suicide. Every year, they invest more and more in developing countries. Every year, more U.S., Japanese, and European manufacturing firms move their factories to developing countries. With extensive new factories and low wages, developing countries now export far more to the industrial countries than they import.

Solving the Problem

Step 1: Review the chapter material. This problem is about the relationship between the current account and the financial account, so you may want to review the section "Why Is the Balance of Payments Always Zero?"

Step 2: Explain the errors in the commentator's argument. The argument sounds plausible. It would be easy to find statements similar to this one in recent books and articles by well-known political commentators. But the argument contains an important error: The commentator has failed to understand the relationship between the current account and the financial account. The commentator asserts that developing countries are receiving large capital inflows from industrial countries. In other words, developing countries are running financial account surpluses. The commentator also asserts that developing countries are exporting more than they are importing. In other words, they are running current account surpluses. As we have seen in this section, it is impossible to run a current account surplus *and* a financial account surplus simultaneously. A country that runs a current account surplus *must* run a financial account deficit and vice versa.

Extra Credit: Most emerging economies that have received large inflows of foreign investment during the past two decades, such as South Korea, Thailand, and Malaysia, have run current account deficits: They import more goods and services than they export. Emerging economies, such as Singapore, that run current account surpluses also run financial account deficits: They invest more abroad than other countries invest in them.

The point here is not obvious; if the point was obvious, it wouldn't confuse so many intelligent politicians, journalists, and political commentators. Unless you understand the relationship between the current account and the financial account, you won't be able to understand a key aspect of the international economy.

Your Turn: For more practice, do related problems 1.7, 1.8, and 1.9 at the end of this chapter.

The Foreign Exchange Market and Exchange Rates

2 LEARNING OBJECTIVE

Explain how exchange rates are determined and how changes in exchange rates affect the prices of imports and exports.

A firm that operates entirely within the United States will price its products in dollars and will use dollars to pay its suppliers' bills, wages and salaries to its workers, interest to its bondholders, and dividends to its shareholders. A multinational corporation such as McDonald's, in contrast, may sell its products in many different countries and receive payments in many different currencies. Its suppliers and workers may also be spread around the world and may have to be paid in local currencies. Corporations may also use the international financial system to borrow in a foreign currency. For example, during a period of rapid expansion in East Asian countries such as Thailand and South Korea during the late 1990s, many large firms received dollar loans from foreign banks. When firms make extensive use of foreign currencies, they must deal with fluctuations in the exchange rate.

The **nominal exchange rate** is the value of one country's currency in terms of another country's currency. Economists also calculate the *real exchange rate*, which corrects the nominal exchange rate for changes in prices of goods and services. We discuss the real exchange rate later in this chapter. The nominal exchange rate determines how many units of a foreign currency you can purchase with $1. For example, the exchange rate between the U.S. dollar and the Japanese yen can be expressed as ¥100 = $1. (This exchange rate can also be expressed as how many U.S. dollars are required to buy 1 Japanese yen: $0.01 = ¥1.) The market for foreign exchange is very active, with the equivalent of more than $3 trillion worth of currency being traded each day. The exchange rates that result from this trading are reported on a number of online sites devoted to economic news and in the business or financial sections of most newspapers.

Banks and other financial institutions around the world employ currency traders, who are linked together by computer. Rather than exchange large amounts of paper currency, they buy and sell deposits in banks. For example, a bank buying or selling dollars will actually be buying or selling dollar bank deposits. Dollar bank deposits exist not just in banks in the United States but also in banks around the world. Suppose that the Crédit Agricole bank in France wants to sell U.S. dollars and buy Japanese yen. The bank may exchange U.S. dollar deposits that it owns for Japanese yen deposits owned by the Deutsche Bank in Germany. Businesses and individuals usually obtain foreign currency from banks in their own country.

Nominal exchange rate The value of one country's currency in terms of another country's currency.

Making the Connection	## Exchange Rate Listings

You can find the exchange rates between the dollar and other major currencies on many online sites, such as wsj.com, Bloomberg.com, or finance.yahoo.com, as well as in the financial pages of most newspapers. The exchange rates in the following table are for August 9, 2013. The euro is the common currency used by 17 European countries, including France, Germany, and Italy.

Exchange Rate between the Dollar and the Indicated Currency		
Currency	**Units of Foreign Currency per U.S. Dollar**	**U.S. Dollars per Unit of Foreign Currency**
Canadian dollar	1.03	0.978
Japanese yen	96.23	0.010
Mexican peso	12.62	0.074
British pound	0.65	1.55
Euro	0.75	1.33

You can find information on exchange rates on many online sites that report economic news and in the financial pages of most newspapers.

Notice that the expression for the exchange rate stated as units of foreign currency per U.S. dollar is the *reciprocal* of the exchange rate stated as U.S. dollars per unit of foreign currency. So, the exchange rate between the U.S. dollar and the British pound can be stated as either 0.65 British pounds per U.S. dollar or 1/0.65 = 1.55 U.S. dollars per British pound.

Banks are the most active participants in the market for foreign exchange. Typically, banks buy currency for slightly less than the amount for which they sell it. This spread between the buying and selling prices allows banks to cover their costs from currency trading. Therefore, when most businesses and individuals buy foreign currency from a bank, they receive fewer units of foreign currency per dollar than would be indicated by the exchange rate shown on online business sites or printed in the newspaper.

Source: *Wall Street Journal*, August 9, 2013.

Your Turn: Test your understanding by doing related problem 2.5 at the end of this chapter.

The market exchange rate is determined by the interaction of demand and supply, just as other prices are. Let's consider the demand for U.S. dollars in exchange for Japanese yen. There are three sources of foreign currency demand for the U.S. dollar:

1. Foreign firms and households that want to buy goods and services produced in the United States.

2. Foreign firms and households that want to invest in the United States either through foreign direct investment—buying or building factories or other facilities in the United States—or through foreign portfolio investment—buying stocks and bonds issued in the United States.

3. Currency traders who believe that the value of the dollar in the future will be greater than its value today.

Equilibrium in the Market for Foreign Exchange

Figure 2 shows the demand and supply of U.S. dollars for Japanese yen. Notice that as we move up the vertical axis, the value of the dollar increases relative to the value of the yen. When the exchange rate is ¥150 = $1, the dollar is worth 1.5 times as much relative to the yen as when the exchange rate is ¥100 = $1. Consider, first, the demand curve for dollars in exchange for yen. The demand curve has the normal downward slope. When the value of the dollar is high, the quantity of dollars demanded will be

Figure 2

Equilibrium in the Foreign Exchange Market

When the exchange rate is ¥150 to the dollar, it is above its equilibrium level, and there will be a surplus of dollars. When the exchange rate is ¥100 to the dollar, it is below its equilibrium level, and there will be a shortage of dollars. At an exchange rate of ¥120 to the dollar, the foreign exchange market is in equilibrium.

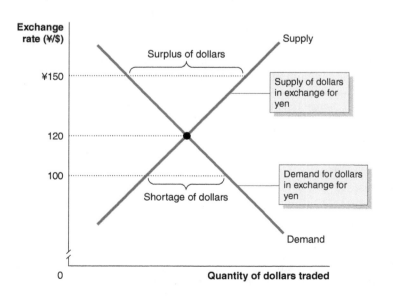

low. A Japanese investor will be more likely to buy a $1,000 bond issued by the U.S. Treasury when the exchange rate is ¥100 = $1 and the investor pays only ¥100,000 to buy $1,000 than when the exchange rate is ¥150 = $1 and the investor must pay ¥150,000. Similarly, a Japanese firm is more likely to buy $150 million worth of microchips from Intel Corporation when the exchange rate is ¥100 = $1 and the microchips can be purchased for ¥15 billion than when the exchange rate is ¥150 = $1 and the microchips cost ¥22.5 billion.

Now consider the supply curve for dollars in exchange for yen. The supply curve has the normal upward slope. When the value of the dollar is high, the quantity of dollars supplied in exchange for yen will be high. A U.S. investor will be more likely to buy a ¥200,000 bond issued by the Japanese government when the exchange rate is ¥200 = $1 and he needs to pay only $1,000 to buy ¥200,000 than when the exchange rate is ¥100 = $1 and he must pay $2,000. The owner of a U.S. electronics store is more likely to buy ¥20 million worth of television sets from the Sony Corporation when the exchange rate is ¥200 = $1 and she only needs to pay $100,000 to purchase the televisions than when the exchange rate is ¥100 = $1 and she must pay $200,000.

As in any other market, equilibrium occurs in the foreign exchange market where the quantity supplied equals the quantity demanded. In Figure 2, ¥120 = $1 is the equilibrium exchange rate. At exchange rates above ¥120 = $1, there will be a surplus of dollars and downward pressure on the exchange rate. The surplus and the downward pressure will not be eliminated until the exchange rate falls to ¥120 = $1. If the exchange rate is below ¥120 = $1, there will be a shortage of dollars and upward pressure on the exchange rate. The shortage and the upward pressure will not be eliminated until the exchange rate rises to ¥120 = $1. Surpluses and shortages in the foreign exchange market are eliminated very quickly because the volume of trading in major currencies such as the dollar and the yen is large, and currency traders are linked together by computer.

Currency appreciation occurs when the market value of a country's currency increases relative to the value of another country's currency. **Currency depreciation** occurs when the market value of a country's currency decreases relative to the value of another country's currency.

Currency appreciation An increase in the market value of one currency relative to another currency.

Currency depreciation A decrease in the market value of one currency relative to another currency.

How Do Shifts in Demand and Supply Affect the Exchange Rate?

Shifts in the demand and supply curves cause the equilibrium exchange rate to change. Three main factors cause the demand and supply curves in the foreign exchange market to shift:

1. Changes in the demand for U.S.-produced goods and services and changes in the demand for foreign-produced goods and services

2. Changes in the desire to invest in the United States and changes in the desire to invest in foreign countries

3. Changes in the expectations of currency traders about the likely future value of the dollar and the likely future value of foreign currencies

Shifts in the Demand for Foreign Exchange Consider how these three factors will affect the demand for U.S. dollars in exchange for Japanese yen. During an economic expansion in Japan, the incomes of Japanese households will rise, and the demand by Japanese consumers and firms for U.S. goods will increase. At any given exchange rate, the demand for U.S. dollars will increase, and the demand curve will shift to the right. Similarly, if interest rates in the United States rise, the desirability of investing in U.S. financial assets will increase, and the demand curve for dollars will also shift to the right. **Speculators** are currency traders who buy and sell foreign exchange in an attempt to profit from changes in exchange rates. If a speculator becomes convinced that the value of the dollar is going to rise relative to the value of the yen, the speculator will sell yen and buy dollars. If the current exchange rate is ¥120 = $1, and the speculator is

Speculators Currency traders who buy and sell foreign exchange in an attempt to profit from changes in exchange rates.

convinced that it will soon rise to ¥140 = $1, the speculator could sell ¥600,000,000 and receive $5,000,000 (= ¥600,000,000/120) in return. If the speculator is correct and the value of the dollar rises against the yen to ¥140 = $1, the speculator will be able to exchange $5,000,000 for ¥700,000,000 (= $5,000,000 × ¥140) for a profit of ¥100,000,000.

To summarize, the demand curve for dollars shifts to the right when incomes in Japan rise, when interest rates in the United States rise, or when speculators decide that the value of the dollar will rise relative to the value of the yen.

During a recession in Japan, Japanese incomes will fall, reducing the demand for U.S.-produced goods and services and shifting the demand curve for dollars to the left. Similarly, if interest rates in the United States fall, the desirability of investing in U.S. financial assets will decrease, and the demand curve for dollars will shift to the left. Finally, if speculators become convinced that the future value of the dollar will be lower than its current value, the demand for dollars will fall, and the demand curve will shift to the left.

Shifts in the Supply of Foreign Exchange The factors that affect the supply curve for dollars are similar to those that affect the demand curve for dollars. An economic expansion in the United States increases the incomes of Americans and increases their demand for goods and services, including goods and services made in Japan. As U.S. consumers and firms increase their spending on Japanese products, they must supply dollars in exchange for yen, which causes the supply curve for dollars to shift to the right. Similarly, an increase in interest rates in Japan will make financial investments in Japan more attractive to U.S. investors. These higher Japanese interest rates will cause the supply curve for dollars to shift to the right, as U.S. investors exchange dollars for yen. Finally, if speculators become convinced that the future value of the yen will be higher relative to the dollar than it is today, the supply curve for dollars will shift to the right as traders attempt to exchange dollars for yen.

A recession in the United States will decrease the demand for Japanese products and cause the supply curve for dollars to shift to the left. Similarly, a decrease in interest rates in Japan will make financial investments in Japan less attractive and cause the supply curve for dollars to shift to the left. If traders become convinced that the future value of the yen will be lower relative to the dollar, the supply curve will also shift to the left.

Adjustment to a New Equilibrium The factors that affect the demand and supply for currencies are constantly changing. Whether the exchange rate increases or decreases depends on the direction and size of the shifts in the demand curve and supply curve. For example, as Figure 3 shows, if the demand curve for dollars in exchange

Figure 3

Shifts in the Demand and Supply Curve Resulting in a Higher Exchange Rate

Holding other factors constant, an increase in the supply of dollars will decrease the equilibrium exchange rate. An increase in the demand for dollars will increase the equilibrium exchange rate. In the case shown in this figure, both the demand curve and the supply curve have shifted to the right. Because the demand curve has shifted to the right by more than the supply curve, the equilibrium exchange rate has increased from ¥120 to $1 at point *A* to ¥130 to $1 at point *B*.

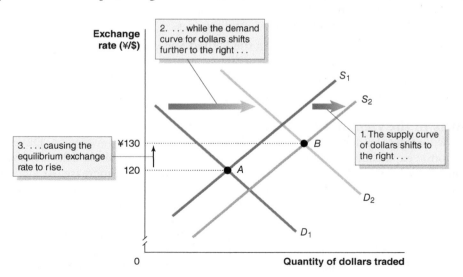

for Japanese yen shifts to the right by more than the supply curve shifts, the equilibrium exchange rate will increase.

Some Exchange Rates Are Not Determined by the Market

To this point, we have assumed that exchange rates are determined in the market. This assumption is a good one for many currencies, including the U.S. dollar, the euro, the Japanese yen, and the British pound. Some currencies, however, have *fixed exchange rates* that do not change over long periods. For example, for more than 10 years, the value of the Chinese yuan was fixed against the U.S. dollar at a rate of 8.28 yuan to the dollar. A country's central bank has to intervene in the foreign exchange market to buy and sell its currency if it wishes to keep the exchange rate fixed.

How Movements in the Exchange Rate Affect Exports and Imports

When the market value of the dollar increases, the foreign currency price of U.S. exports rises, and the dollar price of foreign imports falls. Suppose that initially the market exchange rate between the U.S. dollar and the euro is $1 = €1. In that case, a Blu-ray disc that has a price of $20 in the United States will have a price of €20 in France. A bottle of French wine that has a price of €50 in France will have a price of $50 in the United States. Now suppose the market exchange rate between the U.S. dollar and the euro changes to $1.20 = €1. Because it now takes more dollars to buy a euro, the dollar has *depreciated* against the euro, and the euro has *appreciated* against the dollar. The depreciation of the dollar has decreased the euro price of the Blu-ray disc from €20 to $20/ (1.20 dollars/euro) = €16.67. The dollar price of the French wine has risen from $50 to €50 ×1.20 dollars/euro = $60. As a result, we would expect more Blu-ray discs to be sold in France and less French wine to be sold in the United States.

To generalize, we can conclude that a depreciation in the domestic currency will increase exports and decrease imports, thereby increasing net exports. If real GDP is currently below potential GDP, then, holding all other factors constant, a depreciation in the domestic currency should increase net exports, aggregate demand, and real GDP. An appreciation in the domestic currency should have the opposite effect: Exports should fall, and imports should rise, which will reduce net exports, aggregate demand, and real GDP.

| Making the Connection | Japanese Firms Ride the Yen Roller Coaster |

Bridgestone, headquartered in Tokyo, Japan, is the world's largest tire manufacturer. A 2013 headline in the *Wall Street Journal* read: "Weak Yen Boosts Bridgestone Profits." The headline was not unusual. Many large Japanese firms, including Toyota, Sony, and Nintendo, rely heavily on sales in the United States and other foreign countries. As a result, their profits depend on the exchange rate between the yen and other currencies.

As the following figure shows, the long-run trend has been for the yen to gain value against the dollar. The value of the yen has increased from ¥360 = $1 in 1971 to less than ¥100 = $1 in 2013. There have been substantial swings in the exchange rate around that long-run trend, however. For example, the dollar soared in value against the yen by more than 70 percent between 1995 and 1998. Between 2007 and 2011, the value of the dollar fell by 60 percent against the yen, before increasing by 25 percent between 2012 and 2013. As a result of these exchange rate movements, the late 1990s and 2012–2013 were good years for Japanese exporters, while 2007–2011 were bad years.

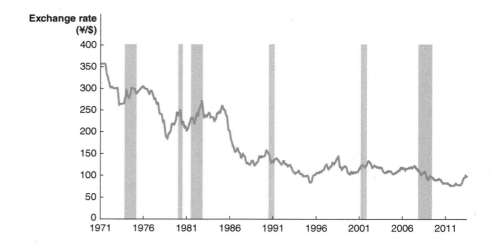

What explains these fluctuations in the yen–dollar exchange rate? We have just seen that an increase in the demand by foreign investors for U.S. financial assets can increase the value of the dollar, and a decrease in the demand for U.S. financial assets can decrease the value of the dollar. The increase in the value of the dollar against the yen in the late 1990s was driven by strong demand by Japanese and other foreign investors for U.S. stocks and bonds, particularly U.S. Treasury securities. This increase in demand was not primarily due to higher U.S. interest rates but to problems in the international financial system. Many investors considered U.S. financial assets a *safe haven* in times of financial problems because the investors believed the U.S. Treasury was unlikely to default on its bonds.

The decline in the value of the dollar against the yen in the years following 2007 began when the Fed started cutting the target for the federal funds rate in response to the beginning of the recession of 2007–2009. When U.S. interest rates are low, investors are likely to buy Japanese and other foreign stocks and bonds rather than U.S. stocks and bonds, which depresses the demand for dollars and lowers the exchange value of the dollar. By 2011, Bridgestone and other Japanese firms were complaining about the losses they were suffering due to the high value of the yen. Some Japanese manufacturers considered moving more of their production capacity out of Japan. The CEO of Nissan stated: "What's taking place now is many projects are now basing their manufacturing outside of Japan because they just cannot survive with this 77 yen to the dollar."

The decline in the value of the yen after 2012 occurred as a result of the Japanese central bank, the Bank of Japan, following an expansionary monetary policy. When Shinzo Abe was elected prime minister in late 2012, he appointed a new governor of the Bank of Japan who pledged to double the Bank's holdings of Japanese government bonds and to buy other assets. Investors expected that the result would be lower nominal Japanese interest rates and a higher inflation rate, reducing the real return from owning Japanese financial assets. In response, investors sold Japanese financial assets and bought U.S. financial assets, causing the value of the yen to decline against the dollar.

The fall in the value of the yen was good news for Japanese firms, but fluctuations in the yen–dollar exchange rate are certain to continue as investors buy and sell currencies in response to changes in monetary policy and other factors.

Sources: Yoree Koh, "Weak Yen Boosts Bridgestone Profits," *Wall Street Journal*, August 9, 2013; "Automakers May Flee Strong Yen," Reuters, November 17, 2011; "Opening the Flood Gates," *Economist*, April 13, 2013; and Federal Reserve Bank of St. Louis.

Your Turn: Test your understanding by doing related problem 2.15 at the end of this chapter.

Don't Let This Happen to You

Don't Confuse What Happens When a Currency Appreciates with What Happens When It Depreciates

One of the most confusing aspects of exchange rates is that they can be expressed in two ways. We can express the exchange rate between the dollar and the yen either as how many yen can be purchased with $1 or as how many dollars can be purchased with ¥1. That is, we can express the exchange rate as ¥100 = $1 or as $0.01 = ¥1. When a currency appreciates, it increases in value relative to another currency. When it depreciates, it decreases in value relative to another currency.

If the exchange rate changes from ¥100 = $1 to ¥120 = $1, the dollar has appreciated and the yen has depreciated because it now takes more yen to buy $1. If the exchange rate changes from $0.010 = ¥1 to $0.015 = ¥1, however, the dollar has depreciated and the yen has appreciated because it now takes more dollars to buy ¥1. This situation can appear somewhat confusing because the exchange rate seems to have "increased" in both cases. To determine which currency has appreciated and which has depreciated, it is important to remember that an appreciation of the domestic currency means that it now takes *more* units of the foreign currency to buy one unit of the domestic currency. A depreciation of the domestic currency means it takes *fewer* units of the foreign currency to buy one unit of the domestic currency. This observation holds no matter which way we express the exchange rate.

Your Turn: Test your understanding by doing related problem 2.6 at the end of the chapter.

Solved Problem 2

Why Did Honda Move Some Production to the United States?

In 2012, an executive at Honda Motor Company announced that the firm would be moving more of its car production from Japan to the United States. A newspaper article stated: "The move, driven by the strength of the Japanese yen, will also result in Honda significantly reducing the number of vehicles it imports into North America from plants in Japan."

a. What does the article mean by the strength of the Japanese yen?
b. Why would a strong yen cause Honda to produce more cars in the United States and fewer cars in Japan?

Solving the Problem

Step 1: **Review the chapter material.** This problem is about changes in the value of a currency, so you may want to review the section "How Movements in the Exchange Rate Affect Exports and Imports."

Step 2: **Answer part (a) by explaining what the article means by the "strength of the yen."** In this case, a strong yen means a yen that is worth more relative to the U.S. dollar. With a stronger yen, fewer yen would exchange for one U.S. dollar.

Step 3: **Answer part (b) by explaining how a strong yen will affect Honda's decision as to where it should base production.** When Honda manufactures cars in Japan, it pays its production costs—including the salaries of its assembly-line workers and payments to its suppliers—with yen. With a strong yen, the dollar price of cars Honda sells in the United States increases. As a result, Honda will lose sales to other companies, particularly those that produce their cars in the United States. By moving more production to the United States, Honda will pay its production costs in dollars, so it will not be affected by fluctuations in the yen–dollar exchange rate.

Extra Credit: Of course, Honda executives were aware that if the value of the yen declined against the dollar—as it did beginning in late 2012—they would be better off producing in Japan the cars they planned to sell in the United States. With a weak yen, they would be able to sell their cars in the United States for a lower dollar price, gaining sales from companies that produce cars in the United States. But the executives also knew that moving more production to the United States would allow them to plan better and to stabilize their profits because their sales would no longer depend on fluctuations in the exchange rate.

Source: Mike Ramsey, "Honda Bolsters Its Production in North America," *Wall Street Journal*, August 12, 2012.

Your Turn: For more practice, do related problem 2.10 at the end of this chapter.

The Real Exchange Rate

Real exchange rate The price of domestic goods in terms of foreign goods.

We have seen that an important factor in determining the level of a country's exports to and imports from another country is the relative prices of each country's goods. The relative prices of two countries' goods are determined by two factors: the relative price levels in the two countries and the nominal exchange rate between the two countries' currencies. Economists combine these two factors in the **real exchange rate**, which is the price of domestic goods in terms of foreign goods. The price level is a measure of the average prices of goods and services in an economy. We can calculate the real exchange rate between two currencies as

$$\text{Real exchange rate} = \text{Nominal exchange rate} \times \left(\frac{\text{Domestic price level}}{\text{Foreign price level}}\right).$$

Notice that changes in the real exchange rate reflect both changes in the nominal exchange rate and changes in the relative price levels. Suppose that the exchange rate between the U.S. dollar and the British pound is $1 = £1, the price level in the United States is 100, and the price level in the United Kingdom is also 100. Then the real exchange rate between the dollar and the pound is

$$\text{Real exchange rate} = 1\,\text{pound/dollar} \times \left(\frac{100}{100}\right) = 1.00.$$

Now suppose that the nominal exchange rate increases to 1.1 pounds per dollar, while the price level in the United States rises to 105 and the price level in the United Kingdom remains 100. In this case, the real exchange rate will be

$$\text{Real exchange rate} = 1.1\,\text{pound/dollar} \times \left(\frac{105}{100}\right) = 1.15.$$

The increase in the real exchange rate from 1.00 to 1.15 tells us that the prices of U.S. goods and services are now 15 percent higher relative to British goods and services.

Real exchange rates are reported as index numbers, with one year chosen as the base year. As with the consumer price index, the main value of the real exchange rate is in tracking changes over time—in this case, changes in the relative prices of domestic goods in terms of foreign goods.

The International Sector and National Saving and Investment

Having studied what determines the exchange rate, we are now ready to explore further the linkages between the U.S. economy and foreign economies. Until 1970, U.S. imports and exports were usually 4 percent to 5 percent of GDP. Imports and exports are now more than three times as large a fraction of U.S. GDP. Imports have also consistently been larger than exports, meaning that net exports have been negative.

Net Exports Equal Net Foreign Investment

If your spending is greater than your income, what can you do? You can sell some assets—maybe those 20 shares of stock in the Walt Disney Company your grandparents gave you—or you can borrow money. A firm can be in the same situation: If a firm's costs are greater than its revenues, it has to make up the difference by selling assets or by borrowing. A country is in the same situation when it imports more than it exports: The country must finance the difference by selling assets—such as land, office buildings, or factories—or by borrowing.

In other words, for any country, a current account deficit must be exactly offset by a financial account surplus. When a country sells more assets to foreigners than it buys from foreigners, or when it borrows more from foreigners than it lends to foreigners—as it must if it is running a current account deficit—the country experiences a net capital inflow and a financial account surplus. Remember that net exports is roughly equal to the current account balance. Remember also that the financial account balance is roughly equal to net capital flows, which are in turn equal to net foreign investment but with the opposite sign. To review these two points, look again at Table 1, which shows that the current account balance is determined mainly by the balance of trade and the balance of services, and the financial account is equal to net capital flows. Also, remember the definition of net foreign investment.

When imports are greater than exports, net exports are negative, and there will be a net capital inflow as people in the United States sell assets and borrow to pay for the surplus of imports over exports. Therefore, net capital flows will be equal to net exports (but with the opposite sign), and net foreign investment will also be equal to net exports (and with the same sign). Because net exports are usually negative for the United States, in most years, the United States must be a net borrower from abroad, and U.S. net foreign investment will be negative.

We can summarize this discussion with the following equations:

$$\text{Current account balance} + \text{Financial account balance} = 0$$

or

$$\text{Current account balance} = -\text{Financial account balance}$$

or

$$\text{Net exports} = \text{Net foreign investment.}$$

The last equation tells us, once again, that countries such as the United States that import more than they export must borrow more from abroad than they lend abroad: If net exports are negative, net foreign investment will also be negative by the same amount. Countries such as China that export more than they import must lend abroad more than they borrow from abroad: If net exports are positive, net foreign investment will also be positive by the same amount.

Domestic Saving, Domestic Investment, and Net Foreign Investment

We can think of the total saving in any economy as equal to saving by the private sector plus saving by the government sector, which we call *public saving*. When the government runs a budget surplus by spending less than it receives in taxes, public saving is positive. When the government runs a budget deficit, public saving is negative. Negative saving is also known as *dissaving*. We can write the following expression for the level of saving in the economy:

$$\text{National saving} = \text{Private saving} + \text{Public saving}$$

or

$$S = S_{\text{private}} + S_{\text{public}}.$$

Private saving is equal to what households have left of their income after spending on consumption goods and paying taxes (for simplicity, we assume that transfer payments are zero):

$$\text{Private saving} = \text{National income} - \text{Consumption} - \text{Taxes}$$

or

$$S_{\text{private}} = Y - C - T.$$

Public saving is equal to the difference between government spending and taxes:

$$\text{Government saving} = \text{Taxes} - \text{Government spending}$$

or

$$S_{\text{public}} = T - G.$$

Finally, remember the basic macroeconomic equation for GDP or national income:

$$Y = C + I + G + NX.$$

We can use this last equation, our definitions of private and public saving, and the fact that net exports equal net foreign investment to arrive at an important relationship, called the **saving and investment equation**:

$$\text{National saving} = \text{Domestic investment} + \text{Net foreign investment}$$

or

$$S = I + NFI.$$

This equation is an *identity* because it must always be true, given the definitions we have used.

The saving and investment equation tells us that a country's saving will be invested either domestically or overseas. If you save \$1,000 and use the funds to buy a bond issued by General Motors, it may use the \$1,000 to partially pay for renovating a factory in the United States (I) or building a factory in China (NFI) as a joint venture with a Chinese firm.

Saving and investment equation An equation that shows that national saving is equal to domestic investment plus net foreign investment.

Solved Problem 3

Arriving at the Saving and Investment Equation

Use the definitions of private and public saving, the equation for GDP or national income, and the fact that net exports (NX) must equal net foreign investment (NFI) to arrive at the saving and investment equation.

Solving the Problem

Step 1: **Review the chapter material.** This problem is about the saving and investment equation, so you may want to review the section "Domestic Saving, Domestic Investment, and Net Foreign Investment."

Step 2: **Derive an expression for national saving (S) in terms of national income (Y), consumption (C), and government purchases (G).** We can bring together the four equations we need:
  1. $S_{\text{private}} = Y - C - T$
  2. $S_{\text{public}} = T - G$
  3. $Y = C + I + G + NX$
  4. $NX = NFI$

Because national saving (S) appears in the saving and investment equation, we need to find an equation for it in terms of the other variables. Adding equation (1) plus equation (2) yields national saving:

$$S = S_{\text{private}} + S_{\text{public}} = (Y - C - T) + (T - G) = Y - C - G.$$

Step 3: **Use the result from Step 2 to derive an expression for national saving in terms of investment (I) and net exports (NX).** Because GDP (Y) does not appear in the saving and investment equation, we need to substitute the expression for it given in equation (3):

$$S = (C + I + G + NX) - C - G$$

and simplify:

$$S = I + NX.$$

Step 4: **Use the results of Steps 2 and 3 to derive the saving and investment equation.** Finally, substitute net foreign investment for net exports:

$$S = I + NFI.$$

Your Turn: For more practice, do related problem 3.8 at the end of this chapter.

A country such as the United States that has negative net foreign investment must be saving less than it is investing domestically. To see this, rewrite the saving and invest-ment equation by moving domestic investment to the left side:

$$S - I = NFI.$$

If net foreign investment is negative—as it is for the United States nearly every year—domestic investment (I) must be greater than national saving (S).

In most years, the level of saving in Japan has been well above domestic invest-ment. The result has been high levels of Japanese net foreign investment. For example, Japanese automobile companies Toyota, Honda, and Nissan have all constructed facto-ries in the United States. Sony purchased the Columbia Pictures film studio. Japan has made many similar investments in countries around the world, which has sometimes caused resentment in those countries. There were some protests in the United States in the 1980s, for example, when Japanese investors purchased the Pebble Beach golf course in California and the Rockefeller Center complex in New York City.

Japan typically needs a high level of net exports to help offset a low level of domestic investment. When exports of a product begin to decline and imports begin to increase, governments are often tempted to impose tariffs or quotas to reduce imports. In fact, some Japanese firms have been urging the Japanese government to impose trade restric-tions on imports from China.

The Effect of a Government Budget Deficit on Investment

4 LEARNING OBJECTIVE

Explain the effect of a government budget deficit on investment in an open economy.

The link we have just developed among saving, investment, and net foreign investment can help us understand some of the effects of changes in a government's budget deficit. When the government runs a budget deficit, national saving will decline unless private saving increases by the amount of the budget deficit, which is unlikely. As the saving and investment equation ($S = I + NFI$) shows, the result of a decline in national saving must be a decline in either domestic investment or net foreign investment. The algebra is clear, but why economically does an increase in the government budget deficit cause a fall in domestic investment or net foreign investment?

To understand the answer to this question, remember that if the federal govern-ment runs a budget deficit, the U.S. Treasury must raise an amount equal to the deficit by selling bonds. To attract investors, the Treasury may have to raise the interest rates on its bonds. As interest rates on Treasury bonds rise, other interest rates, including those on corporate bonds and bank loans, will also rise. Higher interest rates will discour-age some firms from borrowing funds to build new factories or to buy new equipment or computers. Higher interest rates on financial assets in the United States will attract

Figure 4

The Twin Deficits, 1978–2012

During the early 1980s, large federal budget deficits occurred at the same time as large current account deficits, but twin deficits did not occur in most other periods during these years.

Source: U.S. Bureau of Economic Analysis.

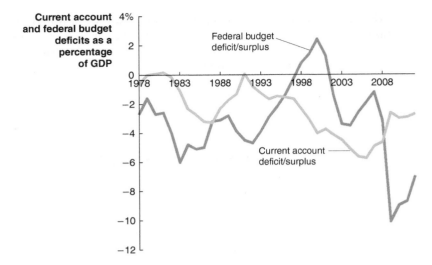

foreign investors. Investors in Canada, Japan, or China will have to buy U.S. dollars to be able to purchase bonds in the United States. This greater demand for dollars will increase their value relative to foreign currencies. As the value of the dollar rises, exports from the United States will fall, and imports to the United States will rise. Net exports and, therefore, net foreign investment will fall.

When a government budget deficit leads to a decline in net exports, the result is sometimes referred to as the *twin deficits*, which refers to the possibility that a government budget deficit will also lead to a current account deficit. The twin deficits idea first became widely discussed in the United States during the early 1980s, when the federal government ran a large budget deficit that resulted in high interest rates, a high exchange value of the dollar, and a large current account deficit.

Figure 4 shows that in the early 1980s, the United States had large federal budget deficits and large current account deficits. The figure also shows, however, that the twin deficits idea does not match the experience of the United States after 1990. The large federal budget deficits of the early 1990s occurred at a time of relatively small current account deficits, and the budget surpluses of the late 1990s occurred at a time of then-record current account deficits. Both the current account deficit and the federal budget deficit increased in the early 2000s, but the federal budget deficit declined in the mid-2000s much more than did the current account deficit. Beginning in 2008, the federal budget deficit soared, more than doubling as a percentage of GDP, while the current account deficit declined.

The experience of other countries also shows only mixed support for the twin deficits idea. Germany ran large budget deficits and large current account deficits during the early 1990s, but both Canada and Italy ran large budget deficits during the 1980s without running current account deficits. The saving and investment equation shows that an increase in the government budget deficit will not lead to an increase in the current account deficit, provided that either private saving increases or domestic investment declines. According to the twin deficits idea, when the federal government ran budget surpluses in the late 1990s, the current account should also have been in surplus, or at least the current account deficit should have been small. In fact, the increase in national saving due to the budget surpluses was more than offset by a sharp decline in private saving, and the United States ran very large current account deficits.

Making the Connection

Why Is the United States Called the "World's Largest Debtor"?

The following graph shows the current account balance as a percentage of GDP for the United States for the period 1960–2012. The United States has had a current account deficit every year since 1982, with the exception of 1991. Between 1960 and 1975, the United States ran a current account deficit in only five years. Many economists believe that the current account deficits of the 1980s were closely related to the federal budget deficits of those years. High interest rates attracted foreign investors to U.S. bonds, which raised the exchange rate between the dollar and foreign currencies. The high exchange rate reduced U.S. exports and increased imports, leading to current account deficits.

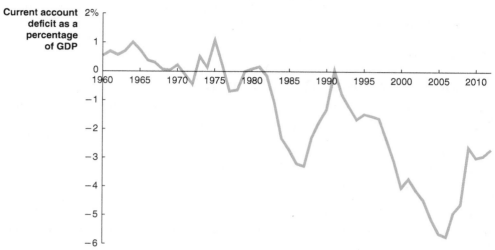

Source: Federal Reserve Bank of St Louis.

As the federal budget deficit narrowed in the mid-1990s and disappeared in the late 1990s, the foreign exchange value of the dollar remained high—and large current account deficits continued—because foreign investors persisted in investing in the United States, despite low interest rates. In the late 1990s, a number of countries around the world, such as South Korea, Indonesia, Brazil, and Russia, suffered severe economic problems. In a process known as a *flight to quality*, many investors sold their investments in those countries and bought investments in the United States. In addition, the strong performance of the U.S. stock market through the spring of 2000 attracted many investors. Finally, the sharp decline in private saving in the United States that began during the late 1990s also contributed to the U.S. current account deficit. The fall in the value of the dollar after 2008 helped reduce the size of the current account deficit, although the deficit still remained substantial.

Are persistent current account deficits a problem for the United States? Current account deficits result in U.S. net foreign investment being negative. Each year, foreign investors accumulate many more U.S. assets—such as stocks, bonds, and factories—than U.S. investors accumulate foreign assets. In 1986, for the first time since the nineteenth century, the value of foreign-owned assets in the United States became larger than the value of U.S.-owned assets abroad. At the end of 2012, foreign investors owned about $3.9 trillion more of U.S. assets than U.S. investors owned of foreign assets, which is why the United States is sometimes called "the world's largest debtor." But the continued willingness of foreign investors to buy U.S. stocks and bonds and foreign companies to build factories in the United States can be seen as a vote of confidence in the strength of the U.S. economy and the buying power of U.S. consumers. When private saving rates declined in the United States to historically low levels in the mid-2000s, only the continued flow of funds from foreign investors made it possible for the United States to maintain the high levels of domestic investment required for economic growth. Beginning in 2009, private saving rates increased, but public saving turned sharply negative as the federal budget deficit soared. Domestic investment in the United States remains reliant on funds from foreign investment.

Source: Elena L. Nguyen, "The International Investment Position of the United States at the End of the First Quarter of 2013 and Year 2012," *Survey of Current Business*, July 2013, pp. 14–25.

Your Turn: Test your understanding by doing related problem 4.7 at the end of this chapter.

5 LEARNING OBJECTIVE

Compare the effectiveness of monetary policy and fiscal policy in an open economy and in a closed economy.

Monetary Policy and Fiscal Policy in an Open Economy

United States is an open economy. Now that we have explored some of the links among economies, we can look at the difference between how monetary policy and fiscal policy work in an open economy as opposed to in a closed economy. Economists refer to the ways in which monetary policy and fiscal policy affect the domestic economy as *policy channels*. An open economy has more policy channels than does a closed economy.

Monetary Policy in an Open Economy

When the Federal Reserve engages in an expansionary monetary policy, it typically buys Treasury securities to lower interest rates and stimulate aggregate demand. In a closed economy, the main effect of lower interest rates is on domestic investment spending and purchases of consumer durables. In an open economy, lower interest rates will also affect the exchange rate between the dollar and foreign currencies. Lower interest rates will cause some investors in the United States and abroad to switch from investing in U.S. financial assets to investing in foreign financial assets. This switch will lower the demand for the dollar relative to foreign currencies and cause its value to decline. A lower exchange rate will decrease the prices of U.S. products in foreign markets and increase the prices of foreign products in the United States. As a result, net exports will increase. This additional policy channel will increase the ability of an expansionary monetary policy to affect aggregate demand.

When the Fed wants to reduce aggregate demand to reduce inflation, it engages in a contractionary monetary policy. The Fed sells Treasury securities to increase interest rates and reduce aggregate demand. In a closed economy, the main effect is once again on domestic investment spending and purchases of consumer durables. In an open economy, higher interest rates will lead to a higher foreign exchange value of the dollar. The prices of U.S. products in foreign markets will increase, and the prices of foreign products in the United States will fall. As a result, net exports will fall. The contractionary policy will have a larger effect on aggregate demand, and therefore it will be more effective in slowing the growth in economic activity. To summarize: *Monetary policy has a greater effect on aggregate demand in an open economy than in a closed economy.*

Fiscal Policy in an Open Economy

To engage in an expansionary fiscal policy, the federal government increases its purchases or cuts taxes. Increases in government purchases directly increase aggregate demand. Tax cuts increase aggregate demand by increasing household disposable income and business income, which results in increased consumption spending and investment spending. An expansionary fiscal policy may result in higher interest rates. In a closed economy, the main effect of higher interest rates is to reduce domestic investment spending and purchases of consumer durables. In an open economy, higher interest rates will also lead to an increase in the foreign exchange value of the dollar and a decrease in net exports. Therefore, in an open economy, an expansionary fiscal policy may be less effective because the *crowding out effect* may be larger. In a closed economy, only consumption and investment are crowded out by an expansionary fiscal policy. In an open economy, net exports may also be crowded out.

The government can fight inflation by using a contractionary fiscal policy to slow the growth of aggregate demand. A contractionary fiscal policy cuts government purchases or raises taxes to reduce household disposable income and consumption spending. It also reduces the federal budget deficit (or increases the budget surplus), which may lower interest rates. Lower interest rates will increase domestic investment and purchases of consumer durables, thereby offsetting some of the reduction in government spending and increases in taxes. In an open economy, lower interest rates will also reduce the foreign exchange value of the dollar and increase net exports. Therefore, in an open economy, a contractionary fiscal policy will have a smaller effect on aggregate demand and therefore will be less effective in slowing an economy. In summary: *Fiscal policy has a smaller effect on aggregate demand in an open economy than in a closed economy.*

Continued

Economics in Your Life

The South Korean Central Bank and Your Car Loan

At the beginning of this chapter, we posed this question: Will the Bank of Korea's decision to sell its U.S. Treasury bonds affect the interest rate you pay on your car loan? To sell its holdings of Treasury bonds, South Korea's central bank may have to offer them at a lower price. When the prices of bonds fall, the interest rates on them rise. As the interest rates on U.S. Treasury bonds increase, the interest rates on corporate bonds and bank loans, including car loans, may also increase. So, the decision of the Bank of Korea has the potential to increase the interest rate you pay on your car loan. In practice, the interest rate on your car loan is likely to be affected only if the Bank of Korea sells a very large number of bonds and if investors consider it likely that other foreign central banks may soon do the same thing. The basic point is important, however: Economies are interdependent, and interest rates in the United States are not determined entirely by the actions of people in the United States.

Conclusion

At one time, U.S. policymakers—and economics textbooks—ignored the linkages between the United States and other economies. In the modern world, these linkages have become increasingly important, and economists and policymakers must take them into account when analyzing the economy.

Visit MyEconLab for a news article and analysis related to the concepts in this chapter.

Chapter Summary and Problems

Key Terms

Balance of payments	Currency appreciation	Net foreign investment	Saving and investment equation
Balance of trade	Currency depreciation	Nominal exchange rate	Speculators
Capital account	Current account	Open economy	
Closed economy	Financial account	Real exchange rate	

 The Balance of Payments: Linking the United States to the International Economy

LEARNING OBJECTIVE: Explain how the balance of payments is calculated.

Summary

Nearly all economies are **open economies** that trade with and invest in other economies. A **closed economy** has no transactions in trade or finance with other economies. The **balance of payments** is the record of a country's trade with other countries in goods, services, and assets. The **current account** records a country's net exports, net investment income, and net transfers. The **financial account** shows investments a country has made abroad and foreign investments received by the country. The **balance of trade** is the difference between the value of the goods a country exports and the value of the goods a country imports. **Net foreign investment** is the difference between capital outflows from a country and capital inflows. The **capital account** is a part of the balance of payments that records relatively minor transactions. Apart from measurement errors, the sum of the current account and the financial account must equal zero. Therefore, the balance of payments must also equal zero.

Visit www.myeconlab.com to complete these exercises online and get instant feedback.

Review Questions

1.1 What is the relationship among the current account, the financial account, and the balance of payments?

1.2 What is the difference between net exports and the current account balance?

1.3 Explain whether you agree with the following statement: "The United States has run a balance of payments deficit every year since 1982."

Problems and Applications

1.4 In 2012, France had a current account deficit of €58.7 billion (approximately $75.6 billion). Did France experience a net capital outflow or a net capital inflow during 2012? Briefly explain.

1.5 Use the information in the following table to prepare a balance of payments account, like the one shown in Table 1. Assume that the balance on the capital account is zero.

Increase in foreign holdings of assets in the United States	$1,181
Exports of goods	856
Imports of services	−256
Statistical discrepancy	?
Net transfers	−60
Exports of services	325
Income received on investments	392
Imports of goods	−1,108
Increase in U.S. holdings of assets in foreign countries	−1,040
Income payments on investments	−315

1.6 **[Related to the** Don't Let This Happen to You**]** In 2012, Germany had a balance of trade surplus of $238 billion and a current account surplus of $208 billion. Explain how Germany's current account surplus could be smaller than its trade surplus. In 2012, what would we expect Germany's balance on the financial account to have been? Briefly explain.

1.7 **[Related to** Solved Problem 1**]** Is it possible for a country to run a trade deficit and a financial account deficit simultaneously? Briefly explain.

1.8 **[Related to** Solved Problem 1**]** Suppose we know that a country has been receiving large inflows of foreign investment. What can we say about the country's current account balance?

1.9 **[Related to** Solved Problem 1**]** The United States ran a current account surplus every year during the 1960s. What must have been true about the U.S. financial account balance during those years?

1.10 An article in the *Economist* quotes Chinese Finance Minister Lou Jiwei as saying that in China, "the ratio of current account surplus [to] GDP has dropped." Briefly explain the implications of this decline in China's current account surplus for the amount that China is investing in foreign countries relative to the amount that foreign countries are investing in China.

Source: "Lou or Louer," *Economist*, June 14, 2013.

1.11 An article in the *Economist* states: "India aims to fund its current account deficit mainly by attracting . . . flows of FDI [foreign direct investment]."
   a. What is foreign direct investment?
   b. In what sense can foreign direct investment "fund" a country's current account deficit?

   Source: "Travellers Checked," *Economist*, May 19, 2012.

---

2 The Foreign Exchange Market and Exchange Rates

LEARNING OBJECTIVE: Explain how exchange rates are determined and how changes in exchange rates affect the prices of imports and exports.

Summary

The **nominal exchange rate** is the value of one country's currency in terms of another country's currency. The exchange rate is determined in the foreign exchange market by the demand and supply of a country's currency. Changes in the exchange rate are caused by shifts in demand or supply. The three main sets of factors that cause the demand and supply curves in the foreign exchange market to shift are changes in the demand for U.S.-produced goods and services and changes in the demand for foreign-produced goods and services; changes in the desire to invest in the United States and changes in the desire to invest in foreign countries; and changes in the expectations of currency traders—particularly **speculators**—concerning the likely future values of the dollar and the likely future values of foreign currencies. **Currency appreciation** occurs when a currency's market value increases relative to another currency. **Currency depreciation** occurs when a currency's market value decreases relative to another currency. The **real exchange rate** is the price of domestic goods in terms of foreign goods. The real exchange rate is calculated by multiplying the nominal exchange rate by the ratio of the domestic price level to the foreign price level.

Visit **www.myeconlab.com** to complete these exercises online and get instant feedback.

Review Questions

2.1 If the exchange rate between the Japanese yen and the U.S. dollar expressed in terms of yen per dollar is ¥95 = $1, what is the exchange rate when expressed in terms of dollars per yen?

2.2 Suppose that the current exchange rate between the dollar and the euro is €0.75 = $1. If the exchange rate changes to €0.80 = $1, has the euro appreciated or depreciated against the dollar? Briefly explain.

2.3 Why do foreign households and foreign firms demand U.S. dollars in exchange for foreign currency? Why do U.S. households and firms supply U.S. dollars in exchange for foreign currency?

2.4 What are the three main sets of factors that cause the supply and demand curves in the foreign exchange market to shift?

Problems and Applications

2.5 **[Related to** Making the Connection: **Exchange Rate Listings]** On January 1, 2002, there were 15 member countries in the European Union. Twelve of those countries eliminated their own individual currencies and began using a new common currency, the euro. For a three-year period from January 1, 1999, through December 31, 2001, these 12 countries priced goods and services in terms of both their own currencies and the euro. During that period, the value of their currencies was fixed against each other and against the euro. So during that time, the dollar had an exchange rate against each of these currencies and against the euro. The following table shows the fixed exchange rates of four European currencies against the euro and their exchange rates against the U.S. dollar on March 2, 2001. Use the following information to calculate the exchange rate between the dollar and the euro (in euros per dollar) on March 2, 2001.

Currency	Units per Euro (Fixed)	Units per U.S. Dollar (As of March 2, 2001)
German mark	1.9558	2.0938
French franc	6.5596	7.0223
Italian lira	1,936.2700	2,072.8700
Portuguese escudo	200.4820	214.6300

2.6 **[Related to the** Don't Let This Happen to You**]** If we know the exchange rate between Country A's currency and Country B's currency and we know the exchange rate between Country B's currency and Country C's currency, then we can compute the exchange rate between Country A's currency and Country C's currency.
   a. Suppose the exchange rate between the Japanese yen and the U.S. dollar is currently ¥95 = $1 and the exchange rate between the British pound and the U.S. dollar is £0.64 = $1. What is the exchange rate between the yen and the pound?
   b. Suppose the exchange rate between the yen and the dollar changes to ¥100 = $1 and the exchange rate between the pound and the dollar changes to £0.55 = $1. Has the dollar appreciated or depreciated against the yen? Has the dollar appreciated or depreciated against the pound? Has the yen appreciated or depreciated against the pound?

2.7 Graph the demand and supply of U.S. dollars for euros and label each axis. Show graphically and explain the effect on the demand and supply of dollars and the resulting change in the exchange rate of euros for U.S. dollars if the European Central Bank takes action to increase interest rates.

2.8 An article in the *Wall Street Journal* in mid-2013 discussed why the exchange value of the U.S. dollar was declining from what it had been earlier in the year. One explanation offered was: "Many investors had piled into the dollar earlier this year on the belief that robust growth in the U.S. would lead the Fed to scale back its bond-purchase program, which has been pumping $85 billion into the economy each month, in the fall." Why might a decision by the Fed to pursue a more expansionary monetary policy cause the exchange value of the dollar to decline?

Source: Nicole Hong, "Doubts Arise over U.S. Dollar's Strength," *Wall Street Journal*, August 11, 2013.

2.9 Use the graph to answer the following questions.

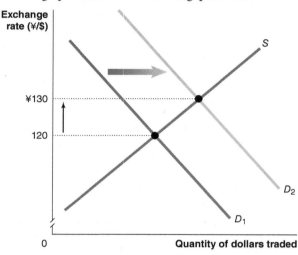

a. Briefly explain whether the dollar appreciated or depreciated against the yen.

b. Which of the following events could have caused the shift in demand shown in the graph?
  i. Interest rates in the United States have declined.
  ii. Income rises in Japan.
  iii. Speculators begin to believe the value of the dollar will be higher in the future.

2.10 **[Related to** Solved Problem 2**]** When a country's currency appreciates, is it generally good news or bad news for the country's consumers? Is it generally good news or bad news for the country's businesses? Explain your reasoning.

2.11 An article discussing the decline in the manufacturing sector in Australia observed that: "The strong Australian dollar has played its part."

a. What does the author mean by a "strong Australian dollar"?

b. Why would a strong Australia dollar cause problems for Australian manufacturers?

Source: Robb M. Stewart, "Ford Won't Rue Aussie Dollar Drop," *Wall Street Journal*, May 29, 2013.

2.12 According to a 2013 article on Top Forex News: "[India's] central bank raised interest rates yesterday in order … to support the weakening currency (the Indian rupee)."

a. What does the article mean by a "weakening currency"?

b. How would the Indian central bank raising interest rates support the weakening Indian rupee?

Source: "RBI Raises Rates, Rupee Stronger," topforexnews.com, July 16, 2013.

2.13 **[Related to the** Chapter Opener**]** In preparing their financial statements, U.S. firms with sales abroad in foreign currencies have to engage in "foreign currency translations"; that is, they have to convert foreign currency values into U.S. dollars. In its *2012 Annual Report*, McDonald's made the following statement: "In 2012, foreign currency translation had a negative impact on [reported revenue and profits] primarily due to the weaker Euro, along with most other currencies."

a. What does the article mean by a weaker euro?

b. As a U.S.-based company, doesn't McDonald's benefit when the U.S. dollar is stronger?

Source: McDonald's, *2012 Annual Report*.

2.14 The humorist Dave Barry once wrote the following: "In economic news, the Federal Reserve Board, responding to recession fears and the continued weakening of the dollar, votes unanimously to be paid in euros." Granted that Barry was joking, what advantages would there be to U.S. citizens being paid in euros at a time when the dollar was "weakening"? Why did the dollar lose value against most other currencies beginning in 2002?

Source: Dave Barry, *Dave Barry's History of the Millenium (So Far)*, New York: Berkeley Books, 2008, pp. 230–231.

2.15 **[Related to** Making the Connection: **Japanese Firms Ride the Yen Roller Coaster]** An article in the *Economist* notes that gasoline prices in Japan were increasing "because of the government's efforts to drive down the yen."

a. Why was the Japanese government trying to drive down the yen?

b. What actions was the Japanese government taking to drive down the yen?

c. Why would driving down the yen have increased gasoline prices in Japan?

Source: "Man with Plan," *Economist*, July 20, 2013.

3   The International Sector and National Saving and Investment

LEARNING OBJECTIVE: Explain the saving and investment equation.

Summary

A current account deficit must be exactly offset by a financial account surplus. The financial account is equal to net capital flows, which is equal to net foreign investment but with the opposite sign. Because the current account balance is roughly equal to net exports, we can conclude that net exports will equal net foreign investment. National saving is equal to private saving plus government saving. Private saving is equal to national income minus consumption and minus taxes. Government saving is the difference between taxes and government spending. GDP (or national income) is equal to the sum of investment, consumption, government spending, and net exports. We can use this fact, our definitions of private and government saving, and the fact that net exports equal net foreign investment to arrive at an important relationship known as the **saving and investment equation**: $S = I + NFI$.

Visit **www.myeconlab.com** to complete these exercises online and get instant feedback.

Review Questions

3.1 Explain the relationship between net exports and net foreign investment.

3.2 What is the saving and investment equation? If national saving declines, what will happen to domestic investment and net foreign investment?

3.3 If a country saves more than it invests domestically, what must be true of its net foreign investment?

Problems and Applications

3.4 Writing in the *New York Times*, Simon Johnson, an economist at MIT, makes the argument that people outside the United States may at some point decide to "save less (in which case they may hold onto their existing United States government debt but not want to buy so much of new issues)." What does saving by people outside of the United States have to do with sales of U.S. government debt? Does the level of domestic investment occurring in foreign countries matter for your answer? Briefly explain.

Source: Simon Johnson, "The Real Fiscal Risks in the United States," *New York Times*, December 6, 2012.

3.5 In 2012, domestic investment in Japan was 21.2 percent of GDP, and Japanese net foreign investment was −2.2 percent of GDP. What percentage of GDP was Japanese national saving?

3.6 In 2012, France's net foreign investment was negative. Which was larger in France in 2012: national saving or domestic investment? Briefly explain.

3.7 Briefly explain whether you agree with the following statement: "Because in 2012 national saving was a smaller percentage of GDP in the United States than in the United Kingdom, domestic investment must also have been a smaller percentage of GDP in the United States than in the United Kingdom."

3.8 **[Related to** Solved Problem 3**]** Look again at Solved Problem 3, where the saving and investment equation $S = I + NX$ is derived. In deriving this equation, we assumed that national income was equal to Y. But Y only includes income *earned* by households. In the modern U.S. economy, households receive substantial transfer payments—such as Social Security payments and unemployment insurance payments—from the government. Suppose that we define national income as being equal to $Y + TR$, where TR equals government transfer payments, and we also define government spending as being equal to $G + TR$. Show that after making these adjustments, we end up with the same saving and investment equation.

3.9 Use the saving and investment equation to explain why the United States experienced large current account deficits in the late 1990s.

3.10 Former congressman and presidential candidate Richard Gephardt once proposed that tariffs be imposed on imports from countries with which the United States has a trade deficit. If this proposal were enacted and if it were to succeed in reducing the U.S. current account deficit to zero, what would be the likely effect on domestic investment spending within the United States? Assume that no other federal government economic policy is changed. (*Hint:* Use the saving and investment equation to answer this question.)

4   The Effect of a Government Budget Deficit on Investment

LEARNING OBJECTIVE: Explain the effect of a government budget deficit on investment in an open economy.

Summary

When the government runs a budget deficit, national saving will decline unless private saving increases by the full amount of the budget deficit, which is unlikely. As the saving and investment equation ($S = I + NFI$) shows, the result of a decline in national saving must be a decline in either domestic investment or net foreign investment.

Visit **www.myeconlab.com** to complete these exercises online and get instant feedback.

Review Questions

4.1 What happens to national saving when the government runs a budget surplus? What is the twin deficits idea? Did it hold for the United States in the 1990s? Briefly explain.

4.2 Why were the early and mid-1980s particularly difficult times for U.S. exporters?

4.3 Why is the United States sometimes called the "world's largest debtor"?

Problems and Applications

4.4 Tim Condon, an economist at the European bank ING, was quoted in the *Wall Street Journal* in 2011 as predicting that "China's current account or saving-investment surplus [will be in] the 1–2% of GDP range." Is he correct in referring to China's current account as being the same as its saving-investment surplus? Briefly explain. If the Chinese government runs a large budget deficit, what will be the likely effect on its current account?

Source: Josh Chin, "Economists React: Chinese Imports Way Up in August," *Wall Street Journal*, September 12, 2011.

4.5 According to an article in the *Economist*: "countries with persistent current-account deficits tend to have higher real interest rates than surplus countries." What do high interest rates have to do with current account deficits?

Source: "Carry on Trading," *Economist*, August 10, 2013.

4.6 The text states: "The budget surpluses of the late 1990s occurred at a time of then-record current account deficits." Holding everything else constant, what would the likely effect have been on domestic investment in the United States during those years if the current account had been balanced instead of being in deficit?

4.7 **[Related to** Making the Connection: **Why Is the United States Called the World's Largest Debtor?]** Why might "the continued willingness of foreign investors to buy U.S. stocks and bonds and foreign companies to build factories in the United States" result in the United States running a current account deficit?

4.8 An article in GulfNews.com noted that in September 2012 the Indian government of Prime Minister Manmohan Singh made "urgently needed reforms to reduce the fiscal deficit and attract foreign investment to help the current account deficit and growth."

   a. Could there be a connection between India's fiscal (budget) deficit and its current account deficit? Briefly explain.

   b. How would attracting foreign investment help the current account deficit and (economic) growth?

   c. The article further notes that the Reserve Bank of India (the central bank) stated that: "Financing the CAD (current account deficit) with increasingly risky and volatile flows increases the economy's vulnerability to sudden shifts in risk appetite and liquidity preference, potentially threatening macroeconomic and exchange rate stability." What does India's central bank mean by "risky and volatile flows" that finance their current account deficit? How could those flows threaten India's macroeconomic stability?

Source: "India's Central Bank Lowers Interest Rate," gulfnews.com, January 29, 2013.

Monetary Policy and Fiscal Policy in an Open Economy

LEARNING OBJECTIVE: Compare the effectiveness of monetary policy and fiscal policy in an open economy and in a closed economy.

Summary

When the Federal Reserve engages in an expansionary monetary policy, it buys government bonds to lower interest rates and increase aggregate demand. In a closed economy, the main effect of lower interest rates is on domestic investment spending and purchases of consumer durables. In an open economy, lower interest rates will also cause an increase in net exports. When the Fed wants to slow the rate of economic growth to reduce inflation, it engages in a contractionary monetary policy by selling government bonds to increase interest rates and reduce aggregate demand. In a closed economy, the main effect is once again on domestic investment and purchases of consumer durables. In an open economy, higher interest rates will also reduce net exports. We can conclude that monetary policy has a greater impact on aggregate demand in an open economy than in a closed economy. To engage in an expansionary fiscal policy, the government increases government spending or cuts taxes. An expansionary fiscal policy can lead to higher interest rates. In a closed economy, the main effect of higher interest rates is on domestic investment spending and spending on consumer durables. In an open economy, higher interest rates will also reduce net exports. A contractionary fiscal policy will reduce the budget deficit and may lower interest rates. In a closed economy, lower interest rates increase domestic investment and spending on consumer durables. In an open economy, lower interest rates also increase net exports. We can conclude that fiscal policy has a smaller effect on aggregate demand in an open economy than in a closed economy.

Visit **www.myeconlab.com** to complete these exercises online and get instant feedback.

Review Questions

5.1 What is meant by a *policy channel*?

5.2 Why does monetary policy have a greater effect on aggregate demand in an open economy than in a closed economy?

5.3 Why does fiscal policy have a smaller effect on aggregate demand in an open economy than in a closed economy?

Problems and Applications

5.4 An article in the *Economist* describes Ireland as "an extraordinarily open economy." Is fiscal policy in Ireland likely to be more or less effective than it would be in a less open economy? Briefly explain.

Source: "Celtic Cross," *Economist*, May 26, 2011.

5.5 Suppose that Federal Reserve policy leads to higher interest rates in the United States.
  a. How will this policy affect real GDP in the short run if the United States is a closed economy?
  b. How will this policy affect real GDP in the short run if the United States is an open economy?
  c. How will your answer to part (b) change if interest rates also rise in the countries that are the major trading partners of the United States?

5.6 An economist remarks: "In the 1960s, fiscal policy would have been a better way to stabilize the economy, but now I believe that monetary policy is better." What has changed about the U.S. economy that might have led the economist to this conclusion?

5.7 Suppose the federal government increases spending without also increasing taxes. In the short run, how will this action affect real GDP and the price level in a closed economy? How will the effects of this action differ in an open economy?

Real-Time Data Exercises

D1 **[Exchange rate movements]** Go to the Web site of the Federal Reserve Bank of St. Louis (FRED) (research.stlouisfed.org/fred2/) and download the most recent value and the value from the same month one year earlier from FRED for the U.S./Euro Foreign Exchange Rate (EXUSEU).
  a. Using these values, compute the percentage change in the euro's value.
  b. Explain whether the dollar appreciated or depreciated against the euro.

D2 **[Exchange rate movements]** Go to the Web site of the Federal Reserve Bank of St. Louis (FRED) (research.stlouisfed.org/fred2/) and download and plot the U.S. dollar-euro exchange rate (EXUSEU), the U.S. dollar-yen exchange rate (EXJPUS), and the U.S. dollar-Canadian dollar exchange rate (EXCAUS) for the period from 2001 to the present. Answer the following questions on the basis of your graphs.
  a. In what year did the euro reach its highest value?

  b. During the financial crisis of 2007–2009, did the yen appreciate or depreciate against the dollar? Briefly explain.
  c. Against which currency did the U.S. dollar depreciate the most during this period?

D3 **[Exchange rate movements]** One way to gauge the general value of one currency relative to other currencies is to calculate the *trade-weighted exchange rate*, which is an index number similar to the consumer price index. The trade-weighted exchange rate for the U.S. dollar weights each individual exchange rate by the share of that country's trade with the United States. Go to the Web site of the Federal Reserve Bank of St. Louis (FRED) (research.stlouisfed.org/fred2/) and download monthly data on the trade-weighted exchange rate for the U.S. dollar against major currencies (TWEXMMTH) from 1973 to the present.
  a. What has been the long-term trend in the exchange value of the dollar? What effect should changes in the exchange rate during this period have had on U.S. net exports? Briefly explain.
  b. What has been the trend in the exchange value of the dollar over the past year? What effect should changes in the exchange rate during the past year have had on U.S. net exports? Briefly explain.

D4 **[Exchange Rates and Exports]** Go to the Web site of the Federal Reserve Bank of St. Louis (FRED) (research.stlouisfed.org/fred2/) and find the two most recent values for the Japan/U.S. Foreign Exchange Rate (DEXJPUS) and the U.S. Exports of Goods to Japan (EXPJP). Given the change in the exchange rate between the two periods, is the change in U.S. exports to Japan consistent with what the analysis in this chapter would predict? Briefly explain.

D5 **[Exchange Rates and Imports]** Go to the Web site of the Federal Reserve Bank of St. Louis (FRED) (research.stlouisfed.org/fred2/) and find the two most recent values from FRED for the Japan/U.S. Foreign Exchange Rate (DEXJPUS) and the U.S. Imports of Goods from Japan (IMPJP). Given the change in the exchange rate between the two periods, is the change in U.S. imports from Japan consistent with what the analysis in this chapter would predict? Briefly explain.

Glossary

Balance of payments The record of a country's trade with other countries in goods, services, and assets.

Balance of trade The difference between the value of the goods a country exports and the value of the goods a country imports.

Capital account The part of the balance of payments that records relatively minor transactions, such as migrants' transfers and sales and purchases of nonproduced, nonfinancial assets.

Closed economy An economy that has no interactions in trade or finance with other countries.

Currency appreciation An increase in the market value of one currency relative to another currency.

Currency depreciation A decrease in the market value of one currency relative to another currency.

Current account The part of the balance of payments that records a country's net exports, net income on investments, and net transfers.

Financial account The part of the balance of payments that records purchases of assets a country has made abroad and foreign purchases of assets in the country.

Net foreign investment The difference between capital outflows from a country and capital inflows, also equal to net foreign direct investment plus net foreign portfolio investment.

Nominal exchange rate The value of one country's currency in terms of another country's currency.

Open economy An economy that has interactions in trade or finance with other countries.

Real exchange rate The price of domestic goods in terms of foreign goods.

Saving and investment equation An equation that shows that national saving is equal to domestic investment plus net foreign investment.

Speculators Currency traders who buy and sell foreign exchange in an attempt to profit from changes in exchange rates.

Credits

Credits are listed in the order of appearance.

Photo

Eye Ubiquitous/Glow Images;
Iain Masterton/Alamy

Index